Lecture Notes in Artificial Intelligence   12163

Subseries of Lecture Notes in Computer Science

More information about this series at http://www.springer.com/series/1244

Ig Ibert Bittencourt · Mutlu Cukurova ·
Kasia Muldner · Rose Luckin ·
Eva Millán (Eds.)

Artificial Intelligence in Education

21st International Conference, AIED 2020
Ifrane, Morocco, July 6–10, 2020
Proceedings, Part I

Springer

Editors
Ig Ibert Bittencourt (iD)
Federal University of Alagoas
Maceió, Brazil

Mutlu Cukurova (iD)
University College London
London, UK

Kasia Muldner (iD)
Carleton University
Ottawa, ON, Canada

Rose Luckin (iD)
University College London
London, UK

Eva Millán (iD)
University of Malaga
Málaga, Spain

ISSN 0302-9743   ISSN 1611-3349 (electronic)
Lecture Notes in Artificial Intelligence
ISBN 978-3-030-52236-0   ISBN 978-3-030-52237-7 (eBook)
https://doi.org/10.1007/978-3-030-52237-7

LNCS Sublibrary: SL7 – Artificial Intelligence

This Springer imprint is published by the registered company Springer Nature Switzerland AG
The registered company address is: Gewerbestrasse 11, 6330 Cham, Switzerland

Preface

The 21st International Conference on Artificial Intelligence in Education (AIED 2020) was held virtually during July 6–10, 2020. AIED 2020 was the latest in a longstanding series of a yearly international conference for high-quality research on ways to enhance student learning through applications of artificial intelligence, human computer interaction, and the learning sciences.

The theme for the AIED 2020 conference was "Augmented Intelligence to Empower Education." As AI in education systems becomes more mature and implemented at scale in real-world contexts, the value of supplementing human intelligence and decision making (e.g., teacher, tutor, peer-tutor) is more apparent than ever. While the paradigm of augmented intelligence is not new to the field, solid theoretical and/or empirical work in the area is limited. Thus, further work is needed to understand the balance of human and AI partnerships in systems that support student learning. The AIED community was convened in 2020 to present solutions for the key questions related to this theme, including the identification of the augmentation opportunities that would empower the stakeholders of education.

AIED 2020 was originally scheduled to visit the African continent for the first time and be co-located with Educational Data Mining (EDM 2020). However, the unprecedented COVID-19 pandemic made international traveling and in-person meetings impossible and AIED joined other conferences in becoming a virtual event. While this certainly brought new challenges, we were humbled by the response of our community during this difficult time. We are extremely grateful to the authors, the keynote speakers, the reviewers, and the other track chairs for making AIED possible. The virtual event included keynotes from Prof. Neil Heffernan on ways that tutoring systems can improve online learning, Prof. Yvonne Rogers on designing interactive technologies that augment humans, and Andreas Schleicher, director for the directorate of education and skills at OECD, with Lord Jim Knight, former school minister from the UK on how AI impacts upon the policymaking landscape in education. We want to extend a special thank you to the AIED Program Committee (PC) members and reviewers – your hard work and commitment was truly appreciated.

There were 184 submissions as full papers to AIED 2020, of which 49 were accepted as full papers (ten pages) with virtual oral presentation at the conference (for an acceptance rate of 26.6%), and 52 were accepted as short papers (four pages). Of the 30 papers directly submitted as short papers, 14 were accepted. Each submission was reviewed by three PC members. In addition, submissions underwent a discussion period (led by a leading reviewer) to ensure that all reviewers' opinions would be considered and leveraged to generate a group recommendation to the program chairs. The program chairs checked the reviews and meta-reviews for quality and, where necessary, requested for reviewers to elaborate their review. Final decisions were made by carefully considering both meta-reviews (weighed more heavily) scores and the discussions. Our goal was to conduct a fair process and encourage substantive and constructive reviews without interfering with the reviewers' judgment. We also took the constraints of the program into account, seeking to keep the acceptance rate within the typical range for this conference.

Beyond paper presentations and keynotes, the conference also included:

- An Industry and Innovation Track, intended to support connections between industry (both for-profit and non-profit) and the research community
- A series of four workshops across a range of topics, such as: empowering education with AI technology, intelligent textbooks, challenges related to education in AI (K-12), and optimizing human learning
- A Doctoral Consortium Track, designed to provide doctoral students with the opportunity to obtain feedback on their doctoral research from the research community

Special thanks goes to Springer for sponsoring the AIED 2020 Best Paper Award. As already mentioned above, we also want to acknowledge the wonderful work of the AIED 2020 Organizing Committee, the PC members, and the reviewers who made this conference possible.

May 2020   Ig Ibert Bittencourt
                                                                          Mutlu Cukurova
                                                                          Kasia Muldner
                                                                          Rose Luckin
                                                                          Eva Millán

Organization

General Conference Chair

Rose Luckin   University College London, UK

Senior Program Chair

Eva Millán   University of Malaga, Spain

Program Chairs

Ig Ibert Bittencourt   Universidade Federal de Alagoas, Brazil
Mutlu Cukurova   University College London, UK
Kasia Muldner   Carleton University, Canada

Advisory Board

Danielle McNamara   Arizona State University, USA
Ido Roll   Technion - Israel Institute of Technology, Israel

Workshop and Tutorial Chairs

Alexandra Cristea   Durham University, UK
Mingyu Feng   WestEd, USA
Richard Tong   Squirrel AI, China

Industry and Innovation Track Chairs

Elle Yuan Wang   ASU EdPlus, USA
Wei Cui   Squirrel AI, China

Doctoral Consortium Chairs

Janice Gobert   Rutgers University, USA
Kaska Porayska-Pomsta   University College London, UK

Program Committee

Adeniran Adetunji   University of Aberdeen, UK
Patricia Albacete   University of Pittsburgh, USA
Vincent Aleven   Carnegie Melon University, USA
Giora Alexandron   Weizmann Institute of Science, Switzerland

Michail Giannakos	Norwegian University of Science and Technology, Norway
Niki Gitinabard	North Carolina State University, USA
Janice Gobert	Rutgers University, USA
Alex Sandro Gomes	Universidade Federal de Pernambuco, Brazil
Monique Grandbastien	Université de Lorraine, France
Nathalie Guin	LIRIS, Université de Lyon, France
Gahgene Gweon	Seoul National University, South Korea
Rawad Hammad	University of East London, UK
Jason Harley	McGill University, Canada
Peter Hastings	DePaul University, USA
Neil Heffernan	Worcester Polytechnic Institute, USA
Martin Hlosta	The Open University, UK
Wayne Holmes	NESTA, UK
Ulrich Hoppe	University of Duisburg-Essen, Germany
Tomoya Horiguchi	Kobe University, Japan
Sharon Hsiao	Arizona State University, USA
Stephen Hutt	University of Colorado Boulder, USA
Paul S. Inventado	California State University Fullerton, USA
Seiji Isotani	University of São Paulo, Brazil
Sridhar Iyer	IIT Bombay, India
Patricia Jaques	UNISINOS, Brazil
Srecko Joksimovic	University of South Australia, Australia
Judy Kay	The University of Sydney, Australia
Carmel Kent	University College London, UK
Simon Knight	University of Technology Sydney, Australia
Kazuaki Kojima	Teikyo University, Japan
Emmanuel Kolog	University of Ghana, Ghana
Amruth Kumar	Ramapo College of New Jersey, USA
Rohit Kumar	Consultant (independent), USA
Jean-Marc Labat	UPMC Paris 6, France
Sébastien Lallé	The University of British Columbia, Canada
Andrew Lan	University of Massachusetts Amherst, USA
Nguyen-Thinh Le	Humboldt-Universität zu Berlin, Germany
Blair Lehman	Educational Testing Service, USA
James Lester	North Carolina State University, USA
Fuhua Lin	Athabasca University, Canada
Zitao Liu	TAL AI Lab, China
Yu Lu	Beijing Normal University, China
Vanda Luengo	Sorbonne Université, LIP6, France
Collin Lynch	North Carolina State University, USA
Michael Madaio	Carnegie Mellon University, USA
Laura Malkiewich	Columbia University, USA
Mavrikis Manolis	UCL Knowledge Lab, UK
Ye Mao	North Carolina State University, USA
Leonardo Marques	University of São Paulo, Brazil

José A. Valiente	University of Murcia, Spain
Vasile Rus	The University of Memphis, USA
Demetrios Sampson	Curtin University, Australia
Olga C. Santos	aDeNu Research Group (UNED), Spain
Mohammed Saqr	University of Eastern Finland, Finland
Flippo Sciarrone	Roma Tre University, Italy
Shitian Shen	North Carolina State University, USA
Yu Shengquan	Beijing Normal University, China
Lei Shi	Durham University, UK
Sean Siqueira	Federal University of the State of Rio de Janeiro, Brazil
Caitlin Snyder	Vanderbilt University, USA
Sergey Sosnovsky	Utrecht University, The Netherlands
Angela Stewart	University of Colorado Boulder, USA
Pierre Tchounikine	University of Grenoble, France
Craig Thompson	The University of British Columbia, Canada
Armando Toda	University of São Paulo, Brazil
Richard Tong	Squirrel AI, China
Maomi Ueno	The University of Electro-Communications, Japan
Felisa Verdejo	Universidad Nacional de Educacin a Distancia, Spain
Rosa Vicari	Universidade Federal do Rio Grande do Sul, Brazil
Erin Walker	Arizona State University, USA
April Wang	University of Michigan, USA
Elle Yuan Wang	ASU EdPlus, USA
Chris Wong	University of Technology Sydney, Australia
Beverly Park Woolf	University of Massachusetts, USA
Sho Yamamoto	Kindai University, Japan
Xi Yang	North Carolina State University, USA
Bernard Yett	Vanderbilt University, USA
Diego Zapata-Rivera	Educational Testing Service, USA
Ningyu Zhang	Vanderbilt University, USA
Guojing Zhou	North Carolina State University, USA
Gustavo Zurita	Universidad de Chile, Chile

Additional Reviewers

Alvarez, Claudio	Herder, Tiffany
Alwahaby, Haifa	Ismail, Daneih
Anaya, Antonio R.	Jensen, Emily
Celepkolu, Mehmet	José, Jario
Corrigan, Seth	Ju, Song
Fraca, Estibaliz	Karp Gershon, Saar
Gao, Ge	Khan, Madiha
Ghosh, Aritra	Krumm
Harrison, Avery	Lee, William
He, Liqun	Li, Warren

Limbu, Bibeg
Mao, Ye
Marwan, Samiha
Medeiros Machado, Guilherme
Mohammadhassan, Negar
Morita, Jun'Ya
Ostrow, Korinn
Pathan, Rumana
Patikorn, Thanaporn
Praharaj, Sambit
Prasad, Prajish
Prihar, Ethan
Rajendran, Ramkumar
Rodriguez, Fernando
Serrano Mamolar, Ana
Shahriar, Tasmia
Shi, Yang

Shimmei, Machi
Singh, Daevesh
T. Lakshmi
Tenório, Thyago
Tobarra, Llanos
Tomoto, Takahito
Tong, Richard
Tsan, Jennifer
Varatharaj, Ashvini
Wang, Emma
Wang, Shuai
Wang, Zichao
Wiggins, Joseph
Yang, Xi
Zhang, Zheng
Zhou, Qi
Zhou, Xiaofei

International Artificial Intelligence in Education Society

Amy Ogan   Carnegie Mellon University, USA
Kaska Porayska-Pomsta   University College London, UK
Mercedes Rodrigo   Ateneo De Manila University, Philippines
Olga Santos   UNED, Spain
Ning Wang   University of Southern California, USA

Keynote Abstracts

How Can Platforms Like ASSISTments Be Used to Improve Research?

Neil Heffernan

Worcester Polytechnic Institute, Worcester, MA 01609, USA
nth@wpi.edu

Abstract. The head of the Institute of Education Sciences is asking about how to use platform to increase education sciences. We have been addressing this. So how do you use platforms like EdX, Khan Academy, Canvas to improve science? There is a crisis in American Science referred to as the Reproducibility Crisis where many experimental results are not able to be reproduced. We are trying to address this crisis by helping "good science" to be done. People that control platforms have a responsibility to try to make them useful tools for learning what works. In Silicon Valley, every company is doing AB Testing to refine their individual products. That, in and of itself, is a good thing and we should use these platforms to figure out how to make them more effective. One of the ways we should do that is by experimenting with different ways of helping students succeed. ASSISTments, a platform I have created, with 50,000 middle-school math students, is used to help scientists run studies. I will explain how we have over 100 experiments running inside the ASSISTments platform and how the ASSISTment-sTestBed.org allows external researchers to propose studies. I will also explain how proper oversight is done by our Institutional Review Board. Further, I will explain how users of this platform agree ahead of time to Open-Science procedures such as open-data, open-materials, and pre-registration. I'll illustrate some examples with the 24 randomized controlled trials that I have published as well as the three studies that have more recently come out from the platform by others. Finally, I will point to how we are anonymizing our data and how over 34 different external researchers have used our datasets to publish scientific studies. I would like to thank the U.S. Department of Education and the National Science Foundation for their support of over $32 million from 40+ grants. I will also address how COVID-19 has driven a ten-fold increase in the number of teachers creating new ASSISTments accounts, and I will give my own personal take on how COVID-19 highlights the need to keep teachers in the loop so that their students know their teachers are paying attention to their work and what it means for the AIED community.

How AI Impacts the Policy Making Landscape in Education

Jim Knight[1], Andreas Schleicher[2]

[1] Tes Global
[2] Organisation for Economic Co-operation and Development (OECD)

Abstract. This keynote aims to provide insights into the criteria that policy makers are looking for when they are advocating for Artificial Intelligence platforms in education. Whilst efficacy and proof of concept of any platform is an obvious need, policy makers have to always consider a world view and consider AI platforms as part of an holistic approach to whole child education and welfare. With a multitude of AI platforms on offer how do they make informed decisions and recognise good from bad. How can policy makers work better with those developing the tools? Since the COVID-19 pandemic what shifts have they seen at state and government level as schools and parents adopt AI platforms as part of the daily education of children worldwide?

The New Zeitgeist: Human-AI

Yvonne Rogers

University College London, London, WC1E 6EA, UK
y.rogers@ucl.ac.uk

Abstract. In place of the Singularity, Superintelligence, and General AI visions that have dominated much of the debate surrounding AI (that predicted that ma-chines will eventually become more intelligent than human beings and take over the world) quite different ways of imagining AI are now emerging that are less dystopian or utopian-driven. A new discourse is emerging that is re-thinking the benefits of future AI advances from a more human perspective. The main thrust of this approach is to orient towards envisioning new forms of human-AI partnerships, where humans collaborate with, talk to, or even confide in AI, and conversely, where AI, through its various guises, becomes a companion, therapist, colleague, assistant, or other. Such a shift in thinking enables researchers and developers to design quite different kinds of intelligent systems – those that augment humans. The implications of doing so are profound; especially when considering how to enhance the way learners, educators, and teachers can collaborate with AI in the future. In my talk I will begin to describe what the opportunities and challenges are with this new framing for AI and Ed.

Contents – Part I

Full Papers

Making Sense of Student Success and Risk Through Unsupervised
Machine Learning and Interactive Storytelling 3
    Ahmad Al-Doulat, Nasheen Nur, Alireza Karduni, Aileen Benedict,
    Erfan Al-Hossami, Mary Lou Maher, Wenwen Dou, Mohsen Dorodchi,
    and Xi Niu

Strategies for Deploying Unreliable AI Graders in High-Transparency
High-Stakes Exams. 16
    Sushmita Azad, Binglin Chen, Maxwell Fowler, Matthew West,
    and Craig Zilles

AI Enabled Tutor for Accessible Training 29
    Ayan Banerjee, Imane Lamrani, Sameena Hossain, Prajwal Paudyal,
    and Sandeep K. S. Gupta

Introducing a Framework to Assess Newly Created Questions
with Natural Language Processing. 43
    Luca Benedetto, Andrea Cappelli, Roberto Turrin, and Paolo Cremonesi

Detecting Off-Task Behavior from Student Dialogue in Game-Based
Collaborative Learning. 55
    Dan Carpenter, Andrew Emerson, Bradford W. Mott, Asmalina Saleh,
    Krista D. Glazewski, Cindy E. Hmelo-Silver, and James C. Lester

Automated Analysis of Middle School Students' Written Reflections
During Game-Based Learning. 67
    Dan Carpenter, Michael Geden, Jonathan Rowe, Roger Azevedo,
    and James Lester

Can Ontologies Support the Gamification of Scripted Collaborative
Learning Sessions? 79
    Geiser Chalco Challco, Ig Ibert Bittencourt, and Seiji Isotani

Predicting Gaps in Usage in a Phone-Based Literacy Intervention System . . . 92
    Rishabh Chatterjee, Michael Madaio, and Amy Ogan

MACER: A Modular Framework for Accelerated Compilation
Error Repair. 106
    Darshak Chhatbar, Umair Z. Ahmed, and Purushottam Kar

Using Motion Sensors to Understand Collaborative Interactions
in Digital Fabrication Labs...................................... 118
   Edwin Chng, Mohamed Raouf Seyam, William Yao,
   and Bertrand Schneider

Student Dropout Prediction 129
   Francesca Del Bonifro , Maurizio Gabbrielli, Giuseppe Lisanti,
   and Stefano Pio Zingaro

Real-Time Multimodal Feedback with the CPR Tutor 141
   Daniele Di Mitri, Jan Schneider, Kevin Trebing, Sasa Sopka,
   Marcus Specht, and Hendrik Drachsler

Impact of Methodological Choices on the Evaluation of Student Models 153
   Tomáš Effenberger and Radek Pelánek

Investigating Visitor Engagement in Interactive Science Museum Exhibits
with Multimodal Bayesian Hierarchical Models 165
   Andrew Emerson, Nathan Henderson, Jonathan Rowe, Wookhee Min,
   Seung Lee, James Minogue, and James Lester

Fooling Automatic Short Answer Grading Systems 177
   Anna Filighera, Tim Steuer, and Christoph Rensing

Using Neural Tensor Networks for Open Ended Short
Answer Assessment.. 191
   Dipesh Gautam and Vasile Rus

The Sound of Inattention: Predicting Mind Wandering with Automatically
Derived Features of Instructor Speech 204
   Ian Gliser, Caitlin Mills, Nigel Bosch, Shelby Smith, Daniel Smilek,
   and Jeffrey D. Wammes

To Tailor or Not to Tailor Gamification? An Analysis of the Impact
of Tailored Game Elements on Learners' Behaviours and Motivation 216
   Stuart Hallifax, Elise Lavoué, and Audrey Serna

Improving Affect Detection in Game-Based Learning with Multimodal
Data Fusion 228
   Nathan Henderson, Jonathan Rowe, Luc Paquette, Ryan S. Baker,
   and James Lester

A Conceptual Framework for Human–AI Hybrid Adaptivity in Education ... 240
   Kenneth Holstein, Vincent Aleven, and Nikol Rummel

Exploring How Gender and Enjoyment Impact Learning
in a Digital Learning Game 255
Xinying Hou, Huy A. Nguyen, J. Elizabeth Richey,
and Bruce M. McLaren

Neural Multi-task Learning for Teacher Question Detection
in Online Classrooms 269
Gale Yan Huang, Jiahao Chen, Haochen Liu, Weiping Fu,
Wenbiao Ding, Jiliang Tang, Songfan Yang, Guoliang Li, and Zitao Liu

A Data-Driven Student Model to Provide Adaptive Support During Video
Watching Across MOOCs 282
Sébastien Lallé and Cristina Conati

Transfer of Automated Performance Feedback Models to Different
Specimens in Virtual Reality Temporal Bone Surgery 296
Jesslyn Lamtara, Nathan Hanegbi, Benjamin Talks,
Sudanthi Wijewickrema, Xingjun Ma, Patorn Piromchai, James Bailey,
and Stephen O'Leary

Use of Adaptive Feedback in an App for English Language
Spontaneous Speech 309
Blair Lehman, Lin Gu, Jing Zhao, Eugene Tsuprun,
Christopher Kurzum, Michael Schiano, Yulin Liu,
and G. Tanner Jackson

Impact of Conversational Formality on the Quality and Formality
of Written Summaries 321
Haiying Li and Art C. Graesser

LIWCs the Same, Not the Same: Gendered Linguistic Signals
of Performance and Experience in Online STEM Courses 333
Yiwen Lin, Renzhe Yu, and Nia Dowell

SoundHunters: Increasing Learner Phonological Awareness in Plains Cree . . . 346
Delaney Lothian, Gokce Akcayir, Anaka Sparrow, Owen Mcleod,
and Carrie Demmans Epp

Moodoo: Indoor Positioning Analytics for Characterising
Classroom Teaching 360
Roberto Martinez-Maldonado, Vanessa Echeverria, Jurgen Schulte,
Antonette Shibani, Katerina Mangaroska, and Simon Buckingham Shum

DETECT: A Hierarchical Clustering Algorithm for Behavioural Trends
in Temporal Educational Data. 374
Jessica McBroom, Kalina Yacef, and Irena Koprinska

Effect of Non-mandatory Use of an Intelligent Tutoring System
on Students' Learning   386
  Antonija Mitrović and Jay Holland

Evaluating Crowdsourcing and Topic Modeling in Generating Knowledge
Components from Explanations.   398
  Steven Moore, Huy A. Nguyen, and John Stamper

Modeling the Relationships Between Basic and Achievement Emotions
in Computer-Based Learning Environments   411
  Anabil Munshi, Shitanshu Mishra, Ningyu Zhang, Luc Paquette,
  Jaclyn Ocumpaugh, Ryan Baker, and Gautam Biswas

Analysis of Task Difficulty Sequences in a Simulation-Based
POE Environment   423
  Sadia Nawaz, Namrata Srivastava, Ji Hyun Yu, Ryan S. Baker,
  Gregor Kennedy, and James Bailey

Affective Sequences and Student Actions Within Reasoning Mind   437
  Jaclyn Ocumpaugh, Ryan S. Baker, Shamya Karumbaiah,
  Scott A. Crossley, and Matthew Labrum

Helping Teachers Help Their Students: A Human-AI Hybrid Approach   448
  Ranilson Paiva and Ig Ibert Bittencourt

Comprehensive Views of Math Learners: A Case for Modeling
and Supporting Non-math Factors in Adaptive Math Software   460
  J. Elizabeth Richey, Nikki G. Lobczowski, Paulo F. Carvalho,
  and Kenneth Koedinger

Exploring the Impact of Simple Explanations and Agency on Batch Deep
Reinforcement Learning Induced Pedagogical Policies   472
  Markel Sanz Ausin, Mehak Maniktala, Tiffany Barnes, and Min Chi

Recommending Insightful Drill-Downs Based on Learning Processes
for Learning Analytics Dashboards   486
  Shiva Shabaninejad, Hassan Khosravi, Sander J. J. Leemans,
  Shazia Sadiq, and Marta Indulska

Using Thinkalouds to Understand Rule Learning and Cognitive Control
Mechanisms Within an Intelligent Tutoring System   500
  Deniz Sonmez Unal, Catherine M. Arrington, Erin Solovey,
  and Erin Walker

Remember the Facts? Investigating Answer-Aware Neural Question
Generation for Text Comprehension   512
  Tim Steuer, Anna Filighera, and Christoph Rensing

Raising Teachers Empowerment in Gamification Design of Adaptive
Learning Systems: A Qualitative Research 524
  Kamilla Tenório, Diego Dermeval, Mateus Monteiro,
  Aristoteles Peixoto, and Alan Pedro

Far from Success – Far from Feedback Acceptance? The Influence
of Game Performance on Young Students' Willingness to Accept Critical
Constructive Feedback During Play 537
  Eva-Maria Ternblad and Betty Tärning

Robust Neural Automated Essay Scoring Using Item Response Theory 549
  Masaki Uto and Masashi Okano

Supporting Teacher Assessment in Chinese Language Learning Using
Textual and Tonal Features 562
  Ashvini Varatharaj, Anthony F. Botelho, Xiwen Lu,
  and Neil T. Heffernan

Early Detection of Wheel-Spinning in ASSISTments 574
  Yeyu Wang, Shimin Kai, and Ryan Shaun Baker

Investigating Differential Error Types Between Human
and Simulated Learners 586
  Daniel Weitekamp, Zihuiwen Ye, Napol Rachatasumrit, Erik Harpstead,
  and Kenneth Koedinger

Studying the Interactions Between Science, Engineering,
and Computational Thinking in a Learning-by-Modeling Environment 598
  Ningyu Zhang, Gautam Biswas, Kevin W. McElhaney, Satabdi Basu,
  Elizabeth McBride, and Jennifer L. Chiu

Exploring Automated Question Answering Methods
for Teaching Assistance 610
  Brian Zylich, Adam Viola, Brokk Toggerson, Lara Al-Hariri,
  and Andrew Lan

Correction to: SoundHunters: Increasing Learner Phonological Awareness
in Plains Cree C1
  Delaney Lothian, Gokce Akcayir, Anaka Sparrow, Owen Mcleod,
  and Carrie Demmans Epp

Author Index 623

Contents – Part II

Short Papers

Modelling Learners in Crowdsourcing Educational Systems 3
  Solmaz Abdi, Hassan Khosravi, and Shazia Sadiq

Interactive Pedagogical Agents for Learning Sequence Diagrams 10
  Sohail Alhazmi, Charles Thevathayan, and Margaret Hamilton

A Socratic Tutor for Source Code Comprehension 15
  Zeyad Alshaikh, Lasagn Tamang, and Vasile Rus

Scientific Modeling Using Large Scale Knowledge 20
  Sungeun An, Robert Bates, Jen Hammock, Spencer Rugaber,
  Emily Weigel, and Ashok Goel

Examining Students' Intrinsic Cognitive Load During Program
Comprehension – An Eye Tracking Approach 25
  Magdalena Andrzejewska and Agnieszka Skawińska

Sequence-to-Sequence Models for Automated Text Simplification 31
  Robert-Mihai Botarleanu, Mihai Dascalu, Scott Andrew Crossley,
  and Danielle S. McNamara

The Potential for the Use of Deep Neural Networks in e-Learning Student
Evaluation with New Data Augmentation Method 37
  Andrzej Cader

Investigating Transformers for Automatic Short Answer Grading 43
  Leon Camus and Anna Filighera

Predicting Learners Need for Recommendation Using Dynamic
Graph-Based Knowledge Tracing 49
  Abdessamad Chanaa and Nour-Eddine El Faddouli

BERT and Prerequisite Based Ontology for Predicting Learner's Confusion
in MOOCs Discussion Forums 54
  Abdessamad Chanaa and Nour-Eddine El Faddouli

Identification of Students' Need Deficiency Through a Dialogue System 59
  Penghe Chen, Yu Lu, Yan Peng, Jiefei Liu, and Qi Xu

The Double-Edged Sword of Automating Personalized Interventions in
Makerspaces: An Exploratory Study of Potential Benefits and Drawbacks . . .   64
  Edwin Chng, Sofya Zeylikman, and Bertrand Schneider

EdNet: A Large-Scale Hierarchical Dataset in Education   69
  Youngduck Choi, Youngnam Lee, Dongmin Shin, Junghyun Cho,
  Seoyon Park, Seewoo Lee, Jineon Baek, Chan Bae, Byungsoo Kim,
  and Jaewe Heo

Exploring Automatic Short Answer Grading as a Tool to Assist
in Human Rating   74
  Aubrey Condor

Multi-document Cohesion Network Analysis: Visualizing Intratextual
and Intertextual Links   80
  Maria-Dorinela Dascalu, Stefan Ruseti, Mihai Dascalu,
  Danielle S. McNamara, and Stefan Trausan-Matu

Mastery Learning Heuristics and Their Hidden Models   86
  Shayan Doroudi

Towards Practical Detection of Unproductive Struggle.   92
  Stephen E. Fancsali, Kenneth Holstein, Michael Sandbothe,
  Steven Ritter, Bruce M. McLaren, and Vincent Aleven

What Happens When Gamification Ends?   98
  Miguel García Iruela, Manuel J. Fonseca, Raquel Hijón-Neira,
  and Teresa Chambel

Using Eye-Tracking and Click-Stream Data to Design Adaptive Training
of Children's Inhibitory Control in a Maths and Science Game.   103
  Andrea Gauthier, Kaśka Porayska-Pomsta, Denis Mareschal,
  and The UnLocke Project Team

Prediction of Group Learning Results from an Aggregation of Individual
Understanding with Kit-Build Concept Map.   109
  Yusuke Hayashi, Toshihiro Nomura, and Tsukasa Hirashima

Automatic Classification for Cognitive Engagement in Online Discussion
Forums: Text Mining and Machine Learning Approach   114
  Hind Hayati

Explaining Errors in Predictions of At-Risk Students in Distance
Learning Education   119
  Martin Hlosta, Tina Papathoma, and Christothea Herodotou

A General Multi-method Approach to Design-Loop Adaptivity
in Intelligent Tutoring Systems   124
    Yun Huang, Vincent Aleven, Elizabeth McLaughlin,
    and Kenneth Koedinger

Towards Improving Sample Representativeness of Teachers on Online
Social Media: A Case Study on Pinterest   130
    Hamid Karimi, Tyler Derr, Kaitlin T. Torphy, Kenneth A. Frank,
    and Jiliang Tang

A Framework for Exploring the Impact of Tutor Practices on Learner
Self-regulation in Online Environments   135
    Madiha Khan-Galaria, Mutlu Cukurova, and Rose Luckin

Automated Personalized Feedback Improves Learning Gains
in An Intelligent Tutoring System   140
    Ekaterina Kochmar, Dung Do Vu, Robert Belfer, Varun Gupta,
    Iulian Vlad Serban, and Joelle Pineau

Allowing Revisions While Providing Error-Flagging Support:
Is More Better?   147
    Amruth N. Kumar

Learner-Context Modelling: A Bayesian Approach   152
    Charles Lang

Distinguishing Anxiety Subtypes of English Language Learners Towards
Augmented Emotional Clarity   157
    Heera Lee, Varun Mandalapu, Andrea Kleinsmith, and Jiaqi Gong

Siamese Neural Networks for Class Activity Detection   162
    Hang Li, Zhiwei Wang, Jiliang Tang, Wenbiao Ding, and Zitao Liu

Deep-Cross-Attention Recommendation Model for Knowledge Sharing
Micro Learning Service   168
    Jiayin Lin, Geng Sun, Jun Shen, David Pritchard, Tingru Cui,
    Dongming Xu, Li Li, Ghassan Beydoun, and Shiping Chen

Investigating the Role of Politeness in Human-Human Online Tutoring   174
    Jionghao Lin, David Lang, Haoran Xie, Dragan Gašević,
    and Guanliang Chen

Raising Academic Performance in Socio-cognitive Conflict Learning
Through Gamification   180
    Zhou Long, Dehong Luo, Kai Kiu, Hongli Gao, Jing Qu,
    and Xiangen Hu

Towards Interpretable Deep Learning Models for Knowledge Tracing   185
   Yu Lu, Deliang Wang, Qinggang Meng, and Penghe Chen

Early Prediction of Success in MOOC from Video Interaction Features   191
   Boniface Mbouzao, Michel C. Desmarais, and Ian Shrier

Predicting Reading Comprehension from Constructed Responses:
Explanatory Retrievals as Stealth Assessment   197
   Kathryn S. McCarthy, Laura K. Allen, and Scott R. Hinze

An Approach to Model Children's Inhibition During Early Literacy
and Numeracy Acquisition   203
   Guilherme Medeiros Machado, Geoffray Bonnin, Sylvain Castagnos,
   Lara Hoareau, Aude Thomas, and Youssef Tazouti

Confrustion and Gaming While Learning with Erroneous Examples
in a Decimals Game   208
   Michael Mogessie, J. Elizabeth Richey, Bruce M. McLaren,
   Juan Miguel L. Andres-Bray, and Ryan S. Baker

Learning Outcomes and Their Relatedness Under Curriculum Drift   214
   Sneha Mondal, Tejas I. Dhamecha, Smriti Pathak, Red Mendoza,
   Gayathri K. Wijayarathna, Paul Gagnon, and Jan Carlstedt-Duke

Promoting Learning and Satisfaction of Children When Interacting
with an Emotional Companion to Program   220
   Elizabeth K. Morales-Urrutia, José Miguel Ocaña Ch.,
   Diana Pérez-Marín, and Celeste Pizarro-Romero

Automatic Grading System Using Sentence-BERT Network   224
   Ifeanyi G. Ndukwe, Chukwudi E. Amadi, Larian M. Nkomo,
   and Ben K. Daniel

Extended Multi-document Cohesion Network Analysis Centered
on Comprehension Prediction   228
   Bogdan Nicula, Cecile A. Perret, Mihai Dascalu,
   and Danielle S. McNamara

Supporting Empathy Training Through Virtual Patients   234
   Jennifer K. Olsen and Catharine Oertel

Generating Game Levels to Develop Computer Science Competencies
in Game-Based Learning Environments   240
   Kyungjin Park, Bradford Mott, Wookhee Min, Eric Wiebe,
   Kristy Elizabeth Boyer, and James Lester

An Evaluation of Data-Driven Programming Hints in a Classroom Setting . . .   246
Thomas W. Price, Samiha Marwan, Michael Winters,
and Joseph Jay Williams

Deep Knowledge Tracing with Transformers   252
Shi Pu, Michael Yudelson, Lu Ou, and Yuchi Huang

Relationships Between Body Postures and Collaborative Learning States
in an Augmented Reality Study   257
Iulian Radu, Ethan Tu, and Bertrand Schneider

Effect of Immediate Feedback on Math Achievement at the High
School Level   263
Renah Razzaq, Korinn S. Ostrow, and Neil T. Heffernan

Automated Prediction of Novice Programmer Performance Using
Programming Trajectories.   268
Miguel A. Rubio

Agent-in-the-Loop: Conversational Agent Support in Service of Reflection
for Learning During Collaborative Programming.   273
Sreecharan Sankaranarayanan, Siddharth Reddy Kandimalla,
Sahil Hasan, Haokang An, Christopher Bogart, R. Charles Murray,
Michael Hilton, Majd Sakr, and Carolyn Rosé

Toward an Automatic Speech Classifier for the Teacher.   279
Bahar Shahrokhian Ghahfarokhi, Avinash Sivaraman,
and Kurt VanLehn

Constructing Automated Revision Graphs: A Novel Visualization
Technique to Study Student Writing   285
Antonette Shibani

When Lying, Hiding and Deceiving Promotes Learning - A Case
for Augmented Intelligence with Augmented Ethics.   291
Björn Sjödén

Understanding Collaborative Question Posing During Computational
Modeling in Science   296
Caitlin Snyder, Nicole M. Hutchins, Gautam Biswas, Mona Emara,
Bernard Yett, and Shitanshu Mishra

Machine Learning and Student Performance in Teams   301
Rohan Ahuja, Daniyal Khan, Sara Tahir, Magdalene Wang,
Danilo Symonette, Shimei Pan, Simon Stacey, and Don Engel

Scanpath Analysis of Student Attention During Problem Solving
with Worked Examples   306
    Samantha Stranc and Kasia Muldner

Helping Teachers Assist Their Students in Gamified Adaptive Educational
Systems: Towards a Gamification Analytics Tool   312
    Kamilla Tenório, Geiser Chalco Challco, Diego Dermeval,
    Bruno Lemos, Pedro Nascimento, Rodrigo Santos,
    and Alan Pedro da Silva

Understanding Rapport over Multiple Sessions with a Social,
Teachable Robot   318
    Xiaoyi Tian, Nichola Lubold, Leah Friedman, and Erin Walker

Exercise Hierarchical Feature Enhanced Knowledge Tracing   324
    Hanshuang Tong, Yun Zhou, and Zhen Wang

Relationships Between Math Performance and Human Judgments
of Motivational Constructs in an Online Math Tutoring System   329
    Rurik Tywoniw, Scott A. Crossley, Jaclyn Ocumpaugh,
    Shamya Karumbaiah, and Ryan Baker

Automated Short-Answer Grading Using Deep Neural Networks
and Item Response Theory   334
    Masaki Uto and Yuto Uchida

Automatic Dialogic Instruction Detection for K-12 Online
One-on-One Classes   340
    Shiting Xu, Wenbiao Ding, and Zitao Liu

Exploring the Role of Perspective Taking in Educational
Child-Robot Interaction   346
    Elmira Yadollahi, Marta Couto, Wafa Johal, Pierre Dillenbourg,
    and Ana Paiva

Evaluating Student Learning in a Synchronous, Collaborative Programming
Environment Through Log-Based Analysis of Projects   352
    Bernard Yett, Nicole Hutchins, Caitlin Snyder, Ningyu Zhang,
    Shitanshu Mishra, and Gautam Biswas

Adaptive Forgetting Curves for Spaced Repetition Language Learning   358
    Ahmed Zaidi, Andrew Caines, Russell Moore, Paula Buttery,
    and Andrew Rice

Learning from Interpretable Analysis: Attention-Based
Knowledge Tracing   364
    Jia Zhu, Weihao Yu, Zetao Zheng, Changqin Huang, Yong Tang,
    and Gabriel Pui Cheong Fung

Industry and Innovation Papers

Identifying Beneficial Learning Behaviors from Large-Scale
Interaction Data   371
   Miruna Cristus, Oscar Täckström, Lingyi Tan, and Valentino Pacifici

A Gamified Solution to the Cold-Start Problem of Intelligent
Tutoring System   376
   Yang Pian, Yu Lu, Yuqi Huang, and Ig Ibert Bittencourt

Bridging Over from Learning Videos to Learning Resources Through
Automatic Keyword Extraction   382
   Cleo Schulten, Sven Manske, Angela Langner-Thiele,
   and H. Ulrich Hoppe

A Large-Scale, Open-Domain, Mixed-Interface Dialogue-Based ITS
for STEM   387
   Iulian Vlad Serban, Varun Gupta, Ekaterina Kochmar, Dung D. Vu,
   Robert Belfer, Joelle Pineau, Aaron Courville, Laurent Charlin,
   and Yoshua Bengio

Doctoral Consortium Papers

Contingent Scaffolding for System Safety Analysis   395
   Paul S. Brown, Anthony G. Cohn, Glen Hart, and Vania Dimitrova

The Exploration of Feeling of Difficulty Using Eye-Tracking
and Skin Conductance Response   400
   Chou Ching-En and Kaska Porayska-Pomsta

Sense of Agency in Times of Automation: A Teachers' Professional
Development Proposal on the Ethical Challenges of AI Applied
to Education   405
   Ana Mouta, Eva Torrecilla Sánchez, and Ana María Pinto Llorente

Improving Students' Problem-Solving Flexibility
in Non-routine Mathematics   409
   Huy A. Nguyen, Yuqing Guo, John Stamper, and Bruce M. McLaren

Workshop Papers

Optimizing Human Learning: Third International Workshop Eliciting
Adaptive Sequences for Learning (WASL 2020)   417
   Jill-Jênn Vie, Fabrice Popineau, Hisashi Kashima, and Benoît Choffin

Empowering Education with AI Technology – IEEE LTSC   420
   Robby Robson, Xiangen Hu, Jim Goodell, Michael Jay, and Brandt Redd

Second Workshop on Intelligent Textbooks 424
  Sergey Sosnovsky, Peter Brusilovsky, Richard G. Baraniuk,
  and Andrew S. Lan

2nd International Workshop on Education in Artificial Intelligence
K-12 (EduAI). 427
  Gerald Steinbauer, Sven Koenig, Fredrik Heintz, Julie Henry,
  Tara Chklovski, and Martin Kandlhofer

Author Index 431

Full Papers

Making Sense of Student Success and Risk Through Unsupervised Machine Learning and Interactive Storytelling

Ahmad Al-Doulat, Nasheen Nur, Alireza Karduni, Aileen Benedict,
Erfan Al-Hossami, Mary Lou Maher$^{(\boxtimes)}$, Wenwen Dou, Mohsen Dorodchi,
and Xi Niu

University of North Carolina at Charlotte, Charlotte NC, USA
{adoulat,nnur,akarduni,abenedi3,ealhossa,
m.maher,wdou1,mdorodch,xniu2}@uncc.edu

Abstract. This paper presents an interactive AI system to enable academic advisors and program leadership to understand the patterns of behavior related to student success and risk using data collected from institutional databases. We have worked closely with advisors in our development of an innovative temporal model of student data, unsupervised k-means algorithm on the data, and interactive user experiences with the data. We report on the design and evaluation of FIRST, Finding Interesting stoRies about STudents, that provides an interactive experience in which the advisor can: select relevant student features to be included in a temporal model, interact with a visualization of unsupervised learning that present patterns of student behavior and their correlation with performance, and to view automatically generated stories about individual students based on student data in the temporal model. We have developed a high fidelity prototype of FIRST using 10 years of student data in our College. As part of our iterative design process, we performed a focus group study with six advisors following a demonstration of the prototype. Our focus group evaluation highlights the sensemaking value in the temporal model, the unsupervised clusters of the behavior of all students in a major, and the stories about individual students.

Keywords: Sensemaking in learning analytics · Data storytelling · Unsupervised machine learning · Data visualization · Interactive user experience · Human-centered design

1 Introduction

As artificial intelligence in education becomes increasingly prominent, there is a growing need to consider augmented intelligence. This is the idea that artificial intelligence can and should be used to enhance human intelligence and

A. Al-Doulat and N. Nur—These authors contributed equally.

© Springer Nature Switzerland AG 2020
I. I. Bittencourt et al. (Eds.): AIED 2020, LNAI 12163, pp. 3–15, 2020.
https://doi.org/10.1007/978-3-030-52237-7_1

abilities rather than attempt to replace it. The 2016 National Artificial Intelligence Research and Development Strategic Plan stated that "the walls between humans and AI systems are slowly beginning to erode, with AI systems augmenting and enhancing human capabilities. Fundamental research is needed to develop effective methods for human-AI interaction and collaboration" [1]. Popenici and Kerr further emphasize the importance of recognizing education as a "human-centred endeavor" and the idea that "solely rely[ing] on technology is a dangerous path, and... that humans should identify problems, critique, identify risks, and ask important questions..." [2]. Therefore, we should take on a human-centered approach in the era of AI. Human centered AI is a viewpoint that AI systems and algorithms "must be designed with an awareness that they are part of a larger system involving humans" [3]. AI research should not just be technological, but humanistic and ethical as well [4]. One aspect of human-centered AI is to create systems that help humans understand the system itself [3]. Therefore, the goal is not simply to provide results through a black-box model. The focus is to help users understand those results and how those results are derived.

We explore sensemaking in Learning Analytics (LA) as an example of human-centered AI and present how we address this challenge for advisors that are presented with large amounts of data and analytics about their students. LA is an interdisciplinary field that emerged to make sense of unprecedented amounts of data collected by the extensive use of technology in education. LA brings together researchers and practitioners from two main fields: data mining and education [5]. Effective presentation of analytical results for decision making has been a major issue when dealing with large volumes of data in LA [6]. Many systems for early alerts on student performance provide results without providing necessary explanations as to how the system derived those results. If an early warning system gives a result that is inconsistent with the expectations of a teacher or an advisor, and there is no information to explain how the system arrived at the prediction, it can easily cause educators to discount or mistrust the prediction [7]. Human sensemaking relies on developing representations of knowledge to help serve a task, such as decision-making, and on the design of AI approaches to better aid these tasks. We discuss the design, implementation, and evaluation of an interactive system designed to help advisors better understand student success and risk. In contrast to many LA systems designed to support student awareness of their performance or to support teachers in understanding the students' performance in their courses, our interactive system is designed to support advisors and higher education leadership in making sense of students' success and risk in their degree programs. Our approach to interactive sensemaking has three main parts: (1) a temporal student data model, (2) data analytics based on unsupervised learning, and (3) storytelling about the student experience.

2   Related Work

In this section, we review related research in two interdisciplinary threads: (1) sensemaking in LA, and (2) data storytelling techniques.

2.1   Sensemaking in Learning Analytics

Sensemaking is process of understanding connections to anticipate their trajectories and to act effectively [8]. Van et al. [9] stated that sensemaking is a core component of LA dashboard interventions, as the purpose of these tools is to provide users with the ability to become aware of, reflect upon, and make data-based decisions. Echeverria et al. [6] proposed a learning design-driven data storytelling approach where they support user sensemaking by directing the user's attention to the critical features of the students' data using visualizations with data storytelling components. Their user study suggests that adding storytelling elements to the LA dashboards has the potential to help users make sense of the critical features of students' data with less effort. CALMSystem [10] is another example of a LA system that supports sensemaking, awareness, and reflection. It was developed on top of an intelligent tutoring system to give a learner insight into the learner model. Klein et al. [11] proposed a model of student sensemaking of LA dashboards to show how data and visualization inform user sensemaking and action. Verbert et al. [11] introduced a LA system for learners and teachers visualizing learning traces with four distinguished stages for the process model - (i) *awareness* is only concerned with the students' data presented using various visualizations, (ii) *reflection* focuses on usefulness and relevance of the queries by the users, (iii) *sensemaking* is concerned with users' responses in the reflection process and the creation of new insights, and (iv) *impact* is concerned with the induction of new meaning or changing behavior by the users. Additionally, researchers made contributions to better prediction and sensemaking of student progress trajectories. Learning Management Systems (LMSs) storing students' temporal data have been leveraged in various works to analyze students' progression throughout their whole program [12–16] and within a course level [12,17–19].

2.2   Sensemaking with Data Storytelling

Stories are capable of conveying essential information to users more naturally and familiarly for them [20]. Data storytelling aims to make data more understandable and memorable by human users by presenting data in the form of stories. Several research studies created natural language presentations of tabular or numeric data ranging from summarizing statistical results [21,22], stock market trends [23], and environmental data [24]. Many applications of Natural Language Generation (NLG) have been used to generate stories from data to promote the user sensemaking. Notable examples of tools that generate textual forecast from structured data include the Forecast Generator (FoG) [25], MUL-TIMETEO [26], and the SumTime system [27]. Such systems increase inter-pretability and reduce routine writing tasks performed by human forecasters. NLG is also used in medicine. TOPAZ [28], creates reports of blood cell and drug dosages for lymphoma patients. It uses a schema-based generation system that generates a textual report read by clinicians. Other systems that gener-ate medical reports include Suregen [29], Narrative Engine [30], and STOP [31]. These systems tend to facilitate the users' sensemaking of homogeneous data through brief textual summaries. FIRST is capable of generating stories to sup-port advisors' sensemaking of complex, temporal, and heterogeneous student data.

3   FIRST: Design and Implementation

The goal of FIRST is to better communicate analytics results by guiding the user through sensemaking tasks and interactive LA. Sensemaking tasks consist of information gathering, developing insights, and performing knowledge discovery [32]. In the sensemaking process, domain experts such as the educational leaders, teachers, and academic advisors decide on the existing challenges and expected outcomes for their institution. Most of the learning management tools involve data scientists in the knowledge discovery process to design the student data model, analytics approach, visualizations, and a reporting system to understand students' patterns of success or failure. Next, domain experts design intervention methods based on the analytics. The analytical process, essential to knowledge discovery, needs substantial data science skills. Domain experts do not engage in the discovery process since the analytical model is a black box to them. In FIRST, domain experts can select features from the temporal data model, see the stories about students, and explore which factors are major contributors to a student's performance and behaviors.

3.1   Interface Design

Our system is designed to allow advisors to engage in sensemaking by inter-acting with temporal data, reviewing aggregate analytics, and reading stories. Figure 1A shows the interface for the user to select the student features in the temporal model. The selected features are used when generating stories for each student. The user can change their preferred features at any point, which will consequently change the content of the stories. It is also possible for the system to automatically generate stories based on what it selects as the most appropri-ate features. However, allowing the user to select the features is important to sensemaking. Figure 1B shows the user experience with the results of unsuper-vised learning, and Fig. 1C shows the user experience for interacting with the automatic story generator. FIRST differs from existing LA tools in the following ways:

- The user can leverage their insights about student behavior and participate in model construction, giving them the flexibility to change the features to be used in the analytic models and automatically generated stories.
- The user is presented with automatically generated stories to complement the results from analytic models.

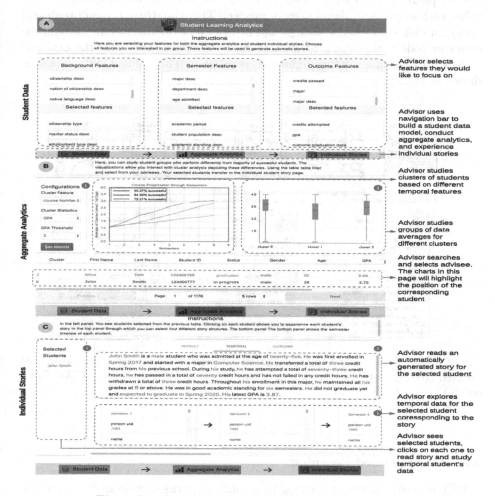

Fig. 1. Interface design for FIRST (Color figure online)

3.2 Temporal Data Model

FIRST uses a temporal data model that uses time segments to group heterogeneous sources of data and form sequences of information for each student [16].

This allows the analytic models to consider the temporal dependencies of students throughout their enrollment. The temporal model gives flexibility in defining the duration of the temporal node, contextualizing information within a node, and interpreting sequences of nodes as stories. The data model contains one sequence per student that starts with their enrollment and ends with when the student graduates or leaves the university. Each node in a sequence represents a period (e.g., a single semester) and contains a vector of features (variables, such as courses taken in that semester). There are three types of temporal nodes for each student: the background node with demographic information, the semester node with semester-wise activities and information, and the outcome node with the value of the performance variable. The student data model is shown in Fig. 2A.

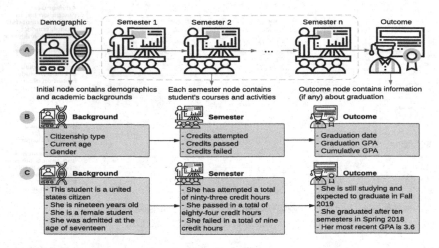

Fig. 2. Components for generating students' stories: (A) temporal data model, (B) selected student features, and (C) examples of sentences in the story (Color figure online)

3.3 Unsupervised Learning

FIRST uses unsupervised learning to identify patterns of student behavior and then maps that behavior onto performance. The user can select from options for the student performance variable, such as GPA, and can select filters to include a subset of the total population, such as male or female students or a period of time. Figure 1B shows the results of clustering all students according to their course progression with the performance variable of GPA, where 2.0 is a minimum value to be successful. Course progression is an example engineered temporal feature, which is the average value of the first digit of a course level for each semester. For example, if a student took three courses with levels 1200, 1212, and 3000 in his/her first semester, this feature will take a value of 1.7 (average of 1, 1, and 3) for the first semester. We then formed a 2D (two-dimensional) feature vector for each student in which each row has the values for one of the engineered features for each semester. We used the K-means clustering algorithm [33] on several engineered features and found that course progression, for example, was able to cluster students with high "purity" in terms of the defined outcome variable. We used the elbow method [34] to determine the optimal number of clusters. We analyzed each cluster to see if they were "coherent" in terms of student performance. For example, after we applied the K-means approach to the "course progression" feature, the result could separate the successful and risky student reasonably clearly. Our primary hypothesis for this feature is that it should be either increasing or steady along the semesters for those successful students. If it is decreasing or steady for a long time, the student did not progress to higher-level courses or the student was repeating lower-level courses.

Figure 1B presents the clustering results with 3 clusters for the engineered feature "Course Progression Through Semesters". In the blue cluster with 483 students, successful students are the most dominant with a percentage of 90.27%. As we see the intercept and the slope of this blue line in Fig. 1B, it has a higher average course level in each semester compared to the other two clusters. In addition, the average course level is consistently increasing. This suggests that this cluster of students consistently takes courses at a higher level and starts to progress early on. The green cluster also has a higher percentage of successful students than the orange cluster. If we compare their intercepts and slopes, the green line stays above the orange one and makes more "linear" progression than the orange counterpart. In this analysis, we define student success as obtaining the final GPA last semester higher than 2.0. If we changed the GPA threshold, the clustering results would be different. The user can select each cluster and further review the data for each student who belongs to that cluster. The bar chart shows the average GPA for each cluster. The user can select an individual student or groups of students in the analytic interface and review their temporal data. The selected students in exploring the analytic results are saved and available on the storytelling page.

We use clustering since more students are successful than unsuccessful:: a supervised learning approach could overfit and impose an accuracy paradox due to a higher number of majority class examples caused by the imbalance. Equalizing class membership by adjusting the within-class imbalance and using random sampling can introduce unrealistic patterns in the data [35]. We use clustering to separate and classify samples. The clustering results provide insight into the engineered features that discriminate on percentages of successful students compared to students at risk. This classification describes characteristics of cohorts of students and how they behave in the clusters. In the future, we will consider a guided re-sampling and classification method to overcome over-fitting. For this reason we adopted an unsupervised clustering approach to find patterns of student behavior that map onto success criteria. In the future, we plan to incorporate the cluster results into a predictive model to apply our knowledge about patterns of behavior in cohorts of students to develop early alerts or predictions for individual students.

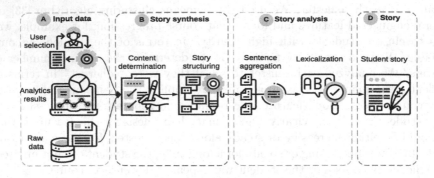

Fig. 3. Process of story generation

3.4   Student Stories

FIRST automatically generates stories for each student using the features selected in the temporal data model. These stories present a summary of the student's experience in a narrative. Figure 1C shows the user experience for interacting with the student stories. When the user selects a student from the left panel, the timeline and story sections are updated. The storytelling algorithm uses user-selected and standard features. The stories are generated from the data in the temporal model shown in Fig. 2. Figure 2A shows the nodes in the temporal data model, Fig. 2B shows the features selected from each node, and Fig. 2C shows the sentences that are constructed from each feature. The text in black is from a predefined template while the text in red is generated from the features. After generating the sentences for each of the selected features, these sentences are used to generate the story as discussed below. An example of a generated story can be shown in Fig. 1C. Figure 3 illustrates the 3 stages in the process of generating stories: raw data source and user selection inputs, story synthesis, and story analysis. We describe each stage of story generation.

Data Source. As shown in Fig. 3A, the input data for story generation comprises: (i) features in the temporal data model, (ii) the results of the analytics, and (iii) the user selected features and outcome. The features in the data model are used in a set of predefined template rules, the analytics results are used to compare the current student with other similar students, and the user-selected variables are used to make the story more customized for the user.

Story Synthesis. The goal of this stage is to determine and sort the content presented in the student's story. As shown in Fig. 3B, synthesis has two tasks: content determination and story structuring.

- Content Determination: this is the task of choosing what is included in the story. The selection is based on these factors:
  - user-selected features: we include the features selected by the user as illustrated in Fig. 1A.
  - performance rules: we identified a set of rules that either inspect any sudden changes of the students' performance over time (e.g., A student's GPA suddenly dropped or increased), or abnormal information compared to most students (e.g., the number of attempted, passed, or failed courses for a semester is higher, or the number of D-scored courses is higher).
  - comparison with other similar students: we used clusters to look for students that are similar and successful to inspect if the student per se is an outlier in terms of some variables.
- Story Structuring: this is the task of deciding the order of information in which it is presented to the reader. We order the information based on the student temporal data model, in which the story starts with the background information about the student, then with the semester information, and ends with the outcome information.

Story Analysis. This stage improves the language of the stories so they are more human-readable and coherent. As shown in Fig. 3C, this includes 2 tasks: sentence aggregation and lexicalization.

- Sentence Aggregation: Clusters multiple pieces of the same kind of information together into a single sentence instead of several ones. For instance, if we have a set of candidate sentences as "student achieved an A in the course X", and "student achieved B in course Y", these sentences should be aggregated into one sentence "student maintained all his grades at B or above".
- Lexicalization and Linguistic Realization: Lexicalization is choosing the proper words and phrases to transform the data into natural language text. Linguistic realization is inserting punctuation, functional words and other elements required for the text to be fluid and coherent.

4 User Study - Focus Group

A focus group study was conducted with the goal of learning what users find important in a tool to support advising. In the focus group session, we demonstrated FIRST and then asked questions about the value of the student data model, analytics, and storytelling. We recruited six professional and faculty advisors whom are already familiar with multiple tools that provide data, analytics, and risk scores for the students that they advise. A focus group study was selected for its effectiveness in collecting user opinions and attitudes through group discussion and dynamic conversations. Some preliminary questions were asked to collect information related to the current technology used during advising and the useful features of those tools. The participants revealed that they often ignored the risk score provided by the analytics in their advising tool because the process behind the calculation is not clear to them. They mentioned that although the student reports generated by the existing tool were useful, they would like more flexibility to customize the information for different cohorts of students. The group discussed that one goal for such tools is to be prepared for advising before the student arrives for the advising appointment. FIRST was demonstrated to the group with scenarios for specific students. The participants asked questions about the system and the facilitator demonstrated additional interactive features. Then the participants were asked to answer questions to assess the sensemaking they performed through the demonstration: (i) What insights were you able to gain about students through viewing this tool? (ii) What are the differences between what you learned about the students from the analytics versus the stories? (iii) What is the value of the analytics results and the stories? (v) How can the student stories help you with advising? And (vi) Can you think of other good predictors(features) of student success? Two researchers reviewed the transcript and identified emerging themes independently and through discussion they agreed on three higher-level themes. These three high-level themes were then used to revisit and code the transcript according to the themes.

- **Selecting Features for Student Models:** Participants appreciated that they could select the features they thought should be part of a predictive model of risk or part of the student story. They also like a number of features that were included, such as students' financial need status, family life, housing options, and mailing addresses. Many expressed surprise that the University actually had a lot of data that would be useful for advising that was not available in the other tools.
- **Value of Aggregate Analytics and Temporal Data:** Participants agreed that aggregate analytics is essential for understanding students, especially a targeted group of students. They found the presentation of the student data as a temporal progression is useful since it presents the overall students' progression through semesters.
- **Value of Student Stories:** The participants agreed that student stories were useful and effective to provide a high-level overview or snapshot of the student. They mentioned that the stories would be helpful for understanding a specific student quickly. They agreed that stories provide a good understanding of students in terms of their demographic information as well as their academic performance. One participant said: "I like the stories the best - knowing that the story was created using analytics is reassuring". One comment to extend FIRST is the suggestion to tell stories about groups of students that lie in a single cluster.

5   Conclusions and Future Work

In this paper, we present FIRST, an interactive LA system designed to support advisors using a temporal data model, unsupervised models, and storytelling. FIRST enables the advisor to select specific features, review the aggregate analytics based on unsupervised learning algorithms, and interact with stories about specific students. The student stories are automatically generated using user-selected features, the features that indicate significant changes, and additional data about the student using rules that present a more complete story. The process for generating stories has 3 stages: sourcing the data, selecting and structuring story components, and text-processing the sentences. A focus group study was conducted to evaluate FIRST and gather feedback. The participants highlighted the sensemaking value of storytelling and the increased access to student data compared to other tools. The aggregate analysis was reported to be enhanced by the storytelling since the user can switch between the story and the visual analytics. The results of the focus group confirm our hypothesis that storytelling complements dashboard-style analytics. In the future, we plan to do a longitudinal study of the use of FIRST to learn more about the changes in the advisors' understanding of their students with and without FIRST.

References

1. Strategic Plan: The national artificial intelligence research and development strategic plan (2016)
2. Popenici, S.A.D., Kerr, S.: Exploring the impact of artificial intelligence on teaching and learning in higher education. Res. Pract. Technol. Enhanc. Learn. **12**(1), 1–13 (2017). https://doi.org/10.1186/s41039-017-0062-8
3. Riedl, M.O.: Human-centered artificial intelligence and machine learning. Hum. Behav. Emerg. Technol. **1**(1), 33–36 (2019)
4. Xu, W.: Toward human-centered AI: a perspective from human-computer interaction. Interactions **26**(4), 42–46 (2019)
5. Gašević, D., Kovanović, V., Joksimović, S.: Piecing the learning analytics puzzle: a consolidated model of a field of research and practice. Learn.: Res. Pract. **3**(1), 63–78 (2017)
6. Echeverria, V., Martinez-Maldonado, R., Granda, R., Chiluiza, K., Conati, C., Shum, S.B.: Driving data storytelling from learning design. In: Proceedings of the 8th International Conference on Learning Analytics and Knowledge, pp. 131–140 (2018)
7. Murphy, R.F.: Artificial intelligence applications to support k-1 2 teachers and teaching. RAND Corporation (2019). https://doi.org/10.7249/PE315
8. Klein, G., Moon, B., Hoffman, R.R.: Making sense of sensemaking 2: a macrocognitive model. IEEE Intell. Syst. **21**(5), 88–92 (2006)
9. Van Harmelen, M., Workman, D.: Analytics for learning and teaching. CETIS Anal. Ser. **1**(3), 1–40 (2012)
10. Kerly, A., Ellis, R., Bull, S.: CALMsystem: a conversational agent for learner modelling. In: Ellis, R., Allen, T., Petridis, M. (eds.) Applications and Innovations in Intelligent Systems XV, pp. 89–102. Springer, London (2008). https://doi.org/10.1007/978-1-84800-086-5_7
11. Verbert, K., Duval, E., Klerkx, J., Govaerts, S., Santos, J.L.: Learning analytics dashboard applications. Am. Behav. Sci. **57**(10), 1500–1509 (2013)
12. Arnold, K.E., Pistilli, M.D.: Course signals at Purdue: using learning analytics to increase student success. In: Proceedings of the 2nd International Conference on Learning Analytics and Knowledge, pp. 267–270 (2012)

13. Essa, A., Ayad, H.: Student success system: risk analytics and data visualization using ensembles of predictive models. In: Proceedings of the 2nd International Conference on Learning Analytics and Knowledge, pp. 158–161 (2012)
14. Chui, K.T., Fung, D.C.L., Lytras, M.D., Lam, T.M.: Predicting at-risk university students in a virtual learning environment via a machine learning algorithm. Comput. Hum. Behav. **107**, 105584 (2018)
15. Nur, N., et al.: Student network analysis: a novel way to predict delayed graduation in higher education. In: Isotani, S., Millán, E., Ogan, A., Hastings, P., McLaren, B., Luckin, R. (eds.) AIED 2019. LNCS (LNAI), vol. 11625, pp. 370–382. Springer, Cham (2019). https://doi.org/10.1007/978-3-030-23204-7_31
16. Mahzoon, M.J., Maher, M.L., Eltayeby, O., Dou, W., Grace, K.: A sequence data model for analyzing temporal patterns of student data. J. Learn. Anal. **5**(1), 55–74 (2018)
17. Wolff, A., Zdrahal, Z., Herrmannova, D., Kuzilek, J., Hlosta, M.: Developing predictive models for early detection of at-risk students on distance learning modules (2014)
18. Choi, S.P.M., Lam, S.S., Li, K.C., Wong, B.T.M.: Learning analytics at low cost: at-risk student prediction with clicker data and systematic proactive interventions. J. Educ. Technol. Soc. **21**(2), 273–290 (2018)
19. Romero, C., Ventura, S., García, E.: Data mining in course management systems: Moodle case study and tutorial. Comput. Educ. **51**(1), 368–384 (2008)
20. Nakasone, A., Ishizuka, M.: Storytelling ontology model using RST. In: Proceedings of the IEEE/WIC/ACM International Conference on Intelligent Agent Technology, pp. 163–169. IEEE Computer Society (2006)
21. Ferres, L., Parush, A., Roberts, S., Lindgaard, G.: Helping people with visual impairments gain access to graphical information through natural language: the *iGraph* system. In: Miesenberger, K., Klaus, J., Zagler, W.L., Karshmer, A.I. (eds.) ICCHP 2006. LNCS, vol. 4061, pp. 1122–1130. Springer, Heidelberg (2006). https://doi.org/10.1007/11788713_163
22. Iordanskaja, L., Kim, M., Kittredge, R., Lavoie, B., Polguere, A.: Generation of extended bilingual statistical reports. In: COLING 1992 Volume 3: The 15th International Conference on Computational Linguistics (1992)
23. Kukich, K.: Design of a knowledge-based report generator. In: Proceedings of the 21st Annual Meeting on Association for Computational Linguistics, pp. 145–150. Association for Computational Linguistics (1983)
24. Bohnet, B., Lareau, F., Wanner, L., et al.: Automatic production of multilingual environmental information. EnviroInfo **2**, 59–66 (2007)
25. Goldberg, E., Driedger, N., Kittredge, R.I.: Using natural-language processing to produce weather forecasts. IEEE Expert **9**(2), 45–53 (1994)
26. Coch, J.: Interactive generation and knowledge administration in MultiMeteo. In: Proceedings of the 9th International Workshop on Natural Language Generation, INLG 1998, August 1998
27. Sripada, S., Reiter, E., Davy, I.: Sumtime-Mousam: configurable marine weather forecast generator. Expert Update **6**(3), 4–10 (2003)
28. Kahn, M.G., Fagan, L.M., Sheiner, L.B.: Combining physiologic models and symbolic methods to interpret time-varying patient data. Methods Inf. Med. **30**(03), 167–178 (1991)
29. Hüske-Kraus, D.: Suregen-2: a shell system for the generation of clinical documents. In: Demonstrations (2003)

30. Harris, M.D.: Building a large-scale commercial NLG system for an EMR. In: Proceedings of the Fifth International Natural Language Generation Conference, pp. 157–160 (2008)
31. Reiter, E., Robertson, R., Osman, L.M.: Lessons from a failure: generating tailored smoking cessation letters. Artif. Intell. **144**(1–2), 41–58 (2003)
32. Russell, D.M., Stefik, M.J., Pirolli, P., Card, S.K.: The cost structure of sensemaking. In: Proceedings of the INTERACT 1993 and CHI 1993 Conference on Human Factors in Computing Systems, pp. 269–276 (1993)
33. MacQueen, J., et al.: Some methods for classification and analysis of multivariate observations. In: Proceedings of the Fifth Berkeley Symposium on Mathematical Statistics and Probability, Oakland, CA, USA, vol. 1, pp. 281–297 (1967)
34. Ng, A.: Clustering with the k-means algorithm. Mach. Learn. (2012)
35. Nickerson, A., Japkowicz, N., Milios, E.E.: Using unsupervised learning to guide resampling in imbalanced data sets. In: AISTATS (2001)

Strategies for Deploying Unreliable AI Graders in High-Transparency High-Stakes Exams

Sushmita Azad[✉], Binglin Chen, Maxwell Fowler, Matthew West, and Craig Zilles

University of Illinois at Urbana-Champaign, Urbana, IL 61801, USA
{sazad2,chen386,mfowler5,mwest,zilles}@illinois.edu

Abstract. We describe the deployment of an imperfect NLP-based automatic short answer grading system on an exam in a large-enrollment introductory college course. We characterize this deployment as both high stakes (the questions were on an mid-term exam worth 10% of students' final grade) and high transparency (the question was graded interactively during the computer-based exam and correct solutions were shown to students that could be compared to their answer). We study two techniques designed to mitigate the potential student dissatisfaction resulting from students incorrectly not granted credit by the imperfect AI grader. We find (1) that providing multiple attempts can eliminate first-attempt false negatives at the cost of additional false positives, and (2) that students not granted credit from the algorithm cannot reliably determine if their answer was mis-scored.

Keywords: Automatic short answer grading · Computer-based exams · Transparency · Code reading · CS1 · EiPE

1 Introduction

Workplace demand for computing skills [19] has led to large enrollments in introductory programming classes [6]. These courses, however, have had historically large failure rates [2,29]. Some evidence suggests that this is due to a premature emphasis on code writing instead of reading-oriented activities [4,14,32]. One important reading skill is the ability to describe the high-level behavior of code [14,17,18,31]. Questions to assess this skill—"Explain in Plain English" (EiPE) questions—aren't widely utilized due to the workload of manually grading natural language responses. Figure 1(A) shows an example prompt of one of our EipE questions.

In this work, we describe our initial efforts in deploying an NLP-based AI grader for EiPE questions and our transition from low-stakes to high-stakes environments. Initially, simple NLP-based AI graders were trained using a small amount of survey data collected from course teaching assistants and upper-level undergraduate computer science students. These simple AI graders were

© Springer Nature Switzerland AG 2020
I. I. Bittencourt et al. (Eds.): AIED 2020, LNAI 12163, pp. 16–28, 2020.
https://doi.org/10.1007/978-3-030-52237-7_2

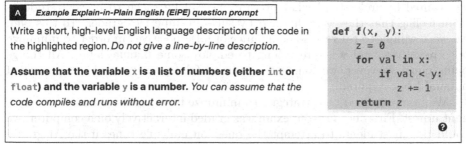

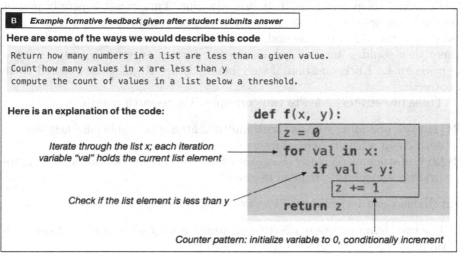

Fig. 1. An example mid-semester automated EiPE exercise (A) in a Python-based intro CS course. After a student submits their answer, they are shown example solutions (B) so that they can learn. Non-trivial code fragments are deconstructed so as to show the correspondence between the code and the natural language description.

deployed in a low-stakes homework context for which we had two goals: 1) we wanted students to improve their ability to provide natural language descriptions of code, so we provided both immediate correct/incorrect feedback and example correct answers as shown in Fig. 1(B) and 2) we wanted to collect additional training data which could be used to train improved NLP-based AI graders.

Positive results with the homework deployment emboldened us to deploy our AI grader on an exam. To our knowledge, this deployment is unique in the research literature for (imperfect) AI-based graders because it was both high stakes—this question was on one of three midterm exams each worth 10% of students' final grades—and high transparency—the question was graded interactively and students are shown correct answers in a way that permits them to evaluate their submitted answer in light of the correct answers.

A high-stakes, high-visibility deployment of an imperfect AI grader, if not well managed, has the potential for student dissatisfaction on a large scale. As such, we wanted to understand what precautions can be taken to prevent students from feeling that they were harmed by such an imperfect grader. To this end, we were willing to tolerate some number of false positives in order to minimize false negatives, and we were willing to employ some manual labor. All things being equal, however, we sought to minimize false positives and the amount of manual labor required.

We brain-stormed two strategies to minimize false negatives and, hence, student unrest. First, because our exam was graded interactively on a computer, we could permit students to attempt the question multiple times if the AI grader didn't award them credit on their first attempt. This would hopefully permit students to re-word their answers into a form that could receive credit automatically from the algorithm. Second, we could provide students an *appeal system* where they could, after they are shown the correct answer, request a manual re-grade for an EiPE question, if they believed the AI grader had scored them incorrectly.

These two strategies led to two corresponding research questions:

RQ1: Does providing students with multiple attempts enable false negatives to earn credit without manual intervention?

RQ2: Can students correctly recognize when the AI grader has failed and appropriately appeal for a manual re-grade?

Our findings can be summarized as follows:

1. The two techniques were effective at avoiding large-scale student dissatisfaction.
2. Re-training the AI grader using student responses drawn from the homework deployment improved the accuracy from 83.4% to 88.8%.
3. Providing three attempts (at full credit) enabled all first-attempt false negatives to automatically earn credit from the algorithm. It did, however, have the consequence of yielding additional false positives.
4. Appeals were useful for morale, but were not effective for distinguishing false negatives from true negatives.
5. Students' perception of the grading accuracy of our NLP-based AI grader was lower than that of deterministically-correct auto-graders for true/false, multiple-choice, and programming questions, but only to a modest degree.

This paper is structured as follows. Section 2 briefly reviews related work. Section 3 describes our data collection and AI grader training, while Sect. 4 reviews the AI grader's performance and results. We conclude in Sect. 5.

2   Related Work

Automatic grading of free response questions is largely split into two areas of focus: automatic short answer grading (ASAG) and automatic essay scoring (AES). We review briefly the recent work in both areas below.

A review of recent, competitive machine learning ASAG shows only 11% of ASAG papers were focused on computer science [11]. Most of the recent studies are laboratory studies or model evaluations on public or sample data sets [11,16,20,22,25,26,33]. The closest to a high-stakes course exam featured automatic grading for *very short answer*—defined as four or less words— questions, but in a not-for-credit exam-like context rather than on a for-credit exam [23]. The Educational Testing Services (ETS) C-rater is deployed for some ETS standardized exams, but is not high-transparency and focuses on concept mapping [13,24]. ASAG feature selection includes lexical, semantic, syntactic, morphological, and surface features [3,11,26]. Most recently, dialog based systems and intelligent tutoring systems [20,22,25] and end-to-end models have been used for ASAG [16,33]. To our knowledge, no ASAG work has reported on the deployment of AI graders in a high-stakes, high-transparency environment like ours.

AES work is more familiar with high-stakes environments. The ETS E-rater receives yearly updates and is used in both high-stakes settings like the GRE and low-stakes such as the SAT online test [21]. However, these systems are not high-transparency as students are provided no means to judge the validity of their scores and there is no process to contest scores. Further, AES' major impact is reduction of human labor, with the evaluation of essays focusing broadly on how essay features correlate to human-grader provided marks rather than specific content grading [12]. Recent AES approaches include GLMMs [8], autoencoders [7], statistical classifiers [15], and various deep-learning neural network approaches [1,9,10,27].

3 Methods

In Fall 2019, we developed and deployed automated EiPE questions in an introductory CS course for non-technical majors at a large U.S. university. This 600-student course introduces basic principles of programming in both Python and Excel to a population largely without any prior programming experience. The course was approaching gender balance with 246 women and 355 men.

We constructed our EiPE AI graders using logistic regression on bigram features. These graders were initially trained with minimal data from a series of surveys. Each survey asked participants to provide two correct responses and two plausible incorrect responses for each of the EiPE questions. These surveys were completed by the course's instructor and TAs and a collection of upper-level CS students who were compensated with an Amazon gift card for each survey. These surveys resulted in approximately 100–200 responses per question. Survey data was manually reviewed by a research team member to perform any necessary re-categorization of the responses.

This survey-data-trained AI grader was deployed on four homework assignments during the first half of the semester. The questions were deployed using the PrairieLearn [30] online learning platform, the course's primary assessment system. Each assignment included a pool of 10–12 EiPE questions, and each time a student attempted a question they were given a random draw from the pool. To tolerate the AI grader's inaccuracy in this low-stakes, formative context, students could attempt the activity as many times as they wanted; points were granted for any correct answers with no penalty for incorrect answers. As such, any false negatives would only delay (rather than prevent) students from getting points. Furthermore, the AI graded EiPE questions were one of many activities on the students' weekly assignment, and they could ignore the activity completely and earn the week's homework points through answering other questions instead.

We next deployed the auto-graded EiPE questions as one of 24 questions on a proctored, computer-based mid-term exam in the 12th week of the course (also run using PrairieLearn). We selected the pool of EiPE questions deployed on the homework during the 5th week of the course. Prior to deployment, two members of the research team manually labeled the students' homework responses to these questions and used as additional training data to improve the grader. The AI graders deployed on the exam were trained with 500–600 labeled responses per question.

Four of the problems in the pool were not included on the exam because they exhibited a noticeable difference in difficulty from the rest. Students were randomly assigned one of the remaining eight problems. Students were given three attempts to submit a correct answer, receiving correct/incorrect feedback on each submission and were shown correct answers (as shown in Fig. 1(B)) once all attempts had been used or their answer was scored as correct.

The students submitted a total of 1,140 responses. After the exam was completed, for the purpose of this research, two members of the research team familiar with the course content independently scored each response without knowing the AI grader's score. For any responses where these two scores matched, the score was considered the final ground truth. Final ground truth for the remaining responses was established by a process of discussion and reconciliation between both scorers and a third research team member until consensus was reached. Necessary grade corrections were made for all students who had incorrectly been denied credit. All further analysis in this paper has been done on this set of 1,140 auto-graded exam responses.

To understand how students perceived the accuracy of auto-graded EiPE questions as compared to other types of auto-graded questions, we asked students to fill out a survey in the week after the exam with the EiPE question. Using a 1–5 Likert scale, students were asked: "For each type of question, rate it based on how reliably accurate you feel the grading for that kind of question is".

4   Results

Comparing AI Grader and Human Performance. 51% of students had their EiPE question scored as correct by the reconciled human graders, and the AI grader achieved an accuracy of 89%, with a 12% False Positive (FP) rate and a 9% False Negative (FN) rate. We used Cohen's kappa to compare the inter-rater reliability of humans and the AI grader. Cohen's kappa between the two experienced human graders was 0.83 ("almost perfect" agreement [28]) and between the AI grader and the ground truth (reconciled human graders) was 0.74 ("substantial" agreement [28]).

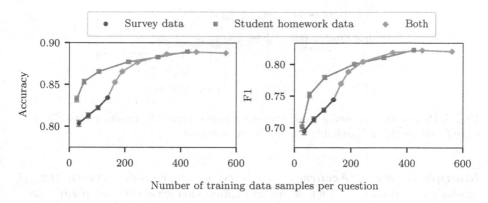

Fig. 2. The performance of the AI grader on the 1,140 exam responses when trained on different combinations of data with different sample sizes.

AI Grader Accuracy Versus Amount of Training Data. To understand how much training data is needed for obtaining a reasonable AI grader and whether there is a qualitative difference between survey data and student homework data, we trained graders with different subsamples of data and show the mean of the grader's performance in Fig. 2. There are three main sources of training data: (1) a subset of the survey data, (2) a subset of the student homework data, and (3) both, meaning all of the survey data and a subset of the student homework data. Although more data consistently lead to better performance, the student homework data seems qualitatively better than survey data, suggesting that the course staff and senior students creating the survey data were only somewhat able to generate realistic training data.

Student Perceptions of Accuracy. Students perceived the grading of AI graded EiPE questions as being less accurate than that of other kinds of questions to a statistically significant degree ($p < 0.001$). Compared to the next-lowest question type (programming), code-reading questions were $d = 0.48$ standard deviations lower, a "medium" effect size [5]. Mean Likert scores for each type of question are shown in Fig. 3 with 95% confidence intervals. We failed to find any correlation between students' perception of the EiPE AI grader and whether it mis-graded their answers on the exam. Instead, a student's perception of accuracy for all kinds of questions is weakly correlated with the student's performance on that kind of question (mean $r = 0.22$).

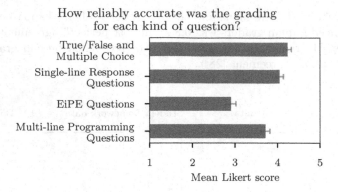

Fig. 3. Responses to a survey question auto-grader accuracy by question type. Choices were from 1 = "Very Unreliable" to 5 = "Very Accurate".

Multiple-Attempt Accuracy. We need to differentiate between the AI grader's performance on a single student submission versus the net performance over all student submissions to a question. To describe the latter, we define the *Multi-Attempt-k* outcomes as shown in Table 1. Whenever we use terms like *False Positive (FP)* without the prefix of "Multi-Attempt", we are referring to the performance on a single-submission level.

Table 1. Definitions of "multi-attempt" terminology.

Term	Definition
Multi-Attempt-k True Positive	Within the first k attempts, student submits at least one correct answer and AI grader awards points for some submission
Multi-Attempt-k False Positive	Within the first k attempts, student submits no correct answer but the AI grader awards points for some submission

We visualized how multiple attempts impact the performance metrics in Fig. 4. We see that as students attempted the question more times (moving from MA-1 to MA-3), the true positive rate increased somewhat (93.2% to 97.7%), but at the expense of a substantially higher multi-attempt false positive rate (14.9% to 32.9%). The reference ROC curve is for the AI grader evaluated on only the first-attempt responses, and we see that the multi-attempt performance is always worse than this.

Trajectories with Multiple Attempts. Figure 5 shows the trajectories students took through the multiple attempts at the EiPE questions. This reveals several features. First, all students who were falsely graded as incorrect (FN) on

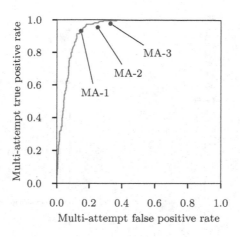

Fig. 4. Multi-attempt AI grader performance (MA-k) using only the first k attempts (see Table 1). The blue ROC curve is for the AI grader on the first-attempt data only. (Color figure online)

the first attempt were able to use the multiple attempts to eventually be graded as correct (as TP or FP). A majority (73%) of these students needed a second attempt to be graded correct, and only 27% needed three attempts. Second, students who were falsely graded as incorrect (FN) re-attempted the question at a higher rate than students who were truly graded as incorrect (TN) (100% versus 96%, $p = 0.013$). Third, the ratio of falsely-graded incorrects (FN) to truly-graded incorrects (TN) decreased as students used more attempts (4.7% to 3.2%, $p = 0.015$).

Strategies with Multiple Attempts. Students marked as incorrect by the AI grader on either first or second attempt deployed two correction strategies: (1) *reword*, where students rephrased their previous answer, and (2) *change*, where students submitted a response different in meaning from their previous answer. Figure 6 plots the paths through these strategies taken by the student population. From a standpoint of strategy *selection*, we see that students who had an actually-correct answer (FN) used the reword strategy at a higher rate than students who did not (TN) (57% vs 42%, $p = 0.022$). Considering strategy *effectiveness*, we observe that for FN students the reword strategy was more successful for receiving points than the change strategy, but not significantly so (75% versus 25%, $p = 0.22$), whereas for TN students the change strategy was significantly more effective (81% vs 19%, $p = 0.036$).

Appeals to Human Graders. Out of the 203 students who were graded as incorrect by the AI grader, 69 appealed for a human re-grade and 4 of these were truly correct (rate of 5.8%). Among those that did not appeal, 3 were truly

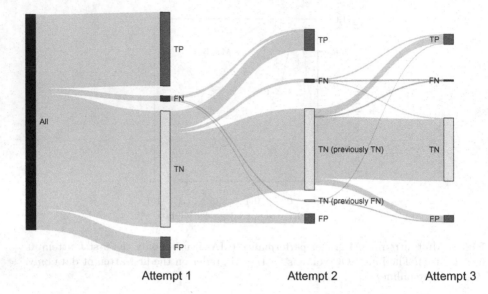

Fig. 5. Trajectories of all students through multiple attempts of the AI graded questions. Students who were scored as correct by the AI grader, either truly (TP) or falsely (FP), do not attempt further.

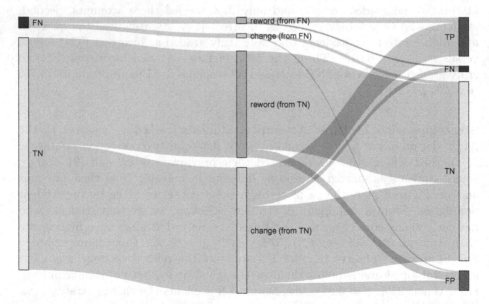

Fig. 6. Strategy selection and effectiveness after a submission was graded as incorrect. There was no significant dependence on attempt number, so this figure collapses all attempts together.

correct (2.2%). The difference in rates of true-correctness was not statistically significant between students who appealed and those that did not ($p = 0.20$).

5 Discussion and Conclusion

These initial results suggest automatically grading "Explain in plain English" (EiPE) questions may be a simpler task than other ASAG contexts. Even using just bigrams, our results (accuracy of 88.78%) are competitive with other ASAG results using much more sophisticated algorithms. We believe that this high accuracy is the result of specific elements of disciplinary vocabulary (e.g., "count", "even") being effective markers of when students have correct answers.

It is not surprising that the student homework responses were more effective than survey data for training the algorithm to predict student exam responses. The surveys did enable us to deploy the algorithm in the low stakes homework context to collect that homework training data, but our conclusion is that we could get by with fewer survey responses, especially if we were to quickly score early homework responses and re-train the model.

While students' perception of accuracy of our NLP model was statistically significantly below their perceptions of accuracy for the other question types, we were surprised by how small the difference in perceptions was. In our minds, the deterministic autograders and our NLP model are categorically different things. The students rated the deterministic autograders much lower than we anticipated (means near 4 out of 5) and the NLP model only $d = 0.48$ standard deviations below the deterministic autograders.

While the answer to RQ1—does providing students with multiple attempts enable false negatives to earn credit without manual intervention?—is yes, there are a number of caveats. First, while all first attempt FN students automatically earned credit on subsequent attempts, a few did so through submitting FP answers, which will potentially hinder those students' learning. Second, rather than merely reword their answer, many students used the multiple attempts to submit conceptually different answers. That is, while FN students primarily used the multiple-attempt feature to rephrase their answer for clarity (as intended by us), TN students appear to be aware that they don't know the answer, and used the multiple-attempt feature as a way to take more "shots in the dark", changing their answer in the hope that they'd strike the correct response and gain credit. Because some of these "shots" resulted in FP, giving students multiple attempts negatively impacted the FP rate.

This distinction between rewording and changing answers is important, because they have different implications on how much credit a student should receive. A student whose answer was correct, but needed rewording to be accepted by the algorithm, presumably deserves full credit. In contrast, a student that hedges by changing their answer on each submission, probably has a more fragile understanding and may deserve only partial credit. If we were to use multiple attempts again, we would probably: 1) provide only two attempts, since the majority of FNs were able to self correct within by their second try, and 2) have a small penalty (10–30%) for credit earned on a second attempt. That said, in our current implementation providing a single attempt and just shifting the implementation along its ROC curve may provide a better FN/FP trade-off.

The answer to RQ2—can students correctly recognize when the AI grader has failed and appropriately appeal for a manual re-grade?—appears to be no. Students that appealed had a statistically equivalent rate of being correct as the whole population of students that didn't earn credit from the algorithm. Relying on students to self report appears to be an inequitable strategy that rewards "noisier" students. One important caveat is that appeals were evaluated in a context with multiple attempts; appeals could be more useful in a single-attempt context where more FNs are present.

In short, in this first report on strategies for deploying imperfect AI graders in high stakes, high visibility contexts, we found that our strategies were ultimately successful. There was no obvious student discontent and only 0.5% (3 out of 600) of students would have incorrectly not received credit (FN) had we not manually scored all responses. While our strategy was passable, there remains a lot of opportunity for improvement. Because perfect auto-graders will not be achievable for many important problems, it is important to explore hybrid AI/human systems that can mitigate algorithmic shortcomings with minimal manual effort.

Acknowledgments. This work was partially supported by NSF DUE-1347722, NSF CMMI-1150490, NSF DUE-1915257, and the College of Engineering at the University of Illinois at Urbana-Champaign under the Strategic Instructional Initiatives Program (SIIP).

References

1. Alikaniotis, D., Yannakoudakis, H., Rei, M.: Automatic text scoring using neural networks. In: Proceedings of the 54th Annual Meeting of the Association for Computational Linguistics (Volume 1: Long Papers), pp. 715–725 (2016)
2. Bennedsen, J., Caspersen, M.E.: Failure rates in introductory programming. SIGCSE Bull. **39**(2), 32–36 (2007). https://doi.org/10.1145/1272848.1272879
3. Burrows, S., Gurevych, I., Stein, B.: The eras and trends of automatic short answer grading. Int. J. Artif. Intell. Educ. **25**(1), 60–117 (2014). https://doi.org/10.1007/s40593-014-0026-8
4. Clancy, M.J., Linn, M.C.: Patterns and pedagogy. In: The Proceedings of the Thirtieth SIGCSE Technical Symposium on Computer Science Education, SIGCSE 1999, pp. 37–42. ACM, New York (1999). https://doi.org/10.1145/299649.299673
5. Cohen, J.: Statistical Power Analysis for the Behavioral Sciences, 2nd edn. Routledge, Abingdon (1988)
6. Computing Research Association: Generation CS: Computer Science Undergraduate Enrollments Surge Since 2006 (2017). https://cra.org/data/Generation-CS
7. Converse, G., Curi, M., Oliveira, S.: Autoencoders for educational assessment. In: Isotani, S., Millán, E., Ogan, A., Hastings, P., McLaren, B., Luckin, R. (eds.) AIED 2019. LNCS (LNAI), vol. 11626, pp. 41–45. Springer, Cham (2019). https://doi.org/10.1007/978-3-030-23207-8_8

8. Crossley, S.A., Kim, M., Allen, L., McNamara, D.: Automated summarization evaluation (ASE) using natural language processing tools. In: Isotani, S., Millán, E., Ogan, A., Hastings, P., McLaren, B., Luckin, R. (eds.) AIED 2019. LNCS (LNAI), vol. 11625, pp. 84–95. Springer, Cham (2019). https://doi.org/10.1007/978-3-030-23204-7_8
9. Dasgupta, T., Naskar, A., Dey, L., Saha, R.: Augmenting textual qualitative features in deep convolution recurrent neural network for automatic essay scoring. In: Proceedings of the 5th Workshop on Natural Language Processing Techniques for Educational Applications, pp. 93–102. Association for Computational Linguistics, Melbourne (2018)
10. Dong, F., Zhang, Y.: Automatic features for essay scoring - an empirical study. In: Proceedings of the 2016 Conference on Empirical Methods in Natural Language Processing, pp. 1072–1077. Association for Computational Linguistics, Austin (2016)
11. Galhardi, L.B., Brancher, J.D.: Machine learning approach for automatic short answer grading: a systematic review. In: Simari, G.R., Fermé, E., Gutiérrez Segura, F., Rodríguez Melquiades, J.A. (eds.) IBERAMIA 2018. LNCS (LNAI), vol. 11238, pp. 380–391. Springer, Cham (2018). https://doi.org/10.1007/978-3-030-03928-8_31
12. Hussein, M.A., Hassan, H., Nassef, M.: Automated language essay scoring systems: a literature review. PeerJ Comput. Sci. 5, e208 (2019). https://peerj.com/articles/cs-208
13. Leacock, C., Chodorow, M.: C-rater: automated scoring of short-answer questions. Comput. Humanit. 37(4), 389–405 (2003). https://doi.org/10.1023/A:1025779619903
14. Lister, R., Fidge, C., Teague, D.: Further evidence of a relationship between explaining, tracing and writing skills in introductory programming. In: Proceedings of the 14th Annual ACM SIGCSE Conference on Innovation and Technology in Computer Science Education, ITiCSE 2009, pp. 161–165. ACM, New York (2009). https://doi.org/10.1145/1562877.1562930
15. Liu, M., Shum, S.B., Mantzourani, E., Lucas, C.: Evaluating machine learning approaches to classify pharmacy students' reflective statements. In: Isotani, S., Millán, E., Ogan, A., Hastings, P., McLaren, B., Luckin, R. (eds.) AIED 2019. LNCS (LNAI), vol. 11625, pp. 220–230. Springer, Cham (2019). https://doi.org/10.1007/978-3-030-23204-7_19
16. Liu, T., Ding, W., Wang, Z., Tang, J., Huang, G.Y., Liu, Z.: Automatic Short Answer Grading via Multiway Attention Networks. arXiv:1909.10166 [cs] (2019). http://arxiv.org/abs/1909.10166
17. Lopez, M., Whalley, J., Robbins, P., Lister, R.: Relationships between reading, tracing and writing skills in introductory programming. In: Proceedings of the Fourth International Workshop on Computing Education Research, pp. 101–112. ACM (2008)
18. Murphy, L., McCauley, R., Fitzgerald, S.: 'Explain in Plain English' questions: implications for teaching. In: Proceedings of the 43rd ACM Technical Symposium on Computer Science Education, SIGCSE 2012, pp. 385–390. ACM, New York (2012). https://doi.org/10.1145/2157136.2157249
19. National Academies of Sciences, Engineering, and Medicine: Assessing and Responding to the Growth of Computer Science Undergraduate Enrollments. The National Academies Press, Washington, DC (2018). https://doi.org/10.17226/24926. https://www.nap.edu/catalog/24926/assessing-and-responding-to-the-growth-of-computer-science-undergraduate-enrollments

20. Ndukwe, I.G., Daniel, B.K., Amadi, C.E.: A machine learning grading system using chatbots. In: Isotani, S., Millán, E., Ogan, A., Hastings, P., McLaren, B., Luckin, R. (eds.) AIED 2019. LNCS (LNAI), vol. 11626, pp. 365–368. Springer, Cham (2019). https://doi.org/10.1007/978-3-030-23207-8_67
21. Ramineni, C., Williamson, D.: Understanding mean score differences between the e-rater® automated scoring engine and humans for demographically based groups in the GRE® general test. ETS Res. Report Ser. **2018**(1), 1–31 (2018). https://onlinelibrary.wiley.com/doi/abs/10.1002/ets2.12192
22. Saha, S., Dhamecha, T.I., Marvaniya, S., Sindhgatta, R., Sengupta, B.: Sentence level or token level features for automatic short answer grading?: Use both. In: Penstein Rosé, C., et al. (eds.) AIED 2018. LNCS (LNAI), vol. 10947, pp. 503–517. Springer, Cham (2018). https://doi.org/10.1007/978-3-319-93843-1_37
23. Sam, A.H., et al.: Very-short-answer questions: reliability, discrimination and acceptability. Med. Educ. **52**(4), 447–455 (2018)
24. Sukkarieh, J.Z., Blackmore, J.: C-rater: automatic content scoring for short constructed responses. In: FLAIRS Conference (2009)
25. Sung, C., Dhamecha, T.I., Mukhi, N.: Improving short answer grading using transformer-based pre-training. In: Isotani, S., Millán, E., Ogan, A., Hastings, P., McLaren, B., Luckin, R. (eds.) AIED 2019. LNCS (LNAI), vol. 11625, pp. 469–481. Springer, Cham (2019). https://doi.org/10.1007/978-3-030-23204-7_39
26. Suzen, N., Gorban, A., Levesley, J., Mirkes, E.: Automatic Short Answer Grading and Feedback Using Text Mining Methods. CoRR (2019). arXiv: 1807.10543
27. Taghipour, K., Ng, H.T.: A neural approach to automated essay scoring. In: Proceedings of the 2016 Conference on Empirical Methods in Natural Language Processing, pp. 1882–1891. Association for Computational Linguistics, Austin (2016)
28. Viera, A.J., Garrett, J.M., et al.: Understanding interobserver agreement: the Kappa statistic. Fam. Med. **37**(5), 360–363 (2005)
29. Watson, C., Li, F.W.: Failure rates in introductory programming revisited. In: Proceedings of the 2014 Conference on Innovation & #38; Technology in Computer Science Education, ITiCSE 2014, pp. 39–44. ACM, New York (2014). https://doi.org/10.1145/2591708.2591749
30. West, M., Herman, G.L., Zilles, C.: PrairieLearn: mastery-based online problem solving with adaptive scoring and recommendations driven by machine learning. In: 2015 ASEE Annual Conference & Exposition. ASEE Conferences, Seattle, Washington (2015)
31. Whalley, J., et al.: An Australasian study of reading and comprehension skills in novice programmers, using the bloom and SOLO taxonomies. In: Eighth Australasian Computing Education Conference, ACE 2006 (2006)
32. Xie, B., et al.: A theory of instruction for introductory programming skills. Comput. Sci. Educ. **29**(2–3), 205–253 (2019)
33. Yang, X., Huang, Y., Zhuang, F., Zhang, L., Yu, S.: Automatic Chinese short answer grading with deep autoencoder. In: Penstein Rosé, C., et al. (eds.) AIED 2018. LNCS (LNAI), vol. 10948, pp. 399–404. Springer, Cham (2018). https://doi.org/10.1007/978-3-319-93846-2_75

AI Enabled Tutor for Accessible Training

Ayan Banerjee[✉], Imane Lamrani, Sameena Hossain, Prajwal Paudyal,
and Sandeep K. S. Gupta

Arizona State University, Tempe, AZ 85281, USA
{abanerj3,ilamrani,shossai5,ppaudyal,sandeep.gupta}@asu.edu

Abstract. A significant number of jobs require highly skilled labor
which necessitate training on pre-requisite knowledge. Examples include
jobs in military, technical field such computer science, large scale fulfill-
ment centers such as Amazon. Moreover, making such jobs accessible to
the disabled population requires even more pre-requisite training such
as knowledge of sign language. An artificial intelligent (AI) agent can
potentially act as a tutor for such pre-requisite training. This will not
only reduce resource requirements for such training but also decrease
the time taken for making personnel job ready. In this paper, we develop
an AI tutor that can teach users gestures that are required on the field
as a pre-requisite. The AI tutor uses a model learning technique that
learns the gestures performed by experts. It then uses a model comparison technique to compare a learner with the expert gesture and provides
feedback for the learner to improve.

Keywords: AI enabled tutor · ASL · Explainable AI

1 Introduction

Advances in machine learning, artificial intelligence (AI) and embedded computing is bringing a revolution in human computer communication, where humans
and computers will operate in symbiosis for collaborative outcomes and cooperative learning. The applications with collaboration can span over robot assisted
military combat [12,22,33], and collaboratory rehabilitation for diseases such
as Parkinson's or Alzheimer's [1,30]. Cooperative learning applications include
computer aided training of military personnel [23], heavy equipment operators
[15], or performance coaching in entertainment applications [29] or tutoring
American Sign Language (ASL) for ease of communication between humans with
various disability profiles such as deaf or hard-of-hearing [7]. In most of these
applications gestures form an important component of communication between
the human and the computer or another human. A gesture is composed of multiple components arranged in temporal order with specific transitions from one
component to the other. There are typically two components: a) gesture recognition, by a machine or a human, and b) replication by an audience (machine/
human). If the audience is a machine, the recognized gesture may not be in any

© Springer Nature Switzerland AG 2020
I. I. Bittencourt et al. (Eds.): AIED 2020, LNAI 12163, pp. 29–42, 2020.
https://doi.org/10.1007/978-3-030-52237-7_3

understandable form since the machine can be programmed to replicate by using the original sensor measurements. But if the audience is a human then gestures need to not only be recognized but understood in more fundamental ways to achieve desired learning outcomes.

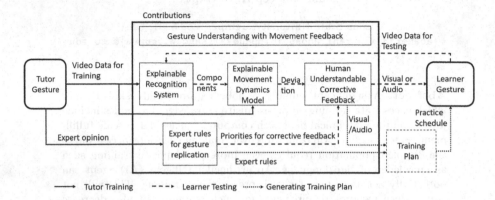

Fig. 1. Co-operative learning application model for understanding and replicating gestures similar to a tutor.

In this work, we consider a co-operative gesture learning application model that not only recognizes errors in a learner but also provides corrective feedback that enables the learner to replicate a gesture with similar qualities of a tutor (Fig. 1). The application model takes multiple iterations of a given gesture from several tutors. It should model not only the individual gesture components potentially using a data-driven machine learning architecture but also the transition from one component to the other. In addition, the tutors will also provide "expert rules" that are essential for expressing the correct or nuanced meaning of a gesture and can be used to guide corrective feedback to the learner. In the testing phase, a learner provides sensor data for a replication of the gesture, which is passed to a recognition system. It results in recognition of the gesture components along with an explanation for correctness. The inter-component movement will be checked against a tutor. The results from the component and movement recognition system will be combined with expert rules to create a prioritized set of corrective feedback for the learner, which will be disseminated through audio-visual means. In an extension of this system, it can also be envisioned that the system generates a personalized training plan for the learner over time. The training plan is considered as an extension for the research.

In this paper, we consider ASL learning example to demonstrate our contributions. ASL signs are poly-componential in nature and is a sophisticated gesture based language [2]. Hence, lessons learned from this example can potentially be applicable to other gesture based communication domains such as ensuring compliance to Center for Disease Control (CDC) guidelines for hand-washing [3].

The ASL tutor is intended to be used in computer science accessible virtual education (CSAVE) architecture for Deaf and Hard of Hearing (DHH) individuals [14]. An IMPACT Lab project, CSAVE architecture facilitates personalized learning environment for deaf and hard of hearing students. It enables DHH students to collaborate with the instructor, interpreter, and their hearing peers seamlessly without them having to reveal their disability. Many of these technical courses require students to work in groups to collaborate on projects. Incorporating ASLTutor within the CSAVE architecture can enable the hearing students with the tool they would need to communicate with their DHH peers.

2   Existing Work and Challenges

To understand the unique challenges associated in answering the above-mentioned question, let us contrast two examples: a) an AI tutor for training a person in a foreign spoken language, and b) an AI tutor for training a person in ASL.

Existing Work: For second spoken language learners, many research works point out to the positive relationship between feedback given through interaction and the learning performance [19,20]. The ability to practice and receive feedback is also a positive aspect of immersive environments for second language learning such as study abroad programs and even classroom environment to some extent [21]. Many software applications for spoken languages incorporate some form of feedback to help improve the pronunciation of learners [36]. Applications like DuoLingo also provide interactive chat-bot like environments with feedback to increase immersion [40]. However, such applications are not available for learners of sign languages. This is in part due to the inherent technical difficulties for providing feedback to sign language learners.

2.1   Challenge 1: Explainable Systems

A simple notion of the correctness of a sign execution can be computed using existing sign language recognition systems [5,6,8,9,16,17,32,34,41]. However, for providing more fine-grained feedback, more details are desirable. This is specially so because sign languages, unlike spoken languages, are multi-modal. Thus, if an error is present in execution, feedback should be given that ties back to the erroneous articulator(s). For instance, if a student executes the movement part of a sign correctly, and performs the sign in the right position relative to her body, but she fails to articulate the right shape of the hand, then feedback should be given regarding the incorrect handshape. Thus, blackbox recognition systems are not very useful for feedback and explainable systems that can recognize conceptual elements of the language must be developed.

2.2   Challenge 2: Determination of Appropriate Feedback

Feedback mechanisms for spoken and sign language differ significantly. The differences arise primarily due to the articulators used for speech versus those used for signing. Apart from some research for feedback in rehabilitation for physical therapy, which is conceptually very dissimilar to sign language learning, there are no existing systems in this domain [42]. Thus, the types of feedback to be given to learners must be determined by referring to the linguistics of sign languages, close work with ASL instructors and referring to academic studies. Codifying and automating the suggested feedback into a usable system is a challenging process and a worthy research undertaking.

2.3   Challenge 3: Extension to Unseen Vocabulary

Sign language recognition differs from speech recognition in one crucial aspect: the number of articulatory channels. This is partially an artifact of the medium used for recognition, i.e. audio vs video. Audio is usually represented as two-dimensional signals in amplitude and time, while colored videos are four-dimensional signals: three spatial dimensions, one channel dimension for color and one time dimension. The consequence of this for speech to text systems for spoken language learning such as Rosetta Stone [36] offers some feedback to a learner based on comparisons between their utterances and those of a native speaker. This one-to-one comparison to a gold standard is a desirable way for learning systems where the learner is attempting to get close in performance to a tutor. Such comparison for gesture learning becomes multi-dimensional spatio-temporal problem and hence is more challenging. Moreover, a tutoring system needs to readily extend to new vocabulary as the learner progresses. To extend the capability of a recognition system that is based on a classifier, the entire system will need to be retrained to account for new signs.

2.4   Challenge 4: Ubiquitous Recognition

The growing usage of self-paced learning solutions can be attributed to the effect of the economy of scale as well as to their flexibility in schedule. To achieve these desired advantages, the barrier to access must be reduced as much as possible. This implies that requiring the usage of specialized sensors such as 3-D cameras will hinder the utility. Thus, a proposed solution that can truly scale and have the maximum impact as a learning tool must be accessible without the need to purchase special sensors or to attend in special environments. The sensing device that is most accessible to any user is the smartphone. This is challenging because there is a huge variance in the type, quality, and feed of smartphone-based cameras and webcams. Furthermore, assumptions on adequate lighting conditions, orientations, camera facing directions and other specific configurations cannot be made, and have to either be verified by quality control or accounted for by the recognition and feedback algorithms.

In this paper, we use concept level learning for gesture understanding that can enable: a) extendable recognition, b) corrective explainable feedback to human learners, c) configurable feedback incorporation based on expert rules, and d) ubiquitous operation on any smartphone.

3   AI Tutor Design Goals

In this section, we discuss the design goals and principles for an AI Tutor and show proof-of-concept studies on an ASL tutor.

3.1   Embedding Movement in Models

Hybrid systems encode transient behavior using a set of differential equations that can potentially be used to represent the kinematics of the gesture. For example, the transient behavior of the movement from one hand shape to other is captured from high definition video and then utilizing Posenet to estimate wrist positions [24]. A kinematic model obtained from expert knowledge of human hand movements [35] can express the transient dynamics of movement in between hand shapes. The recognition result of the explainable machine learning system can then be considered as discrete states while the learned kinematic model can be considered as the dynamical component of the hybrid system representation of the gesture. State transitions can be expressed through temporal constraints.

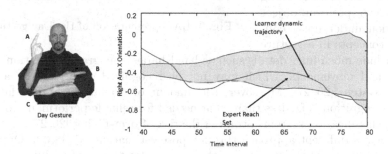

Fig. 2. Day example, the evolution of reach set over time for a tutor, and the execution for a learner.

Proof-of-Concept Example

We consider the gesture for "Day" in ASL. The Day gesture is shown in Fig. 2, it involves two hand shapes: a) the left hand pointing towards the right, and b) the right hand pointing towards the head. Then it has one transient hand movement, where the right arm while pointing pivots on the right elbow and makes a quarter circle and lands on the left elbow.

We generate the hybrid system for Day gesture as shown in Fig. 3. We consider three different components or states of the "Day" gesture: a) Pointing to the head (State A), b) movement from head to the top of the left arm (State B), and c) movement from top of the left arm to the elbow (State C). While transiting from one state to the other, we consider that the center point of the palm of both the left and right arm move following the model described in Eq. 1.

$$\frac{d\vec{p}}{dt} = \vec{v}, \frac{d\vec{v}}{dt} = \vec{a}, \frac{d\vec{a}}{dt} = x_1\vec{a} + x_2\vec{v} + x_3\vec{p} + x_4, \tag{1}$$

where $\vec{p}$ is the position vector for the right arm, $\vec{v}$ is the velocity vector and $\vec{a}$ is the acceleration vector and x_is are parameters of the hand motion. This is an overly simplistic model of the palm movement but is used to generate useful feedback relating to arm acceleration.

3.2   Ubiquitous Recognition of Movement

The need for recognition of concepts from data collected using heterogenous sensors prohibits the usage of traditional machine learning systems, which are affected by camera resolution, lighting condition, as well as distance from the lens. Although Convolutional Neural Networks (CNN) or other deep learning systems can perform object recognition under noisy conditions, concepts in a gesture video include much finer details such as handshapes, fine grained location information, and movements, which may not be recognized effectively by a deep learning system [25–27]. Moreover, the amount of available training data for gesture recognition is far less than what needed for reliable performance of deep learning classification systems avoiding the risk of over-fitting [26,27].

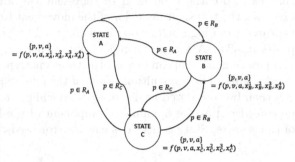

Fig. 3. HA representation of the Day gesture.

We take a different approach through pose estimation [31,38,39]. Our approach is to convert the gesture execution into spatio-temporal evolution of continuous variables. The recognition is a composite outcome of simpler similarity-based comparisons. This can potentially contribute to the robustness to changing environmental conditions since the pose estimation step already eliminates background and only focuses on points of interest.

We considered the "X" and "Y" co-ordinate time series of the right and left wrist normalized with respect to torso height and hip width. The location concept was extracted using six location buckets around the face and the chest of a user. This is because as a concept only the proximity to different body parts are important and not the exact pixel level location.

To extract handshape we utilized the wristpoints to crop the palm of the user. We then used the CNN Inception model trained using the ImageNet dataset and retrained using fingerspelling handshapes [37]. The retrained inception model was not used to classify handshapes but instead was used to compare two handshapes: one from the tutorial video and the other from the test user. Only the outputs of the penultimate layer of the Inception model for both the tutorial and the user was compared using the euclidean distance metric. This not only enables concept matching but also provides extensibility, because to compare with a new tutorial sign no training is required.

We explored two different methods of movement concept recognition: a) direct comparison using segmental dynamic time warping strategy [28], and b) comparison with respect to kinematic model parameters [4]. The first strategy is model agnostic and only gives feedback about the correctness of the movement concept. The second approach utilizes a hybrid dynamical system to model gesture concepts. This model driven approach can provide more granular feedback as discussed in our initial work [4].

We evaluated the concept learning methodology on 100 first time learners of ASL users each of them learned 25 ASL gestures and performed three times each gesture. The videos of the ASL gestures were taken using their own smartphones at home. The system has an overall test accuracy of 87.9% on real-world data [28]. We also evaluated our hybrid dynamical model on 60 first time learners of ASL users each of them learned 20 ASL gestures and performed three times each gesture. Results show that kinematic parameters in Eq. 1 can represent each gesture with precision of 83%, and recall of 80%.

3.3   Movement Matching Between Tutor and Learner

In our approach, the hybrid system based representation of a gesture is instantiated for a tutor. The instantiation procedure involved collecting data using wearable and video based sensors from a tutor and running the following hybrid system mining technique.

Hybrid Mining Technique: The input to the model mining methodology are the input output traces, which may contain timed events, and discrete or continuous inputs.

A) First step is I/O segmentation. The discrete mode changes of the hybrid model is triggered by three main causes: a) user generated external events that are accompanied by time stamps and input configurations, b) system generated timed events, and c) events generated due to threshold crossing of observable parameters of the physical system.

B) Second step is to cluster modes in accordance with their triggering mechanism. This clustering step is required to minimize the redundancy in the number of discrete modes of the mined specification.

C) The third step is mining the kinematic equations. Each trace is passed to a Multi-variate Polynomial Regression to obtain the kinematic equations. For the linear case, we utilize Fischer information and Cramer Rao bound to compute the linear coefficients [18]. The output is the flow equation parameters for each trace between modes. A result of the flow equation extraction mechanism is that different traces may have the same flow equation. The corresponding modes are then clustered together using density based approaches on the flow parameters and assigned the same mode labels.

D) The fourth step is guard mining. We derive the guard conditions for each cluster, where each cluster represents a distinct control switch. If the guard condition is not a constant value of actuation and is varying within each data point in the cluster, we employ Fisher information and Cramer Rao bound to derive the linear relation of the input, output, and internal parameters [18]. The Guard conditions are then used to further refine the mode clustering. The output is a Hybrid automata inferred from the input, output, and internal parameters with modes, flow equations, and guards.

Tutor and Learner Comparison: The natural variation of a tutor is modeled by computing a reach set of the learned hybrid system. The reach set is the set of all continuous states that is observed from simulating the hybrid system over time for a bounded set of initial conditions, which may represent natural variations in the tutor's execution of the gesture.

Given an execution of the gesture by a learner, the video based hand gesture recognition system provides us with executed hand shapes, the times of transition from one shape to the other, and an identification of wrong executions by the learner. The reach set comparison can provide the deviation from a tutor. For instance if the fingertip data is encompassed by the reach set then, it is tutor level. However, if it is outside the reach set at any point in time, then it the learner has differences with the tutor. The time segments where the learner differed from the tutor can then be passed to a dynamical system mining technique that is programmed with the kinematic model of the human arm. The mining technique will provide a new set of parameters for the learner.

Proof-of-Concept: We collected Kinect data including video and bone movement data from 60 subjects for 20 ASL gestures including "Day". We chose one user, who is a lecturer at ASU on sign language and considered the person as a tutor. We collected data for 20 executions of "Day" and computed the variations in initial positions and angles, speeds, and the parameters of Eq. 1. The sensors used were Kinect video and bone data. In addition the tutors wore an armband that collected accelerometer, orientation, gyroscope and Electromyogram data. The traces were used to derive the parameters of the kinematics described in Eq. 1.

We then derived different initial conditions by performing a statistical analysis of the tutor's speed, initial positions and parameters for Eq. 1. These were used to perform the reachability analysis of the hybrid system using the SpaceEx tool [10]. Figure 2 shows the X orientation reach set evolution of the hybrid system. All the different executions of the tutor are inside the gray area. The reach set is an over approximation because exact computing is intractable.

We then considered another subject's execution of the "Day" gesture, where the learner ended the Day gesture with the right palm near to the left. The X orientation of the right palm of the learner is shown in red in Fig. 2. It clearly shows that the learner violates the reach set and hence is not classified as similar to a tutor, although all the hand signs are correctly executed by the learner. However, the learner executes the same sequence of hand shapes. Hence, a knowledge based feedback system will consider this execution as correct. But the execution has clear differences with the tutor in the transition between gestures in the transition from state B to C.

The dynamics of the learner's execution between state B and C is then used to regenerate the parameters of Eq. 1. The learner is seen to have 40% elevated x_3. This means that as the position of the right arm goes closer to the left arm, the acceleration increases resulting in overshooting of the right arm beyond the left arm position. Hence the feedback that is generated for the learner is to control the learner's right arm so that the velocity is uniform. By practicing one can get the right arm velocity uniform and be on par with a tutor.

3.4 Explainable Feedback

A variety of feedback could be constructed using the information available from the results of the location, movement, and handshape modules. In addition to separate feedback for each of the hands, feedback could also be presented in forms of annotated images or by using animations. For location feedback, the correct and the incorrect locations for each of the hands could be highlighted in different colors. For the handshape feedback, the image of the hand that resulted in the highest difference in similarity could be presented. Each of these types of possible feedback is derived from the information available. However, they should be individually tested for usability and care should be taken not to cognitively overload the learner with too much feedback at once.

More granular feedback can be provided using kinematic models if each component of the model has direct correlation with a physical manifestation of the human arm. Such correlations and the parameters estimated for the learner can be used to generate understandable feedback that enables the learner to perfect gesture execution. Such feedback will be guided by the expert rules specified by the tutor. Complex models tend to be less amenable towards feedback generation. Hence our goal will be to best exploit the trade-off between model complexity and explainability.

4   Prototype and Evaluation of Learning Outcomes

We first discuss our experimental setup and then evaluation results.

4.1   Prototype

A chat bot enabled web based gesture learning interface is developed (Fig. 4). In this chatbot, the learner chooses a sign and learns the gesture. Then the learner chooses to practice when the video of the learner executing is recorded and compared with the expert. Textual feedback is then provided to the learner to improve gesture execution capability.

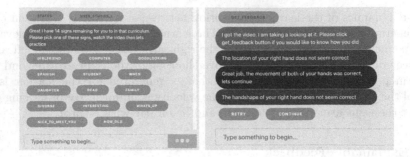

Fig. 4. Interactive chat-bot interface. Right: The movement of both the hands were correct (green), but the location and right hand handshape were not correct. (Color figure online)

4.2   Learning Outcomes

The purpose of assessment tests are to evaluate learning outcomes. Two types of tests are considered: a) retention tests and b) execution tests. We recruited 15 subjects who were tested on 50 ASL signs of their choice from a pool of ASL signs for the states of USA.

Each learner is given randomly selected signs for retention tests. The learner either chose to practice a given sign multiple times or move on. For each test, the learner is shown a video and is asked to choose among 4 options for the correct one. Thus, the baseline performance for random guessing would be 25%. The performance of the learner with and without feedback is used as a metric for feedback effectiveness.

For execution tests each of the learners is given randomly selected signs to execute. During the test the learner is given a sign and asked to begin recording its execution. The execution tests is manually scored offline by the research team. If the learner had any two of location, movement or handshape correct on both hands, then she receives a score of 0.5 for that sign. If all three were correct, she receives 1. Otherwise, she receives 0. The performance on execution tests with and without feedback is considered to evaluate effectiveness of feedback.

Our results show that retention of the signs did not improve with feedback. In fact retention was already upwards of 80% with or without feedback. However, there was significant improvement in execution accuracy. It improved from 63% without feedback to 85% with feedback. This indicates that overall feedback has a significant effect on learning outcome. The effectiveness of different types of feedback however could not be evaluated given the less number of participants. However, an end of study survey showed that majority of the participants preferred fine grained feedback.

5   Conclusions and Discussions

Feedback in gesture based learning is of utmost importance as evidences in our evaluation results. An AI tutor hence not only has to disseminate knowledge and evaluate students, but also provide feedback to ensure learning. In this paper, we have demonstrated through a proof-of-concept study of an AI tutor of ASL, that AI tutor has to be explainable, ubiquitous and extensible. The concepts learned in this project can be employed in other gesture based training applications such as military, physiotherapy, medical surgery training. Through proof-of-concept implementations we have shown the importance of feedback in AI tutor, however, there are significant hurdles before it can be realized in practice.

Usability: The system requires no extra sensor, just a mobile phone camera is enough. The system could achieve this operation, because of the modular representation and identification of gestures in terms of their components.

Extensibility: The system only compares a test gesture to one expert video and does not need training for new gesture classes. Hence it is extensible with only the inclusion of an expert gesture video.

Difference in Feedback Generation Methods: Generation of explanation heavily depends on the model. Complex models may be more accurate but not be explainable. Dynamical models of the human arm of different complexity can be broadly classified into the following categories:

a) Differential equation models derived from kinematics of human fingers and arms: These models are typically derived from Magnetic Resonance Imaging (MRI) [35] or CT [13] scans of the human hand and can go to the level of minute finger movements. In these methods a kinematic model is developed from a general understanding of human hand and the parameters are estimated from the imaging data. Authors in [35] use a parameterized models such that each parameter has a direct visual manifestation. A deviation in a parameter hence can be easily converted into explanations considering the visual signatures. A big problem is that the model is the dimensionality, and learning the appropriate parameters from MRI images is computationally expensive.

b) Data-driven models derived using data glove or frictional sensors: Such models typically utilize predictors such as Kalman filters [11]. The model parameters have no direct relation to any understandable component of the human hand. But the overall model can be used to predict hand motion given a configuration of the parameters. Results from these models are difficult to explain.

Constraints on Generation of Feedback: Another significant hurdle is the feasibility of using the feedback for a person given their unique constraints. A difference in model parameters between the learner and the tutor is intended to be used to generate correctional feedback. However, the low dimensional dynamical model is not accurate for larger time horizons. This means that there can be cases where the model may generate inviable feedback. Such as requesting extremely large acceleration or bending the arm at infeasible angles. Hence, every feedback has to be validated against a set of constraints that express viable feedback. Moreover in case feedback is invalid, we have to modify the model such that it can generate a feasible feedback.

One of the important future work is to apply this AI tutor for training DHH students, gestures related to technical concepts of computer science so that they can then take CS courses in the future and have a career in the technical field. CS courses have several technical terms which do not have gestures for them. Utilizing AI tutor to not only teach but organically generate signs for these technical gestures is one of our future goals.

References

1. Alwardat, M., et al.: Effectiveness of robot-assisted gait training on motor impairments in people with Parkinson's disease: a systematic review and meta-analysis. Int. J. Rehabil. Res. **41**(4), 287–296 (2018)
2. Anthimopoulos, M., Dehais, J., Diem, P., Mougiakakou, S.: Segmentation and recognition of multi-food meal images for carbohydrate counting. In: 13th International Conference on Bioinformatics and Bioengineering (BIBE), pp. 1–4. IEEE (2013)
3. Banerjee, A., Amperyani, V.S.A., Gupta, S.K.: Hand hygiene compliance checking system with explainable feedback. In: 18th ACM International Conference on Mobile Systems Applications and Services, WearSys Workshop (2020)
4. Banerjee, A., Lamrani, I., Paudyal, P., Gupta, S.K.S.: Generation of movement explanations for testing gesture based co-operative learning applications. In: IEEE International Conference on Artificial Intelligence Testing, AITest 2019, Newark, CA, USA, 4–9 April 2019, pp. 9–16 (2019). https://doi.org/10.1109/AITest.2019.00-15
5. Camgöz, N.C., Kındıroğlu, A.A., Karabüklü, S., Kelepir, M., Özsoy, A.S., Akarun, L.: BosphorusSign: a Turkish sign language recognition corpus in health and finance domains. In: Proceedings of the Tenth International Conference on Language Resources and Evaluation, LREC 2016, pp. 1383–1388 (2016)
6. Chai, X., et al.: Sign language recognition and translation with Kinect. In: IEEE Conference on AFGR, vol. 655, p. 4 (2013)
7. Chen, T.L., et al.: Older adults' acceptance of a robot for partner dance-based exercise. PloS One **12**(10), e0182736 (2017)
8. Cooper, H., Bowden, R.: Learning signs from subtitles: a weakly supervised approach to sign language recognition. In: 2009 IEEE Conference on Computer Vision and Pattern Recognition, pp. 2568–2574. IEEE (2009)
9. Forster, J., Oberdörfer, C., Koller, O., Ney, H.: Modality combination techniques for continuous sign language recognition. In: Sanches, J.M., Micó, L., Cardoso, J.S. (eds.) IbPRIA 2013. LNCS, vol. 7887, pp. 89–99. Springer, Heidelberg (2013). https://doi.org/10.1007/978-3-642-38628-2_10
10. Frehse, G., Kateja, R., Le Guernic, C.: Flowpipe approximation and clustering in space-time. In: Proceedings of the Hybrid Systems: Computation and Control, HSCC 2013, pp. 203–212. ACM (2013)
11. Fu, Q., Santello, M.: Tracking whole hand kinematics using extended Kalman filter. In: 2010 Annual International Conference of the IEEE Engineering in Medicine and Biology Society (EMBC), pp. 4606–4609. IEEE (2010)
12. Galliott, J.: Military Robots: Mapping the Moral Landscape. Routledge, Abingdon (2016)
13. Harih, G., Tada, M.: Development of a finite element digital human hand model. In: 7th International Conference on 3D Body Scanning Technologies (2016)

14. Hossain, S., Banerjee, A., Gupta, S.K.S.: Personalized technical learning assistance for deaf and hard of hearing students. In: Thirty Fourth AAAI Conference, AI4EDU Workshop (2020)
15. Jiang, Q., Liu, M., Wang, X., Ge, M., Lin, L.: Human motion segmentation and recognition using machine vision for mechanical assembly operation. SpringerPlus 5(1), 1–18 (2016). https://doi.org/10.1186/s40064-016-3279-x
16. Koller, O., Zargaran, S., Ney, H., Bowden, R.: Deep sign: enabling robust statistical continuous sign language recognition via hybrid CNN-HMMS. Int. J. Comput. Vis. 126(12), 1311–1325 (2018). https://doi.org/10.1007/s11263-018-1121-3
17. Kumar, S.S., Wangyal, T., Saboo, V., Srinath, R.: Time series neural networks for real time sign language translation. In: 2018 17th IEEE International Conference on Machine Learning and Applications (ICMLA), pp. 243–248. IEEE (2018)
18. Lamrani, I., Banerjee, A., Gupta, S.K.: HyMn: mining linear hybrid automata from input output traces of cyber-physical systems. In: IEEE Industrial Cyber-Physical Systems (ICPS), pp. 264–269. IEEE (2018)
19. Lightbown, P.M., Spada, N.: Focus-on-form and corrective feedback in communicative language teaching: effects on second language learning. Stud. Second Lang. Acquisit. 12(4), 429–448 (1990)
20. Mackey, A.: Feedback, noticing and instructed second language learning. Appl. Linguist. 27(3), 405–430 (2006)
21. Magnan, S.S., Back, M.: Social interaction and linguistic gain during study abroad. Foreign Lang. Ann. 40(1), 43–61 (2007)
22. Min, H., Morales, D.R., Orgill, D., Smink, D.S., Yule, S.: Systematic review of coaching to enhance surgeons' operative performance. Surgery 158(5), 1168–1191 (2015)
23. Noble, D.D.: The Classroom Arsenal: Military Research, Information Technology and Public Education. Routledge, Abingdon (2017)
24. Papandreou, G., et al.: Towards accurate multi-person pose estimation in the wild. In: CVPR, vol. 3, p. 6 (2017)
25. Paudyal, P., Banerjee, A., Gupta, S.K.: SCEPTRE: a pervasive, non-invasive, and programmable gesture recognition technology. In: Proceedings of the 21st International Conference on Intelligent User Interfaces, pp. 282–293. ACM (2016)
26. Paudyal, P., Lee, J., Banerjee, A., Gupta, S.K.: DyFAV: dynamic feature selection and voting for real-time recognition of fingerspelled alphabet using wearables. In: Proceedings of the 22nd International Conference on Intelligent User Interfaces, pp. 457–467. ACM (2017)
27. Paudyal, P., Lee, J., Banerjee, A., Gupta, S.K.: A comparison of techniques for sign language alphabet recognition using arm-band wearables. ACM Trans. Interact. Intell. Syst. (TiiS) (2018, accepted)
28. Paudyal, P., Lee, J., Kamzin, A., Soudki, M., Banerjee, A., Gupta, S.K.: Learn2Sign: explainable AI for sign language learning. In: Proceedings of the 24nd International Conference on Intelligent User Interfaces, pp. 457–467. ACM (2019)
29. Riley, M., Ude, A., Atkeson, C., Cheng, G.: Coaching: an approach to efficiently and intuitively create humanoid robot behaviors. In: 2006 6th IEEE-RAS International Conference on Humanoid Robots, pp. 567–574. IEEE (2006)
30. Salichs, M.A., Encinar, I.P., Salichs, E., Castro-González, Á., Malfaz, M.: Study of scenarios and technical requirements of a social assistive robot for Alzheimer's disease patients and their caregivers. Int. J. Soc. Robot. 8(1), 85–102 (2016). https://doi.org/10.1007/s12369-015-0319-6

31. Sarafianos, N., Boteanu, B., Ionescu, B., Kakadiaris, I.A.: 3D human pose estimation: a review of the literature and analysis of covariates. Comput. Vis. Image Underst. **152**, 1–20 (2016)
32. Schmidt, C., Koller, O., Ney, H., Hoyoux, T., Piater, J.: Using viseme recognition to improve a sign language translation system. In: International Workshop on Spoken Language Translation, pp. 197–203 (2013)
33. Sharkey, N.E.: The evitability of autonomous robot warfare. Int. Rev. Red Cross **94**(886), 787–799 (2012)
34. Starner, T., Pentland, A.: Real-time American sign language visual recognition from video using hidden Markov models. Master's Thesis, MIT Program in Media Arts (1995)
35. Stillfried, G., Hillenbrand, U., Settles, M., van der Smagt, P.: MRI-based skeletal hand movement model. In: Balasubramanian, R., Santos, V.J. (eds.) The Human Hand as an Inspiration for Robot Hand Development. STAR, vol. 95, pp. 49–75. Springer, Cham (2014). https://doi.org/10.1007/978-3-319-03017-3_3
36. Stone, R.: Talking back required (2016). https://www.rosettastone.com/speech-recognition. Accessed 28 Sept 2018
37. Szegedy, C., Vanhoucke, V., Ioffe, S., Shlens, J., Wojna, Z.: Rethinking the inception architecture for computer vision. In: Proceedings of the IEEE Conference on Computer Vision and Pattern Recognition, pp. 2818–2826 (2016)
38. Tome, D., Russell, C., Agapito, L.: Lifting from the deep: convolutional 3D pose estimation from a single image. In: CVPR 2017 Proceedings, pp. 2500–2509 (2017)
39. Tompson, J.J., Jain, A., LeCun, Y., Bregler, C.: Joint training of a convolutional network and a graphical model for human pose estimation. In: Advances in Neural Information Processing Systems, pp. 1799–1807 (2014)
40. Vesselinov, R., Grego, J.: Duolingo effectiveness study, vol. 28. City University of New York, USA (2012)
41. Zhang, Q., Wang, D., Zhao, R., Yu, Y.: MyoSign: enabling end-to-end sign language recognition with wearables. In: Proceedings of the 24th International Conference on Intelligent User Interfaces, pp. 650–660. ACM (2019)
42. Zhao, W.: On automatic assessment of rehabilitation exercises with realtime feedback. In: 2016 IEEE International Conference on Electro Information Technology (EIT), pp. 0376–0381. IEEE (2016)

Introducing a Framework to Assess Newly Created Questions with Natural Language Processing

Luca Benedetto[1]([✉])[iD], Andrea Cappelli[2], Roberto Turrin[2],
and Paolo Cremonesi[1][iD]

[1] Politecnico di Milano, Milan, Italy
{luca.benedetto,paolo.cremonesi}@polimi.it
[2] Cloud Academy Sagl, Mendrisio, Switzerland
{andrea.cappelli,roberto.turrin}@cloudacademy.com

Abstract. Statistical models such as those derived from Item Response Theory (IRT) enable the assessment of students on a specific subject, which can be useful for several purposes (e.g., learning path customization, drop-out prediction). However, the questions have to be assessed as well and, although it is possible to estimate with IRT the characteristics of questions that have already been answered by several students, this technique cannot be used on newly generated questions. In this paper, we propose a framework to train and evaluate models for estimating the difficulty and discrimination of newly created Multiple Choice Questions by extracting meaningful features from the text of the question and of the possible choices. We implement one model using this framework and test it on a real-world dataset provided by *CloudAcademy*, showing that it outperforms previously proposed models, reducing by 6.7% the RMSE for difficulty estimation and by 10.8% the RMSE for discrimination estimation. We also present the results of an ablation study performed to support our features choice and to show the effects of different characteristics of the questions' text on difficulty and discrimination.

Keywords: Natural language processing · Item Response Theory · Learning analytics

1 Introduction

Modeling the skill level of students and how it evolves over time is known as Knowledge Tracing (KT), and it can be leveraged to improve the learning experience, for instance suggesting tailored learning content or detecting students in need of further support. KT is most commonly performed with logistic models or neural networks. Although neural models often reach the best accuracy in predicting the correctness of students' answers, they do not provide easy explanations of their predictions. Logistic models such as Item Response Theory (IRT), instead, estimate latent traits of students and questions (e.g., numerical

© Springer Nature Switzerland AG 2020
I. I. Bittencourt et al. (Eds.): AIED 2020, LNAI 12163, pp. 43–54, 2020.
https://doi.org/10.1007/978-3-030-52237-7_4

values representing skill level and difficulty level) and use those to predict future answers. IRT leverages the answers given by a student to a set of calibrated questions (i.e., whose latent traits are known) to estimate her skill level, by finding the skill value that maximizes the likelihood of the observed results. Questions' latent traits are non-observable parameters which have to be estimated and, if such estimation is not accurate, it affects the students' assessment and impacts the overall efficacy of the system (e.g., suggesting wrongly targeted learning content). Also, an accurate calibration of the questions allows to identify the ones that are not suited for scoring students because they cannot discriminate between different skill levels. For instance, questions that are too difficult or too easy are answered in the same way by all the students, and questions that are unclear (e.g., due to poor wording) are answered correctly or wrongly independently of the knowledge of the students. Questions' latent traits are usually estimated with one of two techniques: they are either i) hand-picked by human experts or ii) estimated with pretesting. Both approaches are far from optimal: manual labeling is intrinsically subjective, thus affected by high uncertainty and inconsistency; pretesting leads to a reliable and fairly consistent calibration but introduces a long delay before using new questions for scoring students [29].

Recent works tried to overcome the problem of calibrating newly-generated questions by proposing models capable of estimating their characteristics from the text: with this approach, it is possible to immediately obtain an estimation of questions' latent traits and, if necessary, this initial estimation can be later fine-tuned using students' answers. However, most works targeted either the *wrongness* or the *p-value* of each question (i.e., the fraction of wrong and correct answers, respectively), which are approximations of the actual difficulty; [4] focus on latent traits as defined in IRT (i.e., difficulty and discrimination). This work introduces *text2props*, a framework to train and evaluate models for calibrating newly created Multiple-Choice Questions (MCQ) from the text of the questions and of the possible choices. The framework is made of three modules for i) estimating ground truth latent traits, ii) extracting meaningful features from the text, and iii) estimating question's properties from such features. The three modules can be implemented with different components, thus enabling the usage of different techniques at each step; it is also possible to use predefined ground truth latent traits, if available. We show the details of a sample model implemented with *text2props* and present the results of experiments performed on a dataset provided by the e-learning provider *CloudAcademy*[1]. Our experiments show an improvement in the estimation of both difficulty and discrimination: specifically, reaching a 6.7% reduction in the RMSE for difficulty estimation (from 0.807 to 0.753) and 10.8% reduction in the RMSE for discrimination estimation (from 0.414 to 0.369). We also present an ablation study to empirically support our choice of features, and the results of an experiment on the prediction of students' answers, to validate the model using an observable ground truth. The contributions of this work are: i) the introduction of *text2props*, a framework to implement models for calibrating newly created MCQ, ii) the implementation of

---

[1] https://cloudacademy.com/.

a sample model that outperforms previously proposed models, iii) an ablation study to support our choice of features in the sample model, iv) publication of the framework's code to foster further research[2]. This document is organized as follows: Sect. 2 presents the related works, Sect. 3 introduces *text2props*, Sect. 4 describes the dataset and the sample model, Sect. 5 presents the results of the experiments, Sect. 6 concludes the paper.

2 Related Work

2.1 Students' Assessment

Knowledge Tracing (KT) was pioneered by Atkinson [3] and, as reported in a recent survey [2], is most commonly performed with logistic models (e.g., IRT [27], Elo rating system [25]) or neural networks [1,22]. Recent works on students' performance prediction claim that Deep Knowledge Tracing (DKT) (i.e., KT with neural networks [22]) outperforms logistic models in predicting the results of future exams [1,6,32,33], but this advantage is not fully agreed across the community [8,20,28,31]. Also, DKT predictions do not provide an explicit numerical estimation of the skill level of the students or the difficulty of the questions. Recent works [17,30] attempted to make DKT explainable by integrating concepts analogous to the latent traits used in logistic models, but being much more expensive from a computational point of view and without reaching the same level of explainability as logistic models. Thus, logistic models are usually chosen when interpretable latent traits are needed. In this work, we use Item Response Theory (IRT) [12], that estimates the latent traits of students and questions involved in an exam. We consider the two-parameters model, which associates to each item two scalars: the difficulty and the discrimination. The difficulty represents the skill level required to have a 50% probability of correctly answering the question, while the discrimination determines how rapidly the odds of correct answer increase or decrease with the skill level of the student.

2.2 NLP for Latent Traits Estimation

The idea of inferring properties of a question from its text is not new; however, most of previous works did not focus on difficulty estimation. The first works focused on text readability estimation [9,16]. In [14] the authors use a neural network to extract from questions' text the topics that are assessed by each question. Wang et al. in [26] and Liu et al. in [18] proposed models to estimate the difficulty of questions published in community question answering services leveraging the text of the question and some domain specific information which is not available in the educational domain, thus framing the problem differently. Closer to our case are some works that use NLP to estimate the difficulty of assessment items, but most of them measured questions' difficulty as the fraction of students that answered incorrectly (i.e., the *wrongness*) or correctly (i.e., the

---

[2] https://github.com/lucabenedetto/text2props.

p-value), which are arguably a more limited estimation than the IRT difficulty, as they do not account for different students' skill levels. Huang et al. [13] propose a neural model to predict the difficulty of "reading" problems in Standard Tests, in which the answer has to be found in a text provided to the students together with the question. Their neural model uses as input both the text of the question and the text of the document, a major difference from our case. Yaneva et al. in [29] introduce a model to estimate the *p-value* of MCQ from the text of the questions, using features coming from readability measures, word embeddings, and Information Retrieval (IR). In [23] the authors propose a much more complex model, based on a deep neural network, to estimate the *wrongness* of MCQ. In [4] the authors use IR features to estimate the IRT difficulty and the discrimination of MCQ from the text of the questions and of the possible choices. All relevant related works experimented on private datasets and only [4] focuses on IRT latent traits. In this paper, we make a step forward with respect to previous research by introducing *text2props*, a modular framework to train and evaluate models for estimating the difficulty and the discrimination of MCQ from textual information. Then, we implement a sample model with *text2props* and test is on a sub-sample of a private dataset provided by *CloudAcademy*.

3 The Framework

3.1 Data Format

The *text2props* framework interacts with two datasets: i) the *Questions* (Q) dataset contains the textual information, ii) the *Answers* (A) dataset contains the results of the interactions between students and questions. Specifically, Q contains, for each question: i) ID of the question, ii) text of the MCQ, iii) text of all the possible choices, and iv) which are the correct choices and which the distractors. A, instead, contains for each interaction: i) ID of the student, ii) ID of the question, iii) correctness of student's answer, and iv) timestamp of the interaction. The interactions in A are used to obtain the ground truth latent traits of each question, which are used as target values while training the estimation of latent traits from textual information.

3.2 Architecture

Three modules compose *text2props*: i) an IRT estimation module to obtain ground truth latent traits, ii) a feature engineering module to extract features from text, and iii) a regression module to estimate the latent traits from such features. At training time all the modules are trained, while only the feature engineering module and the regression module are involved in the inference phase.

Figure 1 shows how the three modules interact with the datasets during **training**. A split stratified on the questions is performed on A, producing the dataset for estimating the ground truth latent traits (A_{GTE}) and the dataset for evaluating students' answers prediction (A_{SAP}). This is done in order to have

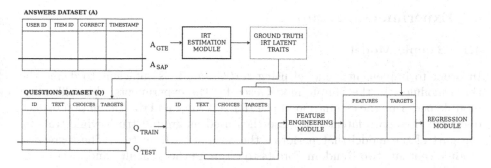

Fig. 1. Framework's architecture and interactions with the datasets during training.

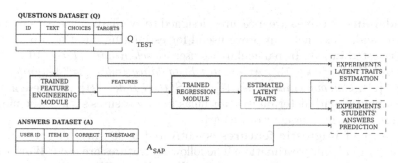

Fig. 2. Framework's architecture and interactions with the datasets during inference.

all the questions in both datasets and, therefore, be able to obtain the ground truth latent traits of all the questions from A_{GTE} and, later, perform the experiments on students' answers prediction using previously unseen interactions. The ground truth latent traits obtained with the IRT estimation module from A_{GTE} are then stored in Q, in order to be used as target values in the regression module. Then, a split is performed on Q, obtaining the dataset used to train the feature engineering and regression modules (Q_{TRAIN}) and the dataset to test them (Q_{TEST}). Lastly, the textual information of Q_{TRAIN} is used by the feature engineering module to extract numerical features, which are then used together with the ground truth latent traits to train the regression module.

During the **inference** phase, pictured in Fig. 2, the trained feature engineering module is fed with the textual information of the questions in Q_{TEST}, and extracts the features that are given to the trained regression module to estimate the latent traits. These estimated latent traits can then be used for evaluating i) latent traits estimation, directly comparing them with the ground truth latent traits (in Q_{TEST}), and ii) students' answers prediction, comparing the predictions with the true answers (in A_{SAP}).

4   Experimental Setup

4.1   Sample Model

In order to implement a model using *text2props*, it is sufficient to define the three modules. In the sample model used for the experiments, the calibration module performs the estimation of the IRT difficulty and discrimination of each question; these two latent traits are then used as ground truth while training the part of the model that performs the estimation from text. The regression module contains two Random Forests to estimate the difficulty and discrimination. The feature engineering module is made of three components to compute: i) readability features, ii) linguistic features, iii) Information Retrieval features.

- **Readability indexes** are measures designed to evaluate how easy a text is to understand, thus they can prove useful for estimating question's properties, as suggested in [29]. In particular, we use: *Flesch Reading Ease* [10], *Flesch-Kincaid Grade Level* [15], *Automated Readability Index* [24], *Gunning FOG Index* [11], *Coleman-Liau Index* [7], and *SMOG Index* [21]. All these indexes are computed with deterministic formulas from measures such as the number of words and the average word length.
- The usage of **linguistic features** is motivated by [9], in which they proved useful for readability estimation. The following features are used: *Word Count Question, Word Count Correct Choice, Word Count Wrong Choice, Sentence Count Question, Sentence Count Correct Choice, Sentence Count Wrong Choice, Average Word Length Question, Question Length divided by Correct Choice Length, Question Length divided by Wrong Choice Length.*
- The choice of **Information Retrieval** (IR) features is supported by previous research [4] and by the idea that there must be a relation between the latent traits of a MCQ and the words that appear in the text. We i) preprocess the texts using standard steps of NLP [19], ii) consider both the text of the question and the text of the possible choices by concatenating them, and iii) use features based on Term Frequency-Inverse Document Frequency (TF-IDF). However, instead of keeping only the words whose frequency is above a certain threshold (as in [4]), we define two thresholds - tuned with cross-validation - to remove i) corpus-specific stop words (i.e., words with frequency above SUP) and ii) very uncommon words (i.e., with frequency below INF).

4.2   Experimental Dataset

All previous works experimented on private data collections [4,13,23,29] and, similarly, we evaluate this framework on a private dataset, which is a sub-sample of real world data coming from the e-learning provider *CloudAcademy*. Dataset Q contains about 11 K multiple-choice questions and they have 4 possible answers; for some questions, there is more than one correct answer and, in that case, the student is asked to select all the correct choices. Dataset A, which is used for estimating the ground truth latent traits and for the experiments on students' answers prediction, contains about 2M answers. Also, it is filtered in order to keep only the students and the questions that appear in at least 100 different interactions; thus we assume that the IRT-estimated latent traits are accurate enough to be used as ground truth for this study.

5 Results

5.1 Latent Traits Estimation

The sample model used for the comparison with the state of the art was chosen from a pool of models, all implemented with *text2props*. All these models had the same IRT estimator module and the same feature engineering module, containing the three components described in Sect. 4.1, but they were implemented with different algorithms in the regression module: specifically, we tested Random Forests (RF), Decision Trees (DT), Support Vector Regression (SVR), and Linear Regression (LR). For each model, hyperparameter tuning was performed via 10-fold randomized cross-validation [5]. The results of this preliminary experiments for choosing the sample model are displayed in Table 1, presenting for each candidate model the Root Mean Square Error (RMSE) and the Mean Absolute Error (MAE) for difficulty estimation and discrimination estimation, separately on a validation set held-out from the test set and on the remaining test set. The two errors measure how accurate the sample model is by comparing the latent traits (i.e., difficulty and discrimination) estimated from text with the ground truth values obtained with IRT estimation. As baseline, we consider a majority prediction, which assigns to all the questions the same difficulty and discrimination, obtained by averaging the training latent traits. All the models outperform the majority baseline, and the RF leads to the best performance in both cases; thus, that is the model which will be used as sample model for the rest of the experiments and the comparison with the state of the art.

Table 1. Preliminary experiments for choosing the sample model.

Regression module	Difficulty estimation				Discrimination estimation			
	Validation set		Test set		Validation set		Test set	
	RMSE	MAE	RMSE	MAE	RMSE	MAE	RMSE	MAE
RF	0.739	0.575	**0.753**	**0.587**	0.393	0.296	**0.369**	**0.287**
DT	0.748	0.586	0.826	0.636	0.393	0.295	0.375	0.290
SVR	0.797	0.632	0.804	0.629	0.394	0.298	0.379	0.296
LR	0.752	0.599	0.779	0.607	0.397	0.298	0.378	0.293
Majority	–	–	0.820	0.650	–	–	0.502	0.427

Table 2. Comparison with state of the art.

Model	Difficulty estimation			Discrimination estimation		
	Range	RMSE	Relative RMSE	Range	RMSE	Relative RMSE
Our model	[−5; 5]	**0.753**	**7.53%**	[−1; 2.5]	**0.369**	**9.22%**
R2DE [4]	[−5; 5]	0.807	8.07%	[−1; 2.5]	0.414	10.35%
Qiu et al. [23]	[0; 1]	0.1521	15.21%	−	−	−
Huang et al. [13]	[0; 1]	0.21	21%	−	−	−
Yaneva et al. [29]	[0; 100]	22.45	22.45%	−	−	−

Table 2 compares the model implemented with *text2props* with the state of the art for difficulty and discrimination estimation. Considering difficulty estimation, our model reduces the RMSE by 6.7% (from 0.807 to 0.753) with respect to R2DE, which was implemented using the code publicly available[3], re-trained and tested on the new dataset. The other works experimented on private datasets and could not be directly re-implemented on our dataset, therefore a comparison on the same dataset was not straightforward; however, as suggested in [4], we can still gain some insight by performing a comparison on the Relative RMSE, which is defined as: $\text{RMSE}/(\text{difficulty}_{max} - \text{difficulty}_{min})$. The Relative RMSE of the sample model is smaller than the ones obtained in previous research and, although this does not guarantee that it would perform better than the others on every dataset, it suggests that it might perform well. The part of the table about discrimination estimation contains only two lines since this and R2DE are the only works that estimate both the difficulty and the discrimination. Again, our model outperforms R2DE, reducing the RMSE from 0.414 to 0.369.

5.2 Students' Answers Prediction

The accuracy of latent traits estimation is commonly evaluated by measuring the error with respect to ground truth latent traits estimated with IRT. However, although IRT is a well-established technique, such latent traits are non observable properties, and we want to validate our model on an observable ground truth as well, therefore we evaluate the effects that it has in predicting the correctness of students' answers. Students' Answers Prediction (SAP) provides an insight on the accuracy of latent traits estimation because questions' latent traits are a key element in predicting the correctness of future answers. Indeed, given a student i with estimated skill level $\tilde{\theta}_i$ and a question j with difficulty b_j and discrimination a_j, the probability of correct answer is computed as

$$P_C = \frac{1}{1 + e^{-1.7a_j \cdot (\tilde{\theta}_i - b_j)}} \tag{1}$$

---

[3] https://github.com/lucabenedetto/r2de-nlp-to-estimating-irt-parameters.

The skill level $\tilde{\theta}_i$ is estimated from the answers previously given by the student:

$$\tilde{\theta}_i = \max_\theta \left[\prod_{q_j \in Q_C} \frac{1}{1 + e^{-1.7a_j \cdot (\theta - b_j)}} \cdot \prod_{q_j \in Q_W} \left(1 - \frac{1}{1 + e^{-1.7a_j \cdot (\theta - b_j)}} \right) \right] \quad (2)$$

where Q_C and Q_W are sets containing the questions correctly and wrongly answered by the student, respectively.

Known the ordered sequence of interactions, SAP is performed as follows:

1. given the latent traits of a question (b_j, a_j) and the student's estimated skill level $(\tilde{\theta}_i$, possibly unknown), the probability of correct answer is computed;
2. if the probability is greater than 0.5 we predict a correct answer;
3. the real answer is observed and compared to the prediction (this is the comparison used to compute the evaluation metrics);
4. the real answer is used to update the estimation of the student's skill level;
5. these steps are repeated for all the items the student interacted with.

By using in the two equations above latent traits coming from different sources, we compare the accuracy of SAP obtained i) with the latent traits estimated with our model, and ii) with ground truth IRT latent traits. Table 3 displays the results of the experiment, showing also as baseline a simple majority prediction. As metrics, we use Area Under Curve (AUC), accuracy, precision and recall on correct answers, and precision and recall on wrong answers. The table shows that our model performs consistently better than the majority baseline and fairly closely to IRT - which is an upper threshold - suggesting that the estimation of latent traits from text can be successfully used as initial calibration of newly generated items. However, it might still be convenient to fine-tune such estimation when the data coming from student interactions becomes available.

Table 3. Students' asnwers prediction.

Model	AUC	Accuracy	Correct		Wrong	
			Precision	Recall	Precision	Recall
IRT	0.74	0.683	0.744	0.735	0.589	0.599
Our model	0.66	0.630	0.707	0.678	0.521	0.555
Majority	0.50	0.613	0.613	1.0	–	0.000

5.3   Ablation Study

The objective of this ablation study is to i) empirically support our choice of features and ii) assess the impact of specific features on the estimation. Table 4 presents the RMSE and the MAE for difficulty estimation and discrimination estimation. In all cases, we use Random Forests in the regression module, since it seemed to be the most accurate and robust approach, according to the preliminary experiments; as baseline, we consider the majority prediction. The combination of all the features leads to the smallest errors, thus suggesting that all the features bring useful information. The IR features seem to provide the most information when considered alone: this is reasonable, since they have two parameters that can be tuned to improve the performance. The smallest error is usually obtained when some terms are removed from the input text; most likely, both corpus specific stop-words and terms which are too rare only introduce noise. It is interesting to notice that readability and linguistic features seem to be more useful for discrimination than difficulty estimation since, when used alone, they perform similarly to the best performing features.

Table 4. Ablation study.

Features	Difficulty estimation				Discrimination estimation			
	INF	SUP	RMSE	MAE	INF	SUP	RMSE	MAE
IR + Ling. + Read.	0.02	0.92	**0.753**	**0.587**	0.02	0.96	**0.369**	**0.287**
IR + Ling.	0.02	0.90	0.754	**0.587**	0.02	0.98	0.370	**0.287**
IR + Read.	0.02	0.94	0.766	0.597	0.02	0.98	0.370	0.288
IR	0.00	0.92	0.758	**0.587**	0.02	0.96	0.372	0.289
Read + Ling	–	–	0.791	0.618	–	–	0.373	0.291
Readability	–	–	0.794	0.619	–	–	0.374	0.292
Linguistic	–	–	0.791	0.620	–	–	0.375	0.292
Majority	–	–	0.820	0.650	–	–	0.502	0.427

6   Conclusions

In this paper we introduced *text2props*, a framework that allows the training and evaluation of models for calibrating newly created Multiple-Choice Questions from textual information. We evaluated a sample model implemented with *text2props* on the tasks of latent traits estimation and students' answers prediction, showing that models implemented with this framework are capable of providing an accurate estimation of the latent traits, thus offering an initial calibration of newly generated questions, which can be fine-tuned when student interactions become available. Our model outperformed the baselines reaching a 6.7% reduction in the RMSE for difficulty estimation and 10.8% reduction in the RMSE for discrimination estimation. As for students' answers prediction, it improved the AUC by 0.16 over the majority baseline, and performed fairly close to the prediction made with IRT latent traits (which is an upper threshold), having an AUC 0.08 lower. Lastly, the ablation study showed that all features are useful for improving the estimation of the latent traits from text, as the best results are obtained when combining all of them. Future works will focus on exploring the effects of other features on the estimation of latent traits (e.g., word embeddings, latent semantic analysis) and testing the capabilities of this framework to estimate other question's properties. Also, future work should focus on the main limitation of *text2props*, consisting in the fact that it forces the implemented models to have the three-modules architecture presented here; in this case the model implemented with this framework proved effective, but it is not guaranteed that it would work similarly well in other situations.

References

1. Abdelrahman, G., Wang, Q.: Knowledge tracing with sequential key-value memory networks (2019)
2. Abyaa, A., Idrissi, M.K., Bennani, S.: Learner modelling: systematic review of the literature from the last 5 years. Educ. Technol. Res. Dev. **67**, 1–39 (2019)
3. Atkinson, R.C.: Ingredients for a theory of instruction. Am. Psychol. **27**(10), 921 (1972)
4. Benedetto, L., Cappelli, A., Turrin, R., Cremonesi, P.: R2DE: a NLP approach to estimating IRT parameters of newly generated questions. In: Proceedings of the Tenth International Conference on Learning Analytics and Knowledge, pp. 412–421 (2020)
5. Bergstra, J., Bengio, Y.: Random search for hyper-parameter optimization. J. Mach. Learn. Res. **13**(Feb), 281–305 (2012)
6. Chen, P., Lu, Y., Zheng, V.W., Pian, Y.: Prerequisite-driven deep knowledge tracing. In: 2018 IEEE International Conference on Data Mining (ICDM), pp. 39–48. IEEE (2018)
7. Coleman, E.B.: On understanding prose: some determiners of its complexity. NSF final report GB-2604 (1965)
8. Ding, X., Larson, E.: Why deep knowledge tracing has less depth than anticipated. In: The 12th International Conference on Educational Data Mining (2019)
9. DuBay, W.H.: The principles of readability. Online Submission (2004)
10. Flesch, R.: A new readability yardstick. J. Appl. Psychol. **32**(3), 221 (1948)
11. Gunning, R.: Technique of clear writing (1968)
12. Hambleton, R.K., Swaminathan, H., Rogers, H.J.: Fundamentals of Item Response Theory. Sage, Thousand Oaks (1991)
13. Huang, Z., et al.: Question difficulty prediction for reading problems in standard tests. In: Thirty-First AAAI Conference on Artificial Intelligence (2017)
14. Huang, Z., Yin, Y., Chen, E., Xiong, H., Su, Y., Hu, G., et al.: EKT: exercise-aware knowledge tracing for student performance prediction. IEEE Trans. Knowl. Data Eng. **PP**, 1 (2019)
15. Kincaid, J.P., Fishburne Jr, R.P., Rogers, R.L., Chissom, B.S.: Derivation of new readability formulas (automated readability index, fog count and flesch reading ease formula) for navy enlisted personnel (1975)
16. Kintsch, W., Vipond, D.: Reading comprehension and readability in educational practice and psychological theory. Perspect. Learn. Mem. 329–365 (2014)
17. Lee, J., Yeung, D.Y.: Knowledge query network for knowledge tracing: how knowledge interacts with skills. In: Proceedings of the 9th International Conference on Learning Analytics and Knowledge, pp. 491–500. ACM (2019)

18. Liu, J., Wang, Q., Lin, C.Y., Hon, H.W.: Question difficulty estimation in community question answering services. In: Proceedings of the 2013 Conference on Empirical Methods in Natural Language Processing, pp. 85–90 (2013)
19. Manning, C.D., Manning, C.D., Schütze, H.: Foundations of Statistical Natural Language Processing. MIT press, Cambridge (1999)
20. Mao, Y., Lin, C., Chi, M.: Deep learning vs. bayesian knowledge tracing: student models for interventions. JEDM J. Educ. Data Min. **10**(2), 28–54 (2018)
21. Mc Laughlin, G.H.: Smog grading-a new readability formula. J. Reading **12**(8), 639–646 (1969)
22. Piech, C., et al.: Deep knowledge tracing. In: Advances in Neural Information Processing Systems, pp. 505–513 (2015)
23. Qiu, Z., Wu, X., Fan, W.: Question difficulty prediction for multiple choice problems in medical exams. In: Proceedings of the 28th ACM International Conference on Information and Knowledge Management, pp. 139–148. ACM (2019)
24. Senter, R., Smith, E.A.: Automated readability index. Technical Report, Cincinnati University, OH (1967)
25. Verhagen, J., Hatfield, D., Arena, D.: Toward a scalable learning analytics solution. In: Isotani, S., Millán, E., Ogan, A., Hastings, P., McLaren, B., Luckin, R. (eds.) International Conference on Artificial Intelligence in Education, vol. 11626, pp. 404–408. Springer, Cham (2019). https://doi.org/10.1007/978-3-030-23207-8_74
26. Wang, Q., Liu, J., Wang, B., Guo, L.: A regularized competition model for question difficulty estimation in community question answering services. In: Proceedings of the 2014 Conference on Empirical Methods in Natural Language Processing (EMNLP), pp. 1115–1126 (2014)
27. Wang, X., Berger, J.O., Burdick, D.S., et al.: Bayesian analysis of dynamic item response models in educational testing. Ann. Appl. Stat. **7**(1), 126–153 (2013)
28. Wilson, K.H., Karklin, Y., Han, B., Ekanadham, C.: Back to the basics: Bayesian extensions of IRT outperform neural networks for proficiency estimation (2016)
29. Yaneva, V., Baldwin, P., Mee, J., et al.: Predicting the difficulty of multiple choice questions in a high-stakes medical exam. In: Proceedings of the Fourteenth Workshop on Innovative Use of NLP for Building Educational Applications, pp. 11–20 (2019)
30. Yeung, C.K.: Deep-IRT: Make deep learning based knowledge tracing explainable using item response theory. arXiv preprint arXiv:1904.11738 (2019)
31. Yeung, C.K., Yeung, D.Y.: Addressing two problems in deep knowledge tracing via prediction-consistent regularization. In: Proceedings of the Fifth Annual ACM Conference on Learning at Scale, p. 5. ACM (2018)
32. Zhang, J., Shi, X., King, I., Yeung, D.Y.: Dynamic key-value memory networks for knowledge tracing. In: Proceedings of the 26th International Conference on World Wide Web, pp. 765–774. International World Wide Web Conferences Steering Committee (2017)
33. Zhang, L., Xiong, X., Zhao, S., Botelho, A., Heffernan, N.T.: Incorporating rich features into deep knowledge tracing. In: Proceedings of the Fourth ACM Conference on Learning@ Scale (2017), pp. 169–172. ACM (2017)

Detecting Off-Task Behavior from Student Dialogue in Game-Based Collaborative Learning

Dan Carpenter[1]([✉]), Andrew Emerson[1], Bradford W. Mott[1], Asmalina Saleh[2],
Krista D. Glazewski[2], Cindy E. Hmelo-Silver[2], and James C. Lester[1]

[1] North Carolina State University, Raleigh, NC 27695, USA
{dcarpen2,ajemerso,bwmott,lester}@ncsu.edu
[2] Indiana University, Bloomington, IN 47405, USA
{asmsaleh,glaze,chmelosi}@indiana.edu

Abstract. Collaborative game-based learning environments integrate game-based learning and collaborative learning. These environments present students with a shared objective and provide them with a means to communicate, which allows them to share information, ask questions, construct explanations, and work together toward their shared goal. A key challenge in collaborative learning is that students may engage in unproductive discourse, which may affect learning activities and outcomes. Collaborative game-based learning environments that can detect this off-task behavior in real-time have the potential to enhance collaboration between students by redirecting the conversation back to more productive topics. This paper investigates the use of dialogue analysis to classify student conversational utterances as either off-task or on-task. Using classroom data collected from 13 groups of four students, we trained off-task dialogue models for text messages from a group chat feature integrated into CRYSTAL ISLAND: ECOJOURNEYS, a collaborative game-based learning environment for middle school ecosystem science. We evaluate the effectiveness of the off-task dialogue models, which use different word embeddings (i.e., word2vec, ELMo, and BERT), as well as predictive off-task dialogue models that capture varying amounts of contextual information from the chat log. Results indicate that predictive off-task dialogue models that incorporate a window of recent context and represent the sequential nature of the chat messages achieve higher predictive performance compared to models that do not leverage this information. These findings suggest that off-task dialogue models for collaborative game-based learning environments can reliably recognize and predict students' off-task behavior, which introduces the opportunity to adaptively scaffold collaborative dialogue.

Keywords: Off-task behavior · Computer-supported collaborative learning ·
Collaborative game-based learning · Game-based learning environments ·
Dialogue analysis

1 Introduction

Computer-supported collaborative learning can create highly effective learning experiences [1, 2]. It has been found that students benefit from learning in groups when

© Springer Nature Switzerland AG 2020
I. I. Bittencourt et al. (Eds.): AIED 2020, LNAI 12163, pp. 55–66, 2020.
https://doi.org/10.1007/978-3-030-52237-7_5

given automated support [3], with conversation between students acting as a stimulus for learning [4]. In digital learning environments, collaboration can be achieved by allowing students to contribute to a group chat conversation [5, 6]. However, students can engage in off-task behavior [7], which can manifest as off-task chat messaging.

Off-task behavior has been identified as a significant challenge [8–10]. Because off-task behavior may be linked to boredom, which has been shown to negatively impact learning outcomes [11], it is important to enable learning environments to respond when students go off task. Although it has been found that off-task behavior can sometimes be beneficial for learning, as students may use off-task time to regulate negative affective states such as frustration [12], it is nonetheless important to identify student behaviors as off-task as such behaviors can be frequently associated with ineffective learning.

Determining when a behavior is off-task is challenging because whether a given behavior is on-task or off-task is highly dependent on the context in which the behavior occurs. To be able to provide adaptive scaffolding that responds to off-task behaviors, learning environments must be able to automatically detect off-task behavior in real-time. While there has been progress on characterizing types of off-task behavior [9, 13] and understanding their impacts on learning [12, 14], limited work has investigated automatically identifying off-task behavior. A particularly intriguing area of unexplored work is on identifying off-task behavior during collaborative learning. In this paper, we investigate off-task dialogue models to classify chat messages from interactions in collaborative game-based learning as off-task or on-task to inform the design of conversational agents that can guide groups that have gone off-task toward more productive dialogue.

Using chat log data collected from middle school students' interactions in CRYSTAL ISLAND: ECOJOURNEYS, a collaborative game-based learning environment for ecosystem science, we investigate off-task dialogue models for classifying students' conversational utterances as off-task or on-task during collaborative game-based learning. We investigate the effects of contextual information by comparing predictive models that only incorporate features derived from the current chat message to models that also include features derived from a context window of previous messages within the chat log. These include both static and sequential modeling techniques that utilize varying amounts of context. Additionally, we compare the use of several word embedding techniques for deriving features. First, we use pre-trained word2vec embeddings [15], which were trained on very large corpora to capture semantic and syntactic features of individual words. Second, we derive embeddings from the ELMo [16] and BERT [17] models, which use sequence-based neural networks to represent lexical semantics. These embeddings also leverage large corpora and augment each word embedding with additional information based on how the word is being used in specific contexts. Results demonstrate that sequential models that incorporate contextual information using both a window of previous dialogue and contextualized word embeddings yield substantial predictive accuracy and precision for detecting off-task student dialogue.

2   Related Work

Computer-supported collaborative learning (CSCL) has been shown to positively impact learning outcomes in a variety of contexts [1, 2]. However, providing students with a means to communicate during learning can potentially lead to off-task conversations. In a study examining discovery learning in a collaborative environment [7], dyads of high school students worked on separate screens in a shared environment and communicated via an integrated chat system. Researchers found that 15.7% of the chat messages were considered to be off-task, which by their definition meant that the messages had nothing to do with the task [7]. And while collaborative game-based learning environments offer the potential to create learning experiences that are engaging on many levels, the combination of collaboration and "seductive details" of game-based learning [8] can potentially exacerbate this issue, leading to off-task behavior.

The majority of previous work investigating off-task behavior in digital learning environments does not seek to automatically detect off-task behaviors. Rather, researchers commonly try to classify the type of off-task behavior and analyze the effects it has on learning [8, 10]. Some work has explored automatically detecting off-task behavior in digital learning environments. Baker [13] sought to detect off-task behavior in an intelligent tutoring system for math education, where off-task behavior was defined as behavior that did not involve the system or the learning task. Field observations of students' behaviors were used as ground truth labels for the machine learning algorithms used by Baker [13] and corresponded to the four categories set forth in Baker et al. [9]. As a baseline, Baker [13] set a threshold for time spent inactive, considering anything above that threshold to be an instance of off-task behavior. Our work extends this line of investigation and focuses on students' textual communication while engaging in collaborative learning.

Little work has analyzed natural language to detect off-task behavior. However, this approach is similar in vein to detecting the topic of students' writing [18–20] and analyzing student dialogue during collaboration [21, 22]. Louis and Higgins [18], Persing and Ng [19] and Rei [20] all used natural language processing methods to determine whether a student's essay is related to a given text prompt. Rei [20] made use of word embeddings for determining if an essay is related to a prompt. Similarly, we use word embeddings to determine if students' dialogue is related to either relevant curricular content or the collaboration process. Focusing more on collaborative learning, Adamson et al. [21] presented a framework for dynamically scaffolding online collaborative learning discussions using conversational agents that analyze students' conversations and respond to certain linguistic triggers. The work by Rodriguez et al. [22] demonstrated that specific characteristics of quality collaboration can be found by examining the contribution of multiple students, which we capture in off-task dialogue models that consider previous messages in the chat log.

3 Off-Task Dialogue Modeling

This work used data collected from CRYSTAL ISLAND: ECOJOURNEYS, a collaborative game-based learning environment on ecosystem science (Fig. 1). Students work together in the game to identify the causes underlying a sudden sickness affecting a fish species on a remote island. Students work at their own computers and share a virtual game environment with the other students in their group. Within each group of students, individual members take on unique roles in the storyline, gathering information that can help them solve the problem along the way. At various points during the story, students gather at an in-game virtual whiteboard to share what they have learned and work together to narrow down the causes of the fishes' sickness. Communication between students is achieved through an in-game chat system (Fig. 1), where they can discuss what they have learned, ask their peers for help, or work together to construct explanations.

In this work, we utilized 4,074 chat messages collected from 13 groups of students. On average, each group sent 313.4 chat messages (min = 118, max = 617, SD = 155.6). Groups consist of four students and a facilitator, who observes students' problem solving and dialogue and guides their discussions. The researcher's role is to keep students on track and to occasionally ask leading questions to nudge them in the right direction. Within each group, students sent an average of 242.3 messages (min = 83, max = 553, SD = 141.9) and the researcher sent an average of 70.1 messages (min = 30, max = 125, SD = 30.1). Individually, students sent an average of 61.8 messages over the course of the study (min = 10, max = 203, SD = 47.7). Messages sent by the researcher were used as context for student messages but were not used as training or testing samples. As a result, the total number of messages available for training and testing was 3,150.

Fig. 1. (Left) CRYSTAL ISLAND: ECOJOURNEYS' gameplay. (Right) CRYSTAL ISLAND: ECOJOURNEYS' in-game chat system.

3.1 Off-Task Message Annotation

We formulate off-task dialogue modeling as a supervised binary classification task. Thus, each message in the chat data is annotated as off-task or on-task. The annotation scheme builds on a classic dialogue act modeling framework [23] as well as dialogue act frameworks related to collaborative learning [22]. Like previous work [24], we label messages as on-task if they address relevant curricular content, foster collaboration, address affective states, or pose relevant questions. These messages are either related to the game's learning goals, self-regulation, or collaborative processes, so we consider them to be on-task. Some examples of chat messages and the labels assigned to them can be seen in Table 1.

To label the chat messages, we first organized the messages by gameplay sessions, which were determined by the day that the students played CRYSTAL ISLAND: ECOJOURNEYS and the group to which they were assigned. This was done so that the sequences of chat messages used to create contextual features were all from the same

Table 1. On-task and off-task chat messages.

	Definition	Examples
On-Task (0)	Productive text: any message that deals with the game's scientific content, fosters collaboration, addresses relevant affective states, or poses a relevant question	"Water temp is warm needs to go in the water cold column" "What do I do I am at the house and have a map"; "Hi" (if the students are introducing themselves)
Off-Task (1)	Text that is not productive	"I notice it seems I am the only one using capital letters around here"; "Nancy and I switched mice and switched back"

group and occurred on the same day. The dataset contains 4,074 messages from 13 groups of students, which are split into 69 gameplay sessions. On average, each session includes approximately 59 messages (min = 1, max = 280, SD = 55.8). Each session, students sent approximately 45.7 messages on average (min = 1, max = 214, SD = 44.9) and the researcher sent approximately 17.1 messages (min = 0, max = 66, SD = 14.4). The data was labeled by two researchers using a rubric that was developed for this task (Table 1). Both researchers labeled 60% of the data, with an overlapping 20% to allow for calculation of inter-rater reliability. The raters achieved a Cohen's kappa of 0.751, indicating substantial agreement. For the messages that the raters did not agree on, labels were reconciled through discussion, and messages that appeared to contain both on-task and off-task dialogue were considered to be on-task. The final message labels contain 1,960 on-task (0) labels and 1,190 off-task labels (37.7% off-task), representing an imbalance. This is significantly higher than the rate of off-task conversation found in some other work [7], which may be because the learning environment combines collaboration and game-related elements.

3.2 Feature Extraction

To evaluate if the context in which a message occurs affects its classification as off-task or on-task, we generated context-based features as well as features that only used information from the current message. The message-specific features were the number of times the student had previously contributed to the group conversation, a score representing the polarity of the message's sentiment, the number of characters in the message, the Jaccard similarity of the message with the game's text content, and the average word embedding for the message [25].

Message sentiment was calculated using NLTK's [26] Vader sentiment analyzer. Because the game is dialogue-driven, information is presented through text-based conversations with in-game characters. We extracted this text from the game and removed stop words, as defined by NLTK's [26] list of English stop words. Then, the complete corpus of game text was compared against each message to calculate Jaccard similarity, which quantifies the similarity between the chat message and the game's text content

Table 2. An example of 21 consecutive chat messages. A window containing a subset of the 20 preceding messages is used as context for predicting whether the last message is on- or off-task.

Number	Group member	Message
1	Wizard (Facilitator)	How are you all doing? It would be great if you could go in and vote once you are done putting your evidence in
2	Student A	We have voted
3	Student B	I am doing very well. I voted for every one and I am also ready for the next chapter. Game on!
4	Student C	And I believe we are done with entering our evidence
5	Wizard	I see that you are all very agreeable!
6	Student B	Great job!
7	Student C	:)
8	Wizard	But we also need to see if we can rule any of our hypotheses out to move on. Let's try to quickly see if we can go through the board. Scientists often have disagreements as they advance their ideas. They will look for evidence both for and against ideas. Let's start on the right with the unsorted ideas. Any suggestions where that might go?
9	Student B	Why thank you kind wizard :)
10	Student B	Ok
11	Student C	Not enough space
12	Student B	Not enough space
13	Wizard	And would that support or not support it? Let's talk about that
14	Student A	If we put that in not enough space then it would kind of be going against it
15	Wizard	What do the rest of you think? How are we then on the 'not enough space' hypothesis?
16	Student B	Yes
17	Student C	Well I think that it should be even though it goes against it it still fits
18	Student A	It has no point in being there because it doesn't affect their health
19	Student A	For not enough space
20	Wizard	[Student A] and [Student B], what do you think? Why would we keep this hypothesis or remove it?
21	Student B	We should actually remove it. It doesn't fit in anything. I thought it over more

[27]. If a message is very similar to the game's text content, then the student is likely talking about something that is relevant to the game and is therefore on-task. Jaccard

similarity, which is the size of the intersection of two sets divided by the size of the union, was preferred over other text similarity metrics like the cosine similarity of tf-idf vectors, because Jaccard similarity only looks at the unique words that are common between two sources of text. This was preferable because many words that are highly related to the game's educational content appear several times in the game's text, and tf-idf would discount these words because they are so common. For the message's average word embedding, we compared word2vec to ELMo and BERT embeddings to evaluate the effects of contextualized embeddings. We used word2vec embeddings with dimensionality 300, ELMo with dimensionality 256, and BERT with dimensionality 768. We used the ELMo embeddings generated from the second LSTM layer (i.e., layer 3 out of 3) to achieve the representation adding contextual information. For the BERT embeddings, we used the average of the token outputs across the 11th layer, which is the last hidden layer. Using these layers for both BERT and ELMo incorporates the richest representation produced by these embedding techniques, allowing for the most contextual information to be used.

For the context-based features, we defined a message's context as a sliding window containing the k previous messages in the chat log. Please see Table 2 for an example of chat dialogue. From these messages, we extracted the number of unique users who contributed to the conversation, the average length of messages in the context, the average time between messages, the number of times the learning facilitator sent a message, the cosine similarity between the current message's average word embedding and the word embedding of the most recent message from the researcher, the cosine similarity between the average word embedding of the current message and the average word embedding for all messages in the context, and the average Jaccard similarity between each previous message and the game's text content. During annotation, researchers noticed that off-task behavior often does not include every student in the team, so keeping track of the number of unique users during this chat window might be an indicator of off-task behavior. That is, if a small number of students are contributing heavily to the chat, it is likely that the messages they are sending are either consistently on-task or consistently off-task. Similarly, message length and time between messages could indicate off-task behavior, since short messages sent in rapid succession likely were not thoughtfully generated and could be off-task. Features related to the researcher's contributions to the chat could indicate off-task behavior, since more messages from the researcher could indicate that they needed to try harder to keep students on-task. Also, given that the facilitator's messages are examples of on-task dialogue, messages that were similar would likely be on-task. Since word embeddings allow words to be represented as real-valued vectors in a high-dimensional space, the cosine similarity between average word embeddings can be used to quantify the similarity of two messages.

3.3 Modeling

We first compared the performance of static models that incorporate contextual information to those that do not. The contextual models include features extracted from the previous 5, 10, 15 or 20 messages within the gameplay session. If there were fewer previous messages than the size of the window, we utilized the most messages available for calculating the features. Additionally, we evaluated the effects of different word embedding techniques (i.e., word2vec, ELMo, and BERT) on the performance of these models. We used logistic regression to perform this binary classification. To ensure a fair feature set comparison, we performed principal component analysis (PCA) on the features for each representation to reduce the feature set to the first 50 principal components. We used standardization of the features before applying PCA, transforming both the training and testing data utilizing the training data's means and standard deviations.

We also investigated the performance of sequential models on this task. We built models that took in different window lengths (i.e., 5, 10, 15, 20) of previous messages, where each message was represented by the set of message-specific features described earlier. Sequences that were shorter than the length of the window were front-padded with zeros. Again, models were evaluated across each word embedding technique. For the sequential modeling task, we adopted LSTM-based sequential models with a single hidden layer. Hyperparameter tuning was performed across the number of nodes in the hidden layer (50, 100, 200, or 300), the activation function (sigmoid, hyperbolic tangent, or rectified linear unit), and the amount of dropout used (0.2, 0.3, 0.4, and 0.5). The optimal configuration was one hidden layer with 50 nodes, sigmoid activation function, and 30% dropout. These models were trained for up to 100 epochs, stopping early if validation loss did not decrease for 15 epochs. Models were trained using group-level 10-fold cross-validation.

4   Results

Results for the off-task prediction task can be found in Table 3. Among the static off-task dialogue models, we found that the most accurate feature configuration used the word2vec embeddings with a context window of size 5 (accuracy = 0.786). We also note that the majority class baseline accuracy for this data is 62.3%, which is the percentage of on-task messages. The improvement over the baseline indicates that the language-based representation of the chat messages does help with determining off-task labels. This same configuration also achieved the highest precision and F1 scores (precision = 0.710, F1 = 0.678). In general, we notice that all three scores tend to be highly related. We also note that, for all embeddings, a context window size of 5 performed the best for these models. Incorporating some amount of contextual information into the model improves performance over relying solely on features derived from the current message, confirming our hypothesis that context can help classify off-task behavior in collaborative game-based learning chat logs.

For the sequential models, the most accurate configuration was the BERT embedding with a window size of 20 (accuracy = 0.791). Both contextual embeddings (i.e., ELMo and BERT) outperformed word2vec across most window sizes. Moreover, these contextual embeddings benefit from longer window sizes, while word2vec still performed best with a window of size 5. While accuracy and F1 score were still correlated, accuracy and precision were less correlated than in the static models, with the most precise configuration being BERT with a window of size 5 (precision = 0.759).

Comparing static and sequential models, we find that the sequential models achieve the best overall performance, both in terms of accuracy and precision. This confirms

Table 3. Results across embedding type, context window length, and model.

Embedding	Context length	Logistic regression			LSTM		
		Accuracy	Precision	F1	Accuracy	Precision	F1
Word2vec	0	0.769	0.691	0.642	–	–	–
	5	**0.786**	**0.710**	**0.678**	0.774	0.710	0.636
	10	0.783	**0.710**	0.676	0.751	0.680	0.609
	15	0.781	0.707	0.670	0.744	0.659	0.604
	20	0.776	0.702	0.660	0.723	0.628	0.591
ELMo	0	0.754	0.662	0.615	–	–	–
	5	0.778	0.696	0.661	0.772	0.693	0.660
	10	0.775	0.701	0.654	0.781	0.707	0.667
	15	0.767	0.687	0.645	0.788	0.714	0.676
	20	0.766	0.681	0.643	0.789	0.720	0.678
BERT	0	0.745	0.664	0.635	–	–	–
	5	0.763	0.684	0.653	0.787	**0.759**	0.660
	10	0.768	0.696	0.659	0.787	0.731	0.674
	15	0.767	0.692	0.657	0.778	0.744	0.670
	20	0.763	0.687	0.651	**0.791**	0.714	**0.686**

our hypothesis that sequential techniques for modeling off-task behavior in student conversations outperform static techniques. While the static models performed best with short context windows, the sequential models make better use of longer context.

4.1 Discussion

For the static models, a short window of context yielded the best performance. A window of size 5 performed better than no context at all, and performance tended to decrease with longer windows. This may be because using too much context relies too heavily on information from the past, whereas information that is more recent can indicate components of the conversation's flow. Longer context windows likely include more information from irrelevant messages, and since the static models summarize previous chat messages by averaging features, relevant and irrelevant information are treated the same. However, the sequential models made better use of more context. The performance of the word2vec embeddings decreased as window size increased, but the contextual embeddings (i.e., ELMo and BERT) performed best with windows of size 20. We speculate that this may be due to the fact that ELMo and BERT create embeddings that, in addition to the syntactic and semantic information transferred from pre-training on large corpora, also encode some information that is related to the specific context in which words were used. Thus, while longer sequences accrue more noise from the solely pre-trained embeddings, the sequential models may be able to focus on context-specific information captured by the contextualized embeddings.

We found that the simpler logistic regression models performed nearly as well as the LSTM models. While we might expect the gap between the static and sequential models to widen given more training data, since the LSTM may be able to pick up on more complex relationships than logistic regression, the static models performed well in this study. This may be due to the set of features that were used to represent the chat's context. In particular, we expect that the cosine similarity with the facilitator's most recent message and the average Jaccard similarity between each previous message and the game's text content could be very helpful in identifying messages as off-task. Since the facilitator's messages are examples of on-task dialogue, messages that are similar will likely be on-task as well. For instance, if a student is responding to the facilitator's question or talking about a similar topic, their messages would likely be similar. In much the same way, if the average Jaccard similarity between the messages in the context window and the game's text content is high, this is an indicator that students are likely talking about things that are related to the game and are thus on-task.

5   Conclusion and Future Work

Collaborative game-based learning environments create learning experiences that feature rich collaborative problem solving. However, students interacting with one another may at times engage in off-task behavior, which can manifest in off-task chat messages. If a collaborative game-based learning environment could utilize an off-task dialogue model to reliably recognize and even predict when students go off-task, it could facilitate more productive conversation. In this work, we have presented predictive off-task dialogue models that analyze students' chat conversations and detect off-task behavior. In particular, LSTM models that use contextualized BERT word embeddings achieve substantial accuracy for detecting off-task messages. These models perform best when provided with a context window of 20 previous messages, since they are able to effectively identify features of the previous messages that may be followed by instances of off-task behavior.

In future work, it will be instructive to investigate additional conversational modeling that considers participant role to determine the most relevant message to send to the students to get them back on task. Additionally, it may be possible to increase the predictive accuracy of models with word-by-word sequential modeling and sentence embedding. Together, these may significantly increase the ability of off-task dialogue models to recognize and predict off-task behavior, which opens the door to real-time adaptive facilitation that supports robust collaborative learning.

Acknowledgements. This research was supported by the National Science Foundation under Grants DRL-1561486, DRL-1561655, SES-1840120, and IIS-1839966. Any opinions, findings, and conclusions expressed in this material are those of the authors and do not necessarily reflect the views of the National Science Foundation.

References

1. Chen, J., Wang, M., Kirschner, P.A., Tsai, C.C.: The role of collaboration, computer use, learning environments, and supporting strategies in CSCL: a meta-analysis. Rev. Educ. Res. **88**(6), 799–843 (2018)
2. Jeong, H., Hmelo-Silver, C.E., Jo, K.: Ten years of computer-supported collaborative learning: a meta-analysis of CSCL in STEM education during 2005–2014. Educ. Res. Rev. **28**, 100284 (2019)
3. Hmelo-Silver, C.E.: Analyzing collaborative knowledge construction: multiple methods for integrated understanding. Comput. Educ. **41**(4), 397–420 (2003)
4. Rosé, C.P., Ferschke, O.: Technology support for discussion based learning: from computer supported collaborative learning to the future of massive open online courses. Int. J. Artif. Intell. Educ. **26**(2), 660–678 (2016)
5. Jeong, H., Hmelo-Silver, C.E.: Technology supports in CSCL. In: The Future of Learning: Proceedings of the 10th International Conference of the Learning Sciences (ICLS 2012), vol. 1, pp. 339–346 (2012)
6. Jeong, H., Hmelo-Silver, C.E.: Seven affordances of computer-supported collaborative learning: how to support collaborative learning? How can technologies help? Educ. Psychol. **51**(2), 247–265 (2016)
7. Saab, N., van Joolingen, W.R., van Hout-Wolters, B.H.: Communication in collaborative discovery learning. Br. J. Educ. Psychol. **75**(4), 603–621 (2005)
8. Rowe, J.R., McQuiggan, S.W., Robison, J.L., Lester, J.: Off-task behavior in narrative-centered learning environments. In: Proceedings of the International Conference on Artificial Intelligence in Education, pp. 99–106 (2009)
9. Baker, R.S., Corbett, A.T., Koedinger, K.R., Wagner, A.Z.: Off-task behavior in the cognitive tutor classroom: when students "game the system". In: Proceedings of the SIGCHI Conference on Human Factors in Computing Systems, pp. 383–390 (2004)
10. Beserra, V., Nussbaum, M., Oteo, M.: On-task and off-task behavior in the classroom: a study on mathematics learning with educational video games. J. Educ. Comput. Res. **56**(8), 1361–1383 (2019)
11. Baker, R.S., D'Mello, S.K., Rodrigo, M.M.T., Graesser, A.C.: Better to be frustrated than bored: the incidence, persistence, and impact of learners' cognitive–affective states during interactions with three different computer-based learning environments. Int. J. Hum.-Comput. Stud. **68**(4), 223–241 (2010)
12. Sabourin, J.L., Rowe, J.P., Mott, B.W., Lester, J.C.: Considering alternate futures to classify off-task behavior as emotion self-regulation: a supervised learning approach. J. Educ. Data Min. **5**(1), 9–38 (2013)
13. Baker, R.S.: Modeling and understanding students' off-task behavior in intelligent tutoring systems. In: Proceedings of the SIGCHI Conference on Human Factors in Computing Systems, pp. 1059–1068 (2007)
14. Cocea, M., Hershkovitz, A., Baker, R.S.: The impact of off-task and gaming behaviors on learning: immediate or aggregate? In: Proceeding of the 2009 Conference on Artificial Intelligence in Education: Building Learning Systems that Care: From Knowledge Representation to Affective Modelling, pp. 507–514. IOS Press (2009)
15. Mikolov, T., Sutskever, I., Chen, K., Corrado, G.S., Dean, J.: Distributed representations of words and phrases and their compositionality. In: Advances in Neural Information Processing Systems, pp. 3111–3119 (2013)
16. Peters, M.E., et al.: Deep contextualized word representations (2018). arXiv preprint arXiv: 1802.05365

17. Devlin, J., Chang, M.W., Lee, K., Toutanova, K.: Bert: pre-training of deep bidirectional transformers for language understanding (2018). arXiv preprint arXiv:1810.04805
18. Louis, A., Higgins, D.: Off-topic essay detection using short prompt texts. In: Proceedings of the NAACL HLT 2010 Fifth Workshop on Innovative Use of NLP for Building Educational Applications, Association for Computational Linguistics, pp. 92–95 (2010)
19. Persing, I., Ng, V.: Modeling prompt adherence in student essays. In: Proceedings of the 52nd Annual Meeting of the Association for Computational Linguistics (Volume 1: Long Papers), pp. 1534–1543 (2014)
20. Rei, M.: Detecting off-topic responses to visual prompts. In: Proceedings of the 12th Workshop on Innovative Use of NLP for Building Educational Applications, pp. 188–197 (2017)
21. Adamson, D., Dyke, G., Jang, H., Rosé, C.P.: Towards an agile approach to adapting dynamic collaboration support to student needs. Int. J. Artif. Intell. Educ. 24(1), 92–124 (2014)
22. Rodriguez, F.J., Price, K.M., Boyer, K.E.: Exploring the pair programming process: characteristics of effective collaboration. In: Proceedings of the 2017 ACM SIGCSE Technical Symposium on Computer Science Education. ACM (2017)
23. Stolcke, A., et al.: Dialogue act modeling for automatic tagging and recognition of conversational speech. Comput. Linguist. 26(3), 339–373 (2000)
24. Mercier, E.M., Higgins, S.E., Joyce-Gibbons, A.: The effects of room design on computer-supported collaborative learning in a multi-touch classroom. Interact. Learn. Environ. 24(3), 504–522 (2016)
25. Sultan, M.A., Bethard, S., Sumner, T.: DLS@CU: sentence similarity from word alignment and semantic vector composition. In: Proceedings of the 9th International Workshop on Semantic Evaluation (SemEval 2015), pp. 148–153 (2015)
26. Bird, S., Loper, E., Klein, E.: Natural Language Processing with Python. O'Reilly Media Inc., California (2009)
27. Niwattanakul, S., Singthongchai, J., Naenudorn, E., Wanapu, S.: Using of Jaccard coefficient for keywords similarity. In: Proceedings of the International Multiconference of Engineers and Computer Scientists, pp. 380–384 (2013)

Automated Analysis of Middle School Students' Written Reflections During Game-Based Learning

Dan Carpenter[1]([✉]), Michael Geden[1], Jonathan Rowe[1], Roger Azevedo[2], and James Lester[1]

[1] North Carolina State University, Raleigh, NC 27695, USA
{dcarpen2,mageden,jprowe,lester}@ncsu.edu
[2] University of Central Florida, Orlando, FL 32816, USA
roger.azevedo@ucf.edu

Abstract. Game-based learning environments enable students to engage in authentic, inquiry-based learning. Reflective thinking serves a critical role in inquiry-based learning by encouraging students to think critically about their knowledge and experiences in order to foster deeper learning processes. Free-response reflection prompts can be embedded in game-based learning environments to encourage students to engage in reflection and externalize their reflection processes, but automatically assessing student reflection presents significant challenges. In this paper, we present a framework for automatically assessing students' written reflection responses during inquiry-based learning in CRYSTAL ISLAND, a game-based learning environment for middle school microbiology. Using data from a classroom study involving 153 middle school students, we compare the effectiveness of several computational representations of students' natural language responses to reflection prompts—GloVe, ELMo, tf-idf, unigrams—across several machine learning-based regression techniques (i.e., random forest, support vector machine, multi-layer perceptron) to assess the depth of student reflection responses. Results demonstrate that assessment models based on ELMo deep contextualized word representations yield more accurate predictions of students' written reflection depth than competing techniques. These findings point toward the potential of leveraging automated assessment of student reflection to inform real-time adaptive support for inquiry-based learning in game-based learning environments.

Keywords: Reflection · Self-regulated learning · Metacognition · Game-based learning · Natural language

1 Introduction

Game-based learning environments provide rich opportunities for students to engage in scientific inquiry by exploring problems that are complex, open-ended, and realistic [1]. Inquiry-based learning has been demonstrated to yield significant improvements

© Springer Nature Switzerland AG 2020
I. I. Bittencourt et al. (Eds.): AIED 2020, LNAI 12163, pp. 67–78, 2020.
https://doi.org/10.1007/978-3-030-52237-7_6

in students' science literacy and research skills [2, 3]. However, the open-ended nature of inquiry learning in game-based environments can prove challenging for many students, which points toward the importance of students effectively regulating their own learning processes [4–6]. Reflection is a key component of self-regulated learning [7]. During reflection, students can become aware of their problem-solving progress and make adaptations to their learning strategies, which can lead to improved learning outcomes [8–10]. We define reflection as a process of introspective consideration of one's own knowledge and learning experiences, which is used to inform strategic revisions for improving learning [11]. During inquiry-based learning, it is important for students to reflect on their knowledge and actions to ensure that they are on track to achieving their desired learning objectives.

A common approach to capturing students' reflections during learning is through free-response reflection prompts [12]. Free-response reflection prompts can be embedded in game-based learning environments to encourage reflection and externalize students' reflection processes. A key dimension of student reflection is reflection depth, which distinguishes between responses that exemplify productive reflection versus surface-level observations or verbatim restatements of content [13, 14].

Assessing students' written responses to reflection prompts can provide insight into the characteristics of students' reflective thinking. However, assessing students' written reflections is often a manual, labor-intensive process. Devising automated methods for assessing reflection is critical for enabling adaptive learning environments that can support students' self-regulatory processes during inquiry-based learning. Approaches to automatically assessing student reflection include expert-crafted rule-based systems, dictionary-based techniques that search for specific words and phrases, and machine learning approaches that are data-driven [15]. Machine learning approaches show particular promise for devising automated reflection assessment models that are accurate, reliable, and can be utilized at run-time [15]. Previous work investigating machine learning approaches to automatically assessing written reflections has used count-based representations of students' natural language reflections [15, 16]. Recent advances in distributed embedding-based representations of natural language show particular promise for encoding students' natural language reflections for automated assessment [17, 18]. Using pre-trained word embeddings, such as GloVe [19] and ELMo [20], syntactic and semantic information captured from large corpora can be leveraged to concisely represent students' written reflections.

In this paper, we present a framework for automatically assessing students' written reflections during inquiry-based learning. Using written reflections of 153 middle school students, we investigate several vector-based representations of students' written reflection responses—unigram, tf-idf, GloVe, and ELMo embedding-based representations—to induce machine learning-based models for measuring the depth of student reflection.

2 Related Work

Reflection plays a critical role in self-regulated learning (SRL). In the Information Processing Theory of SRL [7], reflection is both a backward-looking and forward-looking process [21]. Specifically, students look back at what they have learned and the actions they have taken in the past, and they consider what changes they might need to make to achieve their learning goals moving forward [21]. Reflection is especially important in inquiry-based learning, since it is important for students to understand the relationships between their learning and problem-solving goals [22].

A common approach for assessing students' written reflections is to create a model that distinguishes between varying degrees of reflection depth and different characteristics of reflection breadth [12]. In surveying 34 different models used to analyze reflection, Ullmann [12] found that many models include some notion of reflective depth, often ranging from non-reflective to slightly reflective to highly reflective [13, 23]. Many models also attempt to capture the breadth of reflection, including aspects such as 'attending to feelings' and 'validation' [24] or 'justification' [25]. Students' written responses to reflection prompts embedded in game-based learning environments are often brief, and therefore, inherently limited in reflective breadth. Thus, reflective depth serves as a proxy for measuring the quality of students' reflective thinking during inquiry-based learning in game-based environments.

After establishing a model of reflection, a manual coding process is commonly used to analyze and assess written reflections [15]. Coding students' written reflections can be a labor-intensive process, which has motivated growing interest in automated reflection analysis methods. Approaches to automatic reflection assessment include dictionary-based, rule-based, and machine learning-based systems [15, 16]. Prior work on automated analysis of student reflections has largely used one-hot encodings and features derived from LIWC and Coh-Metrix to represent students' reflections [15, 16]. However, recent advances in natural language understanding and automated essay scoring suggest that pre-trained word embeddings, such as GloVe [19] and ELMo [20], show promise as representations of students' written reflections [17, 18], since they are trained on large corpora and capture both syntactic and semantic aspects of language. Of the work that has been done to automatically assess written reflection, there is a common focus on assessing the written reflections of students in higher education [15, 16]. While supporting reflection in college students is important, substantial benefits can be found when students engage in SRL processes from a young age [26, 27]. Written data from K-12 students presents a distinctive set of challenges, since it is often short and rife with grammatical errors and misspellings [28]. There is a need to investigate more robust techniques for representing written reflections of K-12 students.

Two recent studies, conducted by Kovanovic et al. [16] and Ullmann [15], have investigated machine learning-based approaches for automated assessment of student reflections. Kovanovic et al. [16] coded three different types of reflections (i.e., observations, motives, and goals). To represent written reflections, they extracted the 100 most common unigrams, bigrams, and trigrams (300 total) from their corpus, generated linguistic features using the Linguistic Inquiry and Word Count (LIWC) tool, and extracted several Coh-Metrix features [16]. The model of reflection used by Ullmann [15] included a binary indicator of reflective depth (i.e., reflective versus non-reflective) and seven breadth dimensions that address common components of reflective models (e.g., description of an experience, awareness of difficulties, and future intentions). Ullmann used binary vectors to represent the unique unigrams that occurred in each reflection, ignoring any unigrams that occurred less than ten times throughout the entire corpus [15].

In contrast to this previous work, our model of reflection evaluates reflection depth on a continuous scale. We use Ullmann's binary unigram representation of written reflection as a baseline and investigate the benefits of several language modeling techniques: tf-idf, GloVe, and ELMo. Tf-idf represents a step up in complexity from the binary unigram representation and has been used as a baseline representation for text classification [29]. GloVe [19] and ELMo [20] concisely capture both syntactic and semantic aspects of language. For GloVe and ELMo, we represent student reflections as the average of the embeddings for each word [30]. Furthermore, Kovanovic et al. [16] and Ullmann [15] investigated written reflections collected from undergraduate students, while we explore middle school students' reflections as they engage with a game-based learning environment in their science classrooms.

3   Method

To investigate automated assessment of student reflection, we use data from student inter-actions with CRYSTAL ISLAND, a game-based learning environment for middle school microbiology (Fig. 1). In CRYSTAL ISLAND, students adopt the role of a science detec-tive who has recently arrived at a remote island research station to investigate the cause of an outbreak among a group of scientists. Students explore the open-world virtual environment, gather information by reading in-game books and articles, speak with non-player characters, perform scientific tests in a virtual laboratory, and record their findings in a virtual diagnosis worksheet. Students solve the mystery by submitting a diagnosis explaining the type of pathogen causing the illness, the transmission source of the disease, and a recommended treatment or prevention plan.

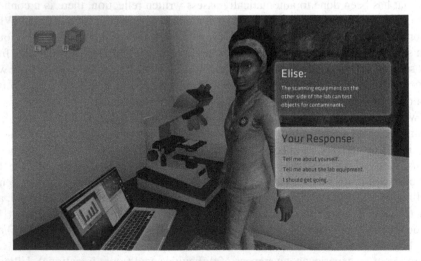

Fig. 1. Crystal Island game-based learning environment.

3.1 Student Reflection Dataset

We analyze a corpus of students' written reflections collected during a pair of classroom studies involving middle school students interacting with CRYSTAL ISLAND during spring 2018 and spring 2019. Data was collected from 153 students in total, but only 118 students reported demographic information. Among these students, 51% identified as female, and ages ranged from 13-14 (M = 13.6, SD = 0.51). 43 students reported being Caucasian/White, 32 reported being African American, 21 students reported being Hispanic or Latino, and 3 reported being of Asian descent. The students did not have prior experience with CRYSTAL ISLAND.

In both studies, students completed a series of pre-study measures the week prior to interacting with CRYSTAL ISLAND, including a microbiology content knowledge test, an emotions, interest, and value instrument, and an achievement goal instrument. Students were briefly introduced to the game by a researcher, and they viewed a short video trailer that provided background on the game's storyline. Afterward, students interacted with CRYSTAL ISLAND until they solved the mystery or when approximately 100 min of gameplay time had elapsed. After finishing the game, students completed a series of post-study materials, which included another microbiology content knowledge test as well as several questionnaires about students' experiences with the game, including sense of presence and engagement.

While interacting with CRYSTAL ISLAND, students were periodically prompted to reflect on what they had learned thus far and what they planned to do moving forward (Fig. 2). These reflection prompts came after major game events, such as talking with the camp nurse, testing objects in the virtual laboratory, or submitting a diagnosis. Students received several prompts for reflection during the game (M = 3.0, SD = 0.95). After completing the game or running out of time, students were asked to reflect on their problem-solving experience as a whole, explaining how they approached the problem

Fig. 2. In-game reflection prompt presented to students.

and whether they would do anything differently if they were asked to solve a similar problem in the future. In total, the data included 728 reflection responses from 153 students. The average length of a reflection response was approximately 19 words (min $= 1$, max $= 100$, SD $= 14.2$). (Please see Table 1 for several example student responses to reflection prompts in CRYSTAL ISLAND.)

3.2 Annotating Students' Written Responses to Reflection Prompts

To measure the depth of students' responses to reflection prompts, a five-point scale was developed by two of the authors using a grounded theory approach [31]. The scale was devised to measure the extent to which students assessed their own knowledge and articulated plans exemplifying high-quality reasoning, hypothesis formation, and

Table 1. Rubric used to annotate students' written responses to reflection prompts. Reflections showing at least one characteristic in the middle column were assigned the associated rating.

Rating	Characteristics	Examples
1	Lacks both a plan and knowledge; abstract and largely meaningless; unactionable	"Each clue will help with solving the problem"; "Yeah cool game I learned science"
2	Presents a vague hypothesis or plan with no clear reasoning; simply restates information that was directly learned in the game, with no abstraction or inference on the part of the student	"That the illness causing the people being sick might be pathogen"; "I found out that the egg has bacteria"; "I think I am going to talk to other people"
3	Presents a clear hypothesis or a plan, but doesn't provide any reasoning for it; demonstrates awareness about gaps in knowledge and presents a plan to fix it; organizes the importance of their knowledge	"Getting more information off the food I think it has something to do with the food"; "The most important thing is how the illness is spreading"
4	Presents a clear hypothesis or plan with reasoning; provides an abstraction of the situation with a plan; addresses what they have learned, why it is important, and what they plan to do with this information	"I plan on questioning the cook as they know more about the food and how it could be contaminated with viruses or bacteria"; "I need to learn more about what the sick people do on a day to day schedule"
5	Presents both a clear hypothesis and plan with reasoning; presents a high-quality sequence of abstract plans	"I think that it might have to do with salmonella because when I tested the milk it was positive with pathogenic bacteria. I think that I will test things that can be contaminated"; "I will continue to test the foods the sick people touched or previously ate to see if it's contaminated"

metacognition. The researchers reviewed 20 reflection responses together, discussing the strengths and weaknesses of each. These reflection responses were individually selected to represent the range of reflection depth in the dataset, with the goal of including several reflections for each of the five ratings. That is, the researchers selected some reflections that seemed to be particularly weak and discussed why they were weak. The observations and insights from these discussions formed the basis for the lowest reflection depth rating. A similar process was used for the other ratings to develop a rubric for evaluating reflection depth (Table 1), providing examples and reasoning for the five possible scores. Once the rubric was developed, the researchers separately annotated another 20 reflections to verify the reliability of the model, then discussed and reconciled incongruent ratings. Finally, the remaining 708 reflections were separately annotated by both researchers and an intraclass correlation of 0.669 was achieved, indicating moderate inter-rater reliability. The final ratings of reflection depth were calculated by averaging the values assigned by the two authors (M = 2.41, SD = 0.86), yielding a continuous measure of reflection. Averaging ratings is a standard approach for reconciling differences between coders' assigned ratings, although it does have limitations. For example, reflections that received the same rating from both coders (e.g., 3 and 3) and reflections that received different ratings (e.g., 2 and 4) would be rated the same even though there is disagreement in the latter case.

3.3 Modeling Reflective Depth Using Natural Language Embeddings

Prior to modeling student reflections, the text responses were normalized using tokenization, conversion to lowercase, and removal of non-grammatical characters. When generating binary unigram vectors, tokens that appeared fewer than ten times throughout the corpus were removed. Similarly, any words that were not found in the GloVe embeddings were ignored when calculating average GloVe and ELMo word embeddings, effectively removing misspelled words from the data. We trained regression models using random forests, SVM, and feedforward neural networks using scikit-learn [32]. Reflection assessment models were trained using nested 10-fold cross-validation at the student level. Within each fold, 10-fold cross-validation was used for hyperparameter tuning. Random forest models were tuned over the number of trees in the forest (100, 200, or 300), the minimum number of samples required to split an internal node (2, 4, or 10), and a the maximum number of features to consider when searching for the best split (log2 or no maximum). SVM models were tuned over the kernel type (rbf or linear) and the regularization parameter (1, 2, 5, 10). Multi-layer perceptron models were tuned over the number of neurons in the hidden layer (50, 100, or 200) and the L2 regularization penalty (0.0001, 0.001, 0.01).

As a baseline, we encoded each natural language reflection as a binary vector representing the unique unigrams that occurred in that reflection (i.e., a one-hot encoding).

This was a 220-dimension vector, where each index represents the presence of a specific word in the corpus vocabulary after infrequent words were removed. We also encoded the student reflections as tf-idf vectors, which are sparse real-valued vectors that represent documents based on the frequency of each term in the corpus, weighted by the uniqueness of that term in the corpus. Since tf-idf accounts for the frequency of each word, unlike the binary unigram representation, infrequent words were not removed. Finally, we examined two different word embedding techniques, GloVe [19] and ELMo [20]. GloVe embeddings are word-based, so it is possible to use pre-trained GloVe embeddings, which have been trained on other corpora (i.e., Wikipedia and Gigaword), and simply look up embeddings by word. We also investigated the benefits of fine-tuning GloVe embeddings. Fine tuning allows you to take the pre-trained embeddings and infuse domain-specific information from an available corpus. Both the pre-trained and fine-tuned GloVe embeddings were 300-dimension real-valued vectors. ELMo, which was also trained on large corpora but uses character-based methods to represent text, is built with the intention that sentences, and not individual words, are used to create embeddings [20]. To maintain a fair comparison between the various representations of students' written reflections, we first embedded entire written reflection responses with ELMo and then extracted individual word embeddings. This allows the embeddings to capture information related to the specific context in which each word was used. The ELMo word embeddings were 256-dimension real-valued vectors. For both GloVe and ELMo, we represented the reflection text as the average embedding across all words in the reflection.

4   Results

To investigate the relationship between student learning outcomes and depth of reflection during inquiry-based learning in CRYSTAL ISLAND, we utilized Pearson correlation analysis. Average reflection depth ratings for all reflections a student wrote were found to be positively correlated with student post-test scores ($r(601) = .29$, $p < .001$).

Next, we compared the accuracy of competing models of reflection depth across five natural language embedding representations and three machine learning-based regression techniques. Models were evaluated using R-squared, mean absolute error, and mean squared error (Table 2).

Table 2. Model results using 10-fold cross-validation. Bold values represent best performance.

Text features	RF			SVM			NN-MLP		
	R^2	MSE	MAE	R^2	MSE	MAE	R^2	MSE	MAE
Binary unigram	0.57	0.32	0.42	0.62	0.28	0.41	0.49	0.37	0.46
TF-IDF	0.53	0.34	0.43	0.40	0.43	0.51	0.43	0.51	0.55
GloVe	0.49	0.38	0.49	0.48	0.38	0.47	0.38	0.67	0.61
GloVe fine-tuned	0.49	0.38	0.49	0.52	0.35	0.45	0.35	0.62	0.62
ELMo	0.55	0.33	0.45	**0.64**	**0.26**	**0.40**	0.26	0.39	0.49

Results indicated that SVM models using average ELMo embeddings to represent students' written reflections achieved the highest predictive accuracy (R-squared = 0.64, MSE = 0.26, MAE = 0.40). While we expected the tf-idf representation to yield improved performance relative to the binary unigram representation, the top performing model using tf-idf vectors performed substantially worse (R-squared = 0.53, MSE = 0.34, MAE = 0.43). This may be due to the fact that, while tf-idf accounts for infrequent terms, keeping words with fewer than ten occurrences in the corpus resulted in a very large and sparse feature space. We also expected GloVe word embeddings, which are able to leverage data from large corpora, to outperform both binary unigram and tf-idf, but the GloVe embedding representations of students' written reflections generally performed the worst out of all feature representations (R-squared = 0.49, MSE = 0.38, MAE = 0.49). Fine tuning GloVe embeddings using the CRYSTAL ISLAND reflection dataset appears to help (R-squared = 0.52, MSE = 0.35, MAE = 0.45), but the improvement is marginal. Notably, the accuracy of the SVM + ELMo approach was greater than all competing methods, including the binary unigram baseline representation, but the improvement was relatively small. A possible explanation is that the information captured by ELMo's character-level embeddings and sentence-based contextualization is critical, especially considering the small size of the dataset used in this work. In comparison, GloVe produces word-level embeddings that are not contextualized, which means that GloVe embeddings encode less fine-grained information as well as less context-based information. The performance of unigram models may be explained by the fact that they use only data from students' natural language responses to reflection prompts in CRYSTAL ISLAND, which removes potential noise from external data sources.

To better understand how the competing models distinguished between different levels of depth in students' written reflections, we qualitatively examined several select assessments generated by the SVM + ELMo model, several of which are shown below in Table 3.

Table 3. Predictions of reflection depth (SVM with ELMo features).

Reflection	Predicted score	Actual score
"The most important things I've learned are that oranges, raw chicken, and tomato were tested positive for nonpathogenic virus. Eggs were tested positive for pathogenic virus. I believe that salmonellosis is the disease that the infected people on Crystal Island have, but I will have to gather some more information on other diseases"	3.3	4
"The egg has a pathogenic virus in it. Influenza is a virus that is spread through direct contact and the only prevention is vaccination"	3.1	3.5
"The milk is contaminated with pathogenic bacteria. To test other foods sick members may have been in contact with"	3.1	3
"I realized that raw chicken has influenza"	1.4	2
"I've learned a lot and my plan moving forward is in progress"	1.4	1

Examples that were assigned higher depth scores appeared to be longer and contain more terms that relate to the microbiology content (e.g., pathogenic, virus, bacteria) in

Crystal Island. This is notable because the ELMo embedding representation should not be sensitive to reflection length; it uses the average word embedding of the reflection response. Reflection responses that were assigned lower scores, on the other hand, are shorter and use fewer terms relevant to the learning scenario's science content. Low-scoring reflections are short, vague, and provide little evidence of deeper reasoning.

5 Conclusion and Future Work

Reflection is critical to learning. Scaffolding student reflection in game-based learning environments shows significant promise for supporting self-regulation and enhancing learning outcomes. By prompting students to engage in written reflection during inquiry-based learning experiences, there is an opportunity to identify when students are not reflecting effectively and scaffold their self-regulated learning processes. This work investigated machine learning-based methods for automatically assessing the depth of student reflection by leveraging natural language embedding-based representations (i.e., GloVe and ELMo) of reflections in a game-based learning environment for middle school microbiology education. Results showed that SVM models using average ELMo embeddings were best able to predict reflection depth compared to competing baseline techniques.

There are several promising directions for future research on automated assessment and support of student reflection during inquiry-based learning. First, investigating methods to address the inherent "noisiness" of middle school students' reflective writings, including misspellings, grammatical errors, non-standard word usage, and other issues of writing quality, shows significant promise, as they are an inevitable feature of K-12 student writing. A related direction is to investigate the relationship between students' English language proficiency and the ratings assigned to their written reflections. Another direction for future work is to investigate alternative machine learning techniques for modeling the depth of student reflections, including deep neural architectures (e.g., recurrent neural networks). Deep recurrent neural networks have been found to be especially effective for capturing sequential patterns in natural language data, and it is possible that they may be well suited for modeling sequential linguistic structures that are more indicative of reflection depth than individual words. Moreover, since deep neural networks can learn abstract representations of data, models of student reflection derived using deep neural networks may be able to generalize to written reflections in different domains. Finally, it will be important to investigate ways in which computational models for automatically assessing student reflection can be used to generate explanations for ratings of reflection depth, which can be provided to learners and teachers to help support the development of reflection and self-regulated learning skills.

Acknowledgements. This research was supported by funding from the National Science Foundation under Grant DRL-1661202. Any opinions, findings, and conclusions expressed in this material are those of the authors and do not necessarily reflect the views of the NSF.

References

1. Plass, J., Mayer, R.E., Homer, B. (eds.): Handbook of Game-Based Learning. MIT Press, Cambridge (2020)
2. Gormally, C., Brickman, P., Hallar, B., Armstrong, N.: Effects of inquiry-based learning on students' science literacy skills and confidence. Int. J. Sch. Teach. Learn. 3(2), n2 (2009)
3. Lazonder, A.W., Harmsen, R.: Meta-analysis of inquiry-based learning: effects of guidance. Rev. Educ. Res. 86(3), 681–718 (2016)
4. Belland, B.R., Walker, A.E., Kim, N.J., Lefler, M.: Synthesizing results from empirical research on computer-based scaffolding in STEM education: a meta-analysis. Rev. Educ. Res. 87(2), 309–344 (2017)
5. Yew, E.H., Goh, K.: Problem-based learning: an overview of its process and impact on learning. Health Prof. Educ. 2(2), 75–79 (2016)
6. Taub, M., Sawyer, R., Smith, A., Rowe, J., Azevedo, R., Lester, J.: The agency effect: the impact of student agency on learning, emotions, and problem-solving behaviors in a game-based learning environment. Comput. Educ. 147, 103781 (2020)
7. Winne, P.H.: Cognition and metacognition within self-regulated learning. In: Handbook of Self-regulation of Learning and Performance, pp. 52–64. Routledge (2017)
8. Azevedo, R., Mudrick, N.V., Taub, M., Bradbury, A.E.: Self-regulation in computer-assisted learning systems. In: Dunlosky, J., Rawson, K. (eds.) The Cambridge Handbook of Cognition and Education, pp. 587–618. Cambridge Press, Cambridge (2019)
9. Joksimović, S., Dowell, N., Gašević, D., Mirriahi, N., Dawson, S., Graesser, A.C.: Linguistic characteristics of reflective states in video annotations under different instructional conditions. Comput. Hum. Behav. 96, 211–222 (2019)
10. Moon, J.A.: A Handbook of Reflective and Experiential Learning: Theory and Practice. Routledge, Abingdon (2004)
11. Boud, D., Keogh, R., Walker, D. (eds.): Reflection: Turning Experience into Learning. Kogan Page, London (1985)
12. Ullmann, T.D.: Automated detection of reflection in texts - a machine learning based approach. Doctoral dissertation, The Open University (2015)
13. Mezirow, J.: Transformative Dimensions of Adult Learning. Jossey-Bass, San Francisco (1991)
14. Tsingos, C., Bosnic-Anticevich, S., Lonie, J.M., Smith, L.: A model for assessing reflective practices in pharmacy education. Am. J. Pharm. Educ. 79(8), 124 (2015). https://doi.org/10.5688/ajpe798124
15. Ullmann, T.D.: Automated analysis of reflection in writing: validating machine learning approaches. Int. J. Artif. Intell. Educ. 29(2), 217–257 (2019)
16. Kovanović, V., et al.: Understand students' self-reflections through learning analytics. In: Proceedings of the 8th International Conference on Learning Analytics and Knowledge, vol. 2, pp. 389–398 (2018)
17. Dong, F., Zhang, Y., Yang, J.: Attention-based recurrent convolutional neural network for automatic essay scoring. In: Proceedings of the 21st Conference on Computational Natural Language Learning (CoNLL 2017), pp. 153–162 (2017)
18. Radford, A., Narasimhan, K., Salimans, T., Sutskever, I.: Improving language understanding by generative pre-training (2018). https://s3-us-west-2.amazonaws.com/openai-assets/research-covers/language-unsupervised/language_understanding_paper.pdf
19. Pennington, J., Socher, R., Manning, C.D.: Glove: global vectors for word representation. In: Proceedings of the 2014 Conference on Empirical Methods in Natural Language Processing (EMNLP), pp. 1532–1543 (2014)

20. Peters, M.E.: Deep contextualized word representations (2018). arXiv preprint arXiv:1802.05365

21. Cui, Y., Wise, A.F., Allen, K.L.: Developing reflection analytics for health professions education: a multi-dimensional framework to align critical concepts with data features. Comput. Hum. Behav. **100**, 305–324 (2019)

22. Hmelo-Silver, C.E.: Problem-based learning: what and how do students learn? Educ. Psychol. Rev. **16**(3), 235–266 (2004)

23. Van Manen, M.: Linking ways of knowing with ways of being practical. Curriculum Inq. **6**(3), 205–228 (1977). https://doi.org/10.1080/03626784.1977.11075533

24. Wong, F.K.Y., Kember, D., Chung, L.Y.F., Yan, L.: Assessing the level of student reflection from reflective journals. J. Adv. Nurs. **22**(1), 48–57 (1995)

25. Poldner, E., Van der Schaaf, M., Simons, P.R.J., Van Tartwijk, J., Wijngaards, G.: Assessing student teachers' reflective writing through quantitative content analysis. Eur. J. Teacher Educ. **37**(3), 348–373 (2014)

26. Zimmerman, B.J., Bonner, S., Kovach, R.: Developing self-regulated learners: beyond achievement to self-efficacy. American Psychological Association, Washington, D.C. (1996)

27. Cleary, T.J., Kitsantas, A.: Motivation and self-regulated learning influences on middle school mathematics achievement. Sch. Psychol. Rev. **46**(1), 88–107 (2017)

28. Riordan, B., Flor, M., Pugh, R.: How to account for misspellings: quantifying the benefit of character representations in neural content scoring models. In: Proceedings of the Fourteenth Workshop on Innovative Use of NLP for Building Educational Applications, pp. 116–126 (2019)

29. Saldaña, J.: The Coding Manual for Qualitative Researchers. Sage, Thousand Oaks (2009)

30. Zhang, W., Yoshida, T., Tang, X.: A comparative study of TF*IDF, LSI and multi-words for text classification. Expert Syst. Appl. **38**(3), 2758–2765 (2011)

31. Sultan, M.A., Bethard, S., Sumner, T.: DLS@CU: sentence similarity from word alignment and semantic vector composition. In: Proceedings of the 9th International Workshop on Semantic Evaluation (SemEval 2015), pp. 148–153 (2015)

32. Pedregosa, F., et al.: Scikit-learn: machine learning in python. J. Mach. Learn. Res. **12**, 2825–2830 (2011)

Can Ontologies Support the Gamification of Scripted Collaborative Learning Sessions?

Geiser Chalco Challco[1,2]($\boxtimes$) (iD), Ig Ibert Bittencourt[2]($\boxtimes$) (iD), and Seiji Isotani[1]($\boxtimes$) (iD)

[1] University of São Paulo, São Carlos, SP 13566-590, Brazil
geiser@usp.br, sisotani@icmc.usp.br
[2] Federal University of Alagoas, Maceió, AL 57072-900, Brazil
ig.ibert@ic.ufal.br

Abstract. In the field of Computer-Supported Collaborative Learning (CSCL), scripts orchestrate the collaborative learning (CL) process to achieve meaningful interactions among the students and so improve the learning outcomes. Nevertheless, the use of scripts may cause motivational problems over time. To deal with this issue, we propose the gamification of scripted CL sessions through an ontology that encodes knowledge from game design practices and theories of motivation and human behavior. This knowledge may be used by intelligent theory-aware systems to avoid the one-size-fits-all approach, providing support for the personalization of gamification. In this paper, we reported the results obtained in an empirical study to validate our ontology-based gamification of scripted CL sessions. Findings from this study indicate that intrinsic motivation, perceived choice, and effort/importance of students were significantly better when our ontology was used to support the gamification. The learning outcomes were significantly better in scripted CL sessions gamified through our approach, with positive correlations to the intrinsic motivation and perceived choice. Based on these results, we can state that the use of ontologies provides adequate support to carry out well-thought-out gamification of scripted sessions.

Keywords: Gamification · Ontologies · Scripted collaboration

1 Introduction

In CL scenarios, the use of CSCL scripts promotes fruitful and significant interactions among students [18,21]. Despite these benefits, motivational problems may occur when a scripted CL session has a high degree of coercion/imposition. For example, when there is an over-scripting [17], the CL sessions limit the students' behaviors and actions, causing a lack of motivation because the students may feel forced to follow an unwilling sequence of interactions. To deal with this motivational problem, and others (such as the lack of interest in the content-domain, and the learners' preference to work individually), Gamification *"as the*

© Springer Nature Switzerland AG 2020
I. I. Bittencourt et al. (Eds.): AIED 2020, LNAI 12163, pp. 79–91, 2020.
https://doi.org/10.1007/978-3-030-52237-7_7

use of game design elements in non-game contexts" [16] has been pointed out as a novelty approach to engaging students in educational contexts [4]. However, gamification is too context-dependent [19,29], so that its benefits depend on how well the game elements are linked with the pedagogical objectives of CL sessions. Gamifying CL sessions is a non-trivial task, and when the game elements are not tailored using the one-size-fits-all approach, as was indicated in other contexts, may cause detrimental to students' motivation [2], cheating [27], embarrassment [28], and lack of credibility [13].

The main difficulty of gamification, in particular for instructional designers who are novices in this approach, is that it needs knowledge from the game design practices and the theories of motivation and human behavior. Without a common representation of this knowledge in a manner that can be understood for computers, we can not build intelligent systems that support the interpretation of theories and practices related to gamification. These intelligent theory-aware systems are also responsible to guide the instructional designers in the personalization of gamification, where the theories and practices of gamification may be used to predict the effects of a gamification design in the students' motivation and engagement, and with this information, these systems can suggest the game-elements and their design that best fit for each student in a scripted CL session. Thus, employing a top-down ontology engineering approach and the model of roles proposed in [26], we developed an ontology named *OntoGaCLeS*[1] (detailed in [8,10]) in which we defined structures to encode theories and practices that support the well-thought-out gamification of scripted CL sessions.

Before spending effort in the development of an intelligent theory-aware system that uses our ontology, we decided to validate the impact of using it in comparison with the approach of one-size-fits-all gamification - a gamification design in which the same game-elements are applied for all the students of CL sessions. We conducted this validation through an empirical study in which the first author mediated the interaction between the instructional designers and our ontology (simulating, thus, an intelligent system that supports the gamification process through ontologies). After to present the related work in Sect. 2, Sect. 3 delineates our ontology-based gamification of scripted CL sessions. Sect. 4 describes the formulation of this empirical study, Sect. 5 shows its operation process, Sect. 6 presents its findings, Sect. 7 discusses the interpretation of these findings, and Sect. 8 presents the conclusion and future works.

2   Related Work

The importance of gamification and its personalization based on game design practices and theories of human motivation and behavior has been demonstrated in different empirical studies [3,5,15,24,25,30]. However, few empirical studies were conducted to evaluate the impact of gamification in scripted CL sessions. We previously conducted two empirical studies [6,9] to explore the benefits of our proposed ontology-based gamification (Sect. 3). Finding in these studies showed

---

[1] Available at https://geiser.github.io/ontogacles/.

that our approach significantly increases students' intrinsic motivation, interest/enjoyment and perceived choice when it is compared with non-gamified CL sessions. These studies also indicated that our approach reduces the students' pressure/tension, and that the dropping-out percentage of students per group is reduced through the gamification of CL sessions.

The gamification of CL session based on profiles of learners' motivation was evaluated through empirical studies conducted by Knutas et al. [22,23]. The results from these studies indicate that gamification could increase interactions, communication, and average grades of students who participated in CL discussions. However, these CL discussions were not mediated by any CSCL script.

3   Ontology-Based Gamification of Scripted CL Sessions

As our ontology was conceived to be the core of intelligent theory-aware systems, at least two steps are needed to gamify a scripted CL session. The 1st step is *to set the player roles & game elements for each student* of the CL session based on motivational theories and player type models. This step is performed by selecting a gamification design that best fits the individual motivational goals and game-player preferences of all the students. In the ontology, the gamification designs are encoded as "Motivational strategy" into ontological structures to represent gamified CL sessions, so that an algorithm may be used to search the ontological structures that have the same pattern of individual motivational goals of students. These goals are represented in these structures as "I-mot goal (I)" - an ontological concept encoded from motivational theories, and in which we represented the expected changes in the students' motivation at the end of the scripted CL session. Figure 1 exemplifies the ontology-based gamification of a scripted CL session inspired by the theory "Cognitive Apprenticeship" [11], and delineated for two students L_A and L_B. For this example, the ontological structure "Gamified Cognitive Apprenticeship for Yee Achiever/Yee Socializer" was selected to gamify this session because the individual motivational goals of the student L_A match with the structures "I-mot goal (I)" shown in the frame (a) of Fig. 1. These structures represent the satisfaction of competence need and the internalization of motivation - both structures encoded from the SDT theory [14] that states that feeling challenged and being effective to do something cause the experience of control, making a person to be intrinsically motivated. Thus, as exemplified in Fig. 1, an adequate gamification design for the student L_A with the need of competence is encoded as the motivational strategy "Gamifying by CMPT/CMPR" (Gamifying a scripted CL session by providing an environment with competition and comparison with others).

After the selection of the gamification design, the necessary and desired conditions to play player roles should be verified employing the game-player preferences of the students, and if all the students can play the roles defined by the gamification design, these roles are assigned to them. These conditions are encoded as "Player role" in the ontology, and they were encoded based on information extracted from player type models. Finally, the game elements for the

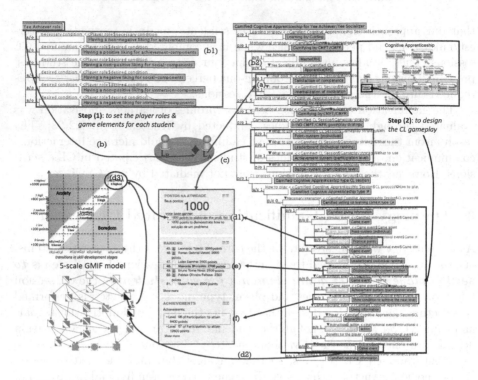

Fig. 1. Example of the ontology-based gamification of a scripted CL session

students come from the ontological structure "Gameplay strategy" - a game design practice that defines the way in which the students should interact with game elements to accomplish the individual motivational goals. The frame (b1) of Fig. 1 exemplifies the verification of necessary and desired conditions to play the player role "Yee Achiever" for the student L_A who has the liking for achievement-components. Assuming that the student L_B can also play the Yee Achiever role, no one restriction is violated in the *Motivational strategy*, as shown in the frame (b2) of Fig. 1. Thus, the Yee Achiever role is assigned to the student L_A, and the game elements selected for him/her are point-systems (individual), leaderboard (individual ranking), and achievement system (participation level) - elements indicated by the structure "I-gameplay" shown in the frame (c) of Fig. 1.

The 2nd step in intelligent theory-aware system that uses our ontology is *to design the CL gameplay* for the CL process based on persuasive game design practices. These practices are encoded as ontological structures "gamified IL events" that describe how the game elements should persuade the students to perform the interactions defined by a CSCL script. Thereby, an intelligent system may use this information to setting up the actions of game elements in the environment where the CL session is executed. This process is exemplified in Fig. 1 in which we present the configuration of game elements selected for the student L_A during the instructional event "Giving information." According to the information encoded in the ontology, to persuade a student to give information, the game element "Point-system (individual)" should perform the game action "Promise points" as shown in the frame (d1), the game element "Leaderboard (individual ranking)" should perform the game action "Display/highlight the current position" as shown in the frame (e), and the game "Achievement system (participation level)" should perform the game action "Show condition to achieve the next level" as shown in the frame (f).

During the second step, we also need to establish a proper balance between ability and challenge. This game design practice comes from the flow theory [12], and to support the application in the gamification of scripted CL session, we developed an algorithm to build n-scale GIMF models [7]. Giving n-levels of challenges, a GIMF model distributes these levels in all the possible transitions of knowledge/skills defined by instructional/learning theories. Figure 1 exemplifies the use of a 5-scale GMIF model in a scripted CL session inspired by the Cognitive Apprentice theory. In the gamification design "Gamifying by CMPT/CMPR," the points to be obtained by a student to perform an instructional and learning actions should be directly related to the challenge levels, so that if a higher challenge is overcome, then a higher amount of points will be earned by the student. The frame (d3) of Fig. 1 shows that the number of points to be promised and given for the student during the transition $s(3, y) \rightarrow s(4, y)$ should be +1000 points based on a 5-scale GIMF model. We defined five challenge levels because this value is the maximum number of interactions defined as *gamified LL events* in this scripted CL session, and the max value of points was 1000 points.

4 Formulation of the Empirical Study

As the empirical study was formulated to validate the impact of our ontology-based gamification (detailed in Sect. 3) in comparison with the one-size-fits-all gamification, we compared the students' motivation and learning outcomes in scripted CL sessions that have been gamified using these two approaches. The scripted CL sessions gamified with our approach will refer hereinafter as *ont-gamified* CL session, whereas the scripted CL sessions gamified with the one-size-fits-all approach will refer as *one-size-fits-all* gamified CL sessions. Thereby, we formulated the following research questions: (1) Is the students' motivation in ont-gamified CL sessions better than in one-size-fits-all gamified CL sessions?; (2) Is the learning outcome in ont-gamified CL sessions better than in one-size-fits-all gamified CL sessions?; and (3) Are the students' motivation and learning outcomes linked on ont-gamified CL sessions?

Hypothesis Formulation: To answer the research question (1), we tested the null hypothesis, there is no significant difference of the students' intrinsic motivation in ont-gamified and one-size-fits-all gamified CL sessions, against the alternative hypothesis, H_1:The students' intrinsic motivation is greater in ont-gamified CL sessions than in one-size-fits-all gamified CL sessions. To answer the research question (2), we tested the null hypothesis, There is no significant difference of the students' skill/knowledge gain in ont-gamified CL sessions or non-gamified CL sessions, against the alternative hypothesis, H_2: The students' skill/knowledge gain is greater in ont-gamified CL sessions than in one-size-fits-all gamified CL sessions. To answer the research question (3), we tested the null hypothesis, There is no significant correlation between the students' intrinsic motivation and the skill/knowledge gain in ont-gamified and one-size-fits-all gamified CL sessions, against the alternative hypothesis, H_3: There are significant correlation between the students' intrinsic motivation and the skill/knowledge gain in ont-gamified and one-size-fits-all gamified CL sessions.

Experiment Design: The empirical study was designed as a controlled experiment conducted in a real situation, in a CL activity of the course of Introduction to Computer Science, with the domain-content of *Recursion*, and using a CSCL script inspired by the Cognitive Apprentice theory to orchestrate the CL process. Based on this script, the students will play the CL roles of *Master* and *Apprentice*, so that this study has a 2×2 factorial design, with a randomized assignment for the types of CL session, and with a theory-driven assignment for the CL roles employing the pseudo-algorithm proposed in [20].

5 Experiment Operation

The empirical study was conducted in three phases (pre-test, intervention, and post-test) with 59 Brazilian undergraduate computer engineering students enrolled in the course of Introduction to Computer Science at the University of São Paulo. These students were part of a homogeneous population in the age range of 17–25 years old, sharing the same religion, social-economy status, and culture. During the conduction of this empirical study, the aspects under study and hypotheses were not informed to the students, but they were aware that the researcher would use their data with anonymity. All the *materials and questionnaires* employed in this study were prepared in advance, and they are available at https://bit.ly/35CpZ88. As part of the course, the students were instructed on how to participate in CL sessions orchestrated by CSCL scripts using the *Scripting-forum module*[2], and they also answered a web-based questionnaire of the QPJ-BR instrument [1]. During this training, the students were also put in contact with the game-elements to avoid the novelty effect.

During the pre-test phase (1 week), the students' initial skill/knowledge was gathered from one programming problem task (P4 - *Calculate fibonacci polynomials*) solved by the students using the *VPL module*[3] in the Moodle platform, and from one multiple-choice knowledge questionnaire (p3a) answered by the students during 2 h at the classroom as formative evaluation.

During the intervention phase (4 weeks & 3 days), the students were formed into 21 groups of 2 or 3 members with 21 masters and 38 apprentices

---

[2] Available at https://github.com/geiser/moodle_scripting_forum.

[3] Available at https://moodle.org/plugins/mod_vpl.

assigned according to the theory-driven group formation proposed in [20]. Thus, when the students know the topic of recursion, and they known how to use recursion in the solution of a programming problem, they played the *master* role. Otherwise, the student played the *apprentice* role. After the CL role distribution, one-half of groups were randomly chosen to participate in one-size-fits-all gamified CL sessions, and the other half was chosen to participate in ont-gamified CL sessions. Thereby, 11 groups participated in ont-gamified CL sessions, and 11 groups were involved in one-size-fits-all gamified CL sessions.

The game elements were setting-up in the ont-gamified CL sessions through the approach detailed in Sect. 3. Based on the individual motivational goals of students who participated in this study, the gamification designs were defined employing two ontological structures: (a) *"Gamified Cognitive Apprenticeship Scenario for Master/Yee Achiever and Apprentice/Yee Achiever,"* and (b) *"Gamified Cognitive Apprenticeship Scenario for Master/Social Achiever and Apprentice/Social Achiever."* Thus, students who had more liking for achievement-components than social-components were assigned to play the *Yee Achiever role*, whereas students who had positive liking for social-components and achievement-components were assigned to play the *Social Achiever role*.

Figure 2 shows the interfaces of scripted CL sessions that have been gamified to conduct our empirical study in the Moodle platform using our plugins[4]: *gamepoints, game-leaderboards, game-achievements*, and *game badges*. In scripted CL sessions that have been gamified using the structure (a), the gamification design intended to support a gameplay of *individual competition* in which the students acted as Yee Achiever. For these students, we provided leaderboards that display individual rankings (a4), point-systems that accumulate rewards for each individual (a3), and the win state that was defined through an achievement-system (a1) and badges of participation (a2). The gamification design for scripted CL sessions that have been gamified using the structure (2) supported a gameplay experience of *individual and cooperative competition* when the students played the Social Achiever role, so that we provided for them leaderboards that displayed individual rankings (b5) and collaborative rankings (b6), point-systems (b4) that accumulateed rewards for the groups and individuals, and the win state that was defined through two achievement-systems (b1) and (b2) with badges of participation and collaboration (b3).

For the one-size-fits-all gamified CL sessions, the game elements were setting-up without using the ontology, so that we established the same game-elements and their design for all the students in the CL sessions, as shown in Fig. 2 (c). In these sessions, we used an individual point-system (c3), an achievement-system (c1) and badge-system (c2) for participation, and a leaderboard with individual rankings (c4). The points to be given when a student perform any interaction were the same (+500 points), and all the students received the same badge of participation at the end of the CL session. The complete setting up of gameelements and their design are detailed in https://bit.ly/3dfZdFg.

---

[4] Available at https://github.com/geiser/gamification-moodle-plugins.

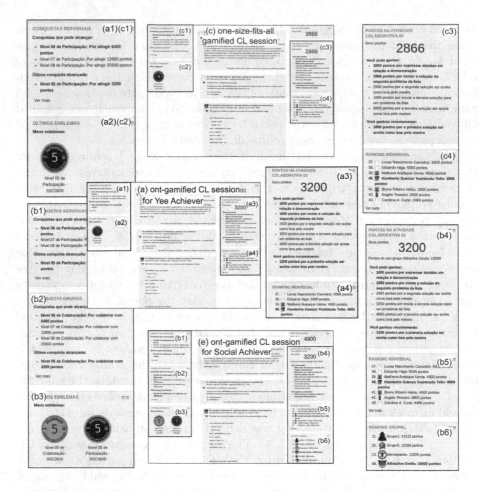

Fig. 2. Interfaces of scripted CL sessions delineated in the empirical study

During the post-test phase (1 week), to gather data related to the skill/knowledge, a multiple-choice knowledge questionnaire of recursion (p3c) has been answered by the students during 2 h at the classroom as part of the formative evaluations in the course, and three programming problem tasks (PF - *Programming Problem: Generation of planning poker sequence*), (PG - *Programming Problem: Counting palindromes*) and (PH - *Programming Problem: Maze solving algorithm*) have been solved by the students in the Moodle platform using the VPL module. To gather data of motivation, the students answered a Web-based adapted Portuguese versions of IMI questionnaire.

6   Findings of the Empirical Study

Employing the responses gathered through the IMI questionnaire, we run two-way ANOVA tests and *Tukey post-hoc comparisons* to find significant differences in the dependent variables of motivation. Before this analysis, we validated the IMI questionnaire to ensure the psycho-metrically sound of its items through a CFA analysis and a reliability test obtaining a Cronbach's $\alpha = 0.85$ (good) - this validation process is detailed at https://bit.ly/2xFsAS8. The students' skill/knowledge gains were estimated through the difference of scores obtained in the post-test and pre-test. With these gains, we run two-way ANOVA tests and Tukey post-hoc comparisons to find significant differences. All the results from these statistical analyses are available at https://geiser.github.io/phd-thesis-evaluation/study03.

Motivation: Results from the ANOVA tests indicated significant differences on the intrinsic motivation ($F(1, 47) = 6.15$, $p = 0.017$), perceived choice ($F(1, 47) = 8.27$, $p = 0.006$), and effort/importance ($F(1, 47) = 7.51$, $p = 0.009$). The tukey post-hoc comparisons show that the students' intrinsic motivation in ont-gamified CL sessions ($lsmean = 4.56$, $SE = 0.149$) was significantly greater than in one-size-fits-all gamified CL sessions ($lsmean = 4.10$, $SE = 0.149$) with a p-adj. value of $p = 0.023$ and Hedges' $g = 0.63$ medium effect size. The perceived choice in ont-gamified CL sessions ($lsmean = 4.80$, $SE = 0.295$) was significantly greater than in one-size-fits-all gamified CL sessions ($lsmean = 3.60$, $SE = 0.295$) with $p = 0.009$ and $g = 0.75$ medium effect size. The effort/importance in ont-gamified CL sessions ($lsmean = 5.32$, $SE = 0.246$) was significantly greater than in one-size-fits-all gamified CL sessions ($lsmean = 4.37$, $SE = 0.245$) with $p = 0.007$ and $g = 0.79$ medium effect size.

Learning Outcomes: According to the ANOVA tests, the effect on the students' skill/knowledge gain yielded $F(1, 45) = 10.77$ with $p = 0.002$ indicating a significant difference between one-size-fits-all gamification and ontology-based gamification of scripted CL sessions. The Tukey post-hoc comparisons indicate that the students' skill/knowledge gain in ont-gamified CL sessions ($lsmean = 1.38$, $SE = 0.578$) was greater than in one-size-fits-all gamified CL sessions ($lsmean = -1.26$, $SE = 0.564$) with $p = 0.002$ and $g = 0.88$ medium effect size. For *Apprentice* students, their skill/knowledge gain in ont-gamified CL sessions ($lsmean = 2.50$, $SE = 0.638$) was also greater than in one-size-fits-all gamified CL sessions ($lsmean = 0.07$, $SE = 0.585$) with $p = 0.036$ and $g = 0.892$ large effect size.

Correlation of Students' Motivation and Learning Outcomes: Spearman's rank-order correlation tests were run to find significant correlations between the students' motivation and learning outcomes. According to these tests, in ont-gamified CL sessions, the skill/knowledge gain of master students was significantly strong correlated to the intrinsic motivation ($\rho = 0.73$, $p = 0.05$), perceived choice ($\rho = 0.85$, $p = 0.023$), and pressure/tension ($\rho = -0.77$, $p = 0.039$).

7 Interpretation and Discussion of Findings

The null hypothesis related to motivation is rejected, so that this study is evidence to support the *alternative hypothesis*, H_1, "the students' intrinsic motivation is greater in ont-gamified CL sessions than in one-size-fits-all gamified CL sessions" in which the students' perceived choice and effort/importance in ont-gamified CL sessions were also greater than in one-size-fits-all gamified CL sessions. This fact is consequence of a well-though-out gamification design that, through the gamification design provided by our ontology, aligns the pedagogical objectives with the students' intrinsic motivation. As was detailed in Sect. 3, the selection of the gamification design is based on the individual motivational goals of students. These effects may also consequence of the personalization of game-elements based on information from player models and the persuasive game design applied to these game-elements. As the game-elements were set up based on a persuasive design, they easily convince the student to follow the sequence of interactions defined by the CSCL scripts during the CL process. The perceived choice and effort/importance of students in ont-gamified were greater in ont-gamified CL sessions than in one-size-fits-all gamified CL sessions. A possible explanation for this fact is that students in our ont-gamified CL sessions put more effort in their actions and behaviors to be properly rewarded by the game elements because the GMIF model provides an adequate balance between the current students' skill/knowledge and perceived challenge, a balance that was not established in one-size-fits-all gamified CL sessions.

Our empirical study also constitutes evidence to support the alternative hypothesis, H_2, "the students' skill/knowledge gain is greater in ont-gamified CL sessions than in one-size-fits-all gamified CL sessions." This finding indicates that, through our gamification approach, the pedagogical benefits of scripted CL sessions are better achieved by the students. Having better pedagogical benefits in our scripted CL session is likely a consequence of increasing the students' intrinsic motivation and their autonomy sense through our ontology-based gamification approach. The evidence that supports this fact is the significant correlations found in the students' intrinsic motivation and perceived choice with the skill/knowledge gains in ont-gamified CL sessions.

8   Conclusion and Future Works

The findings in the empirical study reported in this paper indicate that our ontology-based approach to gamify scripted CL sessions is likely to be an efficient method to deal with motivational problems with the potential to improve the learning outcomes. In scripted CL sessions that have been gamified using our ontology-based approach, students reported to be more intrinsic motivated and with better perceived choice than in scripted CL sessions that have been gamified employing the one-size-fits-all approach. Our approach also demonstrated that raising intrinsic motivation and perceived choice in scripted CL sessions through gamification helps the students to accomplish in better learning outcomes.

Our empirical study was limited to undergraduate students (ages 17–25), to the content-domain of *Recursion*, and using only one CSCL script to conduct the CL sessions. As the gamification is too-context dependent, we can not generalize our findings, so additional empirical studies will be carried to validate the efficiency of our ontology-based approach. These further study should be conducted using other content-domains with different difficulty levels and from different courses, with other participants, and using other CSCL scripts.

References

1. Andrade, F., Marques, L., Bittencourt, I.I., Isotani, S.: QPJ-BR: Questionário para Identificação de Perfis de Jogadores para o Português-Brasileiro. In: XXVII Brazilian Symposium on Computers in Education, vol. 27, pp. 637–646. Maceio (2016)
2. Andrade, F.R.H., Mizoguchi, R., Isotani, S.: The bright and dark sides of gamification. In: Micarelli, A., Stamper, J., Panourgia, K. (eds.) ITS 2016. LNCS, vol. 9684, pp. 176–186. Springer, Cham (2016). https://doi.org/10.1007/978-3-319-39583-8_17
3. Böckle, M., Novak, J., Bick, M.: Towards adaptive gamification: a synthesis of current developments. Research Papers (2017)
4. Borges, S.S., Durelli, V.H.S., Reis, H.M., Isotani, S.: A systematic mapping on gamification applied to education. In: Proceedings of the 29th Annual ACM Symposium on Applied Computing. SAC 2014, pp. 216–222. ACM (2014). https://doi.org/10.1145/2554850.2554956
5. Busch, M., et al.: Personalization in serious and persuasive games and gamified interactions. In: Proceedings of the 2015 Annual Symposium on Computer-Human Interaction in Play, CHI PLAY 2015, pp. 811–816. ACM (2015). https://doi.org/10.1145/2793107.2810260
6. Challco, G.C., Isotani, S., Bittencourt, I.I.: The effects of ontology-based gamification in scripted collaborative learning. In: 2019 IEEE 19th International Conference on Advanced Learning Technologies (ICALT), vol. 2161–377X, pp. 140–144 (2019). https://doi.org/10.1109/ICALT.2019.00043
7. Challco, G.C., Andrade, F.R.H., Borges, S.S., Bittencourt, I.I., Isotani, S.: Toward a unified modeling of learner's growth process and flow theory. Educ. Technol. Soc. 19(2), 215–227 (2016)
8. Challco, G.C., Mizoguchi, R., Bittencourt, I.I., Isotani, S.: Gamification of collaborative learning scenarios: structuring persuasive strategies using game elements and ontologies. In: Koch, F., Koster, A., Primo, T. (eds.) SOCIALEDU 2015. CCIS, vol. 606, pp. 12–28. Springer, Cham (2016). https://doi.org/10.1007/978-3-319-39672-9_2
9. Challco, G.C., Mizoguchi, R., Isotani, S.: Using ontology and gamification to improve students' participation and motivation in CSCL. In: Cristea, A.I., Bittencourt, I.I., Lima, F. (eds.) HEFA 2017. CCIS, vol. 832, pp. 174–191. Springer, Cham (2018). https://doi.org/10.1007/978-3-319-97934-2_11
10. Challco, G.C., Moreira, D.A., Bittencourt, I.I., Mizoguchi, R., Isotani, S.: Personalization of gamification in collaborative learning contexts using ontologies. IEEE Latin Am. Trans. 13(6), 1995–2002 (2015). https://doi.org/10.1109/TLA.2015.7164227
11. Collins, A.: Cognitive apprenticeship and instructional technology. In: Educational Values and Cognitive Instruction: Implications for Reform, pp. 121–138 (1991)
12. Csikszentmihalyi, M.: Flow: The Psychology of Optimal Experience. 1st edn. Harper Perennial Modern Classics, New York, July 2008

13. Davis, K., Singh, S.: Digital badges in afterschool learning: documenting the perspectives and experiences of students and educators. Comput. Educ. **88**, 72–83 (2015). https://doi.org/10.1016/j.compedu.2015.04.011
14. Deci, E.L., Ryan, R.M.: Self-Determination. The Corsini Encyclopedia of Psychology. Wiley, Hoboken (2010)
15. Deterding, S.: Eudaimonic design, or: six invitations to rethink gamification. SSRN Scholarly Paper ID 2466374, Social Science Research Network, Rochester, NY (2014)
16. Deterding, S., Dixon, D., Khaled, R., Nacke, L.: From game design elements to gamefulness: defining gamification. In: Proceedings of the 15th International Academic MindTrek Conference: Envisioning Future Media Environments, pp. 9–15. ACM (2011)
17. Dillenbourg, P.: Over-scripting CSCL: the risks of blending collaborative learning with instructional design. In: Three Worlds of CSCL. Can We Support CSCL? pp. 61–91. Open Universiteit, Nederland (2002)
18. Fischer, F., Kollar, I., Stegmann, K., Wecker, C., Zottmann, J.: Collaboration scripts in computer-supported collaborative learning. In: The International Handbook of Collaborative Learning, pp. 403–419 (2013)
19. Hamari, J., Koivisto, J., Sarsa, H.: Does Gamification Work?–A Literature Review of Empirical Studies on Gamification. In: 47th International Conference on System Sciences, HICSS 2014, pp. 3025–3034. IEEE Computer Society, Hawaii (2014). https://doi.org/10.1109/HICSS.2014.377
20. Isotani, S., Mizoguchi, R.: Theory-driven group formation through ontologies. In: Woolf, B.P., Aïmeur, E., Nkambou, R., Lajoie, S. (eds.) ITS 2008. LNCS, vol. 5091, pp. 646–655. Springer, Heidelberg (2008). https://doi.org/10.1007/978-3-540-69132-7_67
21. Isotani, S., et al.: A semantic web-based authoring tool to facilitate the planning of collaborative learning scenarios compliant with learning theories. Comput. Educ. **63**, 267–284 (2013). https://doi.org/10.1016/j.compedu.2012.12.009
22. Knutas, A., Ikonen, J., Maggiorini, D., Ripamonti, L., Porras, J.: Creating software engineering student interaction profiles for discovering gamification approaches to improve collaboration. In: Proceedings of the 15th International Conference on Computer Systems and Technologies, CompSysTech 2014, pp. 378–385. ACM, New York (2014). https://doi.org/10.1145/2659532.2659612
23. Knutas, A., Ikonen, J., Nikula, U., Porras, J.: Increasing collaborative communications in a programming course with gamification: a case study. In: Proceedings of the 15th International Conference on Computer Systems and Technologies, CompSysTech 2014, pp. 370–377. ACM, New York (2014). https://doi.org/10.1145/2659532.2659620
24. Knutas, A., van Roy, R., Hynninen, T., Granato, M., Kasurinen, J., Ikonen, J.: A process for designing algorithm-based personalized gamification. Multimedia Tools Appl. **78**(10), 13593–13612 (2018). https://doi.org/10.1007/s11042-018-6913-5
25. Koivisto, J., Hamari, J.: The rise of motivational information systems: a review of gamification research. Int. J. Inf. Manag. **45**, 191–210 (2018). https://doi.org/10.1016/j.ijinfomgt.2018.10.013
26. Mizoguchi, R., Sunagawa, E., Kozaki, K., Kitamura, Y.: The model of roles within an ontology development tool: Hozo. Appl. Ontol. Roles Interdisc. Perspect. **2**(2), 159–179 (2007)

27. Nunes, T.M., Bittencourt, I.I., Isotani, S., Jaques, P.A.: Discouraging gaming the system through interventions of an animated pedagogical agent. In: Verbert, K., Sharples, M., Klobučar, T. (eds.) EC-TEL 2016. LNCS, vol. 9891, pp. 139–151. Springer, Cham (2016). https://doi.org/10.1007/978-3-319-45153-4_11

28. Ohno, A., Yamasaki, T., Tokiwa, K.I.: A discussion on introducing half-anonymity and gamification to improve students' motivation and engagement in classroom lectures. In: 2013 IEEE Region 10 Humanitarian Technology Conference, pp. 215–220, August 2013. https://doi.org/10.1109/R10-HTC.2013.6669044

29. Richards, C., Thompson, C.W., Graham, N.: Beyond designing for motivation: the importance of context in gamification. In: Proceedings of the First ACM SIGCHI Annual Symposium on Computer-Human Interaction in Play, CHI PLAY 2014, pp. 217–226. ACM, Canada (2014). https://doi.org/10.1145/2658537.2658683

30. Seaborn, K., Fels, D.I.: Gamification in theory and action: a survey. Int. J. Hum Comput Stud. **74**, 14–31 (2015)

Predicting Gaps in Usage in a Phone-Based Literacy Intervention System

Rishabh Chatterjee, Michael Madaio$^{(\boxtimes)}$, and Amy Ogan

Carnegie Mellon University, Pittsburgh, PA 15213, USA
rishabhc@andrew.cmu.edu, {mmadaio,aeo}@cs.cmu.edu

Abstract. Educational technologies may help support out-of-school learning in contexts where formal schooling fails to reach every child, but children may not persist in using such systems to learn at home. Prior research has developed methods for predicting learner dropout but primarily for adults in formal courses and Massive Open Online Courses (MOOCs), not for children's voluntary ed tech usage. To support early literacy in rural contexts, our research group developed and deployed a phone-based literacy technology with rural families in Côte d'Ivoire in two longitudinal studies. In this paper, we investigate the feasibility of using time-series classification models trained on system log data to predict gaps in children's voluntary usage of our system in both studies. We contribute insights around important features associated with sustained system usage, such as children's patterns of use, performance on the platform, and involvement from other adults in their family. Finally, we contribute design implications for predicting and supporting learners' voluntary, out-of-school usage of mobile learning applications in rural contexts.

Keywords: Machine learning · Dropout · Out-of-school learning

1 Introduction

Access to literacy is critical for children's future educational attainment and economic outcomes [13], but despite an overall rise in global literacy rates, these gains have not been evenly distributed [40]. Educational technologies may help supplement gaps in schooling in low-resource contexts [6,30,32]. However, given that many educational technologies are used in schools [51], children in agricultural communities who are chronically absent from school (e.g., [30]), may be

This research was supported by the Jacobs Foundation Fellowship, Grant No. 2015117013, and the Institute of Education Sciences, U.S. Department of Education, Grant No. R305B150008. We thank our participants, the village chiefs, school leaders, and COGES directors for their time and help, and we are indebted to all of our collaborators at the Jacobs Foundation TRECC Program and Eneza Education.

© Springer Nature Switzerland AG 2020
I. I. Bittencourt et al. (Eds.): AIED 2020, LNAI 12163, pp. 92–105, 2020.
https://doi.org/10.1007/978-3-030-52237-7_8

further denied access to technologies to supplement their learning unless learning technologies are available for use at home (as in [50]).

Côte d'Ivoire is one such context. While enrollment has risen drastically and many more children have access to schooling, nearly a fifth of rural fifth graders are not yet able to read a single word of French (the official national language) [14] and adult literacy rates stand below 50% [25]. Through multiple studies in a years-long research program, we investigated families' beliefs and methods for supporting literacy at home and their design needs for literacy support technology [28], and used these findings as design guidelines to develop an interactive voice response (IVR) literacy system for fostering French phonological awareness [27]. Then, to investigate how and why children and their families adopt and use such a system over several months at their homes, we deployed our IVR system, Allô Alphabet, in a series of studies of increasing size and duration, in 8 rural villages in Côte d'Ivoire [27,29]. We found that there was high variance in the consistency of children's use of the system, with some children who did not access the lessons for several weeks or months at a time [29].

In this paper, in order to understand whether we can predict (and perhaps, ultimately prevent) such gaps before they occur, we explore the efficacy of using system log data to predict gaps in children's system usage. We evaluate the efficacy of multiple models to predict usage gaps for two separate longitudinal deployments of Allô Alphabet and identify features that were highly predictive of gaps in usage. We contribute insights into features that contribute to gaps in usage as well as design implications for personalized reminders to prompt usage for educational interventions in out-of-school contexts. This work has contributions for educational technology usage prediction, as well as for mobile literacy systems more broadly.

2 Related Work

2.1 Educational Technology Used for Out-of-school Learning

While there is prior literature on the use of educational technologies in low-resource contexts [19,34,50], existing solutions are often deployed in schools, where children's use of devices may be controlled by the teacher [39,51]. Given that children in agricultural contexts may have limitations in their ability to consistently access and attend formal schooling [30], there is a need for out-of-school educational technologies for children. Some designers of mobile learning applications suggest children will use their applications to develop literacy skills [17,18,22]. However, as Lange and Costley point out in their review of out-of-school learning, children learning outside of school often have a choice of whether to engage in learning or not—given all of the other options for how to spend their time—a choice which may lead to gaps in their learning [24].

2.2 Predicting Usage Gaps in Voluntary Educational Applications

There is an abundance of prior work on predicting dropout to increase student retention in formal educational contexts like colleges [23,47,48]. Some work has leveraged Machine Learning (ML) to identify predictors of adult learners' dropout from courses, as in work with English for Speakers of Other Languages (ESOL) courses in Turkey [7]. In addition to this work on predicting dropout from in-person courses, prior work has leveraged ML to identify predictors of dropout from Massive Open Online Courses (MOOCs) [4,33,36,45,53] and distance learning for adult learners [2,12,19,49]. Across these studies, a combination of social factors, like age, finances, family and institutional involvement, etc., and system usage data, like correctness, frequency, response log, etc. were found to be predictive of dropout.

While this is informative, much of this prior work is targeted towards distance learning or use of e-learning portals as part of formal instruction, not informal, out-of-school learning at home. Additionally, the type of learners is different—the majority of MOOC learners are between 18 and 35 years old [9], while we are focusing on children as users, who may have less-developed metacognitive abilities for planning and sustaining out-of-school learning. It thus remains to be seen what factors are useful for predicting gaps in children's literacy education with out-of-school use of learning technology. In particular, we are interested in system usage features as those are more easily and automatically acquired than socio-economic data.

Although there is a dearth of research on predicting gaps in children's usage of educational mobile applications, there is a rich legacy of research on mobile app usage prediction more broadly, primarily for adults (e.g., [20,31,43,44]). In both educational and non-educational application use, the engagement is voluntary, initiated by the user, and designers of such systems want to increase usage and retention. Prior research on *churn* prediction in casual and social gaming applications used machine learning models like Support Vector Machines (SVM) and Random Forests (RF) to model system usage. RF is an ensemble learning method, a category of model that has shown good performance for these predictions [37,42]. *Churn* is defined as using an application and then not continuing to use it after a given period of time [20]. Churn prediction allows systems to develop interventions, like reminders or nudges, which are positively related to increasing user retention [31,43,52]. However, there remain differences between casual and social mobile games and educational mobile applications, including the motivation to use the system and the nature of the data. This leads us to investigate the following research questions:

RQ1: Can we use system interaction data to predict gaps in children's usage of a mobile-based educational technology used outside of school in rural contexts?

RQ2: Which features of the users' interaction log data are most predictive of gaps in system usage of a mobile educational technology?

RQ3: How well does this usage gap prediction approach continue to perform for a replication of the same study in similar contexts?

3   Methodology

3.1   Study Design

This study is part of an ongoing research program [14, 27–29] to support literacy in cocoa farming communities, conducted by an interdisciplinary team of American and Ivorian linguists, economists, sociologists, and computer scientists, in partnership with the Ivorian Ministry of Education since 2016, and approved by our institutional review boards, the Ministry, and community leaders. Based on design guidelines identified through co-design research with children, teachers, and families [28], we developed Allô Alphabet, a system to teach early literacy concepts via interactive voice response (IVR) accessible on low-cost mobile devices ubiquitous in the context (described in more detail in [27, 29]). When a user placed a call to the IVR system, they heard a welcome message in French, an explanation of the phonology concept to be taught in that lesson, and were given a question. For each question, the system played a pre-recorded audio message with the question and response options. Students then pressed a touchtone button to select an answer and received feedback on their responses. If incorrect, they received the same question again with a hint, otherwise a selection of the next question was made based on their level of mastery of the concepts.

In this paper, we use data from two deployments of Allô Alphabet. In the first deployment (Study 1), we deployed Allô Alphabet with nearly 300 families with a child in grade CM1 (mean age = 11 years, SD = 1.5) in 8 villages in Côte d'Ivoire for 16 weeks, beginning in February 2019 [29]. Then we deployed it again in a larger randomized controlled trial with 750 children of similar ages (Study 2), beginning in December, 2019 and ongoing at the time of publication. In the beginning of each study we provided a mobile device and SIM card to freely access the system and a one-hour training session for children and a caregiver, in which we explained the purpose of the study and taught the child and caregiver how to access and use the IVR system (described in more detail in [27, 29]. We obtained 16 weeks of system and call data for Study 1 (February - May, 2019), and equivalent data from the first 8 weeks of the ongoing Study 2 (December, 2019 - February, 2020). For our analysis, we use data from the participants who called the system at least once ($N_1 = 165, N_2 = 408$).

3.2   Data Collection and Processing

The data used in training our models was the same for both Study 1 and 2. Each time a user called the system, the call metadata and the interactions during the call were logged on our database. The metadata included call start and end times (in local time), and the interaction data corresponded to a log of events that occurred during the call, such as attempting quiz questions, correctly completing those questions, parents or other caregivers accessing information (e.g., support messages and progress updates) about their child's usage, and more.

Each record in the data was identified by a unique *user-week*. Because we wanted to use all the data up to (and including) a given week to predict a gap in

usage in the subsequent week, we excluded the final week of system usage from
our dataset. For Study 1, we generated a time series with 15 timestamps (one
for each week prior to the final week) and data from 165 children for each timestamp ($N_1 = 2475$). For Study 2, we generated a time series with 7 timestamps
and data from 408 children for each timestamp ($N_2 = 2856$). Each timestamp
corresponded to data up to, and including, the given week. We trained a new
model on the data for each timestamp to avoid future bias, i.e., training on future
data while predicting the same. Based on prior research on dropout prediction in
MOOCs (e.g. [4,33,53]) and churn prediction in mobile applications and social
games (e.g. [20,37]) with a focus on features that could be gleaned solely from
interaction logs, we used a total of 11 features including *call_duration* (average call duration during the week), *num_calls* (total number of calls), *num_days*
(number of days the user called in a given week), *mastery* (percentage of questions attempted correctly), and *main_parent* (number of times a user accessed
the main menu for the parent-facing version of the system). A list of all features
used in the model and their pre-normalized, post-aggregation means and standard deviations can be found in Table 1. We aggregated the features at the week
level, averaging *call_duration* and *mastery*, and summing the others. We decided
to average *mastery* and *call_duration* to better represent the non-uniform distribution of lesson performance and call duration across the calls in a given week.

Table 1. Full set of features used in the predictive model

Feature	Explanation	Mean (SD)
sum_correct	Number of questions correct	8.78 (20.90)
sum_incorrect	Number of questions incorrect	10.38 (24.76)
sum_completed	Total number of questions completed	19.16 (44.48)
mastery	Percentage of questions correct	0.19 (0.26)
nunique_unit_id	Number of distinct units attempted	0.46 (0.53)
nunique_lesson_id	Number of distinct lessons attempted	4.34 (9.34)
num_calls	Number of calls	6.39 (12.01)
num_days	Number of days user called system	1.59 (1.83)
start_child_call_flow	Number of times a child began a lesson	3.78 (7.70)
main_parent	Number of times user accessed	2.02 (5.62)
	Parent-facing version of the system	
call_duration	Average call duration in seconds	137.95 (238.91)

3.3   Problem Formulation

We wanted to predict gaps in usage for our users. Given the distribution of usage
data in our study which related to the school week, we define a gap as a given

user not calling the system for one week. We thus use this gap as the *positive* class in our model (*base rate* = 65%, i.e., 65% of *user_weeks* have a gap). Because we want to be able to predict for out-of-sample users who might begin calling later in the study (i.e., without prior call log data), we use a population-informed week-forward chaining approach to cross-validation [3]. That is, we held out a subset of users and trained the data for all weeks using a k-fold time-series cross-validation [46].

We wanted to use model types that were likely to perform well on smaller, imbalanced datasets as well as models that would allow us to identify feature importance and compare model performance. Prior literature on churn prediction [15,37] identified several model types that might meet these criteria: Random Forests (RF), Support Vector Machines (SVM), and eXtreme Gradient Boosting (XGBoost). Ensemble learning methods (like RF and XGBoost) had been shown to perform well for churn prediction, and SVM's kernel trick had been shown to successfully identify decision boundaries in higher dimensional data. Furthermore, boosted tree algorithms have been shown to perform as well as deep, neural approaches in certain scenarios [11,41], while requiring smaller datasets and compute power, which is of particular interest for predictive models in low-resource, developing contexts [21]. We used Scikit-Learn modules [35] for implementation, and Grid Search for hyper-parameter tuning of the optimisation criterion, tree depth, type of kernel, learning rate, and number of estimators [16].

4   Findings

4.1   Usage Gap Prediction Models for Study 1 (RQ1)

We evaluated the three models (SVM, RF, and XGBoost) models using four metrics—recall, precision, accuracy, and Area Under the Curve (AUC). Of these, we optimised for recall because we wanted to minimize false negatives. That is, we do not want to incorrectly predict that someone will call the next week, and thus miss an opportunity to remind or nudge them to use the system. We report on the mean and standard deviation for the performance metrics for all three models, averaged across all 15 model iterations in Table 2. In Fig. 1, we show the AUC results for each weekly model iteration for all 15 weeks. We found that XGBoost was the best performing model for Study 1, using a tree booster, a learning rate of 0.1, and a maximum depth of 5. We hypothesize that XGBoost performed the best because it was an ensemble learning method (unlike SVM), and used a more regularized model formalization (as opposed to RF), which may be more effective for the nature of our data because it avoids overfitting [5].

Table 2. Performance of Different Models in Study 1: Mean and Standard Deviation

Model	Recall	Precision	Accuracy	AUC
XGBoost	0.93 (σ=0.06)	0.78 (σ=0.13)	0.75 (σ=0.12)	0.68 (σ=0.12)
SVM	0.92 (σ=0.06)	0.78 (σ=0.13)	0.75 (σ=0.12)	0.65 (σ=0.12)
RF	0.90 (σ=0.06)	0.78 (σ=0.13)	0.74 (σ=0.12)	0.60 (σ=0.10)

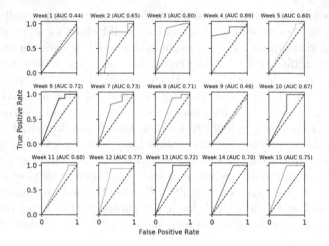

Fig. 1. AUC for each of the 15 iterations of the XGBoost model for Study 1

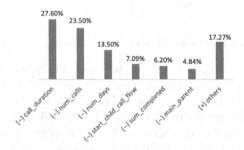

Fig. 2. Feature importance for Study 1, with direction of the feature in parentheses

4.2 Feature Importance in Usage Gap Prediction for Study 1 (RQ2)

We next wanted to estimate feature importance in order to identify the features
most associated with gaps in usage, to suggest potential design implications for
personalized interventions or system designs to promote user retention. The feature importance and the directionality of the top ranked features in the XGBoost
model can be seen in Fig. 2. We obtained the direction of the influence of the
feature (i.e., either positively or negatively associated) using SHAP (SHapley
Additive exPlanation), which allows for post-hoc explanations of various ML
models [26]. We find that the most predictive features associated with gaps in

usage are the call duration, number of calls to the system, number of days with a call to the system, and total number of completed questions in a given week—all negatively predictive of gaps (i.e., positively associated with usage).

Table 3. Performance of Different Models in Study 2: Mean and Standard Deviation

Model	Recall	Precision	Accuracy	AUC
XGBoost	0.69 *(σ=0.18)*	0.58 *(σ=0.19)*	0.66 *(σ=0.07)*	0.73 *(σ=0.09)*
SVM	0.68 *(σ=0.13)*	0.58 *(σ=0.19)*	0.66 *(σ=0.07)*	0.72 *(σ=0.09)*
RF	0.69 *(σ=0.24)*	0.56 *(σ=0.18)*	0.65 *(σ=0.12)*	0.66 *(σ=0.11)*

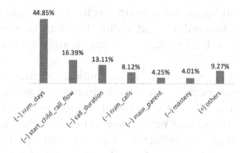

Fig. 3. Feature importance for Study 2, with direction of the feature in parentheses

4.3 Replication of Usage Prediction for Study 2 (RQ3)

In order to evaluate the robustness of our approach, we evaluated the same models on data from the first 8 weeks of Study 2. We used the same features described in Table 1, for the 408 learners with data for the 7 weeks (again leaving out the 8th and final week for testing), as described in Sect. 3.2. We find that our model performance was consistent with the model performance from Study 1. Mean and standard deviation of model performance across the 7 models is reported in Table 3 We find that the AUC values are higher in Study 2 than in Study 1, although recall, precision, and accuracy are lower overall in Study 2. Given that Study 2 (8 weeks) was half the duration of Study 1 (16 weeks), we hypothesize that these prediction performance differences may be due to effects from differences in usage in the beginning of the study. That is, system usage in the first 1–2 weeks of the study was higher than the rest of the duration (for both Study 1 and 2). Thus, the model may fail to minimize the false negatives, as it is inclined to predict that a user will call back, when in reality there may be a gap in usage. The set of important features (seen in Fig. 3) were nearly the same as in Study 1, but their rank order was different in Study 2, with consistency of calling (operationalized by the number of days called in a given week) being the most predictive feature as opposed to average call duration.

5   Discussion and Design Implications

Contextually-appropriate technologies may support learning outside of school for children in rural contexts with limited access to schooling. However, as prior work has demonstrated, in spite of motivation to learn, a variety of exogenous factors may inhibit children and their caregivers from consistently using learning technologies outside of school, limiting their efficacy [27, 29]. While prior research has developed predictive models of the likelihood of dropout, these approaches have historically dealt with adults dropping out from formal in-person or online courses, each of which may have some financial or social cost for dropping out. These factors may not be relevant for children's voluntary usage of a mobile learning application. In rural, low-resource contexts, mobile educational applications may be more accessible than online learning materials, though there may be additional obstacles to consider (e.g., children's agricultural participation [30]).

We have identified a set of system interaction features that are predictive of gaps in calling. Prior work in predicting dropout of adult learners in online courses found that factors like organizational support, time constraints, financial problems, etc. play an important role in predicting dropout [33]. We extend prior literature by finding that the important features associated with system usage were related to patterns of use, such as the duration of the interactions, their consistency of use (e.g., number of calls and number of days called in a week), as well as features related to their performance on the platform, including the number of questions completed and their overall mastery percent across all questions. In addition, we find that involvement of other family members (operationalized as the number of times the informational menu designed for adult supporters was accessed) is a predictive feature associated with system usage, which had not been accounted for in prior literature on app usage prediction.

Designers of voluntary educational systems can leverage these insights on the impact of learners' consistency of use and patterns of performance on future system usage. First, personalized, preemptive usage reminders may support ongoing engagement with the system. While usage reminders, like SMS texts and call reminders, have been associated with increased usage of mobile learning applications, they are often post-hoc (i.e., sent after a usage gap has already been observed) [38], which may be too late if users have already stopped engaging. Alternatively, sending too many reminders has been associated with a decrease in system usage, perhaps due to perceptions of being spammed [38]. Thus, there is a need for personalized, preemptive interventions based on users' likelihood to not persist in using the system. Researchers can use models trained on the aforementioned features to identify those users who are expected to have a gap in usage in the upcoming week. Furthermore, as we found that family involvement was associated with increased student engagement (following other prior work that did not use predictive modeling [10,54]), we suggest that parents or guardians also receive personalized messages to prompt children's use of the system.

Second, analysis from both Study 1 and 2 showed that students' mastery (i.e., percentage of questions attempted correctly) was negatively associated with gaps in system usage. We thus hypothesize that users may feel a sense of achievement, or a positive sense of self-efficacy when they answer questions correctly, thus motivating them to continue learning (as in [1,55]). Voluntary educational applications may leverage mechanisms like dynamic question difficulty depending on correctness of responses, or system elements designed to give users this sense of achievement and mastery (e.g., virtual rewards to promote student engagement [8]). Introducing such features may better motivate students to continue using the system.

Finally, we analyzed these features across two studies with similar results. We did find that consistency (measured by number of days called) plays a more important role in shorter studies, as seen in Study 2, while call duration plays a more important role in longer studies, as seen in Study 1. We confirmed this by running post-hoc analyses on 8 weeks of data from Study 1 and found the same result. We see that in the first few weeks of usage, a user's calling pattern, as opposed to the interactions within each call, is more predictive of gaps, while the opposite is true for longer studies. We hypothesize that this may be due in part to the novelty effect, and suggest that over time, students receive more personalized content support in deployments.

5.1 Limitations and Future Work

This study uses system interaction data to predict gaps in children's use of a mobile literacy learning application. However, there may be other relevant information that may be useful for informing usage prediction—including data on children's prior content or domain knowledge (here, French phonological awareness and literacy more broadly), prior experience with similar types of applications (here, interactive voice response used on feature phones), and, more broadly, data on children's motivations for learning and self-efficacy. Future work may explore how to most effectively integrate such data collected infrequently in a survey or assessment with time-series data such as we have used here. In addition, the studies we trained our models on were in rural communities in low-resource contexts, and future work may investigate how predictive models of voluntary educational technology usage may differ across rural and urban contexts, and across international and inter-cultural contexts. Finally, future work may investigate the efficacy of personalized reminders or nudges to motivate increased use of the system and their impact on consistent system usage and learning.

6   Conclusion

Educational technologies have been proposed as an approach for supporting education in low-resource contexts, but such technologies are often used in schools, which may compound inequities in education for children who may not be able to attend schools regularly. However, when ed tech use is voluntary for children to use outside of school, there may be gaps in their usage which may negatively impact their learning, or lead to them abandoning the system altogether—gaps which may be prevented or mitigated using personalized interventions such as reminder messages. In this paper, we explore the efficacy of using machine learning models to predict gaps in children's usage of a mobile-based educational technology deployed in rural communities in Côte d'Ivoire, to ultimately inform such personalized motivational support. We evaluate the predictive performance of multiple models trained on users' system interaction data, identify the most important features, and suggest design implications and directions for predicting gaps in usage of mobile-based learning technologies. We intend for this work to contribute to designing personalized interventions for promoting voluntary usage of out-of-school learning technologies, particularly in rural, low-resource contexts.

References

1. Bandura, A.: Self-efficacy. In: The Corsini Encyclopedia of Psychology, pp. 1–3 (2010)
2. Berge, Z.L., Huang, Y.P.: 13: 5 a model for sustainable student retention: a holistic perspective on the student dropout problem with special attention to e-learning. DEOSNEWS. www.researchgate.net/profile/Zane_Berge/publication/237429805 (2004)
3. Bergmeir, C., Benítez, J.M.: On the use of cross-validation for time series predictor evaluation. Inf. Sci. **191**, 192–213 (2012)
4. Chaplot, D.S., Rhim, E., Kim, J.: Predicting student attrition in MOOCs using sentiment analysis and neural networks. In: AIED Workshops, vol. 53, pp. 54–57 (2015)
5. Chen, T., Guestrin, C.: XGBoost: a scalable tree boosting system. In: Proceedings of the 22nd ACM SIGKDD International Conference on Knowledge Discovery and Data Mining, pp. 785–794 (2016)
6. Conn, K.M.: Identifying effective education interventions in sub-Saharan Africa: a meta-analysis of impact evaluations. Rev. Educ. Res. **87**(5), 863–898 (2017)
7. Dahman, M.R., Dağ, H.: Machine learning model to predict an adult learner's decision to continue ESOL course. Educ. Inf. Technol. **24**(4), 1–24 (2019)
8. Denny, P.: The effect of virtual achievements on student engagement. In: Proceedings of the SIGCHI Conference on Human Factors in Computing Systems, pp. 763–772 (2013)
9. Glass, C.R., Shiokawa-Baklan, M.S., Saltarelli, A.J.: Who takes MOOCs? New Dir. Inst. Res. **2015**(167), 41–55 (2016)
10. Gonzalez-DeHass, A.R., Willems, P.P., Holbein, M.F.D.: Examining the relationship between parental involvement and student motivation. Educ. Psychol. Rev. **17**(2), 99–123 (2005)

11. Hashim, M., Kalsom, U., Asmala, A.: The effects of training set size on the accuracy of maximum likelihood, neural network and support vector machine classification. Sci. Int. Lahore **26**(4), 1477–1481 (2014)
12. Herbert, M.: Staying the course: a study in online student satisfaction and retention. Online J. Distance Learn. Adm. **9**(4), 300–317 (2006)
13. Ishikawa, M., Ryan, D.: Schooling, basic skills and economic outcomes. Econ. Educ. Rev. **21**(3), 231–243 (2002)
14. Jasińska, K.K., Petitto, L.A.: Age of bilingual exposure is related to the contribution of phonological and semantic knowledge to successful reading development. Child Dev. **89**(1), 310–331 (2018)
15. Jose, J.: Predicting customer retention of an app-based business using supervised machine learning (2019)
16. Joseph, R.: Grid search for model tuning, December 2018. https://towardsdatascience.com/grid-search-for-model-tuning-3319b259367e
17. Kam, M., Kumar, A., Jain, S., Mathur, A., Canny, J.: Improving literacy in rural India: cellphone games in an after-school program. In: 2009 International Conference on Information and Communication Technologies and Development (ICTD), pp. 139–149. IEEE (2009)
18. Kam, M., Rudraraju, V., Tewari, A., Canny, J.F.: Mobile gaming with children in rural India: contextual factors in the use of game design patterns. In: DiGRA Conference (2007)
19. Kemp, W.C.: Persistence of adult learners in distance education. Am. J. Distance Educ. **16**(2), 65–81 (2002)
20. Kim, S., Choi, D., Lee, E., Rhee, W.: Churn prediction of mobile and online casual games using play log data. PLoS ONE **12**(7), e0180735 (2017)
21. Kshirsagar, V., Wieczorek, J., Ramanathan, S., Wells, R.: Household poverty classification in data-scarce environments: a machine learning approach. In: Neural Information Processing Systems, Machine Learning for Development Workshop, vol. 1050, p. 18 (2017)
22. Kumar, A., Reddy, P., Tewari, A., Agrawal, R., Kam, M.: Improving literacy in developing countries using speech recognition-supported games on mobile devices. In: Proceedings of the SIGCHI Conference on Human Factors in Computing Systems, pp. 1149–1158. ACM (2012)
23. Lam, Y.J.: Predicting dropouts of university freshmen: a logit regression analysis. J. Educ. Adm. **22**, 74–82 (1984)
24. Lange, C., Costley, J.: Opportunities and lessons from informal and non-formal learning: applications to online environments. Am. J. Educ. Res. **3**(10), 1330–1336 (2015)
25. Lucini, B.A., Bahia, K.: Country overview: Côte d'ivoire driving mobile-enabled digital transformation (2017)
26. Lundberg, S.M., Lee, S.I.: A unified approach to interpreting model predictions. In: Advances in Neural Information Processing Systems, pp. 4765–4774 (2017)
27. Madaio, M.A., et al.: "you give a little of yourself": family support for children's use of an IVR literacy system. In: Proceedings of the 2nd ACM SIGCAS Conference on Computing and Sustainable Societies, pp. 86–98. ACM (2019)
28. Madaio, M.A., Tanoh, F., Seri, A.B., Jasinska, K., Ogan, A.: "Everyone brings their grain of salt": designing for low-literate parental engagement with a mobile literacy technology in côte d'ivoire. In: Proceedings of the 2019 CHI Conference on Human Factors in Computing Systems, p. 465. ACM (2019)

29. Madaio, M.A., et al.: Collective support and independent learning with a voice-based literacy technology in rural communities. In: Proceedings of the 2020 CHI Conference on Human Factors in Computing Systems, pp. 1–14 (2020)
30. Malpel, J.: Pasec 2014: education system performance in francophone sub-Saharan Africa. Programme d'Analyse des Systèmes Educatifs de la CONFEMEN. Dakar, Sénégal (2016)
31. Maritzen, L., Ludtke, H., Tsukamura-San, Y., Tadafusa, T.: Automated usage-independent and location-independent agent-based incentive method and system for customer retention, US Patent App. 09/737,274, 28 February 2002
32. McEwan, P.J.: Improving learning in primary schools of developing countries: a meta-analysis of randomized experiments. Rev. Educ. Res. **85**(3), 353–394 (2015)
33. Park, J.H., Choi, H.J.: Factors influencing adult learners' decision to drop out or persist in online learning. J. Educ. Technol. Soc. **12**(4), 207–217 (2009)
34. Patel, N., Chittamuru, D., Jain, A., Dave, P., Parikh, T.S.: Avaaj Otalo: a field study of an interactive voice forum for small farmers in rural india. In: Proceedings of the SIGCHI Conference on Human Factors in Computing Systems, pp. 733–742. ACM (2010)
35. Pedregosa, F., et al.: Scikit-learn: machine learning in Python. J. Mach. Learn. Res. **12**(Oct), 2825–2830 (2011)
36. Pereira, F., et al.: Early Dropout prediction for programming courses supported by online judges. In: Isotani, S., Millán, E., Ogan, A., Hastings, P., McLaren, B., Luckin, R. (eds.) AIED 2019. LNCS (LNAI), vol. 11626, pp. 67–72. Springer, Cham (2019). https://doi.org/10.1007/978-3-030-23207-8_13
37. Periáñez, Á., Saas, A., Guitart, A., Magne, C.: Churn prediction in mobile social games: towards a complete assessment using survival ensembles. In: 2016 IEEE International Conference on Data Science and Advanced Analytics (DSAA), pp. 564–573. IEEE (2016)
38. Pham, X.L., Nguyen, T.H., Hwang, W.Y., Chen, G.D.: Effects of push notifications on learner engagement in a mobile learning app. In: 2016 IEEE 16th International Conference on Advanced Learning Technologies (ICALT), pp. 90–94. IEEE (2016)
39. Phiri, A., Mahwai, N., et al.: Evaluation of a pilot project on information and communication technology for rural education development: a cofimvaba case study on the educational use of tablets. Int. J. Educ. Dev. ICT **10**(4), 60–79 (2014)
40. Richmond, M., Robinson, C., Sachs-Israel, M., Sector, E.: The global literacy challenge. UNESCO, Paris (2008). Accessed 23 August 2011
41. Roe, B.P., Yang, H.J., Zhu, J., Liu, Y., Stancu, I., McGregor, G.: Boosted decision trees as an alternative to artificial neural networks for particle identification. Nucl. Instrum. Methods Phys. Res., Sect. A **543**(2–3), 577–584 (2005)
42. Schölkopf, B.: The kernel trick for distances. In: Advances in Neural Information Processing Systems, pp. 301–307 (2001)
43. Shankar, V., Venkatesh, A., Hofacker, C., Naik, P.: Mobile marketing in the retailing environment: current insights and future research avenues. J. Interact. Mark. **24**(2), 111–120 (2010)
44. Shin, C., Hong, J.H., Dey, A.K.: Understanding and prediction of mobile application usage for smart phones. In: Proceedings of the 2012 ACM Conference on Ubiquitous Computing, pp. 173–182 (2012)
45. Tang, C., Ouyang, Y., Rong, W., Zhang, J., Xiong, Z.: Time Series Model for Predicting Dropout in Massive Open Online Courses. In: Penstein Rosé, C., Penstein Rosé, P., et al. (eds.) AIED 2018. LNCS (LNAI), vol. 10948, pp. 353–357. Springer, Cham (2018). https://doi.org/10.1007/978-3-319-93846-2_66

46. Tashman, L.J.: Out-of-sample tests of forecasting accuracy: an analysis and review. Int. J. Forecast. **16**(4), 437–450 (2000)
47. Terenzini, P.T., Lorang, W.G., Pascarella, E.T.: Predicting freshman persistence and voluntary dropout decisions: a replication. Res. High. Educ. **15**(2), 109–127 (1981)
48. Tinto, V.: Research and practice of student retention: what next? J. Coll. Stud. Retent.: Res. Theory Pract. **8**(1), 1–19 (2006)
49. Tyler-Smith, K.: Early attrition among first time elearners: a review of factors that contribute to drop-out, withdrawal and non-completion rates of adult learners undertaking elearning programmes. J. Online Learn. Teach. **2**(2), 73–85 (2006)
50. Uchidiuno, J., Yarzebinski, E., Madaio, M., Maheshwari, N., Koedinger, K., Ogan, A.: Designing appropriate learning technologies for school vs home settings in Tanzanian rural villages. In: Proceedings of the 1st ACM SIGCAS Conference on Computing and Sustainable Societies, pp. 9–20. ACM (2018)
51. Warschauer, M., Ames, M.: Can one laptop per child save the world's poor? J. Int. Aff. **64**(1), 33–51 (2010)
52. Xie, Y., Li, X., Ngai, E., Ying, W.: Customer churn prediction using improved balanced random forests. Expert Syst. Appl. **36**(3), 5445–5449 (2009)
53. Yang, D., Sinha, T., Adamson, D., Rosé, C.P.: Turn on, tune in, drop out: anticipating student dropouts in massive open online courses. In: Proceedings of the 2013 NIPS Data-Driven Education Workshop, vol. 11, p. 14 (2013)
54. Zellman, G.L., Waterman, J.M.: Understanding the impact of parent school involvement on children's educational outcomes. J. Educ. Res. **91**(6), 370–380 (1998)
55. Zimmerman, B.J.: Self-efficacy: an essential motive to learn. Contemp. Educ. Psychol. **25**(1), 82–91 (2000)

MACER: A Modular Framework
for Accelerated Compilation Error Repair

Darshak Chhatbar[1], Umair Z. Ahmed[2], and Purushottam Kar[1(✉)]

[1] Indian Institute of Technology Kanpur, Kanpur, India
{darshak,purushot}@cse.iitk.ac.in
[2] National University of Singapore, Singapore, Singapore
umair@comp.nus.edu.sg

Abstract. Automated compilation error repair, the problem of suggesting fixes to buggy programs that fail to compile, has pedagogical applications for novice programmers who find compiler error messages cryptic and unhelpful. Existing works frequently involve black-box application of generative models, e.g. sequence-to-sequence prediction (TRACER) or reinforcement learning (RLAssist). Although convenient, this approach is inefficient at targeting specific error types as well as increases training costs. We present MACER, a novel technique for accelerated error repair based on a modular segregation of the repair process into repair identification and repair application. MACER uses powerful yet inexpensive learning techniques such as multi-label classifiers and rankers to first identify the type of repair required and then apply the suggested repair. Experiments indicate that this fine-grained approach offers not only superior error correction, but also much faster training and prediction. On a benchmark dataset of 4K buggy programs collected from actual student submissions, MACER outperforms existing methods by 20% at suggesting fixes for popular errors while being competitive or better at other errors. MACER offers a training time speedup of 2× over TRACER and 800× over RLAssist, and a test time speedup of 2 − 4× over both.

Keywords: Introductory programming · Compilation error · Program repair · Multi-label learning · Structured prediction

1 Introduction

Programming environment feedback such as compiler error messages, although formally correct, can be unhelpful in guiding novice programmers on correcting their errors [14]. This can be due to 1) use of technical terms in error messages which may be unfamiliar to beginners, or 2) the compiler being unable to comprehend the intent of the user. For example, for an integer variable i in the C programming language, the statement 0 = i; results in an error that the "expression is not assignable". Although the issue was merely the direction of assignment, the error message introduces concepts of expressions and assignability which may confuse a beginner (see Fig. 1 for examples). For beginners, navigating

I. I. Bittencourt et al. (Eds.): AIED 2020, LNAI 12163, pp. 106–117, 2020.
https://doi.org/10.1007/978-3-030-52237-7_9

```
1  void main(){          1  void main(){              1  void main(){   1  void main(){
2    int i, n=5, s=0;     2    int i, n=5, s=0;         2    int i=0;       2    int i=0;
3    for(i=1, i<n, i++)   3    for(i=1; i<n; i++)       3    if(0 = i)      3    if(0 == i)
4      s = s+i*(i++)/2;   4      s = s+i*(i++)/2;       4    i++;           4    i++;
5    printf ("%d", s);    5    printf ("%d", s);        5  }              5  }
6  }                      6  }
```

| Error Message E6: expected ';' in 'for' statement specifier | Error Message E10: expression is not assignable |
| Repair Class [E6 [,,] [;;]] (see Sec 2 for details) | Repair Class [E10 [=] [==]] (see Sec 2 for details) |

Fig. 1. Two examples of actual repairs by MACER.

such feedback often means seeking guidance from a human mentor which is not scalable [5]. In this work we report MACER, a tool that automatically suggests repairs to programs with compilation errors to reduce loads on human mentors.

Related Works. DeepFix [9] was one of the first methods to use deep learning (sequence-to-sequence models) to jointly locate and repair errors. TRACER [1] reported better performance by segregating the repair pipeline into repair line localization and repair prediction, and introduced the stringent Pred@k metric that compares the predicted repair against the actual repair desired by student, as opposed to the existing *repair accuracy* metric that simply counts reduction in compilation errors. RLAssist [8] introduced the use of reinforcement learning to eliminate the need for labeled training data but suffers from slow training times. Sect. 4 offers explicit experimental comparisons of MACER to DeepFix, TRACER and RLAssist. Apart from this, [10] used variational auto-encoders to introduce diversity in the suggested repairs. [19] considered *variable-misuse* errors that occur due to similar-looking identifier names. TEGCER [2] focused on *repair demonstration* by showing examples of fixes made by other students rather than repairing the error, which can be argued to have greater pedagogical utility.

Our Contributions. In addition to locating lines that need repair, MACER further segregates the repair pipeline by identifying *what* is the type of repair needed on each line (the *repair-class* of that line), and *where* in that line to apply that repair (the *repair-profile* of that line). Methods like TRACER and DeepFix perform the last two operations in a single step using some heavy-duty generative mechanism. MACER's repair pipeline is end-to-end and entirely automated[1] i.e. steps such as creation of repair classes can be replicated for any programming language for which static type inference is possible. In addition to this,

1. MACER is able to pay individual attention to each repair class to offer superior error repair. MACER also introduces the use of highly scalable multi-label learning techniques, such as hierarchical classification and re-ranking. To the best of our knowledge, the use of these techniques is novel in this domain.
2. MACER accurately predicts the repair class (see Table 1). Thus, instructors can manually rewrite helpful feedback (to accompany MACER's suggested repair) for popular repair classes which may offer greater pedagogical value.

---

[1] The MACER tool-chain is available at https://github.com/purushottamkar/macer/.

ErrorID	Error Message	Freq.
E1	Expected □ after expression	4999
E2	Use of undeclared identifier □	4709
E3	Expected expression	3818
E6	Expected □ in □ statement specifier	720
E10	Expression is not assignable	538
E23	Expected ID after return statement	128
E57	Unknown type name □	23
E76	Non-object type □ is not assignable	11
E98	variable has incomplete type ID	3
E148	Parameter named □ is missing	1

ClassID	[ErrorID [Del] [Ins]]	Type	Freq.
C1	[E1 [∅] [;]]	Insert	3364
C2	[E2 [INVALID] [INT]]	Replace	585
C12	[E6 [,] [;]]	Replace	173
C22	[E23 [;] [∅]]	Delete	89
C31	[E6 [,,] [;;]]	Replace	62
C64	[E3 [)] [∅]]	Delete	33
C99	[E45 [==] [=]]	Replace	19
C115	[E3 [∅] ['']]	Insert	16
C145	[E24 [.] [->]]	Replace	11
C190	[E6 [for] [while]]	Replace	9

Fig. 2. (Left) Some of the 148 compiler errorIDs listed in decreasing order of frequency in the train set. Some errorIDs are frequent whereas others are very rare. The symbol □ is a placeholder for program specific tokens such as identifiers, reserved keywords, punctuation marks etc. E.g., an instance of E6 is shown in Fig. 1. An instance of E1 could be "Expected ; after expression". **(Right)** Some of the 1016 repair classes used by MACER listed in decreasing order of frequency in the train set. E.g., ClassID C145 concerns inappropriate use of the dot operator to access member fields of a (pointer to a) structure and requires replacement with the arrow operator. ∅ indicates that no token need be inserted/deleted for that class, e.g., no token need be inserted to perform repair for C22 whereas no token need be deleted to perform repair for C115. Please see the text in Sect. 2 for a description of the notation used in the second column.

2 MACER: Data Pre-processing

The training data for MACER is in the form of (source-target) program pairs where the source program failed to compile and the target is the student-repaired program. Similar to [1], we train only on pairs where the two programs differ in a single line (although MACER is tested on programs where multiple lines require repairs as well). The differing line in the source (resp. target) program is called the *source line* (resp. *target line*) (e.g. line 3 in Fig. 1). With every such program pair, we also receive the errorID and message generated by the Clang compiler [13] when compiling the source program. Figure 2 lists a few errorIDs and error messages. Some error types are extremely rare whereas others are very common.

Notation. We use angular brackets to represent n-grams e.g. the statement $a = b + c$; contains unigrams $\langle a \rangle$, $\langle = \rangle$, $\langle b \rangle$, $\langle + \rangle$, $\langle c \rangle$, $\langle ; \rangle$, and bigrams $\langle a = \rangle$, $\langle = b \rangle$, $\langle b + \rangle$, $\langle + c \rangle$, $\langle c ; \rangle$, $\langle ; \text{EOL} \rangle$. Including an end-of-line character EOL helps MACER distinguish this location since several repairs (such as insertion of expression termination symbols) require edits at the end of the line.

Feature Encoding. Source lines contain user-defined literals and identifiers that are diverse yet uninformative for error repair. Thus, we perform *abstraction* by replacing literals and identifiers with an abstract LLVM token type [13], while retaining keywords and symbols, e.g. the raw/*concrete* statement int abc = 0; is converted to the *abstract* statement int VARIABLE_INT = LITERAL_INT ;. An exception is string literals where format-specifiers (e.g. %d and %s) are retained since these are often a source of error themselves. Such abstraction is common in literature [1,2]. The token INVALID is used for unrecognized identifiers. This gave us a vocabulary of 161 uni and 1930 bigrams (trigrams did not offer significant improvements). A source line is represented as a 2239 (148 + 161 + 1930) dimensional vector storing one-hot encodings of the compiler errorID (see Fig. 2), and uni and bigram feature encodings of the abstracted source line. Note that the feature encoding step does not use the target line in any way.

Repair Class Creation. The *repair class* of a source line encodes *what* repair to apply to that line. The Clang compiler offers 148 distinct errorIDs in our training dataset. However, diverse repair strategies may be required to handle all instances of a single errorID. E.g., errorID E6 can either signal missing semicolons ';' within the for loop statement specifier (as in Fig. 1), or missing semicolon at the end of a do-while block, or missing colons ':' in a switch case block. To address this, similar to TEGCER [2], we expand the 148 compiler errorIDs into 1016 *repair classes*. These repair classes are generated automatically from training data and do not require any manual supervision. For each training example, the diff of the abstracted source and target lines reveals the set of tokens that must be inserted/deleted to/from the abstracted source line to obtain the abstracted target line. The *repair class* of this example is then simply a tuple enumerating the compiler error ID followed by the tokens to be inserted/deleted (in order of their occurrence in the source line from left to right).

$$[\text{ErrID} [\text{TOK}_1^- \ \text{TOK}_2^- \ \ldots][\text{TOK}_1^+ \ \text{TOK}_2^+ \ \ldots]]$$

We identified 1016 such classes (see Fig. 2). Repair classes requiring no insertions (resp. no deletions) are called *Delete* (resp. *Insert*) classes and others are called *Replace* classes. Repair classes, like error IDs, exhibit a heavy tail distribution with a few popular repair classes having hundreds of training examples whereas most repair classes having single digit training examples (see Fig. 2).

Repair Profile Creation. The *repair profile* of a source line encodes *where* in that line to apply the repair encoded in its repair class. For every erroneous program, the diff between its abstracted source and target lines tells us which bigrams in the abstracted source line require edits (insert/delete/replace). The repair profile for a training example is given as a one-hot representation of the set of bigrams i.e. $\mathbf{r} \in \{0,1\}^{1930}$ which require modification. We note that the repair profile is a sparse fixed-dimensional binary vector (that does not depend on the number of tokens in the source line) and ignores repetition information. Thus, even if a bigram requires multiple edit operations, or appears several times in the source line and only one of those occurrences requires an edit, we record a 1 in the repair profile corresponding to that bigram. This was done in order to simplify prediction of the repair profile for erroneous programs at testing time.

Working Dataset. After the above pre-processing steps, we have with us, corresponding to every training source-target example pair, a class-label $y^i \in$ [1016] telling us the repair class for that source line, a feature representation $\mathbf{x}^i \in \{0,1\}^{2239}$ that tells us the errorID along with the uni/bigram representation of the source line, and a sparse Boolean vector $\mathbf{r}^i \in \{0,1\}^{1930}$ that tells us the repair profile. Altogether, this constitutes a dataset of the form $\left\{(\mathbf{x}^i, y^i, \mathbf{r}^i)\right\}_{i=1}^{n}$.

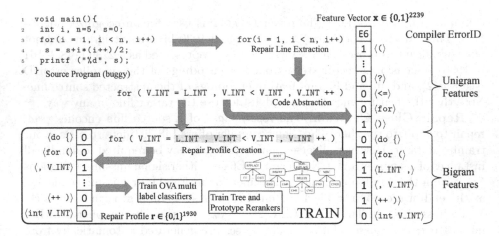

Fig. 3. The training pipeline for MACER, illustrated using the example used in Fig. 1. L_INT and V_INT are shorthand for LITERAL_INT and VARIABLE_INT.

3   MACER: Training and Prediction

MACER segregates the error repair process (at test time) into six distinct steps

1. **Repair Lines:** Locate which line(s) are erroneous and require repair.
2. **Feature Encoding:** A 2239-dimensional feature vector for each such line.
3. **Repair Class Prediction:** Use the feature vector to predict which of the 1016 repair classes is applicable i.e. which type of repair is required.
4. **Repair Localization:** Use the feature vector to predict locations within the source line where repairs should be applied.
5. **Repair Application:** Apply repairs at the predicted locations.
6. **Repair Concretization:** Undo code abstraction and compile.

MACER departs notably from previous works in segregating the repair process into these steps. Apart from faster training and prediction, this allows MACER to learn a customized repair location and repair application strategy for every repair class, e.g. if it is known that the repair requires the insertion of a semi-colon, then the possible repair locations are narrowed down significantly.

Repair Lines. In addition to the compiler reported error line numbers, MACER samples 2 additional lines, one above and one below, as candidate repair lines. The same technique was used by TRACER [1], and achieves a *repair line localization* recall of around 90% on our training dataset.

Repair Class Prediction. Given the large number of repair classes, MACER uses a probabilistic hierarchical classification trees [12,17] for fast and accurate prediction. Given a source line feature vector $\mathbf{x} \in \{0, 1\}^{2239}$, they assign a likelihood score $s_c^{\text{tree}}(\mathbf{x})$ for each repair class $c \in [1016]$ that is used to rank the classes. The tree used by MACER (see Fig. 4) uses a feed-forward network with 2 hidden layers with 128 nodes each at the root node and linear one-vs-rest classifier at other nodes, all trained on cross entropy loss. However, given the large number

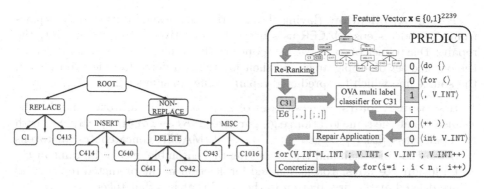

Fig. 4. (Left) The prediction hierarchy used by MACER to predict the repair class. **(Right)** The repair pipeline for MACER, illustrated using the example used in Fig. 1. A situation is depicted where a wrong repair class gets highest score from the classification tree, but reranking corrects the error. Table 1 shows that this is indeed common.

Table 1. Performance benefits of reranking. Here, Top@k reports the fraction of test examples on which the correct errorID/repair tokens were predicted within top k locations of the ranking. MAP refers to mean-averaged precision. Reranking significantly boosts MACER's performance. MAP error indicates that reranking ensures that the correct errorID/repair tokens were almost always predicted within the first two ranks.

	Top@1	Top@3	Top@5	MAP
Reranking Off (use $s_c^{\text{tree}}(\mathbf{x})$ to rank repair classes)	0.66	0.83	0.87	0.40
Reranking On (use $0.8 \cdot s_c^{\text{tree}}(\mathbf{x}) + 0.2 \cdot s_c^{\text{prot}}(\mathbf{x})$ instead)	0.67	**0.88**	**0.90**	**0.50**

of extremely rare repair classes (Fig. 2 shows that only $\approx$150 of the 1016 repair classes have more than 10 training examples), there is room for improvement.

Repair Class Reranking. To improve classification performance on rare repair classes, MACER uses *prototype classifiers* [11,16]. Prototypes vectors are obtained for each repair class $c \in [1016]$ (with say n_c training examples) by clustering training examples associated with that class into $k_c = \left\lceil \frac{n_c}{25} \right\rceil$ clusters with centroids $\tilde{\mathbf{x}}_c^1, \ldots, \tilde{\mathbf{x}}_c^{k_c}$. For a source line $\mathbf{x} \in \{0, 1\}^{2239}$, the prototypes are used to assign a new score to each repair class $s_c^{\text{prot}}(\mathbf{x}) := \max_{k \in [k_c]} \exp\left(-\frac{1}{2} \left\| \mathbf{x} - \tilde{\mathbf{x}}_c^k \right\|_2^2\right)$. This score is combined with the earlier (hierarchical classification tree) score as $s_c(\mathbf{x}) = 0.8 \cdot s_c^{\text{tree}}(\mathbf{x}) + 0.2 \cdot s_c^{\text{prot}}(\mathbf{x})$ and $s_c(\mathbf{x})$ is used to rank the repair classes. Table 1 outlines how the reranking step significantly boosts MACER's ability to accurately predict the relevant compiler errorID and the repair class.

Repair Localization. MACER predicts the repair profile vector by solving a multi-label learning problem with 1930 "labels" corresponding to the bigrams in our vocabulary. MACER trains a separate "one-vs-rest" (OVR) classifier [4] per repair class that allows it to adapt to needs of different repair classes. Only those OVR classifiers that correspond to bigrams actually present in the source line are invoked. This offers good localization with a Hamming loss of just 1.43.

Repair Application. Having obtained the nature and location of the repairs from the above steps, MACER uses frugal but effective techniques to apply the repairs. Due to lack of space, we postpone details to the full version. Let $\mathcal{B}$ denote the ordered set of all bigrams (and their locations, ordered from left to right) in the source line which the predicted repair profile considers edit-worthy.

1. **Insertion Repairs**: In most cases of insertion repair, all tokens need to be inserted at the same location, e.g., `for(i=0;i<5)` → `for(i=0;i<5;i++)` with repair class [E6 [∅] [; VARIABLE_INT ++]]. MACER concatenates all tokens marked for insertion and tries inserting this ensemble into all bigrams in $\mathcal{B}$.
2. **Deletion Repairs**: Tokens marked for deletion in the predicted repair class are deleted at the first bigram in the set $\mathcal{B}$ that has that token.
3. **Replace Repairs**: The repair class specifies a list of pairs of tokens (TOK⁻, TOK⁺) where TOK⁻ needs to be replaced with TOK⁺. Similar to deletion repairs, MACER attempts this edit at the first bigram that contains TOK⁻.
4. **Miscellaneous Repairs**: for unstructured repair classes where insertions and deletions are both required but an unequal number of tokens are inserted and deleted, MACER first ignores insertion tokens and performs edits as if this were a deletion repair class instance and then performs all insertions. This approach leaves room for improvement but nevertheless performs relatively well.

Repair Concretization. To make the repaired program compilable, abstract LLVM tokens such as `LITERAL_INT` are replaced with concrete program tokens such as literals and identifiers. Each abstract token is replaced with the most recently used concrete variable/literal of the same type, that already exists in the current scope. The process, although approximate, nevertheless recovers the correct replacement in 90+% of the instances in our datasets. Each candidate repair line reported by the *repair line localizer* is replaced with MACER's repair prediction, if it reduces the number of compilation errors in the program.

4 Experiments

We compared MACER's performance against previous works, as well as performed ablation studies to study the relative contribution of its components. All MACER implementations[2] were done using standard machine learning libraries such as `sklearn` [15] and `keras` [6]. Experiments were performed on a system with Intel(R) Core(TM) i7-4770 CPU @ 3.40GHz × 8 CPU having 32 GB RAM.

Datasets. We report results on 3 different datasets, all curated from CS-1 course offerings at IIT-Kanpur (a large public university) with 400+ students attempting 40+ programming assignments. The datasets were recorded using Prutor [7], an online IDE. The DeepFix dataset[3] contains 6,971 programs that fail to compile, each with max 400 tokens [9]. The *single-line* (17,669 train + 4,578 test) and *multi-line* (17,451 test programs) datasets[4] contain program pairs where error-repair is required, respectively, on a single line or multiple lines [1].

---

[2] The MACER tool-chain is available at https://github.com/purushottamkar/macer/.

[3] https://www.cse.iitk.ac.in/users/karkare/prutor/prutor-deepfix-09-12-2017.zip.

[4] https://github.com/umairzahmed/tracer.

Metrics. We report i) repair accuracy, the fraction of test programs that were successfully repaired by a tool, and ii) Pred@k, the fraction of programs where at least one of the top k abstract repair suggestions exactly matched the student's own abstract repair. This is a metric introduced in [1] motivated by the fact that the goal of program repair, especially in pedagogical settings, is not to merely generate any program that compiles (see below).

The Importance of Pred@k. We consider a naive method *Kali'* that simply deletes all lines where the compiler reported an error. This is inspired by Kali [18], an erstwhile state-of-art semantic-repair tool that repaired programs by functionality deletion alone. *Kali'* gets 48% repair accuracy on the DeepFix dataset whereas DeepFix [9], TRACER [1] and MACER get respectively 27%, 44% and 56% (Table 3). Although *Kali'* seems to offer better repair accuracy than TRACER, its Pred@1 accuracy on the single-line dataset is just 4%, compared to 59.6% and 59.7% by TRACER and MACER respectively (Table 2). This shows the weakness of the repair accuracy metric and the need for the Pred@k metric.

Results. Of the total 7 min train time (see Table 3), MACER took less than 5 s to create repair classes and repair profiles from the raw dataset. The rest of the training time was taken up more or less evenly by repair class prediction training (tree ranking + reranking) and repair profile prediction training.

Comparisons with Other Methods. The values for Pred@k (resp. Rep@k) were obtained by considering the top k repairs suggested by a method and declaring success if any one of them matched the student repair (resp. removed compilation errors). For Pred@k computations, all methods were given the true repair line and did not have to perform repair line localization. For Rep@k computations, all methods had to localize then repair. Tables 2 and 3 compare MACER with competitor methods. MACER offers superior repair performance at much lesser training and prediction costs. Figure 6 shows that MACER outperforms TRACER by $\approx$ 20% on popular classes while being competitive or better on others.

Ablation studies with MACER. To better understand the strengths and limitations of MACER, we report on further experiments. Figure 6 shows that MACER is effective at utilizing even small amounts of training data and that its prediction accuracy drops below 50% only on repair classes which have less than 30 examples in the training set. Figure 5 offers examples of actual repairs by MACER. Although it performs favorably on repair classes seen during training, it often fails on *zero-shot* repair classes which were never seen during training. Table 4 presents an explicit ablation study analyzing the differential contributions of MACER's individual components on the single-line dataset. Re-ranking gives 10–12% boost to both Pred@k and repair accuracy. Predicting the repair class (resp. profile) correctly accounts for 5–12% (resp. 6%) of the performance. MACER loses a mere 6% accuracy on account of improper repair application. For all figures and tables, details are provided in the captions due to lack of space.

Table 2. TRACER vs MACER on single, multi-line datasets. Although comparable on single line, MACER outperforms TRACER by 14% on multi-line dataset. P@k, R@k are shorthand for Pred@k, Rep@k resp.

Table 3. All methods on the DeepFix dataset. Values take from *[9] and †[8]. MACER offers the highest repair accuracy with a margin of 12.5% over the next best method, a prediction time that is at least 2× faster, and a train time 2× faster than TRACER and 800× faster than RLAssist.

Dataset	Single			Multi
Metric	P@1	P@5	R@5	R@5
TRACER	0.596	0.683	0.792	0.437
MACER	0.597	0.691	0.805	**0.577**

DeepFix	RLAssist	TRACER	MACER
Repair Acc	0.27*	0.267†	0.439	**0.566**
Test Time	<1s†	<1s†	1.66 s	**0.45 s**
Train Time	-	4 Days	14 min	**7 min**

#	Source-line	Target-line	MACER's Top Prediction	Pred?	Repair?	Zero-shot?
1	scanf("%c",&a[i] ;	scanf("%c",&a[i]);	scanf("%c",&a[i]);	Yes	Yes	No
2	for (i =0;i<n;i++)	for(int i=0;i<n;i++)	for (int i=0;i<n;i++)	Yes	Yes	No
3	if(x==y)printf("Y"); break;	if(x==y)printf("Y");	if(x==y)printf("Y") ;	Yes	Yes	No
4	for(i=0; i=<N ;i++)	for(i=0;i<=N;i++)	for(i=0; i<N ;i++)	No	Yes	No
5	if ((a[j]==' ')	if(a[j]==' ')	if((a[j]==' '))	No	Yes	No
6	int n; n=q;	int n;	int n; n=0;	No	Yes	Yes
7	c=sqrt(a^2+b^2);	c=sqrt(a*a+b*b);	c=sqrt(a^2+b^2);	No	No	Yes

Fig. 5. Some examples of repairs by MACER on test examples. Pred? = Yes if MACER's top suggestion exactly matched the student's abstracted fix. Rep? = Yes if MACER's top suggestion removed all compilation errors. ZS? = Yes for "zero-shot" test examples i.e. the corresponding repair class was absent in training data. MACER offers exactly the student's repair for the first three examples. Note that the second example involves an undeclared identifier. For the next three examples, although MACER does not offer exactly the student repair, it nevertheless offers sane fixes that eliminate all compilation errors. The last two are zero-shot examples – MACER handles one of them.

5   Conclusion

We presented MACER, a novel technique that offers superior repair accuracy and increased training and prediction speed by finely segregating error repair into efficiently solvable ranking and labeling problems. Targeting rare error classes and "zero-shot" cases (Fig. 5) is an important area of future improvement. A recent large scale user-study [3] demonstrated that students who received automated repair feedback from TRACER [1] resolved their compilation errors faster on average, as opposed to human tutored students; with the performance gain increasing with error complexity. We plan to conduct a similar systematic user study in the future, to better understand the correlation between our improved Pred@k metric scores and error-resolution efficiency of students.

Acknowledgments. The authors thank the reviewers for helpful comments and are grateful to Pawan Kumar for support with benchmarking experiments. P. K. thanks Microsoft Research India and Tower Research for research grants.

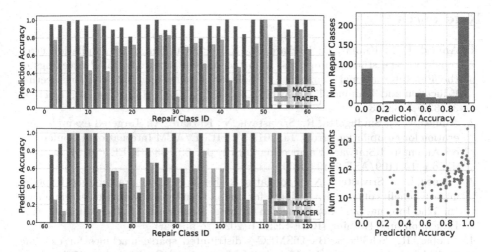

Fig. 6. (Left-Top and Left-Bottom) MACER vs TRACER on the 60 most frequent (head) and top 60–120 (torso) repair classes. To avoid clutter, only 30 classes from each category are shown. MACER outperforms TRACER by around 20% in terms of Pred@k on head classes and is competitive or better on torso classes. **(Right-Top and Right-Bottom)** Prediction (exact match) accuracy for MACER on the 391 repair classes that had at least 3 training points. On a majority of these classes 221/391 = 56%, MACER offers greater than 90% Pred@k. On a much bigger majority 287/391 = 73%, MACER offers more than 50% prediction accuracy. MACER's prediction accuracy drops below 50% only on classes which have less than around 30 points. This indicates that MACER is effective at utilizing even small amounts of training data.

Table 4. An ablation study on the differential contributions of MACER's components. ZS stands for "zero-shot". For the "ZS included" column, all test points were considered while the "ZS excluded" column took only those test points whose repair class was seen at least once in the training data. RR stands for reranking. RCP stands for Repair Class Prediction, RLP stands for Repair Location Prediction. RCP = P (resp. RLP = P) implies that we used the repair class (resp. repair location) predicted by MACER. RCP = G (resp. RLP = G) implies that we used the true (G for gold) repair class (resp. true repair profile vector). The difference in the first two rows shows that reranking gives 10–12% boost to both Pred@k and repair accuracy. Predicting the repair class (resp. profile) correctly accounts for 5–12% (resp. 6%) of the performance. The final row shows that MACER loses 6–8% performance owing to improper repair application/concretization. In the last two rows, Pred@1 is higher than Rep@1 (1–2% cases) owing to concretization failures – even though the predicted repair matched the student's repair in abstracted form, the program failed to compile after abstraction was removed.

			ZS included		ZS excluded	
RR	RCP	RLP	Pred@1	Rep@1	Pred@1	Rep@1
OFF	P	P	0.492	0.599	0.631	0.706
ON	P	P	0.597	0.703	0.757	0.825
ON	G	P	–	–	0.885	0.877
ON	G	G	–	–	0.943	0.926

References

1. Ahmed, U.Z., Kumar, P., Karkare, A., Kar, P., Gulwani, S.: Compilation error repair: for the student programs, from the student programs. In: Proceedings of the 40th International Conference on Software Engineering: Software Engineering Education and Training (ICSE-SEET), pp. 78–87 (2018). https://doi.org/10.1145/3183377.3183383
2. Ahmed, U.Z., Sindhgatta, R., Srivastava, N., Karkare, A.: Targeted example generation for compilation errors. In: 2019 34th IEEE/ACM International Conference on Automated Software Engineering (ASE), pp. 327–338. IEEE (2019). https://doi.org/10.1109/ASE.2019.00039
3. Ahmed, U.Z., Srivastava, N., Sindhgatta, R., Karkare, A.: Characterizing the pedagogical benefits of adaptive feedback for compilation errors by novice programmers. In: 42nd International Conference on Software Engineering: Software Engineering Education and Training (ICSE-SEET) (2020, to appear)
4. Babbar, R., Schölkopf, B.: DiSMEC - distributed sparse machines for extreme multi-label classification. In: 10th ACM International Conference on Web Search and Data Mining (WSDM), pp. 721–729 (2017). https://doi.org/10.1145/3018661.3018741
5. Camp, T., Zweben, S.H., Walker, E.L., Barker, L.J.: Booming enrollments: good times? In: Proceedings of the 46th ACM Technical Symposium on Computer Science Education (SIGCSE), pp. 80–81. ACM (2015). https://doi.org/10.1145/2676723.2677333
6. Chollet, F., et al.: Keras: the python deep learning library (2015). https://keras.io
7. Das, R., Ahmed, U.Z., Karkare, A., Gulwani, S.: Prutor: a system for tutoring CS1 and collecting student programs for analysis (2016). arXiv:1608.03828 [cs.CY]
8. Gupta, R., Kanade, A., Shevade, S.: Deep reinforcement learning for syntactic error repair in student programs. In: 33rd AAAI Conference on Artificial Intelligence (AAAI), pp. 930–937 (2019). https://doi.org/10.1609/aaai.v33i01.3301930
9. Gupta, R., Pal, S., Kanade, A., Shevade, S.: DeepFix: fixing common C language errors by deep learning. In: 31st AAAI Conference on Artificial Intelligence (AAAI), pp. 1345–1351 (2017)
10. Hajipour, H., Bhattacharyya, A., Fritz, M.: SampleFix: learning to correct programs by sampling diverse fixes (2019). arXiv:1906.10502v1 [cs.SE]
11. Jain, H., Prabhu, Y., Varma, M.: Extreme multi-label loss functions for recommendation, tagging, ranking & other missing label applications. In: 22nd ACM SIGKDD Conference on Knowledge Discovery and Data Mining (KDD), pp. 935–944 (2016). https://doi.org/10.1145/2939672.2939756
12. Jasinska, K., Dembczyński, K., Busa-Fekete, R., Pfannschmidt, K., Klerx, T., Hüllermeier, E.: Extreme F-measure maximization using sparse probability estimates. In: 33rd International Conference on Machine Learning (ICML), pp. 1435–1444 (2016)
13. Lattner, C., Adve, V.: LLVM: a compilation framework for lifelong program analysis & transformation. In: Proceedings of the International Symposium on Code Generation and Optimization: Feedback-Directed and Runtime Optimization, p. 75. IEEE Computer Society (2004)
14. McCauley, R., et al.: Debugging: a review of the literature from an educational perspective. Comput. Sci. Educ. 18(2), 67–92 (2008). https://doi.org/10.1080/08993400802114581

15. Pedregosa, F., et al.: Scikit-learn: machine learning in python. J. Mach. Learn. Res. **12**(85), 2825–2830 (2011)
16. Prabhu, Y., et al.: Extreme multi-label learning with label features for warm-start tagging, ranking & recommendation. In: 11th ACM International Conference on Web Search and Data Mining (WSDM), pp. 441–449 (2018). https://doi.org/10.1145/3159652.3159660
17. Prabhu, Y., Kag, A., Harsola, S., Agrawal, R., Varma, M.: Parabel: partitioned label trees for extreme classification with application to dynamic search advertising. In: 27th International World Wide Web Conference (WWW), pp. 993–1002 (2018). https://doi.org/10.1145/3178876.3185998
18. Qi, Z., Long, F., Achour, S., Rinard, M.C.: An analysis of patch plausibility and correctness for generate-and-validate patch generation systems. In: International Symposium on Software Testing and Analysis, pp. 24–36. ACM (2015). https://doi.org/10.1145/2771783.2771791
19. Vasic, M., Kanade, A., Maniatis, P., Bieber, D., Singh, R.: Neural program repair by jointly learning to localize and repair. In: 7th International Conference on Learning Representations (ICLR) (2019)

Using Motion Sensors to Understand Collaborative Interactions in Digital Fabrication Labs

Edwin Chng[✉], Mohamed Raouf Seyam, William Yao, and Bertrand Schneider

Harvard University, Cambridge, MA 02138, USA
chng_weimingedwin@g.harvard.edu, mohamedseyam@gse.harvard.com,
william_yao@college.harvard.edu,
bertrand_schneider@gse.harvard.edu

Abstract. Open-ended learning environments such as makerspaces present a unique challenge for instructors. While it is expected that students are given free rein to work on their projects, facilitators have to strike a difficult balance between micromanaging them and letting the community support itself. In this paper, we explore how Kinect sensors can continuously monitor students' collaborative interactions so that instructors can gain a more comprehensive view of the social dynamics of the space. We employ heatmaps to examine the diversity of student collaborative interactions and Markov transition probabilities to explore the transitions between instances of collaborative interactions. Findings indicate that letting students work on their own promotes the development of technical skills, while working together encourages students to spend more time in the makerspace. This confirms the intuition that successful projects in makerspaces necessitate both individual and group efforts. Furthermore, such aggregation and display of information can aid instructors in uncovering the state of student learning in makerspaces. Identifying the instances and diversity of collaborative interactions affords instructors an early opportunity to identify struggling students and having these data in a near real-time manner opens new doors in terms of making (un)productive behaviors salient, both for teachers and students. We discuss how this work represents a first step toward using intelligent systems to support student learning in makerspaces.

Keywords: Motion sensors · Social interactions · Makerspaces

1 Introduction

Makerspaces are open-ended learning environments that offer students unique learning opportunities for developing a maker's mindset [1] as well as critical 21st century competencies [2]. The nature of makerspace projects allows students with diverse prior knowledge and experiences to come together in pursuit of personally meaningful projects. Such learning opportunities effectively model the demands of a professional workspace and cultivates students with the proper skills and mindset to meet the challenges of the 21st century. As such, makerspaces have become increasingly popular over the last decade.

© Springer Nature Switzerland AG 2020
I. I. Bittencourt et al. (Eds.): AIED 2020, LNAI 12163, pp. 118–128, 2020.
https://doi.org/10.1007/978-3-030-52237-7_10

Open-ended learning environments, however, make it challenging for instructors to continuously monitor students' progress. While there may be pockets of instructional time when instructors explicitly teach students, students are often left to their own devices when it comes to project work. In fact, the many benefits of makerspaces cannot be divorced from the need to leave students to productively struggle on their own. As a result, instructors have to strike a difficult balance between micromanaging students and simply leaving them without any form of support.

The use of minimally invasive sensors such as Kinect can provide instructors with a dual advantage: to unobtrusively monitor student progress without affecting their natural workflow, and to intervene whenever necessary to help struggling students [3]. In particular, the study of students' collaborative interactions within makerspaces can bring a unique insight into students' learning. As proposed by Lave [4], 'learning is a process of becoming a member of a sustained community of practice' (p. 65). By examining how students socially interact within makerspaces, we hope to identify indicators that will inform instructors of students' needs. Thus, the goal of this paper is to examine the instances and diversity of student collaborative interactions within makerspaces using Kinect sensors.

2 Literature Review

Makerspaces embody learning under the long tradition of constructionism [5]. Within makerspaces, students are encouraged to address open-ended problems and figure things out for themselves with minimal aid from instructors. In such learning environments, instructors play the role of facilitators while students are given free rein to explore the space as they construct knowledge for themselves [2, 6].

However, since students are still novices, they may encounter barriers to learning. If struggling students are not promptly identified by instructors, repeated failures may result in them developing a sense of learned helplessness [7]. On the other hand, instructors may not want to intervene too early so that they can fail productively [8]. This creates an inherent tension between instruction and construction in makerspaces [9]. Instructors need to strike a balance between giving direct instruction to help struggling students and leaving students to productively fail and construct knowledge for themselves. This balance in instruction has been discussed by scholars such as Star [10], who pointed out that despite the many benefits of productive failures [8], there are instances when instructors should step in to prevent students from giving up entirely.

Recognizing the need to balance instruction and free exploration presents instructors with a new challenge. Using traditional methods, it is difficult for instructors to monitor students' progress without disrupting their natural workflow. Constructionist researchers like Berland et al. [11] have proposed the use of technology-enabled learning analytics to derive rich inference about learners whilst preserving minimum instructor interference. For the purpose of providing instructional support, several related works have been conducted. For instance, orchestration graphs were created by Prieto et al. [12] to suit teaching needs using data and Behoora and Tucker [13] have examined how body language can expose the emotional states of students, which is suitable for identifying frustration. Such work goes beyond just the simple extraction and assimilation of data for presentation as algorithms used value-added by showing teachers information that is pedagogically meaningful.

A reasonable question is what data our sensors should be collecting within makerspaces. A potential answer comes from Lave's call for situating learning in communities of practice [4]. In his seminal paper, Lave [4] states that 'learning is recognized as a social phenomenon ... the process of changing knowledgeable skill is subsumed in processes of changing identity in and through membership in a community of practitioners; and mastery is an organizational, relational characteristic of communities of practice' (p. 64). When viewed through this lens, makerspaces can be seen as natural grounds for the formation of a community of practice, and students' collaborative interactions become natural targets for data collection. As such, this paper aims to provide instructional support in makerspaces through the examination of the instances and diversity of student collaborative interactions using motion sensors.

3   Context of the Study

This section outlines the curriculum of the makerspace course the students were enrolled in, the infrastructure of the multi-sensor data collection system and the primary research questions for this study.

3.1   Course Overview

Over the course of 15 weeks, the research team collected motion sensor data and survey responses of 16 graduate students enrolled in a hands-on digital fabrication course. The goal of the course was to teach students the usage of modern fabrication technologies such as 3D printers and laser cutters, and their application in educational contexts. Throughout the semester, students were responsible for prototyping educational toolkits using digital fabrication tools, all of which were provided in the makerspace. Students were given access to use the space any time they wanted and collaborate across teams at their discretion, without presence of an instructor required.

The 15-week makerspace course can be divided into four discrete units of 3–4 weeks: 1) Introductory unit where students complete individual tasks, learn about makerspace tools and build up basic technical knowhow. 2) Making focused unit covering microprocessor programming using block-based code, fabrication and robotics 3) Programming focused unit involving the use of more advanced computer applications and techniques such as fiducial marker tracking, MMLA sensing and object-oriented programing basics 4) Final project unit during which students work on their group capstone projects for the class relying on the techniques and principles they learned during the first 3 units. For units 2, 3 and 4, students work in groups of 2–3 and their group members were assigned to them.

3.2   Makerspace Setup

The makerspace was equipped with two Kinect v2 sensors to capture human motion within the space. The sensors were placed on opposing ends of the makerspace lab, collecting data streams independently as shown in Fig. 1.

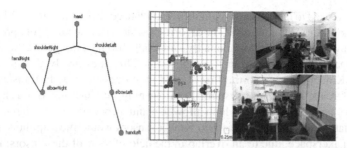

Fig. 1. Skeletal joint data collected by the Kinect (left). Sample frame from the video generation script showing a few students working together after course hours (right).

3.3 Research Questions (RQs)

- **RQ1**: Do the *instances* of collaborative interactions (as detected by Kinect sensors) provide meaningful and accurate information about students' performance in the makerspace?
- **RQ2**: Do the *diversity* of collaborative interactions (as detected by Kinect sensors) provide meaningful and accurate information about students' performance in the makerspace?
- **RQ3**: What can the *transitions between instances of interactions* inform instructors about student learning experiences in the makerspace?

4 Methods

This section describes the data and analysis methods used in this study. Kinect data were collected 24/7 for the duration of the semester, and we obtained information about the collaborative interactions of students using the data collected. Instructors also rated the students based on their perceived levels of collaborative interactions and technical competence. Information was also gathered through surveys given to the students on a weekly basis, asking about the amount of time spent in the space and on solving the weekly assignment, and 5-point Likert items on personal evaluation of levels of challenge, frustration, and engagement.

4.1 Kinect Data

Two Kinect sensors were used to collect motion and posture data in the makerspace. Motion detection and tracking was possible by the embedded IR sensor within each Kinect sensor. Before data were processed, the multi-sensor system collected approximately 1.04 million observations. From those observations, 800,513 were labeled with identity numbers, and after removing non-participants (the teaching team) and performing further preprocessing (as described below), 352,943 observations were used to perform our analysis.

   Kinect Data - Cleaning and Labeling: To detect episodes of collaboration, students and instructors needed to be identified. OpenFace, an open-source facial recognition algorithm was used to label the individuals in each data collection instance. When applied to each week's facial image dataset, the algorithm achieved an accuracy of approximately 88%, which was determined by manually validating 100 face images per week.

Kinect Data - Standardizing and Deduplicating: This study involved the simultaneous use of two Kinect sensors, so the first step in preprocessing was to translate the data into one reference coordinate system. Data cleaning was facilitated via the use of a custom video generation script, which allowed manual checking for further detection of erroneous data. In many cases, the two Kinect sensors would pick up the same person within the makerspace, due to an overlap in the field of view of the sensors. Duplicates were identified by calculating the Euclidean and cosine distances between the head joints of two skeletons and comparing the value to a lower threshold. Upon the identification of a duplicate, a decision tree was used to determine whether to average the data collected between the two sensors or choose one and discard the other.

Kinect Data - Instances of collaborative interactions: A student is said to have collaboratively interacted with another student or instructor if he/she is within one meter to another student or instructor. Even though the choice of using physical proximity is admittedly a necessary but not sufficient condition for collaborative interaction, prior work has demonstrated the reliability and efficacy of using proximity as a proxy for collaborative interactions [14–17]. Furthermore, based on the theory of proxemics, individuals normally interact at an optimal distance of one meter [18]. If the distance is too far, individuals will tend to move closer to facilitate a quality interaction, and if the distance is too near, individuals will tend to move apart to avoid unease in encroaching into each other's personal space. We classify the different instances of collaborative interactions as students working individually, working in a group of students and interacting with an instructor.

4.2 Instructor Rating Data

To gain a complementary perspective of the students' collaborative interactions and learning progress, we invited two senior instructors of the teaching team to assess students on two dimensions at the end of the course: social and technical. For the social dimension, instructors rated each student based on their observed ability to collaborate with others. For the technical dimension, instructors rated each student based on their perceived mastery of makerspace tools and skills. The rating for each student was completed separately by each instructor before they came together to review the given ratings. A rating of 1 on any dimension indicates weak, 2 indicates average, and 3 indicates strong. If any of the ratings differed, the instructors had to negotiate to settle on an agreed score. In this manner, the ratings assigned to the students were the result of deliberations from senior members of the teaching team.

5 Results

RQ 1: Do the *instances* of collaborative interactions (as detected by Kinect sensors) provide meaningful and accurate information about students' performance in the makerspace?

We correlated the time spent by students in each interaction category ("individual": working alone; "instructor": working with an instructor; and "student": working with peers) with the scores assigned by the instructors on each of the performance dimensions. As shown in Table 1, we found that receiving a higher technical score was significantly correlated with spending more time working individually ($r = 0.54$, $p < 0.05$) and spending more time working with other students ($r = 0.64$, $p < 0.01$) – but only in the 4th unit. On the other hand, no significant results were uncovered in the first three units. One interpretation is that the nature of the final projects (which is only executed in the 4th unit) necessitates both individual and group efforts to produce an outcome that meets instructor expectations on the technical dimension.

Similarly, both spending more time interacting with instructors and spending more time interacting with other students were found to significantly positively correlate to social score ($r = 0.60$, $p < 0.05$ and $r = 0.56$, $p < 0.05$ respectively) in the 4th unit. This might suggest that actively seeking help and interacting with others - whether students or instructors - is related to getting assigned a higher score on the social dimension. This finding could also reflect the collaborative and open-ended nature of the final deliverable. As such, it appears that a certain balance of the three interaction types - provided sufficient overall time has been spent by the student - is required to maximize student performance during this course.

Table 1. Correlations between collaborative interaction and performance (* $p < 0.05$; ** $p < 0.01$)

Unit	Interaction type	Performance	Pearson's correlation
4	Individual	Technical	$r = 0.54$*
4	Instructor	Social	$r = 0.60$*
4	Student	Technical	$r = 0.64$**
4	Student	Social	$r = 0.56$*

To further investigate and visualize the instances of collaborative interactions, bar plots (Fig. 2) and line plots (Fig. 3) were created to show the differences in interaction profile. For each dimension of instructor rating, two separate bar plots were generated. Within each bar plot, the students were grouped according to the scores that they received from the instructors. The x-axis reflects instructor-rated scores while the y-axis indicates fluctuations (from class average at $y = 0$) in time spent for each instance of collaborative interaction. Fluctuations were studied because we treated the class average as the baseline amount of time spent and we are interested in the deviations from this baseline.

Examining the social dimension bar plot (Fig. 2), we see that social scores received by the students is proportional to the amount of interaction time with instructors and other students. For instance, students with lower social scores (below 2.0) spent notably less time with instructors and other students. This demonstrates that the Kinect sensor data can indeed reflect students' collaborative interactions within makerspaces. Based on the technical dimension bar plot, students who received an instructor-assigned score of 1.0 spend less time (about 30 min lesser per week) working individually than their peers; and spent nearly the same average time (fluctuation = 0) interacting with an instructor or with other students across the semester. In contrast, students with high technical skills spent a lot of time working individually. Thus, it seems important that students spend sufficient time working alone to hone their technical skills.

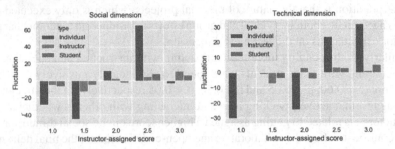

Fig. 2. Bar plots indicating fluctuations (from class average) in time spent (minutes) for students grouped according to instructor ratings. Box colors indicate interaction type. (Color figure online)

Line graphs in Fig. 3 show the weekly time spent for different interaction instances averaged for the whole class and for a student with a low technical score (whose anonymized name is *Pat*). Comparing the general shape of the two-line graphs, it is clear that the interaction profile for *Pat* is distinct from the entire class. In particular, the amount of time committed by *Pat* decreases as the weeks go by, with a relatively low period from week 7 to week 10. The amount of time spent by *Pat* only increased towards the end of the course, presumably because of the final project that he/she has to undertake. In contrast, the interaction profile for the entire class exhibits an ebb and flow that is in line with the demands of the course. For instance, the class' weekly time spent peaks in week 6 and 10 when the midterm and final term projects are ongoing. Overall, these data can aid instructors by providing a clear visualization to indicate which students have interaction instances that are inconsistent with class averages.

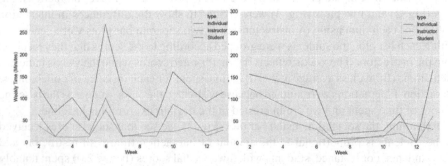

Fig. 3. Class overall (left) compared to *Pat* - student with low technical score (right)

RQ 2: Do the *diversity* of collaborative interactions (as detected by Kinect sensors) provide meaningful and accurate information about students' performance in the makerspace?

To visualize the diversity of student collaborative interactions, we generated heatmaps based on the time that each student spent with each other in the makerspace. A single cell within the heatmap indicates the amount of time (in hours) that student A (on the x-axis) spend with student B (on the y-axis). The longer the amount of time spent, the brighter the color of the cell. Additionally, the students are grouped according to the level of technical ratings that they receive from the instructors on the x-axis and according to the level of social ratings on the y-axis.

Figure 4 shows the generated heatmaps of all students for the duration of the course. The heatmap on the left includes student interactions with their assigned partners while the heatmap on the right leaves out all student interactions with their assigned partners. By comparing the two heatmaps, we see a stark difference between the time spent among partners compared to non-partners: not surprisingly, a lot more time is spent with assigned partners compared to the rest of the student population.

Furthermore, it can be observed from the heatmaps that students with higher social ratings have more diverse collaborative interactions (which is expected), and students with higher technical ratings have less diverse collaborative interactions (which corroborates with the findings in RQ1). The heatmaps allow instructors to directly identify pairs of students who worked closely together. For instance, we see that *Ben* and *Pat* share a close working relationship. *Pat* has been identified previously as someone who might be struggling in the space. On the other hand, *Ben* received a high technical rating. In this case, it is likely that *Pat* has reached out to *Ben* to address his learning challenges.

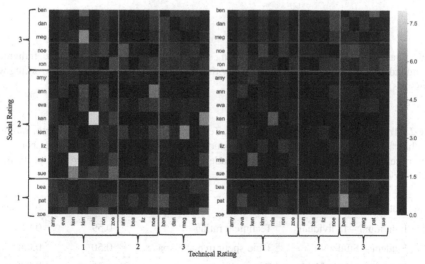

Fig. 4. Heatmaps indicating diversity of interactions. Students are arranged according to the instructor technical ratings on the x-axis and according to the instructor social ratings on the y-axis.

RQ 3: What can the *transitions between instances of interactions* inform instructors about student learning experiences in the makerspace?

Figure 5 displays Markov chains for a well performing student (*Meg*) and for a struggling student (*Pat*). The Markov chains demonstrate the transitions between states over the entire duration of the course. For example, *Meg*'s chain in Fig. 5 indicates that at any given minute of working individually in the makerspace (Individual state), *Meg* has a 81% chance of continuing to work alone, an 13% chance of transitioning to working with others (Student state), and a 6% chance of transition to working with instructors (Instructor state). We notate a state transition probability value by the initial state and the next state. For example, Instructor-Individual corresponds to 0.41 in *Meg*'s diagram. For each state transition, we computed 16 transition probabilities for each student, which were then correlated against the survey and technical skill measures gathered. The significant correlations are reported in Table 2.

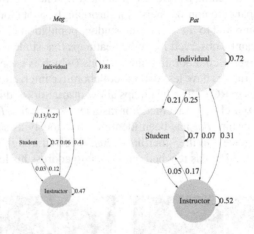

Fig. 5. Examples of Markov chains representing state changes within the makerspace. Individual: working individually state, Student: working with other student(s) state, Instructor: working with instructor(s).

Table 2. Transition probabilities correlations. Technical rating refers to the instructor rating on the technical aspect. Time spent refers to the students' self-reported amount of time spent in the makerspace. Frustration level refers to the students' self-reported level of frustration from the weekly survey.

	State transition	Measure	Correlation	p-value
1.	Individual – Individual	Technical rating	0.59	0.017
2.	Student – Student	Time spent in makerspace	0.50	0.050
3.	Instructor – Individual	Frustration level	−0.52	0.038

1. This correlation indicates a positive relationship between the Individual-Individual transition probability and the technical skills of the student. In other words, students who are more likely to stay in an individual working state, gain greater technical competence. This is an expected finding which corroborates the findings in RQ1, indicating that mastering the tools of the makerspace requires individual practice.
2. This correlation indicates a positive relationship between the Student-Student transition probability and the time spent within the makerspace by the student. In an open-ended learning environment, it is motivating to work in a group, and this correlation aligns with this idea.
3. This correlation indicates a negative relationship between the Instructor-Individual transition probability and the frustration levels of students. It is likely that when an instructor effectively addresses a student's challenges, the student transitions from working with the instructor to working alone once again. This correlation could indicate that the instructors are effective in helping students get unstuck, which is demonstrated by the lower levels of reported frustration.

6 Discussion

The results of our analyses suggest the possibility that letting students work on their own promotes the development of technical skills, while working together encourages students to spend more time in the makerspace. Heatmaps and line charts generated from these data allow instructors to visualize student behavior, and how far each student is from the right balance of collaborative interactions. This is a task that is challenging for an instructor to accomplish based solely on personal observations or interactions with students. Limitations of our study include using a relatively small sample size (16 students over 15 weeks). Additionally, the Kinect sensor data are inherently noisy owing to such aspects as overlapping student bodies, obscured joints, and other errors in skeleton tracking. Lastly, in future analysis we are planning to use a finer grain proxy for collaborative interactions that includes joint visual attention (from head orientation), body gestures and speech data to replace the current coarse proxy for collaborative interaction by physical proximity. Nonetheless, the information and data made available by the Kinect sensor system, paired with analysis techniques and methodologies to understand and interpret the data, opens new doors for both teachers, as classroom facilitators, and students for making (un)productive behaviors salient. For example, teachers will be afforded a greater awareness of how much support each student is receiving and can make informed pedagogical decisions accordingly.

7 Conclusion

While makerspaces hold much promise in providing training grounds for students to emulate the practices of a professional working environment and develop 21st century skills, instructors face the constant tension in deciding when and how to intervene in the pedagogical process. In this respect, we explored the use of Kinect sensors in identifying the instances and diversity of student collaborative interactions to help instructors gain a comprehensive view of student progress and to intervene when necessary. These findings suggest that multimodal sensors have a role to play in aiding instructors in harnessing the full potential of makerspaces and represent initial steps towards the development of a semi-automated teacher dashboard to provide instructional support for makerspaces.

References

1. Clapp, E.P., Ross, J., Ryan, J.O., Tishman, S.: Maker-Centered Learning: Empowering Young People to Shape their Worlds. Jossey-Bass, San Francisco (2016)
2. Martin, L.: The promise of the maker movement for education. J. Pre-Coll. Eng. Educ. Res. (J-PEER) **5**(1), 4 (2015)
3. Blikstein, P., Worsley, M.: Multimodal learning analytics and education data mining: using computational technologies to measure complex learning tasks. J. Learn. Anal. **3**(2), 220–238 (2016)
4. Lave, J.: Situating learning in communities of practice. In: Resnick, L.B., Levine, J.M., Teasley, S. (eds.) Perspectives on Socially Shared Cognition, pp. 63–82. American Psychological Association, Washington (1991)
5. Sheridan, K., Halverson, E.R., Litts, B., Brahms, L., Jacobs-Priebe, L., Owens, T.: Learning in the making: a comparative case study of three makerspaces. Harvard Educ. Rev. **84**(4), 505–531 (2014)
6. Papert, S.: Mindstorms: Children, Computers, and Powerful Ideas, 2nd edn. Perseus Books, New York (1993)
7. Maier, S.F., Seligman, M.E.P.: Learned helplessness: theory and evidence. J. Exp. Psychol. Gen. **105**(1), 3–46 (1976)
8. Kapur, M.: Productive failure. Cogn. Instr. **26**(3), 379–424 (2008)
9. Tan, M.: When makerspaces meet school: negotiating tensions between instruction and construction. J. Sci. Educ. Technol. **28**(2), 75–89 (2018). https://doi.org/10.1007/s10956-018-9749-x
10. Star, J.: When Not to Persevere: Nuances Related to Perseverance in Mathematical Problem Solving. Spencer Foundation, Chicago (2015)
11. Berland, M., Baker, R.S., Blikstein, P.: Educational data mining and learning analytics: applications to constructionist research. Technol. Knowl. Learn. **19**(1-2), 205–220 (2014). https://doi.org/10.1007/s10758-014-9223-7
12. Prieto, L.P., Sharma, K., Kidzinski, L., Rodríguez-Triana, M.J., Dillenbourg, P.: Multimodal teaching analytics: automated extraction of orchestration graphs from wearable sensor data. J. Comput. Assist. Learn. **34**(2), 193–203 (2018)
13. Behoora, I., Tucker, C.S.: Machine learning classification of design team members' body language patterns for real time emotional state detection. Des. Stud. **39**, 100–127 (2015)
14. Echeverria, V., Martinez-Maldonado, R., Power, T., Hayes, C., Shum, S.B.: Where is the nurse? Towards automatically visualising meaningful team movement in healthcare education. In: Proceedings of International Conference on Artificial Intelligence in Education, pp. 74–78 (2018) https://doi.org/10.1007/978-3-319-93846-2_14
15. Martinez-Maldonado, R., Echeverria, V., Santos, O.C., Santos, A.D.P.D., Yacef, K.: Physical learning analytics: a multimodal perspective. In: Proceedings of the 8th International Conference on Learning Analytics and Knowledge, pp. 375–379 (2018)
16. Saquib, N., Bose, A., George, D., Kamvar, S.: Sensei: sensing educational interaction. Proc. ACM Interact. Mobile Wearable Ubiquit. Technol. **1**(4), 1–27 (2018)
17. Martinez-Maldonado, R., Echeverria, V., Schulte, J., Shibani, A., Mangaroska, K., Shum, S.B.: Moodoo: indoor positioning analytics for characterising classroom teaching. In: International Conference on Artificial Intelligence in Education. Springer, Cham (2020)
18. Hall, E.T.: The Hidden Dimension. Doubleday, Garden City (1966)

Student Dropout Prediction

Francesca Del Bonifro[1,2], Maurizio Gabbrielli[1,2], Giuseppe Lisanti[1],
and Stefano Pio Zingaro[1,2(✉)]

[1] University of Bologna, Bologna, Italy
stefanopio.zingaro@unibo.it
[2] INRIA, Sophia-Antipolis, France

Abstract. Among the many open problems in the learning process,
students dropout is one of the most complicated and negative ones, both
for the student and the institutions, and being able to predict it could
help to alleviate its social and economic costs. To address this problem
we developed a tool that, by exploiting machine learning techniques,
allows to predict the dropout of a first-year undergraduate student. The
proposed tool allows to estimate the risk of quitting an academic course,
and it can be used either during the application phase or during the first
year, since it selectively accounts for personal data, academic records
from secondary school and also first year course credits. Our experiments
have been performed by considering real data of students from eleven
schools of a major University.

Keywords: Machine learning · Educational data mining · Decision
support tools

1 Introduction

Artificial Intelligence is changing many aspects of our society and our lives since
it provides the technological basis for new services and tools that help decision
making in everyday life. Education is not immune to this revolution. Indeed AI
and machine learning tools can help to improve in several ways the learning
process. A critical aspect in this context is the possibility of developing new
predictive tools which can be used to help students improve their academic
careers.

Among the many different observable phenomena in the students' careers,
University dropout is one of the most complex and adverse events, both for
students or institutions. A dropout is a potentially devastating event in the life
of a student, and it also impacts negatively the University from an economic
point of view [6]. Furthermore, it could also be a signal of potential issues in the
organisation and the quality of the courses. Dropout prediction is a task that can
be addressed by exploiting machine learning techniques, which already proved to
be effective in the field of education for evaluating students' performance [1,6,8–
10].

© Springer Nature Switzerland AG 2020
I. I. Bittencourt et al. (Eds.): AIED 2020, LNAI 12163, pp. 129–140, 2020.
https://doi.org/10.1007/978-3-030-52237-7_11

In this work, we face the challenge of early predicting the dropout for a freshman by adopting a data-driven approach. Trough an automated learning process, we aim to develop a model that is capable of capturing information concerning the particular context in which dropout takes place.

We built our model by taking into account the following three design principles. First, we want to estimate the risk of quitting an academic course at an early stage, either before the student starts the course or during the first year. Statistical evidence shows that this time frame is one of the most critical periods for dropout. Targeting first-year students means that the data we can use to train our predictive models are only personal information and academic records from high school—e.g. gender, age, high school education, final mark — and the number of credits acquired during the first months of the first year. Second, we do not focus on a specific predictive model; instead, we conducted a thorough study considering several machine learning techniques in order to construct a baseline and assess the challenge of the problem under analysis. Last, we conducted the training and test processes on real data, collecting samples of approximately 15,000 students from a specific academic year of a major University.

The remainder of this paper has the following structure. Related approaches are discussed in Sect. 2. In Sect. 3 we describe the machine learning methods used in our analysis, the dataset we collected and the preprocessing techniques applied to it. In Sect. 4 we evaluate the selected models by comparing their performance: first, with the different values of the models' parameters; second, to the features used in the train and test sets and, finally, considering each academic school separately. Then, we draw final remarks in Sect. 5 and present possible uses and extensions of this work.

2 Related Work

Several papers recently addressed the prediction of students' performances employing machine learning techniques. In the case of University-level education [14] and [1] have designed machine learning models, based on different datasets, performing analysis similar to ours even though they use different features and assumptions. In [1] a balanced dataset, including features mainly about the student provenance, is used to train different machine learning models. Tests report accuracy, true positive rate and AUC-ROC measures. Also in [11] there is a study in this direction but using a richer set of features involving family status and life conditions for each student. The authors used a Fuzzy-ARTMAP Neural Network gaining competitive performances. Moreover, as in our case, they performed the predictions using data at enrollment time. In [12] a set of features similar to the previous work is exploited. An analysis with different classification algorithms from the WEKA environment is performed, in order to find the best model for solving this kind of problem. It turns out that in this case the algorithm ID3 reaches the best performance with respect to the classification task.

Another work on the University dropout phenomenon was proposed in [7]. The proposed solution aim at predicting the student dropout but using a completely different representation for the students. In fact, the approach exploits data acquisition by web cams, eye-trackers and other similar devices in the context of a smart class. Based on these data, it is possible to perform emotion analysis and detection for the students in the room which will be then exploited to predict the dropout. There also exist studies related to high school education [10]. However, in this case, different countries have quite different high school systems, for example, the duration of the high school and the voting system can vary a lot among countries. Due to these differences, datasets from different countries can have very different meanings and, even if they include similar features, these are describing quite different situations. For this reason, works on lower levels of education are much less general and exportable to other systems. On the contrary, University systems are more similar, or it is possible to easily "translate" a system into another. Predictive models for students' final performance in the context of blended education, partially exploiting online platforms [9] or entirely online University courses [8,15], have also been proposed. In these cases, the presence of the technological devices allows the use of an augmented set of data—e.g. consulting homework submission logs—which can improve the quality of the models. However, the aim of these approaches is different from the proposed solution. In fact, besides the analysis of the correlations between the features and the students' performances discovered by the machine learning models, we propose to exploit the prediction at the moment of the students' enrolment in order to prevent the problematic situations that can bring to the dropout occurrences. Prediction at application-time is one of our main contribution, in fact a model exploiting data which are available after the enrolment—e.g. considering the students' performances and behaviour at the University—is certainly more accurate, but the timing for the suggestions is not optimal. Considering to take more courses or to change academic path while the mandatory courses at the University have already started could be highly frustrating for the students and do not enhance motivation in continuing their studies. Another important point in our work is the fact that we aim to perform a careful analysis of fair results with respect to the statistical characteristics of the dataset (in particular dealing with the unbalanced data). On the other hand, most of the previous works while mentioning the problem do not focus on how this unbalance affects the exploited models and may produce misleading results, and often dot not provide a clear justifications for the best performance measures on real data affected by this problem. This lack of extensive statistical analysis and evaluation of the limits and risks of the developed models has also been highlighted in [5], an excellent survey of different techniques for the students' performances prediction and related considerations.

3   Methodology

We considered a specific set of well-known classification algorithms to provide a tool enabling a reasonably accurate prediction of the dropout phenomenon. In particular, we considered the Linear Discriminant Analysis (LDA), Support Vector Machine (SVM) [3] and Random Forest (RF), as they are the most commonly used models in literature to solve similar problems.

LDA acts as a dimensional reduction algorithm, trying to reduce the data complexity, i.e. by projecting the actual feature space on a lower-dimensional one, while trying to retain relevant information; also, it does not involve parameter settings. SVM is a well-established technique for data classification and regression. It finds the best separating hyper-plane by maximising the margin in the feature space. The training data participating in the maximisation process are called support vectors. RF builds a collection of tree-structured classifiers combining them randomly. It has been adopted in the literature for a great variety of regression and prediction tasks [2].

We verified our methodology in three steps, providing a proper set of evaluation measures as we discuss later in this section. First, we assessed the different classifiers performance for the model parameters. In our case, we validated the SVM model over seven different values of C, that is the regularisation parameter, and we analysed the behaviour of four number of estimators in the case of RF. Moreover, we performed each validation considering two different re-scaling techniques of the data instances. Second, we evaluated the classifiers over three training sets that considered different features. For LDA, RF and SVM we only kept the best parameters' choice and monitored their performance on the different datasets.

Dataset. The dataset used for this work has been extracted from a collection of real data. More precisely, we considered pseudo-anonymized data describing 15,000 students enrolled in several courses of the academic year 2016/2017. The decision to focus our research within the limit of the first year lies in the analysis of statistical evidence from the source data. This evidence indicates a concentration of career dropouts in the first year of the course and a progressive decrease of the phenomenon in the following years. More specifically, students who leave within the first year is 14.8% of the total registered, while those who leave by the third year is 21.6%. This is equivalent to saying that the 6.8% of registered abandoned in subsequent years compared with 14.8% who leaves during the first year; confirming the importance of acting within the first year of the program to prevent the dropout phenomenon.

Table 1 shows a detailed description of the information available in the dataset. The first column lists the name of the features, while the second column describes the possible values or range. The first two features represent personal data of students while the third and the fourth are information related to the high school attended by the student.

Concerning the *Age* feature, its three possible values represent three different ranges of ages at the moment of enrolment, the value 1 is assigned to students until 19 years old, 2 for student's age between 20 and 23 years, and 3 otherwise. The values of *High school id* indicate ten different kinds of high school where the student obtained the diploma. The *High school final mark* represents

Table 1. Available features for each student in the original dataset, along with the possible values range

Feature	Value range
Student gender	1, 2
Student age range	1 to 3
High school id	1 to 10
High school final mark	60 to 100
Additional Learning Requirements	1, 2, 3
Academic school Id	1 to 11
Course Credits	0 to 60
Dropout	0, 1

the mark that the student received when graduating in high school. The flag *Additional Learning Requirements* (*ALR*) represents the possibility for mandatory additional credits in the first academic year. In fact, some degree programs present an admission test; if failed, the student has to attend some further specific courses and has to pass the relative examinations (within a given deadline) in order to be able to continue in that program. The values for the *ALR* feature indicate three possible situations: the value one is used to describe degree programs without *ALR*; the value two stands for an *ALR* examination that has been passed while the value three indicates that the student failed to pass the *ALR* examination, although it was required. *Academic school id* represents the academic school chosen by the student: there are eleven possible schools according to the present dataset. *Course Credits* indicates the number of credits acquired by the students. We use this attribute only in the case in which we evaluate the students already enrolled, and we consider only those credits acquired before the end of the first year, in order to obtain indications on the situation of the student before the condition of abandonment arises. The Boolean attribute *Dropout* represents the event of a student who abandons the degree course. This feature also represents the class for the supervised classification task and the outcome of the inference process—i.e. the prediction. Since the dropout assumes values True (1) or False (0), the problem treated in this work is a binary classification one.

It is possible to evaluate the amount of relevant information contained in the presented features by computing the *Information Gain* for each of them. This quantity is based on the concept of entropy, and it is usually exploited to build decision trees, but it also permits to obtain a ranked list of the available features for their relevance. In our case, some of the most relevant ones are (in descending order) *ALR*, *High school final mark*, *High school Id*, *Academic school Id*.

Data Preprocessing. We describe the preprocessing phase, used to clean the data as much as possible in order to maximise their exploitation in the prediction task. Firstly, we observed that in the original dataset, some of the values contain an implicit ordering that is not representative of the feature itself and can bias the model. These are the *High school id*, *Academic school id*, and *ALR*. We represent these three features as categorical—and thus not as numerical—by transforming each value, adopting a One-hot encoding representation. As one can expect, the dataset is highly unbalanced since the students who abandon the enrolled course is a minority, less than 12.3%; in particular, the ratio between the negative (non-dropout) and positive (dropout) examples is around 7 : 1. Even though this is good for the educational institution, training a machine learning model for binary classification with a highly unbalanced dataset may result in poor final performance, mainly because in such a scenario the classifier would underestimate the class with a lower number of samples [16]. For this reason, we randomly select half of the negative samples (i.e., the students who effectively drop) and use it in the train set; an equal number of instances of the other class is randomly sampled from the dataset and added to the train set. In doing so, we obtain a balanced train set, which is used to train the supervised models. The remaining samples constitute an unbalanced test set which we use to measure the performance of the trained models. This procedure is repeated ten times and for each one of these trials we randomise the selection and keep balanced the number of samples for the two classes in the train set. The final evaluation is obtained by averaging the results of the ten trials on the test sets.

Feature Selection and Evaluation Metrics. Concretely, the first group of features that we select is composed by *gender*, *age range*, *high school*, *high school final mark*, and *academic school*. We referred to this set of features as the "basic" set. We performed the other validations by adding to the "basic" set the remaining features incrementally, first, *ALR* (basic + *ALR*) and then *CC* (basic + *ALR* + *CC*). In this way, we were able to check the actual relevance of each feature. Third, considering the best configuration from the analysis above, the performance for each academic school separately has been analysed.

Several evaluation metrics can be used to asses the quality of the classifiers both in the process of selecting the best hyper-parameter configuration and in ranking the different models. The classification produces True Positive (TP), True Negative (TN), False positive (FP) and False Negative (FN) values; in our case, we interpret an FP as the prediction of a dropout that does not occur, and an FN as a student which accordingly to the model's prediction will continue the studies while the dropout phenomenon actually occurs.

In the case of binary classification, accuracy (ACC), specificity (SPEC), and sensitivity (SENS) are used instead of plain TP, TN, FP and FN values to improve experimental results interpretability [4]. ACC is the ratio between correct predictions over the total number of instances. SPEC, or *True Negative Rate* (TNR), is the ratio of TN to the total number of instances that have actual negative class. SENS, also known as recall or *True Positive Rate* (TPR), is the ratio of TP to the total number of instances that have actual positive class.

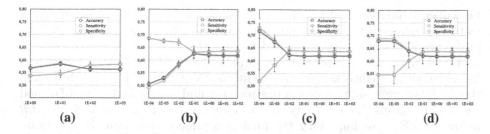

Fig. 1. Results obtained: (a) using RFs with an increasing number of estimators without rescaling the data; (b) using SVM for different values of C without rescaling the data; (c) using SVM for different values of C with standard rescaling; (d) using SVM for different values of C with min-max rescaling.

4   Experimental Result

All the experiments have been performed using the Python programming language (version 3.7) and the `scikit-learn` framework [13] (version $0.22.1$), which provides access to the implementation of several machine learning algorithms. Training and testing run on a Linux Workstation equipped with Xeon 8-Core $2,1$ Ghz processor and 96 GB of memory.

Parameters Selection and Data Scaling. We performed a set of experiments in order to find the best parameters configuration for SVM, and RF. Tests with SVM have been conducted by progressively increasing the penalty term C, ranging over the following set: $\{1E^{-04}, 1E^{-03}, 1E^{-02}, 1E^{-01}, 1E^{+00}, 1E^{+01}, 1E^{+02}\}$. The same applies to the value for the number of estimators in RF algorithm, ranging over the set $\{1E^{+00}, 1E^{+01}, 1E^{+02}, 1E^{+03}\}$. We observe, from Fig. 1, that the best results for both accuracy and sensitivity are obtained with $C = 1E^{-01}$ and with a number of estimators $= 1E^{+03}$. In addition, we assessed whether our dataset may benefit from data re-scaling or not. For this reason, we performed standard and min-max scaling on the data before training to evaluate their effectiveness for the original data—i.e., without scaling. Standard scale acts on numerical data values transforming for each numerical feature the original values distribution into another one with mean equal to zero and standard deviation equal to one, assuming that the values are normally distributed. *Min-Max* scaling aims to transform the range of possible values for each numerical feature from the original one to $[0, 1]$ or $[-1, 1]$. Both standard scaling and min-max scaling are computed on the train set and applied to the test set. We observed that the scaling has no effect on the final performance of LDA and RF. On the contrary, as shown in Fig. 1 the scaling does affect the performance of SVM but it does not seem to add any benefit. This may be related to the fact that most of the features are categorical. For this reason we chose not to re-scale the data in the following tests.

Features Analysis. Table 2 shows the results obtained considering different features combinations while keeping the SVM and RF parameters as described in the previous section and without data rescaling.

Considering the basic set of features LDA and SVM obtain the highest performance with a slightly larger variance for the SVM results. The introduction of the *ALR* feature mainly improves the accuracy and specificity for the LDA and SVM, but it drops the sensitivity. On the contrary, the introduction of the *ALR* feature in RF helps improving the final performance across all the measures, obtaining a higher performance compared to the results of LDA and SVM on the basic set of features.

The relevant gain here is that this work permits to estimate the risk of the dropout at the application time (for the basic and the basic+*ALR* features cases), i.e. before the students' enrolment and examination—which can give a clear indication about the future academic performances. We believe that this possibility is significant since appropriate policy and measures to counter the dropout should be taken by universities very early, possibly at the very beginning of the academic career, in order to maximise the student success probability and to reduce costs.

Finally, when considering the *CC* feature, all the models reach very high performance, with slightly higher results for SVM. However this feature is not available at application time.

Dropout Analysis per Academic School. The results in Table 2 are useful to understand the general behavior of the predictive model, but it may be difficult for governance to extract useful information. The division of results by academic school allows an analysis of the performance of the models with higher resolution. This could be an important feature that facilitates local administrations (those of schools) to interpret the results that concern students of their degree courses. In Table 2, we have selected the best models from those trained with *basic +* *ALR* and *basic + ALR + CC* features. These are RF for the former and SVM for the latter. The results divided by school are shown in Table 3.

For completeness, we report in Fig. 2 an overview of the dataset composition with respect to the school (horizontal axis) and the number of samples (vertical axis), divided by dropouts, in green, and the remaining, in blue. The results of Table 3 highlight a non-negligible variability between the results for each school and suggests that each school contributes differently to the predictive model. For instance, the results for schools 4, 9, and 10 are higher than those of schools 3, 7, and 8 and all of these schools show results that differ significantly from the general ones (Table 2), both for *basic + ALR* and *basic + ALR + CC*. In this case, the number of dropout samples for schools 4, 9, and 10 is 207, 66, and 231 examples—504, in total—respectively, against the number of dropout samples for schools 3, 7, and 8 which is respectively of 76, 63, and 89 examples—139, in total.

Table 2. Experimental results for LDA, SVM and RF classifiers over different feature sets.

Set	Model	ACC	SENS	SPEC
Basic	LDA	0.62 (±0.01)	0.64 (±0.01)	0.62 (±0.01)
	SVM	0.62 (±0.02)	0.65 (±0.02)	0.62 (±0.02)
	RF	0.56 (±0.01)	0.58 (±0.01)	0.56 (±0.01)
+ ALR	LDA	0.75 (±0.01)	0.59 (±0.02)	0.76 (±0.02)
	SVM	0.81 (±0.03)	0.50 (±0.06)	0.83 (±0.04)
	RF	0.63 (±0.01)	0.63 (±0.01)	0.63 (±0.01)
+ CC	LDA	0.85 (±0.00)	0.90 (±0.00)	0.85 (±0.00)
	SVM	0.87 (±0.00)	0.87 (±0.01)	0.87 (±0.01)
	RF	0.87 (±0.01)	0.85 (±0.01)	0.87 (±0.01)

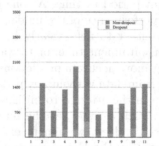

Fig. 2. Number of students per school. Green represents dropout students, blue represents the students which applied to the second academic year. (Color figure online)

Table 3. Experimental results for each academic school: (*left*) RF model trained using *Basic + ALR* features; (*right*) SVM model trained using *Basic + ALR + CC* features.

School	Random Forest ($N = 1E^{+03}$)			SVM ($C = 1E^{-01}$)		
	ACC	SENS	SPEC	ACC	SENS	SPEC
1	0.61 (±0.05)	0.67 (±0.08)	0.61 (±0.06)	0.86 (±0.01)	0.99 (±0.01)	0.85 (±0.01)
2	0.74 (±0,03)	0.63 (±0.07)	0.74 (±0.03)	0.91 (±0.01)	0.84 (±0,01)	0.92 (±0.01)
3	0.45 (±0.04)	0.71 (±0.09)	0.44 (±0.04)	0.84 (±0.02)	0.73 (±0.01)	0.85 (±0.02)
4	0.71 (±0.03)	0.77 (±0.05)	0.70 (±0.03)	0.84 (±0.01)	0.93 (±0.01)	0.83 (±0.01)
5	0.68 (±0.03)	0.56 (±0.05)	0.68 (±0.04)	0.83 (±0.01)	0.91 (±0.01)	0.83 (±0.01)
6	0.58 (±0.03)	0.66 (±0.03)	0.57 (±0.03)	0.86 (±0.01)	0.88 (±0.01)	0.86 (±0.01)
7	0.49 (±0.09)	0.55 (±0.12)	0.49 (±0.10)	0.91 (±0.01)	0.90 (±0.03)	0.91 (±0.01)
8	0.60 (±0.03)	0.46 (±0.06)	0.61 (±0.03)	0.87 (±0.02)	0.87 (±0.05)	0.87 (±0.03)
9	0.80 (±0.03)	0.71 (±0.04)	0.80 (±0.04)	0.94 (±0.01)	0.93 (±0.01)	0.94 (±0.01)
10	0.44 (±0.04)	0.71 (±0.03)	0.41 (±0.04)	0.77 (±0.02)	0.94 (±0.01)	0.76 (±0.02)
11	0.61 (±0.02)	0.64 (±0.03)	0.61 (±0.02)	0.89 (±0.01)	0.83 (±0.01)	0.90 (±0.01)

5   Conclusion and Future Work

In this paper, we have presented an analysis of different machine learning techniques applied to the task of dropout occurrences prediction for university students. The analysis has been conducted on data available at the moment of the enrolment at the first year of a bachelor or single-cycle degree. The analysis made on the model performance takes into account the actual statistical composition of the dataset, which is highly unbalanced to the classes. Considering predictions at the moment of enrolment increases the difficulty of the task (because there are less informative and available data since we cannot use data from the University careers of students) compared to most of the existing approaches. Despite these difficulties, this different approach makes it possible to use the tool in order to actively improve the student's academic situation from the beginning and not only to make predictions and monitoring during the academic career. On the other hand, we also performed a set of tests considering the credits obtained by a students after a certain period of time. As one can expect, this helps in largely improving the final performance of the model. This fact can be used by the institution to decide whether to act as early as possible, on the basis of the information available at enrolment time, or to wait for some more data in the first year thus obtaining more accurate predictions. In any case, the results obtained show that starting from data without any pedagogical or didactic value, our tool can practically help in the attempt to mitigate the dropout problem.

We designed the tool in such a way that the integration with other components can occur seamlessly. Indeed, we aim to extend it to a more general monitoring system, to be used by the University governance, which can monitor students careers and can provide helpful advice when critical situations are encountered. For example, if the tool predicts that for a new cohort of students enrolled in a specific degree program there are many possible dropouts, then specific support services (such as supplementary support courses, personalised guidance, etc) could be organised. We hope and believe that this can be an effective way to decrease the dropout rate in the future years and to avoid the phenomenon since the very beginning of the University careers of the students.

The first natural step in our work is the integration of our tool with other University services as described before. Next we would like to monitor the dropout frequency in the coming years in order to obtain some hint about the effectiveness of our tool. The outcomes of this analysis could guide us to improve the deployment of the tool—e.g. by using different, more robust strategies. To improve the model effectiveness it could also be useful to make predictions for different courses possibly within the same school, possibly integrating this with an appropriate definition of a similarity measure between courses. Another further development could be the inclusion of more data about student performances, for example by considering the results of activities done in Learning Management Systems (LMS) or Virtual Learning Environments (VLE) such as, for example, Moodle, Google Classroom, Edmodo, that could be used in the courses management and organisation. A limitation in our study is in the fact that the tool take advantage of sensitive data, so one has to be very careful with using the classifier, since there is no evidence of the model fairness—e.g., concerning the gender feature.

Finally, given the increasing attention gathered by deep learning models, we would like to extend our analysis in order to include these methods and consider several factors, such as: the depth of the network (e.g., the number of layers) the dimension of each layer, etc.

References

1. Aulck, L., Velagapudi, N., Blumenstock, J., West, J.: Predicting student dropout in higher education. In: 2016 ICML Workshops #Data4Good Machine Learning, New York, vol. abs/1606.06364, pp. 16–20 (2016)
2. Breiman, L.: Random forests. Mach. Learn. **45**(1), 5–32 (2001). https://doi.org/10.1023/A:1010933404324
3. Chang, C.C., Lin, C.J.: LIBSVM: a library for support vector machines. ACM Trans. Intell. Syst. Technol. (TIST) **2**(3), 27 (2011)
4. Freeman, E.A., Moisen, G.G.: A comparison of the performance of threshold criteria for binary classification in terms of predicted prevalence and kappa. Ecol. Modell. **217**(1–2), 48–58 (2008)
5. Hellas, A., et al.: Predicting academic performance: a systematic literature review. In: Proceedings Companion of the 23rd Annual ACM Conference on Innovation and Technology in Computer Science Education, pp. 175–199. ACM (2018)
6. Jadrić, M., Garača, Ž., Ćukušić, M.: Student dropout analysis with application of data mining methods. Manag. J. Contemp. Manag. Issues **15**(1), 31–46 (2010)
7. Kadar, M., Sarraipa, J., Guevara, J.C., Restrepo, E.G.: An integrated approach for fighting dropout and enhancing students' satisfaction in higher education. In: Proceedings of the 8th International Conference on Software Development and Technologies for Enhancing Accessibility and Fighting Info-exclusion, DSAI 2019, Thessaloniki, Greece, 20–22 June 2018, pp. 240–247 (2018)
8. Kotsiantis, S.B., Pierrakeas, C.J., Pintelas, P.E.: Preventing student dropout in distance learning using machine learning techniques. In: Palade, V., Howlett, R.J., Jain, L. (eds.) KES 2003. LNCS (LNAI), vol. 2774, pp. 267–274. Springer, Heidelberg (2003). https://doi.org/10.1007/978-3-540-45226-3_37
9. Li, H., Lynch, C.F., Barnes, T.: Early prediction of course grades: models and feature selection. In: Conference on Educational Data Mining, pp. 492–495 (2018)
10. Márquez-Vera, C., Romero Morales, C., Ventura Soto, S.: Predicting school failure and dropout by using data mining techniques. Rev. Iberoam. Tecnol. del Aprendiz. **8**(1), 7–14 (2013)
11. Martinho, V.R.D.C., Nunes, C., Minussi, C.R.: An intelligent system for prediction of school dropout risk group in higher education classroom based on artificial neural networks. In: 2013 IEEE 25th International Conference on Tools with Artificial Intelligence, pp. 159–166, November 2013
12. Pal, S.: Mining educational data using classification to decrease dropout rate of students. CoRR abs/1206.3078 (2012)
13. Pedregosa, F., et al.: Scikit-learn: machine learning in python. J. Mach. Learn. Res. **12**(Oct), 2825–2830 (2011)
14. Serra, A., Perchinunno, P., Bilancia, M.: Predicting student dropouts in higher education using supervised classification algorithms. In: Gervasi, O., et al. (eds.) ICCSA 2018. LNCS, vol. 10962, pp. 18–33. Springer, Cham (2018). https://doi.org/10.1007/978-3-319-95168-3_2

15. Whitehill, J., Mohan, K., Seaton, D.T., Rosen, Y., Tingley, D.: Delving deeper into MOOC student dropout prediction. CoRR abs/1702.06404 (2017)
16. Zheng, Z., Li, Y., Cai, Y.: Oversampling method for imbalanced classification. Comput. Inform. **34**, 1017–1037 (2015)

Real-Time Multimodal Feedback
with the CPR Tutor

Daniele Di Mitri[1(✉)], Jan Schneider[2], Kevin Trebing[3], Sasa Sopka[4],
Marcus Specht[5], and Hendrik Drachsler[1,2]

[1] Open University of The Netherlands, Valkenburgerweg 177,
6419 AT Heerlen, The Netherlands
daniele.dimitri@ou.nl
[2] DIPF - Leibniz Institute for Research and Information in Education,
Frankfurt, Germany
[3] Maastricht University, Maastricht, The Netherlands
[4] AIXTRA - RWTH Aachen University Hospital, Aachen, Germany
[5] Delft University of Technology, Delft, The Netherlands

Abstract. We developed the CPR Tutor, a real-time multimodal feedback system for cardiopulmonary resuscitation (CPR) training. The CPR Tutor detects mistakes using recurrent neural networks for real-time time-series classification. From a multimodal data stream consisting of kinematic and electromyographic data, the CPR Tutor system automatically detects the chest compressions, which are then classified and assessed according to five performance indicators. Based on this assessment, the CPR Tutor provides audio feedback to correct the most critical mistakes and improve the CPR performance. To test the validity of the CPR Tutor, we first collected the data corpus from 10 experts used for model training. Hence, to test the impact of the feedback functionality, we ran a user study involving 10 participants. The CPR Tutor pushes forward the current state of the art of real-time multimodal tutors by providing: 1) an architecture design, 2) a methodological approach to design multimodal feedback and 3) a field study on real-time feedback for CPR training.

1 Introduction

In learning science, there is an increasing interest in collecting and integrating data from multiple modalities and devices with the aim of analysing learning behaviour [4,15]. This phenomenon is witnessed by the rise of multimodal data experiments especially in the contexts of project-based learning [21], lab-based experimentation for skill acquisition [11], and simulations for mastering psychomotor skills [19]. Most of the existing studies using multimodal data for learning stand at the level of "data geology", investigating whether multimodal data can provide evidence of the learning process. In some cases, machine learning models were trained with the collected data for classifying or predicting outcomes such as emotions or learning performance. At the same time, the

© Springer Nature Switzerland AG 2020
I. I. Bittencourt et al. (Eds.): AIED 2020, LNAI 12163, pp. 141–152, 2020.
https://doi.org/10.1007/978-3-030-52237-7_12

existing research that uses multimodal and multi-sensor systems for training different types of psychomotor skills features neither personalised nor adaptive feedback [18].

In this study, we aimed at overcoming this knowledge gap and by *exploring how multimodal data can be used to support psychomotor skill development by providing real-time feedback*. We followed a design-based research approach: the presented study is based on the insights of [8], in which we demonstrated that it is possible to detect common CPR mistakes regarding the quality of the chest compressions (CC) (CC-rate, CC-depth and CC-release). In [8], we have also shown that it is possible to extend the common mistake detection of commercial and validated training tools like the Laerdal ResusciAnne manikin with the CPR tutor. We were able to detect the correct locking of the arms while doing CPR and the correct use of the body weight when performing the CCs. The mistake detection models were obtained training multiple recurrent neural networks, using the multimodal data as input and the presence or absence of the CPR mistakes as output. This study extends the previous efforts by embedding the machine learning approaches for mistake detection with real-time feedback intervention.

2   Background

2.1   Multimodal Data for Learning

With the term "multimodal data", we refer to the data sources derived from multimodal and multi-sensor interfaces that go beyond the typical mouse and keyboard interactions [16]. These data sources can be collected using wearable sensors, depth cameras or Internet of Things devices. Example of modalities relevant for modelling a learning task is learner's motoric movements, physiological signals, contextual, environmental or activity-related information [7]. The exploration of these novel data sources inspired the Multimodal Learning Analytics (MMLA) researc [15], whose common hypothesis is that combining data from multiple modalities allows obtaining a more accurate representation of the learning process and can provide valuable insights to the educational actors, informing them about the learning dynamics and supporting them to design more valuable feedback [4]. The contribution of multimodal data to learning is still a research topic under exploration. Researchers have found out that it can better predict learning performance during desktop-based game playing [11]. The MMLA approach is also thought to be useful for modelling ill-structured learning tasks [5]. Recent MMLA prototypes have been developed for modelling classroom interactions [1] or for estimating success in group collaboration [21]. Multimodal data were also employed for modelling psychomotor tasks and physical learning activities that require complex body coordination [14]. Santos et al. reviewed existing studies using sensor-based applications in diverse psychomotor disciplines for training specific movements in different sports and martial arts [19]. Limbu et al. reviewed existing studies that modelled the experts to train apprentices using recorded expert performance [13].

2.2   Multimodal Intelligent Tutors

We are interested in the application of multimodal data for providing automatic and real-time feedback. This aim is pursued by the Intelligent Tutoring Systems (ITSs) research. Historically ITSs have been designed for well-structured learning activities in which the task sequence is clearly defined, as well as the assessment criteria and the range of learning mistakes that ITS is able to detect. Related ITS research looked primarily at meta-cognitive aspects of learning, such as the detection of learners' emotional states (e.g. [3,10]). Several ITSs of this kind are reviewed in a recent literature review [2]. Most of these studies employed a desktop-based system where the user-interaction takes place with mouse and keyboard. To find applications of ITSs beyond mouse and keyboard we need to look in the field of medical robotics and surgical simulations into systems like DaVinci. These robots allow aspiring surgeons to train standardised surgical skills in safe environments [22].

2.3   Cardiopulmonary Resuscitation (CPR)

In this study, we focus on one of the most frequently applied and well studied medical simulations: Cardiopulmonary Resuscitation. CPR is a lifesaving technique applied in many emergencies, including a heart attack, near drowning or in the case of stopped heartbeat or breathing. CPR is nowadays mandatory not only for healthcare professionals but also for several other professions, especially those more exposed to the general public. CPR training is an individual learning task with a highly standardised procedure consisting of a series of predefined steps and criteria to measure the quality of the performance. We refer to the European CPR Guidelines [17]. There exists a variety of commercial tools for supporting CPR training, which can track and assess the CPR execution. A very common training tool is the Laerdal ResusciAnne manikins. The ResusciAnne manikins provide only retrospective and non-real-time performance indicators such as CC-rate, CC-depth and CC-release. Other indicators are neglected and that creates a feedback gap for the learner and higher responsibility for the course instructors. Examples of these indicators are the use of the body weight or the locking of the arms while doing the CCs. So far, these mistakes need to be corrected by human instructors.

3   System Architecture of the CPR Tutor

The System Architecture of the CPR Tutor implements the five-step approach introduced by the *Multimodal Pipeline* [9], a framework for the collection, storing, annotation, processing and exploitation of data from multiple modalities. The System Architecture was optimised to the selected sensors and for the specific task of CPR training. The five steps, proposed by the *Multimodal Pipeline* are numbered in the graphical representation of the System Architecture in Fig. 1. The architecture also features three layers: 1) the Presentation Layer interfacing with the user (either the learner or the expert); 2) the Application

Layer, implementing the logic of the CPR Tutor; 3) the Data Layer, consisting of the data used by the CPR Tutor. In the CPR Tutor, we can distinguish two main phases which have two corresponding data-flows: 1) the *offline training* of the machine learning models and 2) the *real-time exploitation* in which the real-time feedback system is activated.

3.1   Data Collection

The first step corresponds to the collection of the data corpus. The main system component responsible for the data collection is the CPR Tutor, a C# application running on a Windows 10 computer. The CPR Tutor collects data from two main devices: 1) the Microsoft Kinect v2 depth camera and 2) the Myo electromyographic (EMG) armband. In the graphic user interface, the user of the CPR Tutor can 'start' and 'stop' the recording of the session. The CPR Tutor collects the data of the user in front of the camera wearing the Myo. The collected data consist of:

- the 3D kinematic data (x,y,z) of the body joints (excluding ankles and hips)
- the 2D video recording from the Kinect RGB camera,
- 8 EMG sensors values, 3D gyroscope and accelerometer of the Myo.

3.2   Data Storing

The CPR Tutor adopts the data storing logic of the *Multimodal Learning Hub* [20], a core component of the *Multimodal Pipeline*. As the sensor applications collect data at different frequencies, at the 'start' of the session, each sensor application is assigned to a *Recording Object* a data structure arbitrary number of *Frame Updates*. In the case of the CPR Tutor, there are two main streams coming from the Myo and the Kinect. The *Frame Updates* contain the relative timestamp starting from the moment the user presses the 'start' until the 'stop' of the session. Each *Frame Update* within the same *Recording Object* shares the same set of sensor attributes, in the case of the CPR Tutor, 8 attributes for Myo and 32 for Kinect, corresponding to the raw features that can be gathered from the public API of the devices. The video stream recording from the Kinect uses a special type of *Recording Object*, specific for video data. At the end of the session, when the user presses 'stop', the data gathered in memory in the *Recording Object*s and the *Annotation Object* is automatically serialised into the custom format introduced by the LearningHub: the *MLT Session* (Meaningful Learning Task). For the CPR Tutor, the custom data format consists of a zip folder containing: the Kinect and Myo sensor file, and the 2D video in MP4 format. Serialising the sessions is necessary for creating the data corpus for the offline training of the machine learning models.

3.3   Data Annotation

The annotation can be carried out by an expert retrospectively using the *Visual Inspection Tool* (VIT) [6]. In the VIT, the expert can load the *MLT Session* files one by one to triangulate the video recording with the sensor data. The user can select and plot individual data attributes and inspect visually how they relate to a video recording. The VIT is also a tool for collecting expert annotations. In the case of CPR Tutor, the annotations were given as properties of every single CC. From the SimPad of the ResusciAnne manikin, we extracted the performance metrics of each recorded session. With a Python script, we processed the data from the SimPad in the form of a JSON annotation file, which we added to each recorded session using the VIT. This procedure allowed us to have the performance metrics of the ResusciAnne manikin as "ground truth" for the training the classifiers. As previously mentioned, the Simpad tracks the chest compression performance monitoring three indicators, the correct CC-rate, CC-release and CC-depth. By using the VIT, however, the expert can extend these indicators by adding manually custom annotations, in the form of attribute-value pairs. For this study, we use the target custom classes *armsLocked* and *bodyWeight* corresponding to two performance indicators, currently not tracked by the ResusciAnne manikins.

3.4   Data Processing

For data processing, we developed a Python script named SharpFlow[1]. This component is used both for the offline training and validation of the mistake detection classifiers as well as for the real-time classification of the single CCs. In the training phase, the entire data corpus (*MLT Sessions* with their annotations) is loaded into memory and transformed into two Pandas data frames, one containing the sensor data the other one containing the annotations. As the sensor data came from devices with different sampling frequencies, the sensor data frame had a great number of missing values. To mitigate this problem, the data frame was resampled into a fixed number corresponding to the median length of each sample. We obtained, therefore, a 3D tensor of shape (#samples × #attributes × #intervals). The dataset was divided in 85% for training and 15% for testing using random shuffling. A part of the training set (15%) was used as validation set. We also applied feature scaling using min-max normalisation with a range of -1 and 1. The scaling was fitted on the training set and applied on the validation and test sets. The model used for classification was a Long-Short Term Memory network [12] which is a special type of recurrent-neural network. Implementation was performed using PyTorch. The architecture of the model chosen was a sequence of two stacked LSTM layers followed by two dense layers:

- a first LSTM with input shape 17×52 (#intervals *times* #attributes) and 128 hidden units;
- a second LSTM with 64 hidden units;
- a fully-connected layer with 32 units with a sigmoid activation function;
- a fully connected layer with 5 hidden units (number of target classes)
- a sigmoid activation.

---

[1] Code available on GitHub (https://github.com/dimstudio/SharpFlow).

All of our classes have a binary class, so we use a binary cross-entropy loss for optimisation and train for 30 epochs using an Adam optimiser with a learning rate of 0.01.

3.5   Real-Time Exploitation

The real-time data exploitation is the run-time behaviour of the System Architecture. This phase is a continuous loop of communication between the CPR Tutor, the SharpFlow application and the prompting of the feedback. It can be summarised in three phases 1) detection, 2) classification and 3) feedback.

1) Detection. For being able to assess a particular action and possibly detect if some mistake occurs, the CPR Tutor has to be certain that the learner has performed a CC and not something different. The approach chosen for action detection is a rule-based approach. While recording, the CC detector continuously checks the presence of CCs by monitoring the vertical movements of the shoulder joints from the Kinect data. These rules were calibrated manually so that the CC detector finds the beginning and the end of the CCs. At the end of each CC, the CPR Tutor pushes the entire data chunk to SharpFlow via a TCP client.

2) Classification. SharpFlow runs a TCP server implemented in Python which is continuously listening for incoming data chunks by the CPR Tutor. In case of a new chunk, SharpFlow checks if it has a correct data format and if it is not truncated. If so, it resamples the data chunks and feeds them into the min-max scaler loaded from memory, to make sure that also the new instance is normalised correctly. Once ready, the transformed data chunk is fed into the layered LSTMs also saved in memory. The results for each of the five target classes are serialised into a dictionary and sent back to the CPR Tutor where they are saved as annotations of the CC. SharpFlow takes on average 70 ms to classify one CC.

3) Feedback. Every time the CPR Tutor receives a classified CC, it computes a performance and an Error Rate (ER) for each target class. The performance is calculated with a moving average with a window of 10 s, meaning it considers only the CCs performed in the previous 10s. The Error Rate is calculated as the inverse sum of the performance: $ER_j = 1 - \sum_{i=0}^{n} \frac{P_{i,j}}{n}$ where j is one of the five target classes, n is the number of CCs in one time window of 10s. Not all the mistakes in CPR are, however, equally important. For this reason, we handcrafted five feedback thresholds of activation in the form of five rules. If the ER is equal or greater than this threshold the feedback is fired, otherwise, the next rule is checked. The order chosen was the following: $ER_{armsLocked} >= 5$, $ER_{bodyWeight} >= 15$, $ER_{classRate} >= 40$, $ER_{classRelease} >= 50$, $ER_{classDepth} >= 60$. Although every CC is assessed immediately after 0.5s we set the feedback frequency to 10s, to avoid overloading the user with too much feedback. The modality chosen for the feedback was sound, as we considered the auditory sense the least occupied channel while doing CPR. We created the following audio messages for the five target classes:

(1) *classRelease*: "release the compression"; (2) *classDepth*: "improve compression depth"; (3) *armsLocked*: "lock your arms"; (4) *bodyWeight*: "use your body weight"; (5) *classRate*: *metronome sound at 110 bpm*.

4 Method

In light of the research gap on providing real-time feedback from multimodal systems, we formulated the following research hypothesis which guided our scientific investigation.

H1: The proposed architecture allows the provision of real-time feedback for CPR training.

H2: The real-time feedback of the CPR Tutor has a positive impact on the considered CPR performance indicators.

4.1 Study Design

To test H1, we developed the CPR tutor with a real-time feedback component based on insights from our design-based research cycle. We planned a quantitative intervention study in collaboration with a major European University Hospital. The study took place in two phases: 1) Expert data collection involving a group of 10 expert participants, in which the data corpus was collected; 2) a Feedback intervention study involving a new group of 10 participants. A snapshot of the study setup for both phases is shown in Fig. 2. All participants in the study were asked to sign an informed consent letter detailing all the details of the experiment as well as the treatment of the collected data in accordance with the new European General Data Protection Regulation (2016/679 EU GDPR).

4.2 Phase 1 - Expert Data Collection

The expert group counted 10 participants (M: 4, F: 6) having an average of 5.3 previous CPR courses per person. We asked the experts to perform 4 sessions of 1 min duration. Two of these sessions, they had to perform correct CPR, while the reminder two sessions they had to perform incorrect executions not locking their arms and not using their body weight. In fact, from the previous study [8] we noticed it was difficult to obtain the full span of mistakes the learners can perform. Asking the experts to mimic the mistakes was, thus, the most sensible option for obtaining a dataset with a balanced class distribution. We, therefore, collected around 400 CCs per participant. The 1 min duration was set to prevent that physical fatigue influenced the novice's performance. Once the data collection was completed, we inspected each session individually using the *Visual Inspection Tool*. We annotated the CC detected by the CPR Tutor, by triangulating with the performance metrics from the ResusciAnne manikin. The *bodyWeight* and *armsLocked* were instead annotated manually by one component of the research team.

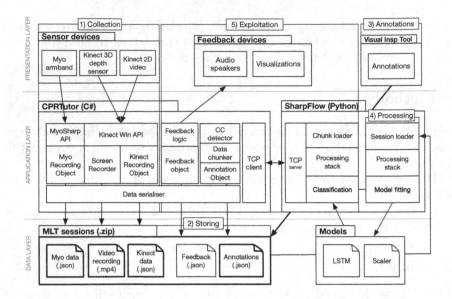

Fig. 1. The system architecture of the CPR tutor

4.3   Phase 2 - Feedback Intervention

The feedback intervention phase counted 10 participants (M: 5, F: 5) having an average of 2.3 previous CPR courses per person. Those were not absolute novices but recruited among the group of students that needed to renew their CPR certificate. The last CPR training for these participants was, therefore, older than one year. Each participant in the feedback intervention group performed 2 sessions of 1 min, one with feedback enabled and one without feedback.

5   Results

The collected data corpus from the expert group consisted of 4803 CCs. Each CC was annotated with 5 classes. With the methodology described in Sect. 3.4, we obtained a tensor of shape (4803, 17, 52). As the distribution of the classes was too unbalanced, the dataset was downsampled to 3434 samples (-28.5%). In Table 1, we report the new distribution for each target class. In addition, we report the results of the LSTM training reporting for each target class the accuracy, precision, recall and F1-score. In the feedback group, we collected a dataset of 20 sessions from 10 participants with 2223 CCs detected by the CPR Tutor and classified automatically. The feedback function was enabled only in 10 out of 20 sessions. The feedback was fired a total of 16 times. In Table 2, we report the feedback frequency for each target class and the class distribution for each target class. We generated Error Rate plots for each individual session. In Fig. 3, we provide an example plot of a session having five feedback interventions (vertical dashed lines) matching the same colours of the target classes. Although

Table 1. Five target classes distribution and performance of corresponding LSTM models trained on the expert dataset.

Class	Class distribution	Accuracy	Precision	Recall	F1-score
classRelease	0: (1475, 42.9%), 1: (1959, 57.1%)	0.905	0.897	0.954	0.925
classDepth	0: (2221, 64.6%), 1: (1213, 35.4%)	0.954	0.955	0.953	0.954
classRate	0: (1457, 42.5%), 1: (1977, 575%)	0.901	0.815	0.819	0.817
armsLocked	0: (1337, 38.9%), 1: (2097, 61.1%)	0.981	0.975	1	0.987
bodyWeight	0: (1206, 35.1%), 1: (2228, 64.9%)	0.97	0.967	0.994	0.98

the Error Rates fluctuate heavily throughout each session, we noticed that nearly every time the feedback is fired the Error Rate for the targeted mistake is subject to a drop. We analysed, therefore, the effect of CPR Tutor feedback by focusing on the short-term changes in Error Rate for the mistakes targeted by the CPR Tutor. In Table 2, we report the average ERs 10s before and 10s after the audio feedback was fired. We report the average delta of these two values for each target class. For *classRelease*, *classDepth* and *classRate* we notice a decrease of the Error Rate, whereas for *armsLocked* and *bodyWeight* an average increase.

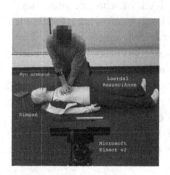

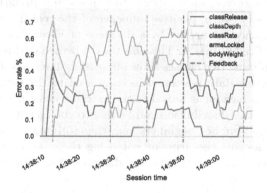

Fig. 2. Study design of the CPR tutor

Fig. 3. Plot of the error rates for one session.

6 Discussion

In H1 we hypothesised that the proposed architecture for a real-time feedback is suitable for CPR training. With the System Architecture outlined in Sect. 3, we implemented a functional system which can be used both for the offline model training of the CPR mistakes as well as for the real-time multimodal data exploitation. The proposed architecture exhibited reactive performances, by classifying one CC in about 70 ms. The System Architecture proposed is the

Table 2. Average Error Rate for each target class 10 s before and 10 s after the audio feedback were fired.

Class	Class distribution	Freq. Feedback	ER 10 s before feedback	ER 10 s after feedback	Delta
classRelease	0: (475, 21.4%), 1: (1746, 78.6%)	2	46.60%	33.50%	−13.10%
classDepth	0: (704, 31.7%), 1: (1517, 68.3%)	5	59.80%	55.00%	−4.80%
classRate	0: (475, 21.4%), 1: (1746, 78.6%)	5	44.20%	34.5%	−9.70%
armsLocked	0: (3, 0.1%), 1: (2218, 99.9%)	1	0.6%	5.1%	4.50%
bodyWeight	0: (69, 3.1%), 1: (2152, 96.9%)	3	10.70%	12.90%	2.20%

first complete implementation of the *Multimodal Pipeline* [9] and it shows that it is possible to close the feedback loop with a real-time multimodal feedback.

In H2 we hypothesised that the CPR Tutor with its real-time feedback function can have a positive impact on the performance indicators considered. With a first intervention feedback study involving 10 participants we noticed that there is a short-term positive influence of the real-time feedback on the detected performance, witnessed by a decrease of Error Rate in the 10 s after the feedback was fired (Table 2). This effect is confirmed in three out of five target classes. The remaining two classes show opposite behaviours. In these two cases, the increase of Error Rate is smaller as compared to the former target classes. We suppose this behaviour is linked to the extreme class distribution of these two classes. In turn, this distribution can be due to the fact that the participants of the second group were not beginners and, therefore, not perform common mistakes such as not locking the arms or not using their body weight correctly. These observations cannot be generalised due to the small number of participants tested for the study.

7   Conclusions

We presented the design and the development of real-time feedback architecture for CPR Tutor. Building upon existing components, we developed an open-source data processing tool (SharpFlow) which implements a neural network architecture as well as a TCP server for real-time CCs classification. The architecture was employed in a first study aimed at expert data collection and offline training and the second study for real-time feedback intervention allowing us to prove our first hypothesis. Regarding H2, we collected observations that, while cannot be generalised, provide some indication that the feedback of the CPR tutor had a positive influence on the CPR performance on the target classes. To sum up, the architecture used for the CPR Tutor allowed for provision of real-time multimodal feedback (H1) and the generated feedback seem to have a short-term positive influence on the CPR performance on the target classes considered.

References

1. Ahuja, K., et al..: EduSense: practical classroom sensing at scale. In: Proceedings of the ACM on Interactive, Mobile, Wearable and Ubiquitous Technologies, vol. 3, no. 3, pp. 1–26 (2019). http://dl.acm.org/citation.cfm?doid=3361560.3351229
2. Alqahtani, F., Ramzan, N.: Comparison and efficacy of synergistic intelligent tutoring systems with human physiological response. Sensors 19(3), 460 (2019)
3. Arroyo, I., Cooper, D.G., Burleson, W., Woolf, B.P., Muldner, K., Christopherson, R.: Emotion sensors go to school. Front. Artif. Intell. Appl. 200(1), 17–24 (2009)
4. Blikstein, P., Worsley, M.: Multimodal learning analytics and education data mining: using computational technologies to measure complex learning tasks. J. Learn. Anal. 3(2), 220–238 (2016)
5. Cukurova, M., Kent, C., Luckin, R.: Artificial intelligence and multimodal data in the service of human decision-making: a case study in debate tutoring. Br. J. Educ. Technol. 50, 3032–3046 (2019). https://onlinelibrary.wiley.com/doi/abs/10.1111/bjet.12829
6. Di Mitri, D., Schneider, J., Klemke, R., Specht, M., Drachsler, H.: Read between the lines: an annotation tool for multimodal data for learning. In: Proceedings of the 9th International Conference on Learning Analytics & Knowledge - LAK19, pp. 51–60. ACM, New York (2019). http://dl.acm.org/citation.cfm?doid=3303772.3303776
7. Di Mitri, D., Schneider, J., Specht, M., Drachsler, H.: From signals to knowledge: a conceptual model for multimodal learning analytics. J. Comput. Assist. Learn. 34(4), 338–349 (2018). http://doi.wiley.com/10.1111/jcal.12288
8. Di Mitri, D., Schneider, J., Specht, M., Drachsler, H.: Detecting mistakes in CPR training with multimodal data and neural networks. Sensors 19(14), 1–20 (2019)
9. Di Mitri, D., Schneider, J., Specht, M., Drachsler, H.: Multimodal pipeline : a generic approach for handling multimodal data for supporting learning. In: AIMA4EDU Workshop in IJCAI 2019 AI-based Multimodal Analytics for Understanding Human Learning in Real-world Educational Contexts, pp. 2–4 (2019)
10. D'Mello, S., et al.: AutoTutor detects and responds to learners affective and cognitive states. IEEE Trans. Educ. 48(4), 612–618 (2008)
11. Giannakos, M.N., Sharma, K., Pappas, I.O., Kostakos, V., Velloso, E.: Multimodal data as a means to understand the learning experience. Int. J. Info. Manag. 48(Feb), 108–119 (2019). https://doi.org/10.1016/j.ijinfomgt.2019.02.003
12. Hochreiter, S., Schmidhuber, J.: Long short-term memory. Neural Comput. 9(8), 1735–1780 (1997). http://www7.informatik.tu-muenchen.de/hochreit%0Awww.idsia.ch/ juergen
13. Limbu, B.H., Jarodzka, H., Klemke, R., Specht, M.: Using sensors and augmented reality to train apprentices using recorded expert performance: a systematic literature review. Educ. Res. Rev. 25(2017), 1–22 (2018). https://doi.org/10.1016/j.edurev.2018.07.001
14. Martinez-Maldonado, R., Echeverria, V., Santos, O.C., Dos Santos, A.D.P., Yacef, K.: Physical learning analytics: a multimodal perspective. In: ACM International Conference Proceeding Series, pp. 375–379 (2018)

15. Ochoa, X., Worsley, M.: Augmenting learning analytics with multimodal sensory data. J. Learn. Anal. **3**(2), 213–219 (2016). http://learning-analytics.info/journals/index.php/JLA/article/view/5081
16. Oviatt, S., Schuller, B., Cohen, P.R., Sonntag, D., Potamianos, G., Krüger, A.: The Handbook of Multimodal-Multisensor Interfaces: Foundations, User Modeling, and Common Modality Combinations, vol. 2, April 2018. https://dl.acm.org/citation.cfm?id=3015783
17. Perkins, G.D., et al.: European resuscitation council guidelines for resuscitation 2015: Section 2. Adult basic life support and automated external defibrillation. Resuscitation **95**, 81–99 (2015). https://doi.org/10.1016/j.resuscitation.2015.07.015
18. Santos, O.C.: Training the body: the potential of AIED to support personalized motor skills learning. Int. J. Artif. Intell. Educ. **26**(2), 730–755 (2016). https://doi.org/10.1007/s40593-016-0103-2
19. Santos, O.C.: Artificial intelligence in psychomotor learning: modeling human motion from inertial sensor data. Int. J. Artif. Intell. Tools **28**(04), 1940006 (2019)
20. Schneider, J., Di Mitri, D., Limbu, B., Drachsler, H.: Multimodal learning hub: a tool for capturing customizable multimodal learning experiences. In: Pammer-Schindler, V., Pérez-Sanagustín, M., Drachsler, H., Elferink, R., Scheffel, M. (eds.) EC-TEL 2018. LNCS, vol. 11082, pp. 45–58. Springer, Cham (2018). https://doi.org/10.1007/978-3-319-98572-5_4
21. Spikol, D., Ruffaldi, E., Dabisias, G., Cukurova, M.: Supervised machine learning in multimodal learning analytics for estimating success in project-based learning. J. Comput. Assist. Learn. **34**(4), 366–377 (2018)
22. Taylor, R.H., Menciassi, A., Fichtinger, G., Fiorini, P., Dario, P.: Medical robotics and computer-integrated surgery. In: Siciliano, B., Khatib, O. (eds.) Springer Handbook of Robotics, pp. 1657–1684. Springer, Cham (2016). https://doi.org/10.1007/978-3-319-32552-1_63

Impact of Methodological Choices on the Evaluation of Student Models

Tomáš Effenberger[✉] and Radek Pelánek

Masaryk University, Brno, Czech Republic
`tomas.effenberger@mail.muni.cz, pelanek@fi.muni.cz`

Abstract. The evaluation of student models involves many methodological decisions, e.g., the choice of performance metric, data filtering, and cross-validation setting. Such issues may seem like technical details, and they do not get much attention in published research. Nevertheless, their impact on experiments can be significant. We report experiments with six models for predicting problem-solving times in four introductory programming exercises. Our focus is not on these models per se but rather on the methodological choices necessary for performing these experiments. The results show, particularly, the importance of the choice of performance metric, including details of its computation and presentation.

1 Introduction

Student modeling [4,12] is at the core of many techniques in the field of artificial intelligence in education. A key element of research and development of student modeling techniques is the comparison of several alternative models. Such comparisons are used to choose models (and their hyper-parameters) to be used in real-life systems, to judge the merit of newly proposed techniques, and to determine priorities for future research.

Results of model comparison can be influenced by methodological decisions made in the experimental setting of the comparison, e.g., the exact manner of dividing data into training and testing set [13], the choice of metrics [10], or the treatment of outliers. These issues do not get much attention unless suspiciously good results are reported, e.g., as in the case of deep knowledge tracing paper [15], which reported significant improvement in predictive accuracy, prompting several research groups to probe the results and to identify several methodological problems in the evaluation [8,16,17].

The importance of methodological choices was recently discussed in [13], but using mostly simplified examples and simulations. We perform an exploration of the impact of methodological choices using real data. We use data from introductory programming exercises, where students are expected to construct a program to solve a given problem. We compare models that predict the problem-solving time for the next item. We use data from four types of exercises with different characteristics—this allows us to explore the generalizability of our observations.

© Springer Nature Switzerland AG 2020
I. I. Bittencourt et al. (Eds.): AIED 2020, LNAI 12163, pp. 153–164, 2020.
https://doi.org/10.1007/978-3-030-52237-7_13

For the data, we perform a comparison of six student models. Our focus is not on these models (which typically get attention in reported results), but rather on the methodological choices done in the experimental setting and on the impact of these choices on results. We explicitly describe the choices that need to be made and show specific examples that illustrate how these choices influence the results of model comparison. Our results highlight the importance of the choice of performance metric, including details of its computation, processing, and reporting.

2 Setting

To analyze the impact of methodological choices, we measure the performance of six student models for predicting the time to solve the next problem in four programming exercises. Predicting problem-solving times is less explored than predicting binary success, yet it is a more informative measure of performance for problems that take more than just a few seconds to solve [14]. As the problem-solving times are usually approximately log-normal [14], our models and evaluations work with the log-transformed times (denoted 'log-time').

2.1 Data

We use data from four introductory programming exercises, each containing 70–100 items divided into 8–12 levels. Table 1 provides an overview of these exercises. In the Arrows exercise, students place commands (usually directions to follow) directly into the grid with the game world. In the Robot exercise [5] and Turtle graphics [2], students create programs using a block-based programming interface [1]. In the last exercise, students write Python code to solve problems with numbers, strings, and lists. In all cases, the problems require at most 25 lines of code and are solved in between 10 seconds and 5 min by most of the students.

Table 1. Programming exercises and data used in experiments.

Exercise	Items	Students	Successful attempts	Median time
Arrows	94	13,000	182,000	32 s
Robot	85	10,800	146,000	51 s
Turtle	77	10,100	87,000	81 s
Python	73	1,400	17,000	174 s

2.2 Student Models

In all experiments, we compare the following student models for predicting problem-solving times. All these models can be first fitted offline and then evaluated online on previously unseen students.

1. *Item average (I-Avg)*: a baseline model predicting average log-time for a given item.
2. *Student-item average (SI-Avg)*: a simple model predicting item average time reduced by a naive estimate of the student's skill. The skill is computed from the previous student's attempts as the average deviation between the observed log-time and the item average log-time. To avoid overfitting, the estimate is regularized by adding five pseudo-observations of zero deviations.
3. *t-IRT*: a one-parameter item response theory model (1PL IRT) adapted for problem-solving times [14]. The model has the same set of parameters as the SI-Avg, but now they are optimized to minimize RMSE (with L2 penalty), using regularized linear least squares regression. The skill, which is assumed to be constant, is in the online evaluation phase estimated using the regularized mean deviation in the same way as in the SI-Avg model.
4. *t-AFM*: an additive factors model [3] adapted for problem-solving times. The Q-matrix is constructed from the levels in each exercise. Three additional modifications to the standard AFM were necessary for a reasonable performance: a difficulty parameter for each item, log-transformation of the practice opportunities counts (only solved attempts are considered), and an online estimate of the prior skill, using the same regularized mean deviation as for the SI-Avg and t-IRT.
5. *Elo*: a model based on the Elo rating system adapted for problem-solving times [11]. It tracks a single skill for each student and a single difficulty for each item. After each observed attempt, the skill and the difficulty are updated in proportion to the prediction error. In contrast to SI-Avg and t-IRT, the Elo model assumes changing skill, which is reflected by holding the learning rate for the estimate of the student's skill constant. On the other hand, the difficulties are assumed not to change over time, so their learning rate is inversely proportional to the number of observations.
6. *Random forest (RF)*: a generic machine learning model utilizing ensemble of decision trees, with the following features: item and level (using one-hot-encoding scheme), problem-solving time on recent items (using exponential moving average), and the numbers of items the student had already solved under and above several time thresholds, both in total and in the individual levels.

To select reasonable hyper-parameters for the models (e.g., the number of pseudo-observations for the online estimate of the prior skill, or the number of trees and the maximum depth for the Random forest), we used a subset of data from the Robot exercise (first 50,000 attempts). These data were not used for the subsequent experiments, and the hyper-parameters were not modified for the other exercises.

2.3   Evaluation Approach

To explore the impact of a set of methodological choices, we compare the results of student models evaluation using these choices. For each exercise and each set of methodological choices, we use the following evaluation approach, which corresponds to a common practice in the evaluation of student models.

First, we apply data preprocessing choices, such as filtering of students with few attempts and capping observed solving times. Then we perform student-level k-fold cross-validation [13], i.e., all attempts of a single student are all assigned to one of the k folds (we use $k = 10$). For each fold and each model, we fit the model parameters on a training set ($k - 1$ folds) and then evaluate the performance of the model on a testing set (the remaining fold). The evaluation phase is online, i.e., the models can update their parameters (e.g., the skill of a student) after each observed attempt. The performance of models is measured by comparing the predicted and observed problem-solving times, using Root Mean Square Error (RMSE) as the default performance metric. Finally, we report the mean value and the standard deviation of the metric across folds and also the average rank of the model according to the metric.

We evaluate the impact of several methodological choices and their interactions: the choice of predictive accuracy metric and the details of the computation and reporting of the metric, division of data into training and testing sets, filtering of the data, and treatment of outliers. When reporting the observed results, we face the trade-off between conciseness and representativeness. Often, we illustrate the impact of a given choice on a single exercise; when we do so, we always report to which extent the trends observed in this exercise generalize to the other three and provide the same plots for the other exercises as a supplementary material available at github.com/adaptive-learning/aied2020.

3   Metrics

Although student models can be evaluated and compared from many perspectives [7], the primary criterion used to compare models is the predictive accuracy. The predictive accuracy is quantified by a performance metric [10], i.e., a function that takes a vector of predictions and a vector of observations and produces a scalar value. The choice of a metric used for model comparison involves quite a large number of (often under-reported) decisions.

3.1   Normalization and Stability of Results

We start by a discussion of the processing and presentation of results since it also influences the presentation of our results in the rest of the paper. To check the stability of model comparisons, it is useful to have not just a single value of a metric but to run repeated experiments and study the stability of results. A straightforward approach is to perform k-fold cross-validation and report the mean value of a metric and its standard deviation.

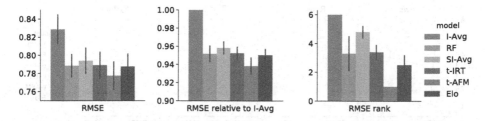

Fig. 1. Comparison of student models for the Robot exercise using RMSE (left), RMSE relative to the baseline (center), and order of the models according to RMSE (right). The vertical bars show standard deviations computed from 10 cross-validation folds.

Such a presentation can be, however, misleading. Figure 1 provides a specific illustration. The left part of the figure shows the basic approach to evaluation where we compare the values of RMSE directly. This presentation shows that the results for individual models overlap to a large degree; we could be tempted to conclude from this that the accuracy of the studied models is not very different. However, it may be that the observed variability is due to variability across folds, not due to the variability of models predictive ability.

The variability caused by data can be, for example, due to the presence of unmotivated students with chaotic and hard to predict behavior and their uneven distribution across folds. To reduce this variability, we can normalize the metric value. In Fig. 1 we report two types of such normalization: A) RMSE relative to a baseline model (per fold), B) RMSE rank among compared models (per fold). As Fig. 1 shows, these normalizations give quite a different picture concerning how consistent are the differences in model performance. Consider, for instance, comparison of SI-Avg and t-AFM. While the distributions of their RMSEs across folds largely overlap, exploring their ranks reveals that t-AFM has consistently better performance than SI-Avg. This is not an isolated case; for all four exercises, there are some pairs of models whose distributions of RMSEs largely overlap, while the distributions of the ranks do not.

We do not claim that the normalized approaches are better. It may be that one model is consistently better (which is highlighted by the rank approach), but the differences are consistently small and thus practically not important. Reporting both the absolute and normalized RMSEs gives a fuller picture than using just one of the approaches alone.

In this paper, we usually report both the absolute RMSEs and the ranks. The ranks often provide more insight into the impact of methodological choices, since they are more robust to the noise within the folds, and this makes the differences between the models more salient. Additionally, the ranking approach allows us to study the impact of different metrics, which we look at next.

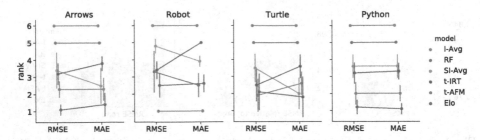

Fig. 2. Comparison of model orderings under RMSE and MAE metrics in four programming exercises. The vertical bars show standard deviations of the ranks computed from 10 cross-validation folds.

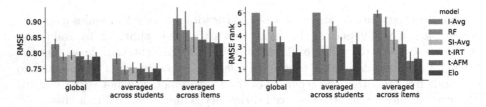

Fig. 3. Comparison of models for the Robot exercise using RMSE averaged either globally, across students, or across items. The vertical bars show standard deviations of the ranks computed from 10 cross-validation folds.

3.2 RMSE Versus MAE

There is a large number of metrics, particularly for the case of models predicting probabilities [10]. Our default choice, RMSE, is a commonly used metric. For the case of predicting continuous values (as is the case of the used logarithm of time), another natural choice is Mean Absolute Error (MAE). To explore the potential impact of metric choice, we compare these two metrics.

Figure 2 shows the results of this comparison across our four datasets. The figure visualizes the ranking of models and shows that the results are mostly stable with respect to the choice of metric. However, there are cases where the choice of metric influences results. Particularly, there is a mostly consistent trend with respect to SI-Avg and t-IRT models: t-IRT achieves better results for the RMSE metric, whereas SI-AVG is better for the MAE metric.

3.3 Averaging

Another decision is the approach to the averaging in the computation [13]. We can use either global computation (treat all observations equally), averaging across students (compute RMSE per student and then compute an average), or averaging across items (compute RMSE per item and then compute an average). These can produce different results, particularly when the distribution of answers is skewed across items or students. For all four datasets we use, that is indeed the case. Figure 3 shows an example of the Robot exercise, where the impact

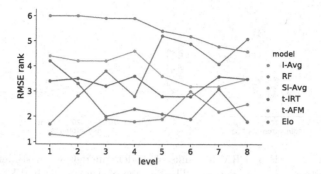

Fig. 4. Average ranks of student models in individual levels of the Robot exercise.

of the averaging is the most pronounced. In this exercise, the averaging across items leads to considerably higher values of RMSE and even to some changes in the ordering of the models.

To get better insight, we can disaggregate RMSE into individual levels (groups of items of similar difficulty) or populations (e.g., groups of students according to their activity or performance). Figure 4 shows an example of such per-level RMSE decomposition for the Robot exercise. Note, particularly, the performance of the Random forest model; it is one of the best models in the initial levels, while one of the worst in the advanced levels. Since students mostly solved items in the first few levels, the global averaging (shown in Fig. 3) favors this model.

We expected that the benefits of the more complex models (like Random Forest and t-AFM) would manifest especially in the last levels, where the complex models can make use of richer students' history. However, the results, for all four programming datasets, show that the trends are exactly opposite: the mean ranks of all models get closer to each other in higher levels. Probably, the skew of the data leads the complex models to overfocus on the first few levels at the expense of the less solved last advanced levels; furthermore, while the models can benefit from more data about the students, they might be seriously hampered by less data for the items.

4   Data Processing

Another set of methodological choices concerns the processing of data: Do we perform some data filtering? How do we treat outliers? How exactly do we divide data into a training and testing set?

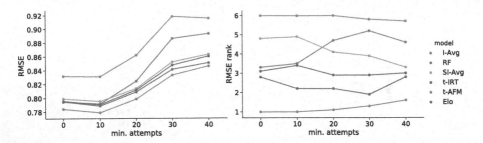

Fig. 5. Average RMSE and RMSE ranks of student models when students with few attempts are filtered (Robot exercise). The filtering of students with at least 10, 20, 30, and 40 attempts results in keeping 86%, 47%, 22%, and 13% of the original attempts.

4.1 Filtering and Outliers

The data from learning systems are noisy, e.g., due to off-task behavior, guessing, or cheating. In order to reduce the impact of this noise on the results of experiments, it may be meaningful to perform some data preprocessing, for example:

- filtering students with small activity (rationale: students with small activity are often just experimenting with the system, and thus there is higher chance that their behavior is noisy),
- filtering items with small activity (rationale: models do not have enough information to provide good predictions for such items),
- removing or capping outliers, i.e., too high problem-solving times (rationale: very high problem-solving times are often caused by some disruption in solving activity, not by poor student skill or high item difficulty).

In some cases, the choice of a filtering threshold can have a pronounced effect on the absolute RMSE, even much higher than the differences in RMSE caused by using a different model. This is illustrated in Fig. 5 for the case of filtering students in the Robot exercise. We observed similar trends in all four datasets and for other data preprocessing choices: high impact on the absolute values of RMSE, but usually a negligible impact on the ranking, unless the thresholds are rather extreme.

As in the case of disaggregating RMSE per level, our initial intuition about the relative merits of the filtering for the simple and complex models was incorrect: we expected the complex models to benefit more from severe filtering since the remaining students have a long history that the complex models can utilize, while the simple models cannot. Nevertheless, both the absolute RMSE and ranks of the complex models actually increase with more severe filtering since the filtering results in an increased proportion of the data for the items with few attempts and less training data overall, which is a more significant issue for the models with many parameters.

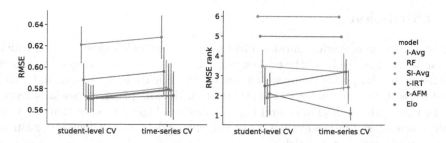

Fig. 6. Comparison of models for the Turtle exercise using either student-level or time-series cross-validation strategy.

4.2 Data Division for Cross-Validation

Reported comparisons of student models often use "k-fold cross-validation" without further specification of the division of data into folds. Since the data from learning systems have an internal structure (mapping to items and students, temporal sequences), there are many ways in which the division of data can be performed [13].

To explore the impact of this choice, we compare two natural choices: student-level cross-validation and time-series cross-validation. In the student-level k-fold cross-validation, all attempts of a single student are assigned randomly to one of the k folds. The relative order of the attempts is preserved (there is no shuffling), and all groups contain approximately the same number of students. This cross-validation strategy ensures that the models cannot use future attempts of a given student to predict her past, but it does not prevent them from using future attempts of the *other* students. In contrast, the time-series cross-validation creates the folds strictly by time, always using only the preceding folds for the training.

Our analysis shows that the choice of cross-validation strategy can influence the results of experiments. Figure 6 shows the results for the Turtle dataset: with respect to ranking, the Elo model is a clear winner when the time-series cross-validation is used, whereas in the case of student-level cross-validation, it has similar results as other models. An analysis of the dataset shows that it contains a temporal pattern—the performance of consecutive students on each item is correlated. Although this correlation is quite weak and the Elo model is not explicitly designed to exploit it, the presence of this pattern is sufficient to impact the results of the comparison.

In the other exercises, especially in the Arrows and Python, the impact of the cross-validation strategy is rather small. However, in these two exercises, the Elo model is already the best model even when the student-level cross-validation is used. In the other five models, the students in the test set cannot influence the predictions for the subsequent students, so these models cannot exploit the described temporal pattern.

5 Discussion

The comparison of student models involves many methodological choices, which can influence the results of the evaluation. This situation is not unique to student modeling; similar problems are well-known in other fields, e.g., Gelman and Loker [6] discuss statistical analysis of experiments with examples from social science.

In this work, we highlight and explore methodological choices that are typically encountered in the evaluation of student models. Insufficient attention to these details poses several risks:

- Possibility of "fishing" for choices that present a researcher's favorite technique (e.g., a newly proposed method) in a favorable light.
- Missing of potentially interesting results due to some arbitrary methodological choice that masks important differences between models.
- Misleading comparisons of models, which were evaluated by slightly different methodologies (differing in details that are undocumented or over which authors gloss over).

The basic step to mitigating these risks is the awareness of the available choices and their explicit and clear description in research papers. Some kind of preregistration procedure [9] can further strengthen the credentials of student model comparisons.

Typically, researchers in student modeling and developers of adaptive learning systems are interested primarily in student models and do not want to spend much time exploring methodological choices. Experiments are not inherently unstable—many decisions have only a small impact on results. It is thus useful to know which choices deserve most focus. This, of course, depends to a large degree on a particular setting and it is unlikely that some completely universal guidelines can be found. However, reporting experience from a variety of comparisons should lead to a set of reasonable recommendations.

We have performed our experiments in the domain of problem-solving activities and for the student models predicting problem-solving times. In this setting, the results show the importance of the choice of a performance metric and of the details of its processing and presentation. Specifically, our results show that there are large differences between the presentation of results of cross-validation across folds in terms of the absolute value of metrics, relative values (normalized by baseline performance per fold), and rankings of performance per fold. On the other hand, filtering of data and treatment of outliers have a relatively small impact on the ranking of models (for reasonable choices of thresholds).

Our results also clearly illustrate that the absolute values of performance metrics depend on details of the evaluation methodology and properties of a specific dataset. The differences in metric values are typically larger among different evaluation settings than among different models. Consequently, it is very dangerous to compare metric values to results reported in research papers even when using the same dataset (as done, for example, in the deep knowledge tracing paper [15]). Comparisons make sense only when we are absolutely sure that the computation of metric values is done in exactly the same way. Since there are many subtle choices that influence metric values, this can be in practice best done by comparing only models that use the same implementation of an evaluation framework.

Supplementary Materials

For all the presented plots, we provide their analogues with all four exercises as supplementary materials at github.com/adaptive-learning/aied2020. The numbering of the supplementary plots corresponds to the numbering in the paper.

References

1. Bau, D., Gray, J., Kelleher, C., Sheldon, J., Turbak, F.: Learnable programming: blocks and beyond. Commun. ACM **60**(6), 72–80 (2017)
2. Caspersen, M.E., Christensen, H.B.: Here, there and everywhere - on the recurring use of turtle graphics in CS1. In: ACM International Conference Proceeding Series, vol. 8, pp. 34–40 (2000)
3. Cen, H., Koedinger, K., Junker, B.: Learning factors analysis – a general method for cognitive model evaluation and improvement. In: Ikeda, M., Ashley, K.D., Chan, T.-W. (eds.) ITS 2006. LNCS, vol. 4053, pp. 164–175. Springer, Heidelberg (2006). https://doi.org/10.1007/11774303_17
4. Desmarais, M.C., Baker, R.S.: A review of recent advances in learner and skill modeling in intelligent learning environments. User Model. User-Adap. Interact. **22**(1–2), 9–38 (2012). https://doi.org/10.1007/s11257-011-9106-8
5. Effenberger, T., Pelánek, R.: Towards making block-based programming activities adaptive. In: Proceedings of Learning at Scale, p. 13. ACM (2018)
6. Gelman, A., Loken, E.: The garden of forking paths: why multiple comparisons can be a problem, even when there is no "fishing expedition" or "p-hacking" and the research hypothesis was posited ahead of time. Columbia University, Department of Statistics (2013)
7. Huang, Y., González-Brenes, J.P., Kumar, R., Brusilovsky, P.: A framework for multifaceted evaluation of student models. International Educational Data Mining Society (2015)
8. Khajah, M., Lindsey, R.V., Mozer, M.C.: How deep is knowledge tracing? In: Proceedings of Educational Data Mining (2016)
9. Nosek, B.A., Ebersole, C.R., DeHaven, A.C., Mellor, D.T.: The preregistration revolution. Proc. Natl. Acad. Sci. **115**(11), 2600–2606 (2018)
10. Pelánek, R.: Metrics for evaluation of student models. J. Educ. Data Min. **7**(2), 1–19 (2015)
11. Pelánek, R.: Applications of the Elo rating system in adaptive educational systems. Comput. Educ. **98**, 169–179 (2016)
12. Pelánek, R.: Bayesian knowledge tracing, logistic models, and beyond: an overview of learner modeling techniques. User Model. User-Adap. Interact. **27**, 313–350 (2017). https://doi.org/10.1007/s11257-017-9193-2
13. Pelánek, R.: The details matter: methodological nuances in the evaluation of student models. User Model. User-Adap. Interact. **28**, 207–235 (2018). https://doi.org/10.1007/s11257-018-9204-y

14. Pelánek, R., Jarušek, P.: Student modeling based on problem solving times. Int. J. Artif. Intell. Educ. **25**, 493–519 (2015). https://doi.org/10.1007/s40593-015-0048-x
15. Piech, C., et al.: Deep knowledge tracing. In: Advances in Neural Information Processing Systems, pp. 505–513 (2015)
16. Wilson, K.H., et al.: Estimating student proficiency: deep learning is not the panacea. In: Proceedings of Neural Information Processing Systems, Workshop on Machine Learning for Education (2016)
17. Xiong, X., Zhao, S., Van Inwegen, E., Beck, J.: Going deeper with deep knowledge tracing. In: Proceedings of Educational Data Mining, pp. 545–550 (2016)

Investigating Visitor Engagement in Interactive Science Museum Exhibits with Multimodal Bayesian Hierarchical Models

Andrew Emerson[✉], Nathan Henderson, Jonathan Rowe, Wookhee Min, Seung Lee, James Minogue, and James Lester

North Carolina State University, Raleigh, NC 27695, USA
{ajemerso,nlhender,jprowe,wmin,sylee,james_minogue,
lester}@ncsu.edu

Abstract. Engagement plays a critical role in visitor learning in museums. Devising computational models of visitor engagement shows significant promise for enabling adaptive support to enhance visitors' learning experiences and for providing analytic tools for museum educators. A salient feature of science museums is their capacity to attract diverse visitor populations that range broadly in age, interest, prior knowledge, and socio-cultural background, which can significantly affect how visitors interact with museum exhibits. In this paper, we introduce a Bayesian hierarchical modeling framework for predicting learner engagement with FUTURE WORLDS, a tabletop science exhibit for environmental sustainability. We utilize multi-channel data (e.g., eye tracking, facial expression, posture, interaction logs) captured from visitor interactions with a fully-instrumented version of FUTURE WORLDS to model visitor dwell time with the exhibit in a science museum. We demonstrate that the proposed Bayesian hierarchical modeling approach outperforms competitive baseline techniques. These findings point toward significant opportunities for enriching our understanding of visitor engagement in science museums with multimodal learning analytics.

Keywords: Museum-based learning · Visitor modeling · Multimodal learning analytics

1 Introduction

Engagement is a critical component of learning in informal environments such as museums [1, 2]. Visitor engagement shapes how learners interact with museum exhibits, navigate the exhibit space, and form attitudes, interests, and understanding of scientific ideas and practices. Recent developments in multimodal learning analytics have significant potential to enhance our understanding of visitor engagement with interactive museum exhibits [3, 4]. Multimodal learning analytics techniques can be utilized to create computational models for uncovering patterns in meaningful visitor engagement through the triangulation of multimodal data streams captured by physical hardware sensors (e.g., webcams, eye trackers, motion sensors). Multimodal learning analytics has

© Springer Nature Switzerland AG 2020
I. I. Bittencourt et al. (Eds.): AIED 2020, LNAI 12163, pp. 165–176, 2020.
https://doi.org/10.1007/978-3-030-52237-7_14

shown significant promise in laboratory and classroom environments [5, 6], but there has been comparatively little work investigating multimodal learning analytics in informal contexts, such as science museums.

Devising computational models of visitor engagement with interactive science museum exhibits poses significant challenges. Visitor interactions with museum exhibits are brief; dwell times with *highly engaging* exhibits often last only 3–4 min [7–9]. Furthermore, museums attract a broad range of visitors of varying age, background, knowledge, and learning objectives. Different types of museum visitors show distinctive patterns of engagement, including how they interact with specific exhibits, as well as how they move about the museum floor [10]. To address these challenges, it is important to utilize computational techniques that make efficient use of available data and account for inherent differences in how visitors engage with interactive exhibits in museums.

In this paper, we present a multimodal learning analytics framework for investigating visitor engagement in science museums that is based upon Bayesian hierarchical models. Bayesian hierarchical models explicitly account for differences in patterns of visitor engagement between separate visitor groups. We focus on visitor interactions with a game-based interactive museum exhibit about environmental sustainability, FUTURE WORLDS. By instrumenting FUTURE WORLDS with multiple hardware sensors, it is possible to capture fine-grained data on visitors' facial expression, eye gaze, posture, and learning interactions to model key components of visitor engagement in science museums. We investigate the relationship between multimodal interactions and visitor engagement by analyzing posterior multimodal parameter distributions of Bayesian hierarchical models that model visitor dwell time with the FUTURE WORLDS interactive exhibit. Results show that Bayesian hierarchical linear models more accurately model visitor dwell time than baseline techniques that do not incorporate hierarchical architectures and yield valuable insights into which features are most predictive for modeling visitor engagement.

2   Related Work

Engagement is a critical mechanism for fostering meaningful learning in museums [7]. Much work on modeling learner engagement has focused on formal educational settings, such as school classrooms [11]. In a museum context, low levels of visitor engagement may appear as shallow interactions with an interactive exhibit, or no interaction at all, whereas high-level engagement can manifest as extended dwell times and productive exploration behaviors. We seek to utilize rich multi-channel data streams to identify patterns of meaningful visitor engagement as defined through visitor dwell time with a game-based interactive exhibit. Dwell time has been used previously to examine visitor engagement with museum exhibits [12, 13].

Multimodal learning analytics techniques show significant promise for capturing patterns of visitor engagement in museums. By taking advantage of information across concurrent sensor-based data channels, multimodal learning analytic techniques have been found to yield improved models in terms of accuracy and robustness compared to unimodal techniques [14]. Although these applications have shown significant promise, the preponderance of work on multimodal learning analytics has been conducted in laboratory and classroom settings [5, 15]. Using multimodal learning analytics to investigate visitor engagement in informal environments is an important next step for the field.

Traditionally, computational models of learner engagement assume relatively high levels of homogeneity across learners in the training data, which is a natural assumption for classroom settings where all learners are approximately the same age and have similar levels of prior knowledge. However, learners express engagement in different ways depending on a range of factors such as prior knowledge and socio-cultural background, suggesting that group-based differences should be considered when modeling engagement [16]. There are limited examples of research on computational models of engagement that account for these differences. Sawyer et al. used Bayesian hierarchical models to investigate models of learner engagement with a game-based learning environment in both classroom and laboratory settings [17]. We build on this work by adopting a Bayesian hierarchical modeling framework for investigating group-level differences in visitor engagement in a museum context.

3 FUTURE WORLDS Testbed Exhibit

To conduct data-rich investigations of visitor engagement in science museums, we utilize a game-based museum exhibit called FUTURE WORLDS. Developed with the Unity game engine, FUTURE WORLDS integrates game-based learning technologies into an interactive surface display to enable hands-on explorations of environmental sustainability [18]. With FUTURE WORLDS, visitors solve sustainability problems by investigating the impacts of alternate environmental decisions on a 3D simulated environment (Fig. 1). Learners interact with the environment through tapping and swiping the display to test hypotheses about how different environmental decisions impact the environment's sustainability and future health. Visitors read about different regions of the virtual environment and observe how they are impacted by the learner's actions. The effects of visitors' decisions are realized in real-time within the simulation.

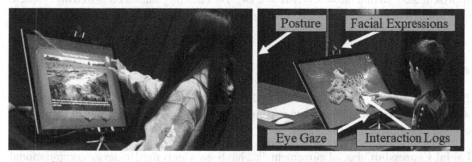

Fig. 1. FUTURE WORLDS museum exhibit capturing multimodal visitor data.

FUTURE WORLDS' focus on environmental sustainability targets three major themes—water, energy (both renewable and non-renewable), and food—and it facilitates exploration of the interrelatedness of these themes. Initial pilot testing with both school and summer-camp groups in a science museum in the southeastern United States has shown that learner interactions with FUTURE WORLDS enhance sustainability content knowledge and yield promising levels of visitor engagement as indicated by observations of learner behavior [18].

4   Multimodal Data Collection

We leverage a suite of multimodal sensors (e.g., video camera, motion tracking sensor, eye tracker, game logs) to capture visitors' facial expression, body movement, eye gaze, and interaction trace data, respectively, to serve as complementary data sources for inducing computational models of visitor engagement with FUTURE WORLDS. In this work, we focus on modeling visitor dwell time, which is a manifestation of visitors' behavioral engagement, as the ground-truth label of visitor engagement.

4.1   Study Participants and Procedure

We conducted a series of three data collections with museum visitors engaging with the FUTURE WORLDS exhibit at the North Carolina Museum of Natural Sciences in Raleigh, North Carolina. The three groups of visitors were recruited from regional elementary schools from different socio-cultural backgrounds (e.g., race/ethnicity, urban vs. rural, language diversity). Each of the schools served populations where 70% of the students are considered economically disadvantaged. In aggregate, participants included 116 visitors between 10–11 years of age. Each visitor completed a series of questionnaires before and after interacting with FUTURE WORLDS, including a demographics survey, science interest scale, sustainability content knowledge assessment, and engagement survey. Fourteen of the participants did not complete the surveys, which left 47 female and 55 male participants. Approximately 21.6% of the visitors were African American, 8% Asian, 3% Caucasian, 32.3% Latino, and 11.8% American Indian. Visitors interacted with FUTURE WORLDS individually until they were finished or up to a maximum of approximately 10 min ($M = 3.97, SD = 2.24$). The resulting dataset consisted of complete multimodal data for 86 visitors, following removal of participants with missing data from one or more modalities.

4.2   Multimodal Data Channels

The study utilized a suite of multimodal sensors to gather data on visitor interactions with FUTURE WORLDS. These data streams included facial expression, eye gaze, posture, gesture, and interaction trace logs.

Facial Expression.   Facial movement data has been widely used to devise computational models for automatically recognizing learning-centered affective states [5]. In our work, we capture facial expression data using video recordings from an externally mounted Logitech C920 USB webcam. The resulting data is analyzed using OpenFace, an open-source facial behavior analysis toolkit that provides automated facial landmark detection and action unit (AU) recognition for 17 distinct AUs [19].

Eye Gaze. A growing body of empirical work has demonstrated the importance of eye gaze for modeling learner interactions [20]. To track visitor eye gaze, we utilize a mounted eye-tracking sensor which uses near-infrared light to track eye movements and gaze points during visitor interactions with the interactive exhibit. We automatically identify in-game targets of visitor attention in FUTURE WORLDS using a gaze target-labeling module that processes eye tracking data using ray casting techniques.

Body Movement. Recent years have seen growing interest in research on affective modeling using human body movement data [21, 22]. To capture data on visitor posture and gesture, we utilize Microsoft Kinect for Windows v2, a dedicated motion sensing camera that provides skeletal tracking for 26 distinct vertices, in addition to raw pixel data for depth and color camera sensors [23]. The Kinect sensor was mounted on a tripod five feet away from the exhibit and allowed for tracking of body movement.

Interaction Trace Logs. FUTURE WORLDS provides support for detailed logs of learner interactions with the digital interactive exhibit software. The log data consists of timestamped records (at the millisecond level) of visitor taps and multitouch gestures, as well as learning events and simulation states, that arise during visitor experiences.

4.3 Multimodal Features

We extracted several features from each modality to serve as predictors of visitor dwell time. We selected a relatively small number of features for each modality due to the limited size of our dataset. For visitor facial expression, we used AU data captured by OpenFace. We calculated the proportional duration that each AU was exhibited throughout the visitor's interaction with FUTURE WORLDS. Each visitor's facial expression data was standardized and the duration of an AU was recorded if its tracked intensity exceeded one standard deviation above the mean intensity for that AU. Each duration was only recorded if it was present for longer than 0.5 s to avoid noise associated with facial micro expressions [24]. We selected 5 AU values: *AU2* (Outer Brow Raiser), *AU7* (Lid Tightener), *AU10* (Upper Lip Raiser), *AU12* (Lip Corner Puller), and *AU14* (Dimpler). These AUs were selected based upon related work on modeling learner engagement with facial expression data [24–26]. We adopted a similar approach to previous work using facial expression for student modeling [24] by scaling the durations of AU data by the total time spent engaging with FUTURE WORLDS.

To capture patterns in visitor attention with FUTURE WORLDS, we used the Tobii EyeX eye tracker to pinpoint areas of interest (AOIs) on the interactive exhibit's display. Visitor fixations on in-game objects exceeding 210 ms in duration were automatically tracked [27]. We aggregated the gaze fixation data to compute the proportion of time visitors spent looking at five categories of in-game objects: virtual locations (AOI-Location), environmental sustainability imagery (AOI-Imagery), environmental sustainability labels (AOI-Labels), environmental sustainability selection menus (AOI-Menu), and user interface elements (AOI-Interface). The *AOI-Location* category included fixations on any of the nine discrete, hexagon-shaped regions of the virtual environment in FUTURE WORLDS. The *AOI-Imagery* category included high-resolution images associated with the exhibit's environmental sustainability content. The *AOI-Labels* category encompassed all textual labels about environmental sustainability topics within FUTURE WORLDS (e.g., text descriptions about renewable vs. non-renewable energy, sustainable farming practices). The *AOI-Menu* category referred to a pop-up menu that appeared when a visitor tapped on a particular location of the virtual environment to learn more about that region or make a change to the region's environmental practices (e.g., add solar panels, introduce organic farming). The *AOI-Interface* category contained user interface elements for navigating the exhibit software (e.g., restart button). Leveraging an approach similar to related work on gaze-enhanced student modeling [28], we calculated the total time spent fixated on each category of in-game element and scaled by the total time spent engaging with FUTURE WORLDS.

To extract features on visitor body movement, we focused on four skeletal vertices tracked by the Microsoft Kinect motion sensor: *Head, SpineShoulder* (upper-back), *SpineMid* (mid-back), and *Neck*. Selection of these vertices was informed by prior work on multimodal affect detection with motion-tracking sensor data [29]. For each skeletal vertex, we calculated the sum variance of its distance from the Kinect sensor across the visitor's entire interaction with FUTURE WORLDS. Additionally, we utilized the four vertices to calculate the total posture change for each visitor based upon the sum movement of all vertices within the Kinect's coordinate tracking space.

For interaction log features, we calculated the total number of times the visitor tapped on the FUTURE WORLDS exhibit's touch display (*Total Taps*) and the total number of times the visitor tapped to examine environmental sustainability imagery and labels (*Total Info Taps*). The two interaction log features were computed by scaling the above measures by the total dwell time for that visitor (i.e., taps per second), which measured how actively participants interacted with FUTURE WORLDS and its embedded environmental sustainability content.

In sum, we extracted five facial expression features, five eye gaze features, five body movement features, and two interaction log features for a total of 17 multimodal features for this analysis.

5 Bayesian Linear Models

To predict visitor dwell time with the FUTURE WORLDS exhibit, we induced linear models using Bayesian Lasso regression. Lasso regression is a regression analysis method that privileges simpler models by forcing a subset of model coefficients to be set to zero, which serves as a form of feature selection and regularization [30]. We utilized a Bayesian framework to incorporate prior distributions for parameter estimation, account for uncertainty in modeling, and share information across groups of data. Because our dataset contained multimodal data from 86 participants, linear models provided a natural machine learning framework to prevent overfitting and support parameter interpretability. We implemented Bayesian linear models using double exponential prior distributions on all feature coefficients, serving as a form of L1 (Lasso) regularization to limit the number of features utilized in the induced models.

In addition to utilizing prior distributions for model parameters, we also used a logarithmic link function in the regression model to better predict visitor dwell time. In standard Bayesian linear regression, a normal distribution is used to model the relationship between the predictor variables and the dependent variable. The mean of this distribution is the linear combination of the input features and their coefficients. Due to use of the normal distribution, the predictions can be negative. In our case, dwell time cannot be a negative value, so we exponentiate the linear combination of features and coefficients before using it as the mean of the normal distribution. Varying the link function is a form of generalized linear modeling [30]. The formulation for the base linear regression used in our analysis is as follows:

$$Y_i \sim Normal(\mu_i, \sigma^2), \text{ where } log(\mu_i) = \alpha + \sum_{k=1}^{p} X_{ik}\beta_k \qquad (1)$$

Y_i is the dwell time for visitor i. α is a fixed intercept added to all predictions in the regression, X_{ik} is the value of the input feature k for student i, β_k is the coefficient for feature k, p is the total number of features (of which there are 17), and σ^2 is the fixed variance used for all predictions.

5.1 Baseline Models

We investigated two baseline models using the regression formula (Eq. 1) described above for modeling visitor dwell time. First, we use a *Pooled Model*, where all visitor data was grouped together and treated equally. Second, we used a *Group-Specific model*, where a separate linear model was trained on each visitor group. The Pooled Model loses information about the individual groups and does not characterize group-based differences in visitor interest, background, or demographics. This can lead to underfitting of the data. The Group-Specific model is a more specialized form of the regression model, where each visitor group has its own distinct set of model parameters. In comparison to the Pooled Model, this approach risks overfitting the data and is unlikely to generalize effectively due to the limited number of data samples per group and inherent differences between the visitor groups.

5.2 Bayesian Hierarchical Model

The regression formula (Eq. 1) assumes that the residual variance for all visitor observations are the same. In many contexts this is a reasonable assumption, but in a museum setting, different groups of visitors may arrive with highly different socio-cultural backgrounds, interests, knowledge levels, and learning objectives, among other relevant characteristics. Different groups of visitors may not only spend different amounts of time at exhibits, but their dwell times may have higher or lower variance depending on the group. Thus, it is important that the multimodal models of visitor engagement account for these differences, and therefore treat the error variances differently in the regression formulation. The assumption of equal variance by standard linear models, or *homoskedasticity*, can result in reduced model fit and information loss when the observations come from groups. We propose an extension to Eq. 1 to incorporate a learned variance parameter that is unique to each visitor group to ensure that the variance of the residual errors is treated differently depending on the group from which the visitor came. To avoid overfitting to the visitor groups, we used a shared latent distribution to model the three groups' variance parameters. This *Bayesian hierarchical model* is shown below:

$$Y_i \sim Normal(\mu_i, \sigma_g^2), \text{ where } log(\mu_i) = \alpha + \sum_{k=1}^{p} X_{ik}\beta_k \qquad (2)$$

The only difference in this regression formulation compared to Eq. 1 is that the variance, σ_g^2, varies based on the school group, g.

6   Results

The predictive models of dwell time were trained and compared using student-level leave-one-out cross-validation. We used cross-validation to compare the performance of the Pooled Model, the Group-Specific Model, and the Hierarchical Model. We report R^2, root mean squared error (RMSE), and mean absolute error (MAE) averaged across each cross-validation fold. The performance of each model is reported on the entire dataset as well as the performance for each visitor group.

Each model was trained using Markov chain Monte Carlo (MCMC) sampling in R using the JAGS framework [31]. To check the convergence of the sampling, we used the Gelman-Rubin diagnostic, which is commonly used for evaluating MCMC convergence [32]. For each of the models, we drew 3,000 MCMC samples after omitting the first 1,000 for burn-in. The process of burn-in is performed to ensure the convergence of the Markov chain in MCMC sampling. The final predictive models used the means of the 3,000 samples for each model parameter. Within each of the predictive models, the coefficients of the features, s, are assigned a prior distribution. For each , we used a double exponential prior with mean 0 to operate in the same manner as Lasso regression priors. This encouraged many of the feature coefficients to be as close to 0 as possible, resulting in only a few selected features as significant. The group-level variance parameters, σ_g^2, also used a shared prior distribution to relate information across groups. We chose the Gamma distribution with shape and scale parameters equal to 0.1. Each of the prior distributions chosen for this work were relatively uninformative and thus weak. This forced the posterior distributions of the model parameters to be largely affected by the data rather than our prior beliefs.

6.1   Predictive Accuracy

We compared the accuracy of the three Bayesian linear models: the Pooled Model, Group-Specific Model, and Hierarchical Model. Table 1 shows the results for each model in predicting visitor dwell time (seconds). The Hierarchical Model outperformed both the Pooled and Group-Specific models for all visitor groups. For Group 1, the Pooled Model outperformed the competing models, but for Groups 2 and 3, the Hierarchical Model performed best with respect to the three evaluation metrics.

The Group-Specific models were each trained on data from a single group, and then each model was evaluated only using data from that group. The total predictive performance of the Group-Specific Models was calculated by aggregating the predictions of each of the three models and calculating R^2, RMSE, and MAE with the total data. An explanation for why this modeling approach performed relatively poorly its risk of overfitting to a specific group; each visitor group only consisted of 20–40 visitors. Pooling the data and ignoring group-level characteristics yield good results but risks underfitting the data by losing group-specific information about the visitors. The Hierarchical Model takes advantage of both modeling approaches by incorporating group-level information

Table 1. Predictive performance of the three linear models.

Model type	Context	R^2	RMSE	MAE
Pooled	*All Groups*	0.514	93.720	68.334
	Group 1	**0.425**	**85.846**	**72.532**
	Group 2	0.727	70.429	47.583
	Group 3	0.370	118.319	82.637
Group-Specific	*All Groups*	0.285	110.882	81.457
	Group 1	0.303	96.270	74.216
	Group 2	0.685	75.616	54.567
	Group 3	−0.116	157.409	117.060
Hierarchical	*All Groups*	**0.536**	**91.593**	**67.690**
	Group 1	0.411	88.488	72.649
	Group 2	**0.742**	**68.444**	**47.338**
	Group 3	**0.428**	**112.713**	**80.582**

but keeping all data instances pooled using a shared prior for the group-level variance. An alternative approach to hierarchical modeling is to train a set of feature coefficients for each visitor group. However, this approach would multiply the number of model parameters by the number of visitor groups, which risks poor performance due to the limited size of the data sample.

6.2 Posterior Distributions of Model Parameters

Bayesian models allow summarization and comparison of model parameters by using the MCMC samples that were directly taken from their posterior distribution. As the Hierarchical Model outperformed both the Pooled and Group-Specific models, we summarize the model parameters' posterior distributions of the Hierarchical Model.

Table 2 displays the mean and standard deviation (SD) for each of the model parameters from the Hierarchical Model. Since each model induced double exponential priors on the feature coefficients, many of the features resulted in non-significant coefficients. We report the 10 features with the largest coefficients in terms of absolute value, including the model intercept, noting that features from each modality were chosen as being significant. The remaining features had posterior distributions that resulted in a mean of 0. The significant features for the posture modality were *Total Position Change* and *Head Variance*. For eye gaze, the significant features were *AOI-Labels* and *AOI-Interface*. For facial expression, the features were *AU12*, *AU7*, and *AU2*. The features for the interaction log modality were *Total Taps* and *Total Info Taps*.

Table 2. Posterior parameter distributions for Bayesian Hierarchical linear model.

	Mean	SD
Intercept	5.344	0.046
AU12	−0.197	0.050
AOI-interface	−0.197	0.080
Total position change	−0.151	0.052
AU7	−0.130	0.049
Head variance	0.082	0.095
AOI-labels	0.081	0.040
AU2	−0.080	0.044
Total info taps	0.068	0.056
Total taps	−0.060	0.043

7   Conclusion and Future Work

Multimodal learning analytics offers significant potential to advance our understanding of museum visitor engagement. However, museums pose distinctive challenges for modeling learner engagement, including the brief duration of visitor dwell times, as well as visitor populations that range broadly in age, prior knowledge, and socio-cultural background. To address these challenges, we have introduced a multimodal Bayesian hierarchical modeling framework for modeling visitor engagement with interactive science museum exhibits. Leveraging multimodal data on visitor interactions with an interactive game-based exhibit for environmental sustainability education across three diverse groups of visitors, we found that Bayesian hierarchical models outperform competing baseline methods. Furthermore, results indicate that features from each modality contributed significantly toward predicting visitor dwell time, underscoring the promise of multimodal learning analytic techniques for modeling visitor engagement.

There are several promising directions for future research. First, extending multimodal models of visitor engagement beyond predicting visitor dwell time to capture patterns of visitors' cognitive, affective, and behavioral engagement is a key next step. Furthermore, adapting multimodal learning analytic techniques to account for the "messiness" of free-choice learning, including fluid grouping at exhibits [12] and complex patterns of movement across the museum floor [10], is an important challenge. Extending this work to other science museums as well as other informal learning contexts (e.g., science centers, aquariums, zoos, and other public spaces) will help reveal and strengthen the generalizability of this approach. Finally, it will be critical to investigate how multimodal learning analytics can inform iterative cycles of design and development by exhibit designers, as well as best practices of museum educators to enhance high-quality visitor engagement in science museums.

Acknowledgements. The authors would like to thank the staff and visitors of the North Carolina Museum of Natural Sciences. This research was supported by the National Science Foundation under Grant DRL-1713545. Any opinions, findings, and conclusions or recommendations expressed in this material are those of the authors and do not necessarily reflect the views of the National Science Foundation.

References

1. Hein, G.: Learning science in informal environments: people, places, and pursuits. Museums Soc. Issues **4**(1), 113–124 (2009)
2. Falk, J., Dierking, L.: Learning from Museums. Rowman & Littlefield (2018)
3. Blikstein, P., Worsley, M.: Multimodal learning analytics and education data mining: using computational technologies to measure complex learning tasks. J. Learn. Anal. **3**(2), 220–238 (2016)
4. Oviatt, S., Grafsgaard, J., Chen, L., Ochoa, X.: Multimodal learning analytics: assessing learners' mental state during the process of learning. In: The Handbook of Multimodal-Multisensor Interfaces: Signal Processing, Architectures, and Detection of Emotion and Cognition, vol. 2, pp. 331–374 (2018)
5. Bosch, N., et al.: Detecting student emotions in computer-enabled classrooms. In: Proceedings of the 25th International Joint Conference on Artificial Intelligence, pp. 4125–4129 (2016)
6. DeFalco, J., et al.: Detecting and addressing frustration in a serious game for military training. Int. J. Artif. Intell. Educ. **28**(2), 152–193 (2018)
7. Diamond, J., Horn, M., Uttal, D.: Practical Evaluation Guide: Tools for Museums and Other Informal Educational Settings. Rowman & Littlefield (2016)
8. Lane, H.C., Noren, D., Auerbach, D., Birch, M., Swartout, W.: Intelligent tutoring goes to the museum in the big city: a pedagogical agent for informal science education. In: Biswas, G., Bull, S., Kay, J., Mitrovic, A. (eds.) AIED 2011. LNCS (LNAI), vol. 6738, pp. 155–162. Springer, Heidelberg (2011). https://doi.org/10.1007/978-3-642-21869-9_22
9. Long, D., McKlin, T., Weisling, A., Martin, W., Guthrie, H., Magerko, B.: Trajectories of physical engagement and expression in a co-creative museum installation. In: Proceedings of the 12th Annual ACM Conference on Creativity and Cognition, pp. 246–257 (2019)
10. Shapiro, B., Hall, R., Owens, D.: Developing and using interaction geography in a museum. Int. J. Comput.-Support. Collaborative Learn. **12**(4), 377–399 (2017)
11. Halverson, L., Graham, C.: Learner engagement in blended learning environments: a conceptual framework. Online Learn. **23**(2), 145–178 (2019)
12. Block, F., et al.: Fluid grouping: quantifying group engagement around interactive tabletop exhibits in the wild. In: Proceedings of the 33rd Annual ACM Conference on Human Factors in Computing Systems, pp. 867–876 (2015)
13. Knutson, K., Lyon, M., Crowley, K., Giarratani, L.: Flexible interventions to increase family engagement at natural history museum dioramas. Curator: Museum J. **59**(4), 339–352 (2016)
14. Baltrušaitis, T., Ahuja, C., Morency, L.: Multimodal machine learning: a survey and taxonomy. IEEE Trans. Pattern Anal. Mach. Intell. **41**(2), 423–443 (2018)
15. Aslan, S., et al.: Investigating the impact of a real-time, multimodal student engagement analytics technology in authentic classrooms. In: Proceedings of the 2019 CHI Conference on Human Factors in Computing Systems, pp. 1–12 (2019)
16. Archambault, I., Dupéré, V.: Joint trajectories of behavioral, affective, and cognitive engagement in elementary school. J. Educ. Res. **110**(2), 188–198 (2017)

17. Sawyer, R., Rowe, J., Azevedo, R., Lester, J.: Modeling player engagement with Bayesian hierarchical models. In: Proceedings of the 14th AAAI Conference on Artificial Intelligence and Interactive Digital Entertainment, pp. 215–221 (2018)

18. Rowe, J.P., Lobene, E.V., Mott, B.W., Lester, J.C.: Play in the museum: design and development of a game-based learning exhibit for informal science education. Int. J. Gaming Comput.-Mediated Simul. **9**(3), 96–113 (2017)

19. Baltrušaitis, T., Robinson, P., Morency, L.: OpenFace: an open source facial behavior analysis toolkit. In: Proceedings of the 2016 IEEE Winter Conference on Applications of Computer Vision, pp. 1–10. IEEE (2016)

20. Aung, A., Ramakrishnan, A., Whitehill, J.: Who are they looking at? Automatic eye gaze following for classroom observation video analysis, pp. 166–170 (2018)

21. Henderson, N., Rowe, J., Mott, B., Brawner, K., Baker, R., Lester, J.: 4D affect detection: improving frustration detection in game-based learning with posture-based temporal data fusion. In: Proceedings of the 20th International Conference on Artificial Intelligence in Education, Chicago, Illinois, pp. 144–156 (2019)

22. Patwardhan, A., Knapp, G.: Multimodal affect recognition using kinect. arXiv preprint arXiv: 1607.02652 (2016)

23. Zhang, Z.: Microsoft kinect sensor and its effect. IEEE Multimedia **19**(2), 4–10 (2012)

24. Sawyer, R., Smith, A., Rowe, J., Azevedo, R., Lester, J.: Enhancing student models in game-based learning with facial expression recognition. In: Proceedings of the 25th Conference on User Modeling, Adaptation and Personalization, pp. 192–201 (2017)

25. Grafsgaard, J., Wiggins, J., Vail, A., Boyer, K., Wiebe, E., Lester, J.: The additive value of multimodal features for predicting engagement, frustration, and learning during tutoring. In: Proceedings of the 16th International Conference on Multimodal Interaction, pp. 42–49 (2014)

26. Vail, A., Wiggins, J., Grafsgaard, J., Boyer, K., Wiebe, E., Lester, J.: The affective impact of tutor questions: predicting frustration and engagement. In: International Educational Data Mining Society (2016)

27. Rayner, K., Li, X., Williams, C., Cave, K., Well, A.: Eye movements during information processing tasks: individual differences and cultural effects. Vis. Res. **47**(21), 2714–2726 (2007)

28. Emerson, A., Sawyer, R., Azevedo, R., Lester, J.: Gaze-enhanced student modeling for game-based learning. In: Proceedings of the 26th ACM Conference on User Modeling, Adaptation and Personalization, Singapore, pp. 63–72 (2018)

29. Grafsgaard, J., Boyer, K., Wiebe, E., Lester, J.: Analyzing posture and affect in task- oriented tutoring. In: Proceedings of the 25th Florida Artificial Intelligence Research Society Conference, pp. 438–443 (2012)

30. Reich, B., Ghosh, S.: Bayesian Statistical Methods. CRC Press, Boca Raton (2019)

31. Plummer, M.: JAGS: a program for analysis of Bayesian graphical models using Gibbs sampling. In: Proceedings of the 3rd International Conference on Distributed Statistical Computing, pp. 1–10 (2003)

32. Gelman, A., Rubin, D.: Inference from iterative simulation using multiple sequences. Stat. Sci. **7**, 457–511 (1992)

Fooling Automatic Short Answer Grading Systems

Anna Filighera(✉)(iD), Tim Steuer(iD), and Christoph Rensing

Multimedia Communications Lab, Technical University of Darmstadt,
Darmstadt, Germany
{anna.filighera,tim.steuer,christoph.rensing}@kom.tu-darmstadt.de

Abstract. With the rising success of adversarial attacks on many NLP tasks, systems which actually operate in an adversarial scenario need to be reevaluated. For this purpose, we pose the following research question: *How difficult is it to fool automatic short answer grading systems?* In particular, we investigate the robustness of the state of the art automatic short answer grading system proposed by Sung et al. towards cheating in the form of *universal adversarial trigger* employment. These are short token sequences that can be prepended to students' answers in an exam to artificially improve their automatically assigned grade. Such triggers are especially critical as they can easily be used by anyone once they are found. In our experiments, we discovered triggers which allow students to pass exams with passing thresholds of 50% without answering a single question correctly. Furthermore, we show that such triggers generalize across models and datasets in this scenario, nullifying the defense strategy of keeping grading models or data secret.

Keywords: Automatic short answer grading · Adversarial attacks · Automatic assessment

1 Introduction

Adversarial data sample perturbations, also called adversarial examples, intending to fool classification models have been a popular area of research in recent years. Many state of the art (SOTA) models have been shown to be vulnerable to adversarial attacks on various data sets [8,44,47].

On image data, the extent of modifications needed to change a sample's classified label are often so small they are imperceptible to humans [2]. On natural language data, perturbations can more easily be detected by humans. However, it is still possible to minimally modify samples so that the semantic meaning does not change but the class assigned by the model does [3,6,13,17, 22,29,30].

While the existence of such adversarial examples unveils our models' shortcomings in many fields, they are especially worrying in settings where we actually expect to face adversaries. In this work, we focus on one such setting: automatic short answer grading (ASAG) systems employed in exams. ASAG systems

I. I. Bittencourt et al. (Eds.): AIED 2020, LNAI 12163, pp. 177–190, 2020.
https://doi.org/10.1007/978-3-030-52237-7_15

take free-text answers and evaluate their quality with regards to their semantic content, completeness and relevance to the answered question. These free-text answers are provided by students and are typically somewhere between a phrase and a paragraph long.

The willingness of college students to cheat has been well-studied [1, 9, 11, 18, 36, 37]. And while the exact percentage of cheating students varies greatly from study to study, Whitley [42] reports a mean of 43.1% of students cheating on examinations over 36 studies in his review. Klein et al. [19] report similar values for cheating on exams in their large scale comparison of cheating behaviors in different schools.

In these studies cheating behavior included copying from other students, getting the exam questions beforehand or bringing a cheat sheet to the exam. We argue that exploiting weaknesses in automatic grading schemes is just another, albeit less explored, form of cheating and expect the students' willingness to exhibit such behavior to be similar. Therefore, if we wish to employ automated grading systems in exams, we should ensure that the perceived cost of cheating them outweighs the benefits.

The perceived cost of cheating is made up of various factors, such as the punishment when caught, moral considerations or the difficulty of cheating in the first place [26]. In this work, we aim to investigate the last factor: *How difficult is it to fool automatic short answer grading systems?*

For this purpose, we first reproduce the SOTA approach to ASAG [39] which is based on the transformer model BERT [10]. Then we subject the reproduced models to adversarial attacks. In particular, we employ and modify the universal trigger attack proposed by Wallace et al. [41]. It generates short sequences of tokens, called *universal adversarial triggers*, which try to make a model predict a target class regardless of the actual sample.

In our context, students could prepend such a universal trigger targeted at the *correct* class to all of their answers in an exam to artificially improve their score. An example of such a trigger can be seen in Table 1. This kind of universal trigger attack is especially critical as such triggers can be easily employed by anyone once they are found.

In this work we make the following novel contributions:

- Application of SOTA natural language processing insights to the educational scenario of exam grading
- Modification of Wallace et al.'s universal trigger attack to make it more targeted at a specific class, namely the *correct* class
- Investigation of trigger transferability across datasets and models

2   Related Work

Two research areas are relevant for our work: automatic short answer grading and adversarial attacks.

Table 1. An example showing how prepending the trigger sequence "none exits" to a student answer - taken from SCiENTSBANK's question EM-21b's unseen answers [12] - changes the prediction from *incorrect* to *correct*.

Question:	Georgia found one brown mineral and one black mineral. How will she know which one is harder?
Reference Answer:	The harder mineral will leave a scratch on the less hard mineral. If the black mineral is harder, the brown mineral will have a scratch
Student Answer:	that it stay the scratch. → *incorrect*
Triggered Answer:	none exits that it stay the scratch. → *correct*

2.1 Adversarial Attacks in NLP

Adversarial attacks can be categorized into input dependent and input independent attacks. Input dependent attacks aim to modify **specific** inputs so that the model misclassifies them. Strategically inserting, deleting or replacing words with their synonyms [29], their nearest neighbors in the embedding space [3] or other words which have a high probability of appearing in the same context [47] are examples of such an attack. Samanta and Mehta [35] also consider typos which in turn result in valid words, e.g. goods and good, for their replacement candidate pool. Modifications can also be made on the character level by inserting noise, such as swapping adjacent characters or completely scrambling words [6]. Finally, the text can also be paraphrased to change the syntactic structure [17].

Input agnostic attacks, on the other hand, aim to find perturbations that lead to misclassifications on **all** samples. For instance, this can be done by selecting a single perturbation in the embedding space which is then applied to all tokens indiscriminately [15]. Alternatively, Ribeiro et al. [30] propose an approach that first paraphrases specific inputs to find *semantically equivalent adversaries* and then generalizes found examples to universal, *semantically equivalent adversarial rules*. Rules are selected to maximize semantic equivalence when applied to a sample, induce as many misclassifications as possible and are finally vetted by humans. An example of such a rule is "What is" → "What's".

Another input independent approach involves concatenating a series of adversarial words - triggers - to the beginning of every input sample [5]. The universal trigger attack [41] utilized in this work also belongs to this category. In Sect. 4 the attack is explained in more detail. Additional information on adversarial attacks can also be found in various surveys [44,48].

2.2 Automatic Short Answer Grading

Systems that automatically score student answers have been explored for multiple decades. Proposed approaches include clustering student answers into groups of similar answers and assigning grades to whole clusters instead of individual answers [4,16,45,46], grading based on manually constructed rules or models of ideal answers [21,43] and automatically assigning grades based on the answer's similarity to given reference answers. We will focus on similarity-based approaches here because most recent SOTA results were obtained using this kind of approach. However, more information on other approaches can be found in various surveys [7,14,32].

The earlier similarity-based approaches involve manually defining features that try to capture the similarity of answers on multiple levels [12,24,25,33,34,38]. Surface features, such as lexical overlap or answer length ratios, are utilized by most feature engineered approaches. Semantic similarity measures are also common, be it in the form of sentence embedding distances or measures derived from knowledge bases like WordNet [28]. Some forms of syntactic features are also often employed. Dependency graph alignment or measures based on the part-of-speech tags' distribution in the answers would be examples of syntactic features. A further discussion of various features can be found in [27].

More recently, deep learning methods have also been adapted to the task of automatic short answer grading [20,31,40]. The key difference to the feature engineered approaches lies in the fact that the text's representation in the feature space is learned by the model itself. The best performing model (in terms of accuracy and F1 score) on the benchmark 3-way SemEval dataset [12] was proposed by Sung et al. [39]. They utilize the uncased BERT base model [10] which was pre-trained on the BooksCorpus [49] and the English Wikipedia. It was pre-trained on the tasks of predicting randomly masked input tokens and whether a sentence is another's successor or not. Sung et al. then fine-tune this deep bidirectional language representation model to predict whether an answer is *correct, incorrect* or *contradictory* compared to a reference answer. For this purpose, they append a feed-forward classification layer to the BERT model. The authors claim that their model outperforms even human graders.

3   Reproduction of SOTA ASAG Model

To reproduce the results reported by Sung et al. [39], we trained 10 models with the hyperparameters stated in the paper. Unreported hyperparameters were selected close to the original BERT model's values with minimal tuning. The models were trained on the shuffled training split contained in the SCIENTS-BANK dataset of the SemEval-2013 challenge. As in the reference paper, we use the 3-way task of predicting answers to be *correct, incorrect* or *contradictory*. Then the models were evaluated on the test split. The test set contains three distinct categories: unseen answers, unseen questions and unseen domains. Unseen answers are answers to questions for which some answers have already been seen during training. Unseen questions are completely new questions and the unseen domains category contains questions belonging to domains the model has not seen during training.

We were not able to reproduce the reported results exactly with this setup. Out of the 10 models, Model 4 and 8 performed best. A comparison of their and the reported model's results can be seen in Table 2. The 10 models' average performance can be seen in Fig. 1. Since the reported results are mostly within one or two standard deviations of the results achieved in our experiments, more in-depth hyperparameter tuning and reruns with different random seeds may yield the reported results. Alternatively, the authors may have taken steps that they did not discuss in the paper. However, as this is not the focus of this work, we deemed the reproduced models sufficient for our experiments.

Table 2. Performance of best reproduced models, Model 4 and 8, compared to the results reported by Sung et al. [39] in terms of accuracy (Acc), macro-averaged F1 score (M-F1) and weighted-averaged F1 score (W-F1). Each category's best result is marked in bold.

	Unseen answers			Unseen questions			Unseen domains		
	Acc	M-F1	W-F1	Acc	M-F1	W-F1	Acc	M-F1	W-F1
#4	0.744	0.703	0.741	*0.675*	0.555	*0.665*	0.624	0.490	0.609
#8	0.737	0.690	0.732	0.674	0.561	0.662	*0.670*	*0.599*	*0.661*
Ref.	*0.759*	*0.720*	*0.758*	0.653	*0.575*	0.648	0.638	0.579	0.634

4   Universal Trigger Attack

In this work, we employ the universal trigger attack proposed by Wallace et al. [41]. It is targeted, meaning that a target class is specified and the search will try to find triggers that lead the model to predict the specified class, regardless of the sample's actual class. The attack begins with an initial trigger, such as "the the the", and iteratively searches for good replacements for the words contained in the trigger. The replacement strategy is based on the HotFlip attack proposed by Ebrahimi et al. [13]. For each batch of samples, candidates are chosen out of all tokens in the vocabulary so that the loss for the target class is minimized. Then, a beam search over candidates is performed to find the ordered combination of triggers which maximizes the batch's loss.

We augment this attack by also considering more target label focused objective functions for the beam search than the batch's loss. Namely, we experiment with naively maximizing the number of target label predictions and the targeted LogSoftmax function depicted in Eq. 1. Here, $L = \{correct, incorrect, contradictory\}$, t is the target label, n denotes the number of samples in the batch $\mathbf{x}$ and $f_l(x)$ represents the model's output for label l's node before the softmax activation function given a sample x.

$$TargetedLogSoftmax(t, \mathbf{x}) = \sum_{i=0}^{n} log \left(\frac{exp(f_t(x_i))}{\sum_{j \epsilon L} exp(f_j(x_i))} \right) \tag{1}$$

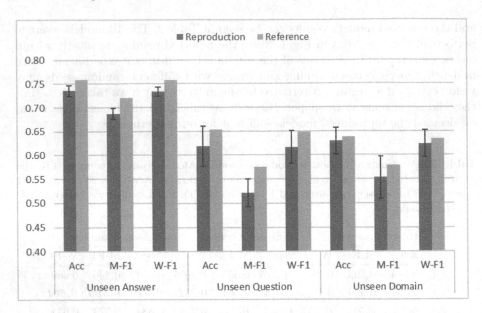

Fig. 1. Average performance of the 10 reproduction models compared to the results reported by Sung et al. [39]. The black bars represent one standard deviation in each direction. Please note that the y axis begins at 0.4 instead of 0.

5   Experiments

In this section, we first give a short overview of the datasets used in our experiments. Then, we present the best triggers found, followed by a short investigation of the effect of trigger length on the number of successful flips. Next, the effect of our modified objective function is investigated. Finally, we report on the transferability of triggers across models.

5.1   Data

The SemEval ASAG challenge consists of two distinct datasets: SCIENTSBANK and BEETLE. While the BEETLE set only contains questions concerning electricity, the SCIENTSBANK corpus includes questions of various scientific domains, such as biology, physics and geography. We do not include the class distribution of the 3-way task here, as it can be found in the original [12] and the ASAG reference paper [39].

5.2   Experiment Setup

Unless explicitly stated, all experiments were conducted in the following way. Model 8 was chosen as the victim model because it has the overall best performance of all reproduction models. See Table 2 for reference. Since the model was trained on the complete SCIENTSBANK training split as stated in the reference paper, we selected the BEETLE training split as basis for our attacks. While the class labels were homogenized for both datasets in the SemEval challenge, the datasets are still vastly different. They were collected in dissimilar settings, by different authors and deal with disparate domains [12]. **This is important, as successful attacks with this setup imply transferability of triggers across datasets.** In practice, this would allow attackers to substitute secret datasets with their own corpora and still find successful attacks on the original data. To the best of our knowledge, experiments investigating the transferability of natural language triggers across datasets are a novel contribution of our work.

From the BEETLE training set all 1227 *incorrect* samples were selected. The goal of the attack was to flip their classification label to *correct*. We would also have liked to try and flip *contradictory* examples. However, the model was only able to correctly predict 18 of the 1049 *contradictory* samples without any malicious intervention necessary. Finally, the triggers found are evaluated on the SCIENTSBANK test split.

5.3 Results

In the related work, the success of an attack is most often measured in the drop in accuracy it is able to achieve. However, this would overestimate the performance in our scenario as we are only interested in *incorrect* answers which are falsely graded as *correct* in contrast to answers which are labeled as *contradictory*. Therefore, we also report the absolute number of successful flips from *incorrect* to *correct*.

During the iterative trigger search process described in Sect. 4 a few thousand triggers were evaluated on the BEETLE set. Of these, the 20 triggers with the most achieved flips were evaluated on the test set and of these, the best triggers can be seen in Table 3. On the unseen answers test split, the model without any triggers misclassified 12.4% (31) of all *incorrect* samples as *correct*. The triggers "none varies" and "none would" managed to flip an additional 8.8% of samples so that 21.3% (53) are misclassified in total. On the unseen questions split, the base misclassification rate was 27.4% (101) and "none would" added another 10.1% for a total of 37.5% (138). On the unseen domains split, "none elsewhere" increased the misclassification rate from 22.0% (491) to 37.1% (826).

Effect of Trigger Length. Wallace et al. [41] state that the trigger length is a trade-off between effectiveness and stealth. They experimented with prepending triggers of lengths between 1 and 10 tokens and found longer triggers to have higher success rates. This differs from observations made in our experiments. When the *correct* class is targeted, a trigger length of two achieves the best results, as can be seen in Table 3. On the unseen answers split, the best trigger of length 3 is "heats affected penetrated" and it manages to flip only 42 samples. The number of successful flips further decreases to 9 for the best trigger of length 4, "##ired unaffected least being". The same trend also holds for the other test

Table 3. The triggers with the most flips from *incorrect* to *correct* for each test split. The number of model 8's misclassifications without any triggers can be found in the last row. For the sake of comparability with related work, the accuracy for *incorrect* samples is also given. UA stands for "unseen answers", UQ denotes "unseen questions" and UD represents "unseen domains".

Triggers	Number of flips			Accuracy		
	UA	UQ	UD	UA	UQ	UD
none varies	53	134	687	71.08	54.62	63.69
none would	53	138	810	41.77	31.25	31.15
none elsewhere	50	121	826	47.79	36.14	37.93
Base misclassification	31	101	491	84.74	70.65	76.93

splits but is omitted here for brevity. This difference in observation may be due to the varying definitions of attack success. Wallace et al. [41] view a trigger as successful as soon as the model assigns **any** class other than the true label, while we only accept triggers which cause a prediction of the class *correct*. The educational setting of this work may also be a factor.

Effect of Objective Function. We compared the performance of the three different objective functions described in Sect. 4, namely the original function proposed by Wallace et al. [41], the targeted LogSoftmax depicted in Eq. 1 and the naive maximization of the number of target label predictions. To make the comparison as fair as possible while keeping the computation time reasonable, we fixed the hyperparameters of the attack to a beam size of 4 and a candidate set size of 100. The attack was run for the same number of iterations exactly once for each function. The best triggers found by each function can be seen in Table 4. The performance is relatively similar, with the targeted function achieving the most flips on all test splits, closely followed by the original function and, lastly, the naive prediction maximization. Qualitative observation of all produced triggers showed that the original function's triggers resulted in more flips from *incorrect* to *contradictory* than the proposed targeted function's.

Table 4. A comparison of the objective functions.

Objective function	Best trigger	Number of flips		
		UA	UQ	UD
Naive	none cause	42	107	647
Original	nobody penetrated	43	121	673
Targeted	none elsewhere	50	121	826

Transferability. One of the most interesting aspects of triggers relates to the ability to find them on one model and use them to fool another model. In this setting, attackers do not require access to the original model, which may be kept secret in a grading scenario. Trigger transferability across models allows them to train a substitute model for the trigger search and then attack the actual grading model with found triggers. We investigate this aspect by applying all good triggers found on Model 8 to Model 4. Note that this also included triggers from a search on the SCIENTSBANK training split and not just the BEETLE training set. The best performing triggers in terms of flips induced in Model 4 can be seen in Table 5. We also included the triggers which performed best on Model 8 here.

Table 5. Performance of the triggers found on Model 8 evaluated on Model 4. For reference, the number of flips originally achieved on Model 8 are also given. The first rows are the best performing triggers on Model 4. The middle block contains the best triggers on Model 8. Finally, the last row gives the number of samples misclassified by Model 4 without any triggers.

Trigger	Number of flips on Model 4 and 8					
	UA		UQ		UD	
	4	8	4	8	4	8
nowhere changes	**81**	51	**184**	135	957	640
anywhere.	58	45	108	105	**1027**	682
none else	73	53	158	136	941	818
none varies	49	53	79	134	576	687
none would	38	53	97	**138**	495	810
none elsewhere	60	50	115	121	701	**826**
Base misclassification	44	31	100	101	646	491

While there are triggers that perform well on both models, e.g. "none else", the best triggers for each model differ. Interestingly, triggers like "nowhere changes" or "anywhere." perform even better on Model 4 than the best triggers found for the original victim model. On UA, "nowhere changes" flips 14.9% of all *incorrect* samples to *correct*. In addition to the base misclassification rate, this leads to a misclassification rate of 32.5%. On UQ, the same trigger increases the misclassification rate by 22.8% to a total of 50%. On the UD split, prepending "anywhere." to all *incorrect* samples raises the rate by 17.1% to 46.1%.

As a curious side note, the trigger "heats affected penetrated" discussed in the section regarding trigger length performed substantially better on Model 4, so that it was a close contender for the best trigger list.

6   Discussion and Conclusion

In our scenario, a misclassification rate of 37.5% means that students using triggers only need to answer 20% of the questions correctly to pass a test that was designed to have a passing threshold of 50%. If an exam would be graded by Model 4, students could pass the test by simply prepending "nowhere changes" to their answers without answering a single question correctly! However, this does not mean that these triggers flip any arbitrary answer, as a large portion of the flipped *incorrect* answers showed at least a vague familiarity with the question's topic similar to the example displayed in Table 1. Additionally, these rates were achieved on the unseen questions split. Translated to our scenario this implies that we would expect our model to grade questions similar to questions it has seen during training but for which it has not seen a single example answer, besides the reference answer. To take an example out of the actual dataset, a model trained to grade the question *What happens to earth materials during deposition?* would also be expected to grade *What happens to earth materials during erosion?* with only the help of the reference answer "Earth materials are worn away and moved during erosion.". The results suggest that the current SOTA approach is ill-equipped to generalize its grading behavior in such a way.

Nevertheless, even if we supply training answers to every question the misclassification rates are quite high with 21.3% and 32.5% for Model 8 and 4, respectively. Considering how easy these triggers are employed by everyone once someone has found them, this is concerning. Thus, defensive measures should be investigated and put into place before using automatic short answer grading systems in practice.

In conclusion, we have shown the SOTA automatic short answer grading system to be vulnerable to cheating in the form of universal trigger employment. We also showed that triggers can be successful even if they were found on a disparate dataset or model. This makes the attack easier to execute, as attackers can simply substitute secret grading components in their search for triggers. Lastly, we also proposed a way to make the attack more focused on flipping samples from a specific source class to a target class.

7   Future Work

There are several points of interest which we plan to study further in the future. For one, finding adversarial attacks on natural language tasks is a very active field at the moment. Exposing ASAG systems to other forms of attacks, such as attacks based on paraphrasing, would be very interesting. Additionally, one could also explore defensive measures to make grading models more robust. An in-depth analysis of why these attacks work would be beneficial here. Finally, expanding the transferability study conducted in this work to other kinds of models, such as RoBERTa [23] or feature engineering-based approaches, and additional datasets may lead to interesting findings as well.

References

1. Ahmadi, A.: Cheating on exams in the Iranian EFL context. J. Acad. Ethics **10**(2), 151–170 (2012). https://doi.org/10.1007/s10805-012-9156-5
2. Akhtar, N., Mian, A.: Threat of adversarial attacks on deep learning in computer vision: a survey. IEEE Access **6**, 14410–14430 (2018)
3. Alzantot, M., Sharma, Y., Elgohary, A., Ho, B.J., Srivastava, M., Chang, K.W.: Generating natural language adversarial examples. In: Proceedings of the 2018 Conference on Empirical Methods in Natural Language Processing, pp. 2890–2896 (2018)
4. Basu, S., Jacobs, C., Vanderwende, L.: Powergrading: a clustering approach to amplify human effort for short answer grading. Trans. Assoc. Comput. Linguist. **1**, 391–402 (2013)
5. Behjati, M., Moosavi-Dezfooli, S.M., Baghshah, M.S., Frossard, P.: Universal adversarial attacks on text classifiers. In: ICASSP 2019–2019 IEEE International Conference on Acoustics, Speech and Signal Processing (ICASSP), pp. 7345–7349. IEEE (2019)
6. Belinkov, Y., Bisk, Y.: Synthetic and natural noise both break neural machine translation. arXiv preprint arXiv:1711.02173 (2017)
7. Burrows, S., Gurevych, I., Stein, B.: The eras and trends of automatic short answer grading. Int. J. Artif. Intell. Educ. **25**(1), 60–117 (2015). https://doi.org/10.1007/s40593-014-0026-8
8. Carlini, N., Wagner, D.: Adversarial examples are not easily detected: bypassing ten detection methods. In: Proceedings of the 10th ACM Workshop on Artificial Intelligence and Security, pp. 3–14. ACM (2017)
9. Danielsen, R.D., Simon, A.F., Pavlick, R.: The culture of cheating: from the classroom to the exam room. J. Phys. Assist. Educ. (Phys. Assist. Educ. Assoc.) **17**(1), 23–29 (2006)
10. Devlin, J., Chang, M.W., Lee, K., Toutanova, K.: BERT: pre-training of deep bidirectional transformers for language understanding. In: Proceedings of the 2019 Conference of the North American Chapter of the Association for Computational Linguistics: Human Language Technologies, Volume 1 (Long and Short Papers), pp. 4171–4186 (2019)
11. Diekhoff, G.M., LaBeff, E.E., Shinohara, K., Yasukawa, H.: College cheating in Japan and the United States. Res. High. Educ. **40**(3), 343–353 (1999). https://doi.org/10.1023/A:1018703217828
12. Dzikovska, M.O., et al.: SemEval-2013 task 7: the joint student response analysis and 8th recognizing textual entailment challenge. Technical report. North Texas State Univ., Denton (2013)
13. Ebrahimi, J., Rao, A., Lowd, D., Dou, D.: HotFlip: white-box adversarial examples for text classification. In: Proceedings of the 56th Annual Meeting of the Association for Computational Linguistics (Volume 2: Short Papers), pp. 31–36 (2018)
14. Galhardi, L.B., Brancher, J.D.: Machine learning approach for automatic short answer grading: a systematic review. In: Simari, G.R., Fermé, E., Gutiérrez Segura, F., Rodríguez Melquiades, J.A. (eds.) IBERAMIA 2018. LNCS (LNAI), vol. 11238, pp. 380–391. Springer, Cham (2018). https://doi.org/10.1007/978-3-030-03928-8_31

15. Gao, H., Oates, T.: Universal adversarial perturbation for text classification. arXiv preprint arXiv:1910.04618 (2019)
16. Horbach, A., Pinkal, M.: Semi-supervised clustering for short answer scoring. In: Proceedings of the Eleventh International Conference on Language Resources and Evaluation (LREC 2018) (2018)
17. Iyyer, M., Wieting, J., Gimpel, K., Zettlemoyer, L.: Adversarial example generation with syntactically controlled paraphrase networks. In: Proceedings of NAACL-HLT, pp. 1875–1885 (2018)
18. King, C.G., Guyette Jr., R.W., Piotrowski, C.: Online exams and cheating: an empirical analysis of business students' views. J. Educ. Online **6**(1), n1 (2009)
19. Klein, H.A., Levenburg, N.M., McKendall, M., Mothersell, W.: Cheating during the college years: how do business school students compare? J. Bus. Ethics **72**(2), 197–206 (2007). https://doi.org/10.1007/s10551-006-9165-7
20. Kumar, S., Chakrabarti, S., Roy, S.: Earth mover's distance pooling over Siamese LSTMs for automatic short answer grading. In: IJCAI, pp. 2046–2052 (2017)
21. Leacock, C., Chodorow, M.: C-rater: automated scoring of short-answer questions. Comput. Humanit. **37**(4), 389–405 (2003). https://doi.org/10.1023/A: 1025779619903
22. Liang, B., Li, H., Su, M., Bian, P., Li, X., Shi, W.: Deep text classification can be fooled. In: Proceedings of the 27th International Joint Conference on Artificial Intelligence, pp. 4208–4215. AAAI Press (2018)
23. Liu, Y., et al.: RoBERTa: a robustly optimized BERT pretraining approach. arXiv preprint arXiv:1907.11692 (2019)
24. Marvaniya, S., Saha, S., Dhamecha, T.I., Foltz, P., Sindhgatta, R., Sengupta, B.: Creating scoring rubric from representative student answers for improved short answer grading. In: Proceedings of the 27th ACM International Conference on Information and Knowledge Management, CIKM 2018, pp. 993–1002. Association for Computing Machinery, New York (2018). https://doi.org/10.1145/3269206. 3271755
25. Mohler, M., Bunescu, R., Mihalcea, R.: Learning to grade short answer questions using semantic similarity measures and dependency graph alignments. In: Proceedings of the 49th Annual Meeting of the Association for Computational Linguistics: Human Language Technologies-Volume 1, pp. 752–762. Association for Computational Linguistics (2011)
26. Murdock, T.B., Anderman, E.M.: Motivational perspectives on student cheating: toward an integrated model of academic dishonesty. Educ. Psychol. **41**(3), 129–145 (2006)
27. Padó, U.: Get semantic with me! the usefulness of different feature types for short-answer grading. In: Proceedings of COLING 2016, the 26th International Conference on Computational Linguistics: Technical Papers, pp. 2186–2195 (2016)
28. Pedersen, T., Patwardhan, S., Michelizzi, J.: Wordnet::similarity: measuring the relatedness of concepts. In: Demonstration Papers at HLT-NAACL 2004, pp. 38–41. Association for Computational Linguistics (2004)
29. Ren, S., Deng, Y., He, K., Che, W.: Generating natural language adversarial examples through probability weighted word saliency. In: Proceedings of the 57th Annual Meeting of the Association for Computational Linguistics, pp. 1085–1097 (2019)

30. Ribeiro, M.T., Singh, S., Guestrin, C.: Semantically equivalent adversarial rules for debugging NLP models. In: Proceedings of the 56th Annual Meeting of the Association for Computational Linguistics (Volume 1: Long Papers), pp. 856–865 (2018)

31. Riordan, B., Horbach, A., Cahill, A., Zesch, T., Lee, C.M.: Investigating neural architectures for short answer scoring. In: Proceedings of the 12th Workshop on Innovative Use of NLP for Building Educational Applications, pp. 159–168 (2017)

32. Roy, S., Narahari, Y., Deshmukh, O.D.: A perspective on computer assisted assessment techniques for short free-text answers. In: Ras, E., Joosten-ten Brinke, D. (eds.) CAA 2015. CCIS, vol. 571, pp. 96–109. Springer, Cham (2015). https://doi.org/10.1007/978-3-319-27704-2_10

33. Saha, S., Dhamecha, T.I., Marvaniya, S., Sindhgatta, R., Sengupta, B.: Sentence level or token level features for automatic short answer grading? Use both. In: Penstein Rosé, C., et al. (eds.) AIED 2018. LNCS (LNAI), vol. 10947, pp. 503–517. Springer, Cham (2018). https://doi.org/10.1007/978-3-319-93843-1_37

34. Sahu, A., Bhowmick, P.K.: Feature engineering and ensemble-based approach for improving automatic short-answer grading performance. IEEE Trans. Learn. Technol. **13**(1), 77–90 (2019)

35. Samanta, S., Mehta, S.: Towards crafting text adversarial samples. arXiv preprint arXiv:1707.02812 (2017)

36. Sheard, J., Dick, M., Markham, S., Macdonald, I., Walsh, M.: Cheating and plagiarism: perceptions and practices of first year IT students. ACM SIGCSE Bull. **34**, 183–187 (2002)

37. Smyth, M.L., Davis, J.R.: An examination of student cheating in the two-year college. Commun. Coll. Rev. **31**(1), 17–32 (2003)

38. Sultan, M.A., Salazar, C., Sumner, T.: Fast and easy short answer grading with high accuracy. In: Proceedings of the 2016 Conference of the North American Chapter of the Association for Computational Linguistics: Human Language Technologies, pp. 1070–1075 (2016)

39. Sung, C., Dhamecha, T.I., Mukhi, N.: Improving short answer grading using transformer-based pre-training. In: Isotani, S., Millán, E., Ogan, A., Hastings, P., McLaren, B., Luckin, R. (eds.) AIED 2019. LNCS (LNAI), vol. 11625, pp. 469–481. Springer, Cham (2019). https://doi.org/10.1007/978-3-030-23204-7_39

40. Tan, C., Wei, F., Wang, W., Lv, W., Zhou, M.: Multiway attention networks for modeling sentence pairs. In: IJCAI, pp. 4411–4417 (2018)

41. Wallace, E., Feng, S., Kandpal, N., Gardner, M., Singh, S.: Universal adversarial triggers for attacking and analyzing NLP. In: Proceedings of the 2019 Conference on Empirical Methods in Natural Language Processing and the 9th International Joint Conference on Natural Language Processing (EMNLP-IJCNLP), pp. 2153–2162 (2019)

42. Whitley, B.E.: Factors associated with cheating among college students: a review. Res. High. Educ. **39**(3), 235–274 (1998). https://doi.org/10.1023/A:1018724900565

43. Willis, A.: Using NLP to support scalable assessment of short free text responses. In: Proceedings of the Tenth Workshop on Innovative Use of NLP for Building Educational Applications, pp. 243–253 (2015)

44. Yuan, X., He, P., Zhu, Q., Li, X.: Adversarial examples: attacks and defenses for deep learning. IEEE Trans. Neural Netw. Learn. Syst. **30**(9), 2805–2824 (2019)

45. Zehner, F., Sälzer, C., Goldhammer, F.: Automatic coding of short text responses via clustering in educational assessment. Educ. Psychol. Meas. **76**(2), 280–303 (2016)

46. Zesch, T., Heilman, M., Cahill, A.: Reducing annotation efforts in supervised short answer scoring. In: Proceedings of the Tenth Workshop on Innovative Use of NLP for Building Educational Applications, pp. 124–132 (2015)
47. Zhang, H., Zhou, H., Miao, N., Li, L.: Generating fluent adversarial examples for natural languages. In: Proceedings of the 57th Annual Meeting of the Association for Computational Linguistics, pp. 5564–5569 (2019)
48. Zhang, W.E., Sheng, Q.Z., Alhazmi, A., Li, C.: Adversarial attacks on deep learning models in natural language processing: a survey (2019)
49. Zhu, Y., et al.: Aligning books and movies: towards story-like visual explanations by watching movies and reading books. In: Proceedings of the IEEE International Conference on Computer Vision, pp. 19–27 (2015)

Using Neural Tensor Networks for Open Ended Short Answer Assessment

Dipesh Gautam and Vasile Rus[✉]

The University of Memphis, Memphis, TN 38152, USA
{dgautam,vrus}@memphis.edu

Abstract. In this paper, we present a novel approach to leverage the power of Neural Tensor Networks (NTN) for student answer assessment in intelligent tutoring systems. The approach was evaluated on data collected using a dialogue based intelligent tutoring system (ITS). Particularly, we have experimented with different assessment models that were trained using features generated from knowledge graph embeddings derived with NTN. Our experiments showed that the model trained with the feature vectors generated with NTN, when trained with a combination of domain specific and domain general triplets, performs better than a previously proposed LSTM based approach.

Keywords: Knowledge graph · Neural Tensor Network · Answer assessment · Open ended short answer assessment · Entity vector embedding

1 Introduction

Natural language understanding is the foundation of assessment in conversational ITSs and other educational technologies that elicit freely generated natural language responses. Typically, automatic answer assessment methods measure the extent to which a given student answer or parts of it related or match some target/benchmark concepts. These benchmark or expected concepts are specified by subject matter experts and other experts (e.g., experts in pedagogy or linguistics). If the student answer or parts of it are semantically similar to the target (reference) concepts then the student response is deemed correct; otherwise, it is deemed incorrect. Semantic similarity methods can be categorized as either knowledge based, such as methods that rely on WordNet for computing similarity among concepts, versus corpus based, such as Latent Semantic Analysis (LSA) [10] and Latent Dirichlet Allocation (LDA) [4]. Another category of methods use a combination of knowledge based and corpus based methods [16,20].

There is a major limitation of similarity based assessment methods: they assume the student answer and the reference answer are self contained. Most often, the student responses are elliptical, contain anaphoras, or depend heavily on a broader context such as the instructional task description or prior dialogue

© Springer Nature Switzerland AG 2020
I. I. Bittencourt et al. (Eds.): AIED 2020, LNAI 12163, pp. 191–203, 2020.
https://doi.org/10.1007/978-3-030-52237-7_16

Table 1. An example of student tutor conversation in DeepTutor

Q: *What forces are acting on the puck while the puck is moving on the ice between the two players?*
A1: *The forces acting on the puck are the gravitational force and the normal force from the ice*
A2: *Normal and gravity*
A3: *The **downward force from the earth** and the normal force from the ice*
E: *The forces acting on the puck are the downward force of gravity and the upward normal force from the ice*

turns (dialogue history) in the case of task-oriented conversational ITSs. For example, in Table 1, student answer A1 is quite self-contained; a semantic similarity approach would lead in this case to a high similarity score to the expected answer (E).

On the other hand, some correct short answers could be elliptical (see answers A2 and A3 in the table) and computing a semantic similarity score between such elliptical answers and the references answer is a challenge simply because the elliptical, shorter answers have many implied parts which a typical semantic similarity approach would fail to account for as such approaches rely mostly on explicitly specified information, i.e., words in this case. The problem with assessing such elliptical answers using a standard semantic similarity approach is that it leads to a low similarity score between the elliptical responses and the expected answers, thus incorrectly assessing elliptical responses even if they are correct.

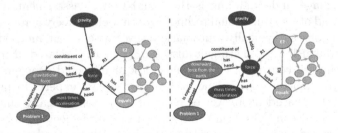

Fig. 1. Portions of knowledge graph that show concepts "gravitational force" (left) and "downward force from the earth" (right)

To address this issue, we propose a knowledge graph based approach by representing the concepts in the student answers and reference answers using embedded vectors that are learned directly from a knowledge graph. The embedded vectors encode indirect relationship between concepts, e.g., they can account for implicit information among concepts in the student answer and the benchmark answer. To this end, we construct a knowledge graph by extracting concepts and their surface relations from reference answers and then train a Neural Tensor Network (NTN; [22]). The idea here is that once the NTN is trained, these concept vectors encode relationships among entities/concepts in the knowledge graph - the more two entities share same or similar neighbors and relations with those entities, the more similar their vector representations are. For instance, in Fig. 1, the entity "gravitational force" and "downward force from the earth" are more likely to have similar vector embeddings since they share same neighbors (*force* and *problem 1*) and relation types (*constituent of, has head* and *is expected concept*).

2   Related Works

Knowledge graphs containing concepts or entities and their relations are important knowledge resources that have been used successfully for various applications such as question answering and information retrieval. However constructing knowledge graphs from unstructured data such as text is challenging. There have been a number prior efforts such as [1,5,9] to extract knowledge graphs from the text. These efforts employed classification approaches to classify whether an entity participates in a particular relation or not. The output of those methods is in the form of triplets specifying two entities and the corresponding relations among those entities (entity 1, relations, entity 2). The OpenIE tool [1] is an example of such an information extraction software system that outputs triplets from a given input text[1].

Often such knowledge graphs do not specify all possible relations between entities and in general they lack reasoning capabilities to infer the unspecified relations. That is, there are many true relations among entities in a given knowledge graphs that are not explicitly encoded in the graph. The task of explicitly inferring those missing relations is called the knowledge completion task. Several attempts have been made to complete knowledge graphs with missing relations among their entities.

One such approach to the task of knowledge completion in knowledge graphs relies on relational learning and was proposed by Nickel and colleagues [18]. They used a tensor model representation of relational data and developed RESCAL, an approach that employs tensor factorization to factorize the tensor obtained from relational data. This approach is comparable to LSA with two dimensional matrices representing relation between entities. However, in the RESCAL approach the representation of relations with three dimensional (3-D) matrices make it possible to have multiple relationships between entity pairs.

Socher and colleagues [22] proposed a neural network approach to represent relations with neural network. They developed a method to represent entities as vectors and relations as neural tensor networks (NTN), a variant of neural networks which combines a feed forward model with a bi-linear tensor product. The parameters of such NTN encode the latent relationship between the entities.

---

[1] https://nlp.stanford.edu/.

One of the important aspects of NTN that attracted our attention towards using the model in answer assessment is that it learns entity embeddings for each concepts as a vector that inherently encodes the relationship with the other entities. Such embeddings of concepts could help infer implied relationships and concepts in knowledge graphs corresponding to student answers. Our work relies on classification method for which concepts in answers are represented by embedding vectors learned while training Neural Tensor Network similar to that proposed by Socher and colleagues [22].

To our knowledge, our work is the first attempt to use knowledge graphs and a knowledge completion mechanism for automated answer assessment. In the past decade, automated assessment systems [6,11,21] were developed for texts of various sizes and generated with different purposes in mind. For instance, SAT-style argumentative essays have a well-defined structure and are 3–5 paragraphs in length on average. On the other hand, in problem-solving conversational tutoring systems students generate short answers in the form of dialogue turns while working with the tutoring system to solve a given problem. Unlike the essay grading, which focuses more on style, coherence, and organization of ideas, the short answer assessment task focuses more on assessing the correctness of the student response. Ziai and colleague [23] pointed the need of publicly available good quality dataset that could arguably enable comparison of such systems that are designed for different purposes. To this end, we focus here on the latter task of short answer assessment and compare result with previous works such as [13,14] that were proposed for same problem as this work. In the past, Latent Semantic Analysis, for instance, was used [7,17] for short answer assessment. However, LSA is an algebraic method that relies on word co-occurrence analysis of large collections of naturally occurring texts and it cannot account for linguistic phenomena such as anaphora resolution which is quite frequent in tutorial dialogues as explained next. While analyzing tutorial dialogues in a dialogue based tutorial system, Niraula and colleague [19] found that a significant portion of student answers contain pronoun that refer entities in the previous utterances. Methods to address such problems were proposed at different times such as [2,3,12,13]. In their methods, they assume that the question and the problem description provide import contextual cues for elliptic answers. In our case, when generating knowledge graphs, pronouns are solved to their corresponding referents.

3   Methods

Our assessment system is based on a multi-class classifier that classifies a student answer into one of the four assessment labels: (i) correct, (ii) correct but incomplete, (iii) incorrect and (iv) contradictory. For this, we extract entities and relations from student answers and reference answers and obtain embedding vector of these entities. In the following sections, we discuss in detail the steps of knowledge graph construction, entity embeddings, and assessment models.

3.1   Entity Relations Extraction

In order to construct the knowledge graph, a large collection of entities and relations triplets are needed. These triplets could then be used to learn latent (implied) relationships and thus discover missing, valid links between the entities. In our work, we use two categories of such entity relations: (i) semantic relations obtained from WordNet [22] and (ii) surface relations defined and extracted from the domain dataset, i.e., the DT-Grade dataset (see later).

While extracting surface relation triplets, we assume that there are a finite number of problems that are authored for training with a given intelligent tutoring system. An entity could be a token, a text chunk, or an unique identification number of the problem. The token entities are obtained by tokenizing the reference answers. From those tokens, we keep only content words such as nouns, verbs, adverbs and adjectives as entities. The text chunks are obtained from dependency parse trees. We used SpaCy [8] for text parsing. Besides that, other kind of entities and binary relationships are extracted using OLLIE [15], a state-of-art tool for information extraction.

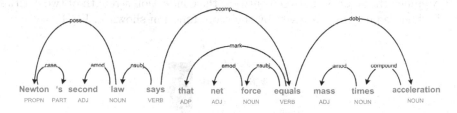

Fig. 2. Example of a sentence parsed with SpaCy dependency parser

In addition to extracting phrases, the dependency parse tree provides a way to obtain syntactic relations between entities. For instance, from Fig. 2 we can obtain several possible relations between entities. We define the following five relation types:

1. **is concept of:** if an entity is an expected concept of a problem. A problem is an abstract entity that represents problem's unique identification number (*"Problem 1"* is an abstract entity; Fig. 1).
2. **is constituent of:** if an entity is constituent of another entity; i.e., if an entity is a part of another entity (*"force"* is constituent of *"gravitational force"*; Fig. 1)
3. **has head text:** if a noun phrase's head word is another entity according to the dependency parse tree.
4. **has ancestor text:** if an entity's ancestor is another entity according to the dependency parse tree.
5. **has child text:** if an entity's child is another entity according to the dependency parse tree.

3.2 Knowledge Graph Embedding

A collection of entity-relation triplets forms a knowledge graph. Such graphs are usually extracted from explicit information in texts. Many valid relationships among the entities in the graph are not explicitly mentioned in those graphs. This is known as the knowledge incompleteness property. Among several approaches proposed previously, we used Neural Tensor Network (NTN) proposed by Socher and colleagues [22], which learns the connection strength between entity pairs, hence discover missing links. The NTN architecture consists of a bilinear tensor layer as well as feed forward layer which makes NTN powerful by harnessing the power of both bilinear and feed forward networks. Here, we present a high level architecture (Fig. 3) of a typical Neural Tensor Network and the scoring function (see Eq. 1) that is originally used in the original paper by Socher et al. Several NTN units (equal to the number of relation types) trained in unison produces a knowledge graph embedding. Since the errors from each unit (i.e error for each relation type) are aggregated while training, the weights of each cell affect each other during training. In other words, the whole knowledge graph represented by neural tensor network gets updated. While after training, the weights of these NTN embed the relation between entities, the connection strength of two entities in the knowledge graph is given by the score function shown in Eq. 1.

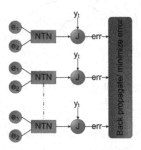

Fig. 3. High level architecture of knowledge graph embedding derived using NTN.

$$g(e_1, R, e_2) = U_R^T f\left(e_1^T W_R^{[1:k]} e_2 + V_R \begin{bmatrix} e_1 \\ e_2 \end{bmatrix} + b_R\right) \tag{1}$$

where $e_1, e_2 \in \mathbb{R}^d$ are d dimensional vectors of entities, $f = tanh$, is a non-linear activation function, $W_R^{[1:k]} \in \mathbb{R}^{d \times d \times k}$ is a tensor and the bilinear tensor product $e_1^T W_R^{[1:k]} e_2$ results in a vector $h \in \mathbb{R}^k$, where each entry is computed by one slice $i = 1, ..., k$ of tensor: $h_i = e_1^T W_R^i e_2$. The other parameters for relation R are the standard form of a neural network: $V_R \in \mathbb{R}^{k \times 2d}$ and $U \in \mathbb{R}^k, b_R \in \mathbb{R}^k$.

To train such NTN, the entity relation triplet such as *"(net force, has head text, equal)"* are labeled as true relation and negative examples such as *"(net force, has head text, friction)"*, created by corrupting one of the entities in each of the positive relation triplets are labeled as false. Then, such negative and positive triplets with corresponding binary labels are used to train the NTN. While training, the network updates its weights as well as the entity vector to obtain better representation of each of the entity after each epoch. The vectors produced as bi-product are useful in our answer assessment method.

3.3   Classifier Using Entity Embedding

Using the entity embeddings obtained after training with NTN, we construct vectors by extracting entities from an answer instance and averaging the entity vectors to get a single vector for the answer instance. We obtain such vectors for both the student answer as well as the reference answer. While computing the average of vector entities, out of vocabulary entities in student answers need to be handled. We address this problem by replacing such out of vocabulary entities with the vectors of potential synonyms or one of its constituents, if the case. If none exists, we simply use the *"NONE"* word vector.

Once the vectors of the student and reference answers are obtained, we feed them onto a classifier. Indeed, our assessment model is a classifier that categorizes the student answer into one of the classes that represent the assessment labels. We used two types of classifiers based on neural networks. The first type is a simple neural network with one input (Fig. 4a), the vector of the student answer. The second type concatenates the reference answer vector and the student answer vector (Fig. 4b). The advantage of the classifier with two input vectors is its ability to learn by comparing the student answers with standard reference answers during training. In other words, such a classifier learns to distinguish between a good answer that is semantically close to the reference answer and incomplete or incorrect answers which are not semantically close to the reference answer. Additionally, the reference answers are generally self contained and complete, hence they can provide contextual cues to the student answer, when used together.

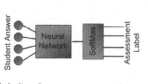

(a) Student answer as input

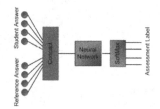

(b) Student answer and reference answer as input

Fig. 4. Student answer classifier

Compared to one input classifier, training and predicting with the two input classifier is different when there are multiple possible reference answers (usually, paraphrases of each other) for same problem. For training, those reference answers, paired with corresponding student answers produce a larger number of training examples, an advantage over the one input classifier. However, while predicting, multiple pairs with same true label but different predicted labels could be possible for a single instance (student answer). In such situations, a majority vote strategy is used to select the predicted assessment label; i.e., the assessment label that is predicted most frequently for a student answer is selected as the final predicted label.

4   Experiments and Results

We performed experiments with two different types of classifiers using entity vectors learned with NTN trained with both semantic (domain general) and surface (domain specific) relation triplets. The two types of classifiers, one input and two inputs trained with different entity vectors obtained from various triplet sources, are shown in Table 2. The domain general triplets are obtained from WordNet relations (prefixed with "WN") whereas the domain specific triplets are obtained from DT-Grade dataset (prefixed with "DT"). We also performed experiments by augmenting the domain general triplets with domain specific triplets (prefixed with "Aug"). For augmentation, we combined the domain general entities and relation obtained from WordNet with entities and triplets obtained from the DT-Grade dataset. In the following sections, we first describe datasets and then present the results obtained in various experimental setups.

Table 2. Experimental models

One input classifier	Two input classifier	Triplet source
WN1IP	WN2IP	WordNet
DT1IP	DT2IP	DT-Grade
Aug1IP	Aug2IP	Augmented (WordNet & DT-Grade combined)

4.1   Dataset

Tutorial Dataset. We used the DT-Grade dataset [3] which contains instances in the form of student answer - ideal answer pairs extracted from logged tutorial interaction of 40 junior level college students and a state-of-the-art intelligent tutoring system. The instructional tasks were conceptual physics problems. The dataset consists of 900 instances. The student responses were labeled with the following four assessment labels (shown in Table 3).

Table 3. DT-Grade dataset

Labels	Description	Distribution
Correct	Covers all the expected concepts	367 (40.77%)
Incomplete	Covers some of the expected concepts	211 (23.44%)
Contradictory	Semantically opposite or contrast to expected answer	84 (9.33%)
Incorrect	Does not include any of the expected concepts	238 (26.44%)
	Total	900

Knowledge Graph Dataset. We used the WordNet knowledge graph dataset described by Socher and colleagues [22]. We preprocess the WordNet triplets to combine the different senses for same word into a single entity for training our neural tensor network. Though the different senses are combined, the relations that those different senses previously participated in was kept unchanged and treated as a separate training instance. This makes the model simple yet enabling the encoding of the relations in the embedding. There are 11 relations categories obtained from WordNet, 33,163 entities, and 109,165 relationship triplets. These categories characterize the semantic relations between the entities in the knowledge graph. Additionally, we created an entity relation triplets dataset from the reference answers in the DT-Grade dataset. The entities we created are of two types: (i) the question itself is the entity, i.e. there are 900 such entities and (ii) the content words, phrases, head words, parents and children obtained by parsing the reference answers using the SpaCy [8] dependency parser. Encoding question as an entity provides contextual information such as the relation *"is concept of "* (see Sect. 3.1) to the knowledge graph. After obtaining the entities, we identified 5 syntactic relations among the entities obtained from reference answers, with 1,263 entities and 22,941 relation triplets. We used these two categories of knowledge graph datasets separately as well as augmenting the syntactic knowledge graph dataset by combining with the semantic knowledge graph dataset.

4.2 Results

The results of 10-folds cross validation training-testing process is summarized in Table 4. We report the performance in terms of accuracy and F1 measure. The result shows that Aug2IP performed best with an average accuracy of 0.644, which is 2.2% better than *LSTM, the previously best performing model (0.622) [13]. Also its F1 score (= 0.642) is 2.2% and Kappa (= 0.482) is 3.2% better, respectively, than that of *LSTM. The *LSTM used the problem description, tutor question, student answer, and reference answer as input, however, and relied on one-hot-encoding inputs for entities to discover general semantic and domain specific linguistic relationships. In fact, our two inputs classifier when used with domain specific vectors (DT2IP & Aug2IP) performed better. This suggests that the NTN model could learn vectors better than the word2vec used in previous approach. The result aligns with our expectation that the knowledge graph inferred with NTN can encode the latent relations between entities.

Table 4. Performance of models

Model	Avg acc	F1	Kappa
*LSTM [13]	0.622	0.620	0.450
DT2IP	**0.626**	**0.624**	0.450
Aug2IP	**0.644**	**0.642**	0.482
WN2IP	0.564	0.569	0.334
DT1IP	0.569	0.569	0.350
Aug1IP	0.604	0.604	0.409
WN1IP	0.551	0.565	0.302

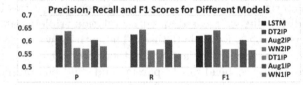

Fig. 5. Comparison of precision, recall and f1 score for different models

Besides performing better than previous model, the result suggests that when trained with vectors created from the same dataset, the classifiers that takes both student answer and reference answer as input perform better compared to models that only take student answer as input. For instance, DT2IP has average accuracy of 0.626 which is 5.7% higher than of DT1IP. Similarly Aug2IP has average accuracy of 0.644 which is 4% higher than Aug1IP. Whereas the performance of WN2IP is higher than that of WN1IP, it is a small improvement (1.3%) when compared to other classifiers.

Table 4 further shows that the classifier when trained on domain specific vectors (prefixed with DT) perform better than when trained on domain general vectors prefixed with WN). Moreover, when the domain specific triplets were augmented with domain general triplets, the performance boosted up significantly (3.5% improvement for Aug1IP than DT1IP, and 1.8% for Aug2IP than DT2IP).

Figure 5 shows the average precision, recall, and F1 score of various models we experimented with. As seen from the figure, our two input classifier trained with augmented vectors performed best in terms of precision (0.639), recall (0.644) and F1 score. Compared to domain specific vectors (DT1IP and DT2IP) the domain general vectors(WN1IP and WN2IP) performed worse. The reason could be because a significant number of the entities extracted from student answers and reference answers from DT-Grade dataset were not present in the domain general vocabulary. And lack of such entities resulted in inaccurate representation of entities. Because such entities need either semantically similar entities or synonym words instead of relying on NONE entity in the vocabulary.

5 Conclusions

In this paper, we proposed several knowledge graph based models to assess freely generated student responses with a focus on short responses generated in tutorial dialogues. The improved performance in terms of accuracy and F1 measures of the propose models suggests knowledge graph based models yield better vectorial representation of student answer and reference answer texts. In addition, the two input classifier always performed better than the one input classifier when trained with the same set of vectors. This is expected, since the two input classifier uses the reference answer as input as well. More importantly, when the two input classifier is trained with augmented vectors, they performed best. This suggest that the relation triplets obtained from actual tutorial data helps to encode highly predictive features when training with NTN. In summary, the NTN model learns entity vectors that help to represent concepts and relations some of which are not explicitly mentioned and therefore benefit methods for answer assessment such as the one we propose here.

Our method has several areas where further improvement is possible. One of those areas is to define more relations among entities that are specific to a target domain, e.g., physics. In this work, we have limited ourselves to general, syntactically-derived relations. In the future, we plan to integrate methods that can automatically discovering domain specific relations from free text, for instance.

Acknowledgements. This research was partially sponsored by the National Science Foundation under award The Learner Data Institute (award #1934745), NSF award Investigating and Scaffolding Students' Mental Models during Computer Programming Tasks (award # 1822816) and an award from the Department of Defense (U.S. Army Combat Capabilities Development Command - Soldier Center). The opinions, findings, and results are solely the authors' and do not reflect those of the funding agencies.

References

1. Angeli, G., Premkumar, M.J.J., Manning, C.D.: Leveraging linguistic structure for open domain information extraction. In: Proceedings of the 53rd Annual Meeting of the Association for Computational Linguistics and the 7th International Joint Conference on Natural Language Processing (Volume 1: Long Papers), vol. 1, pp. 344–354 (2015)

2. Bailey, S., Meurers, D.: Diagnosing meaning errors in short answers to reading comprehension questions. In: Proceedings of the Third Workshop on Innovative Use of NLP for Building Educational Applications, pp. 107–115. Association for Computational Linguistics (2008)

3. Banjade, R., Maharjan, N., Niraula, N.B., Gautam, D., Samei, B., Rus, V.: Evaluation dataset (DT-Grade) and word weighting approach towards constructed short answers assessment in tutorial dialogue context. In: Proceedings of the 11th Workshop on Innovative Use of NLP for Building Educational Applications, pp. 182–187 (2016)

4. Blei, D.M., Ng, A.Y., Jordan, M.I.: Latent dirichlet allocation. J. Mach. Learn. Res. **3**(Jan), 993–1022 (2003)

5. Chan, Y.S., Roth, D.: Exploiting background knowledge for relation extraction. In: Proceedings of the 23rd International Conference on Computational Linguistics, pp. 152–160. Association for Computational Linguistics (2010)

6. Dikli, S.: An overview of automated scoring of essays. J. Technol. Learn. Assess. **5**(1) (2006)

7. Graesser, A.C., Wiemer-Hastings, P., Wiemer-Hastings, K., Harter, D., Tutoring Research Group Tutoring Research Group, Person, N.: Using latent semantic analysis to evaluate the contributions of students in AutoTutor. Interact. Learn. Environ. **8**(2), 129–147 (2000)

8. Honnibal, M., Montani, I.: spaCy 2: natural language understanding with bloom embeddings, convolutional neural networks and incremental parsing (2017, To appear)

9. Jiang, J., Zhai, C.: A systematic exploration of the feature space for relation extraction. In: Human Language Technologies 2007: The Conference of the North American Chapter of the Association for Computational Linguistics; Proceedings of the Main Conference, pp. 113–120 (2007)

10. Landauer, T.K.: Latent Semantic Analysis. American Cancer Society (2006). https://doi.org/10.1002/0470018860.s00561. https://onlinelibrary.wiley.com/doi/abs/10.1002/0470018860.s00561

11. Leacock, C., Chodorow, M.: C-rater: automated scoring of short-answer questions. Comput. Humanit. **37**(4), 389–405 (2003). https://doi.org/10.1023/A:1025779619903

12. Maharjan, N., Banjade, R., Rus, V.: Automated assessment of open-ended student answers in tutorial dialogues using Gaussian mixture models. In: The Thirtieth International Flairs Conference (2017)

13. Maharjan, N., Gautam, D., Rus, V.: Assessing free student answers in tutorial dialogues using LSTM models. In: Penstein Rosé, C., et al. (eds.) AIED 2018. LNCS (LNAI), vol. 10948, pp. 193–198. Springer, Cham (2018). https://doi.org/10.1007/978-3-319-93846-2_35

14. Maharjan, N., Rus, V.: A concept map based assessment of free student answers in tutorial dialogues. In: Isotani, S., Millán, E., Ogan, A., Hastings, P., McLaren, B., Luckin, R. (eds.) AIED 2019. LNCS (LNAI), vol. 11625, pp. 244–257. Springer, Cham (2019). https://doi.org/10.1007/978-3-030-23204-7_21

15. Schmitz, M., Bart, R., Soderland, S., Etzioni, O.: Open language learning for information extraction. In: Proceedings of Conference on Empirical Methods in Natural Language Processing and Computational Natural Language Learning (EMNLP-CONLL) (2012)

16. Mohler, M., Bunescu, R., Mihalcea, R.: Learning to grade short answer questions using semantic similarity measures and dependency graph alignments. In: Proceedings of the 49th Annual Meeting of the Association for Computational Linguistics: Human Language Technologies-Volume 1, pp. 752–762. Association for Computational Linguistics (2011)

17. Mohler, M., Mihalcea, R.: Text-to-text semantic similarity for automatic short answer grading. In: Proceedings of the 12th Conference of the European Chapter of the Association for Computational Linguistics, pp. 567–575. Association for Computational Linguistics (2009)

18. Nickel, M., Tresp, V., Kriegel, H.P.: A three-way model for collective learning on multi-relational data. In: ICML, vol. 11, pp. 809–816 (2011)

19. Niraula, N.B., Rus, V., Banjade, R., Stefanescu, D., Baggett, W., Morgan, B.: The DARE corpus: a resource for anaphora resolution in dialogue based intelligent tutoring systems. In: LREC, pp. 3199–3203 (2014)

20. Pérez, D., Gliozzo, A.M., Strapparava, C., Alfonseca, E., Rodriguez, P., Magnini, B.: Automatic assessment of students' free-text answers underpinned by the combination of a BLEU-inspired algorithm and latent semantic analysis. In: FLAIRS Conference, pp. 358–363 (2005)

21. Shermis, M.D., Burstein, J.C.: Automated Essay Scoring: A Cross-Disciplinary Perspective. Routledge, Abingdon (2003)

22. Socher, R., Chen, D., Manning, C.D., Ng, A.: Reasoning with neural tensor networks for knowledge base completion. In: Advances in Neural Information Processing Systems, pp. 926–934 (2013)

23. Ziai, R., Ott, N., Meurers, D.: Short answer assessment: establishing links between research strands. In: Proceedings of the Seventh Workshop on Building Educational Applications Using NLP, pp. 190–200. Association for Computational Linguistics (2012)

The Sound of Inattention: Predicting Mind Wandering with Automatically Derived Features of Instructor Speech

Ian Gliser[1]([✉]), Caitlin Mills[1], Nigel Bosch[2], Shelby Smith[1], Daniel Smilek[3], and Jeffrey D. Wammes[4]

[1] University of New Hampshire, Durham, NH, USA
ig1018@wildcats.unh.edu
[2] University of Illinois Urbana–Champaign, Champaign, IL, USA
[3] University of Waterloo, Waterloo, ON, Canada
[4] Queen's University, Kingston, ON, Canada

Abstract. Lecturing in a classroom environment is challenging - instructors are tasked with maintaining students' attention for extended periods of time while they are speaking. Previous work investigating the influence of speech on attention, however, has not yet been extended to instructor speech in live classroom lectures. In the current study, we automatically extracted acoustic features from live lectures to determine their association with rates of classroom mind-wandering (i.e., lack of student attention). Results indicated that five speech features reliably predicted classroom mind-wandering rates (Harmonics-to-Noise Ratio, Formant 1 Mean, Formant 2 Mean, Formant 3 Mean, and Jitter Standard Deviation). These speaker correlates of mind-wandering may be a foundation for developing a system to provide feedback in real-time for lecturers online and in the classroom. Such a system may prove to be highly beneficial in developing real-time tools to retain student attention, as well as informing other applications outside of the classroom.

Keywords: Mind-wandering · Attention · Acoustics · Speech · openSMILE

1 Introduction

In the classroom, lecturers are often faced with the challenging task of combatting frequent bouts of student inattention and disengagement. Such inattention often arises in the form of mind-wandering, defined here as thoughts unrelated to the task at hand (e.g., a classroom lecture [31, 32]). When a student mind-wanders, they risk missing out on critical pieces of information and thus can develop an impoverished understanding of the learning material. It is therefore important to find ways to reduce the occurrence of mind-wandering and potentially mitigate its negative impact.

One way to minimize the potential negative influence of mind-wandering is by detecting and responding to it in real-time [20]. However, approaches to date have mostly focused on student-centered models of mind-wandering – where ongoing data specific to each learner (e.g., eye-gaze) are necessary to make predictions about whether or not

© Springer Nature Switzerland AG 2020
I. I. Bittencourt et al. (Eds.): AIED 2020, LNAI 12163, pp. 204–215, 2020.
https://doi.org/10.1007/978-3-030-52237-7_17

they are currently mind-wandering. These attempts have been successful in laboratory contexts, but they are not currently scalable to entire classrooms.

Here we adopt an environment-centered model instead, by focusing on subtle naturalistic fluctuations in the learning environment (i.e., the instructor's speech). We test, for the first time, whether instructor speech patterns are related to classroom mind-wandering – potentially setting the foundation for the development environment-centered models of mind-wandering that can mitigate mind-wandering through scalable automated instructor feedback.

Environment-centered models seem based on the lessons we have already learned from laboratory cognitive psychology studies about when and why mind-wandering occurs. For example, mind-wandering tends to increase over the course of a task [33], and decrease when the task becomes more difficult (but see [13, 29]). Notably, even features like typeface seem to influence how often learners report mind-wandering: participants reported mind-wandering more often when reading a text in grey Comic Sans versus black Arial [11]. Although these studies demonstrate the potential malleability of mind-wandering, it is unclear if subtle environmental features (e.g., instructor behaviors, content changes, speech) may influence mind-wandering in live classrooms.

Here we directly examine how variations in the way information is transmitted through speech relates to students' attention in classroom contexts. This study builds on the environment-centered approach adopted by Bosch et al. [3], which examined how fluctuations in instructor movements were found to successfully predict classroom mind-wandering rates. Our specific focus on the instructor's speech fills an important gap in the literature, as very little research to date has been dedicated to quantifying and understanding how acoustical speech patterns influence student attention (e.g., rates of mind-wandering).

1.1 Background Literature

Acoustical features of speech have previously been linked to listener attention and information retention, albeit outside of the educational realm [4, 24]. For example, both the structure of speech (e.g., pitch contour and trajectory of source location) as well as prosodic quality (e.g., pitch and loudness) appear to reliably predict audience inattention [5, 10]. The emotional tone conveyed through acoustical features also seems to be an important aspect of speech; for example, there are clearly dissociable processing patterns in the brain when people hear angry versus neutral prosody [26]. These studies, though not conducted in the context of a lecture, highlight the potential for acoustic-prosodic features to impact information processing – making it likely that mind-wandering may also be influenced.

Only a few studies have attempted to link acoustic features to mind-wandering specifically. Drummond & Litman [6] asked students to read a paragraph about biology aloud and then perform a learning task (either self-explanation or paraphrasing). Periodically, they were probed to report how frequently they experienced off-task thoughts on a scale from 1 *(all the time)* to 7 *(not at all)* during the task. Students' responses were split into two categories, where 1–3 on the scale was "high" in zoning out, and 5–7 was "low" in zoning out. They trained a supervised machine learning model on the students' acoustic-prosodic features to classify low and high zone out, and achieved an accuracy of 64% in discriminating between the two. This study provides some evidence that individuals' tendencies to mind-wander are related to acoustic-prosodic cues (e.g., percent of silence, pitch, energy) of their own speech. It remains unclear, however, how such acoustic-prosodic features extracted from a *speaker* influence mind-wandering for *listeners*. Establishing associations between these speaker features and listener attention may have direct applications for an environment-centered feedback system in a classroom.

In the current study we sought to bridge the gap in our understanding of possible associations between features of speech and classroom attention. Our goals were (1) to provide a proof-of-concept method for automatically analyzing classroom speech features from low-cost audio recordings, and (2) to elucidate the relationship between acoustical speech features and mind-wandering in the classroom.

To tackle the first goal, we automatically extracted speech features from classroom lecture recordings using an open source software package called open Speech and Music Interpretation by Large-Space Extraction (openSMILE) [9]. We selected a popular feature set provided by openSMILE – the Geneva Minimalistic Acoustic Parameter Set [8]. We then identified and extracted a set of theoretically-relevant acoustic features from nine live classroom lecture recordings.

Next, as a step toward identifying key features to use in an environment-centered model of mind-wandering, we assessed the relation of these features to mind wandering. We focused on mind-wandering because it is consistently reported to be negatively associated with performance and comprehension in complex learning environments [19, 23, 31], including university lectures [34–36]. We aligned speech features in time with students' self-reported mind-wandering rates in order to probe this relationship. Below we describe our method for processing the audio recordings, how we arrived at a set of theoretically-relevant acoustic-prosodic variables, and how we tested for associations with mind wandering behavior.

2 Method

To address our two research goals, we collected data from multiple sources. As an overview, audio was extracted from low-cost video recordings of lectures, and students' attention was polled using a computer application during these same lectures. The two data channels were temporally aligned at 500-second intervals for analyses. Each stage is outlined in greater detail below.

2.1 Classroom Audio and Self-reported Mind Wandering

We extracted audio from recordings of nine different lectures at the University of Waterloo. These lectures were delivered by three different instructors (three lectures each) who were teaching undergraduate psychology courses. The lectures were delivered during normal classroom meeting times and with no manipulations or interference related to our experiments. The lectures took place in two similar classrooms, each with sloped, stadium-style seating and a stage with a podium for the teacher. The audio recording began at the same time as the lecture and lasted for the entirety of the class. For more details on data collection, please refer to Wammes et al. and Bosch et al. [3, 36].

Mind-wandering self-reports were collected from the students who participated in the study during the lecture (N = 76). Students who agreed to participate in the experiment downloaded an application onto their laptop that administered pseudo-randomly scheduled thought probes throughout the lecture. Specifically, the occurrence of each thought probe notification was individually randomized, with the constraint that probes appeared no more than five times throughout the lecture with a range of 15 and 25 min between probes. When a thought probe was scheduled, a small window appeared in the bottom right corner of their computer screen. This prompted participants to introspect about their mental state just prior to the probe, and report their current degree of mind-wandering on a continuous scale ranging from *Completely mind-wandering* to *Completely on task* (reverse scored to correspond numbers between 0 and 1, where higher values refer to more mind-wandering). They were informed that *mind-wandering* was defined as "thinking about unrelated concerns," and *on task* was defined as "thinking about the lecture."

2.2 Audio Processing and Feature Extraction

In order to avoid interference from speech unrelated to lecture delivery, we used Audacity software to trim each audio clip to *only* include the instructor's speech. Trimmed audio was then processed using openSMILE [10]. openSMILE is a flexible, open-source software package and audio toolkit capable of extracting a variety of different sound-based features, tailored for applications ranging from music to speech. The software extrapolates features based upon one's chosen configuration package and returns information about the occurrences of the selected features [10]. In this experiment, the configuration package was an implementation of the GeMAPS, a set of acoustic parameters based upon recent acoustical speech research [8]. GeMAPS was selected as the configuration for openSMILE due to its minimalistic approach to affect-oriented audio feature extraction. These parameters are Pitch, Jitter, Formant 1, 2, and 3 frequencies (F1, F2, and F3, respectively), F1 bandwidth, Shimmer, Loudness, Harmonics-to-noise-ratio (HNR), Alpha ratio, Spectral slope of 0–500 Hz and 500–1500 Hz, F1, F2, and F3 relative energy, Harmonic difference H1-H2, and Harmonic difference H1-A3 [8].

Various relevant summary statistics of these basic parameters are also output by openSMILE. These include coefficient of variation (standard deviation normalized by the mean; SD) and mean for each parameter. For Loudness and Pitch, the following features were additionally included: 20th percentile, 50th percentile, 80th percentile, the range of 20th to 80th percentile, as well as the mean and SD of the slope rising signal and slope falling signal. Lastly, the mean of Spectral slopes (from 0–500 Hz and 500–1500 Hz), the Alpha Ratio, and the Hammarberg Index were included for each recording, resulting in 56 total features for analysis.

Following extraction of audio recordings from lectures and feature extraction, we identified a subset of these GeMAPS features (described in more detail below) for our analysis.

2.3 Selecting Acoustic Features

We identified a set of theoretically-relevant acoustical characteristics based on previous literature. Specifically, we searched for features that have well-established relationships with psychologically-relevant constructs (see Table 1 for a full description of features and corresponding sources). Due to the lack of classroom-based investigations, the majority of literature review focused on studies examining how features of speech relate to attention and emotion, broadly conceived, in laboratory contexts. For example, emotion is considered to be a fundamental aspect of speech, as the delivery of emotional information is tied to inflection of the voice [21]. The following features were identified with the corresponding sources, as described in Table 1.

Table 1. Full list of selected acoustical speech features, description of selected features, rationale for selection and citations of relevant literature

---

Formant 0 (F0) Mean. This feature characterizes the fundamental frequency of voice, which is critical in driving inflection and linked to prosody [18, 22, 27]

Formant 1 (F1) Mean. The first harmonic formant is a determinant of prosodic quality, which drives speech reception [18, 26-27].

Formant 2 (F2) Mean. The second harmonic formant uniquely defines sounds of speech and is an acoustic correlate of resonance and clearness of speech [18, 25-27]

Formant 3 (F3) Mean. The third harmonic formant is present in vowel sounds and is fundamental to reception of clear speech [1, 18, 26-27]

F1 Bandwidth Mean. This is the region of frequency in which amplitudes differ by less than 3 decibels from the center frequency. It is a determinant of nasally/honky qualities of speech [17-18].

Loudness Mean. The average maximum volume of speech indicates more careful and precise speech and is correlated to confident speech as well as compliance [15, 18].

Loudness Standard Deviation. See above (Loudness Mean).

Jitter Standard Deviation. The standard deviation of pitch fluctuations is associated with trembling/tremorous voices, relating it to nervous voice [30].

Shimmer Mean. The average fluctuations of speech loudness are also associated with trembling/tremorous voices, relating it to nervous voice [30].

Voiced Segment Mean Length. The average length of discrete units in a stream of speech is a correlate of confident and compliant speech, indicative of precise and careful speech [15, 18].

Harmonics-to-Noise Ratio. This is the ratio of harmonic energy difference between the fundamental formant (F0), first harmonic (F1) and second harmonic (F2). This is a correlate of rough, uneven, and bumpy speech [7].

Hammarberg Index Mean. The difference in spectral energy between peaks in the 0.2 kHz and 2.5 kHz band [16] is a correlate of low percentile sadness and perceived attractiveness of the speaker [15, 18].

2.3.1 Formants

Formants are descriptions of the high regions of spectral energy that occur in discrete regions of frequency. F1, 2 and 3 are necessary for synthesis of vowels in speech; additionally, the presence of F3 is required for interpretable speech [37]. *F1 Bandwidth Mean* also describes the degree to which speech is nasally and thus is included here (see Table 1).

2.3.2 Voiced Segment Length, Loudness, Jitter and Shimmer

Loudness of Speech is vital in a lecture due to its important role in conveying information to all members of the audience as well as its relation to confident and precise speech [15, 18].

Voiced Segment Length is defined as the length of discrete units in a stream of speech, which is measured by recording the average periods of uninterrupted speech. Similar to loudness of speech, voiced segment length is a correlate of confidence and precision in speech [15, 18].

Shimmer Mean is described as the occurrences of fluctuations in loudness of speech. Somewhat analogous, *Jitter Standard Deviation* is defined as the fluctuations in pitch. Both shimmer and jitter have been found to be correlates of trembling and nervous speech [30].

2.3.3 Harmonics-to-Noise Ratio and Hammarberg Index

Harmonics-to-Noise Ratio (HNR) is the ratio of harmonic energy: the difference between fundamental formant (F0), first formant (F1), and second formant (F2). Previous research has found HNR to be a correlate of rough, uneven, and bumpy speech.

2.4 Predicting Student Mind-Wandering with Acoustic Features

Speech features were processed and extrapolated from the audio recordings in 500 s epochs of time, whereas students' mind-wandering reports were sampled continuously throughout the lecture. To facilitate comparison between these two data channels, speech features were paired with mind-wandering reports within the same 500 s window. To accomplish this, mind wandering reports were aggregated across participants within each time window from which acoustic features were derived. This resulted in 72 time windows per class, which we used in the analyses below. The average rating of mind-wandering (on a continuous scale between 0–1, where higher values mean more mind-wandering) was .499 ($SD = .287$).

Relationships between speech features and mind-wandering rates were assessed using linear mixed-effects models. We used the *lme4* package in R [2]. All models included a random effect of class to control for within-class variability in baseline mind-wandering. All models regressed mind-wandering on each acoustic feature of interest. We used restricted maximum likelihood estimation (REML) with unstructured covariance to avoid biasing the error variance. Tests of model significance were computed using a type II Wald chi-square test with a two-tailed α of .05 from the *car* package to take a conservative approach based on only estimates from the model [14].

3 Results

Descriptive statistics for each theoretically-relevant feature can be found in Table 2. Below we describe how each of these features related to classroom rates of mind-wandering. Effect sizes (i.e., standardized regression coefficients) can be found in Table 3. We checked for normality of the residuals (i.e. an assumption for linear regressions), and the residuals displayed a normal distribution.

Table 2. Mean and standard deviation of speech features and mind wandering reports.

Features	M	SD
Formant 0 Mean	28.3	2.04
Formant 1 Mean	638	55.8
Formant 2 Mean	1683	56.0
Formant 3 Mean	2750	59.0
Formant 1 Bandwidth Mean	1190	34.0
Loudness Mean	.571	.105
Loudness Standard Deviation	.452	.080
Jitter Standard Deviation	1.56	.117
Shimmer Mean	1.40	.027
Voiced Segment Length Mean	.168	.049
Harmonics-to-Noise Ratio	2.01	1.74
Hammarberg Index Mean	.359	.892
# of Mind Wandering in Epoch	11.8	12.6

3.1 Formants

Formant 0 Mean ($\beta = .047$, $p = .494$) and *Formant 1 Bandwidth Mean* ($\beta = .102$, $p = .156$) were not reliably related to mind-wandering. In contrast, *Formant 1 Mean* ($\beta = -.236$, $p = .006$), *Formant 2 Mean* ($\beta = -.188$, $p = .025$) and *Formant 3 Mean* ($\beta = -.239$, $p = .007$) were all significantly negatively related to classroom of mind-wandering.

3.2 Loudness, Voiced Segment Length, Jitter and Shimmer

Mind-wandering was not significantly related to *Loudness Mean* ($\beta = -.094$, $p = .128$) or *Loudness Standard Deviation* ($\beta = .024$, $p = .801$). The same non-significant patterns were observed between mind-wandering and *Voiced Segment Length Mean* ($\beta = .056$, $p = .482$) and *Shimmer Mean* ($\beta = -.051$, $p = .367$). However, *Jitter Standard Deviation* was significantly positively related to mind-wandering ($\beta = .097$, $p = .008$).

Table 3. Linear mixed effects models of relevant acoustical speech features. Standardized regression coefficients and *p*-values listed for each model with significant values (*p* < .05) bolded.

Features	β	p
Formant 0 Mean	.047	.494
Formant 1 Mean	**-.236**	**.006**
Formant 2 Mean	**-.188**	**.025**
Formant 3 Mean	**-.239**	**.007**
Formant 1 Bandwidth Mean	.102	.156
Loudness Mean	-.094	.128
Loudness Standard Deviation	.024	.801
Jitter Standard Deviation	**.097**	**.008**
Shimmer Mean	-.051	.367
Voiced Segment Length Mean	.056	.482
Harmonics-to-Noise Ratio	**.175**	**.009**
Hammarberg Index Mean	.071	.224

3.3 Harmonics-to-Noise Ratio and Hammarberg Index

Harmonics-to-noise Ratio was significantly positively related to mind-wandering (β = .175, *p* = .009), whereas *Hammarberg Index Mean* was not (β = .071, *p* = .224).

3.4 Summary of Results

We show that subtle fluctuations in speech characteristics influence classroom mind-wandering. Findings indicate that higher speech interpretability (higher values of *Formant 1*, *Formant 2*, and *Formant 3 Mean*), stability of pitch inflection (lower *Jitter Standard Deviation*, and the smoothness and evenness of speech (lower *Harmonics-to-noise Ratio*) were associated with lower rates of self-reported mind-wandering. This same pattern of results was unchanged when analyses were repeated with the number of mind-wandering reports as a control variable.

4 Discussion

To date, little research has been devoted to environment-centered models of mind-wandering in classrooms. However, understanding how subtle variations in classroom lectures relate to student attention is important given that students frequently report mind-wandering while listening to lectures. We addressed this gap by assessing the relationship between acoustical speech features and mind-wandering in a classroom setting.

We first detailed a method for automatically extracting a set of psychologically-relevant acoustical speech features from low-cost video recordings in live classrooms. We then related these features to students' self-reported mind-wandering across nine lectures. The data indicate that acoustical characteristics of the instructor's speech matter: we observed significant relationships between mind-wandering and *Formant 1, Formant 2,* and *Formant 3 Mean*s as well as *Jitter Standard Deviation* and *Harmonics-to-noise Ratio*. Of these features, *Jitter Standard Deviation* and *Harmonics-to-noise Ratio* were positively related to student mind-wandering, whereas *Formants 1, 2, and 3 Mean*s were negatively related to mind-wandering.

The negative relationships seen for *Formant 1, Formant 2,* and *Formant 3 Mean*s suggest that students paid more attention when speech was clearer. These three formants are associated with better speech clarity and negative correlates of raspy or hard-to-hear speech [18, 26, 27]. From a cognitive standpoint, mind-wandering may be more likely to occur when speech is less clear because discerning the content of the speech becomes more difficult; students may not have the cognitive resources available to match these increased task demands [13, 38].

The positive relationship observed for *Jitter Standard Deviation* provide some insight into the role of pitch changes in mind-wandering; that is, as the volatility of the instructor's pitch increased, students reported higher rates of mind-wandering. Prior work revealed an association between jitter and trembling or nervous speech [30]. Thus, mind-wandering occurrences may increase when nervousness becomes detectable in an instructor speech. This relationship may be due to how students interpret of the prosody speech; additional sub textual emotional information that is actually irrelevant to the lecture may influence their attention. A similar positive relationship was found for *Harmonics-to-Noise Ratio Mean*: mind wandering increased along with increased magnitude of *Harmonics-to-Noise Ratio* (i.e., rough, uneven speech [15, 18]). In the context of our findings, this suggests that mind-wandering is more likely to occur when the instructor's speech is more rough and uneven. Taken together, these finding highlight promising avenues for improving classroom lectures given that overall clarity of speech may be a simple way to increase student attention.

Our findings serve as a potential basis for an environment-centered system to address mind-wandering that does not require any intrusive or high-cost student measurements. Current developments for such a system are in their infancy and rarely explore raw audio data. For example, Schneider, Borner, Van Rosmalen & Specht [28] developed a real-time feedback system which analyzes nonverbal and verbal behaviors and provides feedback to speakers. This system, while found to increase performance and confidence in speaking, focused on more basic features than the ones used here, such as arm-crossing and volume. This system seeks to ensure that fluid speech is maintained and does not currently incorporate potential predictors of listener attention such as mind-wandering. Our findings suggest that interventions may be effective by targeting acoustical characteristics of instructor speech to improve lecture delivery and reduce classroom mind-wandering.

Our results, when combined with other environment-centered features like movement [3], may provide a crucial step toward the development of a multi-modal feedback system where acoustic properties are considered along with motion, content, and other sources of classroom data. Future research in this area may benefit by repeating the experiment while controlling for lecture content, as content of the presented information is likely to influence off-task though. Next steps include integrating and testing automatically extracted acoustic features into a real-time system. Such a system would require the intake of data in a specified time window, buffering the data in order to allow time for openSMILE computation, then feeding the buffered data to openSMILE for computation and prediction of student attention. Finally, the system will need to return a report that is easily accessible and interpretable by the instructor. While these steps are substantive, they are all attainable and the efficacy of using both video and auditory features has been established. As these tools develop, they provide a promising direction for online real-time intervention in educational settings.

References

1. Barrichelo-Lindström, V., Behlau, M.: Resonant voice in acting students: perceptual and acoustic correlates of the trained Y-buzz by Lessac. J. Voice **23**, 603–609. https://doi.org/10.1016/j.jvoice.2007.12.001
2. Bates, D., Mächler, M., Bolker, B., Walker, S.: Fitting linear mixed-effects models using lme4. J. Stat. Softw. **67**, 201–210 (2015). https://doi.org/10.18637/jss.v067.i01
3. Bosch, N., Mills, C., Wammes, J.D., Smilek, D.: Quantifying classroom instructor dynamics with computer vision. In: Penstein Rosé, C. et al. (eds.) AIED 2018. LNCS, vol. 10947. Springer, Heidelberg (2018). https://doi.org/10.1007/978-3-319-93843-1_3
4. Darwin, C.J., Hukin, R.W.: Effectiveness of spatial cues, prosody, and talker characteristics in selective attention. J. Acoust. Soc. Am. **107**, 970–977 (2000). https://doi.org/10.1121/1.428278
5. Ding, N., Simon, J.Z.: Cortical entrainment to continuous speech: functional roles and interpretations. Front. Hum. Neurosci. 8 (2014). http://doi.org/10.3389/fnhum.2014.00311
6. Drummond, J., Litman, D.: In the zone: towards detecting student zoning out using supervised machine learning. In: Aleven, V., Kay, J., Mostow, J. (eds.) ITS 2010. LNCS, vol. 6095, pp. 306–308. Springer, Heidelberg (2010). https://doi.org/10.1007/978-3-642-13437-1_53
7. Eskenazi, L., Childers, D.G., Hicks, D.M.: Acoustic correlates of vocal quality. J. Speech Hear. Res. **33**, 298–306 (1990). https://doi.org/10.1044/jshr.3302.298
8. Eyben, F., Scherer, K.R., Schuller, B.W., et al. The Geneva Minimalistic Acoustic Parameter Set (GeMAPS) for voice research and affective computing. IEEE Trans. Affect. Comput. **7**, 190–202 (2016). https://doi.org/10.1109/TAFFC.2015.2457417
9. Eyben, F., Weninger, F., Groß, F., Schuller, B.: Recent developments in openSMILE, the Munich open-source multimedia feature extractor categories and subject descriptors. In: Proc 21st ACM International Conference Multimedia, pp. 835–838 (2013). https://doi.org/10.1145/2502081.2502224
10. Eyben, F., Wöllmer, M., Schuller, B.B., et al.: OPENSMILE: open-source media interpretation by large feature-space extraction. In: MM 2010 - Proceedings of ACM Multimedia 2010 International Conference, pp. 1–65 (2015). https://doi.org/10.1145/1873951.1874246
11. Faber, M., Mills, C., Kopp, K., D'Mello, S.: The effect of disfluency on mind wandering during text comprehension. Psychon. Bull. Rev. **24**, 914–919 (2017). https://doi.org/10.3758/s13423-016-1153-z
12. Faber, M., Radvansky, G.A., D'Mello, S.K.: Driven to distraction: a lack of change gives rise to mind wandering. Cognition **173**, 133–137 (2018). https://doi.org/10.1016/j.cognition.2018.01.007
13. Feng, S., D'Mello, S., Graesser, A.C.: Mind wandering while reading easy and difficult texts. Psychon. Bull. Rev. **20**, 586–592 (2013). https://doi.org/10.3758/s13423-012-0367-y

14. Fox, J., Friendly, M., Weisberg, S.: Hypothesis tests for multivariate linear models using the car package. R J. **5**(1), 39–52 (2013)
15. Fernandez Gallardo, L., Weiss, B.: Perceived interpersonal speaker attributes and their acoustic features. In: Proceedings of the Phonetic & Phonologie, pp. 61–64 (2017)
16. Hammarberg, B., Fritzell, B., Gaufin, J., et al.: Perceptual and acoustic correlates of abnormal voice qualities. Acta Otolaryngol. **90**, 441–451 (1980). https://doi.org/10.3109/000164880 09131746
17. Lee, A.S.Y., Ciocca, V., Whitehill, T.L.: Acoustic correlates of hypernasality. Clin. Linguist. Phonetics **17**, 259–264 (2003). https://doi.org/10.1080/0269920031000080091
18. Memon, S.A.: Acoustic Correlates of the Voice Qualifiers Summarizing the Perception of Qatar on Twitter View project Algorithms for Speaker Profiling (2018). https://doi.org/10.13140/RG.2.2.24759.57764
19. Mills, C., Graesser, A., Risko, E.F., D'Mello, S.K.: Cognitive coupling during reading. J. Exp. Psychol. Gen. **146**, 872–883 (2017). https://doi.org/10.1037/xge0000309
20. Mills, C., Gregg, J., Bixler, R., D'Mello, S.K.: Eye-Mind reader: an intelligent reading interface that promotes long-term comprehension by detecting and responding to mind wandering. Hum.–Comput. Interact. 1–27 (2020). https://doi.org/10.1080/07370024.2020.1716762
21. Murray, I.R., Arnott, J.L.: Toward the simulation of emotion in synthetic speech: a review of the literature on human vocal emotion. J. Acoust. Soc. Am. **93**, 1097–1108 (1993). https://doi.org/10.1121/1.405558
22. Paeschke, A., Kienast, M., Sendlmeier, W.F., Berlin, T.U.: F0contours in emotional speech. In: Proceedings of the 14th International Congress of Phonetic Sciences (1999)
23. Randall, J.G., Oswald, F.L., Beier, M.E.: Mind-wandering, cognition, and performance: a theory-driven meta-analysis of attention regulation. Psychol. Bull. **140**, 1411–1431 (2014). https://doi.org/10.1037/a0037428
24. Rimmele, J.M., Zion Golumbic, E., Schröger, E., Poeppel, D.: The effects of selective attention and speech acoustics on neural speech-tracking in a multi-talker scene. Cortex **68**, 144–154 (2015). https://doi.org/10.1016/j.cortex.2014.12.014
25. Robb, M., Blomgren, M.: Analysis of F2 transitions in the speech of stutterers and non-stutterers. J. Fluency Disord. **22**, 1–16 (1997). https://doi.org/10.1016/S0094-730X(96)000 16-2
26. Sander, D., Grandjean, D., Pourtois, G., et al.: Emotion and attention interactions in social cognition: brain regions involved in processing anger prosody. Neuroimage **28**, 848–858 (2005). https://doi.org/10.1016/j.neuroimage.2005.06.023
27. Scherer, K.R., London, H., Wolf, J.J.: The voice of confidence: paralinguistic cues and audience evaluation. J. Res. Pers. **7**, 31–44 (1973). https://doi.org/10.1016/0092-6566(73)900 30-5
28. Schneider, J., Borner, D., Van Rosmalen, P., Specht, M.: Can you help me with my pitch? Studying a tool for real-time automated feedback. IEEE Trans. Learn. Technol. **9**, 318–327 (2016). https://doi.org/10.1109/TLT.2016.2627043
29. Seli, P., Konishi, M., Risko, E.F., Smilek, D.: The role of task difficulty in theoretical accounts of mind wandering. Conscious Cogn. **65**, 255–262 (2018). https://doi.org/10.1016/j.concog.2018.08.005
30. Shao, J., MacCallum, J.K., Zhang, Y., et al.: Acoustic analysis of the tremulous voice: assessing the utility of the correlation dimension and perturbation parameters. J. Commun. Disord. **43**, 35–44 (2010). https://doi.org/10.1016/j.jcomdis.2009.09.001
31. Smallwood, J., Fishman, D.J., Schooler, J.W.: Counting the cost of an absent mind: mind wandering as an underrecognized influence on educational performance. Psychon. Bull. Rev. 230–236 (2007). https://doi.org/10.3758/bf03194057
32. Smallwood, J., Schooler, J.W.: The restless mind. Psychol. Bull. **132**, 946–958 (2006). https://doi.org/10.1037/0033-2909.132.6.946

33. Thomson, D.R., Seli, P., Besner, D., Smilek, D.: On the link between mind wandering and task performance over time. Conscious Cogn. **27**, 14–26 (2014). https://doi.org/10.1016/j.con cog.2014.04.001

34. Wammes, J.D., Seli, P., Cheyne, J.A., et al.: Mind wandering during lectures II: relation to academic performance. Scholarsh. Teach. Learn. Psychol. **2**, 33–48 (2016). https://doi.org/10.1037/stl0000055

35. Wammes, J.D., Smilek, D.: Examining the influence of lecture format on degree of mind wandering. J. Appl. Res. Mem. Cogn. **6**, 174–184 (2017). https://doi.org/10.1016/j.jarmac.2017.01.015

36. Wammes, J.D., Ralph, B.C.W., Mills, C., et al.: Disengagement during lectures: media multitasking and mind wandering in university classrooms. Comput. Educ. (2019). https://doi.org/10.1016/j.compedu.2018.12.007

37. Weiss, B., Burkhardt, F.: Voice attributes affecting likability perception. In: Proceedings of 11th Annual Conference International Speech Communication Association INTERSPEECH 2010 (2010)

38. Xu, J., Metcalfe, J.: Studying in the region of proximal learning reduces mind wandering. Mem. Cognit. **44**, 681–695 (2016). https://doi.org/10.3758/s13421-016-0589-8

To Tailor or Not to Tailor Gamification? An Analysis of the Impact of Tailored Game Elements on Learners' Behaviours and Motivation

Stuart Hallifax[1]([✉])(iD), Elise Lavoué[1](iD), and Audrey Serna[2](iD)

[1] University of Lyon, University Jean Moulin Lyon 3, iaelyon school of Management,
CNRS, LIRIS UMR5205, Lyon, France
{stuart.hallifax,elise.lavoue}@liris.cnrs.fr
[2] INSA de Lyon - CNRS, LIRIS UMR5205, Villeurbanne, France
audrey.serna@liris.cnrs.fr

Abstract. Gamification, defined as the use of game elements in non game situations, is a widely used method to foster learner engagement and motivation. It is generally accepted that in order to be effective, gamification should be tailored to users. Currently, most systems adapt by assigning different game elements based on a single learner profile (e.g. dominant player type, personality or gender). However, there is no study yet that analyse the effect of combining several profiles. In this paper, we study the usage data from 258 students who used a gamified learning environment as a part of their mathematics class. By simulating different adaptation techniques, we show that the learner model chosen to tailor gamification has significant effects on learners' motivation and engaged behaviours depending on the profile(s) used in this context. We also show that tailoring to initial motivation to learn mathematics can improve intrinsic motivation. Finally, we show that tailoring to both player type and motivation profiles can improve intrinsic motivation, and decrease amotivation, compared to a single adaptation only based on learner motivation. We discuss the implications of our findings regarding the choice of a learner model for tailoring gamification in educational environments.

Keywords: Tailored gamification · User modelling · User behaviour · Motivation · User profile

1 Introduction

Gamification, defined as the use of "game design elements in non-game contexts" [3] is widely used in education to foster learner engagement and motivation, and to improve learner performances. Previous studies have shown that to be effective gamification should be tailored to users' expectations, and individual preferences

© Springer Nature Switzerland AG 2020
I. I. Bittencourt et al. (Eds.): AIED 2020, LNAI 12163, pp. 216–227, 2020.
https://doi.org/10.1007/978-3-030-52237-7_18

[8,10,17,20,26]. However, adapting game elements to specific individual preferences can be a complex task, as learners can have different preferences towards games, and different motivations for learning. Most systems therefore use learner profiles to categorise and classify learners, based on information such as their player type [18,22], personality traits [6], more rarely learner motivation [28]), or more context-dependent information, such as learning styles [12]. Existing tailored gamification systems use a single learner profile to recommend relevant game elements. Even if most of these systems have positive results on learner motivation, engagement, and performance, some more recent work shows more mitigated results [16,29]. This raises the question of how effective the profile is at capturing the differences between learners, the nuances in their motivations and preferences when using learning environments and therefore if the impact of tailored game elements provided to learners depends on the profile used.

In this paper, we study the usage data from a gamified learning environment where learners were randomly assigned a game element whilst doing mathematics quizzes. We compare different subsets of learners that used game elements either adapted to their player profile or to their motivation profile. We also evaluate the impact of a dual profile adaptation method based both on player type and learner motivation. We aim to answer two research questions: (1) What are the effects of tailored gamification on users' motivation and engaged behaviours in comparison to non-tailored gamification? (2) Are these effects different depending on the user model chosen for tailoring game elements?

We show that the user model chosen to tailor game elements has significant effects on learners, but on different metrics depending on the chosen profile. We also highlight that tailoring game elements according to initial motivation induces a more positive variation of intrinsic motivation compared to non-tailored game elements. Finally, the dual profile leads to a more positive variation of intrinsic motivation and less amotivation compared to tailoring based only on initial motivation profile.

2   Related Work

2.1   The Impact of Tailored Gamification

The reported effects of tailored gamification can generally be broken down into two categories: effects on learner motivation [12,16,19–21,24,28,29], and effects on learner performance [12–14,19,28]. Regarding motivation, Mora et al. [21] report an increase in behavioural and emotional engagement from students when adapting to their player type. They estimated these engagements using a post test survey. Monterrat et al. [20] showed that learners who used counter adapted elements said that their game elements were more fun and useful, than learners who used adapted elements. In an earlier study [19], they found that learners spent more time using the learning tool with adapted game elements. Lavoué et al. [16] showed that adaptation had little to no effect for the majority of learners, only reducing the amotivation of the more invested ones. Dos Santos et al. [29] showed that for some of the Brainhex [22] player types, adapted game elements increased flow (using the survey proposed by Hamari et al. [11]), whereas for others, the counter adapted game elements increased flow instead. Oliveria et al. [24] also evaluated learners' flow experience. However they found no differences between the adapted and non adapted learners. In previous work [23], the same authors looked at learner concentration when using game elements adapted to player type. They found that for some gamer types, the tailored system was better than the counter-tailored system, however for other player types, the counter-tailored game elements functioned better.

Regarding performance, Kickmeier-rust et al. [14] found that their adaptive badges decreased the amount of errors made by learners. Jagust et al. [13] reported that learners provided with adapted game elements completed more tasks than those who had none. Paiva et al. [27] found that tailored goals were effective when targeting social and collaborative behaviours, but failed when targeting individual learning goals.

Finally two authors showed an effect on both motivation and performance: Roosta et al. [28] found an impact on motivation and quiz results, with adapted learners having better results in both than a non adapted control group. Hassan et al. [12] found an increase of course completion and motivation from their adapted situation (almost twice as much than a non adapted situation).

We can therefore observe that there are many cases where tailoring gamification works, and has positive results on learner motivation, engagement, and performance. However some recent work shows more mitigated results in these categories, raising issues on modeling user and selecting relevant game elements.

2.2   User Models in Education

In a literature review of adaptive gamification in education Hallifax et al. [8] show that most adaptive gamification systems use user profiles to classify users, and adapt game elements to these categories. Of these systems, most use "player types" (reasons why people play and enjoy games as a basis for classification). One commonly used player type is the Hexad typology [18] created specifically for gamification, and has been shown to be more effective for gamification than other player profiles [9]. Based on Self Determination Theory [1], this profile distinguishes six different categories: *Philanthropists*, *Socialisers*, *Free Spirits*, *Achievers*, *Players*, and *Disruptors*, and has been used in several adaptive gamification studies. For example Mora et al. [21] sorted learners into one of four gamified situations based on their Hexad profile scores. Knutas et al. [15] created rules to propose personalised tasks based on Hexad type. Other profiles, that are less "game" centric are also used to tailor gamification. For example Denden et al. [2] base their tailoring system on the Big Five personality traits [6].

Some adaptive systems use profiles focused on more task related information but are far less common. Hassan et al. [12] use various forms of user task motivation as a basis for adaptation. They identify learner motivation based on a questionnaire adapted from the Academic Motivational Scale [31]. Roosta et al. used the framework presented by Elliot et al. [4] to divide learners into four types of motivation based on what is important for them.

All of these different adaptation systems leverage different learner profiles that present interesting ways to categorise learners and their preferences, However, little is known about the relevance of each user model and no work has yet explored the possibility of combining both player preferences and learning motivation to consider different preferences simultaneously.

2.3 Tailoring Algorithms and Methods

Tailoring algorithms and methods aims at assigning specific game elements for each user profile values. Some research explored the use of direct ratings by experts [16] where experts were asked to rank which game elements would be most appropriate for each player type. Otherwise, the most explored approach consists in using statistical techniques to highlight correlations between game elements and user profile values. For instance, Tondello et al. [30] calculate the correlations between Hexad profile and various game elements directly rated by users. Hallifax et al. [9] used a pairwise comparison approach to generate user ratings for a set of game elements. They then performed a Partial Least Squares Path Modelling (PLS-PM [7]) between various profile systems and the game element ratings in order to provide recommendations for the studied profiles. The path analysis performed with PLS-PM allows to evaluate associations between different variables. This technique is thus well adapted to study the influences of each dimension of a profile on specific metrics, as used also in [5,25].

3 Study Framing

3.1 Research Questions

Our analysis of the literature about tailored gamification in education highlights that gamification could be more effective when tailored to learners, however some recent work shows mitigated or negative results. In addition, these results seem very dependent on the user model used to assign most suitable game elements to users. This work intends to fill that gap by investigating different user models, including a combination of two learner profiles. This paper addresses the following research questions: (1) What are the effects of tailored gamification on users' motivation and engaged behaviours in comparison to non-tailored gamification? (2) Are these effects depending on the user model chosen for tailoring game elements? Especially when considering motivation and player types?

3.2 Method

To investigate these questions, we analysed the data collected during the use of a gamified learning platform in ecological conditions. Each learner was randomly assigned a game element without tailoring. We collected metrics about their motivation, player types and engaged behaviours while using the platform. We chose the Hexad player types since recent studies showed that it is the most relevant typology for tailored gamification [9]. To measure motivation, we used the Academic Motivational Scale (AMS) proposed by Vallerand et al. [31]. It can measure learner academic motivation for a specific task, in our case learning Mathematics. It decomposes academic motivation into seven sub scales, assessing *intrinsic* motivations (IM), *extrinsic* motivations (EM), and *amotivation*:

- **IM for Knowledge**: performing an activity simply for the pleasure and the satisfaction of doing something new.
- **IM for Accomplishment**: performing an activity for the pleasure of overcoming a challenge.
- **IM Stimulation**: performing an activity for fun or excitement.
- **EM External Regulation**: performing an activity to gain some kind of external rewards.
- **EM Introjected Regulation**: performing an activity to avoid shame or increase self-esteem.
- **EM Identified Regulation**: performing an activity in order to achieve precise objectives.
- **Amotivation**: absence of intention to perform an activity.

Once the data was collected, we analysed it through the lens of different tailoring simulations. We analysed the effects of three tailored approaches, each one considering a different user model (1) Hexad profile user model, (2) initial motivation user model, and (3) a dual profile user model composed of both previous profiles. For each single profile tailored approach, we generate an affinity matrix (presented in detail in Sect. 5.1) representing how each profile value affects the appreciation for each game element. Thanks to this matrix, we were able to assign a game element for each learner according to the value of their profile. For the dual adapted condition we used an algorithm to find a compromise between the two single profile recommendations (described also in Sect. 5.1). We then built two subsets from the original data for each approach: a subset containing learners whose game element matched with the one recommended and a second subset containing learners that used a non-adapted game element.

To generate these affinity matrices (Hexad profile and motivation profile), we used the statistical approach PLS-PM [7] inspired by several studies in the domain [5,9,25]. PLS PM is a method of structural equation modelling which allows estimating complex cause-effect relationship models. We used it to identify the influences of the values for each user type on the variations for each motivation type. We chose this approach instead of considering pre-existing recommendations from the literature because as shown by Hallifax et al. [9] the context plays a major role in the impact of game elements on user motivation, and we could not ensure that the context of the studies were similar to ours.

Finally, to measure and compare the impacts of each condition, we ran comparisons on the different subsets created using a Wilcoxon rank sum test.

4   Data Collection

The data collection lasted for a total of 6 weeks, with a frequency of 1–2 lessons per week, involving 4 high schools and 12 classes of approximately 25 learners.

After removing learners who failed to correctly fill out either the pre- or post-test motivation questionnaires, or who were absent too many times during the experiment, we were left with data from 258 learners, aged between 13 and 14 (123 self-reported as female and 135 self-reported as male).

4.1 Gamified Learning Platform

The Ludimoodle platform was designed with the help of secondary school teachers who then used it in class. In total, ten lessons were designed to learn basic algebra, each lesson containing between 4 and 10 quizzes. Each quiz had to be correctly answered at least 70% before learners could access the next one. Game elements implemented in the platform were co-designed with the same teachers. Six game elements were implemented in the platform but only one was embedded to the platform interface. Thus at the beginning of the experiment, each learner was randomly assigned a game element for the ten lessons. We chose six different game elements among the most well-identified ones in the literature:

- **Avatar**: As learners progress in a lesson they can unlock a different piece of clothing, or item that a character can be holding.
- **Badges**: Learners can receive badges for a quiz depending on how much of the quiz they get correctly (bronze for 70%, silver: 85%, and gold: 100%).
- **Progress**: It portrays different coloured spaceships that travel from the earth to the moon depending on how many quizzes learners complete.
- **Leaderboard**: It portrays a "race" where as the learners answer questions correctly they can climb higher in the rankings and possibly win the race.
- **Points**: Each lesson has its own score counter, with a detailed view on how many points learners scored for each quiz.
- **Timer**: It shows a timer for each quiz. Learners are asked to try and beat a "reference time" (generally their average response time for each question).

4.2 Measurements

Before the experiment, learners filled out the Hexad [30] and the AMS [31] questionnaires. Both were translated into French, and some vocabulary was slightly adapted to the context (mathematics for secondary school age learners). After the last lesson, learners filled out the AMS questionnaire a second time. We then calculated the variation in intrinsic, extrinsic motivations, and amotivation as the difference in the motivation scores between the pre test questionnaire (initial motivation) and post test questionnaire (final motivation). The metrics we used to analyse engaged behaviours (mostly related to performances as shown in related work) were computed using the logs generated by the learning platform:

- **AvgQTime**: Average time to answer a question
- **QRatio**: Ratio of correct versus incorrect answers to a question
- **NQuiz**: Number of quizzes attempted

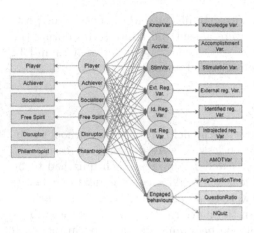

Fig. 1. PLS PM model for creating the Hexad influence matrices.

Table 1. Influence matrix for the Hexad profile on the Avatar game element. Only the significant (p < .05) influences are shown here.

	Pl.	Ac.	So.	FS.	Di.	Ph.
Know.Var.	0.329	-0.356				
Acc.Var.	0.541		-0.521			
Stim.Var.						
Ext.Reg.Var.						
Id.Reg.Var.						
Int.Reg.Var.						
Amot.Var.						
Behaviours						0.396

Table 2. Final affinity matrix for the Hexad profile

	Pl.	Ac.	So.	FS.	Di.	Ph.
Avatar	0.870	-0.356	-0.521			0.396
Badges			-0.548	-1.233		1.229
Progress		-0.011	-0.331		-0.061	
Leaderboards			-0.459		-0.870	
Points	0.490		-0.467			-0.694
Timer		1.772	0.439	0.530	0.398	-1.125

5   Adaptation Simulation

5.1   Data Subsets

For the two single user models, we ran two PLS-PM models between the profile values and the variations of motivations for each subset of learners that used a particular game element (Fig. 1). This gave us a set of 6 matrices of influences for each profile (one per game element, an example for the Avatar game element is given in Table 1). By combining all six of these matrices, we obtained a final affinity matrix, that showed for each game element, how important a given profile metric is in their influences (the full affinity matrix for the Hexad Profile is given in Table 2). By combining these matrices with learner profiles, we generated a recommendation of game element based on the Hexad profile and one based on the initial motivation. For example, a learner with the Hexad profile (Pl:0; Ac:-8; So:2; FS:0; Di:6; Ph:7), would have the following affinity vector ('Avatar': .385, 'Badges': .0364, 'Progress': -.241, 'Leaderboards': -.920, 'Points': -.577, 'Timer': .225) and would therefore be recommended the Avatar game element.

For the dual profile user model, we developed an algorithm that recommends a game element based on both player and motivation profiles. In our original dataset, out of the 258 learners, 87 of them used a game element that was either adapted to their Hexad profile, or adapted to their initial motivation scores (no learners had a game element adapted to both their Hexad profile and initial motivation). The algorithm proposes a compromise between both recommendations: we evaluate if there is a positive overlap between the two affinity vectors, and we take the game element that minimises the ranks in the positive overlap. If there is none, we take the game element that minimises the ranks from both affinity vectors (or maximises the affinities if tied). From our set of 258 learners, we built the following data subsets using the three approaches:

- Hexad data subset: 42 learners used game elements adapted to their Hexad player profile (216 did not).
- Initial motivation data subset: 45 learners used game elements adapted to their initial motivation (213 did not).
- Dual profile data subset: 42 learners used a game element recommended by the dual profile algorithm (216 did not).

5.2 Hexad Adaptation Results

Comparing metrics for the two subsets, we found that learners using an adapted game element spent significantly less average time per question and had a significantly lower correct question ratio (i.e. they got more questions wrong) than learners who had a non adapted game element (see Table 3a). The adaptation process had no significant impact on learners' motivation.

Table 3. Results for different simulations. The values given are the averages for each group. In light grey: no significant differences, in bold and highlighted in grey: significant at p < .05, and highlighted in light grey: almost significant p ≈ .05

Metric	(a) Hexad			(b) Motivation			(C) Dual profile		
	p	Adapted	Non	p	Adapted	Non	p	Adapted	Non
Know.Var.	.233	-1.489	-2.099	.022	**-1.156**	**-2.169**	.052	-1.326	-2.137
Acc.Var.	.289	0.422	-0.352	.008	**0.756**	**-0.423**	.056	0.739	-0.425
Stim.Var.	.458	0.289	-0.263	.335	0.267	-0.258	.045	**0.848**	**-0.387**
Id.Reg.Var	.447	0.289	-0.117	.383	-0.400	0.0282	.691	-0.283	0.005
Int.Reg.Var	.492	0.222	-0.282	.233	0.378	-0.315	.445	0.326	-0.307
Ext.Reg.Var	.482	-1.089	-1.235	.141	-0.667	-1.324	.476	-1.043	-1.245
Amot.Var.	.619	2.267	2.953	.867	2.956	2.808	.012	**1.391**	**3.146**
AvgQTime	.016	**60.73**	**67.78**	.066	71.42	65.51	.812	68.07	66.21
QRatio	.010	**0.608**	**0.665**	.224	0.637	0.659	.137	0.630	0.661
NQuiz	0.792	34.56	35.33	.189	34.18	35.41	.923	36.17	34.98

5.3   Initial Motivation Adaptation Results

Adaptation based on the initial motivation profile had significant positive impacts on the variation of intrinsic motivation (see Table 3b). Learners with adapted game elements lost significantly less Intrinsic Motivation for Knowledge (Know.Var.), i.e. their satisfaction to learn new things decreased less than for learners with non adapted game elements. They also gained significantly more Intrinsic Motivation for Accomplishment (Acc.Var.), i.e. their pleasure for overcoming a challenge increased, whereas it decreased for learners with non adapted game elements. The adaptation process had no significant effects on learner engaged behaviours.

5.4   Dual Profile Adaptation Results

When compared to learners who used a non adapted game element (see Table 3c), we found that learners with adapted game elements gained significantly less amotivation (Amot.Var.), meaning that they were less reluctant to learn mathematics. They also gained significantly more Intrinsic Motivation for Stimulation (Stim.Var.), meaning that they had more fun and excitement performing the maths activities. As with the initial motivation adaptation, we also found that these learners lost less intrinsic motivation to knowledge (Know.Var.) and gained more intrinsic motivation for accomplishment (Acc.Var.) (although these differences were only slightly significant $p \approx .05$).

6   Study Limitations

We identified some limitations to our study related to the context-dependency and generalisability of our results. We employed 6 game elements designed especially for young learners (around 13 years old), for a specific learning environment (secondary school mathematics). First, the influences measured for each game element could be different for other learners. Younger learners may be more receptive to the playfulness induced by our game elements whereas older, or less technology fluent learners, might have been less receptive. Second, we may obtain different results when considering other game elements implementing other game mechanics (such as collaboration or competition). Finally, results could be different for other domains as suggested by [9], some examples of how these results might change in other domains are presented in the following section.

7   Discussion and Conclusion

Our study shows three important findings in the educational field. First, we show that the user model chosen to tailor game elements can have significant effects on learners, but on different metrics (motivation or engaged behaviours) depending on the chosen profile (player profile, initial motivation or both). Second, we highlight that tailoring game elements according to initial motivation can induce a more positive variation of intrinsic motivation compared to un-tailored game elements. Third, a combination of player profile and initial motivation can lead to a more positive variation of intrinsic motivation and less amotivation compared to tailoring based only on initial motivation. We discuss these findings hereafter.

Tailoring gamification based only on the Hexad profile led learners to be more engaged in the learning task, which confirms the results obtained in [21] in a computer network design course regarding learner engagement. However, our study highlights that this engagement is associated with lower performances, which is contradictory with the study reported in [14], where they found that personalised badges and feedback had a positive effect on maths performance. We also show that an adaptation based only on player types has no effect on learner motivation to learn Mathematics, as also observed in [19] when learning French spelling. We can conclude that game elements could be beneficial to engage learners in the learning activity, but only if these elements give direct feedback on their performance.

Providing learners with game elements adapted to their initial motivation led to a positive effect on two kinds of intrinsic motivation to learn Mathematics. This finding is consistent with other studies on the impact of a tailored gamification based on learner motivation in a technical English course [28], and a database management course [12]. More precisely, it reduced the decrease in intrinsic motivation for knowledge and made learners more intrinsically motivated to overcome maths challenges. It therefore seems promising to use learner motivation for the learning subject as a basis to tailor gamification in education, although it was rarely considered in previous studies (see Sect. 2.2).

Finally, combining both profiles for the dual adaptation reinforced the observed results with initial motivation, but also led learners to be more motivated to learn Mathematics for fun or excitement. This finding is in line with previous studies on the impact of tailored gamification that show an increase in perceived fun [19] or flow induced by some game elements depending on the player types [29]. Dual adaptation also reduced learner amotivation to learn Mathematics, which is consistent with the findings of the study conducted in [16] when adapting only to player types. We believe that the dual profile adaptation could be even more reinforced by adding more information on the learners. For example, tailoring to personality traits has shown some promises (see Sect. 2.2). It would therefore be interesting to study whether adding a third or even fourth profile to the learner model would increase the effectiveness of the adaptation. However, it is also possible that adding more profiles to the learner model may dilute the differences between learners, making it more difficult to provide accurate recommendations to tailor gamification.

Acknowledgements. This work is a part of the LudiMoodle project financed by the e-FRAN Programme d'investissement d'avenir.

References

1. Deci, E., Ryan, R.: The "what" and "why" of goal pursuits: human needs and the self-determination of behavior. Psychol. Inquiry **11**(4), 227–268 (2000). https://doi.org/10.1207/S15327965PLI1104_01

2. Denden, M., Tlili, A., Essalmi, F., Jemni, M.: Educational gamification based on personality. In: 2017 IEEE/ACS 14th International Conference on Computer Systems and Applications (AICCSA), pp. 1399–1405, October 2017. https://doi.org/10.1109/AICCSA.2017.87

3. Deterding, S., Dixon, D., Khaled, R., Nacke, L.: From game design elements to gamefulness: defining gamification. In: Proceedings of the 15th International Academic MindTrek Conference: Envisioning Future Media Environments, pp. 9–15. ACM (2011)

4. Elliot, A.J., Murayama, K.: On the measurement of achievement goals: critique, illustration, and application. J. Educ. Psychol. **100**(3), 613 (2008)

5. Fortes Tondello, G., Valtchanov, D., Reetz, A., Wehbe, R.R., Orji, R., Nacke, L.E.: Towards a trait model of video game preferences. Int. J. Hum.-Comput. Interact. 1–17 (2018)

6. Goldberg, L.R.: An alternative "description of personality": the big-five factor structure. J. Pers. Soc. Psychol. **59**(6), 1216 (1990)

7. Hair Jr., J.F., Hult, G.T.M., Ringle, C., Sarstedt, M.: A Primer on Partial Least Squares Structural Equation Modeling (PLS-SEM). Sage Publications (2016)

8. Hallifax, S., Serna, A., Marty, J.C., Lavoue, E.: Adaptive gamification in education: a literature review of current trends and developments. In: Scheffel, M., Broisin, J., Pammer-Schindler, V., Ioannou, A., Schneider, J. (eds.) EC-TEL 2019. LNCS, vol. 11722, pp. 294–307. Springer, Cham (2019). https://doi.org/10.1007/978-3-030-29736-7_22

9. Hallifax, S., Serna, A., Marty, J.C., Lavoue, G., Lavoue, E.: Factors to consider for tailored gamification. In: Proceedings of the Annual Symposium on Computer-Human Interaction in Play, CHI PLAY 2019, pp. 559–572. ACM, New York (2019). https://doi.org/10.1145/3311350.3347167. Event-place: Barcelona, Spain

10. Hamari, J., Koivisto, J., Sarsa, H.: Does Gamification Work? - A Literature Review of Empirical Studies on Gamification, pp. 3025–3034, January 2014. https://doi.org/10.1109/HICSS.2014.377

11. Hamari, J., Koivisto, J.: Measuring flow in gamification: dispositional flow scale-2. Comput. Hum. Behav. **40**, 133–143 (2014)

12. Hassan, M.A., Habiba, U., Majeed, F., Shoaib, M.: Adaptive gamification in e-learning based on students' learning styles. Interactive Learning Environments, pp. 1–21 (2019)

13. Jagušt, T., Botički, I., So, H.J.: Examining competitive, collaborative and adaptive gamification in young learners' math learning. Comput. Educ. **125**, 444–457 (2018)

14. Kickmeier-Rust, M.D., Hillemann, E.C., Albert, D.: Gamification and smart feedback: experiences with a primary school level math app. Int. J. Game-Based Learn. **4**(3), 35–46 (2014). https://doi.org/10.4018/ijgbl.2014070104

15. Knutas, A., et al.: A process for designing algorithm-based personalized gamification. Multimedia Tools Appl. **78**(10), 13593–13612 (2018). https://doi.org/10.1007/s11042-018-6913-5

16. Lavoue, E., Monterrat, B., Desmarais, M., George, S.: Adaptive gamification for learning environments. IEEE Trans. Learn. Technol. **12**(1), 16–28 (2019)

17. Lopez, C., Tucker, C.: Towards personalized adaptive gamification: a machine learning model for predicting performance. IEEE Trans. Games (2018)
18. Marczewski, A.C.: Even Ninja Monkeys like to play. CreateSpace Indep. Publish Platform, Charleston (2015)
19. Monterrat, B., Desmarais, M., Lavoué, É., George, S.: A player model for adaptive gamification in learning environments. In: Conati, C., Heffernan, N., Mitrovic, A., Verdejo, M.F. (eds.) AIED 2015. LNCS (LNAI), vol. 9112, pp. 297–306. Springer, Cham (2015). https://doi.org/10.1007/978-3-319-19773-9_30
20. Monterrat, B., Lavoue, E., George, S.: Adaptation of gaming features for motivating learners. Simul. Gaming **48**(5), 625–656 (2017)
21. Mora, A., Tondello, G.F., Nacke, L.E., Arnedo-Moreno, J.: Effect of personalized gameful design on student engagement. In: 2018 IEEE Global Engineering Education Conference (EDUCON), pp. 1925–1933, April 2018. https://doi.org/10.1109/EDUCON.2018.8363471
22. Nacke, L.E., Bateman, C., Mandryk, R.L.: BrainHex: a neurobiological gamer typology survey. Entertain. Comput. **5**(1), 55–62 (2014)
23. Oliveira, W., Bittencourt, I.I.: Tailored Gamification to Educational Technologies. Springer Singapore (2019). https://doi.org/10.1007/978-981-32-9812-5
24. Oliveira, W., et al.: Does tailoring gamified educational systems matter? The impact on students' flow experience. In: Proceedings of the 53rd Hawaii International Conference on System Sciences (2020)
25. Orji, R., Mandryk, R.L., Vassileva, J.: Improving the efficacy of games for change using personalization models. ACM Trans. Comput.-Hum. Interact. **24**(5), 32:1–32:22 (2017). https://doi.org/10.1145/3119929
26. Orji, R., Nacke, L.E., DiMarco, C.: Towards personality-driven persuasive health games and gamified systems. In: Proceedings of SIGCHI Conference on Human Factors in Computing Systems (2017)
27. Paiva, R., Bittencourt, I.I., Tenório, T., Jaques, P., Isotani, S.: What do students do on-line? Modeling students' interactions to improve their learning experience. Comput. Hum. Behav. **64**, 769–781 (2016)
28. Roosta, F., Taghiyareh, F., Mosharraf, M.: Personalization of gamification-elements in an e-learning environment based on learners' motivation. In: 8th International Symposium on Telecommunications (IST), pp. 637–642 (2016)
29. dos Santos, W.O., Bittencourt, I.I., Vassileva, J.: Gamification design to tailor gamified educational systems based on gamer types. In: SBGames 2018 (2018)
30. Tondello, G.F., Wehbe, R.R., Diamond, L., Busch, M., Marczewski, A., Nacke, L.E.: The gamification user types hexad scale. In: Symposium on Computer-Human Interaction in Play, pp. 229–243. ACM (2016)
31. Vallerand, R.J., Pelletier, L.G., Blais, M.R., Briere, N.M., Senecal, C., Vallieres, E.F.: The academic motivation scale: a measure of intrinsic, extrinsic, and amotivation in education. Educ. Psychol. Measur. **52**(4) (1992)

Improving Affect Detection in Game-Based Learning with Multimodal Data Fusion

Nathan Henderson[1]([✉]), Jonathan Rowe[1], Luc Paquette[2], Ryan S. Baker[3], and James Lester[1]

[1] North Carolina State University, Raleigh, NC, USA
{nlhender,jprowe,lester}@ncsu.edu
[2] University of Illinois at Urbana-Champaign, Champaign, IL, USA
lpaq@illinois.edu
[3] University of Pennsylvania, Philadelphia, PA, USA
rybaker@upenn.edu

Abstract. Accurately recognizing learner affect is critically important for enabling affect-responsive learning environments to support student learning and engagement. Multimodal affect detection combining sensor-based and sensor-free approaches has shown significant promise in both laboratory and classroom settings. However, important questions remain regarding which data channels are most predictive and how they should be combined. In this paper, we investigate a multimodal affect detection framework that integrates motion tracking-based posture data and interaction-based trace data to recognize the affective states of students engaged with a game-based learning environment for emergency medical training. We compare several machine learning-based affective models using competing feature-level and decision-level multimodal data fusion approaches. Results indicate that multimodal affect detectors induced using joint feature representations from posture-based and interaction-based data channels yield improved accuracy relative to unimodal models across several learner-centered affective states. These findings point toward implications for the design of multimodal affect-responsive learning environments that support learning and engagement.

Keywords: Affect detection · Multimodal data fusion · Game-based learning

1 Introduction

Affect is critical in student learning. Automatically recognizing learners' affective states is foundational to the development of affect-responsive learning environments that can support student emotion regulation and promote enhanced learning experiences [1]. Recent years have seen growing interest in the use of *sensor-based* approaches for capturing data on student affect within adaptive learning environments, and in particular, game-based learning environments [1, 2]. An important feature of sensor-based affect detection is its potential for generalizability across a range of domains and learning environments [3]. Sensor-based modalities such as facial expression [4] and posture [5] have been demonstrated to be highly indicative of learner-centered affective states.

© Springer Nature Switzerland AG 2020
I. I. Bittencourt et al. (Eds.): AIED 2020, LNAI 12163, pp. 228–239, 2020.
https://doi.org/10.1007/978-3-030-52237-7_19

An alternative to sensor-based affect detection is utilizing interaction trace log data to induce *sensor-free* affect detectors, which can be used in contexts where it may be difficult or prohibitive to use physical hardware sensors [6]. Sensor-free features are typically derived from trace data generated by learner interactions with adaptive learning environments [7]. Notably, sensor-free affect detectors typically avoid challenges inherent in the use of physical sensors, including calibration issues, hardware failure, and mistracking [8].

A subject of growing interest is the application of multimodal machine learning techniques to develop affect detectors using multiple complementary data sources. Multimodal affect detectors integrate sensor-free (i.e., interaction-based) and sensor-based approaches, capturing multiple simultaneous perspectives on student interactions with adaptive learning environments. Important questions remain about the predictive value of specific modalities and how they should be combined. Prior work has investigated multimodal affect detection across a range of educational subjects, including science [9], math [10], and introductory programming [11]. However, there is a need for continued research on how effectively multimodal affect detection techniques translate to alternative learning environments and educational subjects.

In this work, we present a multimodal affect detection framework that utilizes posture data and interaction-based trace data from college students engaged with a game-based learning environment for emergency medical training called TC3Sim. We extract both spatial and temporal posture features captured by a Microsoft Kinect sensor as well as interaction-based features depicting students' actions within the game-based learning environment. We compare several methods of multimodal data fusion to determine the optimal approach for detecting students' learner-centered affective states using a range of machine learning-based classification techniques. Results indicate that multimodal affect detectors that utilize a combination of posture-based and interaction-based feature representations outperform competing unimodal baseline models on classification accuracy across several affective states. In this work, we focus on variations of both decision-level and feature-level multimodal data fusion to determine the optimal method of combining modalities during the affective modeling process.

2 Related Work

Recent years have seen growing interest in both sensor-free and sensor-based affect detection in adaptive learning environments. Deep neural architectures have shown promise in sensor-free affect detection. Jiang et al. investigated tradeoffs between deep learning-based representation learning and expert feature-engineering in a sensor-free affect detection framework using interaction trace log data [7]. Botelho et al. explored the use of recurrent neural networks in a related sensor-free affect detection task [6]. More recent work has explored improvements in unimodal affect detection with the introduction of sensor-based modalities [12]. For example, Paquette et al. examined the predictive accuracy of several unimodal sensor-free and sensor-based affect detectors that utilized interaction trace log data as well as posture-based data [13], but did not explore multimodal models that integrate multiple modalities simultaneously.

Multimodal affect detection combining sensor-free and sensor-based data channels offers several benefits in terms of model accuracy and robustness. Grafsgaard et al. used multimodal posture and gesture data to model undergraduate students' affect as they engaged in computer-mediated tutoring sessions on introductory programming [14], with results indicating that more shifts in posture corresponds to increased frustration, while stationary posture may be predictive of engagement. Other multimodal affective computing work has investigated the predictive value of combining interaction-based modalities, such as keystroke data or text-based dialogues, with sensor-based modalities such as posture and gesture data [15]. The results of these prior efforts demonstrated the effectiveness and additive value sensor-based modalities contribute compared to unimodal dialogue-only models. Additional work has investigated student affective responses with facial expression data in combination with interaction patterns as a secondary modality [2]. Bosch et al. investigated the combination of facial expression and interaction log data to detect affect in students using an educational game to teach elementary physics, reporting that the facial expression modality was more predictive than the interaction-based modality [16]. However, important questions remain regarding how to most effectively combine independent modalities for affect detection in adaptive learning environments, such as student posture and interaction log data.

3   Multimodal Data Collection

To investigate multimodal affect detection, we utilized an existing dataset containing sensor-based and interaction-based log data from learners engaged with a game-based learning environment for emergency military medical training, *TC3Sim*. In TC3Sim, learners complete a series of simulated medical training scenarios and are tasked with providing adequate medical care to one or more wounded teammates. The dataset consisted of sensor data and interaction trace logs from 119 undergraduate students (i.e., cadets) from the United States Military Academy (83% male, 17% female). During the data collection, participants completed a series of four training scenarios in TC3Sim, which ranged from situations involving the simple application of a tourniquet to simulated scenarios involving severely injured characters expiring regardless of medical care administered (Fig. 1). Each learner engaged with TC3Sim for approximately one hour. Interaction trace log data was captured using *GIFT*, an open-source service-oriented software framework used to develop and deploy adaptive training environments [17]. To facilitate capture of learners' posture data, each participant sat at a laptop connected to a Microsoft Kinect motion-tracking sensor, which was positioned directly in front of the participant to capture skeletal vertex coordinates based on posture and upper-body movement during the session. For additional detail about the dataset, please see DeFalco et al. [1]. We elect to use interaction data due to its ease of collection and cost effectiveness, while also utilizing posture-based data due to its low-cost, non-invasive method of capture.

To obtain ground-truth labels of affect, a pair of trained observers annotated students' affective states and learner behaviors in accordance with the Baker Rodrigo Ocumpaugh Monitoring Protocol (BROMP) [18]. The observations were recorded in 20-second intervals, and they were made using a small handheld device to allow annotations to be recorded discreetly. The two observers recorded an inter-rater agreement on a subset of the data (i.e., data from a single one-hour session) exceeding 0.6 in terms

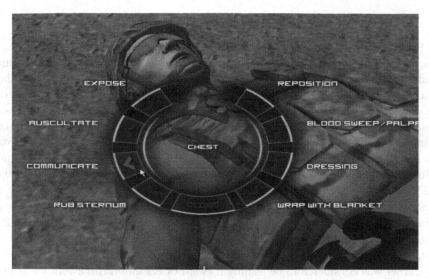

Fig. 1. TC3Sim game-based learning environment.

of Cohen's Kappa [19]. During this study, six affective states were recorded: *bored, confused, engaged concentration, frustration, surprise,* and *anxiety,* with 3,066 distinct BROMP observations captured between the two observers. During the post-processing stage, any observations for which the two observers did not agree were removed from the dataset, as were observations recorded when the students were not actually interacting with the game-based learning environment (i.e., viewing pre- and post-test material or receiving instruction on combat medic procedures). Following post-processing, there were 755 total BROMP observations captured during the study. 435 of the BROMP observations were labeled as *engaged concentration,* 174 as *confused,* 73 as *bored,* 32 as *frustrated,* 29 as *surprised,* and 12 as *anxious.* Due to the low number of observations for *anxious,* we do not consider instances of this affective state in this work.

4 Multimodal Affect Detection

Using the dataset containing synchronized posture data, interaction trace log data, and affect observation data, we induced binary affect detectors for the following learner-centered affective states: *bored, confused, engaged concentration, frustrated,* and *surprised.* We extracted three types of features—posture-based spatial features, posture-based temporal features, and interaction-based features—using feature engineering techniques. The data is upsampled (within the training set only) to resolve imbalances for specific affective states. The features are normalized, and they are utilized to train, validate, and test several machine learning-based models. Due to the multimodal nature of our dataset, we evaluated three variations of data fusion techniques to capture and model information from different modalities, including two feature-level fusion techniques and a decision-level technique [20].

4.1 Posture-Based Spatial Features

The Kinect motion-tracking sensor captures (x, y, z) coordinate information for 91 vertices. We selected the *head, top_skull,* and *center_shoulder* vertices to generate features based on prior work for similar posture-based affect detection tasks [14]. From these vertices, we extracted 73 distinct features to capture the spatial position of each participant's head and upper torso. For each of the three vertices, several positional features were extracted, including current Euclidean distance from the Kinect, current Z-coordinate, minimum observed distance, maximum observed distance, median distance, and variance in observed distance. These features were calculated for each BROMP observation. Additionally, summative features, such as the minimum, maximum, median, and variance in distance, were calculated for the preceding 5, 10, and 20 s time intervals prior to each BROMP observation. In addition to these 54 features, several features were extracted to capture net changes in posture and distance for time windows of 3 and 20 s. Finally, several features were calculated to determine whether a learner was leaning forward, backward, or sitting upright. These features were calculated using the *head* vertex. The learner was considered to be leaning forward or backward if the vertex was more than a single standard deviation from the median head position for that particular workstation. These three posture-based features were calculated over observed sequences of 5, 10, and 20 s, in addition to the entire gameplay session up to the current observation.

4.2 Posture-Based Temporal Features

While skeletal tracking functionalities of motion-tracking sensors, such as Microsoft Kinect, directly capture spatial information about upper body position, temporal information about torso movement is often left implicit despite having been shown to be informative and yield improved accuracy in affect recognition tasks [21]. To address this issue, we extracted several temporal features that capture the "velocity" of skeletal vertices tracked by the Microsoft Kinect sensor. Specifically, the distance between consecutive sensor readings was calculated for the head vertex's positional coordinates. The subsequent delta values were used to generate velocity features calculated across time windows of 3, 5, 10, and 20 s preceding each BROMP observation. Extracted statistical features included the mean, median, max, and variance of each corresponding velocity value, introducing an additional 48 features that served as a form of simulated temporal modality [22]. Because of the large number of features generated per vertex, additional velocity information was not calculated using the *top_skull* and *center_shoulder* vertices.

4.3 Interaction-Based Features

From the gameplay interaction logs, we extracted 39 distinct features centered around the participants' actions in the TC3Sim game-based learning environment, as well as information about the virtual patients treated in the game. Features summarizing the state of virtual patients in TC3Sim included changes in systolic blood pressure and heart rate, number of exposed wounds, lung volume, remaining blood volume, and bleed rate. Additionally, features were extracted based upon actions taken by the learner such as checking a patient's vital signs, conducting a blood sweep, applying a bandage or tourniquet, communicating with the patient, or requesting an evacuation. The resulting interaction-based features were calculated over the 20 s duration prior to the current BROMP observation, using statistical measures such as the sum or current count of a gameplay action, or the standard deviation or average of a metric such as blood pressure.

4.4 Affect Model Evaluation

Following feature engineering, binary datasets were generated for each of the affective states with a variable (i.e., label) denoting whether the record was associated with a positive instance of that particular affective state (e.g., *bored, confused, engaged concentration*). Because of the imbalance between positive and negative instances of several affective states, including *frustrated* and *surprised*, each dataset underwent upsampling using the Synthetic Minority Oversampling Technique (SMOTE) [23], within training sets only. This process selects a positive instance of the minority class at random and linearly interpolates synthetic data points between the selected point and another minority sample chosen by a randomized K-nearest neighbor clustering approach. SMOTE is a common approach to resolving class imbalance issues by bringing the class distribution to a uniform balance while avoiding duplication of minority instances, which can lead to overfitting in affective models.

The datasets for each binary classification task were split into a training set and a held-out test set, containing approximately 80% and 20% of the total dataset, respectively. The datasets were sampled to ensure that the distributions between training and test data were relatively similar. The training set was used to evaluate each of the modeling approaches using 4-fold cross-validation. The splits for both the cross-validation and training/test sets were performed at a student level to avoid data leakage from a single session during either the training or evaluation phases.

Prior to training, each of the datasets was normalized and underwent forward feature selection to allow the models to train using only selected features, eliminating redundant or otherwise uninformative features. Forward feature selection involves iterating through combinations of features in a greedy fashion, beginning with feature vectors of size 1 and continuing until a certain number of features are selected or all combinations of features are exhausted. For this work, we selected 12 features per data channel. In cases involving multimodal input, 6 features were selected per feature type (i.e., spatial and temporal) for the posture-based feature representations, and 4 features were selected per feature type across both of the data channels (i.e., spatial, temporal, and interaction). We used a support vector machine (SVM) to guide feature selection due to its ability to efficiently perform non-linear classification. A feature is selected as "optimal" if its addition to a feature set yields improved accuracy for the SVM model. The computational efficiency of the SVM is important due to the number of times a model is trained during the feature selection process. Feature normalization, upsampling, feature selection, and model training took place within each cross-validation fold to prevent data leakage across the training and validation data.

4.5 Multimodal Data Fusion with Posture- and Interaction-Based Modalities

We investigated several approaches for integrating feature representations from the independent modalities using multimodal data fusion techniques. Two commonly used variations of data fusion include feature-level fusion (early fusion) and decision-level fusion (late fusion). *Early Fusion* (EF) involves the concatenation of features prior to training the models. We evaluated two different configurations of Early Fusion. Early Fusion 1 (EF1) implements feature selection (F. S.) following feature concatenation, and Early Fusion 2 (EF2) implements feature selection prior to feature concatenation. *Late Fusion* (LF) involves independently training a separate model on each modality and subsequently obtaining a single representative prediction through a voting scheme based on the predictions and confidence levels of each model. We used the highest average confidence across each class to determine the final representative prediction within Late Fusion. A visualization of the multimodal data fusion processes is shown in Fig. 2.

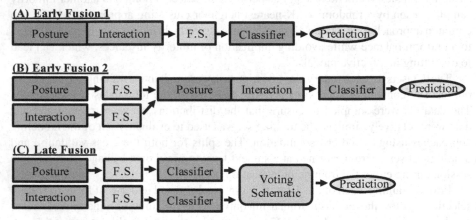

Fig. 2. Visualization of multimodal data fusion pipeline for Early Fusion 1 (2A), Early Fusion 2, (2B), and Late Fusion (2C).

5 Results

We compared five machine learning techniques for inducing detectors of each affective state: Support Vector Machine (SVM), Random Forest (RF), Gaussian Naive Bayes (NB), Logistic Regression (LR), and Multi-Layer Perceptron (MLP). To serve as baselines, we trained unimodal models using either interaction data or posture data, respectively. These models were based upon unimodal affect detectors induced in prior work [1], although we make several methodological refinements related to feature selection, upsampling, cross-validation, evaluation on a held-out test, and implementation of machine learning models. These modifications have a small impact on the results for the baseline models, but overall accuracy trends across affective states remained the same as in prior findings. The posture-only baselines were evaluated using both spatial and temporal modalities using data fusion techniques depicted in Fig. 2, but for this analysis, we consider these models to be "unimodal" because both the spatial and temporal features were extracted from the same sensor-based data channel. Each model's predictive accuracy was examined under cross-validation on the training set to determine which model was "optimal" for the respective combination of feature set, data fusion method, and affective state. The model with highest performance during cross validation was evaluated using data from the held-out test set. Each model was evaluated with Cohen's Kappa as the primary metric, due to its ability to account for positive classifications occurring due to random chance or dataset-induced bias [19]. We also present results in terms of raw classification accuracy (Acc.) and F1. Results from this evaluation are shown in Table 1, with the highest-performing combination of data fusion technique and model for each affective state shown in bold.

Table 1. Optimal models for each combination of modalities and affective states.

Modality		Bored				Confused		
	Model	Kappa	Acc.	F1	Model	Kappa	Acc.	F1
Gameplay	RF	0.3788	0.8579	0.4476	MLP	0.0161	0.4581	0.3232
Posture (EF1)	MLP	0.3147	0.9074	0.3478	SVM	0.1336	0.6975	0.3288
Posture (EF2)	SVM	0.2941	0.9012	0.3334	**MLP**	**0.2206**	**0.7593**	**0.3607**
Posture (LF)	MLP	0.1107	0.8458	0.1935	MLP	0.1141	0.7531	0.2307
Multimodal (EF1)	LR	0.4328	0.8581	0.5106	MLP	0.1181	0.7099	0.2985
Multimodal (EF2)	**SVM**	**0.4664**	**0.9074**	**0.5161**	MLP	0.1023	0.5000	0.4000
Multimodal (LF)	MLP	0.4568	0.9135	0.5000	MLP	0.1329	0.5432	0.4127

Modality		Engaged Concentration				Frustrated		
	Model	Kappa	Acc.	F1	Model	Kappa	Acc.	F1
Gameplay	MLP	0.1047	0.5718	0.6046	MLP	0.0514	0.6643	0.1182
Posture (EF1)	SVM	0.1565	0.5679	0.5205	MLP	0.1492	0.9283	0.1667
Posture (EF2)	RF	0.1566	0.5864	0.6417	SVM	0.0825	0.9135	0.1250
Posture (LF)	MLP	0.1199	0.5741	0.6532	MLP	0.0825	0.9135	0.1250
Multimodal (EF1)	MLP	0.1199	0.5741	0.6532	NB	0.1124	0.7099	0.2034
Multimodal (EF2)	RF	0.1625	0.6049	0.7117	**MLP**	**0.2054**	**0.8951**	**0.2609**
Multimodal (LF)	**SVM**	**0.2544**	**0.6172**	**0.5694**	SVM	0.0028	0.3395	0.1157

Modality		Surprised		
	Model	Kappa	Acc.	F1
Gameplay	RF	0.0797	0.8362	0.1352
Posture (EF1)	MLP	0.0831	0.6605	0.1538
Posture (EF2)	SVM	0.0236	0.8642	0.0834
Posture (LF)	MLP	0.0053	0.0987	0.0875
Multimodal (EF1)	**MLP**	**0.1041**	**0.9259**	**0.1429**
Multimodal (EF2)	MLP	-0.0373	0.9259	0.0000
Multimodal (LF)	MLP	0.0803	0.9135	0.1250

We observe from the results that multimodal affect detectors utilizing a combination of interaction-based and posture-based modalities outperform posture-only baseline and interaction-only baseline models for four out of the five affective states, with the sole exception being the state of *confused*. For the four other affective states, Early Fusion 1 was the best fusion technique for *surprised*, and Early Fusion 2 was the most accurate method for *bored* and *frustrated*. Late Fusion achieved the highest performance for *engaged concentration*. The majority of the affective states produced a relatively high Kappa value (>0.2), excluding *surprised*.

It is noteworthy that the MLP models were the optimal classification model for a majority of cases (60%), potentially due to their ability to robustly model complex, non-linear relationships between modalities. This capability is especially important when modeling data from multiple independent modalities such as Early Fusion and the posture-based models using both spatial and temporal modalities. SVM and RF models were occasionally the best-performing classification techniques for both unimodal and multimodal affect detection. NB and LR models were each selected once as the best-performing model for a certain multimodal configuration, although neither model was the optimally performing model for an entire affective state.

6 Discussion

To conduct a more in-depth analysis of the predictive value of each modality during multimodal data fusion, we recorded the frequency that each feature was selected during cross-validation for each data fusion variation. Although Early Fusion 2 and Late Fusion enforced an inherent balance between modality features, Early Fusion 1 combined all features into a single dataset prior to feature section, resulting in a majority of features being weighted towards the most predictive modality.

We find that the ratio of interaction-based features to posture-based features selected for all 4 folds (48 total features) is 25:23 for *bored*, 18:30 for *confused*, 22:26 for *engaged concentration*, 26:22 for *frustrated*, and 27:21 for *surprised*. The distribution of features was skewed towards interaction-based features for three of the affective states and toward posture-based features for two of the affective states, suggesting a comparable degree of predictive value between modalities across all affective states. This trend may explain why Early Fusion 2 and Late Fusion yielded the best-performing models for three of the five affective states examined (i.e., *bored*, *engaged concentration*, and *frustrated*). Both of these techniques allot equal emphasis on each modality and prevent individual modalities from monopolizing the feature set.

Results indicate that *confusion* was modeled most effectively using posture features only, which suggests that learner posture may be more indicative of confusion than interaction-based features extracted from TC3Sim log data. D'Mello and Graesser previously demonstrated a correlation between students' upright posture and instances of displayed confusion [24]. In aggregate, the results indicate that the predictive value of each modality varies across affective states, which in turn impacts the performance of Early Fusion and Late Fusion techniques. Utilizing dedicated models for each affective state, rather than inducing a single model to classify all affective states, enables the use of different modeling and data fusion techniques to yield improved detector performance.

This also allows the multimodal framework to adapt to variance in feature balances for individual affective states.

It was observed that the most frequently selected features across all of the affective states were *sitmid_freq, sit_forward_freq, Sum of isSafe, CENTER_SHOULDER_max, sitmid_freq_20sec*, and *Min of HeartRate*. This indicates that each modality contributed relatively equally to the performance of the optimal multimodal classifiers. The two most frequent features (*sitmid_freq, sit_forward_freq*) were representative of the frequency that a learner adjusted their posture, while the two interaction-based features (*Sum of isSafe, Min of HeartRate*) were representative of the student's in-game actions and states, respectively. The remaining two features were also posture-based features: *CENTER_SHOULDER_max* focused on the furthest distance of the *CENTER_SHOULDER* vertex from the Kinect sensor over the entire session, and *sitmid_freq_20sec* focused on the learners' frequency of sitting upright for the preceding 20 s. A possible explanation for the improvement of the multimodal models' performance over the unimodal baselines is that the multimodal models were able to obtain a more thorough, comprehensive picture of the learners' behavior, as the most frequently used features were widely varied in the information provided.

7 Conclusion

Accurately detecting learner affect is a critical component of student modeling and has significant potential for guiding adaptive learning environments that support student learning and engagement. In this work, we have demonstrated the effectiveness of a multimodal affect detection framework that integrates interaction-based and posture-based data channels captured from undergraduate students engaging with a game-based learning environment for emergency military medical training. Results indicate that use of multiple independent modalities yields improved performance from multimodal detectors of five affective states compared to unimodal detectors that utilize only interaction-based or posture-based feature representations. We also explored several methods of multimodal data fusion to combine the two modalities and found that feature-level data fusion yielded the greatest predictive accuracy for three of the five affective states.

These results suggest several promising directions for future work. Investigating recent advances in multimodal machine learning techniques, including multimodal neural architectures, has strong potential to yield further improvements to the accuracy of multimodal affect detectors in adaptive learning environments. More sophisticated methods of data upsampling can be explored, as this might have a significant impact on classifier performance due to the pronounced imbalance and relatively small size of many learner-centered affective datasets. Generative models such as generative adversarial networks and variational autoencoders are upsampling methods that show particular promise. Finally, it will be important to investigate the run-time integration of multimodal affect detectors into game-based learning environments to enable adaptive features such as user-sensitive feedback or tailored scaffolding to improve learner engagement and support greater learning outcomes.

Acknowledgements. We wish to thank Dr. Jeanine DeFalco, Dr. Benjamin Goldberg, and Dr. Keith Brawner at the U.S. Army Combat Capabilities Development Command, Dr. Mike Matthews and COL James Ness at the U.S. Military Academy, and Dr. Robert Sottilare at SoarTech for their assistance in facilitating this research. The research was supported by the U.S. Army Research Laboratory under cooperative agreement #W911NF-13-2-0008. Any opinions, findings, and conclusions expressed in this paper are those of the authors and do not necessarily reflect the views of the U.S. Army.

References

1. DeFalco, J., et al.: Detecting and addressing frustration in a serious game for military training. Int. J. Artif. Intell. Educ. **28**(2), 152–193 (2018)
2. Bosch, N., et al.: Detecting student emotions in computer-enabled classrooms. In: Proceedings of the 25th International Joint Conference on Artificial Intelligence, pp. 4125–4129 (2016)
3. Girardi, D., Lanubile, F., Novielli, N.: Emotion detection using noninvasive low cost sensors. In: Proceedings of the 7th International Conference on Affective Computing and Intelligent Interaction, pp. 125–130. IEEE (2017)
4. Soleymani, M., Asghari-Esfeden, S., Fu, Y., Pantic, M.: Analysis of EEG signals and facial expressions for continuous emotion detection. IEEE Trans. Affect. Comput. **7**(1), 17–28 (2015)
5. Grafsgaard, J., Wiggins, J., Boyer, K., Wiebe, E., Lester, J.: Predicting learning and affect from multimodal data streams in task-oriented tutorial dialogue. In: Proceedings of the 7th International Conference on Educational Data Mining, pp. 122–129. International Educational Data Mining Society, London, UK (2014)
6. Botelho, A.F., Baker, R.S., Heffernan, N.T.: Improving sensor-free affect detection using deep learning. In: André, E., Baker, R., Hu, X., Rodrigo, M.M.T., du Boulay, B. (eds.) AIED 2017. LNCS (LNAI), vol. 10331, pp. 40–51. Springer, Cham (2017). https://doi.org/10.1007/978-3-319-61425-0_4
7. Jiang, Y., et al.: Expert feature-engineering vs. deep neural networks: which is better for sensor-free affect detection? In: Penstein Rosé, C., et al. (eds.) AIED 2018. LNCS (LNAI), vol. 10947, pp. 198–211. Springer, Cham (2018). https://doi.org/10.1007/978-3-319-93843-1_15
8. Baker, R., et al.: Towards sensor-free affect detection in cognitive tutor algebra. In: Proceedings of the 5th International Conference on Educational Data Mining, pp. 126–133 (2012)
9. Bosch, N., D'Mello, S., Baker, R., Ocumpaugh, J., Shute, V.: Temporal generalizability of face-based affect detection in noisy classroom environments. In: Conati, C., Heffernan, N., Mitrovic, A., Verdejo, M.F. (eds.) AIED 2015. LNCS (LNAI), vol. 9112, pp. 44–53. Springer, Cham (2015). https://doi.org/10.1007/978-3-319-19773-9_5
10. Arroyo, I., Cooper, D., Burleson, W., Woolf, B., Muldner, K., Christopherson, R.: Emotion sensors go to school. In: Proceedings of the 14th International Conference on Artificial Intelligence in Education, pp. 17–24 (2009)
11. Grafsgaard, J., Wiggins, J., Boyer, K., Wiebe, E., Lester, J.: Automatically recognizing facial expression: predicting engagement and frustration. In: Proceedings of the 6th International Conference on Educational Data Mining, pp. 43–50 (2013)
12. D'Mello, S., Kory, J.: A review and meta-analysis of multimodal affect detection systems. ACM Comput. Surv. (CSUR) **47**(3), 43 (2014)
13. Paquette, L., et al.: Sensor-free or sensor-full: a comparison of data modalities in multichannel affect detection. In: Proceedings of the 8th International Conference on Educational Data Mining, pp. 93–100 (2015)

14. Grafsgaard, J., Boyer, K., Wiebe, E., Lester, J.: Analyzing posture and affect in task-oriented tutoring. In: Proceedings of the International Conference of the Florida Artificial Intelligence Research Society, pp. 438–443 (2012)
15. Grafsgaard, J., Wiggins, J., Vail, A., Boyer, K., Wiebe, E., Lester, J.: The additive value of multimodal features for predicting engagement, frustration, and learning during tutoring. In: Proceedings of the Sixteenth ACM International Conference on Multimodal Interaction, pp. 42–49. ACM (2014)
16. Bosch, N., Chen, H., Baker, R., Shute, V., D'Mello, S.: Accuracy vs. availability heuristic in multimodal affect detection in the wild. In: Proceedings of the 17th ACM International Conference on Multimodal Interaction, pp. 267–274 (2015)
17. Sottilare, R., Baker, R., Graesser, A., Lester, J.: Special issue on the generalized intelligent framework for tutoring (GIFT): creating a stable and flexible platform for innovations in AIED research. Int. J. Artif. Intell. Educ. **28**(2), 139–151 (2018)
18. Baker, R., Ocumpaugh, J., Andres, J.: BROMP quantitative field observations: a review. In: Feldman, R. (ed.) Learning Science: Theory, Research, and Practice, pp. 1–45. McGraw-Hill, New York (2018)
19. Cohen, J.: A coefficient of agreement for nominal scales. Educ. Psychol. Measur. **20**(1), 37–46 (1960)
20. Baltrušaitis, T., Ahuja, C., Morency, L.: Multimodal machine learning: a survey and taxonomy. IEEE Trans. Pattern Anal. Mach. Intell. **41**(2), 423–443 (2018)
21. Sanghvi, J., Castellano, G., Leite, I., Pereira, A., McOwan, P., Paiva, A.: Automatic analysis of affective postures and body motion to detect engagement with a game companion. In: Proceedings of the 6th International Conference on Human-Robot Interaction, pp. 305–312. ACM (2011)
22. Henderson, N., Rowe, J., Mott, B., Brawner, K., Baker, R., Lester, J.: 4D affect detection: improving frustration detection in game-based learning with posture-based temporal data fusion. In: Proceedings of the 20th International Conference on Artificial Intelligence in Education, pp. 144–156 (2019)
23. Chawla, N.V., Bowyer, K., Hall, L., Kegelmeyer, W.: SMOTE: synthetic minority over-sampling technique. J. Artif. Intell. Res. **16**(1), 321–357 (2002)
24. D'Mello, S., Graesser, A.: Mining bodily patterns of affective experience during learning. In: Proceedings of the 3rd International Conference on Educational Data Mining, pp. 31–40 (2010)

A Conceptual Framework for Human–AI Hybrid Adaptivity in Education

Kenneth Holstein[1(✉)], Vincent Aleven[1], and Nikol Rummel[2]

[1] Carnegie Mellon University, Pittsburgh, PA 15213, USA
{kjholste,aleven}@cs.cmu.edu
[2] Ruhr-Universität Bochum, 150, 44801 Bochum, Germany
nikol.rummel@rub.de

Abstract. Educational AI (AIEd) systems are increasingly designed and evaluated with an awareness of the hybrid nature of adaptivity in real-world educational settings. In practice, beyond being a property of AIEd systems alone, adaptivity is often *jointly enacted* by AI systems and human facilitators (e.g., teachers or peers). Despite much recent research activity, theoretical and conceptual guidance for the design of such human–AI systems remains limited. In this paper we explore how adaptivity may be shared across AIEd systems and the various human stakeholders who work with them. Based on a comparison of prior frameworks, which tend to examine adaptivity in AIEd systems or human coaches separately, we first synthesize a set of dimensions general enough to capture *human–AI hybrid adaptivity*. Using these dimensions, we then present a conceptual framework to map distinct ways in which humans and AIEd systems can augment each other's abilities. Through examples, we illustrate how this framework can be used to characterize prior work and envision new possibilities for human–AI hybrid approaches in education.

Keywords: Adaptivity · Human–AI hybrid · Orchestration · Collaboration · Framework

1 Introduction

Moving beyond a focus on adaptivity as a property of AIEd systems alone, AIEd research increasingly acknowledges that, in practice, adaptive learning experiences may be *jointly enacted* by AI and human facilitators (e.g., [7, 15, 24, 30, 47, 58, 70]). For instance, recent work indicates that in K-12 classrooms using AI tutoring software, the sequence of educational activities students receive is often driven by a combination of AI-based activity selection and the dynamic decision-making of classroom teachers (who may selectively override algorithmic recommendations) [53]. Other work has explored the nature and impacts of human–human interactions during AI-supported class sessions, finding that these interactions can play critical roles in mediating AIEd technologies' effectiveness [25, 26, 30, 41, 48, 70]. Building upon such observations, a number of recent projects have begun to explore how AIEd systems might more effectively *work together*

© Springer Nature Switzerland AG 2020
I. I. Bittencourt et al. (Eds.): AIED 2020, LNAI 12163, pp. 240–254, 2020.
https://doi.org/10.1007/978-3-030-52237-7_20

with human facilitators, to amplify their abilities and leverage their complementary strengths [18, 24, 26, 42, 47, 66, 70].

As the AIEd community increasingly turns its attention to *human–AI hybrid* approaches for education, some conceptual guidance may be helpful in navigating this broad design space and in differentiating between fundamentally different kinds of hybrid approaches. Different configurations of AIEd systems and humans, designed to integrate human and AI abilities in different ways, may yield very different outcomes (e.g., [26, 55, 66, 70]). In this paper, we begin to map the diverse ways in which adaptivity may be shared among humans and AIEd systems, to aid the community in (1) organizing *prior work* through the lens of human–AI hybrid adaptivity, and (2) envisioning *new possibilities* for human–AI hybrid approaches in education. To this end, we present a conceptual framework for human–AI hybrid adaptivity in education. Drawing upon multiple existing frameworks for adaptive support—here defined broadly as support that is responsive to unfolding learning situations in pursuit of educational goals—we begin by synthesizing a set of dimensions general enough to capture human–AI adaptivity (Sect. 2). Using these dimensions, we then introduce distinct ways in which humans and AI might augment each other's abilities, illustrating the framework's utility via examples of new directions it surfaces (Sect. 3).

2 Framing "Adaptivity": Synthesizing Existing Frameworks

Several frameworks have been developed to characterize adaptivity in education. In this paper, we build upon a small set of prior frameworks [3, 21, 50, 51, 56, 57, 61, 65] to inform our thoughts about what a more encompassing framework should include. In selecting this set we aimed to consider influential work across multiple research areas, including AIEd [3, 21, 50, 65], computer-supported collaborative learning (CSCL) [56, 61, 65], teacher cognition [57], and classroom orchestration [51]. We searched broadly for theoretically oriented articles that focus on characterizing *adaptive instructional behavior*. While the resulting selection of prior frameworks is not intended to be exhaustive, this set presents several interesting contrasts and overlaps.

Each of the frameworks considered offers a lens to examine particular aspects of adaptive learning systems, while abstracting over others. As discussed below, some frameworks, such as the Adaptivity Grid [3] and Plass's framework [50] provide high resolution lenses to analyze *what* an adaptive system might respond to and *when* an adaptive system might respond, but do not, for example, offer explicit language for describing *how* an adaptive system might respond (see **Action space** below). Meanwhile, other frameworks focus much of their resolution towards characterizing the design space for instructional support actions. For example, VanLehn [65] and Rummel [56] offer ways of characterizing *how* and *when* a system might respond, yet do not offer language for *what* to respond to (see **Perceptual capabilities** below). One possible reason for these differences is that different frameworks have tended to focus on different kinds of adaptive learning systems. A related possibility is that because different frameworks are grounded in different research literatures (e.g., CSCL versus AIEd [65]) they are heavily influenced by the state of the empirical literature within each community. For example, the Adaptivity Grid [3] offered finer-grained distinctions in areas where there was much existing empirical work at the time of writing, but offered coarser-grained distinctions where less prior work existed.

In the remainder of this paper, we adopt a broad framing of adaptivity in terms of *perception-action cycles* [11, 44, 62, 65] enacted by decision-making *agents* or systems of agents (e.g., AI, students, and teachers) [56], in service of specified educational *goals* [56, 65]. Building from prior frameworks, in this section we provide a set of dimensions that are general enough to encompass prior frameworks, while also providing language rich enough to characterize a broad possibility space for human–AI hybrid adaptivity. Whereas prior frameworks focus on providing partial views of agents' adaptive behavior, as discussed above, our dimensions draw from multiple frameworks to provide a more encompassing perspective (cf. [43]). At the same time, we abstract over dimensions from these prior frameworks in the interest of generalizing across a broad range of instructional systems and contexts. For instance, six of the dimensions proposed in [56] are collapsed into the *Actions* dimension below, given that all of these dimensions capture properties of instructional support actions in CSCL.

Goals and Targets: Adaptive instruction presupposes educational goals, or outcomes that the adaptive behavior is intended to bring about (which may vary by student or group and may change over time) [8]. For example, some AIEd systems may be designed to adapt instruction with the ultimate goal of improving student learning outcomes within a domain, whereas others may adapt with the goal of helping students become better self-regulated learners or collaborators. Notably, only some prior frameworks for adaptive instruction provide vocabulary to describe the end goal(s) of the adaptivity. Rummel [56] explicitly names *goals* as the first dimension that needs to be defined upfront of designing any support. Both Rummel [56] and VanLehn [65] further distinguish between the ultimate *goals* of the support (e.g., the kind of change the adaptivity is intended to produce in students), and the immediate *targets* of the support (e.g., whether the support targets cognitive versus metacognitive knowledge).

Perceptual Capabilities: Decision-making agents can adapt to unfolding learning situations only to the extent that they can perceive (i.e., sense and interpret [11, 20]) and represent these situations. An agent's ability to perceive particular variables of a learning situation defines what it can potentially *adapt to*. In addition to variables that are directly observable, this may also include ones that the agent is able to infer from observable attributes (e.g., inferring a student's or teacher's current knowledge from patterns in their recent behavior). In an *Intelligent Tutoring System (ITS)*, the system's perceptual capabilities are defined by its student modeling capabilities, which may include unobservable, inferred constructs such as "help avoidance" or "frustration" [13, 21, 29]. A *human teacher's* perceptual capabilities can be understood as the range of phenomena the teacher is capable of sensing and inferring about a learning situation. In realistic contexts, this may depend on factors such as the teacher's current attentional load [51, 52], as well as the teacher's skill in noticing instructionally relevant events and drawing correct inferences based on potentially limited observations [51, 57, 59]. As noted above, some, but not all prior frameworks included explicit language to characterize an adaptive agent's perceptual capabilities. The Adaptivity Grid [3] categorized previously published empirical evaluations of adaptive learning technologies, in part, based on whether they adapt instruction based on perceptions of students' *prior knowledge & knowledge growth*, their *path through an activity*, their *affective & motivational states*, their *SRL strategies, metacognition, & effort*, or based on a notion of *learning styles*. Similarly, Plass (2016) categorized adaptive learning technologies based on whether they adapt instruction based on perceptions of *affective, cognitive, motivational, or socio-cultural* variables [50].

Action Space: An agent's ability to adapt instruction is also delimited by the set of responses or instructional moves it has at its disposal [56, 57, 61, 62, 65]. For instance, an ITS or a human tutor might try to adapt the kinds of help they provide to a student in their class based on their perceptions of the student's current knowledge state. However, the tutor's ability to adapt will be limited by the instructional moves they currently have in their repertoire (e.g., providing correctness feedback, presenting a worked example, or prompting a self-explanation). Some, but not all, of the frameworks we reviewed included dimensions to characterize an agent's action space. Soller [61] and VanLehn [65] distinguish between actions that *mirror* an agent's perceptions back to students or human facilitators, actions that present an agent's *assessments* of what it perceives, and *coaching* actions (e.g., providing advice). Rummel [56] presents multiple related dimensions classifying instructional support actions, for instance the *directivity* of an action (i.e., whether and to what extent the action presents explicit guidance). In addition, VanLehn [65] and Rummel [56] both characterize instructional actions in terms of their *recipient* or *addressee* (e.g., whether a system presents information to a student, a group of students, or an instructor), and Rummel further specifies whether a student (or group of students) is the direct target of an action, or whether the action is *mediated* through other actors in the learning environment (e.g., where an adaptive system suggests that a teacher or peer tutor help a given student).

Decision Policies: An agent's adaptive behavior can be understood in terms of *decision policies*: sets of rules that map (in a potentially non-deterministic manner) from perceived learning situations or states to particular actions that the agent will take in response [62]. For example, an agent might adaptively respond to detected student frustration by acknowledging or mirroring the student's frustration [21, 50, 65]. However, many alternative decision policies exist. The system might instead respond to detected frustration by selecting alternative activities for the student to work on, or by asking the student whether the system should alert their teacher/peers that they need help [28]. Prior frameworks do not typically provide explicit dimensions to categorize "types" of decision policies (e.g., "responding to affect with affective responses" or "mastery learning based activity selection policies"), although such categorizations often appear in practice when empirically comparing different forms of adaptivity.

Granularity and Timing: Finally, many prior frameworks provide dimensions dedicated to describing *when* a system adapts instruction (e.g., [3, 50, 51, 56, 65]). That is, the frequency or granularity at which the perception-action cycle is enacted. This may occur, for instance, once per *task* or per *step* of a task [3, 56, 65], once per *turn* in a conversation [56], or even once per *design iteration* (when considering systems that are iteratively improved based on data) [3]. Plass [50], Prieto [51], and Rummel [56] also distinguish the *timing* of the adaptation; e.g., whether the adaptation occurs *prior* to the instructional activity, *in the midst* of the activity, or *afterwards* [50, 51, 56].

Many frameworks for adaptive instructional support have been developed, with each offering a lens to examine particular aspects and particular kinds of adaptive learning systems. The set of high-level dimensions presented in this section are intended to capture essential components of adaptive learning systems, informed by a comparison across frameworks (cf. [43]). In the next section, we use these dimensions to explore distinct ways for adaptivity to be *shared* across humans and machines.

3   A Conceptual Framework for Human–AI Hybrid Adaptivity

In the following we present a conceptual framework for human–AI hybrid adaptivity in education, examining the same set of basic components (goals/targets, perception, action, decision policies, and granularity/timing) while broadening our focus. We use this framework both to characterize prior work and to envision new possibilities, based upon distinct ways in which humans and AIEd systems might augment one another: (1) *Goal Augmentation,* (2) *Perceptual Augmentation,* (3) *Action Augmentation,* and (4) *Decision Augmentation.* Within each category, possibilities exist both for *augmenting performance* (in which humans and AI systems, assumed to have complementary strengths and weaknesses, augment one another's abilities at "runtime", but without necessarily producing lasting changes in behavior) and for *co-learning* (in which humans and AI systems help one another improve over time). Finally, we discuss how the *Granularity and Timing* of adaptivity might be understood in human–AI systems.

3.1   Goal Augmentation: Informing Each Other's Instructional Goals

A key way for humans and AIEd systems to support one another is by influencing each other's goals. To a large extent, AIEd technologies encode the assumptions and goals of those who design and develop them—whether explicitly, via objective functions that a system's adaptive policies optimize towards, or implicitly, through design decisions that promote certain goals over others. However, the goals baked into an AIEd system may not always align with those of humans in real-world educational contexts [24, 46, 53]. For example, ITSs used in K-12 school contexts often implement mastery-based activity selection policies, allowing each student to progress through the curriculum at their own pace. Yet prior work suggests that teachers often struggle to balance their desire to implement such personalized classrooms with external pressure to keep classes "on schedule". In practice, teachers often opt to manually push students forward in the curriculum if they are slower to master certain skills [24, 53], sometimes even if they are aware that doing so may harm students' learning [24, 28]. As of yet, little work in AIEd has explored the design of supports for goal augmentation.

AIEd Informing Human Goals. It may not *always* be desirable for AIEd systems to adapt to human facilitators' instructional goals. For instance, in some cases, teachers' or peer tutors' goals may be fundamentally at odds with known instructional best practices. Future systems could play an important role in helping humans productively reflect upon their goals, helping them refine these goals or consider alternatives [4, 19].

Humans Informing AIEd Goals. Human facilitators may hold critical, on-the-ground knowledge about their instructional contexts and personal goals, to which AIEd systems would not typically be privy. Building upon the above example, ITSs might be even more effective in classroom contexts if designed to accept teachers' input regarding the goals they should be optimizing towards. By enabling teachers to help shape the system's goals, the system could in turn help teachers more effectively navigate trade-offs between competing goals (e.g., by supporting teachers in deciding when to push students ahead in the curriculum, while causing minimal harm to their learning [28]).

3.2 Perceptual Augmentation: Leveraging Complementarity in Perception

A second way for AIEd systems and humans to augment one another is by enhancing each other's abilities to perceive instructionally relevant information, or *opportunities for action*. This may take the form of (1) extending what the other is able to *sense* (i.e., what information is made available to them, prior to further interpretation [11, 20]); (2) guiding how the other distributes their *attention*; or (3) guiding how the other *interprets* incoming information. Each of these broad possibilities is discussed in turn, below.

3.2.1 Augmenting Sensing and Attention

AIEd systems can be designed to extend what humans are able to *sense* and *notice* about learners, learning, or their own teaching, or from the other direction, to help humans augment what AIEd systems sense and notice. Thus far, more work in AIEd has focused on supporting *AI→human* than *human→AI* augmentation in this area.

AIEd Augmenting Human Sensing and Attention. A number of AIEd systems have been developed to help human facilitators sense information to which the AI would otherwise have unique access (e.g., [2, 5, 26, 38, 40, 55, 69, 70]). Prior work has focused on augmenting what learners and peer tutors are able to sense and notice about a learning situation. For example, the *Adaptive Peer Tutoring Assistant (APTA)* supports peer tutors in recognizing opportunities for effective intervention, in the context of ongoing peer tutoring [70]. In the context of self-regulated learning with an AI tutor, the *Help Tutor* supports students in monitoring their own help-seeking behavior, and in noticing cases where they may be using the software's help functions in maladaptive ways [2]. More recently, several projects have focused on designing ways to keep human teachers in the loop in AI-supported classrooms (e.g., [27, 40, 47, 68]). For example, the *Lumilo* teacher smartglasses are designed to direct teachers' attention, during a class session, to situations that an AI tutor may be poorly suited to handle on its own, or which require a teacher's further assessment [26, 27]. In each of the above examples, there is potential for future AIEd systems not only to augment human facilitators' abilities in-the-moment, but also to help humans *learn to notice* relevant features of a learning situation even when in-the-moment support is unavailable [2, 19, 59, 70].

Humans Augmenting AIEd Sensing and Attention. From the other side, humans may have relevant on-the-ground knowledge to which AIEd systems are likely to be blind. AIEd systems may be designed so that humans can help them perceive such information. For instance, future systems might be designed to allow teachers and parents to update individual student models with relevant information about the student's broader context; e.g., whether the student is currently facing at-home difficulties that may impact their performance (cf. [9]). Similarly, an AIEd system might be designed to periodically poll students regarding their subjective *feeling of knowing* particular skills that are targeted by the instruction [12, 36]. In addition to having humans input information directly, some research has begun to explore approaches in which humans teach AIEd systems, via demonstration, to perceive instructionally relevant features to which they should attend in the future (e.g., [35]).

3.2.2 Augmenting Interpretation

AIEd systems can also be designed to support humans in *interpreting* and *drawing inferences* from what they notice, or to assist humans in shaping or mediating AIEd systems' interpretations of the events they are able to sense.

AIEd Augmenting Human Interpretation. Beyond extending human sensing capacities, AIEd systems may also support human facilitators in productively interpreting and reflecting upon the information available to them. Whereas some technologies are designed to present information to humans with low-level, minimally pre-interpreted data (e.g., "number of help requests") [4, 5, 16], several of the AIEd systems discussed above, including *APTA*, the *Help Tutor*, and *Lumilo* rely upon advanced student modeling techniques (e.g., automated detectors of "help abuse" or "help avoidance" behaviors). Thus, beyond augmenting human sensing and attention, these systems perform a considerable amount of pre-interpretation on behalf of human facilitators or learners [5]. Emerging lines of research are beginning to explore the design of interfaces that can more actively guide humans towards particular interpretations of learning data (e.g., [17]) or interfaces that can scaffold humans in more productive forms of reflection (e.g., [19]). However, it remains an open question for future research how best to productively guide human interpretation, while still leveraging (rather than diminishing) humans' unique inferential capacities [5, 14, 17, 23, 33].

Humans Augmenting AIEd Interpretation. Future AIEd systems may be designed to support human facilitators in *detecting* cases where the AI misinterprets learning data (e.g., by misclassifying patterns in collaborating groups' behaviors) and to *provide corresponding feedback* in order to shape these interpretations in more meaningful directions. As of yet, the question of how AIEd systems can be designed to effectively elicit and learn from such feedback remains underexplored (cf. [9, 10, 14, 23, 34, 54]).

3.3 Action Augmentation: Leveraging Complementarity in *Action Spaces*

A third way in which AIEd systems and humans can work together to support more adaptive instruction is by augmenting and extending the other's capacities for instructional *action*. In particular, AIEd systems and humans can (1) enhance each other's *ability to perform* particular kinds of instructional actions, and relatedly *expand the range of actions available* to each; and (2) enhance each other's *scalability* and *capacity* for action. Each of these broad possibilities is discussed below.

3.3.1 Enhancing Ability and Expanding the Availability of Actions

Many open research and design opportunities exist for human–AI systems that augment and expand each other's action spaces. Just a few examples are presented below.

AIEd Augmenting Human Actions. AIEd systems may be designed to support human facilitators in providing *more effective* help. For example, while a human coach works with a student, a future AIEd system might follow along with what the coach is doing, and adaptively present educational resources (e.g., relevant readings, videos, or practice materials) that support their current goals [28, 70]. Alternatively, a system may respond during or after human coaching by adaptively providing feedback on the quality of the instruction (e.g., the clarity of a particular explanation the coach provides), to help the coach adjust and improve over time (cf. [19, 28, 70]).

Humans Augmenting AIEd Actions. Humans can also augment the set of instructional moves available to an AIEd system by either *customizing* or creating *new actions* for the system. For example, AIEd systems may be designed to adaptively deliver hints written by peers or instructors (cf. [22, 28, 72]). Authoring tools have been developed to support non-programmer authoring, but further research is needed to support easy authoring in everyday educational settings (e.g., by teachers or students) [1, 29, 37, 39].

3.3.2 Enhancing Scalability and Capacity

Much prior research in AIEd has focused on augmenting human scalability, whereas relatively less research has targeted the reverse direction. However, many open questions remain in each direction, which emerging work is beginning to tackle.

AIEd Augmenting Human Scalability. AIEd systems have often been promoted as "scaling up" some of the benefits of one-on-one tutoring, effectively providing each student with their own, personal AI tutor [6, 31, 58, 64]. In doing so, AIEd systems can serve as *teachers' aides* [24, 73], helping human coaches or teachers personalize instruction beyond what might otherwise be feasible, while also freeing up humans' limited time and attention for other activities (e.g., providing socio-emotional support or coaching for students most in need) [22, 24, 58, 73]. Thus, one way in which AIEd systems can augment human scalability and capacity is through selective *delegation* [27]. Some research has begun to explore the design of AIEd systems that adaptively, dynamically delegate instructional roles between AI systems, teachers, and peers, based upon an awareness of trade-offs between the *instructional ability* and *capacity* of each [28, 47, 49, 63]. A second emerging way for AIEd systems to help human facilitators scale their efforts is by supporting them in *teaching the AI tutor* (as discussed below), transferring their unique expertise and pedagogical preferences into a system that can reach more students than they themselves can [37, 39, 60, 74].

Humans Augmenting AIEd Scalability. It can also be useful to consider the ways in which human facilitators can (and in practice, often do) support AIEd systems in scaling. Increased scalability risks reducing a system's fit with particular educational contexts, as system developers design solutions to fit constraints of multiple contexts simultaneously [32, 45, 46]. On-the-ground facilitators may support AIEd systems in scaling to diverse contexts by adapting the way these systems are implemented in use to the needs of their local contexts (e.g., [24, 30, 46, 58]). For example, when classroom teachers use AIEd systems that are poorly aligned with their school's existing curriculum, they may selectively assign particular modules to students, overriding the systems' built in sequencing algorithms in the interest of providing better aligned learning experiences [23, 45]. Future AIEd systems may be explicitly designed to facilitate such *adaptability* (e.g., local customizations and overrides) [16], improving their chances for adoption across varied contexts of use [22, 24, 28, 45].

3.4 Decision Augmentation: Leveraging Complementarity in *Decision-Making*

Beyond informing each other's goals or augmenting each other's capacities for perception and action, a fourth major way in which AIEd systems and humans can work together is by helping each other make *more effective pedagogical decisions* (i.e., helping each other more effectively link between perception and action). Prior work has explored forms of both *AI→human* and *human→AI* decision augmentation. However, much additional research is needed in order to fully realize the visions of AIEd systems as, for instance, effective *decision support* and *professional development* tools [5, 19, 23, 24, 66] and as *teachable machines* [37, 39, 60, 74].

AIEd Augmenting Human Decision-Making. In addition to providing instruction to students directly, AIEd systems may be designed as decision support for human facilitators, helping humans take more effective instructional actions in particular learning situations [2, 26, 27, 66, 67, 70]. To an extent, all forms of human augmentation discussed thus far can function as forms of decision support. Indeed, decision support is often conceptualized as a continuous spectrum rather than a binary design choice [5, 56, 65, 71]. For instance, perceptual augmentation may enhance decision-making by directing humans' attention towards learning phenomena that require their further assessment or action [5]. However, AIEd systems may also be designed to support human decision-making more directly and explicitly. For example, an AIEd system might automatically suggest effective ways for a human facilitator to help a group of students, in the moment, based on its perceptions of the students' and/or facilitator's current states (effectively functioning as hints or bug messages, targeted for a human in an instructional role rather than a learner; see [27, 28, 68, 70]). With knowledge of a facilitator's instructional goals, future AIEd systems might help the facilitator make more informed trade-offs between competing goals or nudge them away from practices that are at odds with their goals [28]. Such systems could function not only as decision support, but also as professional development, helping humans improve over time, potentially even in the absence of such support [19, 27, 28, 70].

Humans Augmenting AIEd Decision-Making. AIEd systems may also be designed to help human facilitators *mediate* or *shape* these systems' instructional decision-making. Mediation may occur in practice where a facilitator such as a teacher overrides a decision made by an AIEd system (e.g., by selecting an alternative activity for a student to work on, or an alternative group for a student to collaborate with, rather than ones selected by the system) [5, 24, 47, 49]. As discussed under *Goal Augmentation* above, such overriding behavior occurs regularly in K-12 classroom contexts; as noted, although teachers' overrides can often be seen as adaptive, they can also be maladaptive when they detract from (some) goals for the instruction. In addition to mediating AIEd systems' decision-making, humans might also help systems learn more effective policies or ones better suited to their particular educational contexts [23]. Recent work on *machine teaching* for AIEd suggests promise for approaches in which humans *teach the AI to teach* through feedback and demonstrations [37, 39]. However, further research is needed to develop interaction paradigms for machine teaching that are fast and intuitive enough for everyday use in educational settings [60, 74].

3.5 Granularity and Timing in Human–AI Systems

Finally, we briefly discuss how *granularity* and *timing* might be understood in human–AI systems. When AIEd systems and humans work together, they may each adapt instruction at different grain sizes. For instance, in classrooms using step-based tutoring software, teachers may provide *substep* feedback on-the-spot (i.e., feedback on a step while the student is, from the system's perspective, still in the midst of completing the step) [23, 27, 30]. While an AIEd system waits for the student to submit their input, a human facilitator might perceive an opportunity to intervene within a long pause in student typing. The *timing* of adaptation may also vary across humans and machines. For instance, Aleven et al's "design loop adaptivity" [3] can be viewed as involving a form of shared adaptivity in which human facilitators or instructional designers repeatedly adapt an AIEd system's design (informed by educational data and/or their own observations) *before or after* an instructional activity, while the AIEd system in turn takes care of adapting to learning situations *during* the activity.

4 Conclusions

AIEd systems are increasingly designed and evaluated with an awareness of the shared nature of adaptivity in real-world educational settings. Despite much recent research into human–AI hybrid approaches for education, theoretical and conceptual guidance in this area remains limited. Whereas prior frameworks have tended to examine adaptivity in AIEd systems or human coaches separately, in this paper we have explored how adaptivity may be shared across AIEd systems and the various human stakeholders who work with them.

Based on a comparison and synthesis of prior frameworks, we have presented a generalized set of dimensions, with the goal of capturing essential components of adaptive instructional behavior (cf. [43]). Using these dimensions, we have introduced a conceptual framework for *human–AI hybrid adaptivity* in education, suggesting distinct ways in which AIEd systems and human facilitators might augment one another. Throughout the previous section, we have presented several examples to illustrate how this framework can be used both to characterize *prior work* and to surface *new possibilities* and *open questions* for human–AI hybrid approaches in education.

We view the current framework as a step towards the development of richer theory for human–AI hybrid adaptivity in education, and for human–AI hybrid approaches more broadly. As an empirical and design science, AIEd needs theory to productively guide hypothesis generation, prediction, understanding, and design. Theory can help researchers adopt common concepts and vocabulary, which may in turn accelerate communication and innovation. Theory can shape—for better or worse—how researchers and designers see the world, how they make sense of their observations, and what alternatives they are able to envision. The current framework should be viewed as a starting point, not a finished product. We invite others in the community will challenge this framework and expand upon it.

The design space for human–AI hybrid approaches in education is large and combinatorial: almost any real case will involve *combinations* of the categories of human–AI adaptivity specified in this framework (e.g., an AIEd system might augment human decision-making via a human-augmented perceptual model). It is our hope that the present work will help to guide future research and design, assisting others in navigating this broad design space, in formulating more useful hypotheses, and in differentiating among fundamentally different kinds of human–AI hybrid approaches.

Acknowledgements. This work was supported by NSF Grant #1822861 and IES Grant R305A180301. Any opinions expressed in this article are those of the authors and do not represent views of the NSF or IES.

References

1. Aleven, V., et al.: Example-tracing tutors: intelligent tutor development for non-programmers. Int. J. Artif. Intell. Educ. **26**(1), 224–269 (2016)
2. Aleven, V., Roll, I., McLaren, B.M., Koedinger, K.R.: Help helps, but only so much: research on help seeking with intelligent tutoring systems. Int. J. Artif. Intell. Educ. **26**(1), 205–223 (2016)
3. Aleven, V., McLaughlin, E.A., Glenn, R.A., Koedinger, K.R.: Instruction based on adaptive learning technologies. In: Mayer, R.E., Alexander, P. (eds.) Handbook of Research on Learning and Instruction, pp. 522–560. Routledge, New York (2016)
4. An, P., Bakker, S., Ordanovski, S., Taconis, R., Paffen, C.L., Eggen, B.: Unobtrusively enhancing reflection-in-action of teachers through spatially distributed ambient information. In: Proceedings of the 2019 CHI Conference on Human Factors in Computing Systems, pp. 1–14 (2019)
5. An, P., Holstein, K., d'Anjou, B., Eggen, B., Bakker, S.: The TA framework: designing real-time teaching augmentation for K-12 classrooms. In: Proceedings of the 2020 CHI Conference on Human Factors in Computing Systems (CHI 2020) (2020)
6. Anderson, J.R., Corbett, A.T., Koedinger, K.R., Pelletier, R.: Cognitive tutors: lessons learned. J. Learn. Sci. **4**(2), 167–207 (1995)
7. Baker, R.S.: Stupid tutoring systems, intelligent humans. Int. J. Artif. Intell. Educ. **26**(2), 600–614 (2016)
8. Bransford, J.D., Brown, A.L., Cocking, R.R.: How People Learn, vol. 11. National Academy Press, Washington, DC (2000)
9. Bull, S., Kay, J.: SMILI☺: a framework for interfaces to learning data in open learner models, learning analytics and related fields. Int. J. Artif. Intell. Educ. **26**(1), 293–331 (2016)
10. Chen, N.C., Suh, J., Verwey, J., Ramos, G., Drucker, S., Simard, P.: AnchorViz: facilitating classifier error discovery through interactive semantic data exploration. In: 23rd International Conference on Intelligent User Interfaces, pp. 269–280 (2018)

11. Creem-Regehr, S.H., Kunz, B.R.: Perception and action. Wiley Interdisc. Rev. Cogn. Sci. **1**(6), 800–810 (2010)
12. Cromley, J., Azevedo, R., Olson, E.: Self-regulation of learning with multiple representations in hypermedia. In: Proceedings of the International Conference on Artificial Intelligence in Education, pp. 184–191. IOS Press, Amsterdam (2005)
13. Desmarais, M.C., Baker, R.S.: A review of recent advances in learner and skill modeling in intelligent learning environments. User Model. User-Adap. Inter. **22**(1–2), 9–38 (2012)
14. De-Arteaga, M., Fogliato, R., Chouldechova, A.: A case for humans-in-the-loop: decisions in the presence of erroneous algorithmic scores (2020). arXiv preprint arXiv:2002.08035
15. Dillenbourg, P.: The evolution of research on digital education. Int. J. Artif. Intell. Educ. **26**(2), 544–560 (2016)
16. Dillenbourg, P., Nussbaum, M., Dimitriadis, Y., Roschelle, J.: Design for classroom orchestration. Comput. Educ. **69**, 485–492 (2013)
17. Echeverria, V., Martinez-Maldonado, R., Shum, S.B., Chiluiza, K., Granda, R., Conati, C.: Exploratory versus explanatory visual learning analytics: driving teachers' attention through educational data storytelling. J. Learn. Anal. **5**(3), 72–97 (2018)
18. Fancsali, S.E., Yudelson, M.V., Berman, S.R., Ritter, S.: Intelligent instructional hand offs. In: International Educational Data Mining Society (2018)
19. Gerritsen, D., Zimmerman, J., Ogan, A.: Towards a framework for smart classrooms that teach instructors to teach. In Kay, J., Luckin, R. (eds.) Rethinking Learning in the Digital Age: Making the Learning Sciences Count, 13th International Conference of the Learning Sciences (ICLS) 2018, vol. 3. International Society of the Learning Sciences, London (2018)
20. Goldstein, E.B., Brockmole, J.: Sensation and Perception. Cengage Learning, Boston (2016)
21. Harley, J.M., Lajoie, S.P., Frasson, C., Hall, N.C.: Developing emotion-aware, advanced learning technologies: a taxonomy of approaches and features. Int. J. Artif. Intell. Educ. **27**(2), 268–297 (2017)
22. Heffernan, N.T., Heffernan, C.L.: The ASSISTments ecosystem: building a platform that brings scientists and teachers together for minimally invasive research on human learning and teaching. Int. J. Artif. Intell. Educ. **24**(4), 470–497 (2014)
23. Holstein, K.: Designing real-time teacher augmentation to combine strengths of human and AI instruction. Unpublished doctoral dissertation, Carnegie Mellon University (2019)
24. Holstein, K., McLaren, B.M., Aleven, V.: Intelligent tutors as teachers' aides: exploring teacher needs for real-time analytics in blended classrooms. In: Proceedings of the Seventh International Learning Analytics & Knowledge Conference, pp. 257–266 (2017)
25. Holstein, K., McLaren, B.M., Aleven, V.: SPACLE: investigating learning across virtual and physical spaces using spatial replays. In: Proceedings of the Seventh International Learning Analytics & Knowledge Conference, pp. 358–367 (2017)
26. Holstein, K., McLaren, B.M., Aleven, V.: Student learning benefits of a mixed-reality teacher awareness tool in AI-enhanced classrooms. In: Penstein Rosé, C., et al. (eds.) AIED 2018. LNCS (LNAI), vol. 10947, pp. 154–168. Springer, Cham (2018). https://doi.org/10.1007/978-3-319-93843-1_12
27. Holstein, K., McLaren, B.M., Aleven, V.: Co-designing a real-time classroom orchestration tool to support teacher–AI complementarity. J. Learn. Anal. **6**(2), 27–52 (2019)
28. Holstein, K., McLaren, B.M., Aleven, V.: Designing for complementarity: teacher and student needs for orchestration support in AI-enhanced classrooms. In: Isotani, S., Millán, E., Ogan, A., Hastings, P., McLaren, B., Luckin, R. (eds.) AIED 2019. LNCS (LNAI), vol. 11625, pp. 157–171. Springer, Cham (2019). https://doi.org/10.1007/978-3-030-23204-7_14
29. Holstein, K., Yu, Z., Sewall, J., Popescu, O., McLaren, B.M., Aleven, V.: Opening up an intelligent tutoring system development environment for extensible student modeling. In: Penstein Rosé, C., et al. (eds.) AIED 2018. LNCS (LNAI), vol. 10947, pp. 169–183. Springer, Cham (2018). https://doi.org/10.1007/978-3-319-93843-1_13

30. Kessler, A., Boston, M., Stein, M.K.: Exploring how teachers support students' mathematical learning in computer-directed learning environments. Inf. Learn. Sci. **121**, 52–78 (2019)
31. Koedinger, K.R., Anderson, J.R., Hadley, W.H., Mark, M.A.: Intelligent tutoring goes to school in the big city. Int. J. Artif. Intell. Educ. **8**, 30–43 (1997)
32. Kulkarni, C.: Design perspectives of learning at scale: scaling efficiency and empowerment. In: Proceedings of the Sixth (2019) ACM Conference on Learning@ Scale, pp. 1–11 (2019)
33. Lake, B.M., Ullman, T.D., Tenenbaum, J.B., Gershman, S.J.: Building machines that learn and think like people. Behav. Brain Sci. **40**, 258 (2017)
34. Lakkaraju, H., Kamar, E., Caruana, R., Horvitz, E.: Identifying unknown unknowns in the open world: representations and policies for guided exploration. In: Proceedings of the Thirty-First AAAI Conference on Artificial Intelligence (2017)
35. Lee, M.H., Runde, J., Jibril, W., Wang, Z., Brunskill, E.: Learning the features used to decide how to teach. In: Proceedings of the Second (2015) ACM Conference on Learning@ Scale, pp. 421–424 (2015)
36. Long, Y., Aleven, V.: Students' understanding of their student model. In: Biswas, G., Bull, S., Kay, J., Mitrovic, A. (eds.) AIED 2011. LNCS (LNAI), vol. 6738, pp. 179–186. Springer, Heidelberg (2011). https://doi.org/10.1007/978-3-642-21869-9_25
37. Maclellan, C.J., Harpstead, E., Patel, R., Koedinger, K.R.: The apprentice learner architecture: closing the loop between learning theory and educational data. In: International Educational Data Mining Society (2016)
38. Martinez-Maldonado, R., Clayphan, A., Yacef, K., Kay, J.: MTFeedback: providing notifications to enhance teacher awareness of small group work in the classroom. IEEE Trans. Learn. Technol. **8**(2), 187–200 (2014)
39. Matsuda, N., Cohen, W.W., Koedinger, K.R.: Teaching the teacher: tutoring SimStudent leads to more effective cognitive tutor authoring. Int. J. Artif. Intell. Educ. **25**(1), 1–34 (2015)
40. Mavrikis, M., Gutierrez-Santos, S., Poulovassilis, A.: Design and evaluation of teacher assistance tools for exploratory learning environments. In: Proceedings of the Sixth International Conference on Learning Analytics & Knowledge, pp. 168–172 (2016)
41. Miller, W.L., Baker, R.S., Labrum, M.J., Petsche, K., Liu, Y.H., Wagner, A.Z.: Automated detection of proactive remediation by teachers in reasoning mind classrooms. In: Proceedings of the Fifth International Conference on Learning Analytics and Knowledge, pp. 290–294 (2015)
42. Molenaar, I., Horvers, A., Baker, R.S.: Towards hybrid human-system regulation: understanding childrens' SRL support needs in blended classrooms. In: Proceedings of the 9th International Conference on Learning Analytics and Knowledge, pp. 471–480 (2019)
43. Newell, A.: Unified Theories of Cognition. Harvard University Press, Cambridge (1994)
44. Nilsson, N.J.: Artificial Intelligence: A New Synthesis. Morgan Kaufmann, San Francisco (1998)
45. Nye, B.D.: Barriers to ITS adoption: a systematic mapping study. In: Trausan-Matu, S., Boyer, K.E., Crosby, M., Panourgia, K. (eds.) ITS 2014. LNCS, vol. 8474, pp. 583–590. Springer, Cham (2014). https://doi.org/10.1007/978-3-319-07221-0_74
46. Ogan, A., Yarzebinski, E., Fernández, P., Casas, I.: Cognitive tutor use in Chile: understanding classroom and lab culture. In: Conati, C., Heffernan, N., Mitrovic, A., Verdejo, M.F. (eds.) AIED 2015. LNCS (LNAI), vol. 9112, pp. 318–327. Springer, Cham (2015). https://doi.org/10.1007/978-3-319-19773-9_32
47. Olsen, J.: Orchestrating combined collaborative and individual learning in the classroom. Unpublished Doctoral Dissertation, Carnegie Mellon University (2017)
48. Olsen, J.K., Aleven, V., Rummel, N.: Predicting student performance in a collaborative learning environment. In: International Educational Data Mining Society (2015)

49. Olsen, J., Rummel, N., Aleven, V.: Co-designing orchestration support for social plane transitions with teachers: balancing automation and teacher autonomy. In: International Society of the Learning Sciences, Inc. [ISLS] (2018)
50. Plass, J.: Adaptive Learning—Gedankenspiele (2020). http://janplass.com/index.php/2016/07/07/adaptive-learning/ Accessed 20 Feb 2020
51. Prieto, L.P., Dlab, M.H., Gutiérrez, I., Abdulwahed, M., Balid, W.: Orchestrating technology enhanced learning: a literature review and a conceptual framework. Int. J. Technol. Enhanced Learn. 3(6), 583 (2011)
52. Prieto, L.P., Sharma, K., Dillenbourg, P.: Studying teacher orchestration load in technology-enhanced classrooms. In: Conole, G., Klobučar, T., Rensing, C., Konert, J., Lavoué, É. (eds.) EC-TEL 2015. LNCS, vol. 9307, pp. 268–281. Springer, Cham (2015). https://doi.org/10.1007/978-3-319-24258-3_20
53. Ritter, S., Yudelson, M., Fancsali, S.E., Berman, S.R.: How mastery learning works at scale. In: Proceedings of the Third (2016) ACM Conference on Learning @ Scale, pp. 71–79 (2016)
54. Rodríguez-Triana, M.J., Prieto, L.P., Martínez-Monés, A., Asensio-Pérez, J.I., Dimitriadis, Y.: The teacher in the loop: customizing multimodal learning analytics for blended learning. In: Proceedings of the 8th International Conference on Learning Analytics and Knowledge, pp. 417–426 (2018)
55. Roll, I., Wiese, E.S., Long, Y., Aleven, V., Koedinger, K.R.: Tutoring self-and co-regulation with intelligent tutoring systems to help students acquire better learning skills. In: Sottilare, R., Graesser, A., Hu, X., Holden, H. (eds.) Design Recommendations for Intelligent Tutoring Systems, vol. 2, pp. 169–182. US Army Research Laboratory, Orlando (2014)
56. Rummel, N.: One framework to rule them all? Carrying forward the conversation started by Wise and Schwarz. Int. J. Comput. Support. Collab. Learn. 13(1), 123–129 (2018)
57. Schoenfeld, A.H.: How We Think: A Theory of Goal-Oriented Decision Making and Its Educational Applications. Routledge, New York (2010)
58. Schofield, J.W., Eurich-Fulcer, R., Britt, C.L.: Teachers, computer tutors, and teaching: the artificially intelligent tutor as an agent for classroom change. Am. Educ. Res. J. 31(3), 579–607 (1994)
59. Sherin, M., Jacobs, V., Philipp, R. (eds.): Mathematics Teacher Noticing: Seeing Through Teachers' Eyes. Routledge, New York (2011)
60. Simard, P.Y., et al.: Machine teaching: a new paradigm for building machine learning systems (2017). arXiv preprint arXiv:1707.06742
61. Soller, A., Martínez, A., Jermann, P., Muehlenbrock, M.: From mirroring to guiding: a review of state of the art technology for supporting collaborative learning. Int. J. Artif. Intell. Educ. 15(4), 261–290 (2005)
62. Sutton, R.S., Barto, A.G.: Reinforcement Learning: An Introduction. MIT Press, Cambridge (2018)
63. Tissenbaum, M., Slotta, J.: Supporting classroom orchestration with real-time feedback: a role for teacher dashboards and real-time agents. Int. J. Comput. Support. Collab. Learn. 14(3), 325–351 (2019)
64. VanLehn, K.: The relative effectiveness of human tutoring, intelligent tutoring systems, and other tutoring systems. Educ. Psychol. 46(4), 197–221 (2011)
65. VanLehn, K.: Regulative loops, step loops and task loops. Int. J. Artif. Intell. Educ. 26(1), 107–112 (2016)
66. VanLehn, K., et al.: Can an orchestration system increase collaborative, productive struggle in teaching-by-eliciting classrooms? In: Interactive Learning Environments, pp. 1–19 (2019)
67. VanLehn, K., Cheema, S., Wetzel, J., Pead, D.: Some less obvious features of classroom orchestration systems. In: Lin, L., Atkinson, R.K. (eds.) Educational Technologies: Challenges, Applications, and Learning Outcomes, pp. 73–94. Nova Scientific Publisher, New York (2016)

68. van Leeuwen, A., Rummel, N.: Orchestration tools to support the teacher during student collaboration: a review. Unterrichtswissenschaft **47**(2), 143–158 (2019)

69. van Leeuwen, A., Rummel, N., Van Gog, T.: What information should CSCL teacher dashboards provide to help teachers interpret CSCL situations? Int. J. Comput. Support. Collab. Learn. **14**, 261–289 (2019)

70. Walker, E., Rummel, N., Koedinger, K.R.: Adaptive intelligent support to improve peer tutoring in algebra. Int. J. Artif. Intell. Educ. **24**(1), 33–61 (2014)

71. Wickens, C.D., Gordon, S., Liu, Y., Lee, J.: An Introduction to Human Factors Engineering. Longman, New York (1998)

72. Williams, J.J., et al.: Axis: generating explanations at scale with learner sourcing and machine learning. In: Proceedings of the Third (2016) ACM Conference on Learning@ Scale, pp. 379–388 (2016)

73. Yacef, K.: Intelligent teaching assistant systems. In: Proceedings of the 2002 International Conference on Computers in Education, pp. 136–140. IEEE (2002)

74. Zhu, X., Singla, A., Zilles, S., Rafferty, A.N.: An overview of machine teaching (2018). arXiv preprint arXiv:1801.05927

Exploring How Gender and Enjoyment Impact Learning in a Digital Learning Game

Xinying Hou$^{(\boxtimes)}$ ⓘ, Huy A. Nguyen ⓘ, J. Elizabeth Richey ⓘ, and Bruce M. McLaren

Carnegie Mellon University, Pittsburgh, PA 15213, USA
xhou@cs.cmu.edu

Abstract. In digital learning games, do game mechanics that promote learning and those that promote enjoyment have different effects on students' experience? Do males or females learn from or enjoy games more? We explored these questions in *Decimal Point*, a digital learning game that teaches decimal numbers and decimal operations to middle school students. In this work, we conducted a classroom study with two versions of the game, one that encourages students to play to learn and one that encourages students to play for enjoyment. We compared these two conditions to a control condition that is neutral regarding learning and enjoyment. Our results indicated that the enjoyment-focused group learned more efficiently than the control group, and that females had higher learning gains than males across all conditions, particularly on the near and middle transfer learning items. Post hoc analyses also revealed that the learning-focused group engaged in re-practicing the same mini-games, while the enjoyment-focused group demonstrated more exploration of different mini-games. These findings suggest that emphasizing learning or enjoyment can result in distinctive gameplay behaviors from students, and that our game can help bridge the typical gender gap in math education.

Keywords: Digital learning game · Decimals · Learning · Enjoyment · Gender

1 Introduction

Digital learning games are instructional tools that can both engage students and promote learning [20]; however, students may be distracted from learning by the engaging game features [23]. To help students stay on track, modern learning games often incorporate learning-oriented mechanics such as collaborative problem-solving [50], instructional feedback [35] or open learner models [15]. More generally, several frameworks on how to design game features that optimize learning have been proposed [14, 26, 27].

On the other hand, an implicit expectation in digital learning games is that students' enjoyment can serve as a catalyst for their learning motivation and is positively correlated with learning outcomes [2, 19, 30]. Given this expectation, it would be interesting to compare the effects of an enjoyment-focused game environment with those of a learning-focused one, provided that the enjoyment-inducing features are also strongly tied to learning and not just superficial game activities. To our knowledge, only a handful of

© Springer Nature Switzerland AG 2020
I. I. Bittencourt et al. (Eds.): AIED 2020, LNAI 12163, pp. 255–268, 2020.
https://doi.org/10.1007/978-3-030-52237-7_21

prior studies have explicitly compared the learning and enjoyment constructs in the same game context. For example, [17] manipulated how undergraduate students perceived the same multimedia environment as either a learning module or a game, and found that the learning group demonstrated deeper learning while reporting the same level of motivation as the game group. On the other hand, the game group performed better than the learning group when instructional feedback was included in both conditions, implying that a game environment can be helpful if it promotes active learning. Another study by [52] adopted a similar strategy with high school students and found that enjoyment is not affected by playful or serious framing. However, rather than manipulating only the students' a priori perspective of the game as these prior studies did, we believe a more authentic comparison should take place during students' actual gameplay, with different game mechanics designed to emphasize either the learning or enjoyment aspect of the game.

In our work, we explored this idea in the context of *Decimal Point*, a math learning game for middle school students. Our study compared the learning and enjoyment-focused features through three conditions: one that displays the student's current level across different decimal skills and encourages more playing of the mini-games they are weakest at (Learning Condition - LC), one that displays the student's current enjoyment and encourages more playing of the mini-games they enjoy the most (Enjoyment Condition - EC), and one that does not show any learning- or enjoyment-related information (Control Condition - CC). Our research questions are as follows.

RQ1: *Is there a difference in learning outcomes among students in the three conditions?* As the LC design is essentially an open learner model [7, 10], which allows students to see their skill performance and helps regulate their learning, we hypothesized that LC students would achieve the highest learning outcome.

RQ2: *Is there a difference in self-reported enjoyment among students in the three conditions?* Given the emphasis on students playing their most enjoyed mini-games, we hypothesized that the EC group would report the highest enjoyment scores.

RQ3: *Is there a difference in learning outcomes between male and female students?* Given past research showing that females tend to learn more from digital learning games than males [28, 32], we hypothesized that female students would have better learning outcomes than males in our game across all three conditions.

RQ4: *Is there a difference in self-reported enjoyment between male and female students?* Prior research has suggested that males are typically drawn to video game features such as competition [4], achievement [41] and social interaction [22], whereas females tend to prefer engaging with familiar characters in a fantasy setting [49], which aligns more closely with our game environment. Therefore, we hypothesized that females would report higher enjoyment than males across all three conditions.

2   The Digital Learning Game *Decimal Point*

Decimal Point is a web-based single-player digital learning game that helps middle-school students learn about decimal numbers and their operations. The game features an amusement park metaphor (Fig. 1) with 8 theme areas and 24 mini-games that target common decimal misconceptions [25]. Each mini-game also exercises one of the following decimal skills:

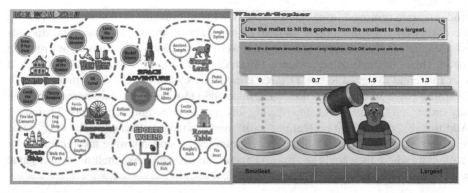

Fig. 1. The main game map where students can select among 24 mini-games to play (left), and an example mini-game in the *Sorting* skill category (right).

1. *Number Line* - locate the position of a decimal number on the number line.
2. *Addition* - add two decimals by entering the carry digits and the sum.
3. *Sequence* - fill in the next two numbers of a sequence of decimal numbers.
4. *Bucket* - compare given decimals to a threshold number and place each decimal in a "less than" or "greater than" bucket.
5. *Sorting* - sort a list of decimal numbers in ascending or descending order.

An initial study of *Decimal Point*, where students had to play all mini-games in a canonical order, showed that the game yielded more learning and enjoyment than a conventional tutor with the same instructional content [33]. Subsequent studies have integrated the element of agency into the game, by allowing students to select which mini-games to play and when to stop [24, 36]. Students who were provided agency acquired equivalent learning gains in less time than those who were not, suggesting that they could self-regulate effectively. Furthermore, a post hoc analysis by [51] reported that certain mini-game sequences which are indicative of students' exercise of agency led to higher self-reported enjoyment than others. However, no effect of agency or other game elements on test performance has been observed so far.

In addition, given an earlier finding that females benefited more from the *Decimal Point* game than males [32], we are interested in further analyses of the gender differences. As agency and learning/enjoyment-focused mechanics are integrated into the game, would the findings from [32] still hold? If a gender effect was present, which factors in the game would likely cause this effect?

3 Method

3.1 Participants and Design

196 fifth and sixth grade students in two public schools in a mid-sized U.S. city participated in our study, which was conducted during students' regular class time and lasted six days. The materials included a pretest, game play, evaluation questionnaire and posttest on the first five days, followed by a delayed posttest one week later. After the study, 35

students were removed from our analyses due to not finishing all the materials. Using the outlier criteria from a prior study in *Decimal Point* [36], we excluded two students whose gain scores from pretest to posttest were 2.5 standard deviations away from the mean. Thus, our final sample included 159 students (82 males, 77 females). Each student was randomly assigned to one of three conditions: Control (CC), Enjoyment (EC) or Learning (LC). In each condition, students could (1) select the mini-games to play in any order, and (2) choose to stop playing any time after completing at least 24 rounds. Additionally, each condition features a different dashboard attached to the main game map shown in Fig. 1. After finishing each mini-game, students were taken back to the main map, where they could see the updated dashboard and make their next mini-game selection.

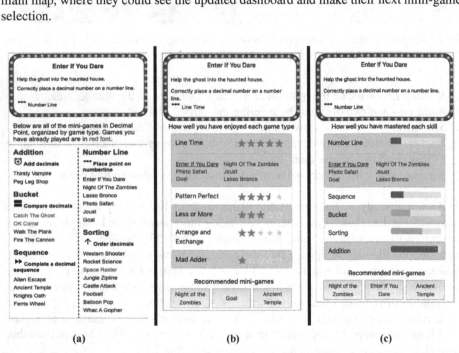

(a)   (b)   (c)

Fig. 2. The dashboards shown along the game map in the Control (a), Enjoyment (b) and Learning (c) condition. The skills in the Enjoyment condition are renamed to appear more playful, e.g., *Addition* becomes *Mad Adder*.

In the CC group (30 males, 20 females), students played two rounds of mini-game per selection (i.e., they played each selected mini-game twice, with different content but the same mechanics). The dashboard listed the mini-games and their corresponding skills, where the completed ones were highlighted in red (Fig. 2a). After finishing the first two rounds of all 24 mini-games, students had the option to play another round of each. This condition is equivalent to the High Agency condition in [24] and [36].

In the EC group (29 males, 25 females), students played one round of mini-game per selection. After each mini-game round, students were asked to rate their enjoyment of that mini-game, on a scale from 1 ("not fun") to 5 ("crazy fun"). The dashboard showed the student's enjoyment rating of each skill, which was averaged over all the mini-game ratings in that skill category so far (Fig. 2b). After the first three rounds, the dashboard would also recommend three mini-games to play next, chosen randomly from the two skills with the highest enjoyment; the student could follow this recommendation or make their own choice. Unlike in CC, EC students could play more rounds of a mini-game any time, without having to complete other mini-games at least once.

In the LC group (23 males, 32 females), students played one round of mini-game per selection. The dashboard showed the game's estimates of the student's mastery of each skill, from 0% to 100% (Fig. 2c), based on Bayesian Knowledge Tracing (BKT) [53]. We set the initial BKT parameters as $p(L_0) = 0.4$, $p(T) = 0.05$, $p(S) = p(G) = 0.299$ [3]. After the first three rounds, the dashboard would also recommend three mini-games to play next, chosen randomly from the two skills with the lowest mastery; the student could follow this recommendation or make their own choice. Similar to those in EC, LC students could play more rounds of a mini-game any time.

3.2 Materials

A web-based learning environment was used in this study. The materials included three tests, the game conditions outlined above, as well as questionnaire/survey items.

Pretest, Posttest, and Delayed Posttest: Each test consisted of 43 items. Most items are worth one point each, while some multi-part items are worth several points, for a total of 52 points per test. The items were designed to probe for specific decimal misconceptions, and involved either the five decimal skills targeted by the game or conceptual questions (e.g., "is a decimal number that starts with 0 smaller than 0?"). Three test forms (A, B and C) that were isomorphic and positionally counterbalanced across conditions were used. One-way ANOVAs showed no differences in terms of performance among the three versions of the test at pretest, $F(2, 156) = 0.480, p = .620$, posttest, $F(2, 156) = 1.496, p = .227$, and delayed posttest, $F(2, 156) = 1.302, p = .275$.

Questionnaires and Survey: Before and after playing the game, students were given demographic questionnaires and asked to rate several statements on a Likert scale from 1 ("strongly disagree") to 5 ("strongly agree"). These statements pertain to factors such as (1) *multidimensional engagement* (6 questions adapted from [6] with $\alpha = .775$ for the affective subscale and $\alpha = .540$ for the behavioral/cognitive engagement subscale), e.g. "I felt frustrated or annoyed," (2) *game engagement* (5 questions adapted from [8] with $\alpha = .736$), e.g., "I lost track of time," and (3) the enjoyment dimension of *achievement emotions* (6 questions adapted from [43] with $\alpha = .891$), e.g. "Reflecting on my progress in the game made me happy." In the multidimensional engagement construct, we excluded the behavioral/cognitive engagement subscale from analysis due to its low α value and only reported the results for affective engagement. After the game, students were also asked to reflect on their game play behavior, e.g. "How many mini-games did you play? Why?"

4 Results

First, a repeated-measures ANOVA showed a significant difference for all students between pretest and posttest scores, $F(1, 158) = 132.882, p < .001$, as well as between pretest and delayed posttest scores, $F(1, 158) = 239.414, p < .001$. In other words, in all three conditions, students' performance improved after playing the game. Next, we investigated our research questions. Given that gender is not a randomly assigned variable and males tend to outperform females in math performance by the end of elementary school [46], we did not expect students to be equivalent across genders at pretest. For this reason, we focused our gender analyses on gain scores [18]. In contrast, because the conditions (CC, LC and EC) were randomly assigned, we expected students to perform equally well on pretest across conditions; therefore, we used analyses of covariance (ANCOVA) to assess condition effects on posttest and delayed posttest.

Table 1. Test performance and self-reported enjoyment scores by condition.

Category	CC	EC	LC
Pretest scores M (*SD*)	26.68 (8.89)	24.76 (9.55)	23.09 (9.65)
Posttest scores M (*SD*)	32.12 (8.01)	29.76 (10.25)	28.42 (11.31)
Delayed posttest scores M (*SD*)	32.84 (8.90)	31.74 (10.12)	30.05 (10.06)
Achievement emotion M (*SD*)	3.46 (1.02)	3.49 (0.88)	3.55 (0.94)
Game engagement M (*SD*)	3.00 (0.90)	3.14 (0.98)	3.18 (0.80)
Affective engagement M (*SD*)	3.66 (0.94)	3.42 (1.04)	3.58 (0.85)

RQ1: *Is there a difference in learning outcomes among students in the three conditions?* Descriptive statistics about students' test scores in each condition are included in Table 1. From a one-way ANOVA, we observed no significant differences across conditions in pretest scores, $F(2, 156) = 1.915, p = .151$. With pretest scores as covariates, an ANCOVA showed no significant condition differences in posttest scores, $F(2, 155) = 0.201, p = .818$, or delayed posttest scores, $F(2, 155) = 0.143, p = .867$.

Following [34], learning efficiency was calculated for each student as the z-score of their pre-post or pre-delayed learning gains minus the z-score of total game time. As the learning efficiency data was not normally distributed, we used Kruskal-Wallis test and found a significant condition effect on learning efficiency for both posttest, $H = 6.30, p = .043$, and delayed posttest, $H = 8.64, p = .013$. Post hoc (Dunn) comparisons indicated that the EC group had significantly higher learning efficiency than CC, $p = .013, d = 0.28$, and delayed learning efficiency, $p = .003, d = 0.33$. There were no significant differences between EC and LC (pre-post: $p = .369$, pre-delayed: $p = .257$) or between CC and LC (pre-post: $p = .466$, pre-delayed: $p = .181$). In summary, there was a condition effect on learning efficiency, where EC students learned more efficiently than CC, but not on test performance, so our hypothesis that LC students would learn the most was not confirmed.

RQ2: *Is there a difference in self-reported enjoyment among students in the three conditions?* Descriptive statistics about students' enjoyment ratings by condition are included in Table 1. Based on one-way ANOVAs, there were no significant differences across conditions in achievement emotions, $F(2, 156) = 0.118$, $p = .889$, game engagement, $F(2, 156) = 0.597$, $p = .552$, or affective engagement, $F(2, 156) = 0.886$, $p = .414$. In other words, there was no condition effect on self-reported enjoyment, so our hypothesis that EC students would report the highest enjoyment was not confirmed.

RQ3: *Is there a difference in learning outcomes between male and female students?* Descriptive statistics about students' test scores by gender are included in Table 2. A one-way ANOVA showed no significant gender differences in pretest performance, $F(1, 157) = 0.534$, $p = .466$. A two-way ANOVA testing effects of condition and gender showed a significant main effect of gender on learning gains, $F(1, 153) = 4.351$, $p = .039$, $d = .33$, and delayed learning gains, $F(1, 153) = 4.431$, $p = .037$, $d = .35$, but no significant gender x condition interaction effect on learning gains, $F(2, 153) = 0.065$, $p = .937$, or delayed learning gains, $F(2, 153) = 0.685$, $p = .506$. Therefore, our hypothesis that females learned more than males across all conditions was confirmed. However, there were no significant gender differences in learning efficiency, $F(1, 157) = 0.259$, $p = .612$, or delayed learning efficiency, $F(1, 157) = 0.301$, $p = .584$.

RQ4: *Is there a difference in self-reported enjoyment between male and female students?* Descriptive statistics about males and females' ratings of the three enjoyment categories are included in Table 2. A two-way ANOVA testing effects of condition and gender revealed no significant main gender effect on achievement emotions, $F(1, 153) = 0.160$, $p = .690$, game engagement, $F(1, 153) = 1.689$, $p = .196$, or affective engagement, $F(1, 153) = 1.390$, $p = .240$. Similarly, there were no significant gender x condition interaction effects on these three constructs: achievement emotions, $F(2, 153) = 0.390$, $p = .678$, game engagement, $F(2, 153) = 0.345$, $p = .709$, and affective engagement, $F(2, 153) = 0.053$, $p = .948$. Thus, our hypothesis that females would enjoy the game more than males was not confirmed.

Table 2. Learning gains and self-reported enjoyment scores by gender.

Category	Males	Females
Pretest M (*SD*)	25.32 (9.74)	24.22 (9.14)
Learning gains M (*SD*)	4.34 (5.71)	6.22 (5.66)
Delayed learning gains M (*SD*)	5.80 (5.27)	7.69 (5.56)
Achievement emotion M (*SD*)	3.46 (1.04)	3.53 (0.83)
Game engagement M (*SD*)	3.01 (0.92)	3.21 (0.85)
Affective engagement M (*SD*)	3.64 (0.99)	3.46 (0.89)

Post Hoc Analyses. We conducted two follow-up analyses to better understand the condition effect on learning efficiency as well as the gender effect on learning gains. In cases where the data is not normally distributed, based on the omnibus test of normality [1], we employed the Kruskal-Wallis test [16] instead of ANOVA.

Condition Effect on Learning Efficiency. We first examined the number of mini-game rounds played in each condition. A Kruskal-Wallis test showed significant differences across conditions in number of rounds, $H = 38.08$, $p < .001$. Post hoc (Dunn) comparisons revealed that the CC ($M = 45.08$, $SD = 18.40$) had significantly more rounds than LC ($M = 33.20$, $SD = 9.86$), $p < .001$, $d = 0.44$, and LC had significantly more rounds than EC ($M = 26.65$, $SD = 4.59$), $p = .007$, $d = 0.33$. Furthermore, a Kruskal-Wallis test showed no significant condition differences in average game time per round, $H = 2.50$, $p = .286$. Therefore, EC students' higher learning efficiency than CC's could be attributed to their similar test scores but fewer mini-game rounds.

Next, we were interested in how varied the mini-games played in each condition were. For this purpose, we defined a new metric for each student called *replay rate*, which is the number of times a student reselected a mini-game beyond the first try divided by their total number of mini-game selections. A high replay rate (close to 1) indicates that the student played more rounds of certain mini-games, while a low rate (close to 0) points to the student playing fewer rounds of more mini-games (i.e., playing a wider variety of mini-games). As CC students could not replay mini-games until after 48 rounds, their replay behaviors were necessarily different from those in LC and EC, so we focused our comparison on the LC and EC groups. We employed a Kruskal-Wallis test and observed significant differences in replay rates between the LC and EC students, $H = 42.41$, $p < .001$; LC students ($M = 0.44$, $SD = 0.20$) had a significantly higher replay rate than EC students ($M = 0.15$, $SD = 0.17$). In other words, LC students tended to replay more rounds of the mini-games they had already played than those in EC. Preliminary analysis of students' reflection on their gameplay behavior revealed a similar picture. Many in the EC group (25/54) and CC group (20/50) mentioned trying out every available mini-game, e.g., "I really wanted to finish the whole map and see all the things filled in with color." On the other hand, fewer LC students (10/55) touched on this idea, while 17 of them instead mentioned the mastery scores as motivation for playing, e.g., "I was trying to get all the decimal category skill bars full."

Gender Effect on Learning Gains. To see where females outperformed males in the tests, we assigned a level of learning transfer to each of the 43 test items: 20 near, 8 middle, 15 far. Following [5]'s taxonomy of transfer along the learned skill dimension [39], we classified test items as near transfer if they could be completed using identical procedures to those practiced in the game, middle transfer if they relied on practiced representations but required modification of procedures, and far transfer if they required students to understand underlying principles of practiced problems. For example, based on the sorting game in Fig. 1, a near transfer problem involves applying the same sorting procedure with new values ("Place the following list of decimals in order, smallest to largest: 0.7, 0, 1.0, 0.35"); a middle transfer problem asks students to apply representations of magnitude using a different procedure ("Which number is closest to 2.8? 2.88888, 2.91, 2.6, or 2.78"), while a far transfer problem tests abstract reasoning about decimal magnitude ("Is a longer decimal number larger than a shorter decimal number?"). Table 3 shows the results of one-way ANOVAs comparing pretest scores, learning gains and delayed learning gains between males and females at each transfer level. For the near and middle transfer items, females had lower scores than males at

Table 3. Comparison of test performance by gender at each transfer level. The mean difference (*MD*) indicates the mean value of males minus mean value of females.

Transfer level	Category	Statistical result
Near	Pretest scores	$F(1, 157) = 3.643, p = .058, MD = 1.399$
	Learning gains	$F(1, 157) = 4.541, p = .035, MD = -1.166$
	Delayed learning gains	$F(1, 157) = 4.020, p = .047, MD = -1.030$
Middle	Pretest scores	$F(1, 157) = 4.474, p = .036, MD = 0.669$
	Learning gains	$F(1, 157) = 4.695, p = .032, MD = -0.784$
	Delayed learning gains	$F(1, 157) = 2.495, p = .116, MD = -0.651$
Far	Pretest scores	$F(1, 157) = 1.569, p = .212, MD = -0.948$
	Learning gains	$F(1, 157) = 0.007, p = .932, MD = 0.047$
	Delayed learning gains	$F(1, 157) = 0.147, p = .702, MD = -0.226$

pretest but outperformed males in learning gains and delayed learning gains; however, there were no significant gender differences in performance on far transfer items.

5 Discussion and Conclusion

In this study, we investigated whether emphasizing the learning or enjoyment aspect of a digital learning game would lead to better outcomes, as well as whether males or females would benefit more from the game. We found that the Enjoyment Condition (EC) students played the least number of rounds but had higher learning efficiency than the Control Condition (CC) students. In addition, females gained more decimal knowledge than males in the posttest and delayed posttest across all conditions.

The condition effect on learning efficiency is an interesting extension to the study by [24], where students in the High Agency conditions (equivalent to our CC) learned more efficiently than those in Low Agency. In our case, since the CC and EC groups had similar test scores and average time per round, the difference in learning efficiency is due to CC students' higher number of rounds, which can be explained by their having to play two rounds per mini-game selection. Focusing on the EC and LC groups' gameplay behavior, we saw that EC students on average played 27 rounds with a replay rate of 0.15, so they chose to stop playing after trying most of the 24 mini-games once. At the same time, LC students had significantly higher number of rounds (33 on average) and replay rates (0.44 on average), indicating that the open learner model was effective in encouraging them to practice for mastery, consistent with prior literature [7, 31]. On the other hand, we found no significant differences between the LC group's learning efficiency and that of EC or CC, suggesting that replaying the mini-games past a certain point may yield diminishing returns. Our post hoc analysis of this study [37] revealed that over-practice, which could negatively impact students' learning efficiency [13], was indeed very common. Therefore, an important enhancement to the open learner model would be to inform students when they have sufficiently practiced one skill and should move on to the next, in order to maximize their learning efficiency.

From the game play perspective, in the CC and EC settings, without the open learner model, students may not have monitored their learning progress [9, 54] and more likely wanted to explore all the mini-games that were offered. In contrast, LC students could see their skill performance and therefore were potentially more motivated to focus on mastering the skills one by one, as this is the traditional approach in school instruction [42]. These conjectures are supported by the students' reflections, which indicated that EC students liked to play all the mini-games while LC students wanted to improve their skill masteries. More generally, this finding suggests that in a game environment where students are free to choose between different types of task, showing an open learner model can encourage re-practicing the tasks one at a time (blocked practice), while not showing the model may result in students engaging in more exploration of the different tasks (interleaved practice). As the effects of these two practice modes depend on the instructional domain [11, 12, 21, 47], game designers should investigate the knowledge content of their game to see which mode is more suitable and, in turn, whether to incorporate an open learner model. In our context, the skills may be sufficiently distinct from one another and each was embedded in a unique interface, so interleaving and blocking, if present, were unlikely to yield differences in learning outcomes. A prior *Decimal Point* analysis similarly reported that students playing the mini-games in different orders still acquired the same knowledge [51].

From the enjoyment perspective, our EC design did not yield the intended effect of maximizing students' enjoyment and engaging them in the game for a longer time. One potential reason is that, while the EC and LC dashboard had similar structures, students were likely not exposed to this "open enjoyment model" before and did not use it effectively. Alternatively, students may have reported similar enjoyment levels because, despite the different dashboards, they still spent the majority of play time in the actual mini-games, which are identical across conditions. Furthermore, our study was conducted in a real classroom environment, where students had limited time per day to play the game and were aware of the posttests; these factors may have negated the playful atmosphere that the Enjoyment condition was intended to induce [40, 44] or caused students to not take the enjoyment model as seriously as the learner model.

For the gender effect, we found that females outperformed males in learning gains at the near and middle transfer items, which most closely resemble those practiced in the game. In addition, females did not differ significantly from males in learning gains on far transfer problems. This outcome can be explained by the game's focus on practicing problems, which is typically beneficial for improving procedural knowledge but not necessarily for abstract knowledge or far transfer [45, 48]. Overall, our findings demonstrate that *Decimal Point* can potentially contribute to bridging the typical gender gap in math education [29, 46]. In addition, there were no gender differences in self-reported enjoyment, suggesting that *Decimal Point* was equally appealing to both genders. This is a positive outcome and likely results from the variety of mini-game themes and activities (Fig. 1), which appeal to both genders even if the game does not contain the features that we hypothesized are critical to the male students' enjoyment.

Our findings open up several avenues for future work. From the learning perspective, we could experiment with different skill mappings or model representation [7, 38] to better observe how students interact with the learner model in *Decimal Point*. From the enjoyment perspective, we plan to implement more in-game measures and survey questions to understand students' perception of game play in the classroom and to optimize enjoyment in *Decimal Point*. Finally, there is potential in further exploration of which game features are conducive to the observed gender effects, and how to extend the game's knowledge content to better support far transfer learning.

In summary, while the learning and enjoyment-focused mechanics in *Decimal Point* had similar impacts on students' outcomes, they yielded two distinct gameplay patterns, one focusing on repeated practice (the Learning Condition) and the other on exploration (the Enjoyment Condition). We also found that females improved in learning from the game more than males. These results in turn lead to the possibility of exploring the effect of emphasizing game-based learning or enjoyment in a classroom environment, as well as the game's potential in bridging the gender gap in math education.

Acknowledgements. This work was supported by NSF Award #DRL-1238619. The opinions expressed are those of the authors and do not represent the views of NSF. Thanks to Jodi Forlizzi, Michael Mogessie Ashenafi, Scott Herbst, Craig Ganoe, Darlan Santana Farias, Rick Henkel, Patrick B. McLaren, Grace Kihumba, Kim Lister, Kevin Dhou, John Choi, and Jimit Bhalani, all of whom made important contributions to the development of and early experimentation with the *Decimal Point* game.

References

1. d'Agostino, R.B.: An omnibus test of normality for moderate and large size samples. Biometrika **58**, 341–348 (1971)
2. Anderman, E.M., Dawson, H.: Learning with motivation. In: Alexander, P., Mayer, R. (eds.) Handbook of Research on Learning and Instruction, pp. 219–241. Routledge, New York (2011)
3. Baker, R.: Personal Correspondence (2019)
4. Bammel, G., Burrus-Bammel, L.L.: Leisure and Human Behaviour. Wm. C Brown Company Publishers, Dubuque (1982)
5. Barnett, S.M., Ceci, S.J.: When and where do we apply what we learn? A taxonomy for far transfer. Psychol. Bull. **128**, 612 (2002)
6. Ben-Eliyahu, A., Moore, D., Dorph, R., Schunn, C.D.: Investigating the multidimensionality of engagement: affective, behavioral, and cognitive engagement across science activities and contexts. Contemp. Educ. Psychol. **53**, 87–105 (2018)
7. Bodily, R., Kay, J., Aleven, V., Jivet, I., Davis, D., Xhakaj, F., Verbert, K.: Open learner models and learning analytics dashboards: a systematic review. In: Proceedings of the 8th International Conference on Learning Analytics and Knowledge, pp. 41–50 (2018)
8. Brockmyer, J.H., Fox, C.M., Curtiss, K.A., McBroom, E., Burkhart, K.M., Pidruzny, J.N.: The development of the Game Engagement Questionnaire: a measure of engagement in video game-playing. J. Exp. Soc. Psychol. **45**, 624–634 (2009)
9. Bull, S., Kay, J.: Metacognition and open learner models. In: The 3rd Workshop on Meta-Cognition and Self-regulated Learning in Educational Technologies, at ITS2008, pp. 7–20 (2008)

10. Bull, S., Nghiem, T.: Helping learners to understand themselves with a learner model open to students, peers and instructors. In: Proceedings of Workshop on Individual and Group Modelling Methods that Help Learners Understand Themselves, International Conference on Intelligent Tutoring Systems. pp. 5–13. Citeseer (2002)
11. Carpenter, S.K., Mueller, F.E.: The effects of interleaving versus blocking on foreign language pronunciation learning. Mem. Cognit. **41**, 671–682 (2013)
12. Carvalho, P.F., Goldstone, R.L.: The benefits of interleaved and blocked study: different tasks benefit from different schedules of study. Psychon. Bull. Rev. **22**, 281–288 (2015)
13. Cen, H., Koedinger, K.R., Junker, B.: Is over practice necessary? Improving learning efficiency with the cognitive tutor through educational data mining. Front. Artif. Intell. Appl. **158**, 511 (2007)
14. Chen, Z.-H.: Exploring students' behaviors in a competition-driven educational game. Comput. Hum. Behav. **35**, 68–74 (2014)
15. Chen, Z.-H., Chou, C.-Y., Deng, Y.-C., Chan, T.-W.: Active open learner models as animal companions: motivating children to learn through interacting with My-Pet and Our-Pet. Int. J. Artif. Intell. Educ. **17**, 145–167 (2007)
16. Daniel, W.W.: Kruskal–Wallis one-way analysis of variance by ranks. In: Applied Nonparametric Statistics, pp. 226–234. PWS-Kent, Boston (1990)
17. Erhel, S., Jamet, E.: Digital game-based learning: impact of instructions and feedback on motivation and learning effectiveness. Comput. Educ. **67**, 156–167 (2013)
18. Fitzmaurice, G.M., Laird, N.M., Ware, J.H.: Applied Longitudinal Analysis. Wiley, Hoboken (2012)
19. Fu, F.-L., Su, R.-C., Yu, S.-C.: EGameFlow: a scale to measure learners' enjoyment of e-learning games. Comput. Educ. **52**, 101–112 (2009)
20. Gee, J.P.: What video games have to teach us about learning and literacy. Comput. Entertain. CIE. **1**, 20 (2003)
21. Goldstone, R.L.: Isolated and interrelated concepts. Mem. Cognit. **24**, 608–628 (1996)
22. Griffiths, M.D., Hunt, N.: Computer game playing in adolescence: prevalence and demographic indicators. J. Community Appl. Soc. Psychol. **5**, 189–193 (1995)
23. Harp, S.F., Mayer, R.E.: How seductive details do their damage: a theory of cognitive interest in science learning. J. Educ. Psychol. **90**, 414 (1998)
24. Harpstead, E., Richey, J.E., Nguyen, H., McLaren, B.M.: Exploring the subtleties of agency and indirect control in digital learning games. In: Proceedings of the 9th International Conference on Learning Analytics & Knowledge, pp. 121–129. ACM (2019)
25. Isotani, S., McLaren, B.M., Altman, M.: Towards intelligent tutoring with erroneous examples: a taxonomy of decimal misconceptions. In: Aleven, V., Kay, J., Mostow, J. (eds.) ITS 2010. LNCS, vol. 6095, pp. 346–348. Springer, Heidelberg (2010). https://doi.org/10.1007/978-3-642-13437-1_66
26. Kiili, K., Lainema, T., de Freitas, S., Arnab, S.: Flow framework for analyzing the quality of educational games. Entertain. Comput. **5**, 367–377 (2014)
27. Kiili, K., Perttula, A.: A design framework for educational exergames. In: de Freitas, S., Ott, M., Popescu, M.M., Stanescu, I. (eds.) New Pedagogical Approaches in Game Enhanced Learning: Curriculum Integration, pp. 136–158. IGI Global, Hershey (2013)
28. Klisch, Y., Miller, L.M., Wang, S., Epstein, J.: The impact of a science education game on students' learning and perception of inhalants as body pollutants. J. Sci. Educ. Technol. **21**, 295–303 (2012)
29. Leahey, E., Guo, G.: Gender differences in mathematical trajectories. Soc. Forces. **80**, 713–732 (2001)
30. Liu, M., Horton, L., Olmanson, J., Toprac, P.: A study of learning and motivation in a new media enriched environment for middle school science. Educ. Technol. Res. Dev. **59**, 249–265 (2011)

31. Malacria, S., Scarr, J., Cockburn, A., Gutwin, C., Grossman, T.: Skillometers: reflective widgets that motivate and help users to improve performance. In: Proceedings of the 26th Annual ACM Symposium on User Interface Software and Technology, pp. 321–330 (2013)

32. McLaren, B., Farzan, R., Adams, D., Mayer, R., Forlizzi, J.: Uncovering gender and problem difficulty effects in learning with an educational game. In: André, E., Baker, R., Hu, X., Rodrigo, M.M.T., du Boulay, B. (eds.) AIED 2017. LNCS (LNAI), vol. 10331, pp. 540–543. Springer, Cham (2017). https://doi.org/10.1007/978-3-319-61425-0_59

33. McLaren, B.M., Adams, D.M., Mayer, R.E., Forlizzi, J.: A computer-based game that promotes mathematics learning more than a conventional approach. Int. J. Game-Based Learn. IJGBL. **7**, 36–56 (2017)

34. McLaren, B.M., Lim, S.-J., Koedinger, K.R.: When and how often should worked examples be given to students? New results and a summary of the current state of research. In: Proceedings of the 30th Annual Conference of the Cognitive Science Society, pp. 2176–2181 (2008)

35. Moreno, R., Mayer, R.E.: Personalized messages that promote science learning in virtual environments. J. Educ. Psychol. **96**, 165 (2004)

36. Nguyen, H., Harpstead, E., Wang, Y., McLaren, B.M.: Student agency and game-based learning: a study comparing low and high agency. In: Penstein Rosé, C., et al. (eds.) AIED 2018. LNCS (LNAI), vol. 10947, pp. 338–351. Springer, Cham (2018). https://doi.org/10.1007/978-3-319-93843-1_25

37. Nguyen, H., Hou, X., Stamper, J., McLaren, B.M.: Moving beyond test scores: analyzing the effectiveness of a digital learning game through learning analytics. In: Proceedings of the 13th International Conference on Educational Data Mining (2020)

38. Nguyen, H., Wang, Y., Stamper, J., McLaren, B.M.: Using knowledge component modeling to increase domain understanding in a digital learning game. In: Proceedings of the 12th International Conference on Educational Data Mining, pp. 139–148 (2019)

39. Novick, L.R.: Representational transfer in problem solving. Psychol. Sci. **1**, 128–132 (1990)

40. Osman, K., Bakar, N.A.: Educational computer games for Malaysian classrooms: issues and challenges. Asian Soc. Sci. **8**, 75 (2012)

41. Paraskeva, F., Mysirlaki, S., Papagianni, A.: Multiplayer online games as educational tools: facing new challenges in learning. Comput. Educ. **54**, 498–505 (2010)

42. Patel, R., Liu, R., Koedinger, K.R.: When to block versus interleave practice? Evidence against teaching fraction addition before fraction multiplication. In: CogSci (2016)

43. Pekrun, R.: Progress and open problems in educational emotion research. Learn. Instr. **15**, 497–506 (2005)

44. Rice, J.W.: New media resistance: barriers to implementation of computer video games in the classroom. J. Educ. Multimed. Hypermedia. **16**, 249–261 (2007)

45. Richey, J.E., Nokes-Malach, T.J.: Comparing four instructional techniques for promoting robust knowledge. Educ. Psychol. Rev. **27**, 181–218 (2015)

46. Robinson, J.P., Lubienski, S.T.: The development of gender achievement gaps in mathematics and reading during elementary and middle school: examining direct cognitive assessments and teacher ratings. Am. Educ. Res. J. **48**, 268–302 (2011)

47. Rohrer, D., Dedrick, R.F., Burgess, K.: The benefit of interleaved mathematics practice is not limited to superficially similar kinds of problems. Psychon. Bull. Rev. **21**, 1323–1330 (2014)

48. Singley, M.K., Anderson, J.R.: The Transfer of Cognitive Skill. Harvard University Press, Cambridge (1989)

49. Subrahmanyam, K., Greenfield, P.M.: Computer Games for Girls: What Makes Them Play? From Barbie to Mortal Kombat: Gender and Computer Games. MIT Press, Cambridge (1998)

50. Sung, H.-Y., Hwang, G.-J.: A collaborative game-based learning approach to improving students' learning performance in science courses. Comput. Educ. **63**, 43–51 (2013)

51. Wang, Y., Nguyen, H., Harpstead, E., Stamper, J., McLaren, B.M.: How does order of gameplay impact learning and enjoyment in a digital learning game? In: Isotani, S., Millán, E., Ogan, A., Hastings, P., McLaren, B., Luckin, R. (eds.) AIED 2019. LNCS (LNAI), vol. 11625, pp. 518–531. Springer, Cham (2019). https://doi.org/10.1007/978-3-030-23204-7_43

52. Wechselberger, U.: Learning and enjoyment in serious gaming-contradiction or complement? In: DiGRA Conference, pp. 26–29 (2013)

53. Yudelson, M.V., Koedinger, K.R., Gordon, G.J.: Individualized bayesian knowledge tracing models. In: Lane, H.C., Yacef, K., Mostow, J., Pavlik, P. (eds.) AIED 2013. LNCS (LNAI), vol. 7926, pp. 171–180. Springer, Heidelberg (2013). https://doi.org/10.1007/978-3-642-39112-5_18

54. Zimmerman, B.J.: Self-efficacy: an essential motive to learn. Contemp. Educ. Psychol. **25**, 82–91 (2000)

Neural Multi-task Learning for Teacher Question Detection in Online Classrooms

Gale Yan Huang[1,3], Jiahao Chen[1], Haochen Liu[2], Weiping Fu[1],
Wenbiao Ding[1], Jiliang Tang[2], Songfan Yang[1], Guoliang Li[3], and Zitao Liu[1(✉)]

[1] TAL Education Group, Beijing, China
{galehuang,chenjiahao,fuweiping,dingwenbiao,
yangsonogfan,liuzitao}@100tal.com
[2] Data Science and Engineering Lab, Michigan State University, East Lansing, USA
{liuhaoc1,tangjili}@msu.edu
[3] Department of Computer Science, Tsinghua University, Beijing, China
liguoliang@tsinghua.edu.cn

Abstract. Asking questions is one of the most crucial pedagogical techniques used by teachers in class. It not only offers open-ended discussions between teachers and students to exchange ideas but also provokes deeper student thought and critical analysis. Providing teachers with such pedagogical feedback will remarkably help teachers improve their overall teaching quality over time in classrooms. Therefore, in this work, we build an end-to-end neural framework that automatically detects questions from teachers' audio recordings. Compared with traditional methods, our approach not only avoids cumbersome feature engineering, but also adapts to the task of multi-class question detection in real education scenarios. By incorporating multi-task learning techniques, we are able to strengthen the understanding of semantic relations among different types of questions. We conducted extensive experiments on the question detection tasks in a real-world online classroom dataset and the results demonstrate the superiority of our model in terms of various evaluation metrics.

Keywords: Question detection · Multi-task learning · Natural language understanding · Online classroom

1 Introduction

Teachers utilize various pedagogical techniques in their classrooms to inspire students' thought and inquiry at deeper levels of students' comprehension. These techniques may include lectures, asking questions, assigning small-group work, etc. [6,9,25]. A large body of research has demonstrated that asking certain types of questions can increase student engagement and it is an important factor of student achievement [1,2,16,20,27,32]. Asking questions has become a central

---

H. Liu—Work was done when the author did internship in TAL Education Group.

© Springer Nature Switzerland AG 2020
I. I. Bittencourt et al. (Eds.): AIED 2020, LNAI 12163, pp. 269–281, 2020.
https://doi.org/10.1007/978-3-030-52237-7_22

component of teachers' dialogic instructions and often serves as a catalyst for in-depth classroom discussions [21, 26, 28].

A large spectrum of approaches have been developed and successfully applied in generating classroom feedback to evaluate teachers' performances and help them improve their pedagogical techniques [15, 19, 26, 28, 31]. For example, the Nystrand and Gamoran coding scheme provides a general template for recording teachers' activities, which are used by trained human judges to manually assess teachers' classroom practices [15, 26]. However, manually analyzing teacher questions is very subjective, expensive, time-consuming and not scalable. Thus, it is crucial to develop computational methods that can automatically detect teacher questions in live classrooms. By automatically analyzing when teachers ask questions and the corresponding question types, we are able to evaluate the question impact on teaching achievements and help teachers make adjustments to improve their pedagogical techniques. Previous endeavors have been conducted to tackle this problem using traditional machine learning (ML) algorithms [4–6, 12, 29]. However, the majority of these methods are not sufficient for teacher question detection due to the following challenges:

- *Question type variation.* Different from questions in daily chatting, routine conversation or other scenarios, teacher questions in classrooms are very diverse and open-ended. There are different types of classroom questions, such as knowledge-solicitation questions (e.g., *"What's the definition of quadrangle?"*), open questions (e.g., *"Could you tell me your thought?"*), procedural questions (e.g., *"Can everyone hear me?"*), and discourse-management questions (e.g., *"What?"*, *"Excuse me?"*) [7, 28]. Traditional methods fail to perform a deep semantic understanding on natural languages, which is necessary for detecting questions of various types.
- *Subject and speaker variability.* Teaching materials and styles vary dramatically for different subjects and teachers, which leads to significantly distinguished classroom question sentences. Traditional methods show poor adaptability. When new subjects or teachers appear, most existing approaches have to be redesigned and retrained with the newly arrived data.
- *Tedious feature engineering.* Traditional ML-based methods detect questions based on complex acoustic and language features. It's time-consuming to construct manually-engineered patterns.

In this work, we aim to investigate accurate teacher question detection in online classrooms. In particular, we study two variants of the teacher question detection problem. One is a two-way detection task that aims to distinguish questions from non-questions. The other is a multi-way detection task that aims to classify different types of questions. Please note that the formal definitions of the above two tasks are introduced in Sect. 3.2. We design a neural natural language understanding (NLU) model to automatically extract semantic features from teachers' sentences for both the two-way task and the multi-way task. Our approach shows a powerful generalization capability for detecting questions of various types from different teaching scenarios. With the neural model as a core component, we build an end-to-end framework that directly takes teacher audio tracks as input and outputs the detection results. Experiments conducted on a real-world online education dataset demonstrate the superiority of our proposed framework compared with competitive baseline models.

2 Related Work

2.1 Teacher Question Detection

Blanchard et al. explore classifying Q&A discourse segments based on audio inputs [4]. A simple amplitude envelope thresholding-based method is developed to detect teachers' utterances. Then the authors extract 11 speech-silence features from detected utterances and train supervised classifiers to differentiate Q&A segments from other segments. Following this work, Blanchard et al. further introduce an automatic speech recognition (ASR) system to convert audio features into domain-general language features for teacher question detection [5,6]. They extract 37 NLP features from ASR transcriptions and train different classical ML models to distinguish questions from non-questions. Besides linguistic features, Donnelly et al. try both prosodic and linguistic features for supervised question classification and conclude that ML classifiers can achieve better performance with linguistic features [12].

The line of research presented above focuses on detecting questions from non-questions, which is a binary classification problem. Besides, we are interested in classifying questions into specific categories. Samei et al. build ML models to predict two properties "uptake" and "authenticity" of questions in live classrooms [29]. They extract 30 linguistic features related to part-of-speech and pre-defined keywords from each individual question. Samei et al. show that ML models are able to achieve comparable question detection performance as human experts.

Different from previous works of building question detection ML models based on manually selected linguistic and acoustic features, our approach eliminates the feature engineering efforts and directly learns effective representations from the ASR transcriptions. Furthermore, we introduce multi-task learning techniques into our model to classify different types of questions.

2.2 Multi-task Learning

Multi-task learning is a promising learning paradigm that aims at taking advantage of information shared in multiple related tasks to help improve the generalization performance of all tasks [8]. In multi-task learning, a model is trained with multiple objectives towards different tasks simultaneously, where all or some of the tasks are related. Researches have shown that learning multiple tasks jointly can achieve better performance than learning each task separately. Yang et al. propose a novel multi-task representation learning model that learns cross-task sharing structures at each layer of a neural network [37]. Hashimoto et al. propose a joint multi-task model for multiple NLP tasks [17]. The authors point out that training a single network to model the hierarchical linguistic information from morphology, syntax to semantics can improve its generalization ability. Kendall et al. observe that the performance of the multi-task learning framework heavily depends on the weights of the objectives for different tasks [22]. They develop a novel method to learn the multi-task weightings by taking the homoscedastic uncertainty of each task into consideration.

3   Problem Statement

The teacher question detection task in live classrooms identifies questions from teachers' speech and classify those questions into correct categories. In this section, we first introduce the method for coding questions and then formulate the problem of teacher question detection.

3.1   Question Coding

By analyzing thousands of classroom recordings and surveying hundreds of instructors and educators, we categorize teacher questions into the following four categories:

- **Knowledge-solicitation Question (KQ)**: Questions that ask for a knowledge point or a factual answer. Some examples include: "What's the solution to this problem?", "What's the distance between A and B?", and "What is the area of this quadrilateral?".
- **Open Question (OQ)**: Questions to which no deterministic answer is expected. Open questions usually provoke a cognitive process of students such as explaining a problem and talking about knowledge points. Some Examples are: "How to solve this problem?", "Can you share your ideas?", and "Why did you do this problem wrong?".
- **Procedural Question (PQ)**: Questions that teachers use to manage the teaching procedure, such as testing teaching equipment, greeting students, and asking them something unrelated to course content. Examples are: "Can you hear me?", "How are you doing?", and "Have I told you about it?".
- **Discourse-management Question (DQ)**: Questions that teachers use to manage the discourses, such as making transitions or drawing students' attention. Examples include: "Right?", "Isn't it?", and "Excuse me?".

We ask crowdsourcing annotators to code each utterance segment as non-question or one of the above four types of questions. The annotators code utterance segments by listening to the corresponding audio tracks. To ensure the coding quality, we first test the annotators on a set of 400 gold-standard examples. The 400 gold-standard examples are randomly sampled from the dataset and annotated by two experienced specialists in education. We only keep the top five annotators who achieve precision scores over 95% and 85% on the two-way and multi-way tasks on the gold-standard set to code the entire dataset.

3.2   Problem Formulation

We define the **two-way** task and the **multi-way** task for the teacher question detection problem as follows. Let $X = (x_1, \ldots, x_n)$ be a transcribed utterance where x_i is the i-th word and n is the length of the utterance. In the two-way task, each utterance X is assigned a binary label $Y \in \{Q, NQ\}$ where Q indicates that X is a question and NQ indicates it is not a question. In the multi-way task, each utterance X is assigned a label $Y \in \{KQ, OQ, PQ, DQ, NQ\}$ where KQ, OQ, PQ, DQ indicate that X is a knowledge-solicitation question, open question, procedural question or discourse-management question, respectively, and NQ denotes that X is not a question. Both the two-way task and the multi-way task are treated as classification problems where we seek for predicting the label Y of a given utterance X.

4   The Proposed Framework

In this section, we present our framework for teacher question detection in both two-way and multi-way prediction settings. We first introduce the overview of the proposed framework. After that, we discuss the details of our neural natural language understanding module, which is a key component in our question detection framework.

4.1   The Framework Overview

The overall workflow of our end-to-end approach is shown in Fig. 1. Similar to [24], we efficiently process the large-volume classroom recordings by utilizing a well-studied voice activity detection (VAD) system to cut an audio recording into small pieces of utterances [30,40]. The VAD algorithm is able to segment the audio stream into segments of utterances and filter out the noisy and silent ones. Then, each utterance segment is fed into an ASR system for transcription. After that, we build a neural NLU model to extract the semantically meaningful information within each sentence and make the final question detection prediction. Please note that as an end-to-end framework, our model can be integrated seamlessly into a run-time environment in the practical usage.

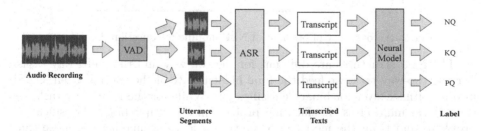

Fig. 1. The overall workflow of our end-to-end question detection framework.

4.2   The Neural Natural Language Understanding Model

In the task of text classification, traditional ML models only use simple word-level features, a.k.a., word embeddings. Due to the fact that such models are not able to extract contextual information, they fail to understand the sentence-level semantics and yield satisfactory detection performance. Therefore, in the work, we propose a neural NLU model to address above issues.

In our NLU module, given a sentence $X = (x_1, \ldots, x_N)$ that contains N tokens, similar to Devlin et al. [11], we first insert a special token $[CLS]$ in front of the token sequence X. Then the sequence of the corresponding token embeddings $E = (E_{[CLS]}, E_1, \ldots, E_N)$ is passed through multiple Transformer encoder layers [35]. Within each Transformer block, each token is repeatedly enriched by the combination of all the words in the sentence so that the contextualized information is captured. At last, we obtain the final hidden states $H = (H_{[CLS]}, H_1, \ldots, H_N)$. We treat the final hidden state $H_{[CLS]}$ of the special token $[CLS]$ as the aggregated representation of the entire sentence and use $H_{[CLS]}$ for our two-way and multi-way prediction tasks. Our neural NLU module is shown in Fig. 2.

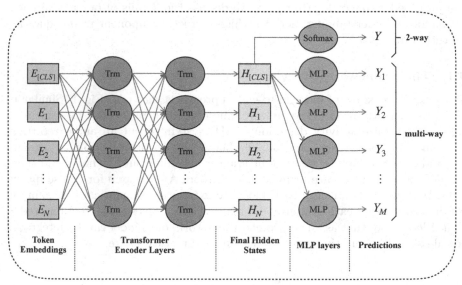

Fig. 2. An overview of our neural NLU module for question detection.

The NLU structures are different for the two-way and the multi-way tasks. For the two-way task, we feed the final hidden state of the special token $[CLS]$ into a Softmax layer for binary classification. While for the multi-way task, we convert the multi-class classification problem into multiple binary classification problems and train the model in a multi-task learning manner. Suppose that the number of classes is M. The final hidden state of $[CLS]$ is fed into M different multi-layer perceptron (MLP) layers to calculate the probabilities of class memberships for each utterance segment. For class c_i, the cross-entropy loss function is

$$L_i = -(\mathbb{I}\{c_i = 0\} \log(1 - p_i) + \mathbb{I}\{c_i = 1\} \log p_i)$$

where $\mathbb{I}\{\cdot\}$ is an indicator function. c_i is 1 if the utterance segment belongs to the i-th class and is 0 otherwise. p_i is the predicted probability that the utterance segment belongs to the i-th class. We minimize the sum of cross-entropy loss functions of the M tasks, which is defined as $L_{multi} = \sum_{i=1}^{M} L_i$. In the inference phase, we make predictions for utterance segments by picking question types with the highest estimated probability.

In this multi-task learning model, multiple binary question classification tasks are learned simultaneously. This method provides several benefits. First, for different tasks, lower layers of the model are shared while the upper layers are different. The shared layers learn to extract the deep semantic features of the input utterance and the upper layers are responsible for making accurate question type predictions. This design yields more modeling capabilities. Second, in teacher question detection, different types of questions share some common patterns, such as interrogative words. But they typically have vastly different contents. When learning a task, the unrelated parts of other tasks can be viewed as auxiliary information, which prevents the model from overfitting and further improves the generalization ability of the model.

5 Experiment

To verify the effectiveness and superiority of our proposed model, we conduct extensive experiments on a real-world dataset. In this section, we first introduce our dataset that is collected from a real-world online learning platform. Then we describe the details of our experimental setup and the competitive baselines. Finally, we present and discuss the experimental results.

5.1 Dataset

We collect 548 classroom recordings of different subjects and grades from a third party K-12 online education platform[1]. Recordings from both teacher and the students are stored separately in each online classroom. Here, we only focus on the teacher's audio recording. The audio recordings are cut into utterance segments by a self-trained VAD system and each audio segment is transcribed by an ASR service (see Sect. 5.2). As a result, we obtain 39313 segments in total that are made up of 5314, 16934, and 17065 segments from classes in elementary school, middle school, and high school respectively. The average length of the segments is 3.5 seconds. The detailed segment-level per school-age and per subject question distribution is shown in Fig. 3(a).

---

[1] https://www.xes1v1.com/.

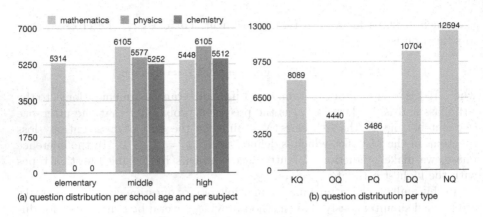

(a) question distribution per school age and per subject

(b) question distribution per type

Fig. 3. Question distributions of our real-world education dataset.

As described in Sect. 3.1, each segment is labeled by five qualified annotators. The average pairwise Cohen's Kappa agreement score is 0.696, which indicates a strong annotator agreement. Therefore, we choose to use majority votes as the final labels. The detailed distribution of questions with different types is shown in Fig. 3(b). We split the whole dataset into a training set, a validation set, and a test set with the proportion of 8:1:1, and the details of data statistics are shown in Table 1.

Table 1. Data statistics of the training set, the validation set, and the test set.

	KQ	OQ	PQ	DQ	NQ	Total
Training	6450	3551	2786	8514	10149	31450
Validation	861	431	328	1104	1207	3931
Test	778	458	372	1086	1238	3932

5.2   Implementation Details

In the work, we train our VAD model by using a four-layer DNN neural network to distinguish normal human utterances from background noises and silences [33]. Similar to Blanchard et al. [3], we find that publicly available ASR service may yield inferior performance in the noisy and dynamic classroom environments. Therefore, we train our own ASR models on the classroom specific datasets based on a deep feed-forward sequential memory network proposed by Zhang et al. [38]. Our ASR has a word error rate of 28.08% in our classroom settings.

Language model pre-training techniques have achieved great improvements on various NLU tasks [11,36]. In the implementation of our neural NLU model, we first pre-train the model with a large-scale language corpus and then use question specific classroom data to conduct the model fine-tuning. Here, we adopt the pre-trained NEZHA-base model released by Wei et al. [36]. In the multi-task setting, we apply a two-layer MLP with hidden sizes 256, 64 for each class. The output is passed through a sigmoid function to calculate the predictive probability. An optimal set of hyper-parameters is picked according to the model's performance on the validation set and we report its performance on the test set.

5.3   Baselines

We compare our approach with the following representative baseline methods: (1) Logistic Regression (LR) [23], (2) K-Nearest Neighbor (KNN) [14], (3) Random Forest (RF) [18], (4) Support Vector Machine (SVM) [10], (5) Gradient Boosted Decision Tree (GBDT) [13] and (6) Bidirectional Long Short Term Memory Network (Bi-LSTM) [39]. For the first five baselines, we use the sentence embedding of a given transcribed utterance as the feature vector for classification. The sentence embedding is computed by taking the average of the pre-trained word embeddings within each sentence. For Bi-LSTM, the word embeddings are fed into an LSTM network sequentially and the concatenation vector of the final hidden states in two directions is fed into a Softmax layer for classification.

5.4   Experimental Results

We show the results of the two-way and the multi-way tasks in Table 2 and Table 3, respectively. In the two-way task, we report the classification results of different models in terms of accuracy, precision, recall, F1 score, and AUC score, respectively. In the multi-way task, we report the classification results on each question type in terms of F1 score, as well as the overall results in terms of precision, recall and F1 scores from both micro and macro perspectives [34]. From Table 2 and Table 3, we make the following observations:

Table 2. Performance comparison of the **two-way task**.

	Accuracy	Precision	Recall	F1 score	AUC
LR	0.724	0.863	0.711	0.779	0.811
KNN	0.740	0.745	0.943	0.832	0.763
RF	0.766	0.758	**0.968**	0.850	0.824
SVM	0.798	0.874	0.824	0.848	0.854
GBDT	0.817	0.826	0.929	0.874	0.837
Bi-LSTM	0.873	0.882	0.940	0.910	0.915
Our Model	**0.885**	**0.888**	0.952	**0.919**	**0.933**

Table 3. Performance comparison of the **multi-way task**. ma-Pre., ma-Rec., mi-F1 and ma-F1 represent the macro precision, macro recall, micro F1 score and macro F1 score respectively.

Type	KQ	OQ	PQ	DQ	NQ	Overall			
	F1	F1	F1	F1	F1	ma-Pre.	ma-Rec.	mi-F1	ma-F1
LR	0.621	0.584	0.532	0.734	0.620	0.611	0.634	0.637	0.618
KNN	0.450	0.461	0.450	0.616	0.540	0.580	0.490	0.540	0.503
RF	0.564	0.454	0.483	0.699	0.632	0.661	0.537	0.612	0.566
SVM	0.644	0.629	0.561	0.791	0.694	0.655	0.681	0.688	0.664
GBDT	0.629	0.583	0.516	0.758	0.676	0.662	0.616	0.668	0.632
Bi-LSTM	0.743	0.751	0.654	0.914	0.778	0.769	0.769	0.794	0.768
Our Model	0.767	0.768	0.686	0.912	0.793	**0.781**	**0.794**	**0.808**	**0.785**

- First, in terms of both the two-way and multi-way tasks and most of the evaluation metrics, our model outperforms all the baseline methods. Due to the fact that our dataset consists of different subjects, school-ages, teachers and question types, we believe that the performance improvements achieved by our approach show the adaptability and robustness towards the real challenging educational scenarios.
- Second, by comparing the performances of the models on different types of questions, we find that procedural questions are relatively harder to identify compared to discourse-management questions. We believe the reason is that procedural questions typically involve a wide range of topics and appear in diverse forms. While discourse-management questions are short and succinct, and their forms are relatively fixed.
- Third, the baselines LR, KNN, RF, SVM, and GBDT achieve unsatisfactory performance in both tasks. Because they simply average the word embeddings as the features for classification, which fail to capture any contextualized information. Bi-LSTM performs better by learning better contextualized representations. The proposed framework outperforms Bi-LSTM because of its powerful ability of deep semantic understanding learned through the Transformer layers, the pre-training procedure, and the multi-task learning technique.

6   Conclusion

In this paper, we present a novel framework for the automatic detection of teacher questions in online classrooms. We propose a neural NLU model, which is able to automatically extract semantic features from teachers' utterances and adaptively generalize across recordings of different subjects and speakers. Experiments conducted on a real-world education dataset validate the effectiveness of our model in both two-way and multi-way tasks. As a future research direction, we are going to explore the relationship between the use of teacher questions and student achievement in live classrooms, thus we can make corresponding suggestions to teachers to improve their teaching efficiency.

Acknowledgements. Haochen Liu and Jiliang Tang are supported by the National Science Foundation of United States under IIS1714741, IIS1715940, IIS1715940, IIS1845081 and IIS1907704.

References

1. Applebee, A.N., Langer, J.A., Nystrand, M., Gamoran, A.: Discussion-based approaches to developing understanding: classroom instruction and student performance in middle and high school English. Am. Educ. Res. J. **40**(3), 685–730 (2003)
2. Beck, I.L., McKeown, M.G., Sandora, C., Kucan, L., Worthy, J.: Questioning the author: a yearlong classroom implementation to engage students with text. Elementary Sch. J. **96**(4), 385–414 (1996)
3. Blanchard, N., et al.: A study of automatic speech recognition in noisy classroom environments for automated dialog analysis. In: Conati, C., Heffernan, N., Mitrovic, A., Verdejo, M.F. (eds.) AIED 2015. LNCS (LNAI), vol. 9112, pp. 23–33. Springer, Cham (2015). https://doi.org/10.1007/978-3-319-19773-9_3
4. Blanchard, N., D'Mello, S., Olney, A.M., Nystrand, M.: Automatic classification of question & answer discourse segments from teacher's speech in classrooms. Int. Educ. Data Mining Soc. (2015)
5. Blanchard, N., et al.: Identifying teacher questions using automatic speech recognition in classrooms. In: Proceedings of the 17th Annual Meeting of the Special Interest Group on Discourse and Dialogue, pp. 191–201 (2016)
6. Blanchard, N., et al.: Semi-automatic detection of teacher questions from human-transcripts of audio in live classrooms. Int. Educ. Data Mining Soc. (2016)
7. Blosser, P.E.: How to Ask the Right Questions. NSTA Press (1991)
8. Caruana, R.: Multitask learning. In: Thrun, S., Pratt, L. (eds.) Learning to Learn, pp. 95–133. Springer, Heidelberg (1998). https://doi.org/10.1007/978-1-4615-5529-2_5
9. Chen, J., Li, H., Wang, W., Ding, W., Huang, G.Y., Liu, Z.: A multimodal alerting system for online class quality assurance. In: Isotani, S., Millán, E., Ogan, A., Hastings, P., McLaren, B., Luckin, R. (eds.) AIED 2019. LNCS (LNAI), vol. 11626, pp. 381–385. Springer, Cham (2019). https://doi.org/10.1007/978-3-030-23207-8_70
10. Cortes, C., Vapnik, V.: Support-vector networks. Mach. Learn. **20**(3), 273–297 (1995)
11. Devlin, J., Chang, M., Lee, K., Toutanova, K.: BERT: pre-training of deep bidirectional transformers for language understanding. In: Proceedings of the 2019 Conference of the North American Chapter of the Association for Computational Linguistics: Human Language Technologies, NAACL-HLT 2019, Minneapolis, MN, USA, 2–7 June 2019, pp. 4171–4186 (2019)
12. Donnelly, P.J., Blanchard, N., Olney, A.M., Kelly, S., Nystrand, M., D'Mello, S.K.: Words matter: automatic detection of teacher questions in live classroom discourse using linguistics, acoustics, and context. In: Proceedings of the Seventh International Learning Analytics & Knowledge Conference, Vancouver, BC, Canada, 13–17 March 2017, pp. 218–227 (2017)

13. Drucker, H., Cortes, C.: Boosting decision trees. In: Advances in Neural Information Processing Systems, pp. 479–485 (1996)
14. Fix, E.: Discriminatory analysis: nonparametric discrimination, consistency properties. USAF school of Aviation Medicine (1951)
15. Gamoran, A., Kelly, S.: Tracking, instruction, and unequal literacy in secondary school English. In: Stability and Change in American Education: Structure, Process, and Outcomes, pp. 109–126 (2003)
16. Graesser, A.C., Person, N.K.: Question asking during tutoring. Am. Educ. Res. J. **31**(1), 104–137 (1994)
17. Hashimoto, K., Xiong, C., Tsuruoka, Y., Socher, R.: A joint many-task model: growing a neural network for multiple NLP tasks. CoRR abs/1611.01587 (2016). http://arxiv.org/abs/1611.01587
18. Ho, T.K.: Random decision forests. In: Proceedings of 3rd International Conference on Document Analysis and Recognition, vol. 1, pp. 278–282. IEEE (1995)
19. Kane, T.J., Staiger, D.O.: Gathering feedback for teaching: combining high-quality observations with student surveys and achievement gains. Research paper. met project. Bill & Melinda Gates Foundation (2012)
20. Kelly, S.: Classroom discourse and the distribution of student engagement. Soc. Psychol. Educ. **10**(3), 331–352 (2007)
21. Kelly, S.: Race, social class, and student engagement in middle school English classrooms. Soc. Sci. Res. **37**(2), 434–448 (2008)
22. Kendall, A., Gal, Y., Cipolla, R.: Multi-task learning using uncertainty to weigh losses for scene geometry and semantics. CoRR abs/1705.07115 (2017). http://arxiv.org/abs/1705.07115
23. Kleinbaum, D.G., Dietz, K., Gail, M., Klein, M., Klein, M.: Logistic Regression. Springer, Heidelberg (2002)
24. Li, H., et al.: Multimodal learning for classroom activity detection. In: 2020 IEEE International Conference on Acoustics, Speech and Signal Processing, pp. 9234–9238. IEEE (2020)
25. Liu, Z., et al.: Dolphin: a spoken language proficiency assessment system for elementary education. In: Proceedings of the Web Conference 2020, pp. 2641–2647. ACM (2020)
26. MacNeilley, L.H.: Opening dialogue: understanding the dynamics of language and learning in the English classroom by Martin Nystrand with Adam Gamoran, Robert Kachur, and Catherine Prendergast. Language **74**(2), 444–445 (1998)
27. Nystrand, M., Gamoran, A.: Instructional discourse, student engagement, and literature achievement. In: Research in the Teaching of English, pp. 261–290 (1991)
28. Nystrand, M., Wu, L.L., Gamoran, A., Zeiser, S., Long, D.A.: Questions in time: investigating the structure and dynamics of unfolding classroom discourse. Discourse Process. **35**(2), 135–198 (2003)
29. Samei, B., et al.: Domain independent assessment of dialogic properties of classroom discourse. In: Proceedings of the 7th International Conference on Educational Data Mining, London, UK, 4–7 July 2014, pp. 233–236 (2014)
30. Sohn, J., Kim, N.S., Sung, W.: A statistical model-based voice activity detection. IEEE Sig. Process. Lett. **6**(1), 1–3 (1999)
31. Stivers, T., Enfield, N.J.: A coding scheme for question-response sequences in conversation. J. Prag. **42**(10), 2620–2626 (2010)
32. Sweigart, W.: Classroom talk, knowledge development, and writing. In: Research in the Teaching of English, pp. 469–496 (1991)
33. Tashev, I., Mirsamadi, S.: DNN-based causal voice activity detector. In: Information Theory and Applications Workshop (2016)

34. Van Asch, V.: Macro-and micro-averaged evaluation measures. Belgium: CLiPS**49** (2013)
35. Vaswani, A., et al.: Attention is all you need. In: Advances in Neural Information Processing Systems, pp. 5998–6008 (2017)
36. Wei, J., et al.: NEZHA: neural contextualized representation for Chinese language understanding. CoRR abs/1909.00204 (2019). http://arxiv.org/abs/1909.00204
37. Yang, Y., Hospedales, T.: Deep multi-task representation learning: A tensor factorisation approach. arXiv preprint arXiv:1605.06391 (2016)
38. Zhang, S., Lei, M., Yan, Z., Dai, L.: Deep-FSMN for large vocabulary continuous speech recognition. In: 2018 IEEE International Conference on Acoustics, Speech and Signal Processing, pp. 5869–5873. IEEE (2018)
39. Zhang, S., Zheng, D., Hu, X., Yang, M.: Bidirectional long short-term memory networks for relation classification. In: Proceedings of the 29th Pacific Asia Conference on Language, Information and Computation, pp. 73–78 (2015)
40. Zhang, X.L., Wu, J.: Deep belief networks based voice activity detection. IEEE Trans. Audio Speech Lang. Process. **21**(4), 697–710 (2012)

A Data-Driven Student Model to Provide Adaptive Support During Video Watching Across MOOCs

Sébastien Lallé[(⊠)] and Cristina Conati

Department of Computer Science, The University of British Columbia, Vancouver, Canada
`{lalles,conati}@cs.ubc.ca`

Abstract. MOOCs have great potential to innovate education, but lack of personalization. In this paper, we show how FUMA, a data-driven framework for student modeling and adaptation, can help understand how to provide personalized support to MOOCs students, specifically targeting video watching behaviors. We apply FUMA across several MOOCs to show how to: *(i)* discover video watching behaviors that can be detrimental for or conductive to learning; *(ii)* use these behaviors to detect ineffective learners at different weeks of MOOCs usage. We discuss how these behaviors can be used to define personalized support to effective MOOC video usage regardless of the target course.

Keywords: Personalization · Student modeling · MOOCs · Data mining

1 Introduction

While the popularity of Massive Open Online Courses (MOOCs) has risen to engage thousands of students in higher-education, there is still limited understanding on how to deliver personalized instruction in MOOCs to accommodate the needs and abilities of their very diverse audience. Research on MOOCs has mostly focused on analyzing the students' logged data to model relevant states or behaviors, such as dropping-out [1–3], learning outcome [4, 5], or browsing strategies [6–8]. There is initial work on how to leverage such models to deliver personalized support in real time, e.g., to recommend better pathways in the course [9, 10] or tailor the course content [11, 12]. Although these studies provided encouraging results, further research is needed to broaden the understanding of which forms of personalization are effective in MOOCs.

In this paper, we contribute to this research by looking at the potential of providing adaptive interventions to support effective usage of MOOCs' *videos*, a form of personalization largely unexplored thus far, except for recommending what videos to watch next [10, 13, 14]. We do so by leverage an existing framework for User Modeling and Adaptation (*FUMA* from now on) that we proposed to learn from data how to provide adaptation in exploratory learning environments [15, 16]. FUMA uses clustering of existing interaction data to learn which student behaviors are more or less conducive to effective learning. Next, association rule mining extracts behavioral patterns that characterize each clustered group of students. These association rules are then used to classify

© Springer Nature Switzerland AG 2020
I. I. Bittencourt et al. (Eds.): AIED 2020, LNAI 12163, pp. 282–295, 2020.
https://doi.org/10.1007/978-3-030-52237-7_23

new students in terms of how well they are learning during interaction, and trigger real-time adaptive interventions designed to encourage effective behaviors and discourage ineffective ones. We have successfully applied FUMA to identify useful adaptations with two different interactive simulations [17, 18]. In this paper, we investigate if FUMA can also identify meaningful forms of adaptive support across several MOOCs.

We focus on video watching behaviors because videos typically account for a significant amount of the learning material in [19]. However, not all students use and benefit from videos at best [20–23], indicating the need for adaptive support that can promote effective video watching for all students. To the best of our knowledge, adaptive support for videos has been limited in MOOCs to recommending a video to watch [10, 13, 14], but not to counteract suboptimal behaviors while watching videos.

In this paper we make a first step toward this direction by providing insights on what forms of adaptation could promote effective video watching behaviors, along with a student model that can be deployed across MOOCs to drive these adaptations. Our results show in particular that FUMA can derive student models that distinguish with high accuracy effective and ineffective learners solely based on their video watching behaviors, indicating that these behaviors can be leveraged for defining the content of adaptive support to video watching during interaction. These results broaden the set of video watching behaviors that have been considered for adaptation in MOOCs, in particular by showing that behaviors related to how selectively the students interact with the videos can identify low learners, thus warranting the design of adaptive support. We also show that a single student model built with FUMA from these behaviors can generalize across several MOOCs, so as to drive adaptation regardless of the target MOOC.

2 Related Work

There has been extensive work on analyzing student clickstream data in MOOCs, typically by using data-mining techniques to identify relevant behaviors and learning strategies. In particular, several of these studies have leveraged the same data-mining techniques used in FUMA offline to mine students' behaviors. For instance, clusters and association rules were mined in [6–8, 24, 25] to identify relationships among student's behaviors and their engagement in the course. Unlike these works, FUMA can not only identify students' behaviors that can be the target of adaptive support, but also detect these behaviors online, to build a student model and drive adaptive support accordingly.

There has been work focused on analyzing video watching behaviors in MOOCs. Li et al. [23] compared video behaviors related to pausing, seeking or replaying videos among effective and ineffective learners to understand what behaviors can hinder the student experience. Interaction data collected during video watching were used to predict performance on quiz in [26, 27] and dropping out in [28]. We contribute to these works by leveraging additional video watching behaviors than the ones they used, in particular related to how consistently students used the different video actions (pausing, seeking...) captured by the standard deviation of these usages across videos. We also contribute to these works by building a student model from these behaviors over multiple MOOC datasets, so as to examine the generality of the resulting student model.

A few other works have evaluated classifiers to predict dropout over several MOOC datasets, using standard classifiers and neural networks [29–32]. We contribute to these works by using solely video watching behaviors and a data-driven approach based on association rules, which are fully interpretable and can guide the design of adaptive support to video watching regardless of the target courses. We also extend [29–32] by modeling students' learning performance across MOOCs rather than dropout.

In non-MOOC settings, previous works have shown that adaptive support can improve the student's engagement and learning with educational videos, e.g., [33, 34]. In MOOCs, a few studies have evaluated the value of adaptive support. Adaptation recommending the next page or video to visit was delivered in [10, 13, 14] based on the previous pages/videos visited by the students, but not based on how students interact with the video. Other work tailored the course content to the students, depending on their learning performance [11] or their learning style [12]. Adaptive feedback has been explored in [35] to encourage students to be more active, when their clickstream data reveal a low level of engagement. Another work [31] provided encouragements to students predicted to be at risk of dropping-out by a classifiers trained on interaction data. Adaptive scaffolding to foster self-regulation can improve the amount of viewed videos in MOOCs [36]. While these works have shown that adaptation is MOOCs can be valuable, they have largely ignored adaptation to promote efficient video watching behaviors (e.g., dedicated adaptation to recommend effective pausing or seeking behaviors), which is the end goal of the data-driven student models we build in this paper.

3   FUMA Framework

FUMA consists of two main phases to guide the delivery of adaptive support, shown in Fig. 1 and described next (for a complete description, see [15, 16]).

In the *Behavior Discovery* phase (Fig. 1, top), interaction data of previous students is first pre-processed into feature vectors. Next, clustering is applied to these vectors to identify students with similar interaction behaviors. The resulting clusters are analyzed by comparing the learning performance of the students in each cluster relatively to the other clusters. Next, association rule mining is used to identify the distinctive behaviors in each cluster. To do so, the values of features are discretized into bins to avoid producing a large number of fine-grained rules that are difficult to interpret, a well-known problem with association rules learnt on continuous features [16]. Hyper-parameters such as the number of clusters, the minimum support of the association rules, and the number of bins to be used for discretization, are learnt as part of the training process.

In the *User Classification* phase (Fig. 1, bottom), the labeled clusters and the corresponding association rules extracted in Behavior Discovery are used to train a classifier student model. As new students interact with the target MOOC, they would be classified in real-time into one of the identified clusters, based on a membership score that summarizes how well the student's behaviors match the association rules for each cluster. In addition to classifying students, this phase returns the subset of association rules satisfied by the students that caused the classification. These rules can be used to trigger adaptation meant to encourage productive behaviors and discourage detrimental ones.

FUMA has been previously applied to two interactive simulations (CSP [15, 16] and CCK [18]), respectively to support learning about constraint satisfaction algorithms

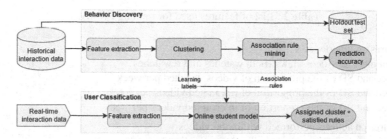

Fig. 1. FUMA's framework

and electric circuits. For both simulations, results showed that FUMA identified two clusters of students, one with significantly higher learning gains than the other, solely by mining interaction behaviors. FUMA then classified unseen students as "low" or "high" learners significantly better than chance and other standard classifiers (e.g., random forests, SVM...), with accuracies above 85% [15, 18]. A user study [17] has shown that a version of the CSP simulation augmented with adaptive support provided by FUMA improved students learning, compared to no support or support provided at random.

4 Applying FUMA to MOOC Data

For this work we leverage four edX MOOC datasets collected at the Stanford University. These MOOCs include two science courses, namely computer science (CS101) and statistics (STAT), as well as two courses on social sciences and humanities, namely economics (ECO101) and the study of ancient texts (ATEXT). Table 1 summarizes the content of each of these MOOCs in terms of number of videos (#video) and quizzes (#quiz). Table 1 also includes number of students who accessed the course at least once (#students) and who passed the course (#passed). Students could pass by obtaining a final grade greater than a threshold set by the instructors, with the final grade defined as the number of successfully completed quizzes divided by the total number of quizzes.

Table 1. Summary of MOOC content and enrollments.

MOOC	Weeks	#video	#quiz	#students	#passed
CS101	6	33	29	114,205	10,311 (9%)
STAT	9	65	69	78,631	5,504 (7%)
ECO101	8	72	34	18,873	1,854 (10%)
ATEXT	6	33	36	98,028	7,842 (8%)

Table 2. List of features used for running FUMA.

---

a) Features on video views
- Total number of videos views (both watches and rewatches)
- Average and SD of the proportion of videos watched per week
- Average and SD of the proportion of rewatched videos per week
- Average and SD of the proportion of interrupted videos per week

---

b) Features on actions performed within the videos
- Frequency and Total number of all video actions performed
- Frequency of video action performed, for each type of video action
- Average and SD duration of: video pauses, seek length, and time speeding-up the video

---

4.1 Features Generated from MOOC's Video Usage

We derived 23 features to capture important aspects of the student interaction with the videos, related to *video views* (Table 2a) and *video actions* performed (Table 2b).

Video view features are meant to capture how engaged were the students in the video content. Specifically, the *total number of video views* indicates the overall level of activity of the students in terms of access to the video content, which is one of the most common measures for capturing video usage in MOOCs, e.g., [1, 6, 8, 24, 25]. Additionally, we leveraged features that characterize these video views in a more fine-grained manner, in terms of the mean and standard deviation (SD) of the proportion of *videos watched*, *rewatched* and *interrupted* per week. The average of these measures indicates how extensively students exhibit these behaviors overall, while the standard deviation shows the consistency of these behaviors across weeks.

Action features capture specific usage of each of the available action clicks from within the video in edX, namely play/resume, pause, seek backward, seek forward, change speed, and stop. Specifically, the *frequency* (number of actions divided by the time spent watching videos) and the total number of all actions performed reveals how active the students are when watching videos, which might indicate how engaged the student is. Furthermore, we distinguish between each type of action by measuring the *frequency* of each action performed, to understand what actions students tend to use more, which might reveal suboptimal usage of the video (e.g., seeking forward too frequently might indicate that the student skipped too much of the material). We also measure features that characterize how the students used some of these actions, which includes the *average* and *standard deviation* of the *length of videos pauses*, of the *length of seeks*, and of the *time spent with a higher-than-normal speed* (last three rows of Table 2b). The average of these measures indicate how students tended to use these actions overall (e.g., make short versus long pauses), while the standard deviation indicates the consistency of these usages across videos, as discussed above for video views features.

4.2 Building Student Models with FUMA

To account for the fact that the number of students changes overtime due to students dropping-out, we apply FUMA to three different sets of data for each MOOC, namely cumulative student activity data up to Week 2, up to Week 3, and up to Week 4. We ignored week 1 because about 50% of the students dropped the course during this week, which is typical in MOOCs and may provide irrelevant behaviors for FUMA. We also did not include weeks beyond week 4 because adaptive assistance is most useful early in the course [37]. We include only students who attempted to complete at least half of the quizzes available, because a portion of the students were active in the course but completed very few quizzes, for example because they did not care to obtain the certification, which would make it hard for FUMA to assess how well they learned.

The set of features in Table 1 are computed at each of the three weeks in each of the target MOOC. Next, we split the datasets into a training and holdout set, and train FUMA with two different setups: within-MOOC and across-MOOC. In the *within-MOOC* setup, FUMA is trained on the data from each MOOC separately, to ascertain how well FUMA can learn useful rules that are specific to the target MOOC. This produces four FUMA's student models (one per MOOC). In the *across-MOOC* setup, FUMA is trained over a *merged* dataset that combines data from all of our MOOCs, to ascertain if FUMA can build a student model that generalizes across multiple MOOCs. Note that FUMA does not know which MOOC each student was taking.

Each of the five FUMA student models learned with these two setups at each week is tested on four holdout sets (one per MOOC). Each holdout set is generated beforehand by randomly sampling 100 students from the corresponding MOOC, so as the distribution of students who passed within the holdout set is the same as in the original dataset. The holdout sets are never seen by FUMA (cf. Fig. 1). 10-fold cross-validation is used on the training data to learn FUMA's hyper-parameters (see Sect. 3).

5 Results

We evaluate the suitability of the student models generated by FUMA in terms of:

(i) The quality of the learned clusters, measured by the difference in learning perfor-mance between students in the different clusters. We measure learning performance as the combination of four indicators that are commonly used in MOOCs, without clear evidence as for which one is most representative of student learning on its own [1, 2, 27, 38]: the *final grade* (defined above); the *proportion of correct first answers to quiz*; whether the student *passed*; whether the student *dropped*. We combine these indicators using a Principal Component Analysis (PCA) with one component (*PCA-Metric* from now on), which explained >80% of the variance as recommended for PCA [39].
(ii) The classification accuracy of FUMA's rule-based classifiers trained on the obtained clusters. We compare FUMA against a majority-class baseline, which always assigns students to the largest cluster, as well as a Support Vector Machine (SVM) and a Random Forest (RF) classifier. All features in the training set are leveraged to train these classifiers, and their accuracy is measured on the same holdout sets as used for FUMA. This is to ensure that the association rules learned by FUMA are accurate enough at assigning students to their relevant cluster, as compared to SVM and RF, which have been extensively used for student modeling in MOOCs [2, 32, 40–42].

Table 3. Statistical comparisons among the clusters (abbreviated *"cl"*).

FUMA's model		Main effect	Pairwise comparisons of clusters		
			Week 2	Week 3	Week 4
Within-MOOC	CS101	$p < .0001$, $\eta^2 = 0.17$	cl1 < cl2 < *cl3*	cl1 < cl2 < *cl3*	cl1 < cl2 < cl3 < *cl4*
	Stat	$p < .0001$, $\eta^2 = 0.19$	cl1 < cl2 < cl3 < *cl4<cl5*	cl1 < cl2 < cl3 < *cl4 < cl5*	cl1 < cl2 < cl3 < *cl4 < cl5*
	Eco101	$p < .0001$, $\eta^2 = 0.15$	cl1 < cl2<cl3 < *cl4*	cl1 < cl2 < cl3 < *cl4*	cl1 < cl2 < cl3 < cl4 < *cl5*
	AText	$p < .0001$, $\eta^2 = 0.16$	cl1 < cl2 < *cl3 < cl4*	cl1 < cl2 < *cl3<cl4*	cl1 < cl2 < *cl3 < cl4*
Across-MOOC		$p < .0001$, $\eta^2 = 0.22$	cl1 < cl2 < *cl3*	cl1 < cl2 < *cl3*	cl1 < cl2 < *cl3*

(*iii*) The potential usefulness of the association rules generated by FUMA in identifying behavior patterns that can be used to design and trigger support to students. In doing so we provide insights about the forms of adaptive support our results suggest.

5.1 Quality of the Clusters

The optimal number of clusters found by FUMA ranges from 3 to 5 depending on the target MOOC and setup (within-MOOCS vs across-MOOCS). To ascertain whether the students' video watching behaviors are representative of their learning performance we run a statistical analysis that compares our measure of students' performance (*PCA-Metric*) across clusters. Specifically, for each of the 5 FUMA's student model and each of the 3 weeks of data, we run a Kruskal–Wallis test with *PCA-Metric* as the dependent variable, and the corresponding clusters as the factor, for a total of 15 tests, adjusted for family-wise error using the Holm adjustment ($\alpha = 15$). The results, shown in Table 2 ("Main effect"), reveal a significant (i.e., p < .05) main effect of clusters in all tests. Effect sizes are reported as large for $\eta^2 > .14$, medium for $\eta^2 > .06$, small otherwise.

Post-hoc pairwise comparisons with Holm-adjusted Mann–Whitney U tests are shown in the right portion of Table 2: the clusters are ranked based on their *mean PCA-Metric*, with underlines indicating clusters that are not statistically different by this measure. Results show that in all datasets the clusters can be further categorized into three main groups based on the levels of PCA-Metric, namely a group representing students with *lower learning* compared to all the others (bold red), a group representing students with *higher learning* (italic blue), and a group representing *moderate learning* in between (regular black), with medium to high effect sizes. Noteworthy, these three main groups are found in all datasets, including across-MOOC, which indicates that these three general levels of performance generalize well across our MOOCs.

5.2 Classification Accuracy of the Online Rule-Based Classifiers

Classification accuracy is measured as percentage of unseen students in the relevant holdout sets that are assigned to their relevant cluster. As a first step, we compare the accuracy of each FUMA student model against the corresponding SVM, RF, and baseline

Table 4. Prediction accuracy of FUMA.

	Within-MOOC			Across-MOOC		
	Week 2	Week 3	Week 4	Week 2	Week 3	Week 4
CS101	88%	88%	78%	82%	83%	75%
Stat	79%	77%	76%	70%	72%	72%
Eco101	83%	84%	80%	78%	79%	73%
AText	87%	82%	82%	82%	77%	76%
Average	*84%*	*82%*	*80%*	*78%*	*77%*	*74%*

classifiers. To do so we run a set of ANOVAs (one per FUMA model) with *classification accuracy* as the dependent variable, and *classifiers* (4 levels) as the factor. After adjustment, all ANOVAs yield a significant main effect of classifiers ($p < 0.001$, η^2 from 0.14 to 0.21). Holm-adjusted pairwise comparisons show that FUMA outperforms all other classifiers ($p < 0.05$, $\eta^2 > .10$) in all cases, including the baseline.

Next, we explore FUMA's accuracy across the two different prediction setups (within- and across-MOOC) and the three weeks. Table 4 reports FUMA's accuracy in each of the four MOOCs (i.e., the corresponding holdout set), with the last row showing the accuracy averaged over all holdout sets. We run an ANOVA with *classification accuracy* as the dependent variable, *week* (3 levels) and *prediction setup* (2 levels: within-MOOC and across-MOOC) as the factors. Results show a significant main effect of prediction setup ($p < .001$, $\eta^2 = 0.09$). A follow-up pairwise comparison among the setups reveals that accuracy for within-MOOC is significantly higher than across-MOOC. This is not surprising given that the within-MOOC setup allows FUMA to learn rules that are fully tailored to a given MOOC, albeit not all of these rules may generalize well. This said, it is noteworthy that even across-MOOC prediction accuracy is much higher than the baseline, and only about 5% below the within-MOOC setup on average. This indicates that FUMA is able to learn a set of rules that can generalize well across our MOOCs, a useful finding since the across-MOOC student model can then be leveraged to drive the delivery of adaptive support regardless of the current MOOC.

The lack of main effect of *week* is also interesting because it means that peak accuracy can be already achieved at week 2, leaving substantial time to provide adaptation.

We report in Table 5 the class accuracy for FUMA at predicting each of the main groups identified in Sect. 5.1, i.e., low, moderate and high learning group. For simplicity, we only report class accuracy averaged over all holdout sets. Results show that FUMA reaches high accuracy at identifying *high* and *low* learning students both within-MOOC (87–88% at week 2) and across-MOOC (84%–85% at week 2), while still being able to predict the in-between clusters with over 60% accuracy. The fact that high accuracy is obtained for the low group is especially important, as these students are the ones who need help and may benefit from adaptive support. These results provide encouraging evidence for the usefulness of association rule mining for building a student model across MOOCs, which is interesting because association rules are interpretable and thus can be used to guide the design of adaptation support, as discussed next.

Table 6. Association rules learnt by FUMA.

Week	Low learning group	High learning group

All Week	1. num_views = Low & avg_pause = Low &
	  └ **a.** sd_seek = Low
	  └ **b.** sd_speed = Low
	2. num_views = Low *and* avg_rewatch = Low
		3. num_views = Med & avg_coverage = [Med, High]

Week 2 & 3 only	4. num_views = Low & sd_pause = Low &
	  sd_seek = Low
		5. avg_coverage = [Med, High] &
		  └ **a.** avg_pause = [Med, High]
		  └ **b.** sd_pause = Med
		6. avg_pause = Medium *and* pause_rate = Med

Week 4 only		7. avg_rewatch = Low & avg_pause = Med &
		  └ **a.** sd_pause = Med
		  └ **b.** sd_speed = Med

Table 5. Class accuracy of FUMA averaged over all holdout sets.

Learner group	Within-MOOC			Across-MOOC		
	Week 2	Week 3	Week 3	Week 2	Week 3	Week 4
Low	88%	86%	87%	84%	84%	80%
Moderate	67%	65%	65%	61%	60%	59%
High	87%	86%	85%	85%	83%	82%

5.3 Implications of the Rules for Adaptation

We discuss how the association rules identified by FUMA can inform the design of adaptive support for video watching. We focus on the rules learned in the across-MOOC setup as they can be used drive adaptation regardless of the target MOOC. Among these, we focus on the rules representative of the "*Lower learning*" and "*Higher learning*" clusters, because they most clearly identify behaviors detrimental vs conductive to learning respectively, and thus can be used to derive adaptive support to discourage the ineffective behaviors and promote instead the effective ones exhibited in the high learning group. Such behavioral recommendations have been successfully applied in previous applications of FUMA to improve students' learning [17, 43].

Table 6 shows these rules grouped as those that generalize across all weeks (first row), rules for week 2 and 3 because they largely overlap (second row), and rules that appear at week 4 only (third raw). As discussed in Sect. 3, FUMA discretizes the features into bins, with the number of bins (6 in our case) being learnt during model training. For ease of interpretation we label the bins for the rules in Table 6 as *Low* for bins 1–2, *Medium (Med)* for bins 3–4, and *High* for bins 5–6. When rules share behaviors they are merged in Table 6 as indicated by the indents, e.g., Rule L1a and L1b differ only in terms of the indented behaviors: '*sd_seek*' for Rule L1a and '*sd_speed*' for L1b.

One trend common to all rules for the lower learning group is that they watch few videos (*num_view = Low*), which intuitively explains their lower learning performance. This low video watching activity however, is always accompanied by other interesting patterns in these rules, especially making short pauses (*avg_pause* = *Low*, rules L1a and L1b) and/or exhibiting a *low standard deviation* for video action features (*seek, speed* and *pause*, rules L1a, L1b and L3). The short pauses suggest that these students may not take the time to think about the few videos they watch. The low standard deviations suggest that they were watching videos in a rather uniform manner, rather than selectively focusing on aspects that might be more challenging or interesting for them.

The fact that most of these behaviors are pervasive in students with lower learning performance at all weeks (see rules L1a and L1b), indicates that these students do not modify these behaviors over the course of the different MOOCs, which makes them a suitable target of adaptive support. This support may leverage the rules discovered in the higher learning groups to identify and promote behaviors that can address some of difficulties in the lower learning group, a strategy that has been successfully applied in previous work on FUMA [17]. As shown in Table 6, these "higher learning" behaviors are not always the exact opposite of those representative of lower learning, indicating that it is important to mine the representative behaviors of each cluster separately.

For instance, as discussed above the lower learning students tend to take short pauses during video watching throughout the weeks. In week 2–3 the high learning group shows the opposite behavior of pausing longer (*avg_pause* = *Medium/High*, rule H2a and H3). These longer pauses are accompanied by *covering more* of the weekly videos available (*avg_coverage* = *Medium/High*, rule H2a) a behavior that does not have a direct opposite in lower learning students. The fact that a high coverage of the weekly videos is linked to higher performance makes sense, because each video often introduces new knowledge that can be the target of a quiz. Thus, it is worth experimenting with adaptive support that, in weeks 2–3, recommends longer pauses to students in the lower learning group who tend to go through videos with little pausing, a help strategy that has been shown to be effective with FUMA [17]. This adaptive support should also promotes good video coverage, e.g., by recommending an unwatched video.

This higher coverage of the higher learning group also appears at week 2 and 3 in conjunction with a higher standard deviation of pausing (*sd_pause* = *Medium*, rule H2b). Because during these weeks the lower learning group shows the opposite behaviors of pausing uniformly (*sd_pause* = *Low*, rule L3), these students could benefit from recommendation to be more selective in how they pause (e.g., by reminding them that it is okay to take their time for pausing to reflect on parts a video that are unclear or interesting), combined with the aforementioned suggestion to cover more of the videos.

In week 4, the high learning group still shows the behavior of pausing longer, but now accompanied by a more selective pause length (*sd_pause* = *Medium*, rule H4a) and video speed (*sd_speed* = *Medium*, rule H4b), suggesting the need to recommend different behaviors to the low learning students later in the course. In particular, the low learning group may still benefit from suggestion to take longer pauses, but also to be more selective in how they use the aforementioned video actions.

6   Conclusion

We have presented an application of FUMA to students' video usage in several MOOCs. FUMA is a framework that uses logged interaction data to learn which student behaviors should trigger adaptive help. Our results show that the behaviors learnt by FUMA can predict student learning performance during interaction with a MOOC with accuracy up to 84% across several MOOC datasets lumped together. In particular, our findings reveal that low learners can be identified by their tendency to watch few videos while making short pauses, as well as by their rather uniform usage of the video actions as shown by the low standard deviation of their pause length, seek length, and video speed. This finding is interesting because, to the best of our knowledge, we are the first to mine behaviors related to the consistency (standard deviation) of some of these video watching behaviors for informing the design of adaptive support in MOOCs. Based on these findings, we provided insights on how these behaviors can guide the design of adaptive support in MOOCs to promote better video watching strategies, based on the opposite behaviors shown by high learning students. Moving forward, we plan to collaborate with MOOC instructors to design and implement adaptive support based on FUMA's rules. We are also deploying FUMA on the cloud so has to drive this adaptive support remotely in several MOOCs, and evaluate the value of such support, an important step toward making MOOCs more personalized using data-driven approaches.

References

1. Li, W., Gao, M., Li, H., Xiong, Q., Wen, J., Wu, Z.: Dropout prediction in MOOCs using behavior features and multi-view semi-supervised learning. In: 2016 International Joint Conference on Neural Networks (IJCNN), pp. 3130–3137. IEEE (2016)
2. Nagrecha, S., Dillon, J.Z., Chawla, N.V.: MOOC dropout prediction: lessons learned from making pipelines interpretable. In: Proceedings of the 26th International Conference on World Wide Web Companion, pp. 351–359. International World Wide Web Conferences Steering Committee (2017)
3. Zhao, C., Yang, J., Liang, J., Li, C.: Discover learning behavior patterns to predict certification. In: 2016 11th International Conference on Computer Science & Education (ICCSE), pp. 69–73. IEEE (2016)
4. Wang, Z., Zhu, J., Li, X., Hu, Z., Zhang, M.: Structured knowledge tracing models for student assessment on Coursera. In: 2016 Proceedings of the Third ACM Conference on Learning@ Scale, pp. 209–212. ACM (2016)
5. Pardos, Z.A., Bergner, Y., Seaton, D.T., Pritchard, D.E.: Adapting Bayesian knowledge tracing to a massive open online course in edX. In: EDM, vol. 13, pp. 137–144 (2013)
6. Liu, S., Hu, Z., Peng, X., Liu, Z., Cheng, H.N., Sun, J.: Mining learning behavioral patterns of students by sequence analysis in cloud classroom. Int. J. Distance Educ. Technol. (IJDET) 15, 15–27 (2017)
7. Boroujeni, M.S., Dillenbourg, P.: Discovery and temporal analysis of latent study patterns in MOOC interaction sequences. In: Proceedings of the 8th International Conference on Learning Analytics and Knowledge, pp. 206–215. ACM (2018)
8. Liu, T., Xiu, L.L.: Finding out reasons for low completion in MOOC environment: an explicable approach using hybrid data mining methods. In: 2017 Proceedings of the International Conference on Modern Education and Information Technology, pp. 376–384. DEStech (2017)
9. Rosen, Y., Rushkin, I., Ang, A., Federicks, C., Tingley, D., Blink, M.J.: Designing adaptive assessments in MOOCs. In: 2017 Proceedings of the Fourth ACM Conference on Learning@ Scale, pp. 233–236. ACM (2017)
10. Ketamo, H.: Learning fingerprint: adaptive tutoring for MOOCs. In: EdMedia: World Conference on Educational Media and Technology. Association for the Advancement of Computing in Education (AACE) (2014)

11. Brinton, C.G., Rill, R., Ha, S., Chiang, M., Smith, R., Ju, W.: Individualization for education at scale: MIIC design and preliminary evaluation. IEEE Trans. Learn. Technol. **8**, 136–148 (2015)

12. Sonwalkar, N.: The first adaptive MOOC: a case study on pedagogy framework and scalable cloud architecture—part I. In: MOOCs Forum, pp. 22–29. Mary Ann Liebert, Inc., New Rochelle (2013)

13. Bhatt, C., Cooper, M., Zhao, J.: *SeqSense*: video recommendation using topic sequence mining. In: Schoeffmann, K., et al. (eds.) MMM 2018. LNCS, vol. 10705, pp. 252–263. Springer, Cham (2018). https://doi.org/10.1007/978-3-319-73600-6_22

14. Cooper, M., Zhao, J., Bhatt, C., Shamma, D.A.: MOOCex: exploring educational video via recommendation. In: Proceedings of the 2018 ACM on International Conference on Multimedia Retrieval, pp. 521–524. ACM, New York (2018). https://doi.org/10.1145/3206025.320 6087

15. Conati, C., Kardan, S.: Student modeling: Supporting personalized instruction, from problem solving to exploratory open ended activities. AI Mag. **34**, 13–26 (2013)

16. Kardan, S., Conati, C.: A framework for capturing distinguishing user interaction behaviors in novel interfaces. In: EDM, pp. 159–168 (2011)

17. Kardan, S., Conati, C.: Providing adaptive support in an interactive simulation for learning: an experimental evaluation. In: Proceedings of the 33rd Annual ACM Conference on Human Factors in Computing Systems, pp. 3671–3680. ACM, Seoul (2015)

18. Fratamico, L., Conati, C., Kardan, S., Roll, I.: Applying a framework for student modeling in exploratory learning environments: comparing data representation granularity to handle environment complexity. Int. J. Artif. Intell. Educ. **27**, 320–352 (2017). https://doi.org/10.1007/s40593-016-0131-y

19. Yousef, A.M.F., Chatti, M.A., Schroeder, U., Wosnitza, M.: What drives a successful MOOC? An empirical examination of criteria to assure design quality of MOOCs. In: 2014 IEEE 14th International Conference on Advanced Learning Technologies (ICALT), pp. 44–48. IEEE (2014)

20. Kim, J., Guo, P.J., Seaton, D.T., Mitros, P., Gajos, K.Z., Miller, R.C.: Understanding in-video dropouts and interaction peaks in online lecture videos. In: Proceedings of the First ACM Conference on Learning @ Scale Conference, pp. 31–40. ACM, New York (2014). https://doi.org/10.1145/2556325.2566237

21. Guo, P.J., Kim, J., Rubin, R.: How video production affects student engagement: an empirical study of MOOC videos. In: Proceedings of the First ACM Conference on Learning @ Scale Conference, pp. 41–50. ACM, New York (2014). https://doi.org/10.1145/2556325.2566239

22. Mitrovic, A., Dimitrova, V., Lau, L., Weerasinghe, A., Mathews, M.: Supporting constructive video-based learning: requirements elicitation from exploratory studies. In: André, E., Baker, R., Hu, X., Rodrigo, M., du Boulay, B. (eds.) AIED 2017. LNCS (LNAI), vol. 10331, pp. 224–237. Springer, Cham (2017). https://doi.org/10.1007/978-3-319-61425-0_19

23. Li, N., Kidziński, Ł., Jermann, P., Dillenbourg, P.: MOOC video interaction patterns: what do they tell us? In: Conole, G., Klobučar, T., Rensing, C., Konert, J., Lavoué, É. (eds.) EC-TEL 2015. LNCS, vol. 9307, pp. 197–210. Springer, Cham (2015). https://doi.org/10.1007/978-3-319-24258-3_15

24. Athira, L., Kumar, A., Bijlani, K.: Discovering learning models in MOOCs using empirical data. In: Shetty, N.R., Prasad, N.H., Nalini, N. (eds.) Emerging Research in Computing, Information, Communication and Applications, pp. 551–567. Springer, New Delhi (2015). https://doi.org/10.1007/978-81-322-2550-8_53

25. Wen, M., Rosé, C.P.: Identifying latent study habits by mining learner behavior patterns in massive open online courses. In: Proceedings of the 23rd ACM International Conference on Conference on Information and Knowledge Management, pp. 1983–1986. ACM (2014)

26. Brinton, C.G., Buccapatnam, S., Chiang, M., Poor, H.V.: Mining MOOC clickstreams: video-watching behavior vs. in-video quiz performance. IEEE Trans. Sig. Process. **64**, 3677–3692 (2016). https://doi.org/10.1109/TSP.2016.2546228
27. Brinton, C.G., Chiang, M.: MOOC performance prediction via clickstream data and social learning networks. In: 2015 IEEE Conference on Computer Communications (INFOCOM), pp. 2299–2307 (2015). https://doi.org/10.1109/INFOCOM.2015.7218617
28. Sinha, T., Jermann, P., Li, N., Dillenbourg, P.: Your click decides your fate: inferring information processing and attrition behavior from MOOC video clickstream interactions. ArXiv preprint arXiv:1407.7131 (2014)
29. Whitehill, J., Mohan, K., Seaton, D., Rosen, Y., Tingley, D.: MOOC dropout prediction: how to measure accuracy? In: 2017 Proceedings of the Fourth ACM Conference on Learning @ Scale, pp. 161–164. Association for Computing Machinery, Cambridge (2017). https://doi.org/10.1145/3051457.3053974
30. Gardner, J., Yang, Y., Baker, R.S., Brooks, C.: Modeling and experimental design for MOOC dropout prediction: a replication perspective. In: International Educational Data Mining Society (2019)
31. Gardner, J., Brooks, C., Andres, J.M., Baker, R.: Replicating MOOC predictive models at scale. In: Proceedings of the Fifth Annual ACM Conference on Learning at Scale, pp. 1–10. Association for Computing Machinery, London (2018). https://doi.org/10.1145/3231644.3231656
32. Gardner, J., Brooks, C., Baker, R.: Evaluating the fairness of predictive student models through slicing analysis. In: Proceedings of the 9th International Conference on Learning Analytics & Knowledge, pp. 225–234. Association for Computing Machinery, Tempe (2019). https://doi.org/10.1145/3303772.3303791
33. Kim, J., Guo, P.J., Cai, C.J., Li, S.-W., Gajos, K.Z., Miller, R.C.: Data-driven interaction techniques for improving navigation of educational videos. In: Proceedings of the 27th Annual ACM Symposium on User Interface Software and Technology, pp. 563–572 (2014)
34. Mitrovic, A., Gordon, M., Piotrkowicz, A., Dimitrova, V.: Investigating the effect of adding nudges to increase engagement in active video watching. In: Isotani, S., Millán, E., Ogan, A., Hastings, P., McLaren, B., Luckin, R. (eds.) AIED 2019. LNCS (LNAI), vol. 11625, pp. 320–332. Springer, Cham (2019). https://doi.org/10.1007/978-3-030-23204-7_27
35. Davis, D., Jivet, I., Kizilcec, R.F., Chen, G., Hauff, C., Houben, G.-J.: Follow the successful crowd: raising MOOC completion rates through social comparison at scale. In: Proceedings of the Seventh International Learning Analytics & Knowledge Conference, pp. 454–463. ACM (2017)
36. Davis, D., Triglianos, V., Hauff, C., Houben, G.-J.: SRLx: a personalized learner interface for MOOCs. In: Pammer-Schindler, V., Pérez-Sanagustín, M., Drachsler, H., Elferink, R., Scheffel, M. (eds.) EC-TEL 2018. LNCS, vol. 11082, pp. 122–135. Springer, Cham (2018). https://doi.org/10.1007/978-3-319-98572-5_10
37. Lallé, S., Conati, C.: A framework to counteract suboptimal user-behaviors in exploratory learning environments: an application to MOOCs. In: Proceedings of the 12th Workshop on Plan, Activity, and Intent Recognition, pp. 1–8. AAAI Press, Honolulu (2019)
38. Andres, J.M.L., Baker, R.S., Gašević, D., Siemens, G., Crossley, S.A., Joksimović, S.: Studying MOOC completion at scale using the MOOC replication framework. In: Proceedings of the 8th International Conference on Learning Analytics and Knowledge, pp. 71–78. ACM, Sydney (2018). https://doi.org/10.1145/3170358.3170369
39. Field, A.: Discovering Statistics Using IBM SPSS Statistics. Sage Publications Ltd., London (2012)
40. Rastrollo-Guerrero, J.L., Gómez-Pulido, J.A., Durán-Domínguez, A.: Analyzing and predicting students' performance by means of machine learning: a review. Appl. Sci. **10**, 1042 (2020). https://doi.org/10.3390/app10031042

41. Kloft, M., Stiehler, F., Zheng, Z., Pinkwart, N.: Predicting MOOC dropout over weeks using machine learning methods. In: Proceedings of the EMNLP 2014 Workshop on Analysis of Large Scale Social Interaction in MOOCs, pp. 60–65 (2014)
42. Hong, B., Wei, Z., Yang, Y.: Discovering learning behavior patterns to predict dropout in MOOC. In: 2017 12th International Conference on Computer Science and Education (ICCSE), pp. 700–704 (2017). https://doi.org/10.1109/ICCSE.2017.8085583
43. Putnam, V., Conati, C.: Exploring the need for explainable artificial intelligence (XAI) in intelligent tutoring systems (ITS). In: IUI Workshops (2019)

Transfer of Automated Performance Feedback Models to Different Specimens in Virtual Reality Temporal Bone Surgery

Jesslyn Lamtara[1]([⊠]) [iD], Nathan Hanegbi[1] [iD], Benjamin Talks[1,2] [iD],
Sudanthi Wijewickrema[1] [iD], Xingjun Ma[1] [iD], Patorn Piromchai[1,3] [iD],
James Bailey[1] [iD], and Stephen O'Leary[1] [iD]

[1] The University of Melbourne, Melbourne, Australia
jlamtara@student.unimelb.edu.au
[2] University of Birmingham, Birmingham, UK
[3] Khon Kaen University, Khon Kaen, Thailand

Abstract. Virtual reality has gained popularity as an effective training platform in many fields including surgery. However, it has been shown that the availability of a simulator alone is not sufficient to promote practice. Therefore, simulator-based surgical curricula need to be developed and integrated into existing surgical training programs. As practice variation is an important aspect of a surgical curriculum, surgical simulators should support practice on multiple specimens. Furthermore, to ensure that surgical skills are acquired, and to support self-guided learning, automated feedback on performance needs to be provided during practice. Automated feedback is typically provided by comparing real-time performance with expert models generated from pre-collected data. Since collecting data on multiple specimens for the purpose of developing feedback models is costly and time-consuming, methods of transferring feedback from one specimen to another should be investigated. In this paper, we discuss a simple method of feedback transfer between specimens in virtual reality temporal bone surgery and validate the accuracy and effectiveness of the transfer through a user study.

Keywords: Virtual reality surgical training · Automated performance feedback · Temporal bone surgery

1 Introduction

Virtual reality (VR) is increasingly being used in surgical training as it offers a risk-free, interactive, repeatable, and easily accessible platform that can be utilised to develop standardised training programs. Despite an emerging body of evidence related to the effectiveness of VR in surgical training [1,10,15,40], it is clear that the availability of a surgical simulator alone cannot promote best practice amongst surgical trainees. For example, a study in the United States observed that only 14% of surgical residents completed VR training when participation was voluntary [3]. Thus, even when facilities for VR training exist, a lack of awareness, trainee motivation, and limited access to simulators inhibit their usage [22,25]. To overcome these barriers, an appropriate VR-based curriculum should be developed and integrated into mandatory competency-based surgical training programs [31,33].

Optimal skill acquisition during simulation-based training relies on the availability of performance feedback, task variety with a range of difficulty levels, and the opportunity for extensive deliberate practice [13,21,33]. The incorporation of the above considerations into a VR-based module of a surgical curriculum is likely to improve trainees' readiness for the operating room. The availability of immediate performance feedback is a required component of deliberate practice [9]. Its purpose is to reinforce strengths, address weaknesses, and foster improvements in the learner by providing insights into the consequences of their actions and by highlighting the differences between intended and actual results [33]. While some simulators provide feedback by means of an expert supervising practice [6,27], others have been developed with in-built real-time procedural feedback. For example, a dental simulator exists that compares the user's tool position, tool orientation and force application to an expert data set, and displays its feedback on the screen [30]. Similarly, Sewell et al. [32] have developed a system that provides real-time feedback on bone visibility, drilling velocity and force. The University of Melbourne VR Temporal Bone Surgery Simulator [26] provides step-by-step procedural feedback [38] and technical verbal feedback on drill handling skills [7,18,19,41,42].

Another important aspect of a surgical curriculum is practice variation, which is essential to prepare trainees for anatomical variation between patients [13,33]. In the context of VR simulation, practice variation refers to the availability of multiple specimens of varying difficulty levels. The availability of such practice variation has been shown to improve surgical performance on previously unseen temporal bone models by Otolaryngology residents [29]. Various VR surgical simulators for laparoscopy [3,27] and temporal bone drilling [5,16,23,34] have been developed to offer a selection of cases with a range of difficulties.

To maximise skill acquisition and support self-directed learning, real-time feedback must be provided when practicing on different specimens. However, performance feedback doesn't appear to be available across the full range of cases on existing surgical simulators, limiting their educational value. Also, at present there are no reported methods that transfer feedback models automatically between different cases, as an alternative to the time consuming and data intensive process of developing feedback models individually for each case.

According to the concepts of transfer learning [28], feedback transfer can be defined as transferring the same task (providing feedback on performance) from a source domain to a target domain. The differences in domains can be characterised as the variations in anatomy. Although the feature space (metrics on which feedback should be provided) is the same, the values that these metrics take may differ according to anatomical variations between specimens. Therefore, the transfer of feedback from one specimen to another can be characterised as a domain adaptation problem [2]. It is not practical to obtain labelled data for each new specimen to train a new model or to retrain an existing one. As such, unsupervised learning (such as, instance weighting for covariate shift, self-labelling methods, changes in feature representation, and cluster-based learning [20]) is commonly used in solving problems of this form.

In contrast to using unsupervised learning for domain adaptation, we investigate a simpler, direct transfer approach supported by a pre-processing task that makes the source and target domains similar. To this end, we define regions of a specimen where surgical skills can be considered to be consistent. By defining these regions, we account for the changes in anatomical variation in specimens. We assume that the source and target specimens are similar enough that changes in the values of metrics (features) that feedback is provided on between specimens are negligible. This enables direct transfer of a feedback model of one region in the original specimen to the corresponding region in another specimen. Using this method, we transfer the neural network based model developed for providing technical feedback in VR temporal bone surgery in Ma et al. [18] to new specimens. We show through a user study that the feedback provided by the transferred models are as accurate as that provided by the original model. We also show that practice on multiple specimens with transferred performance feedback results in positive acquisition of surgical skills.

2   VR Environment

The VR platform used in this research is the University of Melbourne temporal bone surgery simulator temporal bone surgery simulator (see Fig. 1). Virtual models of multiple temporal bones, generated from segmented micro-CT scans of cadaveric bones, are available to drill on this simulator. A haptic device that emulates the operation of a surgical drill provides tactile feedback during an operation. Depth perception is achieved through NVIDIA 3D vision technology. A MIDI controller is used as an input device to change environment variables such as magnification level and burr size. Using the VR simulator, surgeons can perform ear operations to remove disease and improve hearing. The surgery under consideration in this paper is cortical mastoidectomy. This is a common procedure performed to remove mastoid air cells as a treatment for chronic otitis media, with or without cholesteatoma or mastoiditis. It is also performed as an initial step of cochlear implant surgery and various lateral skull base operations. A cortical mastoidectomy requires routine identification of key anatomical structures including the tegmen mastoideum, sigmoid sinus, incus, and facial nerve to be used as landmarks to ensure safe removal of the mastoid bone.

3   Types of Performance Feedback

Surgical skills are multi-faceted. As such, surgeons provide performance feedback and guidance on different aspects of surgical skill during training. To

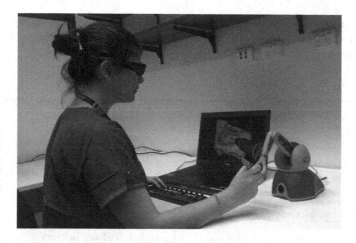

Fig. 1. A surgeon performing an operation on the VR temporal bone surgery simulator.

emulate this, the simulation system considers four main aspects of skill that need to be acquired: procedural knowledge, knowledge of landmarks/boundaries of the operative field, manipulation of environmental variables, and drill handling/technical skills. The effectiveness of these types of feedback/guidance methods on one specimen have been established by Davaris et al. [7].

Procedural guidance is provided using the step-by-step guidance method of Wijewickrema et al. [38]. The steps were obtained by manually segmenting an expert procedure. Each step of the surgery is highlighted sequentially on the temporal bone - the next step is only provided once the current step is completed.

Verbal warnings are provided in the form of verbal advice when nearing an anatomical structure to make trainees aware of the boundaries of the operative field [35]. To this end, distance thresholds per anatomical structure were defined, the crossing of which generated proximity warnings. Further, to enable learning of the anatomical structures, functionality to make the temporal bone transparent, so that the underlying structures can be viewed, is also available.

Feedback on environmental settings such as magnification level and burr size are provided as verbal advice. The ideal values of these settings differ according to where the surgeon is drilling. For example, at the start of a cortical mastoidectomy, an overall view of the surgical space is required, and therefore, a lower magnification level is used. When drilling in tighter spaces, a higher magnification level is required. Advice on how to change these values are provided by comparing against value ranges calculated from pre-collected expert data per surgical region. The region calculation process is discussed in the next section.

For the provision of technical feedback (feedback on surgical technique or motor skills), the method discussed in Ma et al. [18] is used. Similar to environmental setting, surgeons adopt different surgical technique when drilling in different regions of the temporal bone. For example, higher speed and force may be used when drilling in an open area, while lower speed and force may be used when near anatomical structures. As such, different behaviour models were trained for different regions and used to provide technical feedback. Figure 2 shows an overview of the technical feedback generation process.

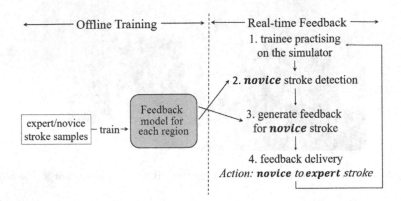

Fig. 2. Method of providing feedback on surgical technique.

For the offline training of the neural network classifier, a dataset of 16 surgeries recorded by 7 experts and 34 surgeries from 18 novices was used. The surgical performances were segmented into strokes - continuous drilling motions without abrupt changes in direction [12]. All strokes in expert and novice performances were considered to be expert and novice strokes respectively. The strokes were separated according to the region. Isolation forests [17] were used to remove outliers. Characteristics (or metrics) of each stroke, such as length, duration, speed, and force were then calculated to represent a stroke. These were used to train a neural network with one hidden layer per region. The number of hidden neurons for each region was chosen using cross validation [18].

In real-time, strokes are segmented from the surgical trajectory, and the neural network classifier for the relevant region is used to identify whether it is an expert or novice stroke. In the case of a novice stroke, an adversarial example [11], a small modification of the metrics that changes the prediction of the model from novice to expert, is generated. The resulting change is recorded in a buffer as an increase or decrease of the metrics that were changed to generate the expert prediction. Once multiple instances of the same change is generated in a row, it is presented to the user as verbal auditory feedback (for example, 'decrease force') [37].

4   Transfer of Feedback Models

As a method of adapting the feedback models to specimens other than the one they were developed on, we explored a method of direct transfer. We assumed that surgical technique (and environmental settings) are similar in the same region on all specimens and that the specimens are similar enough that the values of the metrics (features) that the feedback is provided on remain the same. As such, once the regions are defined on a new specimen, feedback models developed on the original specimen can be transferred to be used on this new specimen without any changes to the models themselves. Note that this assumption is only valid for specimens with no abnormal or pathological anatomy, which is the case for the specimens considered here.

We used the same process used in the generation of regions in the original specimen for this purpose [35]. Regions were identified as the areas surrounding or between anatomical structures. The width of a region was pre-defined and morphological operations were used to generate them. For example, to generate areas around an anatomical structure, we dilated the voxels belonging to that structure and subtracted them from the resulting region. To obtain regions between anatomical structures, we used dilation and erosion in tandem. Figure 3 shows the regions generated for different specimens.

For the generation of proximity warnings on different specimens, we used the same distance thresholds that were defined for the original specimen. We manually segmented steps of an expert procedure for each specimen in order to provide procedural guidance.

5   Validation of the Feedback Transfer

5.1   Study Design

We conducted a user study of 14 medical students to evaluate the accuracy of feedback transfer and to test the effect of the transferred feedback on skill acquisition. The ratio of postgraduate (MD) to undergraduate (MBBS) students was 5:2 and the male to female ratio was 4:3. This study was approved by the Royal Victorian Eye and Ear Hospital Human Ethics Committee (#17/1312H). Written consent was obtained from all participants.

Participants were first shown a video tutorial on how to perform a cortical mastoidectomy on our VR simulator. Then, they were shown how to use the simulator and given five minutes of familiarisation time. Participants then performed the same surgery on the VR simulator with no automated guidance (pre-test). The pre-test was performed in order to gauge their initial skill level, to account for individual variations in aptitude. This is the specimen that the original feedback models were developed on (Bone 0). Next, they underwent training on four specimens (in the same order) with real-time automated guidance. The first of the training sessions was on the original bone. The next three sessions were on different specimens (Bones 1–3) and the automated feedback on these were transferred from the original specimen using the method discussed above. After this, on the same day, the participants performed a post-test: a cortical mastoidectomy without feedback on the original specimen. Note that the 'transfer' temporal bone specimens were from the same side of the head as the original specimen (right-hand side). All procedures were recorded by the simulator and using screen capture software. The study design is shown in Fig. 4.

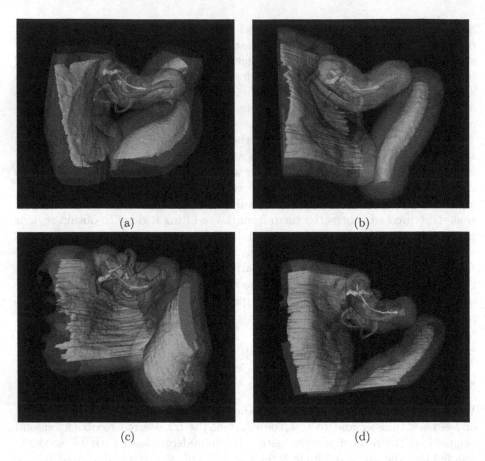

(a)   (b)

(c)   (d)

Fig. 3. Definition of regions where surgical technique is considered to be uniform: (a) original specimen and (b)–(d) transfer specimens. The anatomical structures and the regions defined around them are shown in opaque and transparent colours respectively. (Color figure online)

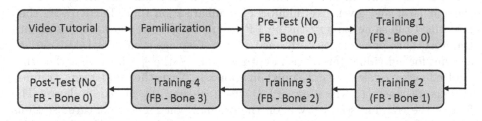

Fig. 4. Design of the validation study.

5.2 Accuracy of Transfer

To determine the accuracy of the provided technical feedback, the errors in the feedback were determined by an expert surgeon through the analysis of anonymised videos based on the following criteria [36].

- False positives (FP): feedback was provided while stroke technique was acceptable.
- Wrong content (WC): participants' technique was accurately detected as poor, but the content of the feedback was inaccurate.
- False negatives (FN): Feedback was not provided while stroke technique was unacceptable.

The accuracy of the feedback (ACC) was calculated for each training session as $ACC = \frac{TF-FP-WC}{TF+FN} \times 100\%$, where, TF is the total feedback provided in a session. Feedback accuracy was compared between specimens using a Kruskal-Wallis test. There was no significant difference in the accuracy level of the feedback provided by the original model when compared to that of the transferred models. Figure 5 illustrates this comparison.

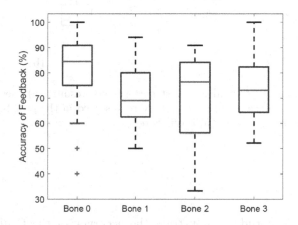

Fig. 5. Accuracy of the technical feedback. Bone 0 is the original specimen on which the feedback models were developed. Bones 1–3 are the new specimens that these models were transferred to. No significant difference was observed in the accuracy levels of the feedback on all specimens.

5.3 Effectiveness of Transfer

To investigate the effect of the transferred feedback on skill acquisition, participant performance in the pre- and post-tests were evaluated by a blinded expert surgeon. To this end, a validated assessment scale designed for temporal bone surgery [14] was used. This scale comprises two parts: checklist and global instruments, and assesses competency of the surgeon in performing the surgery as a whole. This takes into consideration all aspects of surgical skill, for example, knowledge of landmarks and procedure as well as technical skills. The checklist and global instruments consists of 22 and 10 items respectively, each based on a Likert scale ranging from 1 (unable to perform), through 3 (performs with minimal prompting), to 5 (performs easily with good flow). Comparison of pre- and post-test scores using a Wilcoxon signed rank test showed significant improvement in performance (checklist score: $p = 0.001$ and global score: $p = 0.002$). Figure 6 shows the comparison between pre- and post-test scores.

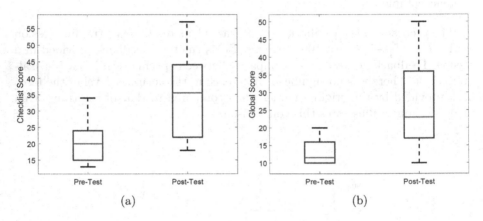

Fig. 6. Comparison of pre- and post-test performance results: (a) checklist score and (b) global score. Significant improvements were observed in the post-test scores when compared to the pre-test scores in both scores.

6   Discussion

The results of this study demonstrate the accuracy of the feedback transfer, as no significant difference was observed between the accuracy of the feedback of the original and transferred models. Furthermore, participants showed significant improvement in surgical performance after training on specimens with transferred feedback models, demonstrating that the transferred feedback (along with other factors such as repeated practice) had a positive impact on skill acquisition. However, it has already been established that repeated practice (without feedback) is not sufficient to impart surgical skills in mastoidectomy in a novice cohort such as the participants in our study [7]. Therefore, we can attribute the improvements in performance to the effectiveness of the feedback.

Successful feedback transfer (of the type outlined in this study) will allow VR simulators to meet the requirement of deliberate practice to have immediate and continuous feedback [9,33]. The provision of instant, unsupervised performance feedback by VR simulators offers a time efficient alternative to the current dependency on continuous expert supervision. Thus, this VR curriculum may serve as a valuable adjunct to current surgical training. In addition, developing a library of virtual temporal bone models covering anatomical variants complete with automated feedback could provide a valuable training resource for rural trainees where exposure to varying cases is limited.

It would also be beneficial to apply feedback transfer to VR simulation in other types of surgery, including laparoscopic surgery [24] and neurosurgery [4], or even endovascular procedures [8,39]. However, a potential barrier to the reapplication of this direct feedback transfer technique would be the ability for comparable pre-processing of the simulation cases, defining different anatomical regions to facilitate the transfer of feedback models.

A limitation of this work is that the developed method was for feedback transfer between specimens with normal anatomy. As surgical behaviour may not be the same when operating on abnormal or pathological specimens, this direct transfer method may not be as accurate for those. For example, for an abnormally large specimen, values of feedback metrics such as stroke length may not be directly transferable. In such cases, the region-based method could be used in conjunction with more complicated domain adaptation techniques and/or a limited amount of labelled data from the abnormal or pathological specimens to overcome this. This may also be used to improve the accuracy of transfer between normal specimens. This is a future avenue of research we will explore.

A further study limitation is that only three of the four types of performance guidance/feedback provided during training were automatically transferred. Procedural guidance was provided by segmenting an expert procedure performed on each specimen. In future work, this process will also be automated, albeit using different techniques to that used for transferring technical feedback. A simulation-based surgical training program that incorporates other concepts of curriculum design that were not considered here (such as practice distribution, task difficulty including pathological cases, and proficiency based training) [33] will also be developed and validated.

The generalisability of our results are limited by the small number of specimens, cohort size, and use of a single expert reviewer. Further studies will be conducted to account for this bias with a larger number of specimens on a larger cohort, including those with intermediate level surgical skills (surgical residents). Assessments by multiple experts will also be performed to reduce the subjectivity of assessment.

7 Conclusion

We introduced a method of transferring technical feedback models from the specimen they were developed on to other specimens and showed that the feedback provided by the transferred models were as accurate as that of the original model. We also showed that the transferred feedback assisted in positive skill acquisition. This enables the development of self-directed, simulation-based surgical curricula that can be used as adjuncts to traditional surgical training methods.

References

1. Andersen, S.A.W., Caye-Thomasen, P., Sorensen, M.S.: Mastoidectomy performance assessment of virtual simulation training using final-product analysis. LARYNGOSCOPE **125**(2), 431–435 (2015)
2. Ben-David, S., Blitzer, J., Crammer, K., Kulesza, A., Pereira, F., Vaughan, J.W.: A theory of learning from different domains. Mach. Learn. **79**(1-2), 151–175 (2010)
3. Chang, L., Petros, J., Hess, D.T., Rotondi, C., Babineau, T.J.: Integrating simulation into a surgical residency program: is voluntary participation effective? Surg. Endosc. **21**(3), 418–421 (2007)
4. Chugh, A., et al.: Use of a surgical rehearsal platform and improvement in aneursym clipping measures: results of a prospective, randomized trial. J. Neurosurg. **126**, 838–844 (2017)
5. Copson, B., et al.: Supporting skill acquisition in cochlear implant surgery through virtual reality simulation. Cochlear Implants Int. **18**(2), 89–96 (2017)
6. Crochet, P., et al.: Deliberate practice on a virtual reality laparoscopic simulator enhances the quality of surgical technical skills. Ann. Surg. (6), 1216 (2011)
7. Davaris, M., et al.: The importance of automated real-time performance feedback in virtual reality temporal bone surgery training. In: Isotani, S., Millán, E., Ogan, A., Hastings, P., McLaren, B., Luckin, R. (eds.) AIED 2019. LNCS (LNAI), vol. 11625, pp. 96–109. Springer, Cham (2019). https://doi.org/10.1007/978-3-030-23204-7_9
8. Desender, L., et al.: Patient-specific rehearsal before EVAR: influence on technical and nontechnical operative performance. a randomized controlled trial. Ann. Surg. **264**(5), 703–709 (2016)
9. Ericsson, K.A.: Deliberate practice and the acquisition and maintenance of expert performance in medicine and related domains. Acad. Med. **79**(10), S70–S81 (2004)
10. Fried, M.P., et al.: From virtual reality to the operating room: the endoscopic sinus surgery simulator experiment. Otolaryngol. - Head Neck Surg. **142**(2), 202–207 (2010)
11. Goodfellow, I.J., Shlens, J., Szegedy, C.: Explaining and harnessing adversarial examples. arXiv preprint arXiv:1412.6572 (2014)
12. Hall, R., et al.: Towards haptic performance analysis using k-metrics. In: Haptic and Audio Interaction Design, pp. 50–59 (2008)
13. Issenberg, S.B., Mcgaghie, W.C., Petrusa, E.R., Gordon, D.L., Scalese, R.J.: Features and uses of high-fidelity medical simulations that lead to effective learning: a beme systematic review. Med. Teach. **27**(1), 10–28 (2005)
14. Laeeq, K., et al.: Pilot testing of an assessment tool for competency in mastoidectomy. Laryngoscope **119**(12), 2402–2410 (2009)
15. Lin, Y., Wang, X., Wu, F., Chen, X., Wang, C., Shen, G.: Development and validation of a surgical training simulator with haptic feedback for learning bone-sawing skill. J. Biomed. Inform. **48**, 122–129 (2014)
16. Linke, R., et al.: Assessment of skills using a virtual reality temporal bone surgery simulator. Acta Otorhinolaryngologica Italica **33**(4), 273–281 (2013)
17. Liu, F.T., Ting, K.M., Zhou, Z.H.: Isolation forest. In: ICDM, pp. 413–422 (2008)
18. Ma, X., et al.: Adversarial generation of real-time feedback with neural networks for simulation-based training. arXiv preprint arXiv:1703.01460 (2017)
19. Ma, X., Wijewickrema, S., Zhou, Y., Zhou, S., O'Leary, S., Bailey, J.: Providing effective real-time feedback in simulation-based surgical training. In: Descoteaux, M., Maier-Hein, L., Franz, A., Jannin, P., Collins, D.L., Duchesne, S. (eds.) MICCAI 2017. LNCS, vol. 10434, pp. 566–574. Springer, Cham (2017). https://doi.org/10.1007/978-3-319-66185-8_64

20. Margolis, A.: A literature review of domain adaptation with unlabeled data. Technical Report, pp. 1–42 (2011)
21. McGaghie, W.C., Issenberg, S.B., Petrusa, E.R., Scalese, R.J.: A critical review of simulation-based medical education research: 2003–2009. Med. Educ. **44**(1), 50–63 (2010)
22. Milburn, J.A., Khera, G., Hornby, S.T., Malone, P.S., Fitzgerald, J.E.: Introduction, availability and role of simulation in surgical education and training: review of current evidence and recommendations from the association of surgeons in training. Int. J. Surg. (8), 393 (2012)
23. Morris, D., Sewell, C., Barbagli, F., Salisbury, K., Blevins, N., Girod, S.: Visuohaptic simulation of bone surgery for training and evaluation. IEEE Comput. Graph. Appl. (6), 48 (2006)
24. Nagendran, M., Gurusamy, K., Aggarwal, R., Loizidou, M., Davidson, B.: Virtual reality training for surgical trainees in laparoscopic surgery. Cochrane Database Syst. Rev. **27**(8), CD006575 (2013)
25. Okuda, Y., et al.: The utility of simulation in medical education: what is the evidence? Mount Sinai J. Med. New York **76**(4), 330–343 (2009)
26. O'leary, S.J., et al.: Validation of a networked virtual reality simulation of temporal bone surgery. Laryngoscope **118**(6), 1040–1046 (2008)
27. Palter, V., Grantcharov, T.: Individualized deliberate practice on a virtual reality simulator improves technical performance of surgical novices in the operating room: a randomized controlled trial. Ann. Surg. (3), 443 (2014)
28. Pan, S.J., Yang, Q.: A survey on transfer learning. IEEE Trans. Knowl. Data Eng. **22**(10), 1345–1359 (2009)
29. Piromchai, P., et al.: Effects of anatomical variation on trainee performance in a virtual reality temporal bone surgery simulator. J. Laryngol. Otol. **131**(S1), S29–S35 (2017)
30. Rhienmora, P., Haddawy, P., Suebnukarn, S., Dailey, M.N.: Intelligent dental training simulator with objective skill assessment and feedback. Artif. Intell. Med. **52**(2), 115–121 (2011)
31. Satava, R.M.: Disruptive visions: surgical education. Surg. Endosc. **18**(5), 779–781 (2004)
32. Sewell, C., et al.: Providing metrics and performance feedback in a surgical simulator. Comput. Aided Surg. **13**(2), 63–81 (2008)
33. Stefanidis, D.: Optimal acquisition and assessment of proficiency on simulators in surgery. Surg. Clin. North America **90**(3), 475–489 (2010)
34. Wiet, G.J., Stredney, D., Kerwin, T., Hittle, B., Fernandez, S.A., Abdel-Rasoul, M., Welling, D.B.: Virtual temporal bone dissection system: Osu virtual temporal bone system: development and testing. Laryngoscope **122**(Suppl 1), S1–S12 (2012)
35. Wijewickrema, S., et al.: Region-specific automated feedback in temporal bone surgery simulation. In: 2015 IEEE 28th International Symposium on Computer-Based Medical Systems (CBMS), pp. 310–315. IEEE (2015)
36. Wijewickrema, S., et al.: A temporal bone surgery simulator with real-time feedback for surgical training. Med. Meets Virtual Real. **21**, NextMed/MMVR21 196, 462 (2014)
37. Wijewickrema, S., et al.: Providing automated real-time technical feedback for virtual reality based surgical training: is the simpler the better? In: Penstein Rosé, C., et al. (eds.) AIED 2018. LNCS (LNAI), vol. 10947, pp. 584–598. Springer, Cham (2018). https://doi.org/10.1007/978-3-319-93843-1_43

38. Wijewickrema, S., Zhou, Y., Bailey, J., Kennedy, G., O'Leary, S.: Provision of automated step-by-step procedural guidance in virtual reality surgery simulation. In: Proceedings of the 22nd ACM Conference on Virtual Reality Software and Technology, pp. 69–72. ACM (2016)

39. Willaert, W., et al.: Simulated procedure rehearsal is more effective than a preoperative generic warm-up for endovascular procedures. Ann. Surg. **255**, 1184–1189 (2012)

40. Zhao, Y.C., Kennedy, G., Yukawa, K., Pyman, B., Stephen, O.L.: Can virtual reality simulator be used as a training aid to improve cadaver temporal bone dissection? Results of a randomized blinded control trial. LARYNGOSCOPE (4), 831 (2011)

41. Zhou, Y., Bailey, J., Ioannou, I., Wijewickrema, S., Kennedy, G., O'Leary, S.: Constructive real time feedback for a temporal bone simulator. In: Mori, K., Sakuma, I., Sato, Y., Barillot, C., Navab, N. (eds.) MICCAI 2013. LNCS, vol. 8151, pp. 315–322. Springer, Heidelberg (2013). https://doi.org/10.1007/978-3-642-40760-4_40

42. Zhou, Y., Bailey, J., Ioannou, I., Wijewickrema, S., O'Leary, S., Kennedy, G.: Pattern-based real-time feedback for a temporal bone simulator. In: Proceedings of the 19th ACM Symposium on Virtual Reality Software and Technology, pp. 7–16. ACM (2013)

Use of Adaptive Feedback in an App for English Language Spontaneous Speech

Blair Lehman[(⊠)], Lin Gu, Jing Zhao, Eugene Tsuprun, Christopher Kurzum, Michael Schiano, Yulin Liu, and G. Tanner Jackson

Educational Testing Service, Princeton, NJ 08541, USA
{blehman,lgu001,jzhao002,etsuprun,ckurzum,mschiano,yliu004,
gtjackson}@ets.org

Abstract. Language learning apps have become increasingly popular. However, most of these apps target the first stages of learning a new language and are limited in the type of feedback that can be provided to users' spontaneous spoken responses. The English Language Artificial Intelligence (ELAi) app was developed to address this gap by providing users with a variety of prompts for spontaneous speech and adaptive, targeted feedback based on the automatic evaluation of spoken responses. Feedback in the ELAi app was presented across multiple pages such that users could choose the amount and depth of feedback that they wanted to receive. The present work evaluates how 94 English language learners interacted with the app. We focused on participants' use of the feedback pages and whether or not performance on spontaneous speech improved over the course of using the app. The findings revealed that users were most likely to access the most shallow feedback page, but use of the feedback pages differed based on the total number of sessions that users completed with the app. Users showed improvement in their response performance over the course of using the app, which suggests that the design of repeated practice and adaptive, targeted feedback in the ELAi app is promising. Patterns of feedback page use are discussed further as well as potential design modifications that could increase the use of feedback and maximize improvement in English language spontaneous speech.

Keywords: MALL · Language learning · Automated speech analysis · Feedback

1 Introduction

Language learning has moved from the traditional classroom-only model to computer-assisted language learning to mobile-assisted language learning (MALL) [1, 2]. MALL apps provide users with flexibility, autonomy, and personalized learning experiences [3]. There are currently over 100 language learning apps in the iOS App Store, and apps have even expanded to smart watches that incorporate exercise into language learning [4]. MALL apps have shown to be an effective method [5, 6]. Duolingo, for example, claims to be as effective as college-level language courses [7], but others report more mixed findings [8]. In this abundance of MALL apps, many have a similar focus in that

I. I. Bittencourt et al. (Eds.): AIED 2020, LNAI 12163, pp. 309–320, 2020.
https://doi.org/10.1007/978-3-030-52237-7_25

they target (a) general language learning and (b) learners at an initially low proficiency level. Thus, there is still a need for the development of apps that provide support to learners at other proficiency levels and with differing goals. For example, recent efforts in MALL app development have focused on the particular language needs of migrants and refugees [9, 10] and low literacy adults [11].

One of the main advantages of MALL apps (and attractions to users) is that they provide immediate, targeted feedback about users' performance on learning activities. This is consistent with years of research that has shown that simply providing feedback is not enough, it must be delivered in a way that is optimally useful for learners [12, 13]. MALL apps are typically able to provide targeted feedback on the quality of selected-response items, grammar and spelling for written responses, and word pronunciation for constrained speaking tasks. However, many MALL apps are limited in the level of detail that can be provided for feedback on speaking tasks [14, 15]. Duolingo, for example, identifies whether or not a user has correctly pronounced a word, but it does not provide feedback about how the user could more accurately pronounce the target word. Given that speaking is often one of the more challenging aspects of learning a language [16–18], it is important for MALL apps to provide feedback in such a way that users feel confident that they can improve their speaking skills.

Given the challenges of providing targeted feedback in real time for speaking tasks, most MALL apps focus only on constrained speaking tasks in which users are provided with a text to read aloud verbatim because automated feedback can be more easily provided. However, our recent user interviews suggested that many language learners would like to practice and receive feedback for spontaneous speaking tasks. Spontaneous speaking tasks involve learners responding to an open-ended prompt (e.g., *Tell me about your favorite vacation.*). This type of task is utilized on many standardized assessments of language skills (e.g., TOEFL®, IELTS™) as it shows an advanced level of speaking proficiency and spontaneous speaking skills are viewed as an important aspect of effective communication [19, 20]. This type of task is often not included in MALL apps because it is difficult to provide immediate, targeted feedback. Spontaneous speaking tasks are typically evaluated by human raters in standardized assessments, which limits the ability to provide feedback to users immediately after responding.

To address the apparent lack of spontaneous speaking practice with immediate feedback for language learners, we have developed the English Language Artificial Intelligence (ELAi) app. The ELAi app was designed to provide users with an opportunity to practice spontaneous speech and receive detailed feedback about the quality of their responses. This learning model is consistent with languaging [21–23] as students are asked to engage in effortful language production that can draw attention to their current weaknesses, but with the added benefit of targeted feedback to help focus efforts for improvement. We utilized an automated speech analysis tool that evaluates spontaneous speech on delivery, language use, and topic development to provide targeted, detailed feedback. However, it is not enough to simply provide feedback [12, 13]. A recent review of research on oral feedback for spoken responses, for example, found that there is a limited understanding of how learners make use of feedback [24]. It is then important that we understand how users interact with the feedback provided. The present work is the first evaluation of the ELAi app and was guided by three research questions: (1)

How do users interact with the app features?, (2) What do users do after viewing feedback?, and (3) Does users' performance improve during app use? We investigated these three research questions with native Mandarin speakers who are learning English for the purpose of attending university in an English-speaking country.

2 ELAi App

The ELAi app was developed to provide an easily accessible resource for English language learners at an intermediate or advanced level, with the goal of attending university in an English-speaking country, to practice spontaneous speech and receive feedback. The development was guided by interviews with potential users from the target audience, which revealed that users were often practicing spontaneous speech on their mobile phone but were unable to receive feedback in the same medium [25]. Users were most interested in feedback that corresponded to standardized English language assessment evaluations. Users also revealed their desire for access to sample responses to compare to their own responses both in terms of delivery and content. The ELAi app was then developed to address the needs of these real-world users.

Users began with the ELAi app by browsing the many prompt options available. Figure 1 shows (from left to right) screenshots of the app splash page as well as the process of selecting a prompt category, responding to a specific prompt (e.g., *Do you think the use of smart watches will increase or decrease in the future? Why?*), and the feedback overview. After completing a new response, users were notified when feedback was available (latency was equivalent to the response length). User responses were evaluated with an automated speech analysis tool that used acoustic and language models to allow for the extraction of acoustic characteristics and creation of a response transcript. The models were based on nonnative English speakers to account for pronunciation differences due to accents. The automated speech analysis tool then evaluated the response on over 100 raw speech features from the acoustic characteristics and transcript. A subset of these features was selected based on their potential for learning feedback and were then combined to provide feedback on six key speech features (filler words, pauses, repeated words, speaking rate, stressed words, vocabulary diversity) to help users improve speaking skills. Users could access feedback on four pages within the app, which allowed for self-selection of the type and amount of feedback provided.

The first feedback page was My History (Fig. 1, rightmost panel), which provided a *Feedback Overview* for each response at a relatively shallow level in that it only identified two speech features that needed improvement (weightlifter icon) and one feature that was done well (thumbs up icon). This was the first instance of feedback that was adaptive to the individual user. For example, in Fig. 1 the user needed to improve on Repeated Words and Vocabulary Diversity, whereas Filler Words was done well in the technology response (top card). Needs work was defined separately for each speech feature with some defined as overuse (filler words, pauses, repeated words, vocabulary diversity), whereas other features had an inverted U-shaped relationship in which too much or too little was problematic (speaking rate, stressed words). However, users were not provided with any explanations or resources to improve future responses on *Overview*. Thus, *Overview* provided minimal feedback on the quality of a response and minimal

Fig. 1. Screenshots of finding and completing a new response in the ELAi app

support for improving future responses but did serve as an organized resource for users to access all of the feedback they had received.

Figure 2 shows the next feedback page that users could access by selecting a specific response card on *Overview* or directly through the feedback ready notification. This next page was *Feedback Summary Report* and was designed to be the main source of feedback for users. On *Summary Report* users could listen to their own response, review explanations for those three speech features that were shown on *Overview*, access additional ideas for how to develop a response to that prompt, and listen to sample responses from both native and nonnative English speakers (from left to right in Fig. 2). The design of *Summary Report* allowed the user to quickly develop an understanding of the quality of their response by focusing on two features that needed improvement and ensured that this feedback was actionable by providing users with additional information and resources to improve their future responses.

Fig. 2. Screenshots of Feedback Summary Report page in the ELAi app

Users could view more detailed feedback on *Feedback Full Report* and *Feedback Details* (see Fig. 3). The *Full Report* provided explanations for all six speech features. For example, in Fig. 3 the two leftmost panels show that the user did well on Filler Words but needed to improve on Repeated Words and Speaking Rate. *Details* provided even more detailed information about four of the six speech features (pauses, repeated words, filler words, vocabulary diversity). *Details* provided a transcript of the response (see second from the right panel in Fig. 3), which highlighted the problematic aspects of the speech feature (e.g., repeated words). *Details* for vocabulary diversity provided suggestions of additional words that could be used to respond to the prompt (see rightmost panel in Fig. 3). *Full Report* and *Details* provided users with a greater amount of and more in-depth feedback, which can be beneficial if users dedicate the time and effort needed to process and apply the information provided [26].

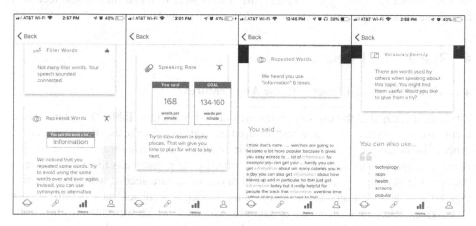

Fig. 3. Screenshots of Feedback Full Report and Details pages in the ELAi app

Users were also able to view information about their app use metrics through the *Me Screen*. Users could see the total amount of time they had recorded responses, total number of responses, the amount of time for recorded responses in the current week, and how many days in a row they had recorded responses. The *Me Screen* also allowed users to *View Badges* that they earned. Users could earn a variety of badges that targeted engagement and performance. Engagement-based badges were designed to encourage persistence and regular practice (e.g., multi-day streaks of recording), whereas performance-based badges allowed users to track their progress over time on a single speech feature (e.g., received "good job" on filler words three times in a row).

3   Method

3.1   Participants

Participants were 94 students from an English language learning program in China that primarily focused on preparation for standardized English language learning assessments. Gender information was obtained from 62 participants: 58% female, 33% male, and 6% preferred not to respond. Participants completed from 1 to 45 sessions with the ELAi app over a one-month period ($M = 8.62$, $SD = 8.56$). Sessions were a little over five minutes on average ($SD = 4.52$) and included an average of 17.2 user-initiated actions ($SD = 14.8$). Users completed an average of 14.4 spoken responses over the course of using the ELAi app ($SD = 24.2$).

3.2 Procedure

Participants were recruited through their English language learning program. Those participants who were interested then completed an informed consent and were provided with the information needed to access the ELAi app. Participants were free to use the app as they wanted for one month. There were no direct instructions about how users should interact with the app; however, participants were told that they would receive a certificate of participation if they recorded at least five spoken responses.

4   Results and Discussion

4.1   How Do Users Interact with the App Features?

First, we investigated the use of app features in four ways (see Table 1): feature access (proportion of participants), average feature time use (in seconds, avg time per access), proportion of total session time (proportion of time), and proportion of total session actions (proportion of actions) [27]. The proportion of participants that accessed each feature at least once revealed a generally high rate of feature access, with the exception that 60% or less of users accessed the more in depth feedback pages (Full Report, Details) and listened to their own or samples responses, which were features that users specifically requested. This contradiction between what users say they want and how they interact with a MALL app has been found in other apps as well [28].

Repeated measures ANOVAs that compared the average time each feature was accessed [$F(10,930) = 11.4$, $p < .001$, $MSe = 1858$, partial $\eta^2 = .109$], the proportion of time spent on each feature [$F(10,930) = 229$, $p < .001$, $MSe = .008$, partial $\eta^2 = .711$], and the proportion of actions that accessed each feature [$F(10,930) = 474$, $p < .001$, $MSe = .005$, partial $\eta^2 = .836$] were significant. Bonferroni corrections were applied to all post hoc analyses and revealed that users spent the most time viewing prompts and the least time viewing badges. Responding to prompts had one of the highest proportions for both time and actions, with only View Prompt having a higher proportion and FB Overview and Me Screen having similar proportions.

Table 1. Use of ELAi features.

	Proportion of Participants	Avg Time per Access		Proportion of Time		Proportion of Actions	
		M	SD	M	SD	M	SD
View Category	.787	8.97	1.11	.034	.056	.032	.041
Low Engagement	.638	5.37	6.29	.037	.072	.032	.051
High Engagement	.936	12.6	13.0	.031	.034	.032	.028
View Prompt	1.00	17.1	2.79	.493	.187	.542	.156
Low Engagement	1.00	12.0	21.3	.514	.211	.564	.173
High Engagement	1.00	22.3	31.2	.472	.157	.520	.135
New Response	.862	58.7	12.8	.114	.113	.057	.051
Low Engagement	.745	30.6	42.7	.115	.144	.055	.056
High Engagement	.979	86.9	167	.114	.071	.059	.046
FB Overview	.947	23.6	4.75	.164	.115	.150	.078
Low Engagement	.915	12.2	19.9	.159	.142	.134	.077
High Engagement	.979	35.0	60.2	.170	.080	.165	.076
FB Summary Report	.723	17.9	2.44	.053	.067	.040	.041
Low Engagement	.532	14.0	23.2	.042	.071	.026	.040
High Engagement	.915	21.8	23.6	.064	.061	.053	.038
FB Full Report	.574	20.2	3.16	.019	.036	.011	.016
Low Engagement	.404	16.1	34.7	.017	.044	.009	.016
High Engagement	.745	24.4	25.6	.021	.025	.013	.015
FB Details	.606	10.8	1.24	.019	.032	.017	.024
Low Engagement	.362	7.71	13.2	.017	.037	.013	.025
High Engagement	.851	13.8	9.86	.021	.026	.020	.023
Listen Own Response	.436	17.3	2.87	.014	.024	.008	.014
Low Engagement	.468	7.68	17.8	.011	.025	.006	.014
High Engagement	.638	27.0	32.5	.017	.023	.010	.014
Listen Sample Response	.457	11.2	1.90	.013	.026	.011	.021
Low Engagement	.255	5.44	11.1	.008	.022	.006	.015
High Engagement	.660	16.9	22.3	.018	.029	.017	.025
Me Screen Viewed	.936	8.20	1.70	.075	.107	.131	.108
Low Engagement	.894	5.89	17.4	.080	.134	.153	.123
High Engagement	.979	10.5	15.5	.070	.073	.109	.085
View Badge	.223	1.38	.327	.001	.004	.003	.008
Low Engagement	.064	.589	2.75	.001	.004	.001	.009
High Engagement	.383	2.18	3.40	.002	.004	.004	.007

Overall the feature use analyses revealed that users spent the majority of their time interacting with the ELAi app browsing for a prompt, responding to prompts, viewing the shallowest level of feedback, and viewing their overall app usage data. This pattern is both consistent and inconsistent with user requests. Users were frequently practicing their spontaneous speech, but they were not typically utilizing the more detailed feedback and learning resources that they requested. It is important to note, however, that the more detailed feedback and learning resources were embedded in the app, meaning that users could only access them via another feedback page. Feedback Overview and Summary Report, on the other hand, could be accessed directly. Thus, the lack of access to the more detailed feedback (Full Report, Details) could represent a lack of user interest or lack of feature awareness. In an effort to consider this dependence between actions, we repeated the proportion of actions analysis with instances in which less detailed feedback page views were removed if they immediately preceded a more detailed feedback page view. This was an overly conservative analysis as it assumed that all of these less detailed feedback page views were only in service of accessing more detailed feedback. The pattern of findings remained the same, which suggests that although we cannot target the exact reason for infrequent access of more detailed feedback, we can feel confident that those pages were accessed less frequently.

The previous analyses considered the sample as a whole; however, there was a wide range in the degree to which users engaged with the ELAi app (1 to 45 sessions), which suggests a potential for different use patterns. Users were divided into low (five or less sessions, $n = 47$) and high engagement groups (more than five sessions, $n = 47$) based on a median split to explore potential feature use differences. Table 1 shows the descriptive statistics for each engagement group. Particularly large differences can be seen for accessing more detailed feedback and learning resources, with high engagement users accessing those features at least once at a higher rate than low engagement users.

The two engagement groups were compared with independent samples t-tests for average time spent on each feature, which revealed that the high engagement group spent more time on all features, except Summary Report, Full Report, and Me Screen. Despite this difference in time spent on features, there were no differences in how users in each engagement group distributed their time (proportion of time, p's > .05) and actions within a session (proportion of actions, p's > .05). The comparison of engagement groups revealed that users who had greater engagement with the ELAi app accessed more features and spent more time on those features, particularly those features that provided more in-depth feedback and support for improving future performance.

4.2 What Do Users Do After Viewing Feedback?

The previous findings led us to question if there were particular patterns of behavior after viewing feedback that were indicative of more or less productive behavior. For example, a productive behavior after viewing FB Overview would be to access FB Summary Report to better understand why certain speech features need improvement and access resources for improvement. Thus, we investigated the next action taken after viewing each type of feedback. We combined several actions into action categories that consisted of Browse Behavior (View Category, View Prompt), Feedback Viewed, Me Screen Viewed (Me Screen, View Badge), and Exit App for these analyses.

Repeated measures ANOVAs compared the prevalence of post-feedback actions for each feedback page (see Table 2) and were significant [Overview: $F(4,352) = 33.6, p < .001, MSe = .044$, partial $\eta^2 = .277$; Summary Report: $F(4,268) = 333, p < .001, MSe = .024$, partial $\eta^2 = .832$; Full Report: $F(4,212) = 313, p < .001, MSe = .026$, partial $\eta^2 = .855$; Details: $F(4,224) = 259, p < .001, MSe = .032$, partial $\eta^2 = .822$]. Bonferroni

Table 2. Proportion of next action type after feedback page view.

| Post-Feedback Page Action | Feedback Page | | | | | | | |
| | Overview | | Summary Report | | Full Report | | Details | |
	M	SD	M	SD	M	SD	M	SD
Browse Behavior	.308	.225	.067	.109	.024	.073	.079	.230
Feedback Viewed	.272	.213	.805	.216	.895	.225	.876	.246
Me Screen Viewed	.277	.241	.014	.052	.003	.023	.008	.028
Exit App	.143	.143	.114	.185	.078	.219	.038	.113

corrections were applied to all post hoc comparisons. The pattern for Overview revealed that all action categories were more likely to occur after viewing Overview than exiting the app. A different pattern emerged for the remaining feedback pages. Specifically, viewing feedback was the most likely action to occur after viewing Summary Report, Full Report, and Details, with at least 80% of next actions involving viewing one of the feedback pages. Exit App and Browse Behavior were the next most likely to occur and Me Screen Viewed was the least likely action to occur after viewing those three feedback pages. These findings suggest that if users can go deeper into the feedback than Overview, they may get into a potentially beneficial feedback loop.

4.3   Does Users' Performance Improve During App Use?

Last, we investigated changes in spoken response performance over the course of app interaction. User sessions (visit to app) were divided into thirds (first, middle, last) and we investigated changes in performance from the first third to the last third. Performance was measured as the proportion of spoken responses that received "Needs Work" feedback on each speech feature in each third of sessions. This investigation reduced the number of users to 27 as users were required to have at least three sessions and to have at least one speech in both the first and last third of sessions. All 27 users included in this analysis were in the high engagement group, which means that they made greater use of the app features, in particular the more detailed feedback and resources for response improvement. Table 3 shows the descriptive statistics and paired samples t-test comparisons for each of the six speech features.

Table 3. Proportion of spoken responses that need work across session phases.

| | Session Phase | | | | | | | |
| | First Third | | Last Third | | | | | |
	M	SD	M	SD	t	df	p	d
Filler Words	.520	.509	.110	.320	4.23	26	<.001	−.964
Pauses	.560	.506	.300	.465	2.56	26	.017	−.535
Repeated Words	.670	.480	.150	.362	4.65	26	<.001	−1.22
Speaking Rate	.930	.267	.520	.509	4.23	26	<.001	−1.01
Stressed Words	.560	.506	.070	.267	4.32	26	<.001	−1.21
Vocabulary Diversity	.810	.396	.300	.465	4.65	26	<.001	−1.18

The comparisons revealed a reduction in the proportion of speech features that needed work, which suggests an overall improvement in performance across use of the ELAi app. The effect size differences between the first and last third of sessions were all large ($d > .8$) [29], with the exception of a medium effect size ($.5 < d < .8$) for Pauses. These findings are very promising as they show large improvements in a variety of speech features over a relatively short period of time. However, the findings should be interpreted with a modicum of caution as a small number of participants were included in these analyses (29% of sample), time on task varied across participants, and we were not able to consider additional resources that users may have accessed during this same time period (e.g., language courses, other MALL apps). It is also important to note that this investigation was limited to performance within the app and a more formal investigation of changes in speaking skills is needed (e.g., pre/posttest design) to determine the true effectiveness of the ELAi app as a learning tool [27].

5   Conclusion

There is currently a plethora of language learning apps available to users. However, these apps are often designed for beginning language learners and are limited in their ability to provide feedback to spoken responses. The ELAi app was developed to provide an easily accessible English language learning app for users that want to receive detailed feedback about their speaking skills during spontaneous speech. The present work was the first evaluation of the ELAi app. Overall, the findings revealed that users spent the majority of their time browsing for prompts, completing new responses, and viewing shallow level feedback. This suggests that users are generally not taking advantage of the more in-depth feedback and resources to facilitate improvement, which were requested by users during interviews [28]. Although the prominence of viewing shallow feedback is disappointing, it could represent productive behavior. Feedback Overview is the only page in which users can compare their performance on multiple speech features across individual responses, which could reveal patterns of improvement or persistent issues [30] by leveraging the benefits of open learner models [31]. Future research is needed to determine if this cross-response comparison is occurring and to explore designs to facilitate these comparisons [32, 33] as language learners may not engage in self-regulated learning behaviors on their own in MALL apps [34].

We also investigated changes in user performance. Our preliminary findings were promising in that more engaged users improved their performance on all six speech features from the beginning to the end of their interaction with the ELAi app. However, these findings are only preliminary and a more rigorous investigation of the impact of the ELAi app on speaking skills is needed. Overall our initial findings suggest that the ELAi app is a promising MALL, but there is still room for improvement. The Feedback Summary Report, for example, could be improved by requiring less scrolling for users to access learning resources and explicitly highlighting the availability of more in-depth feedback to reduce any lack of feature awareness. Tailoring the feedback to user characteristics (e.g., cultural background) could also benefit learning [35]. New in-app incentives (e.g., badges) could encourage more frequent use (e.g., more than five sessions) and use of the in-depth feedback pages and learning resources. Users could also benefit from being shown their improvement over time to implicitly reward continued use of the app. Overall, the ELAi app shows initial promise at creating an easily accessible resource for practicing and receiving feedback on spontaneous speaking tasks, but more research is needed to understand how this app can be the most beneficial to users.

References

1. Kukulska-Hulme, A.: Mobile-assisted language learning. In: Chapelle, C. (ed.) The Encyclopedia of Applied Linguistics, pp. 3701–3709. Wiley, New York (2013)
2. Sharples, M., Taylor, J., Vavoula, G.: A theory of learning for the mobile age. In: Andrews, R., Haythormwaite, C. (eds.) The Sage Handbook of E-Learning Research, pp. 221–247. Sage, London (2007)
3. Sung, Y.T., Chang, K.-E., Yang, J.-M.: Mobile devices for language learning? A meta-analysis. Educ. Res. Rev. **16**, 68–84 (2015)
4. Shadiev, R., Hwang, W.-Y., Shadiev, N., Fayziev, M., Liu, T.-Y., Shen, L.: Smart watches for making EFL learning effective, healthy, and happy. In: Chang, M., et al. (eds.) Challenges and Solutions in Smart Learning. LNET, pp. 73–76. Springer, Singapore (2018). https://doi.org/10.1007/978-981-10-8743-1_11
5. Hanson, A.E.S., Brown, C.M.: Enhancing L2 learning through a mobile assisted spaced-repetition tool: an effective but bitter pill? Comput. Assist. Lang. Learn. **33**, 133–155 (2019)
6. Lin, J.-J., Lin, H.: Mobile-assisted ESL/EFL vocabulary learning: a systematic review and meta-analysis. Comput. Assist. Lang. Learn. **32**, 878–919 (2019)
7. Vesselinov, R., Grego, J.: Duolingo effectiveness study final report (2012). http://static.duolingo.com/s3/DuolingoReport_Final.pdf
8. Loewen, S., Crowther, D., Isbell, D.R., Kim, K.M., Maloney, J., Miller, Z.F.: Mobile-assisted language learning: a Duolingo case study. ReCALL **31**, 293–311 (2019)
9. Demmans Epp, C.: Migrants and mobile technology use: gaps in the support provided by current tools. J. Interact. Media Educ. **2**, 1–13 (2017)
10. Kukulska-Hulme, A.: Mobile language learning innovation inspired by migrants. J. Learn. Dev. **6**, 116–129 (2019)
11. Munteanu, C., et al.: Hidden in plain sight: low-literacy adults in a developed country overcoming social and educational challenges through mobile learning support tools. Pers. Ubiquit. Comput. **18**, 1–15 (2013). https://doi.org/10.1007/s00779-013-0748-x
12. Kluger, A.N., DeNisi, A.: The effects of feedback interventions on performance: a historical review, a meta-analysis, and a preliminary feedback intervention theory. Psychol. Bull. **119**, 254–284 (1996)
13. Shute, V.J.: Focus on formative feedback. Rev. Educ. Res. **78**, 153–189 (2008)
14. Ahn, T.Y., Lee, S.-M.: User experience of a mobile speaking application with automatic speech recognition for EFL learning. Br. J. Edu. Technol. **47**, 778–786 (2016)
15. Kukulska-Hulme, A., Shield, L.: An overview of mobile assisted language learning: can mobile devices support collaborative practice in speaking and listening? Paper presented at EuroCALL 2007 (2008)
16. Horwitz, E.K.: Language anxiety and achievement. Annu. Rev. Appl. Linguist. **21**, 112–126 (2001)
17. Pawlak, M., Mystkowska-Wiertelak, A.: Investigating the dynamic nature of L2 willingness to communicate. System **50**, 1–9 (2015)
18. Von Wörde, R.: Students' perspectives on foreign language anxiety. Inquiry **8**, 1 (2003)
19. Liu, N., Littlewood, W.: Why do many students appear reluctant to participate in classroom learning discourse? System **25**, 371–384 (1997)

20. Yanagi, M., Baker, A.A.: Challenges experienced by Japanese students with oral communication skills in Australian Universities. TESOL J. **7**, 621–644 (2016)
21. Swain, M.: Communicative competence: some roles of comprehensive input and comprehensible output in its development. In: Glass, S.M., Madden, C. (eds.) Input in Second Language Acquisition, pp. 235–253. Newbury House Publishers, Rowley (1985)
22. Swain, M.: Three functions of output in second language learning. In: Cook, G., Seidlhofer, B. (eds.) Principles and Practice in Applied Linguistics, pp. 125–144. Oxford University Press, Oxford (1995)
23. Swain, M.: Languaging, agency, and collaboration in advanced second language proficiency. In: Byrnes, H. (ed) Advanced Language Learning: The Contribution of Halliday and Vygotsky, pp. 95–108. Continuum, New York (2006)
24. Yu, S., Wang, B., Teo, T.: Understanding linguistic, individual and contextual factors in oral feedback research: a review of empirical studies in L2 classrooms. Educ. Res. Rev. **24**, 181–192 (2018)
25. Dourish, P.: The appropriation of interactive technologies: some lessons from placeless documents. Comput. Support. Coop. Work Three Funct. Output Second Lang. Learn. **12**, 465–490 (2003). https://doi.org/10.1023/A:1026149119426
26. Craik, F.I., Lockhart, R.S.: Levels of processing: a framework for memory research. J. Verb. Learn. Verb. Behav. **11**, 671–684 (1972)
27. Demmans Epp, C., Phirangee, K.: Exploring mobile tool integration: design activities carefully or students may not learn. Contemp. Educ. Psychol. **59**, 101791 (2019)
28. Botero, G.G., Questier, F., Zhu, C.: Self-directed language learning in a mobile-assisted, out-of-class context: do students walk the talk? Comput. Assist. Lang. Learn. **32**, 71–97 (2018)
29. Cohen, J.: A power primer. Psychol. Bull. **112**, 155–159 (1992)
30. Demmans Epp, C., McCalla, G.: ProTutor: historic open learner models for pronunciation tutoring. In: Biswas, G., Bull, S., Kay, J., Mitrovic, A. (eds.) AIED 2011. LNCS (LNAI), vol. 6738, pp. 441–443. Springer, Heidelberg (2011). https://doi.org/10.1007/978-3-642-21869-9_63
31. Bull, S., Kay, J.: Open learner models. In: Nkambou, R., Bourdeau, J., Mizoguchi, R. (eds.) Advances in Intelligent Tutoring Systems, vol. 308, pp. 301–322. Springer, Heidelberg (2010). https://doi.org/10.1007/978-3-642-14363-2_15
32. Çakir, I.: Mobile-assisted language learning (MALL). In: Yaman, E., Emekçi, E., Şenel, M. (eds.) Current Trends in ELT, pp. 170–189. NÜANS Publishing, Ankara (2016)
33. Hug, T.: Mobile learning as 'microlearning': conceptual considerations towards enhancements of didactic thinking. Int. J. Mobile Blend. Learn. **2**, 47–57 (2010)
34. Viberg, O., Andersson, A.: The role of self-regulation and structuration in mobile learning. Int. J. Mobile Blend. Learn. **11**, 42–58 (2019)
35. Yang, J.: Learners' oral corrective feedback preferences in relation to their cultural background, proficiency level and types of errors. System **61**, 75–86 (2016)

Impact of Conversational Formality on the Quality and Formality of Written Summaries

Haiying Li[1(✉)] and Art C. Graesser[2]

[1] Department of Applied Research and Services, ACT, Inc., Iowa City, IA 52246, USA
haiying.li@act.org
[2] Department of Psychology, University of Memphis, Memphis, TN 38152, USA
art.graesser@gmail.com

Abstract. This study investigated the impact of conversational agent formality on the quality of summaries and formality of written summaries during the training session and on posttest in a trialog-based intelligent tutoring system (ITS). During training, participants learned summarization strategies with the guidance of conversational agents who spoke one of the following three styles of language: (1) a formal language for both the teacher agent and the student agent, (2) an informal language for both agents, and (3) a mixed language with a formal language for the teacher agent and the informal language for the student agent. Results showed that participants wrote better quality summaries during training than pretest and/or posttest in each condition. Results also showed that agent informal language caused participants to write more informal summaries during training than on pretest. Implications are discussed for the potential application of adaptive design of conversational agents in the ITS.

Keywords: Summary writing · Agent language · Formality

1 Introduction

How to design effective language for instruction and explanations is always a controversial topic for researchers who develop computer-assisted learning environments. The question *"which language better facilitates learning, formal language or informal language"* has been investigated for decades. Formal language and informal language are two opposite ends on a continuum of formality. Formal language is precise, cohesive, and articulate independent of the context and common ground, whereas informal language is conversational, personal, and narrative dependent on the context and common grounds [2, 9, 11–13]. Both formal and informal language could be either in print or oral.

The majority of studies on agent language used personal pronouns to distinguish formal language from informal language. These studies provided empirical evidence that agents' informal language (e.g., first- or second-person pronouns) enhanced learning, reduced perceived difficulties, and increased interests in varied domains such as science

© Springer Nature Switzerland AG 2020
I. I. Bittencourt et al. (Eds.): AIED 2020, LNAI 12163, pp. 321–332, 2020.
https://doi.org/10.1007/978-3-030-52237-7_26

[13, 15–19] and psychology [21, 22], as well as in diverse settings ranging from research labs [21] to massive online open course (MOOC) environments [22] and from intelligent tutoring systems (ITS) [13] to educational games [18]. No studies, to date, have examined the effect of agent language on learners' use of language in writing.

The Common Core State Standards for English Language Arts (CCSS-ELA) [3] require students to develop academic writing skills and to use an academic style in their writing. The National Assessment of Educational Progress [20], however, reports that it is still a daunting challenge for secondary students to meet these standards. Therefore, it is worthwhile to conduct more research on the effect of agent language on students' academic language use to better address this challenge. The present study aimed to investigate how agent language affected participants' learning of summary writing as well as the formality of language in their written summaries.

1.1 Agent Language and Learning

Increasingly, studies have investigated how agent language affects learning through different subject matters and in diverse computer-assisted learning environments. Moreno, Mayer, and colleagues [17–19] conducted a series of experiments to test the effect of informal language (e.g., first- and second-person pronouns) that the agent used to provide instructional explanations for science in an educational game. They found that agent informal language yielded better performance on retention tests and problem-solving transfer tests. These findings were further supported by a meta-analysis study that reviewed 74 empirical studies on agent language published from 1981 to 2012 [5]. A study from a science domain, however, showed an inconsistent finding: agent informal language enhanced retention performance but did not enhance transfer performance [15]. Inconsistent findings are likely due to the different learning environments in the experiments and the different languages in learning. Specifically, the former was in an educational game and the instructional language was in English, while the latter was in a multimedia lesson with a PowerPoint show and the instructional language was in Chinese.

These inconsistent findings were also found in the domain of psychology in different settings. Reichelt et al. conducted a study in the research lab and found that the use of informal language in learning materials yielded better retention performance than the formal language, but this effect was not found on transfer performance [21]. Riehemann and Jucks also used instructional material in psychology but conducted the study in a MOOC [22]. They found that the use of informal language enhanced transfer performance.

We investigated the effect of agent language on summary writing in an ITS and found that the agent informal language enhanced better quality of summary writing [13], but this study is different from previous studies in four ways. First, this study designed a trialog rather than a dialogue or solo narrator. In the trialog, a human learner learned summarization strategies with two computer agents: one was the teacher agent, and another was the student agent. Second, the agent language was designed using three styles rather than two: the formal language for both agents, the informal language for both agents, and the mixed language by merging teacher agent formal language and student agent informal language. Third, the results that the agent informal language facilitated summary writing was on the concentration of the main effect of agent language, namely, formal, informal, and mixed language, but did not consider the effect of agent language on posttest from pretest within each condition. Fourth, this study used multiple textual levels to measure agent language rather than merely personal pronouns as was the case in prior studies. The next section describes the multi-level measure of agent language in detail.

1.2 Measure of Agent Language

Many studies used personal pronouns to distinguish formal language from informal language. Specifically, third-person pronouns were used to produce the formal language, whereas first- and second-person pronouns were used to construct the informal language [17–19]. On one hand, the informal language with greater use of first- and second-person pronouns creates a more social environment that is more engaging for learners. Further, informal language is a familiar and everyday language, which requires less cognitive effort and is much easier to process and comprehend. Even though personal pronouns are an important indicator for formality, we could not ignore the essential roles of other language components that are used to differentiate the formal language from informal language [9, 11, 23].

We used the Coh-Metrix formality to measure agent language at multiple textual levels ranging from word, to syntax, to cohesion, and to genre [13]. Formality increases with the more use of abstract words (e.g., damage vs. hurricane), complex syntactic structures (e.g., subordinate sentences vs. simple sentences), referential cohesion (e.g., repetition of nouns vs. using pronouns to replace the repeated nouns), deep cohesion (e.g., more connectives vs. less/no connectives), and non-narrativity (e.g., third-person pronouns vs. first/second-person pronouns). This multi-level measure considers language in a holistic way rather than with one individual linguistic element. Thus, the agent language that was generated at multi-textual levels was more authentic and natural.

Our previous study examined the effect of agent language on learning. More studies are needed to explore whether agent language affects learners' use of language. The present study aimed to investigate the effect of agent language on both the quality of writing and formality of writing. Agent language was designed and developed into three styles: (1) a *formal* language for both the teacher agent and the student agent, (2) an *informal* language for both agents, and (3) a *mixed* language combining the teacher agent's formal language with the student agent's informal discourse. Specifically, this study addressed two research questions:

(1) Does agent language have an effect on the quality of participants' summary?
(2) Does agent language have an effect on formality in participants' written summaries?

This study advances research on agent language in the following two ways. First, this is the first study to unpack the effect of agent language on both learning outcomes and the use of language in writing. Findings could provide researchers with guidance on how to design language that adapts to the goals of instruction, namely, learning and/or academic writing. Second, this study reveals how agent language affects learning and use of language by comparing not only performance on pretest with posttest but also with training. This method allows for scrutiny of the learning processes from pretest to training (i.e., learning with guidance), and to posttest (i.e., learning with guidance removed) associated with the appropriate and sufficient instructional time for effective learning and the use of academic language during and after the intervention.

2 Method

2.1 Participants

Participants were recruited from Amazon Mechanical Turk (AMT) with $30 compensation for a three-hour experiment [13]. Data collected through AMT are as trusted and reliable as those collected through traditional methods [1, 24]. Qualified participants met the criteria of being English learners and wanted to improve English summary writing. Participants were randomly assigned to three conditions: formal, informal, and mixed conditions (see the Manipulation section for details). Most participants were from India, so this study only used Indian participants to exclude the confounding of participants from different cultures. Ninety-three participants (66.4% male, $M_{Age} = 32.49$ with $SD_{Age} = 8.64$) were in three conditions: 29 in the formal condition, 29 in the informal condition, and 35 in the mixed condition. Participants had learned English for 16.39 years on average ($SD = 8.43$). They first took a demographic survey, then a pretest, training, and finally a posttest.

2.2 Materials

The reading materials were the same as Eight short expository English texts (195–399 words) in our previous study [13]. Four of them were comparison texts and four were causation texts. Two comparison texts (*Butterfly & Moth, Hurricane*) and two causation texts (*Floods, Job Market*) were randomly selected for pretest and posttest and the balanced 4 × 4 Latin-square designs were used to control for order effects. The training session used the remaining four passages (two comparison texts (*Walking and Running, Kobe and Jordan*) and two causation texts (*Effects of Exercising, Diabetes*)) and the same 4 × 4 balanced Latin-square design was applied. The causation texts displayed a causal relationship between ideas and concepts, whereas the comparison texts compared or contrasted ideas or persons and revealed their similarities and differences [20]. These texts were measured by the Coh-Metrix formality scores (.12–.64) and the Flesch-Kincaid grade level (Grade 8–12) and their text difficulties were equivalent to those for students from upper middle school to high school students.

During training, two conversational agents [13] interactively presented a mini-lecture on the function of signal words in comparison and causation texts and lists signals frequently used in comparison texts (e.g., *same/similar* signifying similarity, *differ/but* signifying differences) and in causation texts (e.g., *as/because* signifying causes, *thus/so* signifying effects). Agents then interactively guided participants to read four passages and apply the summarization strategy that they learned. Learning was assessed through five multiple-choice (MC) questions for each passage. The first MC question required participants to identify the text structure of the passage, the second to identify the main ideas, and the last three to distinguish important supporting information from unimportant minor information (see Fig. 1). After completing the MC questions, participants were required to write a summary for the passage they just read. Conversational agents provided real-time feedback and scaffolding for the MC questions, but not for the quality of written summaries due to the lack of accurate real-time automated assessment of summaries [14]. It took participants about one hour to complete the training session in this trialog-based ITS.

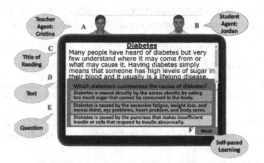

Fig. 1. Screenshot of interface during the training session.

The same procedure was applied to the pretest and posttest sessions, with the only difference in the exclusion of five MC questions along with the real-time feedback and scaffolding. One comparison and one causation texts were used on pretest and another one comparison and one causation texts were used on posttest.

2.3 Manipulation

The agents' conversations were generated by an expert at discourse processing, following a five-step tutoring frame and the expectation and misconception-tailored dialogue (EMT) [6–8]. These conversations were modified by another expert to make them more natural and authentic. Figure 2 presents this conversation mechanism: (1) the teacher agent first asked a main question, (2) the participant initiated an answer, (3) the teacher agent provides feedback and hints to help the participant seek the correct answer, (4) the agent evaluated learning by asking the question again and the participant took another try to answer the question, and (5) the agent wrapped up the question with assertion. This dialogue mechanism has been proven to enhance student learning and engagement [10]. Table 1 displays an example of the conversations that followed this mechanism. Agents delivered the content of their utterances via synthesized speech, but the participants clicked on or typed in their responses.

The agents' conversations involving mini-lecture, asking questions, providing hints, and wrapping-up questions were generated in informal and formal language styles at the multiple text levels of word usage (e.g., less vs. more frequently-used words), syntactic complexity (e.g., simple vs. complex sentences), referential cohesion (e.g., using pronouns to substitute the previous noun vs. repeating nouns), deep cohesion (e.g., less vs. more connectives to make meaning coherently), and genre (e.g., narrative vs. expository

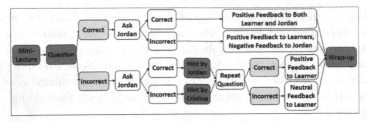

Fig. 2. Trialog moves during the training session.
Note. Conversations in red boxes were manipulated by agents' formality. Participants' responses were in yellow boxes. Jordan was the student agent. (Color figure online)

Table 1. An example of trialog during training.

Cristina: Esther [*Participant*], which statement better summarizes the main idea of this text? [*Main question*]

Esther: (*Click*) Diabetes, a lifelong disease, is caused by too little insulin or resistance to insulin and its symptoms include fatigue, blurry vision, weight loss, and excess thirst. [*First trial: Wrong Answer*]

Cristina: Jordan, it is your turn. What is your answer? [*Ask Jordan*]

Jordan: This is the correct answer. [*Jordan's incorrect response*]

Cristina: The first part of this answer elaborates on the important causes of diabetes, whereas the second part illustrates many specific symptoms, which are inappropriate for the main idea. [*Elaboration*] The main idea in the causation texts should specify the causal relationships. For instance, what causes diabetes and how diabetes affects people's health? [*Hint*] Esther, take another try. I will repeat the question. Which statement better summarizes the main idea of this text? [*Repeat Question*]

Esther: (*Click*) Diabetes is indicated by high levels of sugar in the blood and it has two types: Type 1 happens at any age; Type 2 happens in adulthood. [*Second trial: Incorrect Answer*]

Cristina: Alright. [*Neutral Feedback*] The first part of this answer informs us that people with diabetes have high levels of blood sugar, whereas the second part states two types of diabetes. The second part doesn't demonstrate the causal relationships [*Elaboration*]

Jordan: I see. The text points out two reasons. One is the pancreas. Another is cells. The third answer sums up this information. Therefore, the correct answer should be the first one: Diabetes is caused by too little insulin or resistance to insulin and can cause harmful health complications over the years. [*Wrap-up*]

Cristina: Excellent, Jordan! [*Positive Feedback*] The correct answer should be the first statement: Diabetes is caused by too little insulin or resistance to insulin and can cause harmful health complications over the years. The first part of the statement specifies the causes of diabetes, whereas the second part states the consequences of diabetes. [*Wrap-up*]

style). These conversations were then evaluated by the measure of the Coh-Metrix formality [1, 3]. The mean of agents' formal language was 1.02 and informal, −0.37, which was consistent with humans' perception of formality when they generated conversations. Then the teacher agent formal language and the student agent informal language were mixed, which generated the mixed language. Its formality score was 0.12. The agents' formality in three conditions represents three different levels of formality: informal, medium, and formal [9]. Table 2 illustrates an example of the formal and informal discourse when agents explained why the answer was incorrect. In Table 1, agents used the formal language when they asked the participant the main question, elaborated why the selected answer was incorrect, and provided hints (e.g., *elaboration, hint, question*), whereas they used the informal language for socialization (e.g., *"Jordan, it is your turn"*) or to provide feedback (e.g., *"Excellent"*).

Table 2. Examples of explanations in the formal language and the informal language.

Cristina's Formal discourse:
The third statement specifies that the pancreas produces insufficient insulin and that cells do not respond to insulin normally, which are the right causes of diabetes. Therefore, this statement is correct.
Cristina's Informal Discourse:
The third answer shows how people get diabetes. We can find this information from the text. This answer is correct.

2.4 Measures

Participants were required to write a summary with 50–100 words after reading each passage. They were required to state the main idea and important information with a topic sentence when generating the summaries. They were also encouraged to use signal words to explicitly express their ideas. The summaries were graded based on the rubric used in the previous studies [4, 13] in terms of four components: (1) topic sentence, (2) content inclusion and exclusion, (3) grammar and mechanics, and (4) signal words of text structures [19]. Each component was given 0–2 points, with 0 for the absence of target knowledge, 1 for the partial presence of knowledge, and 2 for the complete presence of knowledge.

Four experts whose native language was English (1 male and 3 females) graded summaries after three rounds of training. For each round of training, they graded 32 summaries that were randomly selected from eight texts and then discussed disagreements until an agreement was reached. The average interrater reliabilities for the three training sets reached the threshold (Cronbach $\alpha = .82$). After training, each rater graded summaries for two source texts. Four raters graded 1,296 summaries in total.

We used the text analysis tool *Coh-Metrix* (3.0) to analyze participants' written summaries. Specifically, Coh-Metrix extracted the five primary Coh-Metrix components: word concreteness, syntactic simplicity, referential cohesion, deep cohesion, and narrativity [9, 13]. We reversed the first two and the last component scores and then computed the formality scores with an average of five scores. The higher scores represented more formal summaries.

3   Results and Discussion

We performed the mixed repeated ANOVA with agent language (informal, mixed, and formal) as a between-subjects factor, text structure (causation and comparison) and time (pretest, training, and posttest) as within-subjects factors (i.e., a repeated measure), and participants' age and year of learning English as covariates. We aimed to examine how agent language affected the quality of summaries and language use from pretest to training and then to posttest. Thus, the design of analyses included three fixed factors: the main-effect of time, the two-way interaction between time and condition, and the three-way interaction among time, condition, and text structure.

Two dependent variables were the quality of written summaries and formality of written summaries. All significance testing was conducted with an alpha level of .05 with Bonferroni correction for multiple analyses. Cohen's d was computed as an appropriate effect size. Table 3 displays the means and standard deviations of summary scores and formality scores of written summaries within each condition in each text structure on pretest, during training, and on posttest.

Table 3. Means and standard deviations of quality and formality of summaries.

Condition	Text structure	Quality of written summaries			Formality of written summaries		
		Pretest	Training	Posttest	Pretest	Training	Posttest
Formal	Causation	3.86(1.35)	4.89(1.55)	3.84(1.45)	0.57(0.58)	0.34(0.51)	0.41(0.51)
	Comparison	3.99(2.01)	4.63(1.71)	4.28(2.05)	0.16(0.47)	0.08(0.43)	0.21(0.58)
	Total	*3.93(1.70)*	*4.76(1.63)*	*4.06(1.77)*	*0.36(0.56)*	*0.21(0.49)*	*0.31(0.55)*
Informal	Causation	4.14(1.38)	5.64(1.54)	4.45(1.38)	0.55(0.52)	0.38(0.45)	0.51(0.44)
	Comparison	4.21(1.70)	4.95(1.49)	4.86(1.85)	0.30(0.56)	0.08(0.35)	0.15(0.48)
	Total	*4.17(1.53)*	*5.29(1.55)*	*4.66(1.63)*	*0.43(0.55)*	*0.23(0.43)*	*0.33(0.49)*
Mixed	Causation	3.69(1.59)	4.71(1.74)	3.79(1.84)	0.49(0.49)	0.35(0.49)	0.32(0.44)
	Comparison	3.54(2.08)	4.76(1.58)	3.97(1.74)	0.17(0.62)	0.05(0.46)	0.26(0.61)
	Total	*3.61(1.84)*	*4.74(1.65)*	*3.88(1.78)*	*0.33(0.57)*	*0.20(0.49)*	*0.29(0.53)*
Total		**3.89(1.71)**	**4.92(1.63)**	**4.18(1.75)**	**0.37(0.56)**	**0.21(0.47)**	**0.31(0.52)**

3.1 Quality of Written Summaries

The mixed repeated ANOVA analysis on the quality of summaries exhibited a significant main effect of time, $F(2, 720) = 26.64$, $p < 0.001$. Pairwise analyses (see the Quality column and the Total row in Bold in Table 3) indicated that participants wrote better quality summaries during the training session when they read the texts with the guidance of conversational agents than when they read by themselves without the guidance of conversational agents on pretest ($p < 0.001$, Cohen's $d = 0.50$) and on posttest ($p < 0.001$, Cohen's $d = 0.35$).

Analyses also displayed a significant two-way interaction for the quality of summaries, $F(6, 720) = 2.91$, $p = 0.008$. Further pairwise analyses showed that participants wrote significantly better quality summaries in each agent formality condition: $F(2, 720) = 6.33$, $p = 0.002$ for the formal condition, $F(2, 720) = 8.88$, $p < 0.001$ for the informal condition, $F(2, 720) = 12.60, p < 0.001$ for the mixed condition. Further analyses (see the Total Row within each condition in Italic in Table 3) revealed that participants wrote significantly better summaries during the training session than on pretest and posttest in both formal condition and mixed condition: $p = 0.005$, Cohen's $d = .41$ for pretest and training and $p = 0.028$, Cohen's $d = .34$ for posttest and training in the formal condition; and $p < 0.001$, Cohen's $d = .52$ for pretest and training and $p = 0.003$, Cohen's $d = .40$ for posttest and training in the mixed condition. In the informal condition, participants wrote significantly better quality summaries during the training session than on pretest, $p < 0.001$, Cohen's $d = .5$. Results did not show a significant three-way interaction.

These findings indicated that conversational agents could facilitate participants writing better summaries when agents guided them to read the texts during training than on pretest and posttest when the guidance was removed. Participants benefited from the guidance provided by agents, no matter what language formality that agents used, formal, informal, or mixed. Unfortunately, when agents' guidance was removed on posttest, participants read and processed texts and then wrote summaries independently, and the quality of their written summaries was not significantly different from that on pretest. These findings imply that intervention on text structure could effectively facilitate summary writing, but would likely be insufficient for participants to master these skills and apply them towards completing summary writing tasks independently. Participants probably need more assistance to complete summary writing tasks successfully.

3.2 Formality of Written Summaries

The analysis on the formality of summaries that participants constructed showed a significant main effect of time, $F(2, 720) = 7.32, p < 0.001$. Pairwise analyses (see the Formality column and the Total row in Bold in Table 3) showed that participants wrote more informal summaries during the training session than on pretest ($p = 0.001$, Cohen's $d = 0.25$). This pattern was not found on posttest and training. Further analyses for each condition (see the Total Row within each condition in Italic in Table 3) showed that this pattern was only found in the informal condition, $F(2, 720) = 3.23, p = .040$. Participants wrote more informal summaries during training than on pretest ($p = .038$, Cohen's $d = 0.32$). Results indicated a significant three-way interaction, $F(9, 720) = 6.73, p < .001$, but further pairwise analyses showed no significant effects.

These findings suggest that the agent informal language more easily influenced participants' use of informal language. Specifically, participants tended to imitate agents' informal discourse when they generated their summaries, possibly because the informal language is more familiar and much easier as it requires less cognitive effort. Fortunately, when participants wrote summaries without agents' guidance, the effect disappeared. We did not find that the agent formal or mixed language affected participants' language use in their written summaries. One explanation is that the training session focused on the instruction of text structures, not the use of formal language in writing. Another explanation is that the directions for summary writing did not require participants to write summaries in the formal language. The third explanation is that the formal language is more complex and using the formal discourse would take more effort and time. Thus, participants tended to use the more familiar language to save effort and time in the situation where they were not explicitly required to write formally.

4 Conclusions and Implications

In this study, we investigated the impact of conversational agent formality on learning of text structures, concentrating on the quality of participants' written summaries and formality of their written summaries during learning processes that included independent reading and writing on pretest, reading with guidance during training, and independent reading and writing on posttest in a trialog-based ITS. During the training session, participants learned with the guidance of conversational agents who spoke one of three styles of language: a formal language for both the teacher agent and the student agent, an informal language for both agents, and a mixed language with the formal language for the teacher agent and the informal language for the student agent.

We found that when participants were guided to read texts, they wrote better quality summaries. When the guidance was removed, they wrote summaries as well as on the pretest. Our findings were inconsistent with prior studies: agents' informal language facilitated learning. The reason for the ineffective intervention on posttest is likely that summary writing involves complex cognitive processes, which may take participants, particularly language learners a longer time to master the skills and successfully apply them to a new task independently. The reason for the effective intervention during training is that even if summary writing is a difficult and complex task, participants could benefit from the intervention no matter what language the agents use. Our findings imply that one-hour intervention is insufficient for summary writing. Further studies are needed to investigate how long participants, including English-native speakers and language learners, need agents' guidance and what is the best time to remove the guidance so that they could successfully complete summary writing tasks independently.

Moreover, we found that participants' use of language was affected by agents' use of language only when agents spoke with the informal language. This finding implies that participants' use of language is potentially affected by the agents' use of language. This study provides evidence that we might facilitate participants' use of language through the use of similar language by agents. The reason for the ineffectiveness of the agents' formal or mixed language on participants' use of formal language is possibly that we did not specify the use of formal language in writing or provide explicit instruction for formal language. Further studies are needed to examine whether agent formal discourse could elicit learners' use of formal language through explicit instruction and requirement in the writing prompts.

This study has some limitations, which could be addressed in future studies, as aforementioned. Another restriction, which has not been mentioned, is the measure of agent language. Previous studies on agent language used personal pronouns, which are easier to manipulate. The present study used multiple textual-level measures to measure agent language, including word abstractness, syntactic complexity, referential cohesion, deep cohesion, and non-narrativity, which are implicit and complex. Future studies will focus on certain specific language and discourse features at each level, provide instruction on the use of these features in academic writing, and investigate the effectiveness of the intervention.

This study contributes to research on agent language in the following three ways. First, this fine-grained analysis unpacked learning processes and informed researchers and educators of the potential for intervention for complex learning tasks. Second, the findings of effective learning during training in all conditions suggest that further studies on agent language need to consider the design of language holistically and comprehensively. Third, this study is the first one to lay a foundation that agent language affects participants' use of language and encourage researchers to design more learning environments to facilitate academic writing.

References

1. Buhrmester, M., Kwang, T., Gosling, S.D.: Amazon's Mechanical Turk a new source of inexpensive, yet high-quality, data? Perspect. Psychol. Sci. **6**, 3–5 (2011). https://doi.org/10.1177/1745691610393980
2. Clark, H.H.: Using Language. Cambridge, New York (1996). https://doi.org/10.1017/cbo9780511620539
3. Common Core State Standards Initiative: Common Core State Standards for English language arts and literacy in history/social studies, science, and technical subjects (2010). http://www.corestandards.org/ELA-Literacy/
4. Friend, R.: Effects of strategy instruction on summary writing of college students. Contemp. Educ. Psychol. **26**, 3–24 (2001). https://doi.org/10.1006/ceps.1999.1022
5. Ginns, P., Martin, A.J., Marsh, H.W.: Designing instructional text in a conversational style: a meta-analysis. Educ. Psychol. Rev. **25**, 445–472 (2013). https://doi.org/10.1007/s.10648-013-9228-0
6. Graesser, A.C., Chipman, P., Haynes, B.C., Olney, A.: AutoTutor: an intelligent tutoring system with mixed-initiative dialogue. IEEE Trans. Educ. **48**, 612–618 (2005). https://doi.org/10.1109/TE.2005.856149
7. Graesser, A.C., Keshtkar, F., Li, H.: The role of natural language and discourse processing in advanced tutoring systems. In: Holtgraves, T. (ed.) The Oxford Handbooks of Language and Social Psychology, pp. 491–509. Oxford, New York (2014)
8. Graesser, A.C., Li, H., Forsyth, C.: Learning by communicating in natural language with conversational agents. Curr. Dir. Psychol. Sci. **23**, 374–380 (2014). https://doi.org/10.1177/0963721414540680
9. Graesser, A.C., McNamara, D.S., Cai, Z., Conley, M., Li, H., Pennebaker, J.: Coh-Metrix measures text characteristics at multiple levels of language and discourse. Elem. Sch. J. **115**, 210–229 (2014). https://doi.org/10.1086/678293
10. Li, H., Cheng, Q., Yu, Q., Graesser, A.C.: The role of peer agent's learning competency in trialogue-based reading intelligent systems. In: Conati, C., Heffernan, N., Mitrovic, A., Verdejo, M. (eds.) AIED 2015. LNCS (LNAI), vol. 9112, pp. 694–697. Springer, Cham (2015). https://doi.org/10.1007/978-3-319-19773-9_94
11. Li, H., Graesser, A.C., Cai, Z.: Comparing two measures of formality. In: Boonthum-Denecke, C., Youngblood, G.M. (eds.) 2013 FLAIRS, pp. 220–225. AAAI Press, Palo Alto (2013)
12. Li, H., Graesser, A.C., Conley, M., Cai, Z., Pavlik, P., Pennebaker, J.W.: A new measure of text formality: an analysis of discourse of Mao Zedong. Discourse Process. **53**, 205–232 (2016). https://doi.org/10.1080/0163853X.2015.1010191
13. Li, H., Graesser, A.: Impact of pedagogical agents' conversational formality on learning and engagement. In: André, E., Baker, R., Hu, X., Rodrigo, M.M.T., du Boulay, B. (eds.) AIED 2017. LNCS (LNAI), vol. 10331, pp. 188–200. Springer, Cham (2017). https://doi.org/10.1007/978-3-319-61425-0_16
14. Li, H., Cai, Z., Graesser, A.C.: How good is popularity? Summary grading in crowdsourcing. In: Barnes, T., Chi, M., Feng, M. (eds.) 2016 EDM, pp. 430–435. EDM Society, Raleigh (2016)

15. Lin, L., Ginns, P., Wang, T., Zhang, P.: Using a pedagogical agent to deliver conversational style instruction: What benefits can you obtain? Comput. Educ. **143**, 103658 (2020). https://doi.org/10.1016/j.compedu.2019.103658

16. Mayer, R.E.: Principles based on social cues: personalization, voice, and presence principles. In: Mayer, R.E. (ed.) Cambridge Handbook of Multimedia Learning, pp. 201–212. Cambridge, New York (2005)

17. Mayer, R.E., Fennell, S., Farmer, L., Campbell, J.: A personalization effect in multimedia learning: students learn better when words are in conversational style rather than formal style. J. Educ. Psychol. **96**, 389–395 (2004). https://doi.org/10.1037/0022-0663.96.2.389

18. Moreno, R., Mayer, R.E.: Personalized messages that promote science learning in virtual environments. J. Educ. Psychol. **96**, 165–173 (2004). https://doi.org/10.1037/0022-0663.96.1.165

19. Moreno, R., Mayer, R.E.: Engaging students in active learning: the case for personalized multimedia messages. J. Educ. Psychol. **92**, 724–733 (2000). https://doi.org/10.1037/0022-0663.92.4.724

20. NAEP: 2015 Reading Assessment [Data file] (2015). http://nces.ed.gov/nationsreportcard/subject/publications/stt2015/pdf/2016008AZ4.pdf

21. Reichelt, M., Kämmerer, F., Niegemann, H.M., Zander, S.: Talk to me personally: personalization of language style in computer-based learning. Comput. Hum. Behav. **35**, 199–210 (2014). https://doi.org/10.1016/j.chb.2014.03.005

22. Riehemann, J., Jucks, R.: "Address me personally!": On the role of language styles in a MOOC. J. Comput. Assist. Learn. **34**, 713–719 (2018). https://doi.org/10.1111/jcal.12278

23. Snow, C.E., Uccelli, P.: The challenge of academic language. In: Olson, D.R., Torrance, N. (eds.) The Cambridge Handbook of Literacy, pp. 112–133. Cambridge, New York (2009)

24. Snow, R., O'Connor, B., Jurafsky, D., Ng, A.Y.: Cheap and fast–but is it good? Evaluating non-expert annotations for natural language tasks. In: Proceedings of the 2008 Conference on Empirical Methods in Natural Language Processing, pp. 254–263. ACM, New York (2008)

LIWCs the Same, Not the Same: Gendered Linguistic Signals of Performance and Experience in Online STEM Courses

Yiwen Lin[✉], Renzhe Yu[✉], and Nia Dowell[✉]

University of California, Irvine, CA 92697, USA
{yiwen121,renzhey,dowelln}@uci.edu

Abstract. Women are traditionally underrepresented in science, technology, engineering, and mathematics (STEM). While the representation of women in STEM classrooms has grown rapidly in recent years, it remains pedagogically meaningful to understand whether their learning outcomes are achieved in different ways than male students. In this study, we explored this issue through the lens of language in the context of an asynchronous online discussion forum. We applied Linguistic Inquiry and Word Count (LIWC) to examine linguistic features of students' reflective posting in an online chemistry class at a four-year university. Our results suggest that cognitive linguistic features significantly predict the likelihood of passing the course and increases perceived sense of belonging. However, these results only hold true for female students. Pronouns and words relevant to social presence correlate with passing the course in different directions, and this mixed relationship is more polarized among male students. Interestingly, the linguistic features per se do not differ significantly between genders. Overall, our findings provide a more nuanced account of the relationship between linguistic signals of social/cognitive presence and learning outcomes. We conclude with implications for pedagogical interventions and system design to inclusively support learner success in online STEM courses.

Keywords: Community of Inquiry · Gender in STEM · Computational linguistics · Linguistic Inquiry and Word Count (LIWC) · Online learning · Higher education

1 Introduction

In higher education, introductory courses have been found to have key influence on students' motivation to major in science, technology, engineering, and mathematics (STEM) disciplines [26,39]. The success in introductory STEM courses is not only determined by academic performance, but also by whether or not students feel supported by the classroom community [19]. While we have

© Springer Nature Switzerland AG 2020
I. I. Bittencourt et al. (Eds.): AIED 2020, LNAI 12163, pp. 333–345, 2020.
https://doi.org/10.1007/978-3-030-52237-7_27

seen an increase in female students' enrollment in STEM disciplines, particularly in online courses [45], more challenges and higher attrition rates were reported among females [3]. It is thus important to understand female students' presence in STEM classrooms and how it affects their learning outcomes and experience. With universities increasingly employing learning management systems and offering STEM classes online, there are more opportunities for learning analytics to offer insights into students' learning processes and for artificial intelligence systems to appropriately scaffold learning behaviors.

Language is a window to learners' social, cognitive, and affective states in learning [8,10,13,42]. The advances of computational linguistics offer a powerful and efficient way to quantify learning behavior at scale [7,9,11,12]. While these methods have been commonly applied to forecast academic achievement and cognitive processes [35,36], there have been fewer instances that focus on non-cognitive outcomes such as learning experience and social identity [1,6]. Moreover, prior research suggests that there are gender differences at the socio-linguistic level in computer-mediated communication [5,29,32]. But it is less known whether these language patterns are associated with outcomes in a different manner for male and female students. As such, we are interested in exploring whether linguistic characteristics of students' discussion forum posts foretell cognitive and non-cognitive outcomes, and what this means for different genders in the context of online STEM courses.

The contributions of this work are as follows. We extend the understanding of gender differences in STEM learning through the lens of language, illustrating the links between linguistics features in students' reflective posting and performance. Further, by incorporating sense of belonging as an additional outcome measure, we demonstrate different ways language is associated with female and male students' experience in class. Lastly, our research contributes to the emerging research around (gender) equity in personalized and adaptive AIED systems. In the conclusion section, we further discuss the theoretical and practical implications for future research and practices in the AIED community.

2   Related Work

The Community of Inquiry (CoI) framework is commonly referenced by works on asynchronous discussion forums. The framework is comprised of three components: cognitive, social, and teaching presence [16]. We primarily focus on the cognitive and social presence in this work. Cognitive presence involves higher-order thinking and constructing meaning through reflection [25]. In the context of our current investigation, the reflection writing assignment highlights two phases of cognitive presence: knowledge integration and resolution. Cognitive presence can be achieved when students link new concepts to past knowledge, and reflect on the application of what they learned in class to real-life scenarios.

Social presence reflects the process when learners interact socially and coordinate efforts with peers [16,31]. In online learning, social presence is further elaborated as "the ability of participants to identify with the community (e.g., course of study)" [15]. Ample evidence from existing literature suggests enhanced academic outcome and educational experience through promoting cognitive and social presence [41]. Prior research also suggests that learning activities promoting social presence may also enhance the learner's satisfaction and a greater sense of belonging to the online community [2,17,37].

There has been extensive research that applies linguistic analysis to reveal social and cognitive presence in online learning. Previously, research has found distinct distributions of psychological categories of words at each level of the cognitive presence in the CoI framework, legitimizing language as a proxy for cognitive engagement [14,24]. Other research combined natural language processing techniques and behavioral data to establish the connection between linguistic features and engagement to predict learning outcomes [4]. The advances in computational techniques and machine learning models have given rise to automatic identifications of activities in discussion forums that require timely intervention [44]. Researchers have also attempted to translate the CoI coding scheme into a artificial intelligence model to capture cognitive presence [27]. However, it has become increasingly evident that the AIED community should progress towards building automated approaches with an eye on equity and inclusivity in order to appropriately address the issue of "one size fits all" [18].

Previous research suggests that linguistics characteristics in computer-mediated communication differ across gender lines [21,22]. In the context of STEM learning, a more recent study also found the ability for language to reveal distinct socio-cognitive processes in male and female students' engagement [29]. With online courses serving as an entryway for female students to pursue STEM disciplines [45], it is important to understand what leads to female students' performance and learning experiences in introductory STEM courses compared to their male counterparts [14,30]. Towards that end, we propose the following research questions:

1. What linguistic features of students' reflective posting are associated with cognitive and non-cognitive outcomes in online STEM courses?
2. Do male and female students exhibit different linguistic features?
3. Do these linguistic features correlate with learning outcomes differently for male and female students?

3 Methods

3.1 Sample and Data

This study was conducted in a fully online, ten-week introductory chemistry course at four-year university in the United States, with a total of 300 students enrolled. The course was administered in the Canvas learning management system (LMS) and students were required to write a reflection post every week in the discussion forum about the assigned reading for that week. This discussion task accounted for 5% of the final course grade and was organized in small groups of ten students. Each student was randomly assigned to a group at the end of

Week 2 and remained in the same group throughout the course. They could only access the posts written by their group members. Beyond the required posts for course credits, students were free to make additional contribution in the discussion forum. For fair comparison, we focused our text analysis on these original reflection posts.

For the linguistic analysis, we obtained students' discussion posts throughout the course along with their metadata (e.g., timestamp, response relationship). In order to address the first research question, we collected the gradebook data to derive performance measures. For the second research question, a pre- and a post-course survey were sent to measure students' sense of belonging, using a validated Classroom Community Scale [37]. The scale contains ten items on a 5-point Likert scale. For each student, the mean of their valid responses across the ten items was calculated as their sense of belonging. Additionally, we collected students' demographic information and academic history data.

We excluded students who did not post at all throughout the course, leaving a total of 238 students for our final analysis. Among them, 53.6% were female, 42.1% were racial/ethnic minorities (African American, Hispanic and Native American), and 58.6% were first-generation college students. These figures suggest that the class had a fair proportion of traditionally underrepresented student populations in STEM fields, so the findings in this study would be especially meaningful for STEM educators in general.

3.2   Linguistic Inquiry and Word Count (LIWC)

Linguistic Inquiry and Word Count (LIWC) is one of the most commonly used dictionary-based tools to evaluate and assess cognitive, social and affective properties in student discourse, as well as educational materials more broadly [34,38]. In the CoI literature, several studies have utilized LIWC to examine the linguistic features associated with social and cognitive presence. In the current research, we focused on a set of LIWC variables that are most representative of cognitive and social presence in students' discussion posts. A brief description of these linguistic features can be found below and in Table 1.

Table 1. Summary of LIWC variables in the analysis

Construct	LIWC variables	Example words
Cognitive presence	Analytic, Tone	–
	Cognitive process	Cause, think, should
Social presence	Clout, Authentic	–
	Social process	Friends, talk
	Personal pronouns	I, we, they, you

Among the four composite variables, two of them are used as proxies of cognitive presence. *Analytic* signifies formal and logical language which results from cognitive processes. *Tone* captures the positive and negative valence in language. Previous research suggests a combination of language valence, pronouns, and cognitive lexicons indicate state of confusion [46]. Academic writing which is less narrative and more cognitively demanding may reside on the negative side of this variable [42]. By contrast, the other two composite variables represent elements relative to social presence. *Clout* is defined as "relative social status, confidence, or leadership displayed through writing" [34]. *Authentic* has been found to signal self-referencing and "humble, vulnerable" positions [33].

The *cognitive process* variable in LIWC includes terms that relate to higher-order thinking and signal cognitive presence [28,31,34]. Research has highlighted subcategories of words under this category to demonstrate different phases of cognitive presence [24]. *Social process* includes content words concerning social support and relationships. While this can be a good indicator for social presence in casual contexts, highly social words might conversely suggest off-topicness in formal chemistry reflections. *Personal pronouns* indicate attentional focus and social relationships [35]. Specifically, the use of "I" represents attention drawn to oneself, in contrast to "we", "you" and "they" which take more "other-oriented" views. Learners who notice and make connections to others' work are likely to use more other-oriented pronouns [33]. For each student, we computed the average of each LIWC variables across all of their discussion posts to reflect their linguistic experience throughout the term.

3.3 Statistical Analysis

We leveraged two models under the framework of generalized linear regressions (GLM) to examine the relationship between linguistic features (all centered and Z-standardized) and students' cognitive and non-cognitive outcomes. For the cognitive aspect, we used logistic regression to regress the log-odds of passing the course (getting a letter grade of D- or above) on LIWC variables. Note that only 76% of the class passed the course. For the non-cognitive outcome, we used multiple regression, where students' change in sense of belonging throughout the course was regressed on LIWC variables. In all regression models, students' background information, including gender, first-generation college status, ethnically underrepresented minority (URM) status and SAT scores, was controlled for, as these variables captured group differences shaped by opportunity gaps prior to their college experience [40]. Also, the four composite LIWC variables were included in separate models from individual LIWC variables (Sect. 3.2) to avoid potential issues of (partial) collinearity.

To compare linguistic features between genders, we used independent t tests to statistically test difference between genders in each of the LIWC variables. Moreover, we reran the previous regression models separately on female and male students, and interpreted the coefficients of LIWC variables to explore potential gender differences in the relationship between linguistic features and student outcomes.

4   Results

4.1   Linguistic Features and Student Outcomes

Table 2 presents the estimated relationships between LIWC variables and cognitive and non-cognitive outcomes. Note that composite and individual LIWC variables were included in separate regression models. For the cognitive outcome (passing the course), raw instead of exponentiated coefficients from logistic regression models are reported. These estimates show that high cognitive complexity, low social content, negative tones, low social-status language and high frequencies of other-oriented pronouns (we/you/they) are associated with a higher likelihood of passing the course. Reflecting on our construction in Sect. 3.2, these results combined suggest a positive relationship between cognitive presence and cognitive outcome but a more complicated one between social presence and the same outcome. In stark contrast, none of the linguistic features succeeds in predicting students' change in sense of belonging after taking the course, or the non-cognitive outcome.

Table 2. Relationship between LIWC variables and cognitive (passing the course) and non-cognitive (change in sense of belonging) outcomes

	Pass		ΔSOB	
	Coef	SE	Coef	SE
Composite LIWC variables				
Analytic	−.164	(.191)	.079	(.0535)
Clout	−.377*	(.195)	−.0192	(.0615)
Authentic	.0861	(.182)	−.0143	(.061)
Tone	−.473***	(.17)	.0041	(.0684)
Individual LIWC variables				
CogProc	.383*	(.211)	.103	(.0805)
SocProc	−1.04***	(.317)	−.119	(.121)
I	−.057	(.207)	−.07	(.0698)
We	.665*	(.343)	−.0188	(.121)
You	.281	(.186)	−.106	(.0746)
They	.352*	(.197)	.0217	(.0704)

* p<0.1 ** p<0.05 *** p<0.01

4.2   Gender Differences in Linguistic Features

Table 3 presents the summary statistics of LIWC variables for male and female students, respectively. All the statistics were calculated before centering and standardization. The last column reports results from independent t tests to show

Table 3. Gender difference in LIWC variables. Format: mean (SD).

	Male	Female	Diff
Composite LIWC variables			
Analytic	83.8 (9.94)	83.8 (10.2)	−.0292
Clout	71.8 (13.4)	72.1 (10.9)	−.325
Authentic	34.6 (15)	36.4 (15.2)	−1.78
Tone	52.1 (16.8)	52.1 (17)	−.0105
Individual LIWC variables			
Cognitive process	11.3 (2.96)	11.3 (2.85)	.04
Social process	6.12 (1.96)	6.16 (1.99)	−.0398
Pronoun: I	.256 (.679)	.237 (.51)	.0191
Pronoun: we	3.35 (1.7)	3.15 (1.53)	.205
Pronoun: you	.176 (.408)	.273 (.431)	−.0973*
Pronoun: they	.558 (.483)	.574 (.514)	−.0166

* $p<0.1$ ** $p<0.05$ *** $p<0.01$

if each variable had a significant gender difference. Contrary to some prior literature [21,22], we did not observe much difference in linguistic features between male and female students. The only differences observed was that male students perceived significantly stronger sense of belonging at the end of the course, and that female students used "you" significantly more in their reflection posts.

4.3 Gender Differences in the Relationship Between Linguistic Features and Student Outcomes

Figure 1 visualizes the estimated coefficients from separate regression models. The visuals depict that the positive relationship between cognitive language and cognitive outcomes is concentrated on female students, evidenced by the significant effects of *tone* (−) and *cognitive process* (+) on the likelihood of passing the course. In contrast, the mixed relationship between social language and cognitive outcomes is more polarized for male students. Specifically, social referencing through other-oriented pronouns (we/you/they) significantly contributes to males' course outcomes but the use of social words has negative effects on the same outcomes.

While the change in sense of belonging is not correlated with any LIWC variables in the overall model, there are some significant relationships among female students. More cognitive language use predicts an increase in women's perceived classroom community, whereas other-oriented pronouns exhibit negative associations.

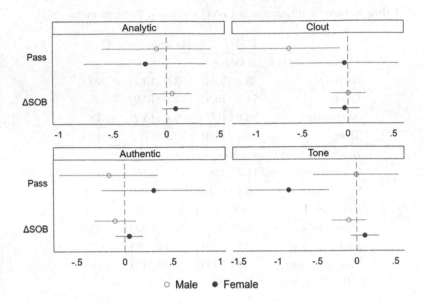

(a) *Composite LIWC variables*

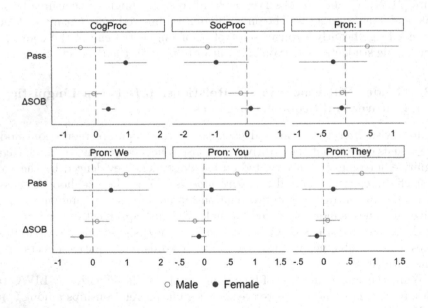

(b) *Individual LIWC varaibles*

Fig. 1. Gender differences in the estimated relationship (regression coefficients) between LIWC variables and cognitive (passing the course) and non-cognitive (change in sense of belonging) outcomes

5   Discussion

In this study, we investigated the relationships between linguistic features of students' reflective posting and student outcomes in an introductory online chemistry class. We further examined the gender differences in these linguistic features, and in the way they associated with outcomes. From our results, the strong positive relationship between cognitive language use and course performance for female students suggests that there might be an underlying need for female students to demonstrate cognitive engagement through language to achieve better outcomes. Additionally, the positive correlation between cognitive language and increased sense of belonging indicate that females are more likely to derive a sense of belonging from making intellectual contributions to the discussion forum. This might imply that cognitive language can improve learning experience and shape STEM identity more for female students than for male students.

The overall negative relationship between social language and passing the course may suggest that being on-topic is an important indicator of grades [43]. A reflection post with too many social signal words could mean a deviation from core content, leading to lower performance on tests. Regarding the use of pronouns, "we" was associated with decreased perceived sense of belonging for female students, which was somewhat surprising. While we expected that the use of an inclusive pronouns such as "we" would create a greater sense of community, this result shows the opposite. This counter-intuitive relationship might be accounted for by group factors. For instance, if a female student is the only person in her discussion group who engages in deep reflection, she may feel disconnected. A weaker sense of belonging may therefore be triggered by using "we" when the personal and group identity do not align. Due to the scope of our analysis, the current study did not take into account of group-level influence, but this remains an important direction for future work.

6   Conclusion

The naturally occurring educational discourse data within online learning platforms presents a golden opportunity for the AIED community to advance the understanding of cognitive and social processes in STEM learning and enables new kinds of personalized interventions focused on increasing inclusivity and equity [20]. Towards these ends, there are several key obstacles including limited analytical approaches to handling the scale of such data and substantive data-driven knowledge that can direct us to cultivate more equitable, respectful, and diverse environments that meaningfully engage all learners. In this context, our findings present some theoretical and practical implications for the AIED community.

For starters, our results alert that transferring and interpreting learner behavior across different types of online environments (i.e., MOOCs versus accredited university classes) or across academic disciplines require careful considerations.

One might assume that increased social presence in asynchronous discussion forums reflected by social language use would benefit learning. Yet the opposite result in the context of this chemistry course suggests that discussing non-academic content may also be irrelevant and undesirable in a formally structured discussion environment. Consequently, contextual information including classroom community and course delivery needs to be considered when deploying AIED applications focused on linguistic analytics. More nuanced considerations should also be given to applying theoretical models to online environments. For the same results above, it is also likely that social presence built upon knowledge construction is more valuable to learners' sense of belonging than that upon shared personal interests. Knowing this differentiation can be particularly informative for designing strategies to reduce the attrition rates of female students in STEM subjects.

Finally, our findings shed light on the emerging discourse around fairness and equity issues in student models [23,47]. Mining educational data should not be left without considerations for equity and inclusivity for different student populations. In our case, although the linguistics features appeared to be indistinguishable for male and female students overall, they were in fact associated with learning outcomes differently at a deeper level. We further highlight concerns about making instructional decisions based on the analysis for an entire student body. Such an approach, as we have found, might inadvertently discount the disparate impact on gender subgroups. Future development of automated analytic tools and machine learning models used to monitor learners' discussion forums activities should thus aim to recognize gender differences in order to close gender gaps in STEM education.

Acknowledgement. This paper is based upon work supported by the National Science Foundation (Grant Number 1535300). We thank Peter McPartlan, Qiujie Li and Teomara Rutherford for providing access to the course information and datasets.

References

1. Abe, J.A.A.: Big five, linguistic styles, and successful online learning. Internet High. Educ. **45**, 100724 (2020)
2. Arbaugh, J., Benbunan-Finch, R.: An investigation of epistemological and social dimensions of teaching in online learning environments. Acad. Manag. Learn. Educ. **5**(4), 435–447 (2006)
3. Chen, X.: Stem attrition: College students' paths into and out of stem fields (nces 2014–001). Technical report (2013)
4. Crossley, S., Mcnamara, D.S., Paquette, L., Baker, R.S., Dascalu, M.: Combining click-stream data with NLP tools to better understand MOOC completion. In: ACM International Conference Proceeding Series, vol. 25–29 April 2016, pp. 6–14. Association for Computing Machinery (2016)
5. Dowell, N., Lin, Y., Godfrey, A., Brooks, C.: Promoting inclusivity through time-dynamic discourse analysis in digitally-mediated collaborative learning. In: Isotani, S., Millán, E., Ogan, A., Hastings, P., McLaren, B., Luckin, R. (eds.) AIED 2019. LNCS (LNAI), vol. 11625, pp. 207–219. Springer, Cham (2019). https://doi.org/10.1007/978-3-030-23204-7_18

6. Dowell, N., Lin, Y., Godfrey, A., Brooks, C.: Exploring the relationship between emergent sociocognitive roles, collaborative problem-solving skills and outcomes: a group communication analysis. J. Learn. Anal. **7**(1), 38–57 (2020)
7. Dowell, N., Poquet, O., Brooks, C.: Applying group communication analysis to educational discourse interactions at scale. International Society of the Learning Sciences (2018)
8. Dowell, N.M., Graesser, A.C., Cai, Z.: Language and discourse analysis with coh-metrix: Applications from educational material to learning environments at scale. J. Learn. Anal. **3**(3), 72–95 (2016)
9. Dowell, N.M., et al.: Modeling learners' social centrality and performance through language and discourse. In: International Educational Data Mining Society (2015)
10. Dowell, N.M.M., Graesser, A.C.: Modeling learners' cognitive, affective, and social processes through language and discourse. J. Learn. Anal. **1**(3), 183–186 (2014)
11. Dowell, N.M., Brooks, C., Kovanović, V., Joksimović, S., Gašević, D.: The changing patterns of MOOC discourse. In: Proceedings of the Fourth (2017) ACM Conference on Learning@ Scale, pp. 283–286 (2017)
12. Dowell, N.M.M., Nixon, T.M., Graesser, A.C.: Group communication analysis: a computational linguistics approach for detecting sociocognitive roles in multiparty interactions. Behav. Res. Methods **51**(3), 1007–1041 (2018). https://doi.org/10.3758/s13428-018-1102-z
13. D'Mello, S.K., Dowell, N., Graesser, A.: Unimodal and multimodal human percep-tionof naturalistic non-basic affective statesduring human-computer interactions. IEEE Trans. Affect. Comput. **4**(4), 452–465 (2013)
14. Fesler, L., Dee, T., Baker, R., Evans, B.: Text as data methods for education research. J. Res. Educ. Eff. **12**(4), 707–727 (2019)
15. Garrison, D.R.: Communities of inquiry in online learning. In: Encyclopedia of Distance Learning, 2nd edn., pp. 352–355. IGI Global (2009)
16. Garrison, D.R., Anderson, T., Archer, W.: Critical thinking, cognitive presence, and computer conferencing in distance education. Int. J. Phytorem. **21**(1), 7–23 (2001)
17. Garrison, D.R., Arbaugh, J.B.: Researching the community of inquiry framework: review, issues, and future directions. Internet High. Educ. **10**(3), 157–172 (2007)
18. Gašević, D., Dawson, S., Rogers, T., Gasevic, D.: Learning analytics should not promote one size fits all: the effects of instructional conditions in predicting academic success. Internet High. Educ. **28**, 68–84 (2016)
19. Gasiewski, J.A., Eagan, M.K., Garcia, G.A., Hurtado, S., Chang, M.J.: From gatekeeping to engagement: a multicontextual, mixed method study of student academic engagement in introductory stem courses. Res. High. Educ. **53**(2), 229–261 (2012). https://doi.org/10.1007/s11162-011-9247-y
20. Goldstone, R.L., Lupyan, G.: Discovering psychological principles by mining naturally occurring data sets. Top. Cogn. Sci. **8**(3), 548–568 (2016)
21. Guiller, J., Durndell, A.: Students' linguistic behaviour in online discussion groups: does gender matter? Comput. Hum. Behav. **23**(5), 2240–2255 (2007)
22. Herring, S.C.: Gender differences in CMC: findings and implications. Comput. Prof. Soc. Responsib. J. **18**(1) (2000). http://archive.cpsr.net/publications/newsletters/issues/2000/winter2000/herring.html. Accessed 23 Jan 2020
23. Hutt, S., Gardner, M., Duckworth, A.L., D'Mello, S.K.: Evaluating fairness and generalizability in models predicting on-time graduation from college applications. In: The 12th International Conference on Educational Data Mining (EDM), Montréal, Canada, pp. 79–88 (2019)

24. Joksimovic, S., Gasevic, D., Kovanovic, V., Adesope, O., Hatala, M.: Psychological characteristics in cognitive presence of communities of inquiry: a linguistic analysis of online discussions. Internet High. Educ. **22**, 1–10 (2014)
25. Kilis, S., Yıldırım, Z.: Investigation of community of inquiry framework in regard to self-regulation, metacognition and motivation. Comput. Educ. **126**, 53–64 (2018)
26. Koenig, K., Schen, M., Edwards, M., Bao, L.: Addressing stem retention through a scientific thought and methods course. J. Coll. Sci. Teach. **41**(4), 23–29 (2012)
27. Kovanovic, V., Joksimovic, S., Gasevic, D., Hatala, M.: Automated Cognitive Presence Detection in Online Discussion Transcripts (2014). http://nlp.stanford.edu/software/corenlp.shtml
28. Kramer, I.M., Kusurkar, R.A.: Science-writing in the blogosphere as a tool to promote autonomous motivation in education. Internet High. Educ. **35**, 48–62 (2017)
29. Lin, Y., Dowell, N., Godfrey, A., Choi, H., Brooks, C.: Modeling gender dynamics in intra and interpersonal interactions during online collaborative learning. In: Proceedings of the 9th International Conference on Learning Analytics & Knowledge, pp. 431–435 (2019)
30. Marie Jackson, S., Marie, S.: The influence of implicit and explicit gender bias on grading, and the effectiveness of rubrics for reducing bias repository citation. Technical report. https://corescholar.libraries.wright.edu/etd_all/1529
31. Moore, R.L., Oliver, K.M., Wang, C.: Setting the pace: examining cognitive processing in MOOC discussion forums with automatic text analysis. Interact. Learn. Environ. **27**(5–6), 655–669 (2019)
32. Nguyen, D., Doğruöz, A.S., Rosé, C.P., de Jong, F.: Computational sociolinguistics: a survey. Comput. Linguist. **42**(3), 537–593 (2016)
33. Oliver, K.M., Houchins, J.K., Moore, R.L., et al.: Informing makerspace outcomes through a linguistic analysis of written and video-recorded project assessments. Int. J. Sci. Math. Educ. (2020). https://doi.org/10.1007/s10763-020-10060-2
34. Pennebaker, J.W., Boyd, R.L., Jordan, K., Blackburn, K.: The development and psychometric properties of LIWC2015. Technical report (2015)
35. Pennebaker, J.W., Chung, C.K., Frazee, J., Lavergne, G.M., Beaver, D.I.: When small words foretell academic success: the case of college admissions essays. PLoS One **9**(12), e115844 (2014)
36. Robinson, C., Yeomans, M., Reich, J., Hulleman, C., Gehlbach, H.: Forecasting student achievement in MOOCs with natural language processing. In: Proceedings of the Sixth International Conference on Learning Analytics & Knowledge, pp. 383–387 (2016)
37. Rovai, A.P.: Development of an instrument to measure classroom community. Internet High. Educ. **5**(3), 197–211 (2002)
38. Sell, J., Farreras, I.G.: Liwc-ing at a century of introductory college textbooks: have the sentiments changed? Procedia Comput. Sci. **118**, 108–112 (2017)
39. Seymour, E., Hewitt, N.M.: Talking About Leaving. Westview Press, Boulder (1997)
40. Shapiro, D., Dundar, A., Huie, F., Wakhungu, P., Bhimdiwala, A., Wilson, S.: Completing college: a state-level view of student completion rates (signature report no. 16a). Technical report, National Student Clearinghouse Research Center, Herndon, VA (2019)
41. Swan, K., Matthews, D., Bogle, L., Boles, E., Day, S.: Linking online course design and implementation to learning outcomes: a design experiment. Internet High. Educ. **15**(2), 81–88 (2012)

42. Tausczik, Y.R., Pennebaker, J.W.: The psychological meaning of words: LIWC and computerized text analysis methods. J. Lang. Soc. Psychol. **29**(1), 24–54 (2010)
43. Wise, A.F., Cui, Y.: Unpacking the relationship between discussion forum participation and learning in MOOCs. In: Proceedings of the 8th International Conference on Learning Analytics and Knowledge - LAK 2018, pp. 330–339. ACM Press, New York (2018)
44. Wise, A.F., Cui, Y., Jin, W.Q., Vytasek, J.: Mining for gold: Identifying content-related MOOC discussion threads across domains through linguistic modeling. Internet High. Educ. **32**, 11–28 (2017)
45. Wladis, C., Hachey, A.C., Conway, K.: Which STEM majors enroll in online courses, and why should we care? The impact of ethnicity, gender, and non-traditional student characteristics. Comput. Educ. **87**, 285–308 (2015)
46. Yang, J.C., Quadir, B., Chen, N.S., Miao, Q.: Effects of online presence on learning performance in a blog-based online course. Internet High. Educ. **30**, 11–20 (2016)
47. Yu, R., Li, Q., Fischer, C., Doroudi, S., Xu, D.: Towards accurate and fair prediction of college success: evaluating different sources of student data. In: Proceedings of the 13th International Conference on Educational Data Mining (EDM 2020) (2020)

SoundHunters: Increasing Learner Phonological Awareness in Plains Cree

Delaney Lothian, Gokce Akcayir⑩, Anaka Sparrow, Owen Mcleod⑩,
and Carrie Demmans Epp⁽✉⁾ ⑩

EdTeKLA Research Group, University of Alberta, Edmonton, AB, Canada
{dlothian,akcayir,asparrow,omcleod,cdemmansepp}@ualberta.ca

Abstract. Indigenous languages have been dying out due to colonial practices that limited and even punished their use. For this reason, there is a need to support the maintenance and revitalization of these languages as part of the reconciliation process. However, there has been little research to guide the use of technology in supporting language revitalization. To contribute to this process, this study investigated the use of a novel e-learning activity for a specific Indigenous language - Plains Cree (nehiyawewin). This activity, SoundHunters, targets the development of learner phonological awareness (i.e., their ability to understand and manipulate sounds in a language) through game play. A mixed-methods study was used to measure learning and explore learner experiences. Learner performance on a transcription task, which required the mapping of sounds to characters, improved following SoundHunters use. The nature of learner errors indicates the development of learners' interlanguage and provides evidence of transfer from English to Cree. Additionally, learners enjoyed the activity while finding it appropriately challenging. These results show the potential for using adaptive technology to support learning in low-resource settings, such as those that exist for most Indigenous languages.

Keywords: Computer assisted language learning · Indigenous languages · Listening skills

1 Introduction

Canada wants to reconcile its previous actions against Indigenous peoples in Canada who have historically been mistreated and oppressed. In 2015, the Truth and Reconciliation Commission of Canada (TRC) released a report calling for the government to take action towards reconciliation [49]. One of the calls to action was the revitalization of the many Indigenous languages and cultures within Canada.

Like with learning any language, learning Indigenous languages includes the acquisition of reading, writing, speaking, and listening skills. Within these, excelling in listening

The original version of this chapter was revised: The reference numbers 28 and 34 have been updated. The correction to this chapter is available at
https://doi.org/10.1007/978-3-030-52237-7_50

and speaking requires phonological awareness which is knowledge of how sounds are used within a language [5]. This awareness gradually develops throughout childhood for one's first language, but it needs to be nurtured when learning additional languages [2]. Phonological awareness facilitates learners' speaking and listening skills. Supporting the development of these skills is of primary importance because of the oral traditions that are common amongst Indigenous cultures in Canada. The need for technologies to support this type of learning is pronounced because of the limited access learners have to instructors or speakers and the prevalence of dictionary-like vocabulary tools that fail to meet this community-identified need [35]. The current lack of ingenuity and adaptivity in the language-learning technologies that are available to learners of Indigenous languages [35] means that there has been little research investigating their effectiveness. Given this lack of investigation, we do not know which approaches support the development of the skills necessary for engaging in the learning practices that are of cultural value to specific Indigenous communities.

One of the approaches that might help learners develop core skills is game-based learning which has been garnering continued attention [10, 56]. Its affordances such as providing immersive exposure to the language and decreasing anxiety [26], as well as creating an entertaining and interactive learning experience have contributed to its use within language learning. These are important factors in language learning because learners' willingness to use a language can foster improvement [1].

In addition to supporting language learning, game-based learning can trigger intrinsic motivation in learners [32] which might help them overcome the barriers that they face during learning. This additional motivation is especially important to Indigenous language learning as there are many social, technical, and access barriers to acquiring these languages [21, 35, 37]. The popularity of Duolingo has demonstrated technology's ability to provide a captivating language learning experience [24]. For these reasons, a game-based e-learning activity that aims to develop learner phonological awareness could support Indigenous language learning as learner knowledge of phonology is predictive of several other language learning tasks [52].

2 Related Literature

Language learning has a long history of using games and simulations in both digital and non-digital learning contexts [12]. Most studies of technology used to support language learning have focused on enhancing the vocabulary knowledge of learners [9, 17, 54], with only a handful of systems using adaptive features to support oral language acquisition. For example, VocabNomad was a mobile communication support tool that enabled listening and pronunciation practice with recommendations being used to expose learners to new vocabulary items [16, 18]. Many other systems focus on supporting grammar instruction [9]. Among the systems and approaches that support learner's grammatical knowledge and writing skills are Grammarly [38] and the use of machine learning approaches for detecting or correcting grammatical errors [48]. When investigating the combined impact of feedback with such approaches, the addition of self-explanation within an adaptive grammar tutor failed to improve retention over practice alone [55]. Other than feedback and practice, a learner's writing abilities benefit from improved reading proficiency as increased receptive knowledge is predictive of productive knowledge [53]. Keeping this in mind, a system that was designed to support English language learners when they are trying to read authentic texts [57] might benefit both skills. However, the effectiveness of this system has yet to be evaluated. As summarized in reviews [45] and demonstrated by the above explorations and system designs, most adaptive computer-assisted language learning applications have focused on receptive skills (e.g., grammar, reading) or text-based approaches. This may be partly due to the technological and other challenges associated with supporting oral and productive language learning activities [31].

While less studied [9, 17], investigations examining how to improve language learners' speaking and listening have used a variety of technologies. One investigation showed that the most common learning activities performed by migrant language learners involved the repurposing of existing technologies to support pronunciation modelling and self-testing [17]. These types of interactions are dependent upon several features that include the ability to record, play audio or produce language through speech synthesis, and automatically analyze learner speech. One commercial technology that aimed to promote the identification and production of sounds used speech recognition to provide feedback on English language learners' pronunciation of single words [47]. Similarly, a game-based adaptive pronunciation tutor provided feedback on learner pronunciation [19]. This tutor was well received by language learners even though it was not shown to improve their phonemic awareness or pronunciation. In contrast, findings from a study where a mobile game was used to promote speaking and listening skills suggested the game only supported the improvement of learners' speaking abilities [28]. In contrast, a popular commercial language-learning application that includes activities which are expected to support the development of phonological awareness (i.e., Duolingo) was associated with improved listening skills [44], and an experimental system, called ToneWars, helped learners develop their declarative knowledge of Chinese tones through collaboration and competition [20]. Going beyond the simpler interactions seen in the above systems, the investigation of one of the few simulation-based systems that effectively supports language learning revealed that those who performed well in foundational skill-based activities, such as phonemic awareness, also performed better in simulation tasks [29]. A more recent example that aims to support communication practice focuses on adding features to agents in a way that will increase learner willingness to communicate [1].

A scoping review on the use of games in language learning revealed that 94% of studies were focused on English as an additional language [26] even though other languages could benefit from these types of approaches. It has even been argued that this class of approaches might help revitalize endangered and threatened Indigenous languages [22]. However, this vision has yet to be realized. In one attempt to support Indigenous language revitalization, Parker and colleagues [39] designed a game to support learners of Blackfoot (an Indigenous language in North America). This game asked players to follow instructions in Blackfoot to achieve a set of sub-goals; however, its effectiveness was not evaluated with users. Another study introduced a computer-based language learning activity to families who want to learn Ojibwe (anishinaabemowin): an Indigenous language spoken in North America. This activity aimed to promote Ojibwe acquisition by incorporating language learning into family activities [25]. An adaptive system for the appropriate use of pronouns in Maori (an Indigenous language in New Zealand) showed similar performance gains as those obtained from standard tutorials [51]. So far, the sole adaptive system for supporting the acquisition of Plains Cree (nehiyawewin) grammar has only been evaluated from the perspective of people's opinion about the system's design [6].

As can be seen in the literature, many technological approaches to supporting language learning can advance learner skills and knowledge. Although, some of them add little benefit over non-adaptive approaches (e.g., [55]). We have yet to see the evaluation of the effectiveness of adaptive or other language learning technologies for Indigenous languages. Given this information and a need for effective educational resources to support Indigenous language learning [34], we created a game that aims to support the development of phonological awareness in Plains Cree (nehiyawewin) with the hope that it would be the first step in a series that supports improved listening and speaking skills among learners.

3   Method

A mixed-methods approach was used where qualitative and quantitative data were triangulated [14]. This approach provided a holistic view of learners' experience and knowledge acquisition [50].

3.1   Learning Technology: SoundHunters

The approach under investigation was inspired by the arcade game called Space Invaders. Instead of defending against an alien invasion, the game asks learners to differentiate between sets of characters and identify the one that matches the sounds they are hearing. Note that there are two common ways that Cree is written, and within this study we will be focusing on the Standard Roman Orthography (SRO) writing system which is composed of eight consonants, two semi-vowels, and seven vowels.

The temporal pressure aspect of the game mechanics was used to help support the development of student fluency [42]. When the game starts, the user sees two to four deer move down the screen (Fig. 1). Each deer has text attached at its side. The learner is then given a sound that corresponds to one of the deer's text (i.e., the correct answer). This sound repeats until the learner identifies and shoots the correct deer.

SoundHunters has four tasks. The first tests the user's knowledge of sound to single character mappings, which is the base unit. The second tests their knowledge of the mapping between sounds and character pairs on the way to developing an understanding of how sound-to-character mappings interact when they are grouped into larger units. The third task tests their ability to distinguish minimal pairs (i.e., two words that are identical except for one sound, such as sun and fun), which is known to support the development of phonological awareness. The fourth task tests the user's ability to identify the word that was said and is the most ecologically valid task as learners will typically have to understand full words when interacting with others. Each task has three difficulty levels: easy, medium, and hard.

The difficulty for the first two tasks is determined in the same way. In both, distractor types are defined based on their similarity to the audio and visual cues associated with the target item (i.e., correct answer). When providing examples, we also provide an international phonetic alphabet (IPA) pronunciation guide. An example of a distractor

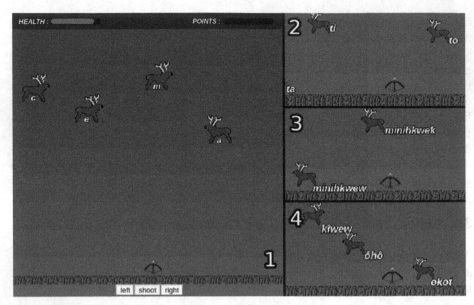

Fig. 1. Screenshots from game play. 1 shows the full screen for task 1. Images 2 through 4 show a close up of the types of stimuli in tasks 2 through 4 respectively.

that includes aspects of both orthography and phonology would be "ô" (as in moose or u in IPA) which is audibly and visually similar to o (as in put or ʊ in IPA). We refer to these types of distractors as bidimensional. A unidimensional distractor would be similar with respect to a single channel (i.e., audio or visual). For example, 'e' (as in bet or ε in IPA) sounds similar to 'â' (as in fa or father - ɑ in IPA) but is not visually similar. A simple distractor would be a distractor that is neither visually nor audibly similar. For example, 't' is neither audibly nor visually similar to 'a' (as in cut or ə in IPA).

For both tasks one and two, the user is presented with two simple distractors and the correct answer at the easy level. At the medium difficulty level, the user is presented with a combination of three simple or unidimensional distractors and the correct answer. At the hard level, the user is presented with a combination of three unidimensional or bidimensional distractors and the correct answer. At the hard level, the speed at which the distractors descend also increases.

The nature of the third task limits the number of potential distractors to one. Consequently, the difficulty of the distractor in this task is based on its length and increased speed for the hard level.

The fourth task requires the user to identify the difference between words. Distractors were randomly chosen. Like task three, the difficulty was determined by the length of the word and the speed at which items descend. The speed increased for the medium level and again for the hard level. At the easy level, the user was presented with the correct answer plus two distractors. At the medium and hard level, they were presented with the correct answer plus three distractors.

3.2 Participants

Participants were recruited via advertisements that included social media posts, posters around campus, and classroom announcements. Participant ages ranged from 19 to 76 (M = 25.9, SD = 11.68); 2 did not provide their age. Of the 25 participants, 13 were female, 11 male, and 1 participant opted not to specify. All were native English speakers who do not know Plains Cree. However, 4 said they can identify Plains Cree when they hear it. Participants were assigned a numeric identifier. This identifier (e.g., P1) is used to indicate which participant a quote originated from.

3.3 Data Collection

This study and its methods were pre-registered (https://osf.io/xjy4v). As planned, we used two measures to evaluate both the effectiveness of SoundHunters and learners' experience. These measures consist of a Cree knowledge test (as pre-test and post-test) and a questionnaire to evaluate player experience.

As a knowledge test, we asked participants to transcribe two short recordings of someone speaking in Cree. Each recording contained approximately 5–10 words in a single sentence. Each recording was 3–5 s long and the participant was allowed to listen to it a maximum of 3 times without pausing. Different recordings were used for the pre- and post-test. Scoring was handled based on correctness of the letters. Each correct letter earned one point. A half point was given to letters that do not exist in Plains Cree when their English sound represents a valid sound in Cree. An example would be if the user wrote 'g' in place of 'k'. The 'k' sound in Cree often sounds like 'g' in English, but 'g' is not used in SRO. The percentage of accumulated scores according to the number of letters in the correct answer (maximum score) are reported.

User experience was evaluated using the Model for Evaluating Educational Games (MEEGA+). This instrument was developed to analyze educational games and was reported to have high reliability (Cronbach's $\alpha = 0.928$) with its subscales established through factor analysis [40].

3.4 Data Analysis

For the knowledge test, the normalized learning gain of each player was calculated [23, 41]. Additionally, using a paired sample t-test, we determined whether performance on the transcription test improved following system use. This test was conducted after determining that data followed a normal distribution. Errors on the pre- and post-test were grouped based on how the participant responded. These errors were compared across tests to identify evidence of changes in participant knowledge of specific sound-to-character mappings.

The analysis of the qualitative data began with reviewing the data from the perspective of participants' learning experience [46]. After that, we conducted thematic analysis to reveal themes within their learning experiences [8]. This process started with identifying codes which are expressions that relate to participants' learning experience. Then, these codes were grouped around themes and data were reviewed to confirm these themes. This process was handled by a researcher who has a PhD in educational technology and is experienced in qualitative data analysis. All steps of the process were reviewed and confirmed by another researcher to increase reliability (as in [43]).

4   Results

4.1   Increased Phonological Awareness

A paired-samples t-test of the phonemic knowledge tests revealed a significant improvement in learner performance ($t(24) = -6.85, p < .001, d = 1.37$) from the pre-test ($M = 49.37, SD = 8.56$) to the post-test ($M = 58.50, SD = 8.74$). Participants' normalized learning gain showed considerable improvement, 95% CI = [0.12, 0.23], given that participants interacted with the system for approximately 49 min ($M = 49$ min. 21 s, $SD = 6$ min. 2 s).

In addition to measurable changes in their knowledge, participants' open-ended responses indicate they learned Cree words or sounds which implies increased phonological awareness of Cree: "As levels progressed, I found I had a better understanding of different sounds" (P16) and "I feel like you get more used to the letters/sounds as you advance" (P14).

An examination of the errors participants made on the pre- and post-tests, indicates many mistakes were consistent across tests. These mistakes included using "e" (as in bet or ɛ in IPA) instead of "i" (as in sit or ɪ in IPA), or "oo" instead of "ô" (as in moose or u in IPA). These mistakes reflect the differences in the sound-to-character mappings between English (participants' native language) and Plains Cree. Along with these persistent errors, there were some types of errors that were different across tests. In the pre-tests, learners did not use accents where they were needed, such as using i and o (as in put or ʊ in IPA) instead of î (as in feel or i in IPA) and ô, whereas accents were observed in the post tests. In some cases, this meant that learners were using accents where they were not needed (e.g., ê instead of e, as e never takes an accent). Similarly, some consonants such as "h" and "w" were absent from the pre-test (e.g., waya was written instead of wâhyaw pronounced wɑhyaʊ in IPA). In contrast, users included these consonants both where they were needed (e.g., mahtesa pronounced məhtesə in IPA) and in other locations which demonstrated negative transfer of sound-to-character mappings from English to Cree. For example, chin was written instead of cin, which is the SRO representation that is pronounced tsɪn in IPA.

4.2   Learner Experience

Figure 2 shows the distribution of participant responses to the learning experience questionnaire. Overall, participants reported positive experiences and positive perceptions of their learning. Their perception that they learned Cree sounds is consistent with the gains seen from the pre-test to the post-test. The themes that emerged from participant comments on their learning experience included the perceived learning of Cree words, having a positive learning experience, and facilitating learner attention.

The questionnaire results indicate that participating learners were challenged, had fun, and were highly satisfied with their learning experiences. Their open-ended comments confirm this finding of the game facilitating a positive learning experience. As participants said,

Fig. 2. Learners' play experience with SoundHunters

P9: "I really enjoyed the game. I thought it was a new and interesting way to help learn some basics on Cree word/sound structure. The game itself was simple enough that it didn't take away from learning but fun enough to keep interest".

P17: "The game was a cool and easy way to learn Cree words/sounds. It was really useful to see both the spelling on screen and hear the sounds."

P13: "Finally hitting the correct target was very satisfying"

Even though participants enjoyed learning in this way, their perceptions with respect to preferred learning approach did not necessarily indicate that using SoundHunters would be their first choice (Relevance, item 1, in Fig. 2). Their responses to the focused attention related items of the questionnaire indicate the game could have better captured their full attention even though their open-ended responses indicate that it helped them to focus on performing the learning task without making them feel like they were engaged in a learning activity: "It did grab my attention throughout playing the game" (P19) and it is a "learning tool where you can forget you're learning" (P12). One learner also stated that "it was simple enough and engaging to play" (P9), suggesting that its simplicity contributed to its capturing their attention.

5 Discussion

We explored the use of a game to improve phonological awareness for Indigenous language learning. The learning observed in this study provides empirical evidence for informal game-based learning practices, which generally lack strong support [7]. The observed improvement in participants' ability to map sounds to characters can be interpreted as a sign of the game's appropriate difficulty levels for the target audience since language-learning technologies that fail to provide the right amount of challenge are associated with a lack of learning [36].

Along with the amount of challenge, the type of interactivity provided could play a role in the activity's effectiveness, as some types of interactions that learners have with games have been associated with increased vocabulary retention [15]. In our game, the primary interaction with the user was through a combination of sounds and text which probably played an important role in the success of the game. These interactions are consistent with the learning objective of increasing learner phonemic awareness, with improvements shown through assessments that required learners to map sounds to characters, which is a fundamental component of phonemic awareness [4]. The repetition involved in the game is likely to have contributed to the measured improvements as repetition provides practice opportunities [13].

Learners' comments and questionnaire responses indicate they responded positively to this learning technology. More specifically, participants said they felt more like they were playing than studying, suggesting that the activity format eliminated the negative emotions, such as anxiety [27, 56], that are associated with foreign language learning as well as the learning of Indigenous languages [35]. As family-based approaches have helped improve Indigenous language learning [25] in other contexts, further game activities can be developed in a way that allows collaborative play so that families can engage with the learning activities together. This would additionally help to mitigate generational differences in Indigenous language learning.

Some of the errors participants made in the post-test indicated negative transfer, which is the expansion and use of existing knowledge from a well-known language to that of another language [3]. In this case, negative transfer was seen through the application of sound-to-character mappings from English during a Cree transcription task. To mitigate negative transfer, further activities can be planned to explicitly point out differences between these two languages [33]. The observed errors additionally provide evidence of the development of learners' interlanguage, which is a part of the language-learning process where learners combine characteristics of the first and additional languages [11] en route to eventual mastery of the target language if they persist.

6 Conclusion

In the last two decades, youth interest in learning their own Indigenous languages has been steadily increasing [21, 30]. However, these languages have few resources [34], research-informed learning activities [37], or personalized systems [6, 35] that learners can access to support their learning. Consistent with this, the need to develop technologies that support Indigenous language learning has been identified by community members [35]. To help meet this need, this study provided a novel instructional activity that promotes listening by developing learners' phonological awareness of Plains Cree using an adaptive game. Increases in learner knowledge as measured through a receptive task, demonstrate the potential for these types of activities, especially when considering how they enable access to learning that may not otherwise be possible, provide a safe practice environment where learners can afford to take risks, and transform the learning of an Indigenous language from something that was previously punishable to something that is enjoyable.

Acknowledgements. We acknowledge the support of the Natural Sciences and Engineering Research Council of Canada (NSERC) [RGPIN-2018-03834] and National Research Council Canada [contract 932832]. As part of our funding agreement, all code will be made publicly available through GitHub: https://github.com/EdTeKLA.

References

1. Ayedoun, E., Hayashi, Y., Seta, K.: L2 learners' preferences of dialogue agents: a key to achieve adaptive motivational support? In: Isotani, S., Millán, E., Ogan, A., Hastings, P., McLaren, B., Luckin, R. (eds.) AIED 2019. LNCS (LNAI), vol. 11626, pp. 19–23. Springer, Cham (2019). https://doi.org/10.1007/978-3-030-23207-8_4
2. Bae, H.S.: Metalinguistic awareness in vocabulary acquisition: evidence from grade six Korean EFL learners. Prim. Engl. Educ. 21(3), 5–22 (2015)
3. Bai, L., Qin, J.: A study of negative language transfer in college students' writing from cultural perspective. Theory Pract. Lang. Stud. 8(3), 306–313 (2018). https://doi.org/10.17507/tpls.0803.05
4. Binder, K.S., Talwar, A., Bond, N.K., Cote, N.G.: From "Degisned" and "Dezine" to "Design". In: Perin, D. (ed.) The Wiley Handbook of Adult Literacy (2020). https://doi.org/10.1002/9781119261407.ch6
5. Blachman, B.A.: Phonological awareness. In: Kamil, M.L., Mosenthal, P.B., Pearson, P.D., Barr, R. (eds.) Handbook of Reading Research, pp. 483–502 Lawrence Erlbaum Associates Publishers, Mahwah (2016)

6. Bontogon, M., Arppe, A., Antonsen, L., Thunder, D., Lachler, J.: Intelligent computer assisted language learning (ICALL) for nêhiyawêwin: an in-depth user-experience evaluation. Can. Mod. Lang. Rev. **74**(3), 337–362 (2018). https://doi.org/10.3138/cmlr.4054

7. Boyle, E.A., et al.: An update to the systematic literature review of empirical evidence of the impacts and outcomes of computer games and serious games. Comput. Educ. **94**, 178–192 (2016). https://doi.org/10.1016/j.compedu.2015.11.003

8. Braun, V., Clarke, V.: Using thematic analysis in psychology. Qual. Res. Psychol. **3**(2), 77–101 (2006). https://doi.org/10.1191/1478088706qp063oa

9. Burston, J.: The reality of MALL: still on the fringes. CALICO J. **31**(1), 103–125 (2014). https://doi.org/10.11139/cj.31.1.103-125

10. Chen, C.H., Liu, J.H., Shou, W.C.: How competition in a game-based science learning environment influences students' learning achievement, flow experience, and learning behavioral patterns. Educ. Technol. Soc. **21**(2), 164–176 (2018). www.jstor.org/stable/26388392

11. Chen, H., Xu, H.: Quantitative linguistics approach to interlanguage development: a study based on the Guangwai-Lancaster Chinese Learner Corpus. Lingua **230**, 1–15 (2019). https://doi.org/10.1016/j.lingua.2019.102736

12. Connolly, T.M., Stansfield, M., Hainey, T.: An alternate reality game for language learning: ARGuing for multilingual motivation. Comput. Educ. **57**(1), 1389–1415 (2011). https://doi.org/10.1016/j.compedu.2011.01.009

13. Coyne, R.: Mindless repetition: learning from computer games. Des. Stud. **24**(3), 199–212 (2003). https://doi.org/10.1016/S0142-694X(02)00052-2

14. Creswell, J.W.: Research Design: Qualitative, Quantitative, and Mixed Methods Approaches. Sage Publications, Thousand Oaks (2014)

15. DeHaan, J., Reed, M.W., Kuwada, K.: The effect of interactivity with a music video game on second language vocabulary recall. Lang. Learn. Technol. **14**(2), 74–94 (2010)

16. Demmans Epp, C., Tsourounis, S., Djordjevic, J., Baecker, R.M.: Interactive event: enabling vocabulary acquisition while providing mobile communication support. In: Lane, H.C., Yacef, K., Mostow, J., Pavlik, P. (eds.) AIED 2013. LNCS (LNAI), vol. 7926, pp. 932–933. Springer, Heidelberg (2013). https://doi.org/10.1007/978-3-642-39112-5_150

17. Demmans Epp, C.: Migrants and mobile technology use: gaps in the support provided by current tools. J. Interact. Media Educ. **1**(2), 1–13 (2017). https://doi.org/10.5334/jime.432

18. Demmans Epp, C.: Mobile adaptive communication support for vocabulary acquisition. In: Lane, H.C., Yacef, K., Mostow, J., Pavlik, P. (eds.) AIED 2013. LNCS (LNAI), vol. 7926, pp. 876–879. Springer, Heidelberg (2013). https://doi.org/10.1007/978-3-642-39112-5_135

19. Demmans Epp, C., McCalla, G.: ProTutor: historic open learner models for pronunciation tutoring. In: Biswas, G., Bull, S., Kay, J., Mitrovic, A. (eds.) AIED 2011. LNCS (LNAI), vol. 6738, pp. 441–443. Springer, Heidelberg (2011). https://doi.org/10.1007/978-3-642-21869-9_63

20. Fan, X., Luo, W., Wang, J.: Mastery learning of second language through asynchronous modeling of native speakers in a collaborative mobile game. In: Proceedings of the CHI Conference on Human Factors in Computing Systems, pp. 4887–4898. ACM, New York (2017). https://doi.org/10.1145/3025453.3025544

21. Galla, C.K.: Indigenous language revitalization, promotion, and education: function of digital technology. Comput. Assist. Lang. Learn. **29**(7), 1137–1151 (2016). https://doi.org/10.1080/09588221.2016.1166137

22. Galla, C.K.: Indigenous language revitalization and technology from traditional to contemporary domains. In: Reyhner, J., Lockard, L. (eds.) Indigenous Language Revitalization: Encouragement, Guidance & Lessons Learned, pp. 167–182. Northern Arizona University, Flagstaff (2009)

23. Hake, R.R.: Interactive-engagement versus traditional methods: a six-thousand-student survey of mechanics test data for introductory physics courses. Am. J. Phys. **66**(1), 64–74 (1998). https://doi.org/10.1119/1.18809

24. Hampton, A.J., Nye, B.D., Pavlik, P.I., Swartout, W.R., Graesser, A.C., Gunderson, J.: Mitigating knowledge decay from instruction with voluntary use of an adaptive learning system. In: Penstein Rosé, C., et al. (eds.) AIED 2018. LNCS (LNAI), vol. 10948, pp. 119–133. Springer, Cham (2018). https://doi.org/10.1007/978-3-319-93846-2_23

25. Hermes, M., King, K.A.: Ojibwe language revitalization, multimedia technology, and family language learning. Lang. Learn. Technol. **17**(1), 125–144 (2013). https://dx.doi.org/10125/24513

26. Hung, H.-T., Yang, J.C., Hwang, G., Chu, H., Wang, C.: A scoping review of research on digital game-based language learning. Comput. Educ. **126**, 89–104 (2018). https://doi.org/10.1016/j.compedu.2018.07.001

27. Hwang, G.J., Hsu, T.-C., Lai, C.-L., Hsueh, C.-J.: Interaction of problem-based gaming and learning anxiety in language students' English listening performance and progressive behavioral patterns. Comput. Educ. **106**, 26–42 (2017). https://doi.org/10.1016/j.compedu.2016.11.010

28. Hwang, W.-Y., Shih, T.K., Ma, Z.-H., Shadiev, R., Chen, S.-Y.: Evaluating listening and speaking skills in a mobile game-based learning environment with situational contexts. Comput. Assist. Lang. Learn. **29**(4), 639–657 (2016). https://doi.org/10.1080/09588221.2015.1016438

29. Johnson, W.L., Wu, S.: Assessing aptitude for learning with a serious game for foreign language and culture. In: Woolf, B.P., Aïmeur, E., Nkambou, R., Lajoie, S. (eds.) ITS 2008. LNCS, vol. 5091, pp. 520–529. Springer, Heidelberg (2008). https://doi.org/10.1007/978-3-540-69132-7_55

30. Krauss, M.: The condition of Native North American languages: the need for realistic assessment and action. Int. J. Soc. Lang. **132**, 9–21 (1998). https://doi.org/10.1515/ijsl.1998.132.9

31. Levy, M., Hubbard, P., Stockwell, G., Colpaert, J.: Research challenges in CALL. Comput. Assist. Lang. Learn. **28**, 1–6 (2015). https://doi.org/10.1080/09588221.2014.987035

32. Lin, C.H., Huang, S., Shih, J., Covaci, A., Ghinea, G.: Game-based learning effectiveness and motivation study between competitive and cooperative modes. In: Proceedings of 17th International Conference on Advanced Learning Technologies (ICALT), pp. 123-127. IEEE, Timisoara (2017). https://doi.org/10.1109/ICALT.2017.34

33. Linck, J., Michael, E., Golonka, E., Twist, A., Schwieter, J.W.: Moving beyond two languages: the effects of multilingualism on language processing and language learning. In: Schwieter, J. (ed.) The Cambridge Handbook of Bilingual Processing, pp. 665–694 (2015). https://doi.org/10.1017/cbo9781107447257.030

34. Littell, P., Kazantseva, A., Kuhn, R., Pine, A., Arppe, A., Cox, C., Junker, M.-O.: Indigenous language technologies in Canada: assessment, challenges, and successes. In: Proceedings of the 27th International Conference on Computational Linguistics. pp. 2620–2632. Association for Computational Linguistics, Santa Fe, New Mexico, USA (2018). https://www.aclweb.org/anthology/C18-1222/

35. Lothian, D., Akcayir, G., Demmans Epp, C.: Accommodating Indigenous people when using technology to learn their ancestral language. In: McCalla, F., Gutierrez, J., Olakanmi, O., Ishola, O. (eds.) International Workshop on Supporting Lifelong Learning co-located with the 20th International Conference on Artificial Intelligence in Education, vol. 2395, pp. 16–22 (2019). http://ceur-ws.org/Vol-2395/

36. Ma, Z.-H., Hwang, W., Chen, S., Ding, W.: Digital game-based after-school-assisted learning system in English. In: 2012 International Symposium on Intelligent Signal Processing and Communications Systems, pp. 130–135. IEEE, Taipei (2012). https://doi.org/10.1109/ISP ACS.2012.6473466

37. McIvor, O.: îkakwiy nîhiyawiyân : I am learning [to be] Cree. University of British Columbia (2012). https://doi.org/10.14288/1.0078368

38. ONeill, R., Russell, A.: Stop! Grammar time: university students' perceptions of the automated feedback program Grammarly. Australas. J. Educ. Technol. 35(1), 42–56 (2019). https://doi.org/10.14742/ajet.3795

39. Parker, J.R., Heavy Head, R., Becker, K.: Technical aspects of a system for teaching aboriginal languages using a game boy. In: Future Play, the International Conference on the Future of Game Design and Technology (2005)

40. Petri, G., Wangenheim, C.G., Borgatto, A.F.: MEEGA+, systematic model to evaluate educational games. In: Lee, N. (ed.) Encyclopedia of Computer Graphics and Games, pp. 1–7. Springer, Cham (2018). https://doi.org/10.1007/978-3-319-08234-9_214-1

41. Prather, E.E., Rudolph, A.L., Brissenden, G.: Teaching and learning astronomy in the 21st century. Phys. Today 62(10), 41–47 (2009). https://doi.org/10.1063/1.3248478

42. Presson, N., MacWhinney, B., Tokowicz, N.: Learning grammatical gender: The use of rules by novice learners. Appl. Psycholinguist. 35(4), 709–737 (2014). https://doi.org/10.1017/S01 42716412000550

43. Psaila, K., Fowler, C., Kruske, S., Schmied, V.: A qualitative study of innovations implemented to improve transition of care from maternity to child and family health (CFH) services in Australia. Women Birth 27(4), e51–e60 (2014). https://doi.org/10.1016/j.wombi.2014.08.004

44. Putri, L.M., Islamiati, A.: Teaching listening using Duolingo application. Proj. (Prof. J. Engl. Educ.) 1(4), 460 (2018). https://doi.org/10.22460/project.v1i4.p460-465

45. Schulze, M., Heift, T.: Intelligent CALL. In: Thomas, M., et al. (eds.) Contemporary Computer-Assisted Language Learning, pp. 249–265. Bloomsbury, London (2012)

46. Strauss, A.L.: Qualitative Analysis for Social Scientists. Cambridge University Press, San Francisco (1987). https://doi.org/10.1017/CBO9780511557842

47. Tao, R.: Eyespeak. CALICO J. 25(1), 126–136 (2008)

48. Troussas, C., Chrysafiadi, K., Virvou, M.: Machine learning and fuzzy logic techniques for personalized tutoring of foreign languages. In: Penstein Rosé, C., et al. (eds.) AIED 2018. LNCS (LNAI), vol. 10948, pp. 358–362. Springer, Cham (2018). https://doi.org/10.1007/978-3-319-93846-2_67

49. Truth and Reconciliation Commission of Canada: Truth and reconciliation commission of Canada: Calls to action (2015). http://trc.ca/assets/pdf/Calls_to_Action_English2.pdf

50. Turner, S.F., Cardinal, L.B., Burton, R.M.: Research design for mixed methods: a triangulation-based framework and roadmap. Organ. Res. Methods 20(2), 243–267 (2017). https://doi.org/10.1177/1094428115610808

51. Vlugter, P., Knott, A., McDonald, J., Hall, C.: Dialogue-based CALL: a case study on teaching pronouns. Comput. Assist. Lang. Learn. 22(2), 115–131 (2009). https://doi.org/10.1080/095 88220902778260

52. Wade-Woolley, L., Geva, E.: Processing novel phonemic contrasts in the acquisition of L2 word reading. Sci. Stud. Read. 4(4), 295–311 (2000). https://doi.org/10.1207/S1532799X SSR0404_3

53. Wagner, R.K., Muse, A.E., Tannenbaum, K.R.: Vocabulary Acquisition: Implications for Reading Comprehension. Guilford Press, New York (2007)
54. Wang, S., Wu, H., Kim, J.H., Andersen, E.: Adaptive learning material recommendation in online language education. In: Isotani, S., Millán, E., Ogan, A., Hastings, P., McLaren, B., Luckin, R. (eds.) AIED 2019. LNCS (LNAI), vol. 11626, pp. 298–302. Springer, Cham (2019). https://doi.org/10.1007/978-3-030-23207-8_55
55. Wylie, R., Sheng, M., Mitamura, T., Koedinger, K.R.: Effects of adaptive prompted self-explanation on robust learning of second language grammar. In: Biswas, G., Bull, S., Kay, J., Mitrovic, A. (eds.) AIED 2011. LNCS (LNAI), vol. 6738, pp. 588–590. Springer, Heidelberg (2011). https://doi.org/10.1007/978-3-642-21869-9_110
56. Yang, Q.-F., Chang, S., Hwang, G., Zou, D.: Balancing cognitive complexity and gaming level: Effects of a cognitive complexity-based competition game on EFL students' English vocabulary learning performance, anxiety and behaviors. Comput. Educ. **148**, 103808 (2020). https://doi.org/10.1016/j.compedu.2020.103808
57. Zilio, L., Fairon, C.: Adaptive system for language learning. In: 17th International Conference on Advanced Learning Technologies (ICALT), pp. 47–49. IEEE, Timisoara (2017). https://doi.org/10.1109/ICALT.2017.46

Moodoo: Indoor Positioning Analytics for Characterising Classroom Teaching

Roberto Martinez-Maldonado[1], Vanessa Echeverria[2,3], Jurgen Schulte[4], Antonette Shibani[4], Katerina Mangaroska[1,5], and Simon Buckingham Shum[4(✉)]

[1] Monash University, Melbourne, VIC, Australia
Roberto.MartinezMaldonado@monash.edu
[2] Escuela Superior Politécnica del Litoral, ESPOL, Guayaquil, Ecuador
[3] Human-Computer Interaction Institute, Carnegie Mellon University, Pittsburgh, PA, USA
[4] University of Technology Sydney, Ultimo, NSW, Australia
Simon.BuckinghamShum@uts.edu.au
[5] Norwegian University of Science and Technology, NTNU, Trondheim, Norway

Abstract. This paper presents Moodoo, a system that models how teachers make use of classroom spaces by automatically analysing indoor positioning traces. We illustrate the potential of the system through an authentic study aimed at enabling the characterisation of teachers' instructional behaviours in the classroom. Data were analysed from seven teachers delivering three distinct types of classes to + 190 students in the context of physics education. Results show exemplars of how teaching positioning traces reflect the characteristics of the learning designs and can enable the differentiation of teaching strategies related to the use of classroom space. The contribution of the paper is a set of conceptual mappings from $x - y$ positional data to meaningful constructs, grounded in the theory of Spatial Pedagogy, and its implementation as a composable library of open source algorithms. These are to our knowledge the first automated spatial metrics to map from low-level teacher's positioning data to higher-order spatial constructs.

Keywords: Spatial modelling · Indoor localisation · Learning spaces

1 Introduction

Classroom activity is ephemeral, and has largely remained opaque to computational analysis [38], with only a small number of artificial intelligence (AI) innovations targeting physical aspects of teaching and learning [16, 38, 47, 54]. However, despite the online learning revolution, physical classrooms remain pervasive across all educational levels [7]. There is a growing interest in using novel sensing technologies (e.g. wearable and computer vision systems) to automatically analyse classroom activity traces to model behaviours such as engagement [30], teacher-student interactions [10] and students' physical activity [1, 53]. Previous research has found that teachers' positioning in the classroom and proximity to students can strongly influence critical aspects such as students' engagement [14], motivation [19], disruptive behaviour [27], and self-efficacy

© Springer Nature Switzerland AG 2020
I. I. Bittencourt et al. (Eds.): AIED 2020, LNAI 12163, pp. 360–373, 2020.
https://doi.org/10.1007/978-3-030-52237-7_29

[31] (see review in [43]). Yet, most research focused on studying spatial aspects of teaching rely on observations or peer/self-assessments [11] that are hard to scale up [21], with the purpose supporting teachers, and are susceptible to bias [49].

Tracking systems have emerged recently, enabling the automated capture of positioning and proximity traces from authentic classrooms using wearables attached to students' shoes [48], computer-vision [1] and positioning trackers [18]. Some systems even summarise the time a teacher has spent in close proximity to a student or group of students, to raise an alarm if a threshold is reached (e.g. [5, 37]). However, very little work has been done in exploring what kinds of metrics researchers can generate from low-level $x - y$ positioning data that could be useful to characterise classroom activity in ways that are meaningful to educators.

This paper presents Moodoo, a system for modelling spatial teaching dynamics. We build on the foundations of Spatial Analysis [20] and Spatial Pedagogy [33] (SP), to explore and propose a set of metrics that can identify teaching positioning strategies in a classroom space. We set the system in an authentic physics education study, in which seven teachers wore indoor positioning trackers while teaching in pairs (see Fig. 1). In total we analysed 18 classes and used the findings to map the $x - y$ positional data to higher-order spatial constructs and propose a composable library of algorithms that can be used to study instructional behaviour of teachers in different teaching scenarios.

Fig. 1. Physics laboratory classroom taught by two teachers while wearing indoor positioning sensors contained in a badge (bottom-right).

2 Background and Related Work

2.1 Foundations of Spatial Pedagogy

Although fragmented across multiple areas [40], research investigating the relationship between classroom spaces and teaching processes has a long history. In the 19th century, observational studies by Barnard [8] informed the design of the teacher-centric lecture classroom to maximise surveillance of students. More contemporary works also used systematic observations to investigate how teachers' proximity to students influences aspects that can impact learning such as effective communication [46], disruptive behaviours [27, 32], sense of ownership of students' own work [25], and motivation [12].

Lim et al. [33] recently coined the term *Spatial Pedagogy* (SP) to refer to the meaning of certain spaces in the classroom depending on the positions and distances between teachers, students and classroom resources. Authors observed two teachers using the same classroom to differentiate pedagogical strategies and created state diagrams to represent the spaces of the classroom in which the teacher was moving, frequency to which a space was visited, and transitions. Chin et al. [14] conducted a similar study with four teachers. The authors of these studies suggested the need for automated approaches that could help scale up their analysis, given the potential to support teachers.

In sum, although the literature suggests that teachers' classroom positioning can have a significant effect on learning, most analyses have been based on self-report questionnaires, and observations made on some classes, visualised until recently mostly through manually produced diagrams (e.g. [33]). Automating the analysis of spatial classroom dynamics has the potential to enable new research in learning spaces that can directly support teachers with objective, accurate, and timely feedback. In the next section, we elaborate on current approaches that automatically study teachers' positioning.

2.2 Spatial Analysis and Positioning Technology in the Classroom

There has been a growing interest in exploring physical aspects of the classroom [16]. For example, authors have used automated video analysis to model students' posture [45] and gestures [1], teacher's walking [10], interactions between teachers and students [1, 53] during a lecture, and characterising the types of social interactions of students in makerspaces [15]. Wearable sensors have also been used to track teachers' orchestration tasks by using a combination of sensors (eye tracker, accelerometer, and a camera) [44] and students' mobility strategies while working in teams in the contexts of primary education [48], healthcare simulation [18] and firefighting training [51]. Some work has attempted to close the feedback loop by displaying some positioning traces back to teachers. For example, ClassBeacons [5] summarises the amount of time a teacher has spent in close proximity to groups of students and displays it through a lamp located at each group's table. Similar work displayed the same information on a screen with alarms indicating potentially neglected students [37], or simple graphs [48] and heatmaps [4] showing what parts of the classroom teachers visited the most.

The above studies indicate that there is an emerging interest in using sensing technologies to analyse teachers' positioning traces. Yet, none of these works have addressed the need for creating spatial metrics (beyond counting the times a teacher comes close to certain students) from the large amounts of indoor positioning data, that may be relevant for teachers' professional development. Whilst we can learn from metrics used in broader areas such as Spatial Analysis [20], these are commonly applied to outdoor data, in which the granularity of the positioning is coarse and the particularities of the educational context are not considered. In fact, there is an identified dearth of indoor positioning analytics tools also in non-educational contexts [13, 35, 42]. To the best of our knowledge, this paper is the first to document the implementation, and empirical validation, of automated spatial metrics that map from low-level $x - y$ teacher's positioning data to higher-order spatial constructs.

3 The Learning Context

The authentic learning situation the illustrative study focuses on was part of the regular classes of a first-year undergraduate unit at the University of technology Sydney. This includes weekly 2½ h laboratory classes (labs) in which students run experiments. A teacher and a teaching assistant both co-teach each lab in the physical classroom (see Fig. 1). Each lab typically has between 30 and 40 students working in 10–13 small teams of 2–3 students each. Eighteen labs were randomly chosen (1–18) for the study. All labs were conducted in the same (16.8 × 10 m) classroom equipped with workbenches, a lectern, a whiteboard, and multiple laboratory tools. Seven teachers (T1-T7) were involved in these classes. T1, the *unit coordinator*, designed the learning tasks and did not teach any class. T2 and T3 were the *main teachers* for 12 and 6 classes respectively, and T4-T7 supported T2 and T3 as *teaching assistants* in various combinations.

Each lab exhibited one of three possible learning designs (LD1-3). LD1 was a *prescribed lab*, in which all students had to do the same experiment following a step-by-step guide. LD2 was a *project-based lab*, in which students were asked to formulate a testing project, with each team working with a different appliance, such as vacuum cleaners or pedestal fans. Finally, LD3 was a *theory-testing lab*, in which 4–5 experiments were set up by the teacher and students had to move to one experiment at a time and predict the outcome of each without further guidance.

The labs were conducted with the same students (and not necessarily with the same teachers) in the same classroom for three consecutive weeks (enacting a different LD in each). This means LD1 was enacted in classes 1–6 in week 4 of the term. LD2 was enacted in classes 7–12 in week 5 with the same students from week 4. LD3 was enacted in classes 13–18 in week 6 with the same students from the previous two weeks.

4 Apparatus

The x and y positions of the two teachers in each lab were automatically recorded through wearable *badges* (Fig. 1, right) based on the Pozyx ultra-wideband (UWB) system, at a 2 Hz average sampling rate (with an error rate of 10 cm). Eight *anchors* were affixed to the classroom walls to estimate the positions of the badges. UWB sensors do not require a straight line of sight and are not affected by signals of students' personal devices [2]. The cost of the equipment is relatively low (~1.5 K AUD) making it affordable and portable. Given the large number of teams in each lab (10–12), the positions of students' experiments were captured by an observer using an observation tool (i.e., iPad) whenever there was a change in the position of teams. For LD1 and LD2, students mostly stayed at the benches where they installed their experiments. For LD3, students moved to each experiment setup, so these were recorded by the observer (Fig. 2).

5 Moodoo: Indoor Positioning Metrics

This subsection presents the metrics defined for teachers' positioning, grounded in the notion of SP [33]. The metrics have been implemented into a composable open source library in Python (https://gitlab.erc.monash.edu.au/rmat0024/moodoo).

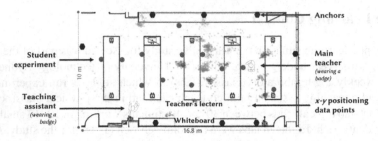

Fig. 2. Floor plan of the classroom with data points from two teachers (in blue and orange).

5.1 Metrics Related to Teachers' Stops

A teacher's *stop* can be defined as a sequence of positioning data points that are short distance apart in space and time. According to the notion of SP, this can denote a period in which the teacher is "*positioned to conduct formal teaching*" or stands "*alongside the students' desk or between rows*" of seats to interact with students ([33], pp. 237).

Thus, a stop can be modelled from $x - y$ teacher's data grouping data points based on a centroid $C(x, y)$ point, distance d and time t parameters; where d is the maximum distance from the current data point to C, and t is the minimum time to group consecutive points (see Fig. 3). For example, for our illustrative study we chose $d = 1$ m, since this distance is considered within a teacher's personal space [50]; and $t = 10$ s to disregard very short stops. These parameters can be further calibrated according to the context and the tracking technology used. From the defined stop construct, other metrics can be calculated, such as the total or partial number of stops, average stopping time; or more complex metrics in relation to other sources of evidence, such as student locations and classroom resources (e.g. work-benches).

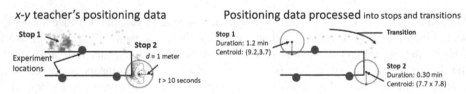

Fig. 3. Modelling from raw $x - y$ positioning data (left) to teachers' stops and transitions (right).

5.2 Metrics Related to Teachers' Transitions

A teacher's *transition* is defined as a sequence of positioning data points that follow a trajectory between two stops. This includes all those positioning traces generated while, for example, the teacher moves from attending one group of students to another group, or, according to the notion of SP, the teacher paces "*alongside the rows of students' desks as well as up and down the side of the classroom transforming these sites into supervisory spaces*" ([33], pp. 238).

Although a smoothing algorithm can be used by the sensing software when capturing positioning data [41], each data point is always an estimate (with its associated error) of the actual position. Hence, a linear quadratic estimation algorithm [52] (i.e. Kalman filtering) was applied to the $x - y$ data points as a pre-processing step. Then, the teacher's walking trajectory is modelled as the transition between two consecutive stops in relation to their centroids (see Fig. 3, right). From teachers' transitions, other related metrics can also be calculated, such as the distance walked, speed and acceleration, and the transitions between specific groups of students or classroom areas.

5.3 Metrics Related to Teacher-Student Interactions

Lim et al. [33] proposed that a space in the classroom becomes *interactional* when the teacher is in close proximity to students to enable conversations or consultation. Although this space may be shaped by the learning task, furniture, and preferences [6], extensive work studying cultural aspects of space has identified that a distance from 0.75 to 1.2 m creates optimal opportunities for social interaction [28, 36]. Hence, a teacher standing within the interactional space of students (*iDis*) can be considered as a potential teacher-student interaction. In our study, we accounted for the parameter *iDis* = 1 m (based on [36]) as the maximum distance to define a teacher's stop within certain students' interactional space. From this construct, other metrics can be calculated, such as teachers' total attention time per student/group, frequency and duration of teachers attending certain students, and sequencing of teacher-student interactions.

Additionally, an index of *dispersion* can be calculated to identify how evenly teachers' attention was distributed in terms of the number of visits and the total time teachers spent with each student or group. In our illustrative study, we calculated the Gini index [23], which is commonly used to model inequality or dispersion (with a single coefficient output ranging from 0 to 1, where 0 represents perfect equality).

5.4 Metrics Related to Proximity to Classroom Resources of Interest

Teachers' proximity to certain resources in the classroom also gives meaning to $x - y$ data. For example, "*the space behind the teacher's desk can be described as the personal space where the teacher ... prepares for the next stage of the lesson*" ([33], pp. 238) similarly, a space can become *authoritative "where the teacher is positioned to conduct formal teaching as well as to provide instructions to facilitate the lesson* ([33], pp. 237). In our study, close proximity to teacher's lectern or a whiteboard, can be indicative of particular activities such as lecturing to the whole class or explaining formulas. For this purpose, the parameter *dObj* delimits the proximity of objects of interests that are close to the teacher (calibrated to 1 m in the study).

5.5 Metrics Related to Co-teaching

Having more than one teacher in the classroom is not an uncommon practice [22]; an example is our illustrative study where pairs of teachers co-taught classes in different combinations. Modelling the instances when both teachers are within each other's interpersonal spaces (*dTeacher*) can assist teachers to reflect how often and where these events happen in the classroom space, or whether the teachers jointly attend a team of students (i.e. parameter *dTeacher* = 1 following the same heuristic as above [36]).

5.6 Metrics Related to Focus of Positional Presence (Spatial Entropy)

In a qualitative study [39], teachers contrasted two extreme mobility behaviours: 1) a teacher walking around the classroom mostly supervising, without engaging much with students (unfocused positional presence), and 2) a teacher focusing most of his/her attention on a small number of students or remaining only in specific spaces of the classroom (focused presence). From the $x - y$ positioning data, the spectrum between these two extreme behaviours can be modelled based on the notion of *spatial entropy* [9] which has been used to measure information density in spatial data [3]. To calculate the entropy, we create a m-by-m grid ($m = 1$ m in our illustrative study) from the two-dimensional $x - y$ data. The proportion of data points in each cell of the grid is calculated, creating a matrix of proportions. This is then vectorised and Shannon entropy is calculated (resulting into a positive number in bits). The closer the number is to zero, the more focused teacher's positioning was to specific students or spaces in the classroom.

6 Illustrative Study: Analysis and Results

This section demonstrates the potential of the metrics related to the constructs presented above through exemplars of how positioning traces i) reflect the characteristics of the learning design, and ii) can be used to characterise contrasting instructional behaviours.

6.1 Dataset, Pre-processing and Analysis

A total of 835,033 datapoints were captured by the indoor positioning system used in the 18 classes taught by pairs of teachers. Each datapoint consisted of i) an identifier of the teacher, ii) a timestamp and iii) $x - y$ coordinates of the classroom position of that teacher in millimetres (e.g., {teacher1, 18/02/2019 9:39:20.34, 5600, 8090}).

Three pre-processing steps were conducted before analysing the data using Moodoo. 1) *Sampling normalisation*: the positioning data was down sampled to 1 Hz by calculating the average position of a teacher per second. 2) *Interpolation*: as sensors are susceptible to missing readings for a few seconds [26], a linear interpolation was applied to fill gaps for cases in which there was not at least 1 datapoint per second. The resulting dataset contained 60 positioning data points per minute and per teacher. 3) *Segmentation*: each class was segmented into three phases according to a common macro-script for the three LDs defined by the unit coordinator. Phase 1 includes the main teacher of the class giving instructions from the lectern (average duration 13 ± 8 min, n = 18). Phase 2 corresponds to the period in which all students start working on the experiment(s) of the day in small teams (1.5 h ± 18 min). Phase 3 corresponds to the time when some teams complete their experiments and start leaving the class (33 ± 22 min). The analysis of this paper focuses on Phase 2, which enables comparison across the classes considered. The resulting dataset comprised a total of 290,228 datapoints.

The data analysis involves processing the $x - y$ positioning data from teachers enacting each learning design (LD1-3) using Moodoo. We report Moodoo's metrics for each teacher by LD, and normalising the results according to the class with the shortest Phase 2 which lasted 1:07 h. We ran a Mann-Whitney's U test to evaluate differences in the metrics among each pair of learning designs (i.e. LD1-LD2; LD1-LD3 and LD2-LD3). Therefore, the median and interquartile range (IQR) values are reported accordingly.

6.2 Results

An overview of the resulting teachers' positioning metrics per learning design (LD) are presented in Tables 1 and 2, below. The median and IQR (Q3-Q1) values are presented by metric (columns/cols) and LD (rows). Bar charts are shown at the bottom of each table to facilitate comparison. Significant differences among pairs of LDs ($p < 0.05$) are emphasised in blue and orange (representing higher and lower values, respectively).

Table 1. Positioning metrics related to teachers' stops and transitions – median (Q3-Q1).

	Stops	Total stop time (mins)	Time per stop (min)	Distance walked (m)	Speed (m/s)	Dispersion (gini index)
LD1	42 (44-40)	**52.5 (56-47)**	**0.8 (1-0.7)**	370 (502-340)	0.5 (0.6-0.4)	0.5 (0.6-0.3)
LD2	35 (43-31)	58.4 (61-54)	1.4 (1.6-1)	303 (389-272)	0.6 (0.6-0.5)	0.4 (0.5-0.3)
LD3	35 (44-26)	58.1 (62-50)	1.1 (1.5-1)	440 (618-177)	0.5 (0.6-0.4)	0.4 (0.5-0.2)

Table 2. Metrics related to teacher-student interactions and proximity to objects in the classroom.

	Attention time (min)	Visits to experiments	Visit duration	Visits per experiment	Time at lectern	Time at whiteboard
LD1	41.5 (50-38)	37 (40-30)	0.9 (1.4-0.7)	3 (3-2.4)	0.6 (5.3-0)	0.3 (1-0)
LD2	42.7 (57-37)	29 (33-26)	1.3 (2-1)	2.5 (3-2)	3.5 (12-0.5)	1 (2-0)
LD3	34 (44-24)	23 (27-13)	0.9 (1.4-0.6)	5 (7-3)	7.3 (16-3)	2.9 (5.9-0.6)

Overall, when teachers enacted LD1 they featured a higher number of stops (median 45 stops) than when enacting LD2 and LD3 (35 stops). This difference was not significant given the high variability of teachers' behaviours (see col 1, IQR values, in Table 1).

Yet, stops were significantly longer for LD2 (U = 35, p = 0.02) and LD3 (U = 37, p = 0.02). For example, every time a teacher stopped while enacting LD2 s/he spent a median of 1.4 (IQR 1.6-1) minutes in that position before moving to the next space in the classroom. In contrast, most of the stops during LD1 were briefer (0.8, 1–0.7 min). This can be explained by the nature of students' task. In LD2 and LD3, students worked on more complex projects. In LD1, all students conducted the same (prescribed) experiment with teachers mostly providing corrective feedback, resulting in shorter pauses.

In terms of distance walked and speed, there were no significant differences by learning design (cols 4 and 5). This means that the learning designs did not strongly shape the way the teachers walked in the classroom as a cohort, in this study. However, there were differences between teachers at a per case (exemplified below).

Table 2 shows more results for those cases in which teachers were in close proximity to students (cols 1–4) and classroom resources (5–6). There was a significant difference between the three LDs regarding the number of visits to students' experiments (LD1-LD2, U = 36, p = 0.02; LD2-L3, U = 33, p = 0.01; LD1-LD3, U = 13, p = 0.001).

There was a larger number of visits for LD1, in comparison to LD2 (col 2), which contributes to describing a *supervisory* pedagogical approach [9] provoked by the prescribed learning task. However, the total attention time to experiments was very similar between LD1 and LD2 (column 1, 41.5 and 42.7 min, respectively). In contrast, for the *theory-testing lab* (LD3) teachers acted as demonstrators, dividing their attention (34, 44–24 min, col 1) visiting around 5 times each of the 4–5 experiments (col 4).

Regarding proximity to objects of interest, teachers significantly spent more time at the lectern and the whiteboard for LD3 compared to LD1 (U = 28, p = 0.01) and LD2 (U = 42, p = 0.04). This can be because in LD1 classes the task is prescribed so teachers did not need to show additional information through the computer (lectern) or whiteboard. For LD2 and LD3, teachers commonly had to explain formulas using the whiteboard. Additionally, classes enacting LD3 occurred later in the semester after student partial results were published, with students often asking clarification questions regarding these LD3 classes. This explains the longer presence of teachers at the lectern.

Finally, the computed index of dispersion (Table 1, col 6) and entropy, did not show any significant difference between LDs. Yet, they enabled the characterisation of contrasting instructional approaches of individual teachers. For example, Fig. 4 shows heatmaps and selected metrics obtained from positioning data of a focused (T6) and an unfocused teacher (T5) in Phase 2 of two LD2 classes. T6 focused on two benches of the classroom (Fig. 4, left), stopping almost half the number of times compared to T5 (25 versus 46 stops). Evidently, the main teacher had to attend students sitting at the remaining desks. This was captured by the metric that counted the times both teachers got close to each other (3 versus 10) suggesting two different co-teaching strategies.

In contrast, T5 remained constantly circulating (see Fig. 4, right), making the space between the work-benches his *supervisory* zone. The measure of spatial entropy captured this behaviour. T6 featured the lowest entropy among the teachers in the dataset (3.2 bits) whilst for T5 it was the second highest (6.2 bits), pointing at the more spread distribution of datapoints in the classroom space. The index of dispersion, calculated in relation to students' experiments, contributes to characterise the contrasting behaviours with a resulting coefficient very close to 1 for T6 (0.83 - highly unequal distribution of

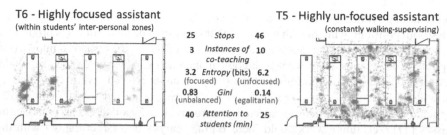

Fig. 4. Contrasting spatial pedagogical approaches. Left: a teacher focusing on certain students during a class. Right: a second teacher mostly walking around the classroom, supervising.

teacher's attention) compared to T5 (0.14 – more even distribution of attention). Finally, teacher-student attention time was higher for the first teacher, who spent much of his time attending 3-4 teams out of the 12 in the class.

In sum, this characterisation of instructional behaviour should provoke reflection among teachers about the different teaching approaches, as it has been previously performed from observations (e.g. [14, 33]). Due to space limitations, providing additional metrics and examples is beyond the purpose of this paper. Yet, some additional illustrative examples are provided in the library documentation.

7   Discussion and Conclusion

Metrics proposed in the paper helped characterise three learning designs using quantifiable observations of classroom positioning data. Such metrics can uncover and bring to the attention of teachers and learning designers certain characteristics that are inherent to learning activities – for instance, increased teacher-student time ratio for a hands-on experiment design versus a lecture delivery.

Our work conveys several *implications* for research and practice. Teachers can use the resulting metrics to reflect on the proportion of different types of learning activities comprising a teaching session, which can then lead to changes in the learning design as needed. Decisions to intervene and make changes are not automated by algorithms deliberately, as this involves another layer of human interpretation and understanding that suits the learning context in hand. Rather, the metrics can act as tools to aid teachers to make informed decisions [24], which can contribute to the expansion of teachers' classroom capabilities, as envisaged in Luckin's work [34] regarding AI in education. While we note that the teachers would require some form of training to best utilise SP, we also identify the potential for teachers and other stakeholders to identify best teaching practices, as illustrated in our example of contrasting the different pedagogical approaches of two teachers. Finally, the data provided by emerging indoor positioning, along with the metrics proposed in this paper, can contribute to the assessment of specific learning spaces, which is an identified gap in learning spaces research [29].

In terms of *limitations* of our illustrative study, we note that the parameters might need tuning to work with other types of learning spaces and learning designs, in particular, the thresholds set for defining certain metrics might vary across contexts. For this reason, other classroom spaces that make use of the metrics need to test them for the right fit in their learning contexts. This points at the opportunity to generate learning design-aware classroom positioning metrics, that can guide instructional behavior in ways productive for learning. Moreover, the analysis of significance of the metrics was not intended to support strong claims about what pedagogical approach is better given the size of the dataset and the authentic conditions of the study which introduced several confounding variables. Controlled experimental studies are not recommended as they can hardly replicate emergent and often unexpected classroom situations that occur in authentic classes [17]. Yet, future work could focus on the analysis of a larger dataset with the aim of mining the positioning data to identify patterns that could be used to differentiate instructional behaviours.

In *conclusion*, this paper presented a set of conceptual mappings from x − y positional data of teachers to higher-order spatial constructs (namely: teacher's stops, transitions, teacher-student interactions, proximity to objects of interest, instances of co-teaching and entropy of teachers' movement), informed by the concept of Spatial Pedagogy [33]. The resulting metrics related to such constructs can facilitate the study of classroom activity in novel ways, which can lead to the expansion of current knowledge about teacher-student proximity and physical behaviours at various learning settings. Future research should certainly further test the applicability of the metrics in other learning settings (i.e. in multi-class open spaces or lecture halls) and, expand the library with metrics that can better model how teachers and students move in such classrooms.

References

1. Ahuja, K., et al.: EduSense: practical classroom sensing at scale. Proc. ACM Interact. Mob. Wearable Ubiquit. Technol. **3**(3), 1–26 (2019)
2. Alarifi, A., et al.: Ultra wideband indoor positioning technologies: analysis and recent advances. MDPI Sens. **16**(5), 1–36 (2016)
3. Altieri, L., Cocchi, D., Roli, G.: A New Approach to Spatial Entropy Measures. Environ. Ecol. Stat. **25**(1), 95–110 (2018). https://doi.org/10.1007/s10651-017-0383-1
4. An, P., Bakker, S., Ordanovski, S., Paffen, C.L., Taconis, R., Eggen, B.: Dandelion diagram: aggregating positioning and orientation data in the visualization of classroom proxemics. In: CHI 2020 Extended Abstracts (2020, in press)
5. An, P., Bakker, S., Ordanovski, S., Taconis, R., Eggen, B.: ClassBeacons: designing distributed visualization of teachers' physical proximity in the classroom. In: Proceedings of the International Conference on Tangible, Embedded, and Embodied Interaction. TEI 2018, pp. 357–367 (2018)
6. Andersen, P.: Proxemics. In: Littlejohn, S.W., Foss, K.A. (eds.) Encyclopedia of Communication Theory, p. 808. SAGE Publications, Inc., Thousand Oaks (2009)
7. Asino, T.I., Pulay, A.: Student perceptions on the role of the classroom environment on computer supported collaborative learning. TechTrends **63**(2), 179–187 (2019). https://doi.org/10.1007/s11528-018-0353-y
8. Barnard, H.: Practical Illustrations of the Principles of School Architecture. Norton, Ann Arbor (1854)
9. Batty, M., Morphet, R., Masucci, P., Stanilov, K.: Entropy, complexity, and spatial information. J. Geogr. Syst. **16**(4), 363–385 (2014). https://doi.org/10.1007/s10109-014-0202-2
10. Bosch, N., Mills, C., Wammes, J.D., Smilek, D.: Quantifying classroom instructor dynamics with computer vision. In: Penstein Rosé, C., et al. (eds.) AIED 2018. LNCS (LNAI), vol. 10947, pp. 30–42. Springer, Cham (2018). https://doi.org/10.1007/978-3-319-93843-1_3

11. Britton, L.R., Anderson, K.A.: Peer coaching and pre-service teachers: examining an underutilised concept. Teach. Teach. Educ. **26**(2), 306–314 (2010)

12. Burda, J.M., Brooks, C.I.: College classroom seating position and changes in achievement motivation over a semester. Psychol. Rep. **78**(1), 331–336 (1996)

13. Cheema, M.A.: Indoor location-based services: challenges and opportunities. SIGSPATIAL Spec. **10**(2), 10–17 (2018)

14. Chin, H.B., Mei, C.C.Y., Taib, F.: Instructional proxemics and its impact on classroom teaching and learning. Int. J. Mod. Lang. Appl. Linguist. **1**(1), 1–20 (2017)

15. Chng, E., Seyam, R., Yao, W., Schneider, B.: Examining the type and diversity of student social interactions in makerspaces using motion sensors. In: Proceedings of the International Conference on Artificial Intelligence in Education. AIED 2020 (2020, in press)

16. Chua, Y.H.V., Dauwels, J., Tan, S.C.: Technologies for automated analysis of co-located, real-life, physical learning spaces: where are we now?. In: Proceedings of the International Learning Analytics and Knowledge Conference. LAK 2019, pp. 11–20 (2019)

17. Dillenbourg, P., et al.: Classroom orchestration: the third circle of usability. In: Proceedings of the International Conference on Computer Supported Collaborative Learning. CSCL 2011, pp. 510–517 (2011)

18. Echeverria, V., Martinez-Maldonado, R., Power, T., Hayes, C., Shum, S.B.: Where is the nurse? Towards automatically visualising meaningful team movement in healthcare education. In: Penstein Rosé, C., et al. (eds.) AIED 2018. LNCS (LNAI), vol. 10948, pp. 74–78. Springer, Cham (2018). https://doi.org/10.1007/978-3-319-93846-2_14

19. Fernandes, A.C., Huang, J., Rinaldo, V.: Does where a student sits really matter?-the impact of seating locations on student classroom learning. Int. J. Appl. Educ. Stud. **10**(1), 66–77 (2011)

20. Fischer, M.M.: Spatial Analytical Perspectoves on GIS. Routledge, London (2019)

21. Fletcher, J.A.: Peer observation of teaching: a practical tool in higher education. J. Fac. Dev. **32**(1), 51–64 (2018)

22. Friend, M., Embury, D.C., Clarke, L.: Co-teaching versus apprentice teaching: an analysis of similarities and differences. Teach. Educ. Spec. Educ. **38**(2), 79–87 (2015)

23. Gastwirth, J.L.: The estimation of the Lorenz curve and Gini index. Rev. Econ. Stat. **54**, 306–316 (1972)

24. Gerritsen, D., Zimmerman, J., Ogan, A.: Towards a framework for smart classrooms that teach instructors to teach. In: Proceedings of the International Conference of the Learning Sciences. ICLS 2018, pp. 1779–1782 (2018)

25. Giangreco, M.F., Edelman, S.W., Luiselli, T.E., Macfarland, S.Z.C.: Helping or hovering? Effects of instructional assistant proximity on students with disabilities. Except. Child. **64**(1), 7–18 (1997)

26. Gløersen, Ø., Federolf, P.: Predicting missing marker trajectories in human motion data using marker intercorrelations. PloS One **11**(3), e0152616 (2016)

27. Gunter, P.L., Shores, R.E., Jack, S.L., Rasmussen, S.K., Flowers, J.: On the move using teacher/student proximity to improve students' behavior. Teach. Except. Child. **28**(1), 12–14 (1995)

28. Hall, E.T., et al.: Proxemics [and comments and replies]. Curr. Anthropol. **9**(2/3), 83–108 (1968)

29. Higgins, S., Hall, E., Wall, K., Woolner, P., Mccaughey, C.: The impact of school environments: a literature review. Report. Design Council, London, UK, pp. 1–45 (2005)

30. Hutt, S., et al.: Automated gaze-based mind wandering detection during computerized learning in classrooms. User Model. User-Adap. Inter. **29**(4), 821–867 (2019). https://doi.org/10.1007/s11257-019-09228-5

31. Koh, J.H.L., Frick, T.W.: Instructor and student classroom interactions during technology skills instruction for facilitating preservice teachers' computer self-efficacy. J. Educ. Comput. Res. **40**(2), 211–228 (2009)
32. Kounin, J.S.: Discipline and Group Management In Classrooms. Holt, Rinehart and Winston, Oxford (1970)
33. Lim, F.V., O'halloran, K.L., Podlasov, A.: Spatial pedagogy: mapping meanings in the use of classroom space. Camb. J. Educ. **42**(2), 235–251 (2012)
34. Luckin, R.: Machine Learning and Human Intelligence: The Future of Education for the 21st Century. UCL IOE Press (2018)
35. Marini, G.: Towards indoor localisation analytics for modelling flows of movements. In: Proceedings of the Adjunct Proceedings of the 2019 ACM International Joint Conference on Pervasive and Ubiquitous Computing and Proceedings of the 2019 ACM International Symposium on Wearable Computers, pp. 377–382 (2019)
36. Martinec, R.: Interpersonal resources in action. Semiotica **135**(1/4), 117–146 (2001)
37. Martinez-Maldonado, R.: I spent more time with that team: making spatial pedagogy visible using positioning sensors. In: Proceedings of the International Conference on Learning Analytics & Knowledge. LAK 2019, pp. 21–25 (2019)
38. Martinez-Maldonado, R., Echeverria, V., Santos, O.C., Dos Santos, A.D.P., Yacef, K.: physical learning analytics: a multimodal perspective. In: Proceedings of the 8th International Conference on Learning Analytics and Knowledge. LAK 2018, pp. 375–379 (2018)
39. Martinez-Maldonado, R., Mangaroska, K., Schulte, J., Elliott, D., Axisa, C., Buckingham Shum, S.: Teacher tracking with integrity: what indoor positioning can tell about instructional proxemics. Proc. ACM Interact. Mob. Wearable Ubiquit. Technol. (UBICOMP) **4**(1), 1–27 (2020)
40. Mcarthur, J.A.: Matching instructors and spaces of learning: the impact of space on behavioral, affective and cognitive learning. J. Learn. Spaces **4**(1), 1–16 (2015)
41. Melamed, R.: Indoor localization: challenges and opportunities. In: Proceedings of the International Conference on Mobile Software Engineering and Systems, pp. 1–2 (2016)
42. Nandakumar, R., et al.: Physical analytics: a new frontier for (indoor) location research. Technical report MSR-TR-2013-107. Microsoft, Redmond, WA, USA (2013)
43. O'Neill, S.C., Stephenson, J.: Evidence-based classroom and behaviour management content in Australian pre-service primary teachers' coursework: wherefore art thou? Aust. J. Teach. Educ. **39**(4), 1–22 (2014)
44. Prieto, L.P., Sharma, K., Kidzinski, Ł., Rodríguez-Triana, M.J., Dillenbourg, P.: Multimodal teaching analytics: automated extraction of orchestration graphs from wearable sensor data. J. Comput. Assist. Learn. **34**(2), 193–203 (2018)
45. Raca, M., Kidzinski, L., Dillenbourg, P.: Translating head motion into attention-towards processing of student's body-language. In: Proceedings of the 8th International Conference on Educational Data Mining. EDM'15, pp. 320–326 (2015)
46. Rubin, G.N.: A naturalistic study in proxemics: seating arrangement and its effect on interaction, performance, and behavior. Ph.D. Bowling Green State University, United States (1972)
47. Santos, O.C.: Training the body: the potential of AIED to support personalized motor skills learning. Int. J. Artif. Intell. Educ. **26**(2), 730–755 (2016). https://doi.org/10.1007/s40593-016-0103-2
48. Saquib, N., Bose, A., George, D., Kamvar, S.: Sensei: sensing educational interaction. Proc. ACM Interact. Mob. Wearable Ubiquit. Technol. **1**(4), 1–27 (2018)
49. Shortland, S.: Peer observation: a tool for staff development or compliance? J. Further High. Educ. **28**(2), 219–228 (2004)

50. Sousa, M., Mendes, D., Medeiros, D., Ferreira, A., Pereira, J.M., Jorge, J.: Remote proxemics. In: Anslow, C., Campos, P., Jorge, J. (eds.) Collaboration Meets Interactive Spaces, pp. 47–73. Springer, Cham (2016). https://doi.org/10.1007/978-3-319-45853-3_4
51. Wake, J., Heimsæter, F., Bjørgen, E., Wasson, B., Hansen, C.: Supporting firefighter training by visualising indoor positioning, motion detection, and time use: a multimodal approach. In: Proceedings of the LASi-NORDIC 2018, vol. 1601, pp. 87–90 (2018)
52. Wang, J., Hu, A., Li, X., Wang, Y.: An improved PDR/magnetometer/floor map integration algorithm for ubiquitous positioning using the adaptive unscented Kalman filter. ISPRS Int. J. Geo-Inf. 4(4), 2638–2659 (2015)
53. Watanabe, E., Ozeki, T., Kohama, T.: Analysis of interactions between lecturers and students. In: Proceedings of the International Conference on Learning Analytics and Knowledge. LAK 2018, pp. 370–374 (2018)
54. Zawacki-Richter, O., Marín, V.I., Bond, M., Gouverneur, F.: Systematic review of research on artificial intelligence applications in higher education – where are the educators? Int. J. Educ. Technol. High. Educ. 16(39), 1–27 (2019)

DETECT: A Hierarchical Clustering Algorithm for Behavioural Trends in Temporal Educational Data

Jessica McBroom[✉], Kalina Yacef, and Irena Koprinska

School of Computer Science, University of Sydney, Sydney, Australia
{jmcb6755,kalina.yacef,irena.koprinska}@sydney.edu.au

Abstract. Techniques for clustering student behaviour offer many opportunities to improve educational outcomes by providing insight into student learning. However, one important aspect of student behaviour, namely its evolution over time, can often be challenging to identify using existing methods. This is because the objective functions used by these methods do not explicitly aim to find cluster trends in time, so these trends may not be clearly represented in the results. This paper presents 'DETECT' (*D*etection of *E*ducational *T*rends *E*licited by *C*lustering *T*ime-series data), a novel divisive hierarchical clustering algorithm that incorporates temporal information into its objective function to prioritise the detection of behavioural trends. The resulting clusters are similar in structure to a decision tree, with a hierarchy of clusters defined by decision rules on features. DETECT is easy to apply, highly customisable, applicable to a wide range of educational datasets and yields easily interpretable results. Through a case study of two online programming courses ($N > 600$), this paper demonstrates two example applications of DETECT: 1) to identify how cohort behaviour develops over time and 2) to identify student behaviours that characterise exercises where many students give up.

Keywords: Hierarchical clustering · Student behaviour · Intelligent tutoring systems · Behavioural trends · Time series clustering

1 Introduction

In recent decades, educational datasets have become increasingly rich and complex, offering many opportunities for analysing student behaviour to improve educational outcomes. The analysis of student behaviour, particularly temporal trends in this behaviour, has played a major role in many recent studies in areas including automated feedback provision [8,12,16,19], dropout analysis [17,18,22], collaborative learning [4,21,23] and student equity [6,9,13].

However, a significant challenge in analysing student behaviour is its complexity and diversity. As such, clustering techniques [24], which organise complex data into simpler subsets, are an important resource for analysing student

© Springer Nature Switzerland AG 2020
I. I. Bittencourt et al. (Eds.): AIED 2020, LNAI 12163, pp. 374–385, 2020.
https://doi.org/10.1007/978-3-030-52237-7_30

behaviour, and have been employed in many recent studies [5]. For example, in [1] and [3] K-means clustering and a self-organising map, respectively, are used to group students based on their interactions with an educational system. In addition, in [7] student programs are clustered to identify common misconceptions.

One limitation of standard clustering techniques is that they are not well-suited to detecting behavioural trends in time. One solution is to use time-series clustering techniques, which typically combine standard techniques with extra processing steps [2]. For example, [15] uses dynamic time warping in conjunction with K-means clustering to cluster time series' of student Moodle activity data. Alternatively, temporal information is often considered only after all student work samples or behaviours have been clustered. For example, in [14] student work is clustered to allow an interaction network over time to be built and in [10] clusters of student behaviour over time are used in a second round of clustering.

Although it is possible to gain insight into student behavioural changes using these techniques, one important limitation is that temporal trend detection is not explicitly incorporated into the objective function when clustering. For example, consider the case where K-means is first used to cluster student behaviours, and then cluster changes over time are observed, as in [10]. Since the objective of K-means is to minimise the distance between points (which in this case represent student behaviours), the process will prioritise grouping behaviours that match on as many features as possible. However, this may obscure important trends, especially if many of the features are unrelated to these trends.

The contribution of this paper is 'DETECT' (*Detection of Educational Trends Elicited by Clustering Time-series data*), a novel divisive hierarchical clustering algorithm that incorporates trend detection into its objective function in order to identify interesting patterns in student behaviour over time. DETECT is highly general and can be applied to many educational datasets with temporal data (for example, from regular homework tasks or repeated activities). In addition, it can be customised to detect a variety of trends and produces clusters that are well-defined and easy to understand. Moreover, it does not require that the features be independent, or that the objective function be differentiable.

Broadly, DETECT has similar properties to the classification technique of decision trees [20]. In particular, it produces a hierarchy of clusters distinguished by decision rules. However, whereas decision trees are a supervised technique requiring the existence of classes in order to calculate entropy, DETECT is unsupervised and uses an objective function completely unrelated to this measure.

This paper is set out as follows: Sect. 2 describes the DETECT algorithm, including the input it takes, its flexibility and how the output is interpreted. Section 3 then shows example usage of the algorithm through a case study and Sect. 4 concludes with a summary of the main ideas of the paper.

2   DETECT Algorithm

2.1   Overview

DETECT produces clusters of student behaviour that reveal cohort behavioural trends in educational datasets. Such trends can include changes in behaviour over time, anomalous behaviours at specific points in the course or a variety of other customisable trends. This is achieved by iteratively dividing student behaviours into clusters that maximise a time-based objective function. The clusters found can then be interpreted by teachers and course designers to better understand student behaviour during the course.

DETECT can be applied to a wide range of datasets, of the form described in Table 1. In particular, the data should be *temporal* - that is, able to be divided into a series of comparable time steps. For example, a series of homework tasks or fixed time periods during an intervention could be considered as comparable time steps. In addition, for each student and time period, there should be a set of features describing the behaviour of the student during that time period. These features could be numeric, such as the number of exercise attempts, or categorical, such as a label for the style of their work. Note that features are not required to be independent or equally important, since the objective function can determine the quality of features and penalise less useful ones.

Table 1. Structure of input data, where the number of cells in the table is equal to S (number of students) × T (number of time periods) × M (number of features). F1, ..., FM are different feature names.

Student	Time	F1	F2	...	FM
1	1	v_{111}	v_{112}	...	v_{11M}
1	2	v_{121}	v_{122}	...	v_{12M}
...	...	...	...	...	...
1	T	v_{1T1}	v_{1T2}	...	v_{1TM}
...	...	...	...	...	...
S	1	v_{N11}	v_{N12}	...	v_{N1M}
...	...	...	...	...	...
S	T	v_{NT1}	v_{NT2}	...	v_{NTM}

DETECT outputs clusters of student behaviour explicitly defined by rules on feature values. For example, a cluster may be defined as all rows of the input data where *'num_submissions'* ≤ 7 and *'completed'* == *'yes'*. These clusters are organised into a hierarchical structure where, in each successive level, an additional condition is added, similarly to a decision tree. Examples of this are given in Sect. 3, as part of the case study.

It is important to note that the clusters are not clusters of students but rather clusters of the input data rows (which each represent the behaviour of one student at one time period). This means students are in many clusters - one for each time period. By observing changes to the distributions of clusters over time, trends in student behaviour can be identified (see Sect. 3).

2.2   Cluster Formation

Clusters are formed divisively through an iterative process with four main steps, as summarised in Fig. 1. Initially, all examples are placed in the same cluster. Then, during each iteration, a search is performed to find the best feature and value to split this cluster on. If this split would result in new clusters that are larger in size than a specified lower-limit (e.g. at least 100 examples each), then the split it performed, creating two new clusters, and the process is repeated recursively on the new clusters. Otherwise, the split is not performed. The algorithm terminates when no cluster can be split further.

Using the given objective functions and assuming the cluster size threshold scales proportionally with the number of examples (which places a constant upper bound on the number of clusters), the time complexity of this process is $O(nm \log n)$, where m is the number of features and n the number of examples.

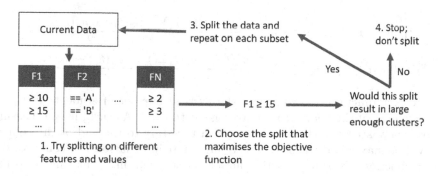

Fig. 1. A summary of the steps involved in DETECT.

Feature and Value Search. Before a cluster is divided, a search is performed to find the best feature and value to split on. For each feature, this can be performed in $O(n \log n)$ time (where n is the cluster size) using the given objective functions in the next subsection. For numeric features, the process is as follows:

1. Sort the examples in ascending order based on the feature value.
2. Create two new clusters, one containing no examples (C_a) and the other containing all (C_b).
3. Set a threshold, t, that is lower than the smallest feature value.
4. While there are still examples in C_b, increase t to the next smallest feature value (or larger) and add all examples $\leq t$ from C_b to C_a, each time checking if this improves the objective function value (and, if so, remembering t).

The best feature and split will then be the one that optimises the function values. Similarly, for categorical features, each category can be iterated through to find the best one to split off from the rest. Note that we recommend minimising the amount of missing data (e.g. by selecting subsets of students or making time periods relative to students as in [11]). However, if required, missing values can be treated as another category if the feature is categorical, or, if the feature is numeric, the process can be repeated twice – once where the missing value examples are always in C_a, and once where they are always in C_b.

Objective Function. The objective function is used to determine the quality of potential cluster divisions using temporal information, thereby controlling the types of trends detected by the algorithm. More specifically, this function maps the distributions of C_a and C_b over time, along with optional additional parameters, to a score. It can be customised to suit different purposes and there are no constraints such as differentiability on the function. Two examples of an objective function are defined here:

Let $\mathbf{n} = [n_a(t_i), n_b(t_i)]$ be the number of students in clusters C_a and C_b respectively at time i and T be the number of time steps in total. In addition, for f_2, let x be a time step of interest. Then:

$$f_1(\mathbf{n}(t_1), \mathbf{n}(t_2), ..., \mathbf{n}(t_T)) = \left| \frac{n_a(t_1) + n_a(t_2)}{2} - \frac{n_a(t_T) + n_a(t_{T-1})}{2} \right|$$

$$f_2(\mathbf{n}(t_1), \mathbf{n}(t_2), ..., \mathbf{n}(t_T), x) = \frac{|n_a(t_x) - n_a(t_{x+1})| + |n_a(t_x) - n_a(t_{x-1})|}{2}$$

The first function, f_1, compares the average number of students in C_a at the beginning of the course to the average at the end. As such, it is a measure of how many students change cluster from the start to the end of the course, and will be maximised when there is a large shift in behaviour. In contrast, the second function, f_2, compares the number of students in C_a at time x to the adjacent time periods and finds the average difference. As such, it is maximised when behaviours at time x vary greatly from those at neighbouring times.

3   Case Study

This section demonstrates two example applications of DETECT using the two objective functions introduced in Sect. 2.2. Specifically, in the first example we apply DETECT to an intermediate course using f_1 to find behavioural trends over time. In the second example, we then apply DETECT to a beginner course using f_2 to find behaviours that characterise an exercise where many students give up. While the data come from programming courses, we only use general features not specific to this domain to demonstrate the generality of the approach.

3.1   Data

Our data come from school students participating in two online Python programming courses of different difficulty levels: intermediate ($N = 4213$[1]) and beginners ($N = 7164$(see footnote 1)). These courses were held over a 5-week period during 2018 as part of a programming challenge held primarily in Australia. The courses involved weekly notes, which introduced students to new concepts, and programming exercises to practice these skills. Students received automated feedback on their work from test cases and were able to improve and resubmit their work.

From this data, we extracted 10 features per student per exercise: 1–3) the number of times the student viewed, failed and passed the exercise, 4) the number of times their work was automatically saved (triggered when unsaved work was left for 10 s without being edited), 5–8) the time of the first view, autosave, fail and pass relative to the deadline, 9) the average time between successive fails and 10) the time between the first fail and passing. Note that these features did not need to be independent (see Sect. 2.1).

3.2   Example 1: Using f_1 to Detect Changes over Time

When analysing student behaviour during a course, one important question is how this behaviour changes in time. To answer this, f_1 was applied to the data from the intermediate course. Since exercises from the last week differed in structure from the others (i.e. students were given significantly less time to complete them), these were excluded, leaving a total of 20 exercises. Each of the remaining exercises were then considered as a time period. The resulting behavioural clusters are given in Table 2 and the number of students in each of the final clusters at each time period is shown in Fig. 2. Note that only data from completing students ($N = 658$) was used to minimise the amount of missing data.

Table 2. Clusters formed by applying f_1 to the intermediate course, using a minimum cluster size threshold of 400 - i.e. an average of 20 students per time period. The clusters are defined by the number of autosaves (level 1) and how long before the deadline the exercise was completed (level 2).

Level 1	Level 2	Label
autosaves ≤ 9	Completed 7.25 days or more before deadline	C_{11}
	Completed within 7.25 days of deadline	C_{12}
autosaves > 9		C_2

From Fig. 2 and Table 2, the most important difference in behaviour between the beginning and end of the course was the number of autosaves, which increased over time. In particular, Fig. 2 shows that most students began in C_{11} (with ≤ 9

---

[1] These refer to the number of students who attempted at least the first exercise.

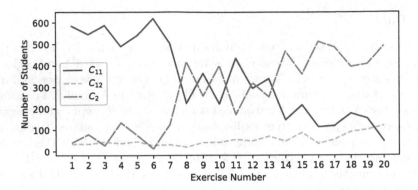

Fig. 2. The distribution of final clusters over time when f_1 is applied to data from all students who completed the course. Most students begin in C_{11}, but transition to other clusters over time.

autosaves) and ended in C_2 (with > 9 autosaves). Since these autosaves were triggered when a student paused for 10 or more seconds, this could indicate increased difficulty (if the students were pausing to read notes or think) or increased disengagement (if they were frequently stopping to do other activities).

Interestingly, even the students who had a smaller number of autosaves changed in behaviour over time, with an increasing proportion completing the exercises closer to the deadline as the course progressed. This can be seen by the increasing proportion of students in C_{12} compared to C_{11} over time. For the importance of this change to be apparent, note that passing these exercises within 7 days of the deadline actually indicates that a student is behind schedule. This is because each week of exercises is intended to take one week, but the deadlines for the first four weeks allow two weeks. If students were falling behind over time, this may suggest that the course content was too dense, and perhaps reducing the amount of content or spreading the course over a larger time period could be beneficial for students.

Furthermore, the distribution of clusters does not change smoothly over time. In particular, the plot lines are jagged, indicating that student behaviour varies a lot even between adjacent exercises. This is particularly interesting considering the features the clusters are defined by. For example, the fact that the number of autosaves varies a lot between adjacent exercises indicates that some exercises may be more interesting or difficult than similar exercises. For instance, the number of students in C_{11} (where there are ≤ 9 autosaves) drops by almost 100 from Exercise 3 to Exercise 4, then increases again at Exercise 5, even though all three exercises involve if-else statements. This could indicate that Exercise 4 is more difficult or less interesting than the others, since students pause more here (either because they are thinking or doing something else).

Another interesting observation is that there are three general and overarching changes to the cluster distributions over the course. In particular, from around Exercises 1 to 7, C_{11} is most dominant. Upon inspection, these exercises are primarily revision exercises (e.g. printing, variables and if-statements). After this period, there is an immediate shift in cluster distributions, with C_{11} and C_2 becoming similar in size, as students begin to learn about string slicing and loops. This general change suggests that students may find these topics more challenging than the previous ones. After Exercise 13, C_2 becomes dominant and C_{12} overtakes C_{11} in size as students learn about list operations, dictionaries and files. Since these general changes in student behaviour seem to occur as the topics become increasingly complex, perhaps the course could be improved by condensing the large revision period and expanding the other topics to allow for a more gradual difficulty change.

In summary, even by using DETECT with a simple objective function, f_1, and a highly general set of features, distinct and interpretable clusters can be found that coherently represent changes in student behaviour over time. By observing how the distributions of these clusters change at different scales (i.e. over the whole course, over groups of exercises or between individual exercises), important insights into student behaviour can be easily gained, and then used for purposes such as informing course development.

3.3 Example 2: Using f_2 to Analyse Behaviour Where Many Students Quit

Another topic of interest when analysing a course is the exercises that students have difficulty completing. In particular, if students attempt an exercise but cannot complete it, this can discourage them from continuing and lead to increased disengagement. This is particularly concerning in a beginner course, where students may not yet have confidence and could be dissuaded from pursuing further study in the area. This section provides an example of how DETECT could be used with objective function f_2 to explore such issues.

During the beginner course, 761 students attempted but could not complete Exercise 29 - the highest out of any exercise during the first four weeks. To understand how student behaviour differed during this exercise compared to others, we applied DETECT to the data using f_2 (setting $x = 29$), which identified clusters that distinguished this exercise from adjacent ones. The clusters formed and their distributions over time are shown in Table 3 and Fig. 3 respectively.

Table 3. Clusters formed by applying f_2 to data from completing beginner students ($N = 635$) with parameter $x = 29$ and minimum size threshold of 660 (i.e. an average of 20 students per time period). The clusters are defined by the number of autosaves and the time between a student's first failure and completion of the exercise.

Level 1	Level 2	Label
autosaves ≤ 8	Time from first fail to completion $\leq 48\,$s, or no fails	C_{11}
	Time from first fail to completion $> 48\,$s	C_{12}
autosaves > 8		C_2

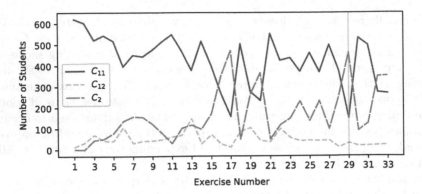

Fig. 3. The distribution of final clusters over time when f_2 is applied to data from all students who completed the course using Exercise 29 (marked in grey) as a parameter.

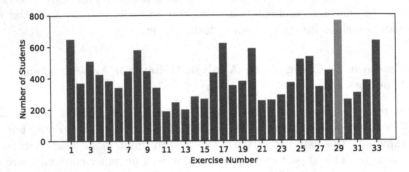

Fig. 4. The number of students who attempt but do not complete each of the beginner exercises from the first four weeks. Exercise 29, used for clustering, is marked in grey.

By comparing the cluster distribution at Exercise 29 to the adjacent exercises in Fig. 3, three general differences can be observed. Firstly, the proportion of students in C_2 ($>$ 8autosaves) is much higher for Exercise 29, indicating that students paused more often. In addition, the proportion of students in C_{11} is much lower. Since this cluster describes behaviour where students quickly solve the task (i.e. with few pauses, and either no failed submissions or a short time from their first fail to passing), a decrease in its frequency suggests this exercise is especially challenging compared to the adjacent tasks. The slight increase in the frequency of C_{12} (where the time from first failing to passing is $>$ 48 s) supports this, suggesting students take longer to correct their work after failing.

Interestingly, the pattern of C_2 sharply increasing and C_{11} sharply decreasing is not limited to Exercise 29. For example, this change also occurs at Exercises 17 and 20. From Fig. 4, which shows the number of students who unsuccessfully attempted each exercise, Exercises 17 and 20 also appear to have resulted in a large number of students giving up, especially relative to the adjacent exercises. Since information about these exercises was not used in the clustering, this is a strong indication that the cluster changes are not simply noise, but meaningful behaviour associated with times when students give up.[2]

Since the clusters are distinguished by the number of autosaves and also the time between a student's first fail and completion, one potential use of this information could be to improve interventions. For example, additional feedback or support messages could be triggered if a student pauses too many times or is unsuccessful in correcting their work for too long after their first fail. In addition, since students already receive automated feedback after failing an exercise, perhaps longer correction times could indicate that this feedback is unclear and could be revised. Finally, perhaps the information could be a useful tool when testing future courses. For example, senior students or a teacher could test-run a course, and the relative differences in the number of autosaves or time taken after failing could be used to highlight potential issues in advance.

In summary, this example has demonstrated how DETECT can be used to find different kinds of trends in educational data by changing the objective function. This customisable feature allows for great flexibility so that DETECT can be used for a range of interesting purposes.

4 Conclusion

This paper has presented a novel hierarchical clustering algorithm, DETECT, for identifying behavioural trends in temporal educational data. In contrast to current clustering approaches, DETECT incorporates temporal information into its objective function to prioritise the detection of behavioural trends. It can be applied to a wide range of educational datasets, produces easily interpretable results and is easy to apply, since the input features do not need to be independent. Two examples of objective functions have been provided, but these can be customised to identify different trends with few constraints (e.g. the functions do not need to be differentiable).

Through a case study, this paper has shown how DETECT can be used to identify interesting behavioural trends in educational data, even when the features are simple and not domain-specific. In particular, it can detect general changes in student behaviour over time or highlight behaviours characterising exercises where students give up. Such information is invaluable to teachers, course designers and researchers, who can use it to understand student behaviour, stimulate further investigation and ultimately improve educational outcomes.

In future, we hope to further develop DETECT by considering a greater range of objective functions and stopping conditions, and exploring the impact of additional domain-specific features and missing data on trend detection. In addition, it would be interesting to consider how DETECT could be used in conjunction with other techniques to, for example, analyse individual student

---

[2] Indeed, regression analysis finds that the correlation between the percentage of students in C_2 and the number of students unsuccessfully attempting each exercise is statistically significant with a p-value of 0.008.

trajectories. Ultimately, in a time when educational data are becoming increasingly abundant, this work aims to contribute to better-understanding student behaviour in order to improve educational outcomes.

References

1. Adjei, S., Ostrow, K., Erickson, E., Heffernan, N.T.: Clustering students in assistments: exploring system-and school-level traits to advance personalization. In: The 10th International Conference on Educational Data Mining, pp. 340–341 (2017)
2. Aghabozorgi, S., Shirkhorshidi, A.S., Wah, T.Y.: Time-series clustering-a decade review. Inf. Syst. **53**, 16–38 (2015)
3. Alias, U.F., Ahmad, N.B., Hasan, S.: Mining of E-learning behavior using SOM clustering. In: 2017 6th ICT International Student Project Conference (ICT-ISPC), pp. 1–4. IEEE (2017)
4. Barros, B., Verdejo, M.F.: Analysing student interaction processes in order to improve collaboration. The degree approach. Int. J. Artif. Intell. Educ. **11**(3), 221–241 (2000)
5. Dutt, A., Aghabozrgi, S., Ismail, M.A.B., Mahroeian, H.: Clustering algorithms applied in educational data mining. Int. J. Inf. Electron. Eng. **5**(2), 112–116 (2015)
6. Finkelstein, S., Yarzebinski, E., Vaughn, C., Ogan, A., Cassell, J.: The effects of culturally congruent educational technologies on student achievement. In: Lane, H.C., Yacef, K., Mostow, J., Pavlik, P. (eds.) AIED 2013. LNCS (LNAI), vol. 7926, pp. 493–502. Springer, Heidelberg (2013). https://doi.org/10.1007/978-3-642-39112-5_50
7. Joyner, D., et al.: From clusters to content: using code clustering for course improvement. In: Proceedings of the 50th ACM Technical Symposium on Computer Science Education, pp. 780–786 (2019)
8. Keuning, H., Jeuring, J., Heeren, B.: A systematic literature review of automated feedback generation for programming exercises. ACM Trans. Comput. Educ. (TOCE) **19**(1), 1–43 (2018)
9. Makhija, A., Richards, D., de Haan, J., Dignum, F., Jacobson, M.J.: The influence of gender, personality, cognitive and affective student engagement on academic engagement in educational virtual worlds. In: Penstein Rosé, C., et al. (eds.) AIED 2018. LNCS (LNAI), vol. 10947, pp. 297–310. Springer, Cham (2018). https://doi.org/10.1007/978-3-319-93843-1_22
10. McBroom, J., Jeffries, B., Koprinska, I., Yacef, K.: Mining behaviours of students in autograding submission system logs. In: The 9th International Conference on Educational Data Mining, pp. 159–166. International Educational Data Mining Society (2016)
11. Mcbroom, J., Koprinska, I., Yacef, K.: How does student behaviour change approaching dropout? A study of gender and school year differences. In: the 13th International Conference on Educational Data Mining (Upcoming)
12. McBroom, J., Koprinska, I., Yacef, K.: A survey of automated programming hint generation-the hints framework. arXiv preprint arXiv:1908.11566 (2019)
13. McBroom, J., Koprinska, I., Yacef, K.: Understanding gender differences to improve equity in computer programming education. In: Proceedings of the Twenty-Second Australasian Computing Education Conference, pp. 185–194 (2020)

14. McBroom, J., Yacef, K., Koprinska, I., Curran, J.R.: A data-driven method for helping teachers improve feedback in computer programming automated tutors. In: Penstein Rosé, C., et al. (eds.) AIED 2018. LNCS (LNAI), vol. 10947, pp. 324–337. Springer, Cham (2018). https://doi.org/10.1007/978-3-319-93843-1_24

15. Młynarska, E., Greene, D., Cunningham, P.: Time series clustering of moodle activity data. In: Proceedings of the 24th Irish Conference on Artificial Intelligence and Cognitive Science (AICS'16), University College Dublin, Dublin, Ireland, 20–21 September 2016, pp. 104–115 (2016)

16. Paassen, B., Mokbel, B., Hammer, B.: Adaptive structure metrics for automated feedback provision in intelligent tutoring systems. Neurocomputing **192**, 3–13 (2016)

17. Pal, S.: Mining educational data to reduce dropout rates of engineering students. Int. J. Inf. Eng. Electron. Bus. 4(2), 1–7 (2012)

18. Pereira, F.D., et al.: Early dropout prediction for programming courses supported by online judges. In: Isotani, S., Millán, E., Ogan, A., Hastings, P., McLaren, B., Luckin, R. (eds.) AIED 2019. LNCS (LNAI), vol. 11626, pp. 67–72. Springer, Cham (2019). https://doi.org/10.1007/978-3-030-23207-8_13

19. Price, T.W., et al.: A comparison of the quality of data-driven programming hint generation algorithms. Int. J. Artif. Intell. Educ. **29**(3), 368–395 (2019)

20. Safavian, S.R., Landgrebe, D.: A survey of decision tree classifier methodology. IEEE Trans. Syst. Man Cybern. **21**(3), 660–674 (1991)

21. Talavera, L., Gaudioso, E.: Mining student data to characterize similar behavior groups in unstructured collaboration spaces. In: Workshop on Artificial Intelligence in CSCL. 16th European Conference on Artificial Intelligence, pp. 17–23 (2004)

22. Tang, C., Ouyang, Y., Rong, W., Zhang, J., Xiong, Z.: Time series model for predicting dropout in massive open online courses. In: Penstein Rosé, C., et al. (eds.) AIED 2018. LNCS (LNAI), vol. 10948, pp. 353–357. Springer, Cham (2018). https://doi.org/10.1007/978-3-319-93846-2_66

23. Villamor, M., Paredes, Y.V., Samaco, J.D., Cortez, J.F., Martinez, J., Rodrigo, M.M.: Assessing the collaboration quality in the pair program tracing and debugging eye-tracking experiment. In: André, E., Baker, R., Hu, X., Rodrigo, M.M.T., du Boulay, B. (eds.) AIED 2017. LNCS (LNAI), vol. 10331, pp. 574–577. Springer, Cham (2017). https://doi.org/10.1007/978-3-319-61425-0_67

24. Xu, D., Tian, Y.: A comprehensive survey of clustering algorithms. Ann. Data Sci. **2**(2), 165–193 (2015)

Effect of Non-mandatory Use of an Intelligent Tutoring System on Students' Learning

Antonija Mitrović$^{(\boxtimes)}$ (iD) and Jay Holland

Intelligent Computer Tutoring Group, University of Canterbury, Christchurch, New Zealand
tanja.mitrovic@canterbury.ac.nz

Abstract. Numerous controlled studies prove the effectiveness of Intelligent Tutoring Systems (ITSs). But what happens when ITSs are available to students for voluntary practice? EER-Tutor is a mature ITS which was previously found effective in controlled experiments. Students can use EER-Tutor for tutored problem solving, and there is also a special mode allowing students to develop solutions for the course assignment without receiving feedback. In this paper, we report the observations from two classes of university students using EER-Tutor. In 2018, the system was available for completely voluntary practice. We hypothesized that the students' pre-existing knowledge and the time spent in EER-Tutor, mediated by the number of attempted EER-Tutor problems, contribute to the students' scores on the assignment. All but one student used EER-Tutor to draw their assignment solutions, and 77% also used it for tutored problem solving. All our hypotheses were confirmed. Given the found benefits of tutored problem solving, we modified the assignment for the 2019 class so that the first part required students to solve three problems in EER-Tutor (without feedback), while the second part was similar to the 2018 assignment. Our hypothesized model fits the data well and shows the positive relationship between the three set problems on the overall system use, and the assignment scores. In 2019, 98% of the class engaged in tutored problem solving. The 2019 class also spent significantly more time in the ITS, solved significantly more problems and achieved higher scores on the assignment.

Keywords: Intelligent Tutoring System · Conceptual database design · Learning analytics · Voluntary practice · Learning effect

1 Introduction

Intelligent Tutoring Systems (ITSs) have been shown in controlled studies to produce significant improvements in learning in comparison to the classroom, e.g. [1–3]. Such randomized studies are usually based on the pre/post-test design, which allows for measuring learning gains. VanLehn [4] in his meta-review reported the effect size of d = 0.76 for ITSs, comparable to the effect sizes achieved in 1:1 human tutoring. Other recent meta-analyses of reported evaluations of ITSs show similar findings [5, 6].

But what happens when ITSs are available for voluntary practice? Existing literature suggests only a fraction of students typically engages with educational systems when their use is completely voluntary. For example, Gašević et al. [7] write that over 60% of

© Springer Nature Switzerland AG 2020
I. I. Bittencourt et al. (Eds.): AIED 2020, LNAI 12163, pp. 386–397, 2020.
https://doi.org/10.1007/978-3-030-52237-7_31

students are limited users of educational technology. Similarly, Denny and colleagues [8] report that only one third of students used PeerWise, a system that supports peer learning by allowing students to pose questions and to answer/rate questions written by their peers. Brusilovsky and colleagues [9] report that only one half of students engaged in voluntary practice in Python grids, a system that provides several types of activities for learning Python.

In this paper, we investigate the effect of EER-Tutor, a mature ITS that teaches conceptual database design. Different versions of EER-Tutor have been used in courses at the University of Canterbury since 2001. The system is available to students for voluntary practice, as a supplement to lectures and labs. The system has previously been evaluated in several studies, which proved its effectiveness. In this paper, we focus on two questions: how students use this ITS, as well as its effect on students' learning.

In Sect. 2, we briefly introduce EER-Tutor, while the following Section presents out hypothesized model. Section 4 presents the findings from the 2018 class. We then made a modification to the assignment, by requiring students to solve three problems in EER-Tutor in addition to a more open-ended problem, and developed a new hypothesized model. We present the findings from the 2019 class in Sect. 5. Finally, we reflect on the findings and discuss the limitations.

2 EER-Tutor

EER-Tutor is a mature ITS, that teaches conceptual database design using the Enhanced Entity-Relationship (EER) data model [10, 11]. Different versions of EER-Tutor have been available to students enrolled in a second-year relational database course since 2001. The system has also been used by numerous students world-wide[1].

We have presented the architecture, the student modeler and the adaptive features of EER-Tutor in previous papers [12–14]; here we briefly summarize its features necessary to understand the analyses we performed. Figure 1 shows a screenshot of EER-Tutor, with the text of the problem at the top, the drawing area in the middle pane, and the feedback area on the right. The student can select any problem he/she wants, or ask for a problem to be selected adaptively by the system (on the basis of the student model). The current version of the system contains 57 problems, which are ordered by their complexity. The student draws the diagram by selecting tools representing the components of the EER model, and names them by selecting words or phrases from the problem text. EER-Tutor highlights the names of created entity types in blue, the names of attributes in green and the names of relationships in magenta, thus providing an easy way for the student to see how much of the requirements have been covered. When the student submits the solution, EER-Tutor evaluates it and presents the feedback. In the situation shown in Fig. 1, the student specified the participation of the SENSOR entity type as partial (single line), while it should be total (double line). EER-Tutor highlights the relevant components of the solution in red to make it easier for the student to focus on the error.

---

[1] EER-Tutor was available on the Addison-Wesley's DatabasePlace portal from 2003 to 2016.

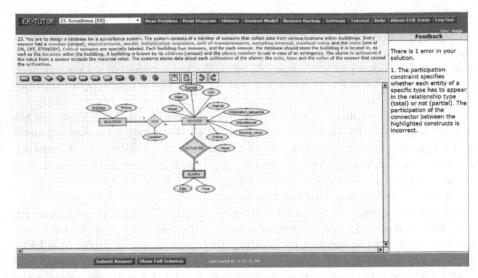

Fig. 1. The screenshot of EER-Tutor

We have implemented many versions of EER-Tutor, in order to evaluate some of its features, such as the open learner model [15–17], affect-aware animated pedagogical agent [18] and tutorial dialogues [19]. In all controlled studies, we have found significant improvements in learning.

3   2018 Database Course and Hypothesized Model

COSC265 is a single-semester (12 weeks) course on Relational database systems at the University of Canterbury, with three lectures and two lab hours per week. In 2018, there were 201 students enrolled in the course, who were completing Bachelor degrees in Computer Science (65%), Software Engineering (32%) or Information Systems (3%). Most of the students were in their second year, but there were 16 students repeating the course, and also some students taking the course in their first year (6%).

After a general introduction to databases (two lectures), the following four lectures were on conceptual database design using the EER model. At the end of the second week of the course (on July 27), the students were given an assignment worth 25% of the final grade, requiring them to develop an EER schema based on the given requirements. The assignment was due on August 24, which is the last day of week 6 (followed by a two-week break). Late submissions were allowed until August 31, in which case the students received a penalty of 15 marks.

EER-Tutor was introduced to the students briefly in a lecture in the second week, and the system was used in labs in the third week. The use of EER-Tutor was completely voluntary; the students did not receive any marks for solving problems in the ITS. The pre-test was given to students immediately after logging in, while the post test was given on a specific date. In addition to the 57 available problems, there is also a special mode of the tutor (referred to as mode 99), which allows students to draw EER diagrams without feedback. All students used

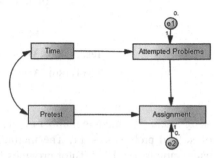

Fig. 2. Hypothesized path analytic model

this mode to draw their solutions for the assignment. The assignment was similar to the most complex problems in EER-Tutor. The final exam covered the whole course (50% of the final grade).

Figure 2 presents our path analytic model, based on previous research. Our first hypothesis is that the pre-existing knowledge (the pre-test score) will have a positive effect on the assignment score (*Assignment*). Positive correlation between pre-existing knowledge and the score after training (in our case the assignment score) is commonly found in the literature (e.g. [9]). Another common finding in the literature is that learning time is positively correlated with the final score. In our case, the time students spent in EER-Tutor was divided between working on assignment (i.e. drawing the diagram in mode 99) and tutored problem solving. The more time students spend in EER-Tutor, the more problems they attempt. We also hypothesize that attempted problems contribute to learning, as have been shown in previous studies with EER-Tutor. Therefore, the number of attempted problems mediates the relationship between time and the assignment score.

4 Findings from the 2018 Course

The pre-test contained seven questions (multiple choice or true/false), worth one mark each. Three questions asked to select correct definitions of EER concepts, while the remaining four questions required the student to select correct diagrams matching given requirements. There were two tests of similar complexities, which were randomly given to students as the pre-test. A student who received Test A as the pre-test, received Test B as the post-test and vice versa. Since there are two different tests used as the pre/post-test, we analysed the students' scores at the pre-test time, to make sure they were of similar difficulty. We report the statistics on pre-test scores in Table 1. There were 89 students who completed test A, and 86 completed test B. We found no significant difference between the pre-test scores on the two tests ($t = 1.46$, $p = 0.15$). The internal validity is acceptable for both tests, given the limited number of test questions and the broad range of tested knowledge [20].

Table 2 report statistics of how students interacted with EER-Tutor. The number of sessions and time are presented for 200 students, while the remaining rows present the values for the 153 students who attempted problem solving. One student never logged onto EER-Tutor. Forty-six students have only used the tutor to work on their

Table 1. 2018 pre-test scores

	Mean score (sd)	Cronbach's alpha
Test A (89)	3.62 (1.79)	0.59
Test B (86)	3.99 (1.56)	0.52

assignment. The median number of attempted problems is 13, while the median number of solved problems is 11. The median number of attempts per student was 34. For each submission, EER-Tutor provides feedback (as shown in Fig. 1). The pedagogical strategy implemented in the current version of EER-Tutor provides positive feedback on correct submissions, or provides up to three messages on mistakes when the submission is incorrect. The last row of Table 2 (*Hints*) reports the total number of error messages provided to the student.

Table 2. Summary statistics of EER-Tutor usage in 2018

	Min	Max	Median	Mean (sd)
Sessions	0	72	14	16.11 (11.84)
Time (min)	0	1285	125	189.85 (218.27)
Attempted problems	1	55	13	14.64 (10.47)
Solved problems	0	54	11	13.04 (10.09)
Attempts	1	364	34	49.95 (52.95)
Hints	0	614	43	75.58 (97.76)

Figure 3 (left) shows the number of students solving problems with EER-Tutor in weeks 2–7. Nineteen students started solving problems as soon as EER-Tutor was introduced in lectures in week 2. The highest number of students solving problems was recorded in week 3, when they used the ITS in the scheduled lab for the course. In weeks 5 and 6, 41 and 67 respectively worked on problems, in preparation for the assignment. There were few problems solved after week 7 until weeks 14–16, when students again solved problems in preparation for the exam. On average, students completed 78.55% of problems they attempted. Figure 3 (right) shows the number of students working on the assignment in weeks 3–7, with the average time (in minutes). Fourteen students started working on their assignment in the second week of the course. The peak in week 6 corresponds to the assignment deadline. Students who were late submitting the assignment used the system substantially in week 7.

Table 3 presents several performance measures. As EER-Tutor was available for voluntary practice, not all students started using it immediately, and consequently the date when students completed the pre-test ranged from July 23 to August 31. There were 16 students who either completed the pre- and post-test on the same day (because they started using the system late), or completed the two tests without attempting any

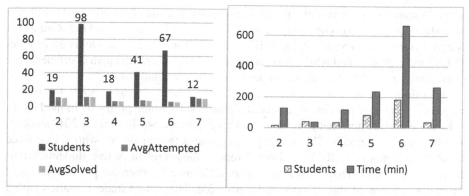

Fig. 3. Left: Number of students and attempted/solved problems. Right: Number of students and average time spent in mode 99

problems in between. For that reason, we did not include those students when calculating the normalized learning gain. Additionally, many students did not complete the post-test, so the number of students for whom we computed the normalized learning gain is 57. On average, the students achieved higher scores on the post-test compared to the pre-test scores, with the effect size (Cohen's d) of 0.38. One possible reason for the low value of the normalized gain is that students did not take the post-test seriously, as it did not contribute to the final grade. Additionally, the students were focused on completing their assignment at the time the post-test was administered.

Table 3. 2018 performance measures

	Min	Max	Median	Mean (sd)
Pretest % (180)	0	100	57.14	53.97 (24.33)
Normalized gain (57)	−1	1	0	0.17 (0.46)
Assignment % (198)	17	96	58.50	59.37 (13.20)

The path analytic model was evaluated with IBM SPSS Amos version 25, using the data collected from 179 participants for whom all relevant data were available (Fig. 4). The number of the parameters to be estimated in this model is 12. The amount of data we have is appropriate for this kind of analysis, as the recommendation is that there are at least ten participants per parameter [21]. All the variables in the path model are observed. Chi-square test (1.62) for this model

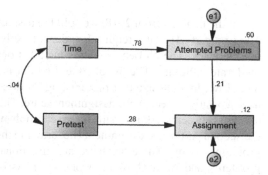

Fig. 4. 2018 model with path coefficients

(df $= 2$) shows that the model's predictions are not statistically significantly different from the data (p $= .44$). The Comparative Fit Index (CFI) was .99, and the Root Mean Square Error of Approximation (RMSEA) was .01. Therefore the model is acceptable: CFI is greater than .9 and RMSEA is less than .06 [22, 23]. All the path coefficients are significant at p $< .005$. Therefore, all our hypotheses are confirmed.

Therefore, tutored problem solving is important. One way to improve the performance of the class would be to require students to solve some problems in the ITS. In order to investigate how many problems make a difference, we divided the 2018 students post-hoc into two groups. The *Active* group contains those students who solved three or more problems in EER-Tutor. Table 4 reports the scores of Active students versus the rest of the class. There was a significant difference between the pre-test scores of the two subgroups of students (t $= 2.32$, p $< .05$). The Active students started with a higher level of knowledge, and used the system more, which may be the effect of those students being more motivated. There was no significant difference on the normalized gain, but the number of students who completed the post-test in both subgroups is small. This may show that the students have not taken post-test seriously; at that time of the course they were focused on completing their assignments, and taking a non-mandatory post-test was low priority. There were significant differences between the two subgroups on both assignment (t $= 3.01$, p $< .005$) and exam marks (t $= 4.72$, p $< .001$).

Table 4. Comparing the two 2018 subgroups

	Pretest	Norm. gain	Assignment	Exam
Active	57.02 (22.95)	0.18 (0.44)	61.44 (12.09)	73.97 (16.14)
	n $= 120$	n $= 51$	n $= 127$	n $= 121$
Others	47.86 (26.01)	-0.03 (0.44)	55.68 (14.34)	62.37 (16.14)
	n $= 60$	n $= 19$	n $= 71$	n $= 67$

5   2019 Course

Given the findings from 2018, we split the assignment into two parts for the 2019 class. The first part (*Assign1*) required students to solve three problems in EER-Tutor, without feedback. The chosen problems included one easy problem, and two problems of moderate difficulty. The hypothesized model is shown in Fig. 5. Similar to the 2018 model, we hypothesize that pre-existing knowledge and time spent in EER-Tutor will have a positive effect on the assignment score. The time students spent in EER-Tutor was divided between working on the three set problems in EER-Tutor (Assign 1), working on the second part of the assignment (i.e. drawing the solution using mode 99), and tutored problem solving. Therefore there are directional links between Time and Attempted problems, and Assign1. While working on Assign1, the students would improve their knowledge of database design; therefore we hypothesized a positive effect of Assign1 on Assign2. As in the previous model, we again hypothesize that the number of attempted problems would have a positive effect on the second part of the assignment (*Assign2*). Assign1 mediates the relationship between the pre-test and attempted problems, as well as between pre-test and Assign2. The number of attempted problems mediates the relationship between the time spent in the system and Assign2, because students' knowledge would increase as they attempt problems in EER-Tutor.

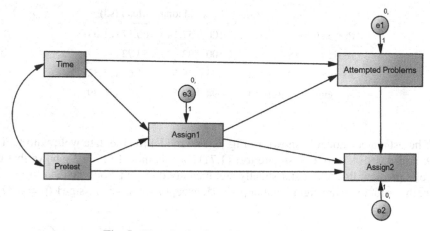

Fig. 5. Hypothesized model for the 2019 class

The only difference between the 2018 and 2019 instances of the course was in the assignment. The first part of the assignment was due at the end of week 4, while the second part was due at the end of week 6. There were 198 students enrolled in 2019, five of which have not engaged with the course at all. Out of the remaining 193 students, only one has not logged onto EER-Tutor. Table 5 presents some statistics of how students interacted with EER-Tutor. The number of sessions and the time in EER-Tutor are reported for 193 students, while the remaining rows of the table present the values for the 189 students who have attempted problem solving. Three students have not attempted problem solving, and used EER-Tutor solely to draw the solution for Assign2.

Table 5. Summary statistics of EER-Tutor usage in 2019

	Min	Max	Median	Mean (sd)
Sessions	0	74	15	17.22 (11.14)
Time (min)	0	2147	382	488.69 (355.89)
Attempted problems	1	57	22	22.11 (11.03)
Solved problems	0	50	18	17.53 (10.90)
Attempts	2	303	62	79.41 (60.93)
Hints	1	613	91	128.38 (117.91)

Table 6 presents the summary results about students' performance. Assign1 was worth 8% and Assign2 was worth 17% of the final grade. The last row in Table 6 presents the overall score for the assignment.

Table 6. 2019 performance measures (in percentages)

	Min	Max	Median	Mean (sd)
Pretest (184)	14.29	100	57.14	60.17 (21.03)
Assign 1 (188)	21	100	92	83.72 (16.29)
Assign 2 (189)	12	93	76.5	71.69 (15.32)
Assignment (192)	14	94	79.5	73.74 (16.39)

The estimated model is shown in Fig. 6. The model fits the data well, with CFI = 0.99, and RMSEA = 0. Chi-square test (1.71) for this model (df = 2) shows that the model's predictions are not statistically significantly different from the data (p = .43). All path coefficients are significant at p < .05, except *Pretest - >* Assign1 (p = .077).

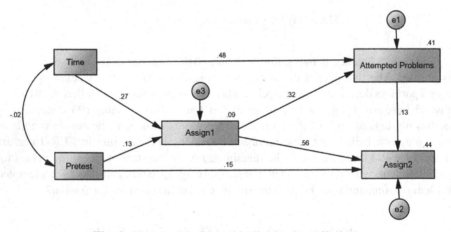

Fig. 6. 2019 model with standardized path coefficients

For the reader's convenience, we present the 2019 data on weekly use of EER-Tutor together with the 2018 data in Fig. 7. In 2019, students used EER-Tutor for the first time in week 3, and therefore we present the data for weeks 3 to 7 only. Many more students engaged in tutored problem solving in weeks 3 and 4 in 2019 in comparison to 2018. We believe the reason for that is the requirement for three problems to be solved in 2019 by week 4, which motivated students to practice more. In 2018, students have spent more time in mode 99 (working on the assignment) than in 2019; that might be because the 2019 students learnt more from tutored problem solving in early weeks and were therefore able to complete the assignment faster.

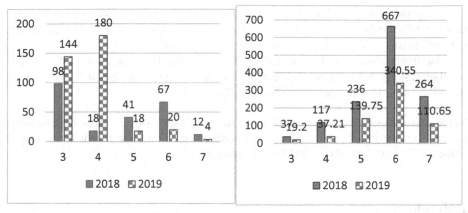

Fig. 7. Left: the number of students solving problems in EER-Tutor; Right: time spent in mode 99

6   Conclusions

In this paper we reported how students used EER-Tutor for voluntary practice in two consecutive years of the same course. Our findings are in contrast to the finding from the literature which shows that many students (50% or more) do not engage in voluntary practice with educational technology [7–9]. On the contrary, in our 2018 cohort, 23% of students used the tutor only to draw their assignments, and have not attempted any problem solving. The majority of the class (77%) used EER-Tutor both to work on the assignment, and for tutored problem solving.

One of the reasons for limited use of educational technology reported in the literature is the low levels of self-regulation skills and motivation [9, 24]. Since tutored problem solving in EER-Tutor was voluntary, it may be the case that the students who solved a lot of problems are more motivated students. We did, however, find that the number of attempted problems and time spent with EER-Tutor are significant predictors of their performance on the assignment. Students who solved at least three problems in EER-Tutor in 2018 received significantly higher marks on the assignment than the rest of the class.

Therefore, one straightforward recommendation for improving students' learning is to introduce a degree of mandatory problem solving. We have made that change in 2019, when the students were required to solve three problems in EER-Tutor as the first part of the assignment. In 2019, only three students have used EER-Tutor solely to draw the EER diagram; therefore, the percentage of students who used EER-Tutor for tutored problem solving increased from 77% in 2018 to 98% in 2019. In 2018, 69.5% of students solved at least one problem in EER-Tutor, while in 2019 that percentage increased to 91.71% (this is one problem in addition to the three mandatory problems). Therefore, requiring students to solve three problems increased their voluntary use of EER-Tutor in 2019. Comparing the two classes, we found that the 2019 class spent significantly more time in the tutor ($t = 10.03$, $p < .001$), solved significantly more problems in EER-Tutor ($t = 7.03$, $p < .001$) and achieved significantly higher marks on the assignment ($t = 9.52$, $p < .001$). Comparing the 2018/2019 assignment scores may not be fair, as the two assignments may not have been of the same complexity, but the other two measures (time and the number of solved problems) show evidence that the intervention (requiring students to solve three prescribed problems) has made a difference.

One limitation of our study is that we have not collected data about students' self-regulation skills and motivation. We plan to collect such data in the 2020 class, which will allow us to look deeper into individual differences.

Acknowledgements. This research would not have been possible without support of all members (past and present) of the Intelligent Computer Tutoring Group. We are also grateful for the support of the University of Canterbury and COSC265 students.

References

1. Anderson, J.R., Corbett, A., Koedinger, K., Pelletier, R.: Cognitive tutors: lessons learned. J. Learn. Sci. **4**(2), 167–207 (1995)
2. VanLehn, K.: The behavior of tutoring systems. Artif. Intell. Educ. **16**(3), 227–265 (2006)
3. Mitrovic, A.: Fifteen years of constraint-based tutors: what we have achieved and where we are going. User Model. User-Adap. Inter. **22**(1–2), 39–72 (2012)
4. VanLehn, K.: The relative effectiveness of human tutoring, intelligent tutoring systems, and other tutoring systems. Educ. Psychol. **46**(4), 197–221 (2011)
5. Ma, W., Adesope, O.O., Nesbit, J.C., Liu, Q.: Intelligent tutoring systems and learning outcomes: a meta-analysis. J. Educ. Psychol. **106**(4), 901 (2014)
6. Kulik, J.A., Fletcher, J.: Effectiveness of intelligent tutoring systems: a meta-analytic review. Rev. Educ. Res. **86**(1), 42–78 (2016)
7. Gašević, D., Mirriahi, N., Dawson, S.: Analytics of the effects of video use and instruction to support reflective learning. In: Proceedings of the 4th International Conference on Learning Analytics and Knowledge, pp. 123–132. ACM (2014)
8. Denny, P., McDonald, F., Empson, R., Kelly, P., Petersen, A.: Empirical support for a causal relationship between gamification and learning outcomes. In: Proceedings of CHI Conference on Human Factors in Computing Systems, p. 311. ACM (2018)
9. Brusilovsky, P., Malmi, L., Hosseini, R., Guerra, J., Sirkiä, T., Pollari-Malmi, K.: An integrated practice system for learning programming in Python: design and evaluation. Res. Pract. Technol. Enhanced Learn. **13**(1), 18 (2018)
10. Chen, P.: The entity relationship model - toward a unified view of data. ACM Trans. Datab. Syst. **1**, 9–36 (1976)
11. Elmasri, R., Navathe, S.B.: Fundamentals of Database Systems. Addison Wesley (1994)
12. Suraweera, P., Mitrovic, A.: KERMIT: a constraint-based tutor for database modeling. In: Cerri, S.A., Gouardères, G., Paraguaçu, F. (eds.) ITS 2002. LNCS, vol. 2363, pp. 377–387. Springer, Heidelberg (2002). https://doi.org/10.1007/3-540-47987-2_41
13. Suraweera, P., Mitrovic, A.: An intelligent tutoring system for entity relationship modelling. Artif. Intell. Educ. **14**(3–4), 375–417 (2004)
14. Zakharov, K., Mitrovic, A., Ohlsson, S: Feedback micro-engineering in EER-Tutor. In: Looi, C.-K., McCalla, G., Bredeweg, B., Breuker, J. (eds.) Proceedings of International Conference Artificial Intelligence in Education. IOS Press, pp. 718–725 (2005)
15. Hartley, D., Mitrovic, A.: Supporting learning by opening the student model. In: Cerri, S.A., Gouardères, G., Paraguaçu, F. (eds.) ITS 2002. LNCS, vol. 2363, pp. 453–462. Springer, Heidelberg (2002). https://doi.org/10.1007/3-540-47987-2_48

16. Duan, D., Mitrovic, A., Churcher, N.: Evaluating the effectiveness of multiple open student models in EER-Tutor. In: Wong, S.L. et al. (eds.) Proceedings of 18th International Conference on Computers in Education, pp. 86–88 (2010)
17. Mathews, M., Mitrovic, A., Lin, B., Holland, J., Churcher, N.: Do your eyes give it away? Using eye tracking data to understand students' attitudes towards open student model representations. In: Cerri, S.A., Clancey, W.J., Papadourakis, G., Panourgia, K. (eds.) ITS 2012. LNCS, vol. 7315, pp. 422–427. Springer, Heidelberg (2012). https://doi.org/10.1007/978-3-642-30950-2_54
18. Zakharov, K., Mitrovic, A., Johnston, L.: Pedagogical agents trying on a caring mentor role. In: Luckin, R., Koedinger, K., Greer, J. (eds.) Proceedings of 13th International Conference on Artificial Intelligence in Education, Los Angeles, pp. 59–66 (2007)
19. Weerasinghe, A., Mitrovic, A., Martin, B.: Towards individualized dialogue support for ill-defined domains. Artif. Intell. Educ. 19(4), 357–379 (2009)
20. Taber, K.S.: The use of Cronbach's alpha when developing and reporting research instruments in science education. Res. Sci. Educ. 48(6), 273–1296 (2018)
21. Raykov, T., Widaman, K.F.: Issues in applied structural equation modeling research. Struct. Eqn. Model. 2(4), 289–310 (1995)
22. Hu, L.T., Bentler, P.M.: Cutoff criteria for fit indexes in covariance structure analysis: conventional criteria versus new alternatives. Struct. Eqn. Model.: Multidiscip. J. 6(1), 1–55 (1999)
23. Teo, T., Tsai, L.T., Yang, C.C.: Applying structural equation modeling (SEM) in educational research: an introduction. In: Application of Structural Equation Modeling in Educational Research and Practice, pp. 1–21. Brill Sense (2013)
24. Lust, G., Elen, J., Clarebout, G.: Regulation of tool use within a blended course: Student differences and performance effects. Comput. Educ. 60(1), 385–395 (2013)

Evaluating Crowdsourcing and Topic Modeling in Generating Knowledge Components from Explanations

Steven Moore$^{(\boxtimes)}$ ⓘ, Huy A. Nguyen ⓘ, and John Stamper

Carnegie Mellon University, Pittsburgh, PA 15213, USA
StevenJamesMoore@gmail.com

Abstract. Associating assessment items with hypothesized knowledge components (KCs) enables us to gain fine-grained data on students' performance within an ed-tech system. However, creating this association is a time consuming process and requires substantial instructor effort. In this study, we present the results of crowdsourcing valuable insights into the underlying concepts of problems in mathematics and English writing, as a first step in leveraging the crowd to expedite the task of generating KCs. We presented crowdworkers with two problems in each domain and asked them to provide three explanations about why one problem is more challenging than the other. These explanations were then independently analyzed through (1) a series of qualitative coding methods and (2) several topic modeling techniques, to compare how they might assist in extracting KCs and other insights from the participant contributions. Results of our qualitative coding showed that crowdworkers were able to generate KCs that approximately matched those generated by domain experts. At the same time, the topic models' outputs were evaluated against both the domain expert generated KCs and the results of the previous coding to determine effectiveness. Ultimately we found that while the topic modeling was not up to parity with the qualitative coding methods, it did assist in identifying useful clusters of explanations. This work demonstrates a method to leverage both the crowd's knowledge and topic modeling to assist in the process of generating KCs for assessment items.

Keywords: Knowledge component · Knowledge component modeling · Crowdsourcing · Topic modeling · Intelligent tutoring systems

1 Introduction

The combination of data-driven knowledge tracing methods and cognitive-based modeling has greatly enhanced the effectiveness of a wide range of educational technologies, such as intelligent tutoring systems and other online courseware. In particular, these systems often employ knowledge component modeling, which treats student knowledge as a set of interrelated KCs, where each KC is "an acquired unit of cognitive function or structure that can be inferred from performance on a set of related tasks" [14]. Operationally, a KC model is defined as a mapping between each question item and a

© Springer Nature Switzerland AG 2020
I. I. Bittencourt et al. (Eds.): AIED 2020, LNAI 12163, pp. 398–410, 2020.
https://doi.org/10.1007/978-3-030-52237-7_32

hypothesized set of associated KCs that represent the skills or knowledge needed to solve that item. This mapping is intended to capture the student's underlying cognitive process and is vital to many core functionalities of educational software, enabling features such as adaptive feedback and hints [22].

While machine learning methodologies have been developed to assist in the automatic identification of new KCs, prior research has shown that human judgment remains critical in the interpretation of the improved model and acquisition of actionable insights [19, 24]. An emerging area that has the potential to provide the human resources needed for scaling KC modeling is crowdsourcing. Naturally, the challenge with this approach is that the population of crowdworkers is highly varied in their education level and domain knowledge proficiency. Therefore, as a first step towards examining and promoting the feasibility of crowdsourced KC modeling, we studied how crowdworkers can provide insights into different word problems that might suggest areas of improvements and generating KCs for the questions. We took these insights via explanations, coded them and ran them through two topic models to analyze how they might be utilized for the task. Our research questions are as follows:

RQ1: Are the explanations provided by crowdworkers indicative of any KCs that the problems require?
RQ2: How effective is topic modeling compared to qualitative coding in identifying explanations indicative of KCs?
RQ3: Do the explanations provide insights into how the presented assessment items may be improved?

2 Related Work

KC models are typically developed by domain experts through Cognitive Task Analysis methods [29], which lead to effective instructional designs but require substantial human efforts. Fully automated methods can potentially discover models with better performance than human-generated ones (in terms of statistical metrics such as AIC, BIC and cross validation score), but they suffer from a lack of interpretability [31]. Other efforts of automatic cognitive model discovery make use of student data, such as the Q-matrix algorithm [2]. On the other hand, [13] showed that a refined KC model that results from both human judgment and computational metrics can help students reach mastery in 26% less time. More generally, as pointed out in [18] the inclusion of human factors in the KC modeling process can be advantageous, leading to lessons that can be implemented in follow-up studies.

Recently, crowdsourcing has become increasingly popular for content development and refinement in the education domain [21, 27]. The process of crowdsourcing data from learners, or learnersourcing, has been used to identify which parts of lecture videos are confusing [12], and to describe the key instructional steps and subgoals of how-to videos [11]. In particular, [33] explored a crowdsourcing-based strategy towards personalized learning in which learners were asked to author explanations on how to solve statistics problems. The explanations generated by learners were found to be comparable in quality to explanations produced by expert instructors.

As the fields of natural language processing and text mining continue to advance, they are being increasingly leveraged by education to help automate arduous tasks [6]. Previous work has looked at using different machine learning models [25, 26] and utilizing a search engine [10] to tag educational content with KCs. Recent efforts have utilized topic modeling on a set of math problems from an intelligent tutoring system to assist in the labeling of KCs [30]. While their initial model had promising results, there was an issue of human interpretability for the topics it produced, that may be relieved by different models [17]. Much of the work in this space is focused towards predicting KCs for content, after being trained on similarly KC tagged problem. Few studies have tried to leverage text mining techniques to generate KCs for content, with no training or prediction modeling involved.

3 Methods

Our study consists of two experiments with the same procedure, but involve different domain knowledge. The first domain is mathematics, with a focus on the area of shapes; the second is English writing, with a focus on prose style involving agents and clause topics. In both domains, we deployed an experiment using Amazon's Mechanical Turk (AMT). Forty crowd workers on AMT, known as "turkers," completed the math experiment, and thirty turkers completed the writing experiment, for a total of 70 participants. In each domain, the tasks took roughly five minutes. Participants were compensated $0.75 upon completion, providing a mean hourly wage of $9.

The main task of the experiment presented participants with two word problems positioned side by side, labeled Question 1 and Question 2. In the math experiment, both problems involve finding the area of two different structures. In the writing experiment, both problems involve identifying the agents and actions of two different sentences. Participants were truthfully told that past students were tested on these problems and that the collected data indicates Question 2 is more difficult than Question 1. They were then asked to provide three explanations on why this is the case. The specific question prompt stated: *"Data shows that from the two questions displayed above, students have more difficulty answering Question 2 than Question 1. Please list three explanations on why Question 2 might be more difficult than Question 1".*

3.1 Math and Writing Experiments

The two mathematics word problems used for the explanation task can be seen in Fig. 1. These problems come from a previous study of a geometry cognitive tutor [32], where the data indicates that students struggle more with the problem involving painting the wall (the right side of Fig. 1). Both problems are tagged with the same three KCs by the domain experts that created the problems, so they assess the same content. These KCs are: Compose-by-addition, Subtract, and Rectangle-area.

Both problems used in the writing experiment come from an online prose style course for freshman and sophomore undergraduates (Fig. 2). Similar to the math problems, student data collected from the online course indicates students struggle more with one problem over the other. The KCs were generated by domain experts and are: Id-clause-topic, Discourse-level-topic, Subject-position, and Verb-form.

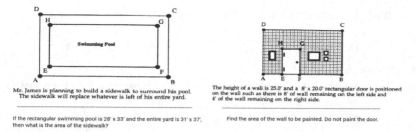

Fig. 1. The two word problems for which participants provided three explanations in the math experiment, with the one on the right being more difficult.

Question 1

Identify the clause-level topic of the first clause in the following sentence:

The archives were created by dictator Joseph Stalin, who assiduously gathered compromising material on his opposition and colleagues.

○ The archives ○ were created ○ by dictator ○ Joseph Stalin ○ who ○ assiduously ○ gathered
○ compromising material ○ on his opposition ○ and colleagues

Question 2

Revise the sentence below so that the agent is in the subject position of a complete sentence. Use the same verb tense in your revision as in the original. If the agent is unstated, supply a plausible one. Try to retain as much of the original sentence's meaning as you can.

Various directions for future research are suggested by this study.

Answer space

Fig. 2. The two problems for which participants provided three explanations in the writing experiment, with the one on the right being more difficult.

3.2 Categorization of Explanations

We collected three explanations from each of the 40 participants in the math experiment, for a total of 120, and three explanations from each of the 30 participants in the writing experiment, for a total of 90. Overall there were 210 explanations, where each explanation is defined as the full text provided by a participant into the answer space. These mostly consisted of sentence fragments or full sentences, but there were several that had multiple sentences. Such explanations were still treated as a single unit, to which the best fitting code was applied [9].

Using data collected from a brief pilot study, two researchers followed the process in [7] to develop a codebook from the explanations in the math experiment, and a separate codebook for the writing experiment. This involved assigning the participant explanations to a set of codes based on their interpreted meaning. These codebooks were iteratively refined until agreement on the codes was achieved. Two research assistants then applied the codebook to the pilot data and discussed discrepancies, seeking clarity for any codes they were unfamiliar with. Table 1 shows the finalized version of the codebook applied to the collected math and writing explanation data. The codebook was then applied to the full dataset from each domain by the two research assistants. Next, we measured the code agreement via Inter-Rater Reliability (IRR). The coders achieved a Cohen's kappa $\kappa = 0.813$ for the math experiment and $\kappa = 0.839$ for the writing experiment, which indicates a high level of agreement [15].

3.3 Topic Modeling Explanations

Topic models estimate latent topics in a document from word occurrence frequencies, based on the assumption that certain words will appear depending on potential topics in

Table 1. Coding dictionary for the math and writing experiment responses.

Code	Definition	Example explanation
Math experiment		
Calculation	Mentions the computational aspects involved in the problem, e.g., subtraction or use of area	"Because they don't know how to calculate the area"
Clarity-Shape	Relates to the understanding of the depicted shape	"It may be less clear which part should be calculated because of shading"
Clarity-Text	Relates to the understanding of the text	"Wording is kinda confusing"
Complexity	Claiming that one problem is more complicated than the other, without further clarification	"Problem two is more complicated than problem one"
Composite	Addresses an embedded shape used in the problem	"The picture itself shows other objects such as windows and this might throw off the student"
Content	General remarks about the problem content that are not captured by other content subcategories	"The numbers displayed have decimal points"
Meta	A mention of general skills needed to solve any type of word problem, such as focusing, reading, and attention	"It takes more time to read in problem 2 so students are more prone to getting discouraged"
N/A	Does not provide any sensible explanation	"340"
Shape-Layout	Mentions the visual element of the word problem's shapes	"It is more difficult based on the shapes presented in question two"
Step-Num	Indicates one problem requires a certain number of steps/more steps	"There are more steps to complete in problem 2"
Value-Num	Indicates one problem has more variables/values to work with	"It has more variables"
Writing experiment		
Answer #	Relating to the number of answer choices present in the question	"In option one there is only one right answer"
Complexity	Discusses the general difficulty/complexity	"More complex knowledge needed"
Content	Touches on the content of the question	"They have to revise it instead of just saying what is wrong"
Meta	Describing a skill required by similar problems, at a more meta level	"It is hard to write"

(*continued*)

Table 1. (*continued*)

Code	Definition	Example explanation
N/A	Not applicable or relevant	"Poor communication with suppliers"
Prework	Discusses the prior knowledge or prework that might be required to answer	"The second isn't explained in the coursework"
Question-type	Addresses the question's type (MCQ or free response) in the explanation	"Written answer instead of multiple choice"
Question-text	Mentions the question's text in some capacity, e.g., longer/confusing	"Sentence 2 is more vague"
Rules	Mentions the rules a student would need to know to solve the problem	"Problem one only requires an understanding of grammar"
Technical	Mentions a specific technical term that might be required to answer	"In problem two, the subject is not in the beginning of the sentence"

the text. We used two topic modeling techniques, Latent Dirichlet Analysis (LDA [5]) and Non-negative Matrix Factorization (NMF [16]), to further analyze the explanations. LDA maps all documents, in this case the explanations, to a set number of topics in a way such that the words in each document are captured by the topics [1]. NMF uses linear algebra for topic modeling by identifying the latent structure in data, the explanations, represented as a non-negative matrix [20]. The explanation text was lemmatized and stop words were removed, using a common NLP library in Python [4]. No further text processing was performed on the explanation data before running them through the models, as we wanted results without fine-tuning any parameters or heavily processing the data. The results of the topic models were then evaluated against the researcher-generated codes, categorizations, and the expert generated KCs for the problems, in order to gauge their effectiveness for this task.

4 Results

RQ1: Are the explanations provided by crowdworkers indicative of any KCs that the problems require? From the coded explanations in the math and writing experiments, we constructed a set of themes, shown in Table 2, formed by grouping several of the related codes within each experiment together [28]. In the math experiment the first three themes, Greater Quantity, Shapes Present, and Domain Knowledge, all comprise explanations which address features of the given problems and are indicative of a KC required to solve the problem. Explanations that are grouped into these three themes can be translated into KCs that fit the problem and are indicative of the underlying skill(s) required to solve it. However, the only explanations that suggested a KC that matched any of the expert ones (Compose-by-addition, Subtract, and Rectangle-area) came from the *Calculation* code. The fourth theme, Clarity/Confusion, pertains to the problem's question text or visuals being unclear and hard to decipher. This theme contains explanations that relate to what makes the problems particularly difficult outside of the knowledge required to solve it; from these explanations, one could also derive ways to improve the assessment, such as making the question text more explicit or clarifying the depicted image. The fifth theme, Irrelevant, holds the remaining explanations – those that do not address the problem in a meaningful way, i.e., they are too general or abstract.

Table 2. Themes for the math (above) and writing (below) experiments created from the coded data and if the theme is akin to a KC or an area of problem improvement.

Theme (# of explanations)	Codes	KC	Improvement
Greater quantity 27	Step-num, value-num	✔	
Shapes present 30	Shape-layout, composite	✔	
Domain knowledge 33	Content, calculation	✔	
Clarity/confusion 15	Clarity-text, clarity-shape		✔
Irrelevant 15	Complexity, meta, N/A		
Process to solve 13	Rules, content	✔	
Domain knowledge 07	Prework, technical	✔	
Question specific attributes 42	Question-text, question-type, answer-num		✔
Irrelevant 28	Complexity, meta, N/A		

In the writing experiment the first two themes, Process to Solve and Domain Knowledge, are indicative of KCs that were required to solve the problems. The only explanations that matched any of the expert generated KCs (Id-clause-topic, Discourse-level-topic, Subject-position, and Verb-form) for the problems came from the *Rules* and *Technical* codes. The third theme, Question Specific Attributes, discusses the relative level of difficulty between problems, due to one being multiple-choice and the other being free-response, or the question text differences between the two. This theme relates explanations that address ways to improve the assessment, such as simplifying the answer choices. Finally, the Irrelevant theme again consists of explanations that are not meaningful or overly general.

RQ2: How effective is topic modeling compared to qualitative coding in identifying explanations indicative of KCs? The 10 topics identified by both the LDA and NMF models, along with the five most common words associated with them, are presented in Table 3. From the math experiment data, both the LDA and NMF models had comparable results to one another. They share the same set of topic interpretations and an equally low number of N/A topics. While certain topics in both models are attributed to KC codes, it would be challenging to discern the explicit KC just from the terms. The three primary themes across the ten topics from each model are calculation of area, the visual nature of the shapes in the problems' figures, and how one problem is generally more complicated than the other. We expected some of the expert-generated KCs for the math problems (Compose-by-addition, Subtract, & Rectangle-area) to be identifiable in the topics. Surprisingly *'subtract'* was not a top five term for any topic nor was *'area'* a term alongside *'rectangle'* for any topics.

Similar to the math topics, both the LDA and NMF models produced comparable results for the writing experiment, with slightly different terms used for the topics between the two. The predominant topic in both models is related to the question type, which is appropriate as it was a dominating category from the qualitative coding. Interestingly, there are not as many topics involving *Complexity* or *N/A*, both irrelevant codes that attribute little to no meaning. The majority of the topics focus on the high-level features of the questions, such as the wording or type. Topic 9 from the LDA model and topic 7 from the NMF one include vocabulary used in two of the expert generated KCs (Id-clause-topic, Discourse-level-topic, Subject-position, and Verb-form). However, these topics and the others are not interpretable enough to discern such KCs explicitly from the terms.

RQ3: Do the explanations provide insights into how the presented assessment items may be improved? In addition to some of the explanations being indicative of a KC, such as ones that fall into the *Calculation* or *Technical* codes, many of the other explanations suggested complications with the word problems. In the math experiment, 15 of the 120 total explanations (12.5%) fall into the *Clarity/Confusion* theme from Table 2. Additionally, only 15 of the 120 (12.5%) were deemed *Irrelevant* to the problems, meaning that in general the majority of the explanations were either suggestive of an improvement that could be made or a KC required to solve them. The writing experiment had a greater number of explanations, 42 out of 90 (46.67%), that fell into the *Question Specific Attributes* theme in Table 2. Only 28 of the 90 (31.11%) explanations in this experiment were deemed *Irrelevant* to the problems.

5   Discussion and Implications

Firstly, we wanted to see if the provided explanations could be used to generate fitting KCs for the problems. We found that many of the provided explanations did address the underlying concepts required to solve a problem, more so in the math domain than the writing domain. For example, explanations from the math experiment in the *Greater Quantity* theme often discuss how one problem required the area calculation of more shapes than the other. Solving a problem that involves the area of multiple shapes instead of just a single one has been identified as a knowledge component for similar problems from a previous study [32]. This type of difficulty may be overlooked due to expert blindspot, as the explicit steps taken to solve a problem can get grouped together when it becomes second nature [23]. Eliciting the crowd for explanations such as these can help bring in a diverse level of knowledge, ranging from novice to expert, that can help to make this KC explicit.

From the writing experiment, the *Process to Solve* theme consists of the most KC indicative explanations. These often discuss a step required to solve one of the problems, which was usually at the granularity that would make it a fitting KC. Unfortunately the explanations contributed by participants that were indicative of KCs were relatively rare, making up only 20 of 90 (22.22%) of the total explanations from the writing data,

Table 3. Top 5 terms from 10 topics identified by the LDA and NMF topic models

Topic #	LDA terms	LDA topic interpretation	NMF terms	NMF topic interpretation
Math experiment				
1	Figure, question, hard, shape, confusing	Clarity-shape	Problem, longer, figure, steps, lines	Step-Num
2	Problem, complicated, 1, complex, 2	Complexity	Area, windows, given, figure, door	Calculation
3	Step, calculation, need, require, work	Step-num	Confusing, wording, question, painted, wall	Complexity
4	Consider, answer, visually, complicated, simple	Shape-layout	Shapes, deal, irregular, question, rectangles	Shape-Layout
5	Width, 223, calculate, problem, attention	Calculation	Numbers, deal, size, work, need	N/A
6	Area, complicated, window, 143, 2	Clarity-shape	Complicated, calculation, somewhat, problem, involves	Complexity
7	Confusing, know, abstract, somewhat, term	Complexity	Simple, question, involves, consider, shape	Complexity
8	Accommodate, time, difficult, shading, shape	Clarity-shape	Harder, visually, figure, shape, make	Clarity-Shape
9	Instruction, measurement, equal, forward, straight	N/A	Areas, account, figure, need, just	Calculation
10	Detail, variable, 340, long, contain	N/A	Difficult, calculate, solve, door, width	Calculation
Writing experiment				
1	Answer, prework, specific, pick, confine	Prework	Choice, multiple, problem, allows, simple	Question-type

(continued)

Table 3. (*continued*)

Topic #	LDA terms	LDA topic interpretation	NMF terms	NMF topic interpretation
2	Multiple, choice, 1, problem, thinking	Question-type	Sentence, meaning, needs, subject, problem	Rules
3	Sentence, vague, problem, option, right	Question-text	Problem, requires, understanding, rules, thinking	Meta
4	Long, response, 1, free, variable	Question-type	Answer, free, easier, pick, right	Question-type
5	Know, comment, paraphrase, range, contain	Rules	People, writing, hard, write, questions	Meta
6	People, write, simplified, question, multiple	N/A	Comments, written, eliminate, like, level	N/A
7	Need, complex, written, knowledge, number	Complexity	Know, subject, verb, tense, agent	Technical
8	Comment, problem, choice, multiple, complex	Question-type	Answers, correct, just, questions, incorrect	Question-type
9	Comment, clause, look, agent, suggest	Technical	Clause, concept, agent, ended, like	Technical
10	Concept, rewrite, choose, sentence, end	Content	Complex, concept, written, ended, like	Complexity

compared to 73 of 120 (60.83%) from the math domain. We attribute this difference between domains due to the knowledge required for them, as the math problems were from a middle school class and the writing questions from a college-level writing course.

The two topic models were only able to identify a few topics, each relating to *Calculation*, that fit into a code indicative of a KC that matched one an expert generated. While the terms for the topics can be gleaned for words that suggest a KC such as "area" or "window", they still lack interpretability and a direct translation into a KC. This is also true of the two models' results in the writing domain, which identified several topics relating to the *Rule* and *Technical* codes. Without further interpretation, the terms suggest some vocabulary used in the problems, but they are insufficient to derive an actionable KC without further human processing.

Secondly, we wanted to see if the explanations provided insights into how the assessment items might be improved. Both experiments had one theme directly related to improving the surface level features of the problems, such as the question text or images. For instance, in the math experiment, the theme *Clarity/Confusion* addresses the confusion caused by the visual elements of the problems. The included images for the questions are a key aspect to the assessment and beneficial to problem solving, but may be misinterpreted in a way the content creators may not have intended [8]. Correcting the images can allow for better assessments; based on the explanations we received, a student may answer incorrectly purely based on the poor image design.

Across both domains, the 10 topics identified by each model are mostly comprised of those that indicate areas of problem improvement. While the models performed poorly at generating KCs from the explanations, many of the topics and terms were indicative of student struggle due to confusion with the text or image of the problems. In total, 12.5% of the explanations in math and 31.11% in writing were considered irrelevant to the task and presented problems. Even with limited instruction and the varying backgrounds, participants were able to provide insights into the problems that could be used for baseline KC generation or identifying areas of assessment refinement.

6   Conclusion and Future Work

In this study, we gathered explanations for the relative difficulty between two mathematics questions and between two English writing questions from crowdworkers. We found that crowdworkers were able to generate valuable explanations that were indicative of a KC required to solve the problems or a suggestion for how to make the problems clearer. Understandably, they were able to provide better explanations in the easier domain of middle school math than in an undergraduate English writing domain. However, in both experiments, a majority of the explanations either pertained to identifying a KC or area of improvement, rather than being irrelevant. The LDA and NMF models created topics akin to the researcher generated codes, although the interpretability of these topics based solely on the terms is limited in usefulness. Nevertheless, the categories from the coding and topic models ultimately assisted in clustering explanations that were either indicative of a KC or an aspect of the problem that could be improved.

For future work, we plan to integrate this process in a learner-sourced context, where participants (i.e., students) potentially have more commitment and domain knowledge that could be leveraged [27]. This would enable us to properly train them to provide such explanations throughout the course, rather than completing the task once with only a brief instruction like the crowdworkers did in this study. Ultimately, we envision a workflow in which students submit explanations for why certain problems are difficult; these explanations are then peer reviewed and presented to the teachers (or relevant parties) to help them identify potential KCs and improve the assessment items. This procedure is analogous to the find-fix-verify pattern in crowdsourcing, which has been shown to be effective [2]. However, before reaching this point, the interpretability of the models will need to be improved or another technique should be utilized. This study demonstrates a first step in developing such a workflow, providing initial insights into how crowdsourced explanations might be leveraged for KC generation and assessment content refinement.

Acknowledgements. The research reported here was supported in part by a training grant from the Institute of Education Sciences (R305B150008). Opinions expressed do not represent the views of the U.S. Department of Education.

References

1. AlSumait, L., Barbará, D., Gentle, J., Domeniconi, C.: Topic significance ranking of LDA generative models. In: Buntine, W., Grobelnik, M., Mladenić, D., Shawe-Taylor, J. (eds.) ECML PKDD 2009. LNCS (LNAI), vol. 5781, pp. 67–82. Springer, Heidelberg (2009). https://doi.org/10.1007/978-3-642-04180-8_22
2. Barnes, T.: The Q-matrix method: mining student response data for knowledge. In: American Association for Artificial Intelligence 2005 Educational Data Mining Workshop, pp. 1–8 (2005)
3. Bernstein, M.S., et al.: Soylent: a word processor with a crowd inside. In: Proceedings of the 23nd Annual ACM Symposium on User Interface Software and Technology, pp. 313–322 (2010)
4. Bird, S., et al.: Natural Language Processing with Python: Analyzing Text with the Natural Language Toolkit. O'Reilly Media, Inc. (2009)
5. Blei, D.M., et al.: Latent Dirichlet allocation. J. Mach. Learn. Res. **3**, 993–1022 (2003)
6. Brack, A., et al.: Domain-independent extraction of scientific concepts from research articles. arXiv Prepr. arXiv:200103067 (2020)
7. DeCuir-Gunby, J.T., et al.: Developing and using a codebook for the analysis of interview data: an example from a professional development research project. Field Methods **23**(2), 136–155 (2011)
8. Edens, K., Potter, E.: How students "unpack" the structure of a word problem: graphic representations and problem solving. Sch. Sci. Math. **108**(5), 184–196 (2008)
9. Elliott, V.F.: Thinking about the coding process in qualitative data analysis. Qual. Rep. **23**, 11 (2018)
10. Karlovčec, M., Córdova-Sánchez, M., Pardos, Z.A.: Knowledge component suggestion for untagged content in an intelligent tutoring system. In: Cerri, S.A., Clancey, W.J., Papadourakis, G., Panourgia, K. (eds.) ITS 2012. LNCS, vol. 7315, pp. 195–200. Springer, Heidelberg (2012). https://doi.org/10.1007/978-3-642-30950-2_25
11. Kim, J., et al.: Learnersourcing subgoal labeling to support learning from how-to videos. In: CHI 2013 Extended Abstracts on Human Factors in Computing Systems, pp. 685–690. ACM (2013)
12. Kim, J., et al.: Understanding in-video dropouts and interaction peaks in online lecture videos. In: Proceedings of the First ACM Conference on Learning@ Scale Conference, pp. 31–40. ACM (2014)
13. Koedinger, K.R., et al.: Automated student model improvement. 5th Int. Educ. Data Min. Soc. (2012)
14. Koedinger, K.R., et al.: The knowledge-learning-instruction framework: bridging the science-practice chasm to enhance robust student learning. Cogn. Sci. **36**(5), 757–798 (2012)
15. Landis, J.R., Koch, G.G.: The measurement of observer agreement for categorical data. Biometrics **33**, 159–174 (1977)
16. Lee, D.D., Seung, H.S.: Algorithms for non-negative matrix factorization. In: Advances in Neural Information Processing Systems, pp. 556–562 (2001)
17. Lee, T.Y., et al.: The human touch: how non-expert users perceive, interpret, and fix topic models. Int. J. Hum.-Comput. Stud. **105**, 28–42 (2017)

18. Liu, R., et al.: Interpreting model discovery and testing generalization to a new dataset. In: Educational Data Mining 2014. Citeseer (2014)
19. Liu, R., Koedinger, K.R.: Closing the loop: automated data-driven cognitive model discoveries lead to improved instruction and learning gains. J. Educ. Data Min. **9**(1), 25–41 (2017)
20. Luo, M., et al.: Probabilistic non-negative matrix factorization and its robust extensions for topic modeling. In: Thirty-First AAAI Conference on Artificial Intelligence (2017)
21. Moore, S., et al.: Crowdsourcing explanations for improving assessment content and identifying knowledge components. In: Proceedings of the 14th International Conference of the Learning Sciences (2020)
22. Moore, S., Stamper, J.: Decision support for an adversarial game environment using automatic hint generation. In: Coy, A., Hayashi, Y., Chang, M. (eds.) ITS 2019. LNCS, vol. 11528, pp. 82–88. Springer, Cham (2019). https://doi.org/10.1007/978-3-030-22244-4_11
23. Nathan, M.J., et al.: Expert blind spot: when content knowledge eclipses pedagogical content knowledge. In: Proceedings of the Third International Conference on Cognitive Science (2001)
24. Nguyen, H., et al.: Using knowledge component modeling to increase domain understanding in a digital learning game. In: Proceedings of the 12th International Conference on Educational Data Mining, pp. 139–148 (2019)
25. Pardos, Z.A., Dadu, A.: Imputing KCs with representations of problem content and context. In: Proceedings of the 25th Conference on User Modeling, Adaptation and Personalization, pp. 148–155 (2017)
26. Patikorn, T., Deisadze, D., Grande, L., Yu, Z., Heffernan, N.: Generalizability of methods for imputing mathematical skills needed to solve problems from texts. In: Isotani, S., Millán, E., Ogan, A., Hastings, P., McLaren, B., Luckin, R. (eds.) AIED 2019. LNCS (LNAI), vol. 11625, pp. 396–405. Springer, Cham (2019). https://doi.org/10.1007/978-3-030-23204-7_33
27. Paulin, D., Haythornthwaite, C.: Crowdsourcing the curriculum: redefining e-learning practices through peer-generated approaches. Inf. Soc. **32**(2), 130–142 (2016)
28. Saldana, J.: An introduction to codes and coding. Coding Man. Qual. Res. **3**, 1–31 (2009)
29. Schraagen, J.M., et al.: Cognitive Task Analysis. Psychology Press (2000)
30. Slater, S., et al.: Using correlational topic modeling for automated topic identification in intelligent tutoring systems. In: Proceedings of the Seventh International Learning Analytics & Knowledge Conference. pp. 393–397 (2017)
31. Stamper, J., et al.: A comparison of model selection metrics in datashop. In: Educational Data Mining 2013 (2013)
32. Stamper, J.C., Koedinger, K.R.: Human-machine student model discovery and improvement using datashop. In: Biswas, G., Bull, S., Kay, J., Mitrovic, A. (eds.) AIED 2011. LNCS (LNAI), vol. 6738, pp. 353–360. Springer, Heidelberg (2011). https://doi.org/10.1007/978-3-642-21869-9_46
33. Williams, J.J., et al.: Axis: generating explanations at scale with learnersourcing and machine learning. In: 2016 Proceedings of the Third ACM Conference on Learning@ Scale, pp. 379–388. ACM (2016)

Modeling the Relationships Between Basic and Achievement Emotions in Computer-Based Learning Environments

Anabil Munshi[1(✉)], Shitanshu Mishra[1], Ningyu Zhang[1], Luc Paquette[2], Jaclyn Ocumpaugh[3], Ryan Baker[3], and Gautam Biswas[1]

[1] Vanderbilt University, Nashville, TN, USA
{anabil.munshi,shitanshu.mishra,ningyu.zhang,
gautam.biswas}@vanderbilt.edu
[2] University of Illinois at Urbana-Champaign, Champaign, IL, USA
lpaq@illinois.edu
[3] University of Pennsylvania, Philadelphia, PA, USA
jlocumpaugh@gmail.com, ryanshaunbaker@gmail.com

Abstract. Commercial facial affect detection software is typically trained on large databases and achieves high accuracy in detecting basic emotions, but their use in educational settings is unclear. The goal of this research is to determine how basic emotions relate to the achievement emotion states that are more relevant in academic settings. Such relations, if accurate and consistent, may be leveraged to make more effective use of the commercial affect-detection software. For this study, we collected affect data over four days from a classroom study with 65 students using Betty's Brain. Basic emotions obtained from commercial software were aligned to achievement emotions obtained using sensor-free models. Interpretable classifiers enabled the study of relationships between the two types of emotions. Our findings show that certain basic emotions can help infer complex achievement emotions such as confusion, frustration and engaged concentration. This suggests the possibility of using commercial software as a less context-sensitive and more development-friendly alternative to the affect detector models currently used in learning environments.

Keywords: Affective modeling · Basic emotions · Achievement emotions

1 Introduction

Detecting student emotions in computer-based learning environments (CBLEs) is central to the development of pedagogical interventions that respond to students' emotional needs during learning. With the growth of the affective computing field [31] and the inclusion of *emotion* as an important aspect of self-regulated learning (SRL) [1], researchers studying SRL and affect regulation have emphasized the development of affect detection technologies [7] that can be integrated with CBLEs to obtain automated measures

© Springer Nature Switzerland AG 2020
I. I. Bittencourt et al. (Eds.): AIED 2020, LNAI 12163, pp. 411–422, 2020.
https://doi.org/10.1007/978-3-030-52237-7_33

of student emotions during learning. However, the focus of researchers studying affect detection in the learning context has been different from other fields.

A majority of affective computing research outside education has emphasized the detection of the prototypical *basic emotions* that are considered fundamental to human psychology [17, 20]. This has led to the development of affect detectors that capture a person's basic emotions using models trained on data from multimodal sources, such as facial expressions (cf., FACS in [14]), physiological sensors (EEG), and bodily gestures. There are commercially available affect detector models, such as Affectiva [26], that are trained and tested on large datasets (~10,000 labeled facial images - see [33]). These systems predict basic emotions from face video frames with high accuracy, using only facial features as action units (AUs) [25]. Therefore, they can be integrated with any webcam-equipped computer to offer accurate and non-intrusive emotion detection.

However, most affect detection with CBLEs has been limited in tapping into the power of commercial software. In complex learning settings, learners face achievement scenarios that are hypothesized to elicit the experience of *achievement emotion* states (such as confusion, frustration, and engaged concentration), which are more complex than basic emotions (such as joy, anger, fear, and sadness). Achievement emotions reflect how learners cope with cognitive difficulties in different learning situations as they progress towards their achievement goals [30]. Therefore, research needs to focus more on detecting achievement emotions rather than basic emotions.

In recent years, AIED researchers have built classifiers to detect students' achievement emotions from features available during learning, such as learner activities [22] or facial expressions [5]. While these non-intrusive models are usable in real classrooms [28], the models driven by activity-based features are context-sensitive, since the features are based on activities specific to the learning environment. Therefore, these models require considerable effort to develop and the features have to be recomputed (or even re-designed) every time the models are deployed in new learning environments. While facial feature-based models are more generally applicable, current models for detecting achievement emotions using facial features are limited by a lack of large testing datasets across diverse populations. In general, they have a lower accuracy for predicting specific affective states [5].

Therefore, an alternate approach is to develop methods to link achievement and basic emotions so that the commercial software output can be transformed to report academic achievement emotions. After discussing our framework and the Betty's Brain system, this paper presents a first attempt at this approach. We report findings from data on learners' emotions collected from a classroom study.

2   Background

Emotions have been widely studied in psychology. Plutchik [32, p. 345] describes *emotion* as "a complex chain of loosely connected events that begins with a stimulus and includes feelings, psychological changes, impulses to action and specific, goal-directed behavior", thereby suggesting that an emotion is not an isolated event but more of a human response to certain actions or situations.

2.1 Basic Emotions

Over time, researchers have defined a set of *basic* emotions that deal with universal human situations [14] or have served certain fundamental biological and social functions through human evolution [20], e.g., as the basis for coping strategies and adaptation. Multiple research studies support this concept of basic emotions, e.g., how *sadness* elicits empathy [4] or *fear* elicits protection behaviors [6]. Another view of basic emotions deals with their fundamental role in *'universal human predicaments'* [15, p. 46]. These emotions can be distinguished from each other and from other emotions [14]. Ekman's list of seven basic emotion states are: *anger, contempt, disgust, fear, joy, sadness,* and *surprise* [16]. Ekman [14] claimed that there is robust and consistent evidence of distinctive facial expressions for each basic emotion. Currently, commercial software, such as iMotions AffDex, predicts these basic emotions from facial features with high accuracy by using the Emotional Facial Action Coding System (EMFACS) [18] that provides a comprehensive taxonomy for coding facial behaviors. The AffDex SDK uses binary support vector machine classifiers that compute the likelihood values of the seven basic emotions by detecting facial landmarks from video frames, extracting features, classifying facial action units (AUs), and then modeling emotion expressions using EMFACS. While iMotions does not provide public information about the accuracy of their emotion prediction models, they report very high accuracy (with ROC values ranging from 0.75 to 0.96 for AU-classifiers) for the identification of AUs [26].

2.2 Achievement Emotions

Achievement emotions are tied directly to students' achievement activities and outcomes in learning situations [30]. Since students' learning activities and outcomes are often judged with respect to achievement standards (e.g.., the COPES SRL model [34]), emotions pertaining to these learning situations may be seen as *achievement emotions*. Individuals experience specific achievement emotions based on their perceived control of the achievement activities and the personally meaningful outcomes (cf., control-value theory [30]). Researchers also constitute these emotions as *cognitive-affective states* [3] due to the relevance of learner cognition to these emotional experiences. Several studies (e.g., [11, 27]) have shown the relation of these emotions to cognitive activities and performance in the learning environment. These achievement emotion states include *boredom, confusion, frustration, engaged concentration,* and *delight.* D'Mello et al. [12] have explored the transitions between emotion states during learning. Affect observation methods such as BROMP [29] have facilitated the observation and coding of these emotions in classrooms. Classifier models trained on BROMP affect labels can capture the probability of occurrence of the emotion states during learning from log data [22] and facial AUs [5]. However, these models may not be as robust as commercial models that detect basic emotions (cf. Sect. 1). In this paper, we apply methods for basic and achievement emotion detection to collect both types of affect data for students working in Betty's Brain, a learning-by-teaching environment [24].

3   The Betty's Brain Learning Environment

Betty's Brain adopts a learning-by-teaching method to teach complex scientific processes, such as climate change or thermoregulation, to middle school students. Students teach the virtual pedagogical agent Betty by building causal (cause-and-effect) relationships between concepts, and they have access to a set of hyperlinked *science book* pages to learn the science topic. A *causal map* equipped with a palette of editing tools helps them build and annotate their causal map. A *quiz* module offers students the ability to let Betty take a quiz on causal relationships she has been taught. A *mentor agent* named Mr. Davis helps students evaluate the quiz results by comparing their causal model to an *expert model* that is hidden from the student's view. These tools allow the student to constantly refine their maps and engage in learning and understanding of the scientific process as they teach Betty.

The learning environment supports SRL as students engage in cognitive activities and develop strategies to teach Betty a correct causal model. This enables achievement scenarios, which elicit the experience of achievement emotions. Prior research [27] has explored the relationships between students' cognitive and affective experiences in Betty's Brain and emphasized how automated affect detector models can be beneficial for providing students with personalized guidance that respond to their affective-cognitive states during learning.

In the following section, we describe our classroom study and data collection procedures. We analyze and relate two types of emotion data obtained from separate automated affect detector models in Betty's Brain.

4   Methodology

4.1   Study Design and Data Collection

The classroom study involved 65 sixth-grade students in an urban public school in the southeastern USA. The study was conducted over a period of 7 days. *Day*1 included a pre-test of domain knowledge and causal reasoning skills. *Day*2 familiarized students with the features of Betty's Brain. For the next four days, students built causal models of climate change, and then took a post-test (identical to pre-test) on *Day*7.

In addition to pre-post test scores that showed statistically significant learning gains ($p < 0.05$, $Cohen's\ sd = 1$), we collected timestamped logs of students' activities in Betty's Brain over 4 days. Our action-view logging mechanism (based on the cognitive task model in [23]) captured and categorized student activities. Affect detector models (binary classifiers trained on BROMP affect labels aligned to learners' activity sequences - cf., [22]) were used to measure students' achievement emotion probabilities at a 20-s interval based on a sliding window of their cognitive activities within the learning environment. Individual students worked on their own webcam-enabled laptops, and their facial videos were processed *post hoc* using iMotions AffDex [26] to obtain basic emotion likelihoods at a 30 Hz frequency. (Our facial videos suffered from occasional data loss when students moved or changed their laptop orientations.)

4.2 Data Analysis

Data Processing Stages. The basic emotion likelihood scores (between 0(absent) to 1(present)) for *joy, anger, surprise, contempt, fear, sadness,* and *disgust* were obtained from AffDex [26] at the frame rate of 30 Hz. Separate classifiers detect likelihood values for each facial AU, and emotion likelihoods are calculated by weighting averages of the relevant AU likelihood scores for each basic emotion.

The achievement emotions (*confusion, frustration, engaged concentration, boredom, delight*) were obtained at a 0.05 Hz frequency (i.e., one set of emotion likelihood values every 20 s), as probability scores (between 0 to 1) from the affect detector models (originally validated using BROMP data) integrated with Betty's Brain.

Data Synchronization. We aligned the two affect data streams using logged timestamps. Since achievement emotions were available at a coarser time scale (*one set of likelihood values every 20 s*) than basic emotions (*30 likelihood values per emotion every 1 s*), the two data streams were aligned at the coarser granularity, i.e., one set of emotion likelihood values every 20-s. We extracted the sets of basic emotion likelihoods for 20-s intervals and picked the set with the highest sum of likelihoods for that interval. (This set represented the most *pronounced* likelihood predictions from the iMotions software for that time interval). Assuming at *time* $= t$ *secs*, the set of likelihood values of the 7 basic emotions is denoted by $LB_{time\,=\,t} = [L_{B1}, L_{B2}, \ldots, L_{B7}]_{time=t}$, then the representative set of basic emotion likelihoods for the time interval $\{t, \ t + 20\}secs$ can be obtained as the set $LB_{time\,=\,T}$, where $\sum_{i=1}^{7} LB_{i_{time\,=\,T}} = max_{t\in\{t,t+20\}}\left[\sum_{i=1}^{7} LB_{i_t}\right]$ and $t \le T \le t + 20$. The joined likelihood set $\left\{LB_{time\,=\,T}, LA_{time\,=\,T}\right\}$ is the representative set of basic and achievement emotions after the selection and merging of data at the 20-s time interval. This set was then aligned with the set of achievement emotion likelihoods that the BROMP detector provided for the same interval.

Data Filtering. We applied norm-based thresholding to the aggregated data to filter out the instances that had a very low likelihood of detecting a basic or achievement emotion. This was achieved by filtering out data points where the norm of emotion likelihoods for basic or achievement emotions was below the first quartile, i.e. keeping only those instances at which $Norm_{bB} > Q_1(Norm_B)$ and $Norm_{aA} > Q_1(Norm_A)$, where $Norm_B = \sqrt{\sum_{i=1}^{7} L_{Bi}^2}$ and $Norm_A = \sqrt{\sum_{i=1}^{5} L_{Ai}^2}$.

The norm-filtered data contained 5152 of the original 9198 data points. This included 4607 instances where the dominant achievement emotion was *confusion*, 157 instances of dominant *engaged concentration*, 360 instances of dominant *frustration*, 28 instances of *boredom, and* 0 instances of *delight*. (The dominant achievement emotion at each data-point was obtained as $max(L_{Ai})$). Due to the lack of sufficient training instances to model delight or boredom, data instances with dominant delight or boredom were excluded from subsequent analyses. We re-sampled the three other labels to remove class imbalance biases and then proceeded to build binary classifier models (with target class prediction label = TRUE or FALSE for each classifier).

We note here that the distribution of data instances above is dependent on prediction rates of the BROMP-trained affect detector models, and while these models predict the classes with high AUC ROC, they are not representative of the exact frequency of each affective state occurring in the classroom. These detectors attempt to identify rare situations – using re-sampling to succeed in this goal [22], and may be more biased towards preferring false positives to false negatives, which may lead to over prediction in certain situations. This limitation, likely caused by re-sampling, is addressed by using more sophisticated re-sampling to address the imbalance created.

Specifically, classifier bias due to imbalanced target classes (i.e., a large difference in the proportion of target class labels) in the training data for each binary classifier was handled by (1) under-sampling majority-class cases using random sampling and (2) synthetic oversampling minority-class cases using the SMOTE algorithm [8]. The re-sampled data, containing 7 numeric features (implying likelihood of basic emotions) and one nominal binary target class, was used to train classifier models.

Training Classifier Models. We used 10-fold stratified cross-validation to build binary classifiers for predicting *engaged concentration, frustration,* and *confusion.* The classifier models selected for this purpose included Random Forest (RF), Decision Tree (DT), Neural Network (NN), Naïve Bayes (NB), and Logistic Regression (LR). The Naïve Bayes and Logistic Regression models were selected to serve as baselines for establishing model performance. While our model selection criteria considered both interpretability and performance, since our intended research objective with this analysis was to interpret how the basic emotion features predict achievement emotion classes, our selection of classifier models was biased towards interpretable models like logistic regression and decision trees over more complex and less interpretable models (cf., [9]). In practice, complex models (viz., Neural Networks) did not produce very notable differences in predictive accuracy for this data set (see Table 1), likely due to the relatively small sample size. In the next section, we present our findings from five different classifier models and study the best-performing interpretable model to determine relations between basic and achievement emotions in learning.

5 Results and Discussion

5.1 Model Performance

Table 1 lists the performance metrics for five classifier models (Random Forest (RF), Decision Tree (DT), Neural Network (NN), Naïve Bayes (NB), and Logistic Regression (LR)). NB and LR served as baselines for establishing model performance. AUC was used as the primary performance metric, since it provides a better measure of model performance than classification accuracy in a skewed dataset. From Table 1, Random Forest outperformed other models for all three prediction classes.

5.2 Model Interpretation

Random forest was the highest performing algorithm, followed closely by the decision tree with forward pruning (Table 1). The high performance of random forest can be attributed to averaging over multiple generated random trees, thereby achieving a model with low bias and low variance. Despite its high predictive efficiency, interpreting a random forest model is considerably difficult, especially compared to 'glass-box' approaches like decision tree. In Table 1, we observe that the decision tree model (with Gini-index for feature selection and forward pruning to prevent overfitting the feature space) achieved the second-highest performance for all target classes. Since decision trees provide better interpretability, we choose to study and interpret the decision tree models for each predicted class in greater detail, given that the purpose of this research is to relate the predicted achievement emotions to the basic emotion detectors.

Table 1. Performance metrics (average over classes) for classifier models predicting achievement emotion (AE) classes (class label = TRUE or FALSE) from basic emotion features

AE	Confusion					Frustration					Engaged concentration				
Classifier	RF	DT	NN	NB	LR	RF	DT	NN	NB	LR	RF	DT	NN	NB	LR
AUC	0.73	0.70	0.60	0.56	0.58	0.76	0.73	0.59	0.58	0.54	0.85	0.83	0.66	0.62	0.58
F1	0.64	0.64	0.53	0.45	0.45	0.69	0.68	0.56	0.56	0.50	0.78	0.76	0.61	0.58	0.57
Accuracy	0.66	0.66	0.59	0.56	0.56	0.69	0.69	0.57	0.57	0.52	0.78	0.76	0.62	0.58	0.58

Figures 1 and 2 present the visualization of the decision tree models for predicting *confusion* and *frustration*. (The figure for *engaged concentration* is not presented due to space constraints in the paper.). In each figure, the color of a tree node indicates the predicted class labels at that node (*'red'* = TRUE, *'blue'* = FALSE), the strength of the colors indicates the predictive power of the model at that node, the width of the edge indicates the proportion of instances classified along a branch with respect to total instances in the training data. The root node at the top is both the most individually predictive and most meaningful for interpretation.

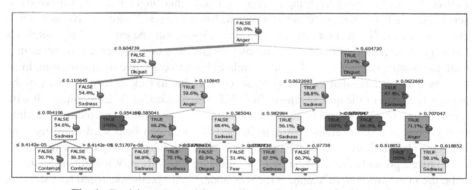

Fig. 1. Decision tree model to predict confusion from basic emotions

Figure 1 presents the decision tree model to predict confusion. From the first two splits, we find that the two most informative features are *anger* and *disgust*. Figure 1 shows a stark contrast between the left and right halves of the tree, right from the first split. We note how the right half of the tree, with higher values for anger and disgust, has more 'red' nodes predictive of *confusion* = *TRUE*, with a recall value of 87% at the

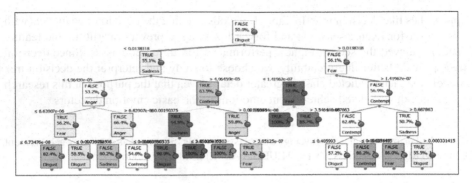

Fig. 2. Decision tree model to predict frustration from basic emotions

decision node $L_{Anger} \geq 0.6 \& L_{Disgust} \geq 0.06$ at *depth* $= 3$. Moving further down to depth $= 4$ gives more pronounced predictions of confusion $=$ TRUE, where the decision nodes $L_{Anger} \geq 0.6 \& L_{Disgust} \geq 0.06 \& (L_{Sadness} \geq 0.98 || L_{Contempt} \leq 0.71)$ show that higher likelihood of *anger* and *disgust*, together with high *sadness* or low *contempt*, predict *confusion* with a recall value upwards of 98%. When we shift our focus to the left half of the tree, we see that low anger and low disgust are mostly predictive of a lack of confusion. The only low anger-low disgust situation that is predictive of confusion $=$ TRUE is when this lack of anger and disgust is present together with high likelihood of sadness ($L_{Anger} \leq 0.6 \& L_{Disgust} \leq 0.06 \& L_{Sadness} \geq 0.95$).

We interpret these findings based on the affect literature in learning. *Confusion* has been linked to 'cognitive disequilibrium triggered by contradictions, conflicts, ...' [13, p. 10]. In an agent-based learning environment (like Betty's Brain), this disequilibrium could be socio-cognitive [13, p. 10], e.g., when the learner disagrees with agent feedback. In this context, the close mapping of *confusion* to higher *anger* likelihood make more sense, especially when we note 'interference with one's activity' is a cognitive antecedent event to anger [17]. The relation of *confusion* to *disgust* may be explained by Plutchik's circumplex model of emotions, which notes disgust as a complementary (contrasting) state to *trust/acceptance* [32]. This again relates back to cognitive disequilibrium, in an achievement scenario that may incorporate conflict due to lack of trust, perhaps in the agent's feedback or the quiz results in Betty's Brain, or a student's disappointment with himself/herself. This suggests that investigating the socio-cognitive processes leading to each basic or achievement emotion in Betty's Brain can help shed more light on finer-grained relations between the two types of emotions during complex learning tasks.

Figure 2 presents the decision tree for predicting frustration. While disgust appears to be the most informative feature at the root node, higher predictive recall (cf., strength of colors in the tree nodes in Fig. 2) is obtained at lower levels of the tree, where disgust is combined with other states such as fear, sadness or contempt. For example, in the right half of the tree (where $L_{Disgust} \geq 0.014$), we find a 92.9% recall for frustration $=$ TRUE at the decision node $L_{Disgust} \geq 0.014 \& L_{Fear} \leq 1.4 * 10^{-7}$ at *depth* $= 3$. In the left half of the tree ($L_{Disgust} \leq 0.014$), we find higher recall ($= 94.5\%$) for confusion prediction when the low disgust likelihood is combined with high sadness and low contempt (refer to Fig. 2 at depth $= 4$ where $L_{Disgust} \leq 0.014$ & $L_{Sadness} \geq 4.9 * 10^{-5}$ & $L_{Contempt} \leq 0.002$).

From the above, frustration seems to closely map to two complex states: (1) a state of high disgust + low fear, and (2) a state of low disgust + possibility of sadness + low contempt. Affect dynamics models in learning [12] show two affect transition scenarios leading to a state of frustration: (1) *confusion* → *frustration*, where disequilibrium associated with confusion remains unresolved and leads to failure/blocked goals. Such a transition into frustration may be related to the *[high disgust + low fear]* state noted above, which is associated with low trust/acceptance and high annoyance (cf. [32], where disgust is complementary to trust/acceptance & submissive states like fear are complementary to aggressive states like annoyance & anger). A prolonged non-acceptance of agent feedback or quiz results due to conflict with expectations may translate into a state of frustration for the learner. (Negative feedback from a tutor has been previously established as possible antecedent of frustration [10]); (2) *boredom* → *frustration*, where having to endure a learning session despite disengagement may translate into frustration. This state may be related to the *[low disgust + sadness + low contempt]* state we find from the decision tree model, suggesting an affective state that is still negative in valence, but with lower activation than the [high disgust + low fear] state.

Predicting Engaged Concentration from Basic Emotion Likelihoods. In the decision tree that predicts engaged concentration, *joy* is the most informative feature, and a very high joy likelihood ($L_{Joy} \geq 0.84$) is associated with a prediction of *engaged concentration = FALSE* with a recall of 72.7%. This implies that *engaged concentration* was not the dominant emotion here; so the dominant emotion could be any of the other achievement emotion states, including *delight*, an achievement emotion state whose definition closely matches that of joy but which could not be modeled here due to insufficient data instances. Indeed, <u>*engaged concentration* is often seen as having neutral activation whereas joy and *delight* are often seen as high activation [3].</u>

The second most predictive feature for engaged concentration is *sadness*. A closer analysis of the model shows that, when joy is low, a greater likelihood of *sadness* is a stronger predictor of *engagedconcentration = TRUE*. However, a more acceptable predictive recall is obtained at *depth = 4*, where a combination of low to medium *joy*, low to medium *sadness* and a possibility of *fear* predict *engagedconcentration = TRUE* with a recall value of 70.7%. This situation is obtained by the decision node $L_{Joy} \leq 0.84$ & $L_{Sadness} \in (3.1 * 10^{-6}, 0.78)$ & $L_{Fear} \geq 3.4 * 10^{-3}$.

Engaged concentration being an affect state of neutral activation and mildly positive valence [3] is not associated with high positive valence and high activation emotions like joy or negative valence, low activation emotions like sadness. The association of engaged concentration with lower joy and a possibility of fear may also be related to the fact that engaged concentration associated with the high competence and high challenge scenario of flow (cf. [3, 29]).

6   Conclusion and Future Scope

This research uses interpretable prediction models built from classroom data to suggest links between fundamental *basic emotions* and complex *achievement emotions* during learning in a CBLE. To summarize, we found that the achievement emotion state of *confusion* seems to map most closely to basic emotion states like [high *anger* + high *disgust*], while *frustration* maps closely to states like [*high disgust* + *low fear*] or [low *disgust* + *sadness* + low *contempt*], and *engaged concentration* maps closely to low/moderate levels of joy, sadness and a possibility of fear.

While data collection in a classroom setting suggests that our findings have the potential to generalize across natural learning settings, the non-constrained setting adds its own limitations, as discussed in Sect. 4.1 and in prior research on collecting affect data in real classrooms [5].

Since our research objective was to map basic and achievement emotions, we could use only the subset of our collected data, where both basic and achievement emotion likelihoods were high. Moreover, our emotion logs were likelihood measures that were not direct human-observed emotions but obtained from affect detector models trained on codes obtained from human observations. While these detector models allow for automated detection of affect at scale in a noisy classroom environment, they are likely to be less reliable than human observations. We intend to further validate our findings by replicating our methods with human-coded emotion labels in future classroom studies. Furthermore, since our affect detectors were built off action sequences and performance data in Betty's Brain, it is hard to claim generality for these results.

Despite the data limitations, the research methods and findings reported in this work have implications for shaping future research directions on affect modeling in AIED. First, our approach using interpretable classifiers to model affect in learning accords with prior work [9] that underlines the importance of interpretable ML in AIED. Secondly, this paper presents a scalable and accessible way to identify achievement emotions whose instructional implications have been studied extensively by prior work in the field. Moreover, since commercial software packages for detecting basic emotions are trained on much larger and more varied data than the affect detector models currently used in education, understanding the relations between basic and achievement emotions can help education researchers make use of these commercial software to detect achievement emotions during learning in a computer-enabled classroom.

In future research, beyond addressing limitations noted earlier, we hope to collect affect data from a wider variety of samples and investigate cross-cultural differences in the presentation of affect [19, 21], including achievement emotions [2]. We also intend to conduct further analyses into the cognitive-affective relationships in Betty's Brain, such as how students' socio-cognitive states during agent interactions influence affect.

Acknowledgements. This research was supported by NSF ECR Award #1561676. The authors thank all researchers, students, and teachers who participated in the data collection process.

References

1. Azevedo, R., Behnagh, R., Duffy, M., Harley, J., Trevors, G.: Metacognition and Self-regulated Learning in Student-Centered Leaning Environments, Theoretical Foundations of Student-Centered Learning, pp. 171–197 (2012)

2. Baker, R.S., Ogan, A.E., Madaio, M., Walker, E.: Culture in computer-based learning systems: challenges and opportunities. Comput.-Based Learn. Context **1**(1), 1–13 (2019)
3. Baker, R.S.D., D'Mello, S., Rodrigo, M.M.T., Graesser, A.: Better to be frustrated than bored: The incidence, persistence, and impact of learners' cognitive–affective states during interactions with three different computer-based learning environments. Int. J. Hum.-Comput. Stud. **68**(4), 223–241 (2010)
4. Barnett, M.A., King, L.M., Howard, J.A., Dino, G.A.: Empathy in young children: Relation to parents' empathy, affection, and emphasis on the feelings of others. Dev. Psychol. **16**(3), 243–244 (1980)
5. Bosch, N., et al.: Detecting student emotions in computer-enabled classrooms. In: IJCAI 2016 (2016)
6. Bowlby, J.: Attachment and loss. In: Separation, vol. 2. Basic Books, New York (1973)
7. Calvo, R.A., D'Mello, S.: Affect detection: an interdisciplinary re-view of models, methods, and their applications. IEEE Trans. Affect. Comput. **1**(1), 18–37 (2010)
8. Chawla, N.V., Bowyer, K.W., Hall, L.O., Kegelmeyer, W.P.: SMOTE: synthetic minority over-sampling technique. J. Artif. Intell. Res. **16**(2002), 321–357 (2002)
9. Conati, C., Porayska-Pomsta, K., Mavrikis, M.: AI in education needs interpretable machine learning: lessons from open learner modelling. In: 2018 ICML Workshop on Human Interpretability in Machine Learning (WHI 2018), Stockholm, Sweden (2018)
10. D'Mello, S., Craig, S., Sullins, J., Graesser, A.: Predicting affective states expressed through an emote-aloud procedure from AutoTutor's mixed-initiative dialogue. Int. J. Artif. Intell. Educ. **16**(1), 3–28 (2006)
11. D'Mello, S., Graesser, A.: The half-life of cognitive-affective states during complex learning. Cogn. Emot. **25**(7), 1299–1308 (2009)
12. D'Mello, S., Graesser, A.: Dynamics of affective states during complex learning. Learn. Instr. **22**(2), 145–157 (2012)
13. D'Mello, S., Lehman, B., Pekrun, R., Graesser, A.: Confusion can be beneficial for learning. Learn. Instr. **29**, 153–170 (2014)
14. Ekman, P.: Are there basic emotions? Psychol. Rev. **99**(3), 550–553 (1992)
15. Ekman, P.: Basic emotions. In: Handbook of Cognition and Emotion, pp. 45–60, Chapter 3 (1999)
16. Ekman, P., Cordaro, D.: What is meant by calling emotions basic. Emot. Rev. **3**(4), 2011 (2011)
17. Ekman, P., Friesen, W.V.: Unmasking the Face. Prentice-Hall, Englewood Cliffs (1975)
18. Ekman, P., Friesen, W.: facial action coding system: a technique for the measurement of facial movements. Consult. Psychol. (1978)
19. Elfenbein, H.A., Ambady, N.: Cultural similarity's consequences a distance perspective on cross-cultural differences in emotion recognition. J. Cross-Cult. Psychol. **34**(1), 92–110 (2003)
20. Izard, C.E.: Basic emotions, relations among emotions, and emotion-cognition relations. Psychol. Rev. **99**(3), 561–565 (1992)
21. Jack, R.E., Garrod, O.G., Yu, H., Caldara, R., Schyns, P.G.: Facial expressions of emotion are not culturally universal. Proc. Nat. Acad. Sci. **109**(19), 7241–7244 (2012)

22. Jiang, Y., et al.: Expert feature-engineering vs. deep neural networks: which is better for sensor-free affect detection? In: Penstein Rosé, C., et al. (eds.) AIED 2018. LNCS (LNAI), vol. 10947, pp. 198–211. Springer, Cham (2018). https://doi.org/10.1007/978-3-319-93843-1_15

23. Kinnebrew, J., Segedy, J.R., Biswas, G.: Integrating model-driven and data-driven techniques for analyzing learning behaviors in open-ended learning environments. IEEE Trans. Learn. Technol. **10**(2), 140–153 (2017)

24. Leelawong, K., Biswas, G.: Designing learning by teaching agents: the Betty's brain system. Int. J. Artif. Intell. Educ. **18**(3), 181–208 (2008)

25. Lien, J.J., Kanade, T., Cohn, J.F., Li, C.C.: Automated facial expression recognition based on FACS action units. In Proceedings In: Third IEEE International Conference on Automatic Face and Gesture Recognition, pp. 390–395. IEEE, April 1998

26. McDuff, D., Amr, M., Mahmoud, A., Turcot, J., Mavadati, M., Kaliouby, R.: AFFDEX SDK: a Cross-platform realtime multi-face expression recognition Toolkit. In: CHI 2016 Extended Abstracts, San Jose, CA, USA. ACM (2016)

27. Munshi, A., Rajendran, R., Ocumpaugh, J., Biswas, G., Baker, R.S., Paquette, L.: Modeling learners cognitive and affective states to scaffold SRL in open ended learning environments. In: Proceedings of the International Conference on User Modelling, Adaptation and Personalization (UMAP), Singapore, pp. 131–138 (2018)

28. Munshi, A., Biswas, G.: Personalization in OELEs: developing a data-driven framework to model and scaffold SRL processes. In: Isotani, S., Millán, E., Ogan, A., Hastings, P., McLaren, B., Luckin, R. (eds.) AIED 2019. LNCS (LNAI), vol. 11626, pp. 354–358. Springer, Cham (2019). https://doi.org/10.1007/978-3-030-23207-8_65

29. Ocumpaugh, J., Baker, R.S., Rodrigo, M.M.T.: Baker Rodrigo Ocumpaugh Monitoring Protocol (BROMP) 2.0 technical and training manual. Technical Report. New York, NY: Teachers College, Columbia University. Manila, Philippines: Ateneo Laboratory for the Learning Sciences (2015)

30. Pekrun, R.: The control-value theory of achievement emotions: assumptions, corollaries, and implications for educational research and practice. Educ. Psychol. Rev. **18**(2006), 315–341 (2006)

31. Picard, R.W.: Affective computing. M.I.T Media Laboratory Perceptual Computing Section Technical Report No. 321 (1997)

32. Plutchik., R.: The nature of emotions. Am. Sci. **89**(4) (2001)

33. Senechal, T., McDuff, D., Kaliouby, R.: Facial action unit detection using active learning and an efficient non-linear kernel approximation. In: Proceedings of ICCV IEEE 2015 (2015)

34. Winne, P.H., Hadwin, A.F.: The weave of motivation and self-regulated learning. In: Schunk, D.H., Zimmerman, B.J. (eds.) Motivation and Self-Regulated Learning: Theory, Research and Applications, pp. 297–314. Lawrence Erlbaum Associates, New York (2008)

Analysis of Task Difficulty Sequences
in a Simulation-Based POE Environment

Sadia Nawaz[1][(✉)] [iD], Namrata Srivastava[1], Ji Hyun Yu[2], Ryan S. Baker[3],
Gregor Kennedy[1], and James Bailey[1]

[1] The University of Melbourne, Parkville, VIC 3010, Australia
nawazs@student.unimelb.edu.au
[2] The University of Michigan, Ann Arbor, MI 48109, USA
[3] University of Pennsylvania, Philadelphia, PA 19104, USA

Abstract. Task difficulty (TD) reflects students' subjective judgement on the
complexity of a task. We examine the task difficulty sequence data of 236 undergraduate students in a simulation-based *Predict-Observe-Explain* environment.
The findings suggest that if students perceive the TDs as *easy* or *hard*, it may
lead to poorer learning outcomes, while the *medium* or moderate TDs may result
in better learning outcomes. In terms of TD transitions, difficulty level *hard* followed by a *hard* may lead to poorer learning outcomes. By contrast, difficulty
level *medium* followed by a *medium* may lead to better learning outcomes.

Understanding how task difficulties manifest over time and how they impact
students' learning outcomes is useful, especially when designing for real-time
educational interventions, where the difficulty of the tasks could be optimised for
students. It can also help in designing and sequencing the tasks for the development
of effective teaching strategies that can maximize students' learning.

Keywords: Task difficulty · Task complexity · Predict-Observe-Explain ·
Learning outcomes · *L*-statistic · Intervention · Flow · Zone of proximal
development

1 Introduction

Students' perceptions of tasks can influence their learning behaviours [4, 6]. For example,
when a task is challenging yet attainable, students may invest effort and persist at it. In
contrast, students may not engage in a task if they repeatedly fail at it [28, 49]. This,
then, engenders the question: how can instructors design optimal learning conditions
where students get challenged but feel confident in accomplishing the task? To address
this question, we analyse the relation of task difficulties (TDs) with students' learning
outcomes. Further, we observe how TDs vary in a simulation-based learning environment
(e.g., is it more probable for TDs to transition from *easy* to *hard* or vice-versa). Lastly, we
assess whether students' sequences of TDs can be indicative of their learning outcomes.

In this paper, TDs are analysed in a digital simulation-based *Predict-Observe-Explain*
(POE) learning environment by using the likelihood statistic (*L*-stat). The AIED community has frequently used *L*-stat for studying students' affective dynamics [18, 19, 21,

© Springer Nature Switzerland AG 2020
I. I. Bittencourt et al. (Eds.): AIED 2020, LNAI 12163, pp. 423–436, 2020.
https://doi.org/10.1007/978-3-030-52237-7_34

22, 36, 37]. Compared to a traditional classroom environment, a benefit of analyzing TDs in a digital setting is that students can receive just-in-time support. For instance, the level of TDs can be adjusted by the instructors to match student's level of understanding or individual students may also choose and change the level of TD in a self-controlled setting [3, 25, 30, 62]. We believe that a better understanding of students' TDs will enable interventions to improve students' learning [1, 53, 55] and reduce undesirable behaviours such as gaming the system [2] and disengagement [29].

2   Related Work

Task complexity and task difficulty (TD) are often used interchangeably. However, they are two different constructs [51, 52]. Task difficulty refers to a person's subjective judgment on the complexity of a task, whilst task complexity represents the characteristics or cognitive demands of a task [9].

Different learners can perceive the same tasks differently [9]. Researchers have shown that TDs can influence students' motivation [32] and self-regulation [4]. TDs can also affect problem-solving strategies and tactics. For example, DeLoache, Cassidy and Brown [24] suggest that "problems that are too *easy* or too difficult are less likely to elicit strategic behaviour than the problems that present a moderate degree of challenge" (1985, p. 125). Further, the "law of optimum perceived difficulty" states that, if the tasks are perceived very *easy* or very *hard*, they can result in lower levels of engagement than the moderately difficult tasks – which may lead to higher levels of engagement [6]. Vygotsky [60] suggested that for instruction to be effective it must be aimed at learners' proximal level of development (where learners can succeed with assistance; a difficulty that is somewhat more challenging than an exact match to a student's skill level, but not so challenging that the student cannot succeed). Csikszentmihalyi in his works [14, 58] talks about TDs and their influence on emotions. He suggests that a person may feel worried and anxious when presented with overly challenging tasks and may feel bored if the tasks are too *easy*. However, when the tasks are moderately difficult, or they offer just the right challenge, a positive 'flow' experience may occur [15, 16]. Therefore, different emotions can be encountered based on how an individual perceives a given task.

This, then raises the question: what relation do TDs have to students' learning outcomes? The data is not entirely clear on these theoretical perspectives. Some studies report that TDs have a negative association with students' self-efficacy and performance [44, 45], yet [7] states that 'certain difficulties can enhance learning'. Several studies have indicated that students can learn from challenges that lead them to identify and articulate their current views, examine their ideas and clarify their misconceptions [34, 35]. To sum up, we investigate the following questions in this paper:

RQ1: What relation do task difficulties have with students' learning outcomes?
RQ2: How do task difficulties vary over time?
RQ3: Is there a sequence of task difficulties that is indicative of better learning?

3 Learning Environment

3.1 Predict Observe Explain (POE) Simulations

This study is built on an underlying educational framework known as the *Predict-Observe-Explain* (POE) paradigm [61]. POE is a three-phase, iterative design [23].

1. During *Prediction*, students formulate a hypothesis. They are often asked to provide the reasons as to why they committed to it.
2. During *Observation*, students test their hypothesis by changing parameters or variables in a simulation. They can then see the effects of their manipulations. This phase is especially crucial for those who make incorrect hypotheses, as they can see a mismatch between their predictions and observations [26].
3. During the *Explanation* phase, clarifications are provided to students detailing the relationship between variables or parameters that represent the conceptual phenomenon under investigation. This phase assists students to reconcile any discrepancies between what they predicted and what they observed in the simulation [31].

POEs can be applied in face-to-face, online and computer lab contexts [13]. They can promote student discussion [61], probe into their prior knowledge and help them update prior conceptions [12, 39, 59]. POE learning designs can make digital environments more engaging [39, 57]. Recently, POE environments have been analysed to examine students' affective experience [38] and their behaviours relating to struggle and confusion [47, 48].

To the best of our knowledge, TDs have not yet been investigated within POE based environments. Understanding how TDs manifest over time and how they impact students' learning outcomes is useful, especially when designing for real-time interventions. Therefore, it is essential that we examine how TDs vary in these environments.

3.2 Course and Module Description

The data in this study is taken from an online project-based **course** called *Habitable Worlds*. It aims to introduce the foundational concepts of Physics, Chemistry and Biology [33]. It intends to develop problem-solving and logical reasoning skills in students through immersive and interactive tasks in a guided discovery environment. *Habitable Worlds* is built using Smart Sparrow's eLearning platform[1], which records moment by moment activity of students. This adaptive learning environment allows the provision of feedback based on students' responses or lack of responses. This course is offered to non-science major undergraduate students over a duration of 7.5 weeks, and it consists of 67 interactive **modules**.

The current study focuses on an introductory module called *Stellar Lifecycles*. The concept under investigation is the relation between a star's mass and its lifespan. There

---

[1] https://www.smartsparrow.com/research/.

are several **tasks** within this module which involve one or more of the following activities: providing free-text answers to a question, watching videos, responding to multiple-choice questions or the 'submissions' associated with simulations. In this module, students follow the prescribed sequence of tasks or activities. Occasionally, however, there is pathways adaptivity for the remediation of students who make errors. Further, the students cannot proceed onto the next tasks unless the current task is completed.

3.3 Tasks Description

Of the 23 tasks within this module, we utilize the following POE based tasks:

- *Prediction*: Students need to select a hypothesis from five possible choices regarding the relationship between stellar mass and lifespan. Then, they need to report their reasons (through free text) for selecting that hypothesis.
- *Observation 1*: During the first stage of the *Observe* task, students explore the stellar nursery simulator to create virtual stars, manipulate their mass and run them (as many times as they wish). Through this simulator, students can study and hopefully understand the relation between stellar mass and its lifespan.
- *Observation 2*: During the second stage of the *Observe* task, students need to create at least three different stars within a specified mass range. They need to record the mass and associated lifespan of these stars. Next, given their observations, they need to either accept or reject their earlier proposed hypotheses.
- *Explanation 1*: This task is only available to the students who make incorrect predictions and endorse them or those who make correct predictions but reject them. This task can assist students in rectifying their hypotheses.
- *Explanation 2:* This task requires the students to report the minimum and the maximum lifespan of seven different stellar classes. Students can again create and run stars within the stellar nursery simulator. Most students seem to struggle at this task as they need to manipulate several different stellar classes. This struggle is reflected in students making repeated attempts. Those who manipulate only one stellar class at a time (more systematic) are more likely to complete this task than those who manipulate more than one stellar classes (less systematic) [48].
- *Post POE*: At the final stage, students are provided with a short lecture-style video to explain to them why low mass stars live longer and how a star's mass and internal pressure contribute in the nuclear fusion process which fuels the burning of stars.

3.4 Participants

The data in this study is taken from the October 2017 offering of the course *Habitable Worlds*. A total of 236 non-science major undergraduate students attempted this module. Of these students, 50% were females, 46% were males, and 4% did not respond. In terms of age, 33% of students were younger than 20, 46% were between the age range of 21 and 30 both inclusive. The remaining 21% were older than 30.

3.5 Measures

Learning Outcomes. We analyse students' scores at the transfer task – the *Stellar Applications* module, which immediately follows the *Stellar Lifecycles* module. It tests students on the concepts that were already introduced to them. The maximum achievable score is ten; with each incorrect attempt, students are penalized by two marks.

Perceived Difficulty During-Task. During each phase of the POE tasks, to infer students' perceived difficulty, they are asked to report their levels of confidence and challenge on a 6-point scale: from 1 (not at all) to 6 (extremely). Following questions are asked:

- How confident are you that you understand the task right now?
- How challenging do you find the task right now?

Perceived Difficulty After-Task. At the end of the POE sequence, students can again report their confidence and challenge on a 6-point scale when asked these questions:

- Overall, how confident are you that you understood the material in the preceding tasks?
- Overall, how challenging was the material in the preceding tasks?

The response to these survey items is voluntary. In terms of participation, *during-task,* 186 students report their perceived TD during the *Prediction* task, 151 and 146 during the *Observe-1* and *Observe-2* tasks respectively, 74 and 146 during the *Explain-1* and *Explain-2* tasks. Lastly, 185 students report their perceived TD *after-task.*

4 Data Pre-processing

4.1 Levels of Task Difficulty

For analyzing the TD dynamics, we include those students who respond to one or more of the task-based surveys. As mentioned, survey items are related to students' confidence and challenge for a given task. To infer TDs, we assign following (3) labels:

- *Easy (E)*: if reported confidence exceeds reported challenge,
- *Hard (H)*: if reported confidence is lower than the reported challenge,
- *Medium (M)*: if reported confidence matches the reported challenge

Note that our TD labels match with Csikszentmihalyi's flow theory [17]. While the flow theory reports on students' affects in terms of their challenge and skills; we use these measures (challenge and confidence) to infer students' perceptions of difficulties.

4.2 Task Difficulties and Learning Outcomes

Learning outcomes reflect students' scores at the transfer task. The maximum achievable score is 10, and for each repeated attempt at this task two points are deducted. *High* achieving students are those who score above the mean (M = 9.21, SD = 0.92), while, the students scoring below the mean are considered *low* achievers (M = 3.64, SD = 4.58).

To compare the above two student groups, we perform Pearson's Chi-square test (or Fisher's exact test when the entries in the contingency table are less than 5). Comparisons are presented for each level of TD and during each phase of the POE cycle.

4.3 Task Difficulty Sequences

During each phase of the POE tasks, as students report their confidence and challenge, we infer their TD sequences. Later, we use these TD sequences to estimate the likelihood statistics (*L*-stat) as well as the bigram sequences.

Calculating L-stat. After obtaining students' TD sequences, we compute the likelihoods of transitions between any two possible states using the transition metric L [21], with self-transitions included in the calculation. This metric specifies the probability of a transition from a level at time t to t + 1, after correcting for the base rate at time t + 1. We can represent this as L (*difficulty$_t$* → *difficulty$_{t+1}$*), where *difficulty$_t$* is the difficulty level at the current task and *difficulty$_{t+1}$* is the difficulty level at the next task:

$$L\left(\text{difficulty}_t \rightarrow \text{difficulty}_{t+1}\right) = \frac{P\left(\text{difficulty}_{t+1}/\text{difficulty}_t\right) - P\left(\text{difficulty}_{t+1}\right)}{1 - P\left(\text{difficulty}_{t+1}\right)}$$

The value of L may vary from $-\infty$ to 1. For a given transition, if $L \approx 0$, we say that the transition occurs at chance level, if $L > 0$, we say that the transition is more likely than chance. Finally, if $L < 0$ then the transition is less likely than chance [20].

For calculations, the L-statistic is computed separately for each student and for each possible transition. The transitions where L is undefined are excluded from further analysis. Later, one-sample (two-tailed) t-tests are conducted on the calculated L values to measure whether each transition is significantly more or less likely than chance. Next, the Benjamini-Hochberg (BH) post-hoc correction is applied to control for false positives, as the analysis involves multiple comparisons [36].

Generating Bi-gram Sequences. We process students' TD sequences to generate TD bigrams. We only consider the students who respond to all task-based surveys and who also attempt the transfer task – there are 63 such students.

In this regard, given a sequence: '*easy-medium-medium-hard-hard-easy*', the associated bigrams are: '*easy-medium*', '*medium-medium*', '*medium-hard*', '*hard-hard*' and '*hard-easy*'. After this, we compare the students who report a given bigram sequence versus those who do NOT report it. For this, we perform t-tests and report the results in terms of *p-value* statistic and *t-value* statistic. Test result is considered significant if *p-value* < 0.05 (*) and marginally significant if *p-value* < 0.10 (·). As the analysis also involves multiple comparisons, BH post-hoc correction is applied.

5 Results

5.1 Task Difficulties Across Different Achievement Levels

A comparison of perceived difficulties, between the *high* achieving students and the *low* achieving students, is presented in Fig. 1. The high achievers are more likely to perceive the tasks as *medium* or moderately difficult than the low achievers – who seem to perceive the tasks as either *hard* or *easy*. Overall, the proportion of students who respond during the *Explain-1* is the lowest, as this task is only available to the incorrect predicting students. Further, during the *Post POE* phase, many of the high achievers did not respond to the surveys. Therefore, the patterns during this task (where each TD category is more likely to be reported by the low achievers) differ from the overall trend.

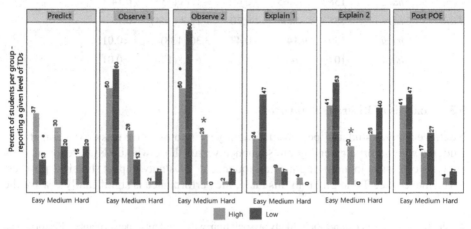

Fig. 1. Comparison of TDs between the high and low achievers using Pearson's Chi-square test (or the Fisher's exact test when the counts in the contingency table are less than 5). High-achievers tend to report *medium* TDs; in contrast, low-achievers tend to report the TDs as either *easy* or *hard*. Results are significant if p-value < 0.05 (*)and marginally significant if p-value < 0.10 (·).

5.2 Analysis of Task Difficulty Sequences

Table 1 presents the TD dynamics in terms of D'Mello's L statistic. For self-transitions, the shift from *easy* → *easy* is not significantly more or less likely than chance, in contrast, the shift from *hard* → *hard* and from *medium* → *medium* are significantly less likely than chance. In terms of increasing TDs, a transition from *easy* → *medium* is less likely than chance, from *easy* → *hard* is more likely than chance and from *medium* → *hard* is not different from chance level. Finally, in terms of decreasing TDs, the transitions from *hard* → *easy* and from *medium* → *easy* are not different from chance level, however, from *hard* → *medium* is more likely than chance.

Table 1. Dynamics of TDs, using D'Mello's L-Statistic. L_{MEAN} in **bold** indicates the transition is more likely and L_{MEAN} in *Italics* indicates that the transition is less likely than chance.

Transitions		Descriptives			One-sample t-test		
from	*to*	*N*	L_{MEAN}	L_{SD}	*T (df)*	*p-value*	*sig after BH correction*
easy	*easy*	101	−0.01	0.63	−0.15 (100)	0.88	
	medium	121	*−0.44*	1.00	−4.85 (120)	<0.01	*
	hard	133	**0.25**	0.74	3.85 (132)	<0.01	*
medium	*easy*	130	−0.11	1.01	−1.24 (129)	0.22	
	medium	110	*−0.65*	1.27	−5.43 (109)	<0.01	*
	hard	138	−0.05	0.43	−1.48 (137)	0.14	
hard	*easy*	135	−0.08	0.70	−1.33 (134)	0.19	
	medium	139	**0.14**	0.47	3.36 (138)	<0.01	*
	hard	107	*−0.77*	1.28	−6.20 (106)	<0.01	*

5.3   Analysis of Bi-gram Sequences

Next, we analyze students' perceived difficulty over consecutive tasks. We compare the students who report a given bigram sequence versus those who do NOT report it. This analysis can assist in analyzing how a sequence of TDs may impact students' post-test performance (see Table 2). From this table, the performance is significantly low for the

Table 2. TD sequences and their likely association with students' performance. Performance seems to be lower for the bigram sequence *hard-hard*, and it appears to be higher for the sequence *medium-medium*.

TD Bigram sequence	Bigram reporting students		T (59)	p-value	sig after BH correction
	Yes	*No*			
	Post-test (Mean ± SD)	*Post-test (Mean ± SD)*			
easy-easy	7.81 ± 3.08	8.34 ± 3.01	−1.12	0.26	
easy-medium	6.96 ± 4.48	8.01 ± 2.86	−1.34	0.18	
easy-hard	6.35 ± 5.04	8.08 ± 2.86	−1.86	0.06	
medium-easy	7.68 ± 3.63	7.79 ± 3.18	−0.15	0.88	
medium-medium	9.81 ± 0.57	7.19 ± 3.70	3.44	<0.01	*
medium-hard	8.67 ± 1.70	7.66 ± 3.60	0.62	0.54	
hard-easy	7.03 ± 3.53	8.04 ± 3.48	−1.22	0.22	
hard-medium	8.33 ± 1.81	7.66 ± 3.71	0.57	0.57	
hard-hard	6.35 ± 5.58	8.18 ± 2.49	−2.61	0.01	*

students who report the TD sequence *hard-hard* than those who do not report it. In contrast, the students who report the TD sequence *medium-medium* have significantly high scores than those who do not report it.

6 Discussion

The goal of this study is to analyse the perceptions of difficulties or TDs. For analysis, we use three labels namely: *easy*, *medium* and *hard*.

RQ1. The first research question examines the relationship between students' TDs and their learning outcomes. From Fig. 1 it is observed that during the POE sequence of tasks, the low achieving students mostly report the tasks as either *easy* or *hard*. For the low achievers who report the tasks as *hard*, it could be that they struggled with the learning content, the environment or both. However, for the students who perceive the tasks as *easy* and yet achieve poorer learning outcomes, a possible explanation for this could be their self-efficacy beliefs. Self-beliefs may influence students' performance [4, 5]. The students with unrealistic and overly optimistic opinions may have difficulty aligning their efforts with the desired performance levels and that can subsequently deteriorate their performance [10, 11, 46].

Figure 1 further suggests that the high achieving students mostly report the TDs as *medium*. A plausible explanation for this outcome is that students tend to engage more in the tasks that are perceived moderately difficult than the tasks that are perceived too *easy* or too *hard* [6]. Therefore, for curricula design, the instructors should plan the tasks that are within the learners' zone of proximal development (ZPD) [60]. If learners are taught a skill that is within their ZPD, it can lead to better performance than when the skill is not [62]. In this regard, [15] suggests that subjects can perform at their optimal capabilities when they experience 'flow', which is likely to happen when their challenge regarding the tasks matches with their skills (confidence in this case).

It is important to mention that students' TDs from Fig. 1 seem to differ at the start of the POE tasks – the *Prediction* phase, where the high achieving students are more likely (*p-value* < 0.10) to indicate that the TDs are *easy*. This difference during the *Prediction* task is important as this task probes students' prior knowledge. Reporting this task *easy* could mean that these students have higher prior knowledge or higher confidence in prior knowledge which contributed to their performance [40, 41].

Further, in a POE context, the *Observe* phase is crucial, it may provide valuable insights into students' prior held beliefs [26]. Confusion may be triggered for students who make incorrect *Predictions* [47]. Interestingly, there were more low achievers who made incorrect *Predictions*; yet the low achieving students were more likely to report this task as *easy* (*p-value* = 0.08). Thus, knowledge of students' TDs at specific moments can help identify the students who require interventions.

RQ2. The second research question analyses the dynamics of TDs – how students' perceptions of difficulties change within this environment. Prior research on task-based instruction suggests that pedagogic tasks should be sequenced in increasing order of their demands or complexity [43, 52, 56]. For example, the cognition hypothesis suggests that a gradual increase in task complexity can prepare students for more advanced problems and can lead them to achieve better performance and development [50–52]. Within the current simulation environment, as the students progressed, the tasks became more complex (in terms of the required actions and activities). The impact of task complexity on TDs is presented in Table 1. From this table, the transition from *hard* → *medium* is more likely than chance, while from *easy* → *medium* is less likely than chance.

When the findings from RQ1 suggest that *medium* or moderate difficulty may lead to better learning outcomes, the results from RQ2 suggest that *harder* tasks are likely to be followed by moderate difficulty. This, then raises the question of how we can make all students experience difficulties of moderate level – should we intentionally make *harder* or complex tasks as they seem to precede TDs of *medium* level? Or should we make the follow-up tasks feel easier by comparison? We believe that this question may benefit from further studies where, e.g., we compare two groups, a treatment group may be offered less guidance from the system so that the tasks become more complex.

RQ3. The last research question analyses the association between sequences of TDs and students' learning outcomes. Research on the sequential effects of TDs suggests that a learner's performance on a given task (regardless of whether the task is *easy* or *hard*) may be affected by the TDs on the preceding task [8, 54]. In their work, Schneider and Anderson [54] report that when an individual faces a *hard* task, a greater amount of cognitive resources may be allocated to it, and as they proceed to the next task there may be a depletion in the available resources. Hence, the performance in the next task may be affected. To inspect this in more detail, we analyse the impact of TD sequences (over consecutive tasks) on students' learning outcomes. From Table 2, the students with perceived difficulty of *hard* on two or more consecutive tasks are significantly more likely to have poorer learning outcomes than those who do not report such a transition. On the one hand, it could mean that these students are weak and therefore perceive the tasks as *hard*. On the other hand, it could also mean that perhaps there was a depletion of resources as students progressed from a *hard* task – which is in agreement with [54].

The next significant finding from Table 2 is that the students who report *medium* difficulty on two or more consecutive tasks are likely to have better learning outcomes than other students. What implications do these findings have for learning design? We find that *medium* TDs may lead to better learning outcomes and they often follow *hard* TDs. However, if tasks get too difficult for students, e.g., reporting *hard* on two or more consecutive tasks, then it can adversely affect students' performance. A knowledge of such perceptions of TDs, early on, may enable us to provide timely interventions to students.

7 Conclusion

In this study, we use task difficulties (TDs) as a factor of analysis. Researchers [27, 28] have acknowledged that only limited studies have investigated the role of students' TDs on their learning outcomes. We examine the effects of increasing as well as decreasing TDs on students' performance. Students who find the tasks *easy* or *hard* generally have poorer learning outcomes. However, if a task is perceived *easy* and it is the prior knowledge task, it may lead to better learning outcomes. Furthermore, in accordance with ZPD [60] and the flow theory [15], we find that TDs of *medium* level can lead to better performance. An implication for AIED researchers is that, TDs are based on students' subjective judgement of the task rather than task complexity. This creates a possibility of individualized predictions of better paths to learning for each student.

An unexpected finding was that the students who find the current task to be *hard* are more likely to perceive the following task as *medium* than the students who find the current task to be *easy*. This suggests that *hard* and challenging TDs have the potential to engage students and lead them to achieve better scores, as well as potentially influencing perception of following tasks. However, when tasks become too *hard* (difficulty sustains over two or more tasks) then it can adversely affect students' performance. To control for the negative effects of TDs, one approach is to detect these difficulties early on so that personalised interventions are provided to enhance students' learning.

A potential future direction for this work could be the analysis of students' learning behaviours to see how some students who find the current task to be *hard* can overcome their challenges and then report the following task to be *easy* or *medium*. Understanding how task difficulties manifest over time and how they impact students' learning outcomes is useful especially when designing for real-time educational interventions, where the difficulty of the tasks could be optimised for the learners. It can also help in designing and sequencing the tasks, for the development of effective teaching strategies that can maximize students' learning [42] and reduce undesirable behaviours such as gaming the system [2] and disengagement [29].

Acknowledgements. We wish to thank Prof. Arial Anbar, Dr Lev Horodyskyj and Dr Chris Mead for providing us with the Habitable Worlds data for this research. We also thank Dr. Linda Corrin, Donia Malekian and Anam Khan for the useful discussion on this work. This research is supported by the Research Training Program (RTP) Scholarship, Melbourne Research Scholarship and the Science of Learning Research Center (SLRC) top-up scholarship.

References

1. Arroyo, I., Woolf, B.P., Cooper, D.G., et al.: The impact of animated pedagogical agents on girls' and boys' emotions, attitudes, behaviors and learning. In: International Conference on Advanced Learning Technologies (ICALT), pp. 506–510. IEEE, Athens (2011)
2. Baker, R., Corbett, A.T., Koedinger, K.R., et al.: Off-task behavior in the cognitive tutor classroom: when students "game The system". In: SIGCHI Conference on Human Factors in Computing Systems, pp. 383–390. ACM (2004)
3. Baker, R., D'Mello, S., Rodrigo, M.M.T., et al.: Better to be frustrated than bored: the incidence, persistence, and impact of learners' cognitive–affective states during interactions with three different computer-based learning environments. Int. J. Hum.-Comput. Stud. **68**(4), 223–241 (2010)
4. Bandura, A.: Self-efficacy: The Exercise of Control. Freeman, New York (1997)
5. Bandura, A.: Social Learning Theory. Prentice Hall, Englewood Cliffs (1977)
6. Belmont, J.M., Mitchell, D.W.: The general strategy hypothesis as applied to cognitive theory in mental retardation. Intelligence **11**(1), 91–105 (1987)
7. Bjork, R.A.: Desirable difficulties perspective on learning. Encycl. Mind **4**, 134–146 (2013)
8. Campbell, D.J.: Subtraction by addition. Memory Cogn. **36**(6), 1094–1102 (2008)

9. Campbell, D.J.: Task complexity: a review and analysis. Acad. Manage. Rev. **13**(1), 40–52 (1988)
10. Carpentar, V.L., Friar, S., Lipe, M.G.: Evidence on the performance of accounting students: race, gender and expectations. Issues Acc. Educ. **8**(1), 1–17 (1993)
11. Christensen, T.E., Fogarty, T.J., Wallace, W.A.: The association between the directional accuracy of self-efficacy and accounting course performance. Issues Acc. Educ. **17**(1), 1–26 (2002)
12. Coştu, B., Ayas, A., Niaz, M.: Investigating the effectiveness of a POE-based teaching activity on students' understanding of condensation. Instr. Sci. **40**(1), 47–67 (2012)
13. Craig, S., Graesser, A., Sullins, J., et al.: Affect and learning: an exploratory look into the role of affect in learning with AutoTutor. J. Educ. Med. **29**(3), 241–250 (2004)
14. Csikszentmihalyi, M.: Beyond Boredom and Anxiety. Jossey-Bass, San Francisco (2000)
15. Csikszentmihalyi, M.: Finding Flow: The Psychology of Engagement with Everyday Life (1997)
16. Csikszentmihalyi, M.: The Flow Experience. Consciousness: Brain and States of Awareness and Mysticism, pp. 63–67 (1979)
17. Csikszentmihalyi, M.: Flow: The Psychology of Optimal Experience. Harper Perennial, New York (1990)
18. D'Mello, S., Graesser, A.: Confusion and its dynamics during device comprehension with breakdown scenarios. Acta Psychol. **151**, 106–116 (2014)
19. D'Mello, S., Graesser, A.: Modeling cognitive-affective dynamics with Hidden Markov Models. In: Annual meeting of the Cognitive Science Society, pp. 2721–2726 (2010)
20. D'Mello, S., Person, N., Lehman, B.: Antecedent-consequent relationships and cyclical patterns between affective states and problem solving outcomes. In: Artifical Intelligence in Education (AIED), pp. 57–64 (2009)
21. D'Mello, S., Taylor, R.S., Graesser, A.: Monitoring affective trajectories during complex learning. In: Annual Meeting of the Cognitive Science Society, pp. 203–208 (2007)
22. D'Mello, S., Graesser, A.: Dynamics of affective states during complex learning. Learn. Instr. **22**(2), 145–157 (2012)
23. Dalziel, J.: Practical eTeaching strategies for predict – observe – explain, problem-based learning and role plays. LAMS International, Sydney (2010)
24. Deloache, J.S., Cassidy, D.J., Brown, A.L.: Precursors of mnemonic strategies in very young children's memory. Child Dev. **56**(1), 125–137 (1985)
25. Dowell, N.M.M., Graesser, A.: Modeling learners' cognitive, affective, and social processes through language and discourse. J. Learn. Anal. **1**(3), 183–186 (2014)
26. Driver, R.: The Pupil as Scientist?. Open University Press, UK (1983)
27. Eccles, J.S., Adler, T.F., Futterman, R., et al.: Expectancies, values and academic behaviors. In: Spence, J.T. (ed.) Achievement and Achievement Motives, pp. 75–146. W.H. Freeman, San Francisco (1983)
28. Eccles, J.S., Wigfield, A.: Motivational beliefs, values, and goals. Ann. Rev. Psychol. **53**, 109–132 (2002)
29. Gobert, J.D., Baker, R., Wixon, M.B.: Operationalizing and detecting disengagement within online science microworlds. Educ. Psychol. **50**(1), 43–57 (2015)
30. Guadagnoli, M.A., Lee, T.D.: Challenge point: a framework for conceptualizing the effects of various practice conditions in motor learning. J. Motor Behav. **36**(2), 212–224 (2004)
31. Gunstone, R., White, R.: A matter of gravity. Res. Sci. Educ. **10**, 35–44 (1980)
32. Hom, H.L., Maxwell, F.R.: The impact of task difficulty expectations on intrinsic motivation. Motiv. Emot. **7**, 19–24 (1983)
33. Horodyskyj, L.B., Mead, C., Belinson, Z., et al.: Habitable worlds: delivering on the promises of online education. Astrobiology **18**(1), 86–99 (2018)

34. Kapur, M., Bielaczyc, K.: Designing for productive failure. J. Learn. Sci. **21**(1), 45–83 (2012)
35. Kapur, M., Rummel, N.: Productive failure in learning and problem solving. Instr. Sci. **40**(4), 645–650 (2012)
36. Karumbaiah, S., Andres, J.M.L., Botelho, A.F., et al.: The implications of a subtle difference in the calculation of affect dynamics. In: International Conference for Computers in Education (2018)
37. Karumbaiah, S., Baker, R., Ocumpaugh, J.: The case of self-transitions in affective dynamics. In: Artificial Intelligence in Education (AIED), pp. 172–181 (2019)
38. Kennedy, G., Lodge, J.M.: All roads lead to Rome: tracking students' affect as they overcome misconceptions. In: 33rd International Conference of Innovation, Practice and Research in the Use of Educational Technologies in Tertiary Education (ASCILITE), Adelaide, AU, pp. 318–328 (2016)
39. Kibirige, I., Osodo, J., Tlala, K.M.: The effect of predict-observe-explain strategy on learners' misconceptions about dissolved salts. Mediterr. J. Soc. Sci. **5**(4), 300–310 (2014)
40. Kulhavy, R.W.: Feedback in written instruction. Rev. Educ. Res. **47**(2), 211–232 (1977)
41. Kulhavy, R.W., Yekovich, F.R., Dyer, J.W.: Feedback and response confidence. J. Educ. Psychol. **68**(5), 522–528 (1976)
42. Li, W., Lee, A., Solmon, M.: The role of perceptions of task difficulty in relation to self-perceptions of ability, intrinsic value, attainment value, and performance. Eur. Phys. Educ. Rev. **13**(3), 301–318 (2007)
43. Long, M.H., Crookes, G.: Three approaches to task-based syllabus design. TESOL Q. **26**(1), 27–56 (1992)
44. Mangos, P.M., Steele-Johnson, D.: The role of subjective task complexity in goal orientation, self-efficacy, and performance relations. Hum. Perform. **14**(2), 169–185 (2001)
45. Maynard, D.C., Hakel, M.D.: Effects of objective and subjective task complexity on performance. Hum. Perform. **10**(4), 303–330 (1997)
46. Mooi, T.L.: Self-efficacy and student performance in an accounting course. J. Financ. Report. Acc. **4**(1), 129–146 (2006)
47. Nawaz, S., Kennedy, G., Bailey, J., et al.: Moments of confusion in simulation-based learning environments. J. Learn. Anal. (in review) (2020)
48. Nawaz, S., Kennedy, G., Bailey, J., et al.: Struggle town? Developing profiles of student confusion in simulation-based learning environments. In: Campbell, M. (eds.) 35th International Conference on Innovation, Practice and Research in the Use of Educational Technologies in Tertiary Education, ASCILITE 2018, pp. 224–233. Deakin University, Geelong (2018)
49. Pintrich, P.R., Schunk, D.H.: Motivation in Education: Theory, Research, and Applications. Prentice Hall, Upper Saddle River (2002)
50. Robinson, P.: Cognitive complexity and task sequencing: a review of studies in a componential framework for second language task design. Int. Rev. Appl. Linguist. Lang. Teach. **43**(1), 1–33 (2005)
51. Robinson, P.: Task complexity, cognitive resources and syllabus design: a triadic framework for examining task influences on SLA. In: Robinson, P. (ed.) Cognition and Second Language Instruction, pp. 185–316. Cambridge University Press, New York (2001)
52. Robinson, P.: Task complexity, task difficulty, and task production: exploring interactions in a componential framework. Appl. Linguist. **22**(1), 27–57 (2001)
53. Rodrigo, M.M.T., Baker, R., Agapito, J., et al.: The effects of an interactive software agent on student affective dynamics while using an intelligent tutoring system. IEEE Trans. Affect. Comput. **3**(2), 224–236 (2012)
54. Schneider, D.W., Anderson, J.R.: Asymmetric switch costs as sequential difficulty effects. Q. J. Exp. Psychol. **63**(10), 1873–1894 (2010)

55. Shute, V.J., D'Mello, S., Baker, R., et al.: Modeling how incoming knowledge, persistence, affective states, and in-game progress influence student learning from an educational game. Comput. Educ. **86**, 224–235 (2015)
56. Skehan, P.: A Cognitive Approach to Language Learning. Oxford University Press, Oxford (1998)
57. Sreerekha, S., Arun, R.R., Sankar, S.: Effect of predict-observe-explain strategy on achievement in chemistry of secondary school students. Int. J. Educ. Teach. Anal. **1**(1), 1–5 (2016)
58. Stephanou, G., Kariotoglou, P., Dinas, K.D.: University students' emotions in lectures: the effect of competence beliefs, value beliefs and perceived task-difficulty, and the impact on academic performance. Int. J. Learn. **18**(1), 45–72 (2011)
59. Tao, P.K., Gunstone, R.F.: The process of conceptual change in force and motion during computer-supported physics instruction. J. Res. Sci. Teach. **36**(7), 859–882 (1999)
60. Vygotsky, L.S.: Mind and Society: The Development of Higher Mental Processes. Harvard University Press, Cambridge (1978)
61. White, R., Gunstone, R.: Probing understanding. Routledge, Abingdon (1992)
62. Zou, X., Ma, W., Ma, Z., Baker, R.S.: Towards helping teachers select optimal content for students. In: Isotani, S., Millán, E., Ogan, A., Hastings, P., McLaren, B., Luckin, R. (eds.) AIED 2019. LNCS (LNAI), vol. 11626, pp. 413–417. Springer, Cham (2019). https://doi.org/10.1007/978-3-030-23207-8_76

Affective Sequences and Student Actions Within Reasoning Mind

Jaclyn Ocumpaugh[1]([envelope]), Ryan S. Baker[1], Shamya Karumbaiah[1], Scott A. Crossley[2], and Matthew Labrum[3]

[1] University of Pennsylvania, Philadelphia, USA
ojaclyn@upenn.edu
[2] Georgia State University, Atlanta, Georgia
[3] Imagine Learning, Provo, USA

Abstract. Now that the modeling of affective states is beginning to mature, understanding affect dynamics has become an increasingly realistic endeavor. However, the results from empirical studies have not always matched those of theoretical models, which raises questions as to why. In this study, we explore the relationship between affective sequences that have been previously explored in the literature and the activities students may engage in when interacting with Reasoning Mind, a blended learning system for elementary mathematics. The strongest correlations are found for students who shift from engaged concentration to frustration, making fewer actions in the system. While confusion is generally associated with positive patterns, and frustration and boredom have unexpectedly similar implications for student activity.

Keywords: Affect dynamics · Mathematics learning · Educational affect

1 Introduction

Efforts to understand the relationship between affective states and learning have been underway in earnest since researchers were first able to model affective constructs through the use of sensors (e.g., Grafsgaard et al. 2014; Bosch et al. 2016) and interaction-based modeling (e.g., Baker and Ocumpaugh 2014). Theoretical models of how students' experiences of affect change over time, such as those suggested by D'Mello and Graesser (2012), have guided much of the discussion, but empirical findings have also had considerable impact on the literature, with researchers suggesting, for example, that brief instances of confusion and frustration may have different effects than extended confusion and frustration (Liu et al. 2013), that different affective states tend to persist for different amounts of time (D'Mello and Graesser 2011; Botelho et al. 2018), and that differences in affective sequences can have substantial impacts on learning (Andres et al. 2019). Work has suggested that affect can influence how students choose to interact with a learning system. For instance, researchers have found that negative affective states such as boredom tend to precede disengaged behaviors such as gaming the system (Baker et al. 2010; Sabourin et al. 2011).

© Springer Nature Switzerland AG 2020
I. I. Bittencourt et al. (Eds.): AIED 2020, LNAI 12163, pp. 437–447, 2020.
https://doi.org/10.1007/978-3-030-52237-7_35

The field has studied how affect manifests within AIED systems, and there have been several attempts to influence affect through the design of AIED systems (Arroyo et al. 2011; Grawemeyer et al. 2017, Karumbaiah et al. 2017). However, there has been relatively limited work to determine how the existing design of AIED systems interacts affect – i.e. how features not specifically intended to be affect-responsive nonetheless connect with the affect students experience. In one example, Slater and colleagues (2016) investigated how the textual features of math problems within the ASSISTments platform. They found relatively minor effects, perhaps due to the relatively minor differences in content they studied. However, for systems that alternate between very different pedagogies (e.g., shifting between games and workbook-style content), it is reasonable to expect that affective experiences may be influenced more substantially by the kinds of tasks students are being asked to complete and that affect may also drive students' choices.

This paper looks at the affective sequences of students using one such system, Imagine Learning's Reasoning Mind, which provides a blended learning curriculum in mathematics that engages elementary-aged students in tasks that range from basic instruction to challenge problems to speed games to non-academic activities. Specifically, this study looks at how the prevalance of affective patterns that have been studied in previous research—including D'Mello and Graesser (2012) and Andres et al. (2019)—correlates with different activities students may engage in when using Reasoning Mind.

2 Previous Research

Theorists working on the role of academic emotions have long suggested the need to understand both their antecedents and their consequences (see discussion in Pekrun 2006; Pekrun and Linnenbrink-Garcia 2012). Therefore, it is becoming increasingly important to understand how student affect relates to their engagement within different kinds of learning environments.

Empirical investigations of academic emotions have produced a number of interesting results, including findings that it is better to be frustrated than bored (Baker et al., 2010). Researchers have also shown that both confusion and frustration appear to have Goldilocks effects on learning, where either too little or too much can be detrimental (Liu et al. 2013). These lead to important questions about when a system should intervene to resolve confusion and frustration and when a student should be allowed or even guided to shift into these affective states (Lehman and Graesser 2015).

As AIED environments have developed as research tools that can provide fine-grained temporal data on the shifts in student cognition and emotion, there has emerged a growing interest in *affect dynamics*— the study of how affect shifts and develops over time. One of the most prominent models of affective dynamics comes to us from D'Mello and Graesser (2012). In this model, two sequences are hypothesized to be related to learning. The first, which is thought to encourage learning, involves a student cycling between engaged concentration and confusion (and back again). The second, which is thought to inhibit learning, involves a student cycling from engaged concentration to confusion to frustration, and finally to boredom.

Subsequent research has sometimes found evidence for the two cycles proposed by D'Mello and Graesser (2012), and in fact, efforts to promote confusion actually lead to positive learning outcomes (Lehman and Graesser 2015), but the cycles themselves are less common than had originally been thought. A recent synthesis of published research on affective dynamics (Karumbaiah et al. 2018) shows that the relative frequency of the transitions captured by these sequences is often below chance. This raises important questions for those hoping to build interventions triggered by affective sequences. If these sequences are tied to learning outcomes, but they are unlikely to occur, we need to know what behaviors within a learning environment might mediate their appearance.

3 Reasoning Mind

3.1 Reasoning Mind

Imagine Learning's Reasoning Mind is an intelligent tutoring system for mathematics that was used by over 100,000 pre-K to 8th grade students, primarily in the Southern United States. Research has shown that Reasoning Mind is associated with higher state standardized test scores (Waxman and Houston 2012) and engagement measures (Ocumpaugh et al. 2013).

Reasoning Mind activities are organized within the context of a virtual environment known as *RM City*, where students can navigate from building to building to participate in multiple modes, including: *City Landscape* (navigation page), *Guided* Study (theory and tests on math concepts), *Office* (teacher-assigned topics), *My Place* (students use points to purchase decorations for their virtual room) and *Game Room* (students participate in speed games, that require them to race against a speed meter, or solve math puzzles, like those found in the *Riddle Machine*). Content is further classified according to function and difficulty. *Theory* problems guide students to learn math concepts through animations and exercises. *Notes Test* check comprehension at the end of segments of theory material, requiring a review crucial concepts while reinforcing good note-taking practices. A-*level* problems reflect a fundamental understanding of basic material, while B-*level* problems may require multiple skills to complete multiple steps. C-*level* problems are conceptually advanced, requiring higher order thinking skills (Fig. 1).

Fig. 1. Reasoning Mind's pedagogical agent, the Genie (left) and *RM City* (where *City Landscape Actions* happen, right)

4   Methods

4.1   Students

This study examines data from 796 Texas students who used Reasoning Mind as part of their regular 2nd to 6th-grade mathematics instruction during the 2017–18 school year.

4.2   Activities (Type of System Usage) Considered

Reasoning Mind students are offered a wide range of activities within the system. These include activities related to the primary modes of instruction, from the most basic problems (*A-level* Actions, *A-level* Accuracy, and *Guided Study* Actions) that all students must complete to more challenging problems (*B/C-level* Actions) which are often optional. They also include measures related to behaviors that vary in terms of their instructional content. For example, the speed-drills (*Game Room Actions*) review learning modules but do not provide instruction on new content. Meanwhile, the number of actions spent in the *RM City,* (or *City Landscape Actions*) tell us how often a student is switching between tasks, which may indicate either completion or dissatisfaction with the learning environment. Finally, we also consider the how students are spending the points they earn in Reasoning Mind's virtual store (*Items Purchased*).

Four activities chosen for this analysis represent a range in the type of usage that students using Reasoning Mind encounter: *Guided Study Actions, B/C-Level Actions, City Landscape Actions,* and *Items Purchased.* The first two represent actions that involve learning, while the latter may be less indicative of learning (although students are not able to purchase items unless they have earned points through positive learning behaviors). These activities also represent a range in the amount of choice a student has in whether they participate in that activity. Finally, they were carefully selected in order to exclude any actions that might have contributed to the BROMP-based interaction detectors developed by Kostyuk et al. (2018). (A-level Actions, for example, are a part of several of Kostyuk's affect detectors, and so they were excluded in order to avoid circularity problems in the analysis.)

4.3   Affective Models and Sequences Considered

Models of Affective States. Affective states studied in this paper are modeled using detectors built by Kostyuk et al. (2018). These cross-validated, interaction-based detectors (e.g., Baker and Ocumpaugh 2014) were developed using the BROMP protocol for classroom observation (Ocumpaugh et al. 2015). Table 1 shows detectors for four academic emotions (boredom, confusion, engaged concentration, and frustration) and for off-task behavior. Although detector performance was relatively weak, the scale of data was sufficient to derive theoretically expected predictions for learning outcomes (Kostyuk et al. 2018). The distribution of affect predictions were re-scaled to bring the low incidence affective states back to the original distributions: Bor (13.7%), Eng (78.8%), Con (31.1%), and Fru (1.1%).

Table 1. Affective Models (from Kostyuk et al. 2018).

	Algorithm	AUC
Boredom (Bor)	Random Forest	0.60
Engaged Concentration (Eng)	Gradient Boosting Machine (GBM)	0.61
Confusion (Con)	Stepwise forward selection linear regression	0.53
Frustration (Fru)	Random Forest	0.65
Off-task (Off)	Stepwise forward selection linear regression	0.64

Affective Sequences. A considerable body of research has emerged using D'Mello's L, a likelihood metric for studying individual transitions (D'Mello and Graesser 2012). However, this metric does not handle multi-state sequences, and recent research suggests that L requires corrections in order to be valid (Karumbaiah et al. 2019). Therefore, we take a different approach.

Instead, this study investigates affective sequences that were selected based on two previous publications. Specifically, we include the two cycles from D'Mello and Graesser's (D'Mello and Graesser 2012) theoretical model, as well as include 16 sequences found to be important in Andres et al.'s (2019) exploration of affective dynamics in Betty's Brain, which (like this study) also made use of BROMP-based detectors.

Specifically, Andres et al. (2019) examined 12 "three-step" transitions where the first step was repeated (e.g., Eng-Eng-Bor, or Fru-Fru-Con) as well as four homogenous "four-step" transitions, which repeated the same affective state across the entire sequence (e.g., Bor-Bor-Bor-Bor). We also investigate two four-step sequences that involve off-task behavior (also modeled using Kostyuk's et al. (2018) BROMP-based detectors), based on evidence that off-task behavior is more strongly negatively correlated with learning outcomes in Reasoning Mind than other interactive learning environments (Kostyuk et al. 2018). In total, this study investigates 20 affect sequences.

For each affect sequence, prevalence is computed using the method in Andres et al. (2019). Prevalence is the total number of times a pattern occurred within a given student's data divided by the total number of times it could have occurred in that data. The sequences involving only engaged concentration or confusion show the highest prevalence with Eng-Eng-Eng-Eng at 63.4% and Con-Con-Con-Con at 13.1%. This is followed by the sequences that have Bor with Eng-Eng-Bor at 6.2% and Bor-Bor-Con at 1.3%. Lastly, the sequences with frustration show the lowest prevalence with Eng-Eng-Fru at 0.29% and Eng-Con-Fru-Bor at 0.02%.

4.4 Analysis

Spearman's Rho (ρ) was used to correlate the prevalence of 20 affect sequences studied to the 4 types of student activities (types of usage) within Reasoning mind. Spearman's Rho is a non-parametric correlation coefficient that is often used when assumptions of normality cannot be applied across an entire data set. Because this analysis resulted in 80 separate statistical tests (20 affective states ×4 activity types within the system), Benjamini and Hochberg's (Benjamini and Hochberg 1995) post-hoc FDR correction was applied. P-values in the results section are only marked as significant if they remained significant after the B&H procedure was applied.

5 Results

Results for the relationship between the prevalence of affective sequences and the different types of activities within Reasoning Mind are given in Table 2, where they are organized by the type of affective sequence being considered. These include (1) the D'Mello and Graesser cycles (both the facilitative and the inhibitory), (2) the sequences using the BROMP-based off-task detector, and then (3) the sequences studied by Andres et al., (2019). The latter is organized by the dominant affect in each sequence (i.e., the one that appears most frequently), with the homogenous four-step sequences (i.e., Eng-Eng-Eng-Eng) given in the order of the D'Mello and Graesser's inhibitory cycle (i.e., engaged, followed by confusion, followed by frustration, followed by boredom). However, readers will see that the results do not fully fit this model's predictions.

Table 2. Correlations between prevalence of affective sequences and types of student actions. Items that are non-significant after the B&H correction was applied are given in gray-scale.

| | Learning Actions | | | | Non-Learning Actions | | | |
| | Guided Study Problems | | B/C-Level Problems | | City Landscape | | N of Items Purchased | |
	Rho	p	Rho	p	Rho	p	Rho	p
Eng-Con-Con-Eng	-0.02	0.4	-0.02	0.54	0.03	0.32	-0.06	0.06
Eng-Con-Fru-Bor	-0.21	0	-0.1	0.01	-0.17	0	0.04	0.24
Off-Off-Off-Off	-0.23	0	-0.09	0.01	-0.19	0	0.03	0.45
Off-Off-Off-Eng	-0.13	0	-0.03	0.33	-0.18	0	-0.02	0.52
Eng-Eng-Eng-Eng	0.16	0	0.09	0	0.05	0.14	-0.05	0.18
Eng-Eng-Bor	-0.16	0	-0.08	0.01	-0.11	0	0.09	0.01
Eng-Eng-Con	0	0.83	0	0.97	0.06	0.1	-0.07	0.03
Eng-Eng-Fru	-0.29	0	-0.12	0	-0.31	0	0.11	0
Con-Con-Con-Con	-0.13	0	-0.07	0.03	-0.04	0.26	-0.02	0.66
Con-Con-Bor	-0.22	0	-0.13	0	-0.08	0.01	0.07	0.03
Con-Con-Eng	-0.05	0.13	-0.03	0.31	0.03	0.48	-0.04	0.21
Con-Con-Fru	-0.28	0	-0.13	0	-0.2	0	0.11	0
Fru-Fru-Fru-Fru	-0.24	0	-0.09	0.01	-0.18	0	0.07	0.05
Fru-Fru-Bor	-0.23	0	-0.1	0	-0.17	0	0.05	0.18
Fru-Fru-Con	-0.28	0	-0.12	0	-0.21	0	0.08	0.02
Fru-Fru-Eng	-0.27	0	-0.1	0	-0.23	0	0.08	0.02
Bor-Bor-Bor-Bor	-0.26	0	-0.13	0	-0.13	0	0.07	0.03
Bor-Bor-Con	-0.25	0	-0.13	0	-0.09	0	0.1	0
Bor-Bor-Eng	-0.21	0	-0.12	0	-0.11	0	0.06	0.08
Bor-Bor-Fru	-0.28	0	-0.14	0	-0.17	0	0.07	0.02

5.1 Off-Task Sequences

Two sequences that were constructed using the BROMP-based off-task detectors were included in these analyses in order to explore findings suggesting that off-task behavior is correlated more negatively in learning in Reasoning Mind than in other interactive learning environments (Kostyuk et al. 2018). The first, Off-Off-Off-Off, was negatively correlated with three of the activity types: *City Landscape Actions* ($\rho = -.19$), *Guided Study Actions* ($\rho = -.23$), and *B/C-Level Actions* ($\rho = -.09$). Interestingly, this effect was nearly twice as strong for *Guided Study Actions* as it was for *B- and C-Level Actions*, which may be because students spend less time in that mode overall. Off-Off-Off-Off was not, however, significantly correlated with the *Number of Items Purchased*, perhaps because students can only purchase items if they spend enough time on task to earn the points to do so.

When we changed the fourth step from off-task to engaged, only two of the correlations remained significant. While the *City Landscape Actions* correlation only changed slightly ($\rho = -.18$), the *Guided Study Actions* correlation was half as strong for Off-Off-Off-Eng ($\rho = -.13$) as it was for the homogenous four-step sequence. This suggests that even a slight reduction in the duration of off-task behavior improves the outcomes for Reasoning Mind students, in line with Pardos et al.'s (2014) findings.

5.2 D'Mello and Graesser's (2012) Sequences

As discussed above, D'Mello and Graesser (2012) they theorized a number of different transitions between affective states that were thought to be relevant to learning. In this section, we explore results related to their facilitative and inhibitory sequences.

D'Mello and Graesser's facilitative sequence, in which a student cycles between engaged concentration and confusion, is operationalized here as Eng-Con-Con-Eng. As the results in Table 2 show, this sequence has no statistically-significant relationship to any of the activities within Reasoning Mind. Likewise, the three-step patterns related to this sequence, Eng-Eng-Con and Con-Con-Eng, show similar results. The former is only weakly significantly related to the *Number of Items Purchased* ($\rho = -0.07$), where it shows the only negative correlation with that activity. The latter, like the main D'Mello and Graesser facilitative sequence, has no significant relationships with any of the activity types.

D'Mello and Graesser's inhibitory sequence is operationalized here as Eng-Con-Fru-Bor. Its results are similar to Off-Off-Off-Eng, as it shows non-significant relationships with two of the action types (*B/C-Level Actions* and *Number of Items purchased*) and negative relationships for the other two ($\rho = -.17$ for *City Landscape Actions* and $\rho = -.21$ for *Guided Study Actions*).

5.3 Engaged Concentration Sequences

Four sequences in this study are composed primarily of engaged concentration, and these sequences demonstrate some of the most divergent results. Much of this divergence is driven by results from Eng-Eng-Fru, which, when compared to all other affective sequences in this study, shows the strongest (negative) correlations with *City Landscape*

Actions ($\rho = -.31$) and with *Guided Study Actions* ($\rho = -.29$). Eng-Eng-Fru also shows one of the strongest correlations with *B/C-Level Actions* ($\rho = -.12$ compared to max $\rho = -.14$). These results are stronger than those of Eng-Eng-Bor: *City Landscape Actions* ($\rho = -.11$), *Guided Study Actions* ($\rho = -.16$), and *B/C-Level Actions* ($\rho = -.08$). Compared to Eng-Eng-Con, which does not have significant relationships with these actions, the results for Eng-Eng-Fru and Eng-Eng-Bor suggest that students who skip confusion when transitioning from engaged concentration have lower levels of positive behaviors.

Skipping confusion (i.e., not going through the Eng-Eng-Con transition) and going to boredom (i.e., Eng-Eng-Bor) or frustration (i.e., Eng-Eng-Fru) also shows differences for the *Number of Items Purchased*. While the sequence with confusion shows a negative relationship with this action type ($\rho = -.07$), the sequences with boredom and frustration are positive ($\rho = .09, .11$, respectively).

Finally, Eng-Eng-Eng-Eng is significant for only two activity types. Notably, in contrast to the results for Eng-Eng-Fru and Eng-Eng-Bor, Eng-Eng-Eng-Eng is positively correlated with *Guided Study Actions* ($\rho = .16$), and *B/C-Level Actions* ($\rho = .09$). In fact, these are the only positive correlations in the whole study that are not related to the *Number of Items Purchased*.

5.4 Confusion Sequences

Sequences involving confusion also show some divergence in their relationships with activity types, though not as extreme as those for engaged concentration. Most of the significant relationships between sequences composed primarily of confusion and activity types are negative. As with the results for the engaged concentration sequences, the exceptions to this pattern are for the *Number of Items Purchased*, which may sometimes be driven by a desire to go off-task, but also require a student to have successfully completed a significant amount of work.

In general, these results show that Con-Con-Con-Con is weakly negatively correlated to learning activities ($\rho = -.16$ for *Guided Study Actions* and $\rho = -.07$ for *B/C-Level Actions*). (The relationship between Con-Con-Con-Con and *City Landscape Actions* is not significant.) The relationships for Con-Con-Bor and Con-Con-Fru are slightly stronger: *City Landscape Actions* ($\rho = -.08, -.20$, respectively), *Guided Study Actions* ($\rho = -.22, -.28$, respectively), and *B/C-Level Actions* ($\rho = -.13, -.13$, respectively). These results are not inconsistent with findings that confusion is beneficial to learning (i.e. Lehman and Graesser 2015; Liu et al. 2013), but contrast with findings that suggest that it is better to be frustrated than bored (i.e. Baker et al. 2010). Interestingly, Con-Con-Eng is not significantly related to these learning activities. While this result is surprising, it is consistent with the results for the facilitative D'Mello and Graesser sequence.

5.5 Frustration and Boredom Sequences

Nearly all of the relationships between sequences composed primarily of frustration and activity types are significantly significant, and the same is true for those sequences composed primarily of boredom. As with the results for confusion sequences, these show negative relationships with *City Landscape Actions*, *Guided Study Actions*, and *B/C-Level Actions* and positive relationships with the *Number of Items Purchased*.

For *City Landscape Actions* and *Guided Study Actions,* the relationships with frustration sequences tend to be stronger than those with boredom sequences, which also contradicts the idea that frustration is better for learning than boredom. However, this difference is small, and for *B/C-Level Actions*, that relationship is reversed. That is, frustration and boredom both appear to be negatively associated with learning-related activities (and positively associated with non-learning activities), but overall there is little separation between them.

6 Conclusion

In this paper, we investigate how affective patterns connect to student activity choices within Reasoning Mind. We find that the strongest patterns involve students who shift from engaged concentration to frustration. These students interact less with the environment than other students, although they do spend more of their points purchasing virtual decorations for their *My Place* room. We also find that confusion is generally associated with positive behavioral patterns. Somewhat surprisingly, frustration and boredom generally correlate to the same usage patterns. Also, inhibitive sequences emerging from D'Mello and Graesser's (2012) theoretical model are relatively weakly associated with activities within the system, while the facilitative sequence is not significantly associated with any of the activities considered in this study.

The findings here, in concert with Karumbaiah et al.'s (2018) research synthesis of affect dynamics research, which found that few patterns were more likely than chance across studies, potentially raise concerns about the generalizability of findings from previous research. However, they also point to the need for a more comprehensive understanding of the relationship between affective dynamics, behavioral patterns, and learning outcomes, as these findings suggest that these relationships may not be as straight-forward as we once thought.

Overall, the findings here suggest that there are relationships between student affect and the activities they engage in within a learning system. It is not entirely clear what the direction of the effects is from our current evidence – are students with specific affective patterns choosing different activities? Or are the activities driving the affective patterns? A more in-depth temporal analysis may be able to shed more light on this issue, but these issues are complex; affect may develop, and shape interaction choices but also shape the future affect itself (i.e. D'Mello and Graesser 2012; Botelho et al. 2018). What our findings indicate is that usage choices and affect are connected in many ways.

Overall, these findings point to the need for a more comprehensive understanding of the relationship between affective dynamics, behavioral patterns, and learning outcomes, as the findings here suggest that the relationship may not be as straight-forward as might have been thought. Fully understanding these interconnections – and the role that the design of AIED systems plays – is an important area for future research, and an important step towards AIED systems that are fully sensitive to the shifts in students' affect and how these shifts in turn impact behavior.

Acknowledgements. Our thanks to the NSF (Cyberlearning Award #1623730) for their funding of this project. All opinions (and any mistakes) are, of course, our own.

References

Andres, J.M.A.L., et al.: Affect sequences and learning in Betty's brain. In: Proceedings of the 9th International Learning Analytics and Knowledge Conference, pp. 383–390 (2019)

Arroyo, I., Woolf, B.P., Cooper, D.G., Burleson, W., Muldner, K.: The impact of animated pedagogical agents on girls' and boys' emotions, attitudes, behaviors and learning. In: 2011 IEEE 11th International Conference on Advanced Learning Technologies, pp. 506–510. IEEE, July 2011

Baker, R.S., D'Mello, S.K., Rodrigo, M.M.T., Graesser, A.C.: Better to be frustrated than bored: the incidence, persistence, and impact of learners' cognitive-affective states during interactions with three different computer-based learning environments. Int. J. Hum.-Comput. Stud. **68**(4), 223–241 (2010)

Baker, R.S., Ocumpaugh, J.: Interaction-based affect detection in educational software. In: Calvo, R.A., D'Mello, S.K., Gratch, J., Kappas, A. (eds.) The Oxford Handbook of Affective Computing. Oxford University Press, Oxford (2014)

Benjamini, Y., Hochberg, Y.: Controlling the false discovery rate: a practical and powerful approach to multiple testing. J. Roy. Stat. Soc. Ser. B (Methodol.) 289–300 (1995)

Bosch, N., D'Mello, S.K., Ocumpaugh, J., Baker, R.S., Shute, V.: Using video to automatically detect learner affect in computer-enabled classrooms. ACM Trans. Interact. Intell. Syst. **6** (2) (2016)

Botelho, A.F., Baker, R., Ocumpaugh, J., Heffernan, N.: Studying affect dynamics and chronometry using sensor-free detectors. In: Proceedings of the 11th International Conference on Educational Data Mining, pp. 157–166 (2018)

Crossley, S., Bradfield, F., Ocumpaugh, J., Dascalu, M., Labrum, M., Baker, R.S.: Modeling math identity and math success through sentiment analysis and linguistic features. In: International Conference on Educational Data Mining, pp. 11–20. EDM Society Press (2018)

DeFalco, J.A., et al.: Detecting and addressing frustration in a serious game for military training. Int. J. Artif. Intell. Educ. **28**(2), 152–193 (2017). https://doi.org/10.1007/s40593-017-0152-1

D'Mello, S., Graesser, A.: The half-life of cognitive-affective states during complex learning. Cogn. Emot. **25**(7), 1299–1308 (2011)

D'Mello, S., Graesser, A.: Dynamics of affective states during complex learning. Learn. Instr. **22**(2), 145–157 (2012)

Grafsgaard, J., Wiggins, J., Boyer, K.E., Wiebe, E., Lester, J.: Predicting learning and affect from multimodal data streams in task-oriented tutorial dialogue. In: Educational Data Mining 2014, July 2014

Grawemeyer, B., Mavrikis, M., Holmes, W., Gutiérrez-Santos, S., Wiedmann, M., Rummel, N.: Affective learning: improving engagement and enhancing learning with affect-aware feedback. User Model. User-Adapt. Interact. **27**(1), 119–158 (2017). https://doi.org/10.1007/s11257-017-9188-z

Hake, R.R.: Interactive-engagement versus traditional methods: a six-thousand-student survey of mechanics test data for introductory physics courses. Am. J. Phys. **66**(1), 64–74 (1998)

Karumbaiah, S., Lizarralde, R., Allessio, D., Woolf, B., Arroyo, I., Wixon, N.: Addressing Student Behavior and Affect with Empathy and Growth Mindset. International Educational Data Mining Society (2017)

Karumbaiah, S., Andres, J.M. A.L., Botelho, A.F., Baker, R.S., Ocumpaugh, J.: The implications of a subtle difference in the calculation of affect dynamics. In 26th International Conference for Computers in Education (2018)

Karumbaiah, S., Baker, R.S., Ocumpaugh, J.: The case of self-transitions in affective dynamics. In: Proceedings of the 20th International Conference on Artificial Intelligence in Education, pp. 172–181 (2019)

Kostyuk, V., Almeda, M.V., Baker, R.S.: Correlating affect and behavior in reasoning mind with state test achievement. In: Proceedings of the International Conference on Learning Analytics and Knowledge, pp. 26–30 (2018)

Lehman, B., Graesser, A.: To resolve or not to resolve? That is the big question about confusion. In: Conati, C., Heffernan, N., Mitrovic, A., Verdejo, M.Felisa (eds.) AIED 2015. LNCS (LNAI), vol. 9112, pp. 216–225. Springer, Cham (2015). https://doi.org/10.1007/978-3-319-19773-9_22

Liu, Z., Pataranutaporn, V., Ocumpaugh, J., Baker, R.S.: Sequences of frustration and confusion, and learning. In: Proceedings of the 6th International Conference on Educational Data Mining, pp. 114–120 (2013)

Mulqueeny, K., Kostyuk, V., Baker, R.S., Ocumpaugh, J.: Incorporating effective e-learning principles to improve student engagement in middle-school mathematics. Int. J. STEM Educ. 2(15) (2015)

Ocumpaugh, J., Baker, R.S., Rodrigo, M.M.T.: Baker Rodrigo Ocumpaugh Monitoring Protocol (BROMP) 2.0 Technical and Training Manual. Technical Report. New York, NY: Teachers College, Columbia University. Manila, Philippines: Ateneo Laboratory for the Learning Sciences (2015)

Ocumpaugh, J., Baker, R.S., Gaudino, S., Labrum, Matthew J., Dezendorf, T.: Field observations of engagement in reasoning mind. In: Lane, H.Chad, Yacef, K., Mostow, J., Pavlik, P. (eds.) AIED 2013. LNCS (LNAI), vol. 7926, pp. 624–627. Springer, Heidelberg (2013). https://doi.org/10.1007/978-3-642-39112-5_74

Pardos, Z.A., Baker, R.S., San Pedro, M.O., Gowda, S.M., Gowda, S.M.: Affective states and state tests: investigating how affect and engagement during the school year predict end-of-year learning outcomes. J. Learn. Anal. 1(1), 107–128 (2014)

Pekrun, R.: The control-value theory of achievement emotions: assumptions, corollaries, and implications for educational research and practice. Educ. Psychol. Rev. 18(4), 315–341 (2006)

Sabourin, J., Rowe, J.P., Mott, Bradford W., Lester, James C.: When off-task is on-task: the affective role of off-task behavior in narrative-centered learning environments. In: Biswas, G., Bull, S., Kay, J., Mitrovic, A. (eds.) AIED 2011. LNCS (LNAI), vol. 6738, pp. 534–536. Springer, Heidelberg (2011). https://doi.org/10.1007/978-3-642-21869-9_93

Slater, S., Ocumpaugh, J., Baker, R., Scupelli, P., Inventado, P.S., Heffernan, N.: Semantic features of math problems: relationships to student learning and engagement. In: Proceedings of the 9th International Conference on Educational Data Mining., pp. 223–230 (2016)

Waxman, H.C., Houston, W.R.: Evaluation of the Reasoning Mind program in Beaumont ISD. Unpublished manuscript (2012)

Helping Teachers Help Their Students: A Human-AI Hybrid Approach

Ranilson Paiva$^{(\boxtimes)}$ ⓘ and Ig Ibert Bittencourtⓘ

Instituto de Computação - IC, Universidade Federal de Alagoas - UFAL, Av. Lourival Melo Mota, S/N - Cidade Universitária, Maceió, Alagoas 57072-970, Brazil
{ranilsonpaiva,ig.ibert}@ic.ufal.br
http://www.ufal.edu.br/unidadeacademica/ic

Abstract. There is a global interest in artificial intelligence to support online learning, but little increase in support for online professors, teachers and tutors (instructors). Over time, more students join online learning, but instructors have no equivalent increase in support to manage their online classes, leaving students under-served. This is evidenced by the number of students who dropout or fail online courses, blaming the "lack of support" from instructors. Interactions in such courses generate considerable quantity and diversity of data, allowing the extraction of pedagogically relevant information. However, instructors do not master the techniques and technologies needed to do it, and it is not practical to train them to do so. In this work, we propose an authoring tool (called T-Partner) that implements a process we created to deal with educational data. The objective is to support instructors making informed pedagogical decisions to manage their online course. T-Partner promotes the cooperation between artificial and human intelligences, however we do not know the appropriate balance between these "intelligences". We then created two versions of the T-Partner to help instructors to: (1) find relevant pedagogical situations occurring within their online courses; (2) understand these situations; (3) create interventions (study plans, for example) to address these situations; (4) monitor and evaluate the impact of these interventions. We evaluated if both versions allowed instructors to make pedagogical decisions and their perceptions regarding this support to decision-making. The results show that both versions brought benefits to pedagogical decision-making, and were positively perceived by the participants.

Keywords: Pedagogical Decision-Making · Data-informed decisions · Authoring tools · On-line learning environments

1 Introduction

Technology can influence the processes and outcomes of education, and many countries are investing in technological support for teaching and learning [20]. Online education is one such example and the number of courses offered online

I. I. Bittencourt et al. (Eds.): AIED 2020, LNAI 12163, pp. 448–459, 2020.
https://doi.org/10.1007/978-3-030-52237-7_36

increase constantly and worldwide [8,19]. Besides that, some countries are passing laws to regulate online learning, while others are investing considerable amounts to stimulate its use[1]. These facts evidence that online education is a viable approach to propagate and democratize education, and there is demand for it.

However, professors, teachers and tutors (we will refer to them as instructors) face challenges with online education. One such challenge is to make (course) decisions using educational data. Doing so requires instructors to quickly and continually deal with these data [21], which can be diverse and in considerable volume. Training them to analyze these data would require lots of time, effort and resources, with uncertain results [7,11]. This highlights the importance to provide instructors the necessary technological support [5,10]. These information indicate the need to: (1) help instructors extract relevant information from educational data; (2) Provide them means to create personalized interventions to address issues discovered and; (3) Check the success of these interventions [14,15].

Complimentary, there is a new research branch in the AIED field: the creation of artificial intelligence to **collaborate** with human intelligence [2,4]. This should position professors, teachers and tutors as the main decision-makers [3,20] in the online "classroom". However, there are no scientific works regarding how much of each of these "intelligences" (artificial and human), should be used in this collaboration. Based on these information, we ask the following research question: how can we balance artificial and human intelligence in order to help instructors manage their online courses while they are occurring? Researching about this problem, we found the definition for authoring tools, which is a tool to help users (professors, teachers and tutors), allowing them to create, sequence and publish content (to students), without requiring advanced technical knowledge or training [6,12].

In this work, we evaluate two versions of an authoring tool (we called it Teachers' Partner or T-Partner). The two versions were named: lightweight and heavyweight, and they were created to present different combinations of artificial and human intelligences in order to assist online instructors manage their courses. In the lightweight version, users make simple choices, with the artificial intelligence having more control over the decisions. In the heavyweight version, users are required to make more choices, giving them more control over the decisions. The trade-off is: simplicity vs. control.

T-Partner was designed to assist online instructors to: (1) search for relevant pedagogical situations in the learning environment (using educational data); (2) Use these data to generate visualizations of patterns and trends in order to understand what is happening with their students/courses; (3) Create personalized study plans (interventions) and deliver them to the target students; (4) Check whether these study plans helped students or not.

We evaluated both versions of T-Partner by asking instructors to complete the four tasks listed above, for a specific scenario, which was to evaluate how the students' interactions affect their performance. The results show the participants

---

[1] Available at: https://bit.ly/2zM3JKp and https://bit.ly/2FX7saW.

(instructors) were able to properly complete the proposed tasks and had positive perceptions about the T-Partner, considering it easy to use, helpful and interesting. The results also show that the participants preferred the heavyweight version, suggesting that the balance between artificial and human intelligence should be designed in favor of human control on the decision-making process.

2   Proposal

In this section, we present the Process (Pedagogical Decision-Making Process), and the two versions (lightweight and heavyweight) of the authoring tool (T-Partner) created.

2.1   Pedagogical Decision-Making Process (PDMP)

The T-Partner follows a process where: (1) educational data is analyzed in search for pedagogical situations; (2) Relevant issues are presented to the instructors as easy-to-understand and interactive visualization; (3) The educational resources (videos, texts, questions, etc.) are organized (domain, curriculum and knowledge component), allowing instructors to devise pedagogical interventions for the pedagogical situations found and; (4) The instructor defines the criteria to measure if the interventions were effective or not (Fig. 1).

The Pedagogical Decision-Making Process (PDMP) is a cyclical process and its objective is to guide instructors (from online learning environments) to: (1) discover issues/situations, with pedagogical value, occurring in their online courses; (2) Understand these situations; (3) Make decisions to address them; (4) Monitor and evaluate the impact of the decisions made. The PDMP has two phases: the construction phase and the execution phase. In the construction phase, human and artificial intelligences collaborate to specify (1) which, among some defined pedagogical situations, they want to search for in the learning environment; (2) What decision they want to make, considering the learning environment's capabilities, to address a pedagogical situation found; (3) How they want to measure the effectiveness of the decision made [16,17]. In the execution phase, the successful definitions made in the construction phase are automatically repeated, if the same pedagogical situation is found again.

In previous works, we used the PDMP to: (1) evaluate the effectiveness of gamification elements in an OLE [13]; (2) Measure differences between male and female students' interactions in an online learning environment (OLE) [18]; (3) Improve students' interactions in an OLE [16]; (4) Recommend topics learners should study to improve their writing performance [1], among other uses[2].

2.2   T-Partner

In order to avoid the error-prone and repetitive task of manually following the PDMP, we created an authoring tool named T-Partner (Teachers' Partner). The T-Partner needs to be integrated to a learning environment in order to access

---

[2] Detect and recommend actions to disengaged learners; Recommend educational resources to practice a specific math topic etc. These works are not published, yet.

Pedagogical Decision-Making Process

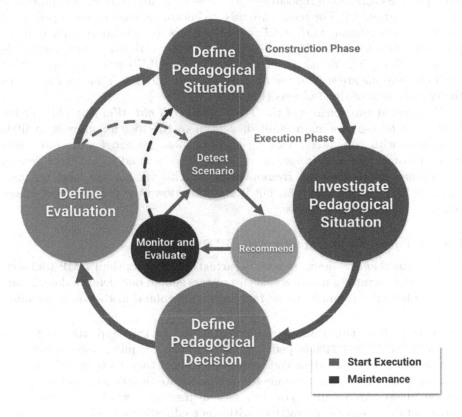

Fig. 1. The Pedagogical Decision-Making Process.

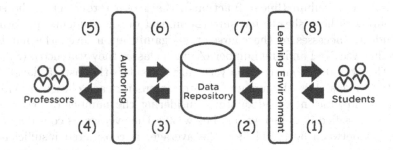

Fig. 2. T-Partner communication with an online learning environment.

its educational data[3]. Basically: (1) learners interact with the online learning

---

[3] Data about learners, educational resources, interaction data (user-user, user-content and user-environment interactions), and other data to support instructors' pedagogical decision making.

environment (OLE); (2) These interactions generate (educational) data that are stored in the OLE's data repository; (3) These data are retrieved and processed by the T-Partner; (4) The results are used to inform instructors about pedagogical situations occurring in the OLE; (5) Instructors use this information to make pedagogical decisions; (6) These decisions use the educational resources available in the OLE; (7) The decisions should consider the OLE's interface capabilities; (8) The decisions are sent to the targeted learners; (9) The T-Partner measures the effectiveness of the decisions (Fig. 2).

We created two versions of the T-Partner: (1) **Light Weight**: This version is an easy to use, but more limited, version of the tool for users with little experience with computers, allowing them to make pedagogical decisions easier and faster, but more constrained. It can also be used as an entry version for training instructors; (2) **Heavy Weight**: This version has more features, allowing finer-grained decisions, but it may slow down the process and be more complex/demanding to the user[4].

2.3   T-Partner Implementing the PDMP

In this subsection we describe how T-Partner implements the PDMP (Subsect. 2.1). It is important to mention that instructors should first define a domain and a curriculum. For example: linear functions (curriculum) in the math domain.

Step 1: Define the Pedagogical Situation. In this step, the instructors choose among the available pedagogical situations, defining some parameters in order to personalize data collection. After that, they must specify how T-Partner must classify each parameter as inadequate, insufficient and adequate, named **classes of results**. For example: an instructor wants to evaluate the impact of the students' interactions with some educational resources, for a particular subject, in the previous 15 days. The instructor chooses the domain (math), the curriculum (linear functions), the group (group 1). (S)he selects the resources (s)he wishes to measure the impact on the students' performance (the students' accesses to the course, their gamification level, the number of badges they received and the number of video classes they watched). (S)he also defines the period of time the analysis must consider (the last 15 days). Next, the instructor classifies the amount of interactions for each chosen resources as inadequate, insufficient or adequate. Considering the number of accesses, the instructor classified it as follows: (1) below 30% the average, is considered inadequate; (2) between 30% and 59% the average, is considered insufficient; (3) above 59% the average, is considered appropriate. The instructor classified level, badges and videos with the same values as the number of accesses. The T-Partner searches the data, following the parameters defined, and classifies the resulting data according to the classification values provided by the instructor.

---

[4] Due to the restricted number of pages, it was not possible to add pictures of T-Partner in this paper. However, we created a website where we present images and detailed descriptions of both versions. It is available at: http://tpartner. ranilsonpaiva.com.

Step 2: Investigate Pedagogical Situation. In this step, the T-Partner groups the students according to the way instructors classified the resources. In this part of the tool, data is processed using an algorithm associated with the pedagogical situation chosen in step 1 (for example: if the instructor chose to evaluate the students' interactions impact on their performance, the algorithm used is a Decision Tree). Before data processing, instructors select how to pre-process the data (imputation, remove registries with missing values, remove outliers etc.), and how they wish to visualize the data processing result. The resulting visualization uses different colors to represent different result classes: inadequate - red, insufficient - yellow and adequate - green. The aim is to provide instructors with information extracted from the educational data, in order to aid their decision process.

Step 3: Define Pedagogical Decisions. In this step, instructors create a personalized intervention (for example: a study plan) for each class of results (inadequate, insufficient and adequate). For each intervention, instructors must give it a name and define: (1) the activities learners should do (texts, videos, questions etc., depending on what is available in the OLE); (2) The amount for each activity; (3) The order the activities should be arranged; (4) The desired modifiers for the activity (for multiple choice questions, a modifier can be its difficulty); (5) The target class of results; (6) The amount of time learners have to complete the task; and (7) The pedagogical approach learners should follow to finish the task (for example: do it individually, do it in group, peer-evaluate colleagues answers, receive points or badges for doing it in case of gamified learning environments etc. It depends on what the OLE offers). For example, an intervention can be, for **linear function** in the **math domain**, to **read *one* text, watch *one* video-class, answer *one* easy multiple-choice question, answer *three* difficult multiple-choice questions (in this order)**. This must be sent to students in the **insufficient** result class, who must do it **individually** and in the **next 10 days**.

Step 4: Define Assessment. In this step, instructors set the desired percentage for *adherence*[5] and the *desired outcome* from those who followed the recommended intervention. This is done for each class of results. For example: an instructor defines, for the inadequate result class, 50% adherence and an 20% increase in the students' performance (number of correct answered divided by the number of questions answered).

3   Experimentation

In this experiment, we invited professors, teachers and tutors to evaluate the T-Partner. This experiment was available on-line for a 30 days period. After this period, we collected the participation data, cleaned them, removing test data,

---

[5] The amount of learners that completed the intervention recommended by the instructor.

empty and incomplete records. Next, we performed the data analysis following the guidelines proposed by [9].

Part 1 - Using T-Partner to Solve a Pedagogical Issue. Participants were randomly assigned to one of the two versions of the T-Partner[6]. They had to read a description of a real education scenario, guiding them to perform the following tasks: (1) evaluate the performance of the students based on their interactions in the OLE; (2) Create a study plan for each class of results; (3) Define the criteria of a successful intervention.

Based on the scenario, we asked participants to: (1) choose the issue they wanted to search for in the learning environment. The available options were: evaluate students' failing probability; evaluate students' dropping out probability and evaluate students' interactions with the educational resources; (2) Choose one of the pre-processing techniques available. Some available options were: remove empty and null registries and apply imputation technique. Next, choose the way they wanted to visualize results[7]; (3) Create a study plan, to address the issue, for each class of results and define how long students had to complete it; (4) Define the adherence and the desired outcome.

Participants could make different choices (decisions). Some were appropriate, some were not. We calculated a **score**, for each step, which was the sum of the tasks completed appropriately, divided by the total amount of tasks, according to the formula:

$$SCORE = \frac{\sum_{i=1}^{n} e_i}{MAX} \tag{1}$$

Part 2 - The Participants' Perceptions About the T-Partner. We asked the participants' perceptions, regarding the following metrics: (1) Perceived utility (PU) - if participants considered the tool useful to manage their courses; (2) Perceived ease of use (PEU) - if participants considered the tool easy to use; (3) Attitude towards use (ATU) - if participants had a positive attitude towards using the tool; (4) Intention to use (IU) - if participants would use the tool if it was available in their workplace; (5) Visualizations used (VIZ) - if the visualizations used were informative; (6) Color scheme used (COL) - if the colors used (red, yellow and green) to represent the classes of results, helped participants understand the situation learners were facing; and (7) vocabulary used (VOC) - if the vocabulary used was appropriate. The first 4 metrics were **based** on the Technology Acceptance Model [22] and the others were created for the purpose of this experiment. Participants had to assign a score for each criteria, according to a Likert scale from 0 to 6, where: 0 = I strongly disagree; 1 = I disagree; 2 = I slightly disagree; 3 = I neither agree nor disagree (indifferent); 4 = I slightly agree; 5 = I agree; 6 = I strongly agree.

---

[6] We used anonymized data from a high school level online learning environment with more than 6000 active Brazilian students.

[7] The available visualizations depended on the pedagogical issue chosen in step 1.

Table 1. Scores for accomplishing the tasks (LW = Light Weight and HW = Heavy Weight).

PDMP	MIN LW/HW	MAX LW/HW	MED LW/HW	AVG LW/HW	SD LW/HW
Step 1	0/0.67	1/1	1/1	0.94/0.97	0.15/0.10
Step 2	0/0	1/1	0.93/1	0.84/0.93	0.3/0.19
Step 3	0/0	1/1	0/0.55	0.33/0.52	0.44/0.49
Step 4	1/0.1	1/1	1/1	1/0.7	0/0.84
All tasks	0/0	1/1	1/1	0.84/0.87	0.32/0.29

Table 2. Score comparison for completing the tasks (Wilcoxon-Mann-Whitney test).

PDMP	P-VALUE	HIGHER SCORE
Step 1	0.0001984*	*HW*
Step 2	0.08513	No difference
Step 3	0.01698*	*HW*
Step 4	0.0004147*	*LW*
All tasks	0.02922*	*HW*

* = Statistically significant; LW = Light Weight; HW = Heavy Weight.

4   Results and Discussion

Regarding the participants, we had 45 complete and valid participations, with n = 20 for the Light Weight version and n = 25 for the Heavy Weight version. They were all higher education professors from Brazil, with ages ranging from 32 to 63 years old. Their years of experience ranged from 6 years to more than 15 years as higher education professors. Their level of familiarity and professional use of educational technologies ranged from good to very good.

For part 1, the Score for each step was normalized[8]. We calculated the minimum score (MIN), maximum score (MAX), median score (MED) average score (AVG) and the standard deviation (SD) for each step. The results are shown in Table 1. In Table 2 we applied the Wilcoxon-Mann-Whitney to test for statistical relevance of the differences in scores for the two versions.

The results show that, regarding the tasks in Steps 1, 2 and the sum of the tasks in all steps, the scores in the Heavy Weight version (HW) were higher, suggesting the HW version allowed instructors to make better decisions (score higher in doing what was expected from them) than the LW version. The Heavy Weight version offers greater detailing and control to instructors (human intelligence), which is represented by more options to make more detailed decisions. In the Light Weight version this control and detailing is mostly done by the system. We believe that having the system handle some parts of the decision confused the participants, affecting their comprehension and proper completion of the task.

---

[8] All scores are in the 0 to 1 interval.

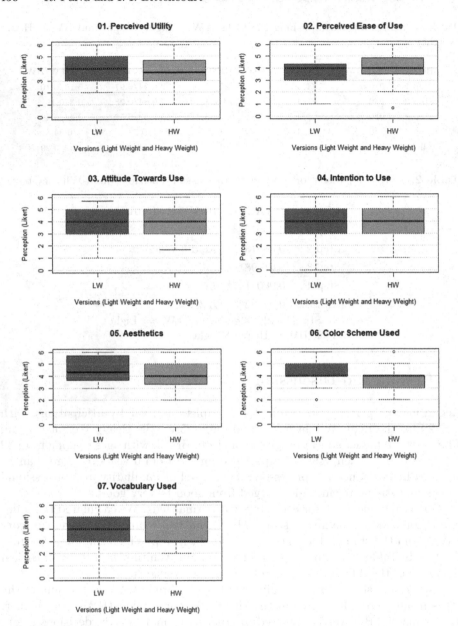

Fig. 3. Participants' perceptions about the T-Partner's versions.

We need to further investigate other variations of this human/computer balance for each step of the process.

The results show higher standard deviation, regarding the scores in Steps 3 and 4 in the Heavy Weight version, suggesting participants had difficulties completing the respective tasks. This may be due to these steps were the ones with a higher amount of tasks to complete (in the HW version). It may be the case to improve clarity of the steps and/or divide these steps into sub-steps (further investigation is necessary).

The results of the participants' perceptions for all metrics of both versions (heavy weight and light weight) were positive and similar (Fig. 3), which is a good and desired result, showing that the participants had a favourable perception regarding the T-Partner and the process, independent of the version. The median value was 4, which corresponds to the answer "I slightly agree." This shows that participants' perceptions were positive (above neutral/indifferent).

5 Conclusion

We proposed the Pedagogical Decision-Making Process (PDMP) and an authoring tool (T-Partner) that implements it. The objective was to have artificial and human intelligence work, collaboratively, to help online instructors managing their courses/students, offering personalised assistance. However, we did not know how to balance these two "intelligences" in the final tool. Therefore, we created two versions of T-Partner: the light weight version, where most part of the decisions are made by the system, and the heavy weight version, where most part of the decisions are made by the instructors (professors, teachers and tutors). We evaluated both versions of T-Partner, regarding its capacity to support instructors' pedagogical decision-making as well as their perceptions on its utility and use.

Overall, the results showed that the participants were able to properly perform the demanded tasks, supporting online instructors' pedagogical decision-making, with some minor issues in the tasks for steps 3 and 4 from the Heavy weight version (with higher number of tasks to complete). Instructors show positive perceptions regarding all the metrics considered, independent of the version, stating that: (1) the tool would be useful to help them manage their courses/students; (2) The tool was easy to use; (3) They had a positive perception towards using the tool; (4) They would use the tool if it was available in their workplace; (5) The visualizations provided were informative; (6) The color scheme helped them understand how serious the students' situation was and; (7) The vocabulary used was appropriate.

We believe the proposed process and tool are a step towards augmenting human intelligence with artificial intelligence in the education area. However, we noticed that some situations require more research and experiments, for example: what is the ideal balance between human and artificial intelligence for making pedagogical decisions? Does this balance change in different contexts? Does the experience of the instructor affect his/her interest in more or less control over the pedagogical decisions they make and the technology support they receive? We will research these and other questions in future works.

Acknowledgements. We would like to thank EyeDuc® team for granting us access to the data used in this research. We acknowledge the financial support from FAPEAL and CAPES/CNPq.

References

1. Abreu, D., Bittencourt, I., Paiva, R., Dermeval, D.: Pedagogical recommendation to improve the quality of writing: a case study in a public school. In: 2018 IEEE 18th International Conference on Advanced Learning Technologies (ICALT), pp. 75–76. IEEE (2018)
2. Baker, R.S.: Stupid tutoring systems, intelligent humans. Int. J. Artif. Intell. Educ. **26**(2), 600–614 (2016)
3. Burden, P., Fuller, A.: The teacher as a decision maker. In: Methods for Effective Teaching Meeting the Needs of All Students (2014)
4. Chou, C.Y., Huang, B.H., Lin, C.J.: Complementary machine intelligence and human intelligence in virtual teaching assistant for tutoring program tracing. Comput. Educ. **57**(4), 2303–2312 (2011)
5. Dağ, F., Durdu, L., Gerdan, S.: Evaluation of educational authoring tools for teachers stressing of perceived usability features. Proc.-Soc. Behav. Sci. **116**, 888–901 (2014)
6. Dermeval, D., Paiva, R., Bittencourt, I.I., Vassileva, J., Borges, D.: Authoring tools for designing intelligent tutoring systems: a systematic review of the literature. Int. J. Artif. Intell. Educ. **28**(3), 336–384 (2018)
7. Duhaney, D.C.: Teacher education: preparing teachers to integrate technology. Int. J. Instruct. Med. **28**(1), 23 (2001)
8. AC EAD: Br: Online learning in Brazil - analytic report 2017/2018. Ibpex, Curitiba (2018)
9. Jain, A.K.: Data clustering: 50 years beyond k-means. Pattern Recogn. Lett. **31**(8), 651–666 (2010)
10. Kim, C., Kim, M.K., Lee, C., Spector, J.M., DeMeester, K.: Teacher beliefs and technology integration. Teach. Teach. Educ. **29**, 76–85 (2013)
11. Kopcha, T.J.: Teachers' perceptions of the barriers to technology integration and practices with technology under situated professional development. Comput. Educ. **59**(4), 1109–1121 (2012)
12. Murray, T.: An overview of intelligent tutoring system authoring tools: updated analysis of the state of the art. In: Murray, T., Blessing, S.B., Ainsworth, S. (eds.) Authoring Tools for Advanced Technology Learning Environments, pp. 491–544. Springer, Dordrecht (2003). https://doi.org/10.1007/978-94-017-0819-7_17
13. Paiva, R., Barbosa, A., Batista, E., Pimentel, D., Bittencourt, I.I.: Badges and XP: an observational study about learning. In: Frontiers in Education Conference (FIE), pp. 1–8. IEEE (2015)
14. Paiva, R., Bittencourt, I.I.: The authoring of pedagogical decisions informed by, data, on the perspective of a MOOC. In: Anais dos Workshops do Congresso Brasileiro de Informática na Educação, vol. 6, p. 15 (2017)
15. Paiva, Ranilson, Bittencourt, Ig Ibert: Helping MOOC teachers do their job. In: Cristea, Alexandra Ioana, Bittencourt, Ig Ibert, Lima, Fernanda (eds.) HEFA 2017. CCIS, vol. 832, pp. 52–67. Springer, Cham (2018). https://doi.org/10.1007/978-3-319-97934-2_4

16. Paiva, R., Bittencourt, I.I., Tenório, T., Jaques, P., Isotani, S.: What do students do on-line? Modeling students' interactions to improve their learning experience. Comput. Hum. Behav. **64**, 769–781 (2016). https://doi.org/10.1016/j.chb.2016.07. 048, http://www.sciencedirect.com/science/article/pii/S0747563216305386

17. Paiva, R.O.A., Bittencourt, I.I., da Silva, A.P., Isotani, S., Jaques, P.: Improving pedagogical recommendations by classifying students according to their interactional behavior in a gamified learning environment. In: Proceedings of the 30th Annual ACM Symposium on Applied Computing, pp. 233–238. ACM (2015)

18. de Santana, S.J., Ranilson Paiva, I.I.B.e.a.: Evaluating the impact of mars and Venus effect on the use of an adaptive learning technology for Portuguese and mathematics. In: The 16th IEEE International Conference on Advanced Learning Technologies - ICALT2016 (2016)

19. Seaman, J., Allen, I., Seaman, J.: Grade increase: tracking distance education in the United States. Babson Survey Research Group, Oakland (2019)

20. Sheridan, S., Mouza, C., Pollock, L.: Professional development for computer science education: design and outcomes from a case study teacher. In: Society for Information Technology & Teacher Education International Conference, pp. 1115–1123. Association for the Advancement of Computing in Education (AACE) (2019)

21. Stephenson, J.: Teaching & Learning Online: New Pedagogies for New Technologies. Routledge, Abingdon (2018)

22. Teo, T.: Factors influencing teachers' intention to use technology: model development and test. Comput. Educ. **57**(4), 2432–2440 (2011)

Comprehensive Views of Math Learners: A Case for Modeling and Supporting Non-math Factors in Adaptive Math Software

J. Elizabeth Richey[✉] ⓘ, Nikki G. Lobczowski ⓘ, Paulo F. Carvalho ⓘ, and Kenneth Koedinger

Carnegie Mellon University, Pittsburgh, PA 15213, USA
jelizabethrichey@cmu.edu

Abstract. Adaptive math software supports students' learning by targeting specific math knowledge components. However, widespread use of adaptive math software in classrooms has not led to the expected changes in student achievement, particularly for racially minoritized students and students situated in poverty. While research has shown the power of human mentors to support student learning and reduce opportunity gaps, mentoring support could be optimized by using educational technology to identify the specific non-math factors that are disrupting students' learning and direct mentors to appropriate resources related to those factors. In this paper, we present an analysis of one non-math factor—reading comprehension—that has been shown to influence math learning. We predict math performance using this non-math factor and show that it contributes novel explanatory value in modeling students' learning behaviors. Through this analysis, we argue that educational technology could better address the learning needs of the whole student by modeling non-math factors. We suggest future research should take this learning analytics approach to identify the many different kinds of motivational and non-math content challenges that arise when students are learning from adaptive math software. We envision analyses such as those presented in this paper enabling greater individualization within adaptive math software that takes into account not only math knowledge and progress but also non-math factors.

Keywords: Math education · Reading comprehension · Opportunity gap · Cognitive tutor · Additive Factors Model · Gaming · Wheel spinning

1 Introduction

1.1 Opportunity Gaps in Mathematics Education

Math software can accelerate—and even double—the rate of student learning in mathematics by identifying the specific knowledge components students have not mastered and delivering individualized instruction accordingly [1, 2]. These types of gains have been replicated across topics and contexts [3–6], leading to increasingly widespread use

© Springer Nature Switzerland AG 2020
I. I. Bittencourt et al. (Eds.): AIED 2020, LNAI 12163, pp. 460–471, 2020.
https://doi.org/10.1007/978-3-030-52237-7_37

in schools [7]. Based on such results and a sense of excitement around the possibilities of individualized learning through technology, many school districts have invested significant resources to bring educational technology into classrooms.

As schools adopt educational technology, however, many are not seeing the changes in student achievement expected based on results from laboratory and controlled classroom experiments. Despite the success of adaptive math software in supporting learning outcomes, there is evidence that challenges in math learning go well beyond issues with math [8, 9], particularly for racially minoritized students and students situated in poverty. Racial and economic opportunity gaps prevent millions of American students from realizing their potential, but researchers have struggled to identify effective solutions to these longstanding problems [10–12]. Although some studies have found that math software supports learning outcomes for all students [13], educational technology is rarely designed to address existing inequities in access and opportunity, and high variation in students' use of educational technology produces additional opportunity gaps. This suggests an important gap in current research: although we have powerful adaptive methods to teach students math, these programs are typically based solely on math performance even though we know that students' math knowledge is not the only factor in understanding math outcomes.

1.2 AI Support for Personalized Mentoring

Recent research suggests that intensive, personalized mentoring may provide a fruitful avenue for reducing racial and economic gaps in learning opportunities and outcomes. In one study, fifth through seventh-grade students who participated in a two-year mentoring program targeting attendance and engagement were absent less often and failed fewer courses by the end of the program [14]. Another mentoring study that focused on intensive instructional support significantly improved students' math achievement test scores and grades while reducing course failure rates [15]. Both studies took place in Chicago Public Schools with predominantly racially minoritized students and students situated in poverty. These effects are encouraging, but the large resources required for such intensive mentoring are prohibitive to many districts.

Mentoring support could be optimized by using artificial intelligence (AI) to help mentors and caregivers assess the specific non-math factors that are disrupting students' learning and direct them to appropriate resources related to those factors. In other words, we could use the same kind of AI that currently assesses and responds to math knowledge to address the non-math factors influencing student learning. To provide this type of individualized non-math support, we must build better models.

In this paper, we present an analysis of one non-math factor—reading comprehension—that has been shown to influence math learning [16–20]. Through this analysis, we argue that educational technology could better address the learning needs of the whole student by modeling non-math factors. We undertook this analysis in the context of developing the Personalized Learning^2 (PL^2) app, which is designed to supplement the individualized cognitive tutoring provided in existing adaptive math software with the motivational and learning support capabilities of human mentors [21]. Data generated through students' use of math software could provide evidence for differentiating motivational and cognitive barriers to engagement and learning. Using this data, we aim to identify the many different kinds of motivational and non-math content challenges that arise when students are learning from adaptive math software and to adapt the PL^2 app to help mentors support students through those challenges. The app currently focuses on data about students' *math performance* in math software to guide mentors to appropriate resources, but analyses such as those presented in this paper could enable greater individualization that takes into account not only math knowledge and progress but also non-math factors.

1.3   Reading Comprehension and Math Performance

We focus on reading because comprehending math text requires more than numerical fluency. Although reading a math story problem is different from reading a work of fiction, reading comprehension plays an important role in comprehending math texts [16]. Students' technical reading skills (i.e., word recognition and decoding, adaptive reading method, speed) predict their skills solving math word problems [17]. The role of reading comprehension in understanding math texts without symbols is similar to its role in understanding non-math texts, but math texts with symbols appear to require more specialized reading skills [18] and present more challenges than non-math texts [19]. This suggests the importance of both generalized reading skills and content-specific math reading skills for understanding symbolic math story problems.

Reading comprehension may have a cumulative effect in constraining math learning. A study that used third-graders' reading comprehension scores to predict math problem solving, math conceptual knowledge, and math computation skills through eighth grade showed that reading comprehension predicted the rate of growth across all three math components, even when controlling for third-grade math achievement [20]. These results suggest that failure to support students' reading comprehension can impact the trajectory of their math learning, but the role of reading comprehension in learning from math software is still an open question. In the current study, we aim to further examine the hypothesized role reading comprehension may have in constraining math learning.

1.4   Current Study

Our data were gathered through a popular educational technology platform used in classrooms around the United States that serves as a good example of an evidence-based, adaptive math software. Although we use reading comprehension in this adaptive math software as a test case, the ultimate goal is that our approach could be used to identify a range of non-math factors across many educational technologies. We explore the following research questions:

RQ1: *Does a measure of reading comprehension extracted from math software relate to math performance in the software?* We hypothesize that reading comprehension, as measured by performance in a non-math software tutorial, will be correlated with performance in the math modules of the same software. We predict that our measure of reading comprehension will not be correlated with non-performance behaviors, such as math hint use, because we hypothesize that we are not measuring an underlying, general behavior in the math software.

RQ2: *Does the reading performance measure constrain growth from math learning opportunities?* We will assess students' learning by modeling growth from each additional practice opportunity, and we hypothesize that our measure of reading comprehension will be associated with less growth.

RQ3: *Is the reading performance measure distinct from established measures of student behaviors in math software?* To determine whether the reading performance measure is simply capturing other student behaviors, we will assess the relation between our measure of reading comprehension and wheel spinning and gaming. Wheel spinning occurs when a student fails to demonstrate mastery of a skill after a long time, typically indicating that they do not have the skills or support to advance [22]. Gaming occurs when students attempt to take advantage of the design of the software to get the correct answer without thinking carefully or learning, such as exploiting hints or clicking through multiple-choice answers until they find the correct response, and it typically involves making a large number of mistakes in a short amount of time [23]. If reading comprehension is highly correlated with these other measures, it may suggest that our measure of reading comprehension is simply detecting wheel spinning or gaming behaviors, since both can be associated with poor performance and learning. We hypothesize that our measure may be moderately correlated with gaming, as poor reading comprehension could lead to attempts to solve the problems without carefully reading them, but that it will not be strongly correlated with either, suggesting it is also detecting something unique.

2 Methods

2.1 Participants and Design

We analyzed two datasets: a smaller dataset with more detailed step-level data from the math software (Dataset 1) and a larger dataset with less detailed, problem-level data from the same software (Dataset 2). Dataset 1 contained data from 67 students from seven schools, including one public school and six charter schools in an urban area in the United States. Within the participating schools, more than 80% of students identified as racially minoritized and 80% qualified for free or reduced lunch. Students were in 6th, 7th, 8th, or 10th grade. Dataset 2 contained data from 197,139 students enrolled in middle school math across multiple schools across the United States. All students in both datasets used the same adaptive math software.

2.2 Materials and Procedure

Anonymized data were collected from students' math software use. Our analysis focused on two module types in the software. The first was an introductory module focused on orienting students to the software through brief instructional text and questions about the text. Performance on the tutorial questions was selected as a measure of reading comprehension because it contained no math content; instead, students read about the math software and answered comprehension questions. For example, one page of the tutorial contained the following: "An Explore Tool is an interactive model that lets you explore math ideas on your own. These tools let you see different ways to model your mathematical thinking." After reading the full text, students saw a list of questions including the following: "I can learn by playing with an Explore Tool, which is a(n) _____ that can help me model mathematical thinking," with "interactive model" available as one of five multiple-choice answers. There were 24 tutorial questions, and most students completed all of them.

Performance on all other modules was used as a measure of math comprehension. Questions targeted a variety of math concepts depending on students' grade level and instructors' choices of assignments. Content across modules was typically presented in the form of math story problems. The number of math problems completed varied by student depending on a number of factors including time spent in the math software and problem type.

3 Results

3.1 Student Performance in Math and Reading Content

First, we examined Dataset 1 students' performance on the math content and reading (non-math tutorial) content separately, looking at the number of problems completed, accuracy, and hint use. This initial inspection of the data allowed us to determine whether both sources of data (Math and Reading Content) provided adequate individual variation to allow for investigation of the RQs in the following sections.

All data focused on students' first attempt on a problem. On math problems, students completed an average of 218.9 problems with an average accuracy rate of .54 and an average of 36.4 hints requests on their first attempts (Fig. 1a–c, Fig. 2a). On the reading problems, only four students completed fewer than the full 24 items available. Students had an average accuracy rate of .67 and used an average of only 1.27 hint requests on their first attempts (Fig. 1d–f, Fig. 2c). Two-tailed, paired-sample t-tests indicated that students had significantly higher accuracy rates, $t(66) = 4.38, p < .001$, and significantly lower hint use, $t(66) = 5.55, p < .001$, when they were completing the reading content compared to the math content. Overall, these analyses suggest students' behavior in both reading and math portions of the tutor is sufficiently varied, and that the reading content is sufficiently different from the math content as demonstrated by differences in accuracy and hint behavior.

3.2 Is Reading Performance Related to Math Performance?

First, we assessed whether reading assistance scores predicted math assistance scores (RQ1). Assistance scores represent the level of support a student required to complete a learning opportunity. If the student completed the step correctly the first time, the assistance score would be 0; every hint or incorrect answer until the correct response added one assistance point to the score. Thus, higher scores mean greater assistance to complete the step, whereas lower scores mean lower assistance levels and potentially correct responses on the first try. A linear regression showed that assistance scores on the reading content explained 10% of the variance in assistance scores on the math content, $r^2 = .51, t(65) = 2.74, p = .008$ (Fig. 2a). We also examined the relation between reading

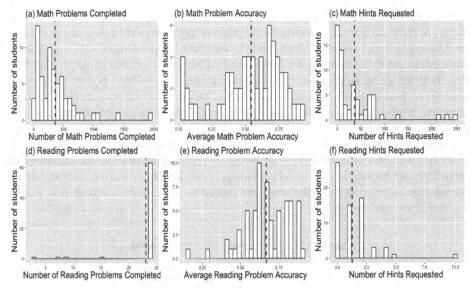

Fig. 1. Histograms for the number of math (a) and reading (d) problems completed, overall math (b) and reading (e) accuracy, and math (c) and reading (f) hints requests in Dataset 1.

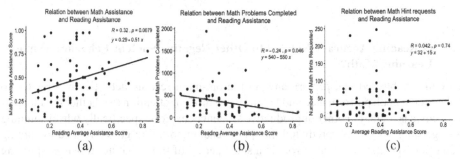

Fig. 2. Correlation between reading assistance score and (a) math assistance score, (b) number of math problems completed in Dataset 1, and (c) math hint use.

assistance and progress, as measured by the number of math problems completed. A linear regression showed that reading assistance explained 6% of the variance in the number of math problems completed, $r^2 = .548$, $t(65) = 2.04$, $p = .046$ (Fig. 2b). Finally, to test whether reading assistance would fail to predict something that we did not hypothesize to be dependent on reading comprehension, we assessed the relation between reading assistance and math hint requests. Reading assistance did not explain a significant level of variance in average number of math hint requests on first attempt, $r^2 = .51$, $t(65) = -0.34$, $p = .74$ (Fig. 2c).

To further understand how performance in the reading tutorial module relates to or constrains later performance during math learning (RQ2), we investigated how well students learned math from each added math practice opportunity using regression models. We investigated student learning using the Additive Factors Model (AFM), which extends item-response theory to include a growth or learning term. In short, AFM predicts, for each assessment opportunity, the probability of correctly answering a problem given the student's baseline easiness and the number of opportunities with each knowledge component. We compared a baseline of AFM with a version of AFM (AFM-R) that included an added parameter to take into account the student's performance in the reading tutorial section of the tutor. In essence, this model took into account not only students' a priori easiness with knowledge components but also a priori easiness with reading materials.

Overall, AFM-R provided a better fit to the data than the baseline AFM (X^2 (1) = 19.61, $p < .001$; see Table 1), suggesting that reading assistance has an impact on math learning. Moreover, consistent with the previous finding, requiring more assistance during the reading portion of the tutor was related to worse math learning, $\beta = -2.55$, $z = 4.82, p < .001$.

Table 1. Model comparison for AFM vs. AFM-R.

Model	DF	AIC	BIC	logLik
AFM	6	31191	31240	−15590
AFM-R	7	31174	31231	−15580

3.3 Is Reading Accuracy Related to Other Negative Student Behaviors While Learning Math?

Having established that performance in the pre-math reading activities was related to subsequent math performance and learning, we turn our attention to whether reading performance is related to other unproductive student behaviors, specifically wheel spinning and gaming (RQ3). We predicted that poor reading ability might be related to gaming behavior (specifically many errors in a short period of time), but not to wheel spinning (specifically indicators of effort without progress). Students with poor reading comprehension may advance in the tutor without trying, making them likely to display gaming behaviors but not wheel spinning.

For this analysis, we used existing models of wheel spinning [22] and gaming [24, 25] to determine for each knowledge component whether each student's behavior could be classified as wheel spinning or gaming. We calculated a proportion of wheel spinning and gaming events out of all knowledge components for each student and related that proportion to performance in the reading portion of the tutor. As predicted, we saw that worse reading performance was related to more gaming events, $r^2 = .45, p < .001$, but not related to wheel spinning behavior, $r^2 = .05, p = .69$ (see Fig. 3).

3.4 Does This Relation Scale and Generalize?

To test the generalizability of our results, we investigated whether the relation between reading and math performance that we observed in the small dataset generalized and scaled to a larger sample.

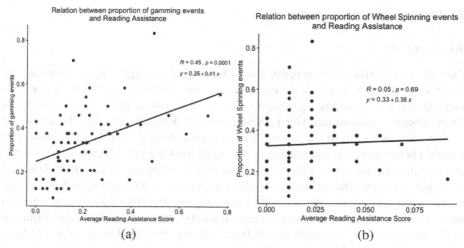

Fig. 3. Correlation between reading assistance score and (a) the proportion of gaming events and (b) the proportion of math wheel spinning events in Dataset 1.

Using Dataset 2, we extracted the same measures of reading and math performance used for our Dataset 1 analyses. Overall, our findings generalized to a larger dataset (see Fig. 4). Students with higher assistance scores during the reading section performed worse (higher assistance scores) in the subsequent math section, $r^2 = 0.39$, $t(197136) = 186.35$, $p < .001$ (Fig. 4a), and completed fewer problems, $r^2 = -0.07$, $t(197136) = -30.433$, $p < .001$ (Fig. 4b). However, contrary to what we saw in the small Dataset 1, we found that students who required greater assistance during the reading portion also requested more hints during the math portion, $r^2 = 0.27$, $t(197136) = 127.03$, $p < .001$ (Fig. 4c).

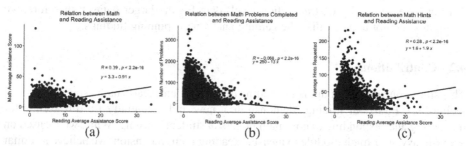

Fig. 4. Correlation between reading assistance score and (a) math assistance score, (b) number of math problems completed, and (c) math hint use in Dataset 2.

4 Discussion and Conclusion

4.1 Overview

Educational technology offers opportunities for students to engage in adaptive learning but does not always lead to positive learning gains. When the technology does not consider the whole student, ignoring key factors that influence learning, it often falls short of helping students reach their optimal potential. Racially minoritized students and students situated in poverty are especially susceptible to being left behind. Technologies must do better to go beyond math content and address the other factors that influence performance. In this study, we provide a first look at using a non-math module within a prominent educational technology to identify an important factor that may negatively impact math learning: reading comprehension. In doing so, our goal was to determine if a measure of reading comprehension within a math software predicted math performance in the same software, restricted growth from learning opportunities, and differed from other measures of student behaviors.

Overall, our results regarding reading comprehension and math learning were similar to those found in previous literature: reading accuracy has an impact on math performance [16–20]. Our study expands on this literature, however, by demonstrating that a module within an adaptive educational technology platform can be used to identify students who may need assistance during reading, which, if provided, could support future math learning. Typical software of this nature falls short in identifying potential issues beyond content understanding. Our results show the importance of integrating novel modules that target other non-content aspects of math learning. Moreover, we were able to show that lower reading performance was related to more gaming behavior, but not to wheel spinning behavior. This suggests that students may attempt to take advantage of the system (e.g., exploiting multiple-choice responses) due to difficulties in reading. Finally, we were able to scale up and generalize our findings related to performance from our original dataset ($n = 67$) to a much larger dataset ($n = 197,139$). Unfortunately, we did not have detailed (i.e., transaction-level) data for the larger dataset; therefore, we could not attempt to generalize the gaming and wheel spinning findings.

4.2 Contributions

This study contributes to our understanding of how students learn math using educational technology. First, our findings demonstrate a new and potentially fruitful avenue for measuring and responding to non-math factors in student learning. While we focused on a text-heavy, non-math module to measure reading comprehension, we believe a similar approach could detect other non-math factors in student data captured by educational technology. Second, these results contribute to the theoretical understanding of how non-math factors influence math learning. Our findings expand on prior research to demonstrate that poor reading comprehension relates to fewer problems solved, less learning from each new learning opportunity, and more gaming behaviors in online math learning. Third, we have highlighted the benefit of adding a non-math, introductory module to existing math content lessons to help identify potential issues with reading comprehension. Doing so introduces a powerful resource to detect possible reading comprehension issues, which in turn could help designers and developers build and refine tutoring systems that better consider the whole student. Finally, our study helps create a way for tutors, mentors, and teachers (i.e., practitioners) to identify students whose literacy needs may negatively affect their math performance. This practical application addresses a need that is often overlooked in math learning. Moreover, a technological solution to identifying these students frees up the time and resources of busy practitioners who may need assistance in identifying these students on their own.

This is a first step toward supporting practitioners as they help students learn math by addressing the needs of the whole student. Programs like PL^2 can create support features (e.g., resources, remediation) for students based on their needs [21]. Supporting reading comprehension as well as students' motivational and social needs could positively affect educational factors such as attendance [26], enrollment in future math courses [27], and performance on college admissions tests [28], which could in turn help address opportunity gaps for marginalized populations of students.

4.3 Limitations

We argue that the results from the non-math (i.e., reading) module can be attributed to reading comprehension due to the nature of the content. One limitation and idea for future research is the unknown effect of motivated attention on learning math-free content. Future researchers could measure the students' attention during these sections (e.g., through eye-tracking) to determine how attention factors into the results. Given that there were no available student performance data outside the math software, we could not validate our measures of reading and math performance with other measures; future work would benefit from comparing these within-software measures to other reading comprehension assessments and measure of math knowledge and growth. Due to the lack of transaction data in the larger dataset, we were unable to generalize our findings on gaming and wheel spinning. Nevertheless, we were still able to scale up our findings related to reading and performance. Future research could examine more comprehensive datasets as well as other educational technology software to assess the scalability and generalizability of these measures and results.

4.4 Next Steps

Future research should focus on adding modules into new and existing tutor systems and using them as detectors for students who may need help with reading comprehension. Once students have been identified, researchers and practitioners need to develop support to address issues with reading comprehension. Researchers could then test the effectiveness of the support and develop formulas for both detecting and improving reading comprehension in adaptive math software, similar to the way such technologies currently detect and support math knowledge. Similarly, research can focus on the specific pieces of word problems (e.g., length, individual word difficulty) that are most detrimental to student performance. Using this information, designers and developers can provide more support when students encounter these problems or structure modules to reduce these issues (e.g., reduce wordiness). Researchers could also experiment with the effectiveness of flagging students based on their performance and hint use in the non-math modules to determine if awareness of additional literacy needs can improve later math performance. Finally, more research should take this learning analytics approach to identify additional detectors to address the needs of the whole student. There are many other important learning factors that can affect math performance (e.g., utility value, technological literacy), and building detectors for these factors increases the likelihood of addressing challenges and improving math learning.

4.5 Conclusion

In this study, we were able to connect reading comprehension to math learning, measuring both constructs within an adaptive math software. This type of analysis will improve our understanding of how math learning interacts with non-math factors and individual differences among students. Building a better theory of how math and non-math factors predict learning will help to clarify the best forms of support for student learning and provide a roadmap for developing tutoring systems that consider the whole student when creating adaptation.

Acknowledgements. This work is supported by the Chan Zuckerberg Initiative (CZI) Grant # 2018-193694. Any opinions, findings, and conclusions or recommendations expressed in this material are those of the authors and do not necessarily reflect the views of the Chan Zuckerberg Initiative.

References

1. Koedinger, K.R., Anderson, J.R., Hadley, W.H., Mark, M.A.: Intelligent tutoring goes to school in the big city. IJAIED **8**, 30–43 (1997)
2. Pane, J.F., Griffin, B.A., McCaffrey, D.F., Karam, R.: Effectiveness of cognitive tutor algebra I at scale. Educ. Eval. Policy Anal. **36**(2), 127–144 (2014)
3. Aleven, V., McLaughlin, E.A., Glenn, R.A., Koedinger, K.R.: Instruction based on adaptive learning technologies. In: Handbook of Research on Learning and Instruction, pp. 522–560. Routledge (2016)
4. Koedinger, K.R., Brunskill, E., Baker, R.S.J.d., McLaughlin, E.A., Stamper, J.: New potentials for data-driven intelligent tutoring system development and optimization. AI Mag. **34**(3), 27–41 (2013)
5. Lovett, M., Meyer, O., Thille, C.: The open learning initiative: measuring the effectiveness of the OLI learning course in accelerating student learning. J. Interact. Media Educ. **2008**, 1 (2008)
6. Ritter, S., Anderson, J.R., Koedinger, K.R., Corbett, A.: Cognitive tutor: applied research in mathematics education. Psychon. Bull. Rev. **14**(2), 249–255 (2007)
7. Calderon, V.J., Carlson, M.: Educators agree on the value of Ed Tech. Gallup Education (2019). https://www.gallup.com/education/266564/educators-agree-value-tech.aspx. Accessed 02 Mar 2020
8. Carnevale, A.P.: Education = success: empowering Hispanic youth and adults. Educational Testing Service and the Hispanic Association of Colleges and Universities. Washington, DC (1999)
9. Lee, J.: Racial and ethnic achievement gap trends: reversing the progress toward equity? Educ. Res. **31**(1), 3–12 (2002)

10. Autor, D.H.: Skills, education, and the rise of earnings inequality among the "other 99 percent". Science **344**(6186), 843–851 (2014)
11. Davis, J.E.: Early schooling and academic achievement of African American males. Urban Educ. **38**(5), 515–537 (2003)
12. Milner, H.R.: Beyond a test score: explaining opportunity gaps in educational practice. J. Black Stud. **43**(6), 693–718 (2012)
13. Setren, E.M.: Essays on the economics of education. Ph.D. dissertation. Massachusetts Institute of Technology, Cambridge, MA (2017)
14. Guryan, J., et al.: The effect of mentoring on school attendance and academic outcomes: a randomized evaluation of the Check & Connect Program. Northwestern University Institute for Policy Research Working Paper No. 16-18. Northwestern University, Evanston, IL (2017)
15. Cook, P.J., et al.: Not too late: improving academic outcomes for disadvantaged youth. Northwestern University Institute for Policy Research Working Paper No. 15-01. Northwestern University, Evanston, IL (2015)
16. Fuentes, P.: Reading comprehension in mathematics. Clearing House **72**(2), 81–88 (1998)
17. Vilenius-Tuohimaa, P.M., Aunola, K., Nurmi, J.E.: The association between mathematical word problems and reading comprehension. Educ. Psychol. **28**(4), 409–426 (2008)
18. Österholm, M.: Characterizing reading comprehension of mathematical texts. Educ. Stud. Math. **63**(3), 325–346 (2006)
19. Koedinger, K.R., Nathan, M.J.: The real story behind story problems: effects of representations on quantitative reasoning. J. Learn. Sci. **13**(2), 129–164 (2004)
20. Grimm, K.J.: Longitudinal associations between reading and mathematics achievement. Dev. Neuropsychol. **33**(3), 410–426 (2008)
21. Lobczowski, N.G., et al.: Building strategies for a personalized learning mentor app: a design case. Poster Accepted for the 2020 Annual Meeting of the American Education Research Association (AERA), San Francisco (2020)
22. Beck, J.E., Gong, Y.: Wheel-spinning: students who fail to master a skill. In: Lane, H.C., Yacef, K., Mostow, J., Pavlik, P. (eds.) AIED 2013. LNCS (LNAI), vol. 7926, pp. 431–440. Springer, Heidelberg (2013). https://doi.org/10.1007/978-3-642-39112-5_44
23. Baker, R., Walonoski, J., Heffernan, N., Roll, I., Corbett, A., Koedinger, K.: Why students engage in "gaming the system" behavior in interactive learning environments. J. Interact. Learn. Res. **19**(2), 185–224 (2008)
24. Paquette, L., Baker, R.S., Moskal, M.: A system-general model for the detection of gaming the system behavior in CTAT and LearnSphere. In: Penstein Rosé, C., et al. (eds.) AIED 2018. LNCS (LNAI), vol. 10948, pp. 257–260. Springer, Cham (2018). https://doi.org/10.1007/978-3-319-93846-2_47
25. Holstein, K., Yu, Z., Sewall, J., Popescu, O., McLaren, B.M., Aleven, V.: Opening up an intelligent tutoring system development environment for extensible student modeling. In: Penstein Rosé, C., et al. (eds.) AIED 2018. LNCS (LNAI), vol. 10947, pp. 169–183. Springer, Cham (2018). https://doi.org/10.1007/978-3-319-93843-1_13
26. Rogers, T., Feller, A.: Reducing student absences at scale by targeting parents' misbeliefs. Nat. Hum. Behav. **2**, 335–342 (2018)
27. Harackiewicz, J.M., Rozek, C.S., Hulleman, C.S., Hyde, J.S.: Helping parents to motivate adolescents in mathematics and science: an experimental test of a utility-value intervention. Psychol. Sci. **23**(8), 899–906 (2012)
28. Rozek, C.S., Svoboda, R.C., Harackiewicz, J.M., Hulleman, C.S., Hyde, J.S.: Utility-value intervention with parents increases students' STEM preparation and career pursuit. PNAS **114**(5), 909–914 (2017)

Exploring the Impact of Simple Explanations and Agency on Batch Deep Reinforcement Learning Induced Pedagogical Policies

Markel Sanz Ausin[✉][iD], Mehak Maniktala, Tiffany Barnes, and Min Chi

North Carolina State University, Raleigh, NC 27695, USA
{msanzau,mmanikt,tmbarnes,mchi}@ncsu.edu

Abstract. In recent years, Reinforcement learning (RL), especially Deep RL (DRL), has shown outstanding performance in video games from Atari, Mario, to StarCraft. However, little evidence has shown that DRL can be successfully applied to real-life human-centric tasks such as education or healthcare. Different from classic game-playing where the RL goal is to make an agent smart, in human-centric tasks the ultimate RL goal is to make the *human-agent interactions* productive and fruitful. Additionally, in many real-life human-centric tasks, data can be noisy and limited. As a sub-field of RL, batch RL is designed for handling situations where data is limited yet noisy, and building simulations is challenging. In two consecutive classroom studies, we investigated applying batch DRL to the task of pedagogical policy induction for an Intelligent Tutoring System (ITS), and empirically evaluated the effectiveness of induced pedagogical policies. In Fall 2018 (F18), the DRL policy is compared against an expert-designed baseline policy and in Spring 2019 (S19), we examined the impact of *explaining* the batch DRL-induced policy with student decisions and the expert baseline policy. Our results showed that 1) while no significant difference was found between the batch RL-induced policy and the expert policy in F18, the batch RL-induced policy *with simple explanations* significantly improved students' learning performance more than the expert policy alone in S19; and 2) no significant differences were found between the student decision making and the expert policy. Overall, our results suggest that pairing simple explanations with induced RL policies can be an important and effective technique for applying RL to real-life human-centric tasks.

Keywords: Deep reinforcement learning · Pedagogical policy · Explanation

1 Introduction

In interactive learning environments such as Intelligent Tutoring Systems (ITSs) and educational games, the human-agent interactions can be viewed as a temporal sequence of steps [2, 20]. Most ITSs are *tutor-driven* in that *the tutor* decides

© Springer Nature Switzerland AG 2020
I. I. Bittencourt et al. (Eds.): AIED 2020, LNAI 12163, pp. 472–485, 2020.
https://doi.org/10.1007/978-3-030-52237-7_38

what to do next. For example, the tutor can *elicit* the subsequent step from the student either with prompting or without (e.g., in a free form entry window where each equation is a step). When a student enters an entry on a step, the ITS records its success or failure and may give feedback (e.g. correct/incorrect markings) and/or hints (suggestions for what to do next). Alternatively, the tutor can choose to *tell* them the next step directly. Each of such decisions affects the student's successive actions and performance. *Pedagogical policies* are used for the agent (tutor) to decide what action to take next in the face of alternatives.

Reinforcement Learning (RL) offers one of the most promising approaches to data-driven decision-making for improving student learning in ITSs. RL algorithms are designed to induce effective policies that determine the best action for an agent to take in any given situation so as to maximize a cumulative reward. In this work, we use *batch RL*, an RL sub-field that deals with the inability to explore the environment. In batch RL, all the learning is done from a fixed-length dataset of samples that were obtained by interacting with the environment using some unknown behavior policy. A number of researchers have studied applying RL to improve the effectiveness of ITSs (e.g. [7,8,11,21,25,38,39,46,47]). While promising, prior work has two limitations: *communication* and *agency*.

One limitation of applying RL to ITSs is *communication*. In recent years, RL, especially Deep RL, has achieved superhuman performance in several complex games [3,49,50,55]. However, different from the classic game-play situations where the ultimate goal is to make the agent effective, in human-centric tasks such as ITSs, the ultimate goal is for the agent to make the *student-system interactions* productive and fruitful. Thus, we argue it is important to communicate the agent's pedagogical decisions to students. Prior work on applying RL to ITSs primarily focused on inducing effective pedagogical policies *for the tutor to act*, but the tutor rarely explains to students *why* certain pedagogical decisions are made. As far as we know, no prior research has been done on exploring the effectiveness of explaining pedagogical policies to students. On the other hand, prior research in Self-Determination Theory (SDT) suggests that explanations could be a powerful tool to increase student engagement and autonomy in learning. For example, it was shown that explaining the benefits of learning a specific task to students would increase their sense of control over their own learning [9,19,22,43,48,57], which can improve their learning outcomes.

The other limitation of RL in ITSs is *agency*. Rather than inducing effective pedagogical policies for the tutor to act, would it be more effective if we just let students make certain pedagogical decisions? Prior research has shown that it is desirable for students to experience a sense of control over their own learning, which could enhance their motivation and engagement [9,19] and improve their learning experience [43,57]. People are more likely to persist in constructive activities, such as learning, exercising, or quitting smoking, when they are given choices and make decisions. Thus, we investigated the effectiveness of letting students make pedagogical decisions vs. the traditional tutor-driven approach.

In short, we 1) examined the impact of *simple* explanations of tutor pedagogical decisions on student learning, and 2) investigated the effectiveness of letting students be the decision makers. Through two empirical classroom studies, our results show that batch RL-induced policies could improve students' learning performance more than our expert-designed baseline policy *only if* simple explanations are present; and no significant difference was found between the student decision making and the baseline policy. In summary, our work suggest that neither letting the tutor make effective pedagogical policy alone nor letting students make decisions alone may be sufficient to improve student learning, a more effective way is to let the tutor make effective pedagogical decisions while communicating some of the decisions to students through simple explanations.

2   Background and Related Work

Prior Research in Applying RL to Pedagogical Policy Induction can be roughly divided into classic RL vs. Deep RL approaches. The latter is highly motivated by the fact that the combination of deep learning (neural networks) and novel reinforcement learning algorithms has made solving complex problems possible in the last decade. For instance, the Deep Q-Network (DQN) algorithm [29] takes advantage of convolutional neural networks to learn to play Atari games observing the pixels directly. Since then, DRL has achieved success in various complex tasks such as the games of Go [49], Chess/Shogi [50], Starcraft II [55], and robotic control [3]. One major challenge of these methods is *sample inefficiency* where RL policies need large sample sizes to learn optimal, generalizable policies. Batch RL, a sub-field of RL, aims to fix this problem by learning the optimal policy from a fixed set of a priori-known transition samples [24], thus efficiently learning from a potentially small amount of data and being able to generalize to unseen scenarios.

Prior research using classic RL approaches has applied both online and batch/offline approaches to induce pedagogical policies for ITSs. Beck et al. [6] applied temporal difference learning to induce pedagogical policies that would minimize the students' time on task. Similarly, Iglesias et al. applied Q-learning to induce policies for efficient learning [15,16]. More recently, Rafferty et al. applied an online partially observable Markov decision process (POMDP) to induce policies for faster learning [33]. All of the models described above were evaluated via simulations or classroom studies, yielding improved student learning and/or behaviors as compared to some baseline policies. Offline or batch RL approaches, on the other hand, "take advantage of previous collected samples, and generally provide robust convergence guarantees" [44]. Thus, the success of these approaches depends heavily on the quality of the training data. One common convention for collecting an exploratory corpus is to train students on ITSs using *random yet reasonable* policies. Shen et al. applied value iteration and least square policy iteration on a pre-collected exploratory corpus to induce a pedagogical policy that improved students' learning performance [46,47]. Chi et al. applied policy iteration to induce a pedagogical policy aimed at improving students' learning gain [7]. Mandel et al. [25] applied an offline POMDP to induce a policy which aims to improve student performance in an educational game. All the models described above were evaluated in classroom studies and were found to yield certain improved student learning or performance relative to a baseline policy. Wang et al. applied an online DRL approach to induce a policy for adaptive narrative generation in educational game using simulations [56]; the resulting DRL-induced policies were evaluated via simulations only. In this work, based on the characteristics of our task domain, we focus on batch RL with neural networks, also known as batch Deep Reinforcement Learning (batch DRL) [13,18] and evaluate their effectiveness in classroom studies.

The Impact of Explanation on Learning: This work is highly motivated by large amount of research in Self-Determination Theory (SDT) investigating the benefit of explanations [10,17,35,41,42]. When teaching correlations to college students in a teacher training program, Jang et al. found that the students who were told the benefit of learning correlation (Explanation), were significantly more engaged than those who were not told (No-Explanation), in that the former showed more on-task attention, effort, and persistence than the latter [17]. Similarly, on a routine tedious task of letter copying, the Explanation students were significantly more engaged in the task than the No-Explanation peers who were not told [42]. Additionally, Reeve et al. compared the impact of Explanation vs. No-Explanation [35] on learning Chinese and found that the former self-reported significantly higher engagement in the task on a post-survey.

While explanations in much of the prior work above were human generated, in recent years an increasing amount of research has explored on how to automatically generate explanations. For example, Eslami et al. [12] investigated users' perspective on revealing advertisement algorithms and personal information used for generating personalized advertisements. As expected, users preferred interpretable explanations about how and why an ad was personalized to their identity. Additionally, Rago et al. [34] and Palanca et al. [31] explored using argumentation to provide explanations for recommender systems. More closely to this work, Barria-Pineda & Brusilovsky [5] and Tsai & Brusilovsky [52] explored explaining recommendations in education and social recommender systems and showed great promises. Despite these results, Kunkel et al. [23] showed human-generated explanations were rated more highly for recommendations and trustworthiness than machine-generated explanations based on item similarity. In [10], Deci et al. examined the impact of several factors on the effectiveness of explanations. As an example, they investigated two levels of controllingness: a high controlling statement would be something like "You *must* watch me solve this problem" while a low controlling counterpart sentence would be "Now you *can* watch me solve this problem". Results showed that low controlling explanations can be significantly more effective to enhance participants' engagement than high controlling ones and more importantly, the former can lead to a *positive correlation* between engagement and the desired learning outcomes. Inspired by this result, in this work our simple explanations are human-generated and to do so, we followed the low controlling principle.

Students as Decision Makers on ITS: While engaging students in decision-making within an ITS is not novel, prior research has focused on letting students dictate content by letting them decide *what problem* they wish to solve [20] but not *how* they wished to solve it. On one hand, letting students make their own decisions would allow them to experience a sense of control over their learning, which could enhance their motivation and engagement [9,19] and further improve their learning experience [43,57]. On the other hand, prior research has shown that students, especially low performing ones, may not always have the necessary meta-cognitive skills to make effective pedagogical decisions [1]. In that research, Aleven & Koedinger studied students' help-seeking behaviors in the Cognitive Tutor where students request help when they do not know what step to take next. Help is provided via a sequence of hints that progress from general top-level hints to bottom-out hints that tell them exactly what action to take. They found that students do not always have the necessary metacognitive skills to know when they need help. Roll et al., by contrast, examined the relationship between students' help-seeking patterns and their learning [37], and found that asking for help on challenging steps was productive while help-abusing behavior (asking for help as a way to avoid work) was correlated with poor learning.

3   Methods

In the conventional RL, an agent interacts with an environment $\mathcal{E}$ over a series of decision-making steps, which can be framed as a Markov Decision Process (MDP). At each timestep t, the agent observes $\mathcal{E}$ in state s_t; it chooses an action a_t from a discrete set of possible actions; and $\mathcal{E}$ provides a scalar reward r_t and evolves into next state s_{t+1}. The future rewards are discounted by the factor $\gamma \in (0,1]$. The return at time-step t is defined as $R_t = \sum_{t'=t}^{T} \gamma^{t'-t} r_{t'}$, where T is the last time-step in the episode. The agent's goal is to maximize the expected discounted sum of future rewards, also known as the return, which is equivalent to finding the optimal action-value function $Q^*(s, a)$ for all states. Formally, $Q^*(s, a)$ is defined as the highest possible expected return starting from state s, taking action a, and following the optimal policy π^* thereafter. It can be calculated as $Q^*(s, a) = \max_{\pi} \mathbb{E}[R_t | s_t = s, a_t = a, \pi]$ and $Q^*(s, a)$ must follow the *Bellman Equation*. We follow the batch RL formulation in that we have a fixed-size dataset $\mathcal{D}$ consisting of all historical sample episodes, each formed by a sequence of state, action, reward tuples $(s_0, a_0, r_0, ..., s_T, a_T, r_T)$. We assume that the state distribution and behavior policy that were used to collect $\mathcal{D}$ are both unknown. We explored two batch DRL algorithms: *Deep Q-Network* (DQN) and *Double Deep Q-Network* (Double DQN).

DQN [29] is fundamentally a version of Q-learning which uses neural networks to approximate the true Q-values. In order to train the DQN algorithm, two neural networks with equal architectures are employed: one for calculating the Q-value of the current state and action $Q(s, a)$, and another neural network to calculate the Q-value of the next state and action $Q(s', a')$. The former is the main network and its weights are denoted θ and the latter is the target network, and its weights are denoted θ^-. Equation 1 shows its corresponding *Bellman Equation*. It is trained through gradient descent to minimize the squared difference of the two sides of the equality. Online DQN uses an experience replay buffer to store the recently collected data and to uniformly sample (s, a, r, s') steps from it. When inducing our batch RL policy, the whole $\mathcal{D}$ is in the experience replay buffer.

$$Q(s, a; \boldsymbol{\theta}) = \mathop{\mathbb{E}}_{s' \sim \mathcal{E}}[r + \gamma \max_{a'} Q(s', a'; \boldsymbol{\theta}^-)] \tag{1}$$

Double-DQN was proposed by Van Hasselt et al. [53] by combining the idea behind Double Q-Learning [14] with the neural network advances of the DQN algorithm to form Double-DQN. The intuition behind it is to decouple the action selection from the action evaluation. To achieve this, the Double-DQN algorithm uses the main neural network for action selection first, and then the target network evaluates its Q-value. This trick has been proven to significantly reduce overestimations in Q-value calculations, resulting in better final policies. With this technique, the modified *Bellman Equation* becomes:

$$Q(s, a; \boldsymbol{\theta}) = \mathop{\mathbb{E}}_{s' \sim \mathcal{E}}[r + \gamma Q(s', \mathop{\mathrm{argmax}}_{a'} Q(s', a', \boldsymbol{\theta}); \boldsymbol{\theta}^-)] \tag{2}$$

Last but not least, in order to address the credit assignment problem caused by having delayed rewards in our ITS, we used the Gaussian Processes (GP) approach in [4] to estimate immediate rewards based on delayed rewards.

4 Pedagogical Decisions and Pedagogical Policy Induction

Pedagogical Decisions: When comparing the effectiveness of students' pedagogical decision-making vs. batch DRL, we strictly control the instructional content to be equivalent for all students in that our ITS gives students the same training problems and we focused on tutorial decisions that cover the same domain content: Problem-Solving (PS) versus Worked Examples (WE). In PS, students are given tasks or problems to complete either independently or with assistance of ITSs while in WE, students are given detailed solutions.

A great deal of research has investigated the impacts of WEs vs. PSs on learning. [26–28,30,36,40,45,51]. Generally speaking, it is shown that studying WEs can significantly reduce the total time on task while keeping the learning performance comparable to doing PS [26–28]; alternating WE and PS can be *more effective* than PS only [26,30,36,40,45,51]. Despite prior work, there is little consensus on how they should be combined effectively and thus when deciding between PS and WE, most existing ITSs always choose PS [20,54]. Since there is no widespread consensus on how or when each alternative should be used, we apply batch DRL to derive pedagogical strategies directly from empirical data.

Training Corpus: Our training corpus consists of 786 historical student-ITS trajectory interactions over 5 different semesters, one trajectory per student. All students go through a standard pretest, training on ITS, and posttest procedure and each student spent around 2–3 h on the ITS, completing around 20 training problems. To represent the learning environment, 142 state features from five categories were extracted. More specifically, we have 10 Autonomy features describing the amount of work done by the student; 29 Temporal features including average time per step, the total time spent, the time spent on PS, the time spent on WE, and so on; 35 Problem Solving features describing the difficulty of the problem, the number of easy and difficult problems solved, and so on; 57 Performance features including the number of incorrect steps, and the ratio of correct to incorrect rule applications and so on; 11 Hint-related features including the total number of hints requested etc. The primary goal of our RL-induced pedagogical policy is to improve student Learning Gain, measured by the difference between the posttest and the pretest scores with a range of $[-200, +200]$. Since in RL immediate rewards are often more efficient than delayed ones, here we applied Gaussian Processes (GP) [4] to infer the immediate rewards for non-terminal states from the final delayed reward (students' Learning Gain).

Policy Induction: For both DQN and Double DQN, we explored using Fully Connected (FC) vs. Long Short Term Memory (LSTM) to estimate the action-value function Q. Our FC network consists of four fully connected layers of 128 units each, with Rectified Linear Unit (ReLU) as the activation function. Our LSTM architecture consists of two layers of 100 LSTM units each with ReLU activation functions, and a fully connected layer as output. Additionally, for both FC and LSTM, for a given time t, we explored three input settings: 1) $k = 1$ that use only the last state s_t; 2) $k = 2$ that uses to use the last two states: s_{t-1} and s_t; and 3) $k = 3$ for using s_{t-2}, s_{t-1} and s_t. L2 regularization was employed to get a model that generalizes better to unseen data and avoid overfitting. We trained our models for 50,000 iterations, using a batch size of 200. To select the best pedagogical policy, we compared all of the different models (FC vs. LSTM, DQN vs. Double-DQN, k = {1, 2, 3}) using Per-Decision Importance Sampling (PDIS), which is one of the most robust off-policy evaluation methods [32]. The policy with highest PDIS value was selected to be our final pedagogical policy. In this work, our final pedagogical policy was DQN with an LSTM network using $k = 3$ observations.

Simple Explanations: The design of our explanation is rather straightforward. We followed the "low-controllingness" principle described in [10]. Our explanations are *action-based* in that they focused on explaining the *benefit of taking the subsequent tutorial actions*. Our simple, action-based explanations were primarily based on the prior research on learning science and cognitive science. For example, a large amount of research showed that studying WEs can be more beneficial if it is a problem involving new level of difficulty or content [27,28] and thus if the current problem was the first problem in a level, our action-based explanation for WE would state "The AI agent thinks you should view this problem as a Worked Example to learn how some new rules work." Our simple action-based explanation for other WE states: "The AI agent thinks you would benefit from viewing this problem as a worked example." Similarly, if the policy decided that the next problem should be a PS, then the message shown stated something like: "The AI agent thinks you should solve this problem yourself."

5 Experiment Setup

Our ITS is a graph-based logic tutor named Deep Thought, which is used in the undergraduate Discrete Mathematics class at North Carolina State University. In this ITS, students must sequentially apply rules to logic statement nodes in order to derive the conclusion node and solve the problem. The tutor consists of seven levels, with three to four problems per level. Here level 1 is our pretest and level 7 is our the posttest. All students experience the exact same problems in the same way in the pretest and posttest. The pedagogical policy decides whether to represent each problem in the training levels 2–6 as a Worked Example (WE) or as a Problem Solving (PS). Our baseline policy is designed by the instructor who has more than 20 years experience on the subject, referred to as the *Expert-designed baseline policy* in the following. Based on our ITS, prior instructional experience, and prior research on WE vs. PS, our Expert Baseline policy is basically an alternative WE-PS policy with additional constraints: on each level, students must complete at least one PS and one WE.

Two studies were conducted: one in Fall 2018 and the other in Spring 2019, denoted F18 and S19 respectively. In both studies, our ITS was given as one of the regular homework assignments and students had one week to complete it.

For **F18**, 84 students were randomly assigned to the two conditions using stratified sampling based on the pretest score to ensure that the two conditions had similar prior knowledge. As a result, we have $N = 41$ students for the *DQN* condition and $N = 43$ for the *Expert* baseline condition. Here the tutor in the *DQN* condition followed the induced *DQN* policies described in Sect. 5 *without* explanations. Our stratified sampling resulted in balanced incoming competence in that no significant difference between the pretest scores for the *DQN* ($M = 59.23$, $SD = 30.63$) and the *Expert* conditions ($M = 57.42$, $SD = 30.95$): $t(82) = 0.27$, $p = 0.79$. For **S19**, 83 students were randomly assigned to three conditions through stratified sampling: *DQN + Explanation* (*DQN+Exp*) (N = 30), *Student Choice* (N = 30), and the *Expert* baseline (N = 23). In the Student Choice condition, once a next problem is presented the students will make decisions on whether they want *the ITS to show* them how to solve the next problem (WE) or they want *to solve* the next problem themselves (PS). A one-way ANOVA test showed no significant difference in the pretest scores among the three conditions: $F(1, 81) = 0.26, p = 0.61$. More specifically, we have *DQN+Exp* ($M = 54.2$, $SD = 30.0$), *Student Choice* ($M = 50.3$, $SD = 31.3$), and *Expert* Baseline ($M = 49.9$, $SD = 35.8$). In short, our results suggested that all conditions were balanced in incoming competence in both F18 and S19.

6 Results

6.1 F18 Study

Overall, no significant difference was found on the posttest between DQN ($M = 48.6, SD = 22.7$) and Expert-Baseline ($M = 54.0, SD = 18.3$). A one-way ANCOVA analysis on posttest scores using Condition as factor and

Table 1. Results of S19 study by condition.

	PostTest	Training time (mins.)	PS count	WE count
DQN+Exp	**41.61** (25.07)	93.0 (109.6)	9.40 (2.42)	6.10 (1.21)
Student choice	34.24 (20.09)	75.5 (104.0)	8.06 (3.15)	7.46 (2.14)
Expert baseline	29.44 (16.43)	65.8 (87.7)	8.13 (1.74)	7.34 (1.26)

pretest scores as a covariate shows that there was no significant difference: $F(1, 81) = 1.76, p = 0.19$. Moreover, much to our surprise, no significant differences were found on the total training time nor on the total number of WE and PS students experienced between the two conditions. So, our DQN-induced bath DRL policy is as effective as the Expert baseline policy.

6.2 S19 Study

The S19 study had two goals: one was to determine whether DQN with simple explanations (DQN+Exp) can be more effective than the Expert baseline policy, and the other was to determine whether Student Choice can be more effective than either the DQN+Exp or the Expert baseline policy. In the following, we will first compare the three conditions in terms of learning performance and then perform a log analysis. Table 1 shows a comparison of the posttest, total training time, the total number of PSs, and the total number of WEs among the three conditions, showing the mean (and SD) for each value.

Learning Performance. A one-way ANOVA test using the condition as a factor showed a significant difference in the posttest scores: $F(1, 81) = 4.47, p = 0.037$, with means (SD) shown in the first column in Table 1 for each condition. Furthermore, a one-way ANCOVA analysis on posttest scores using Condition as factor and pretest scores as a covariate confirms a significant difference in the posttest scores: $F(1, 80) = 4.25, p = 0.042$. Contrast analysis revealed that the *DQN+Exp* condition significantly outperformed the *Expert* condition: $t(79) = 2.02, p = 0.046$; but no significant difference was found between the *DQN+Exp* and *Student Choice* conditions: $t(79) = 1.30, p = 0.20$ or between the *Student Choice* and *Expert* conditions: $t(79) = 0.81, p = 0.42$. In short, our results showed that on the posttest scores, *DQN+Exp* significantly our-performs the *Expert* condition, and no significant difference was found between the *Student Choice* and *Expert* conditions.

Training Time and Log Analysis. The second column in Table 1 shows the average amount of total training time (in minutes) students spent on the tutor for each condition. Despite the differences among the three conditions, a one-way ANOVA test using the condition as a factor showed no significant difference in time on task among them: $F(1, 81) = 0.97, p = 0.33$.

The last two columns in Table 1 show the average number of WEs and PSs that each condition experienced in S19. When comparing the *DQN+Exp* and the *Expert* conditions, a t-test showed a significant difference in the number of PS: $t(51) = 2.22, p = 0.031$, and a significant difference in the number of WE: $t(51) = 3.62, p = 0.0007$, with the *DQN* condition seeing about one more PS and one less WE than the *Expert* condition. When comparing the *DQN+Exp* and *Student Choice* conditions, a t-test showed a marginal difference in the number of PS $t(58) = 1.84, p = 0.07$, and a significant difference in the number of WE $t(58) = -3.04, p = 0.003$, with the *DQN+Exp* condition seeing about one more PS and one less WE than the Student Choice group. A contrast analysis also showed a significant difference in the number of PS $(t(80) = 2.02, p = 0.047)$ and in the number of WE $t(80) = -3.26, p = 0.001$ between the *DQN+Exp* and *Student Choice* conditions.

Much to our surprise, the *Student Choice* condition behaved in a very similar way to the *Expert* condition in that no significant difference was found between the two conditions on the number of PS: $t(51) = -0.09, p = 0.93$. Similarly, no difference was found on the number of WE: $t(51) = -0.251, p = 0.802$. To summarize, our log analysis shows that *DQN+Exp* generated more PS and less WE than the other two conditions and no significant difference was found between the *Student Choice* and *Expert* conditions.

7 Discussion and Conclusion

This work demonstrates one potential way to combine data-driven methods such as DRL with other educational strategies that increase student autonomy and agency, and observe that it can benefit student learning in our Intelligent Tutoring System. In this work, we investigated the impact of 1) providing students with simple explanations for the decisions of a batch DRL policy and 2) the impact of students' pedagogical decision-making on learning. We focused on whether to give students a WE or to engage them in PS. We strictly controlled the domain content to isolate the impact of *pedagogy* from *content*.

In two classroom studies, we compared the batch DRL policy (with and without explanations), the Student Choice pedagogical decision making and the Expert baseline. Overall, our results show that when deciding whether to approach the next problem as PS or WE, both batch DRL-induced policies and Student Choice can be as effective as the Expert baseline policy; however by combining batch DRL-induced policies with simple explanations, we can significantly improve students' learning performance more than our expert-designed baseline policy. One potential hypothesis is that simple explanations can promote students' buy-in to pedagogical decisions made by batch DRL induced policies. However, further survey studies are needed to determine this hypothesis. Interestingly, our results showed that students can make as effective problem-level decisions as the Expert baseline policy. Surprisingly, students selected as many PSs and WEs as the Expert policy but the variance of decisions in Student Choice is larger than those of Expert Baseline.

We believe that the results from this research can shed some light on how to apply DRL for human-centric tasks such as an ITS, and further research is needed to fully understand why simple explanations work and whether they can indeed be applied effectively to other domains. Furthermore, in this work, we have only explored straightforward, human-expert designed explanations, which can sometimes be limiting. In the future, personalized, data-driven explanations, will make the system more powerful and provide more accurate explanations.

Acknowledgements. This research was supported by the NSF Grants: #1726550, #1651909 and #1937037.

References

1. Aleven, V., Koedinger, K.R.: Limitations of student control: do students know when they need help? In: Gauthier, G., Frasson, C., VanLehn, K. (eds.) ITS 2000. LNCS, vol. 1839, pp. 292–303. Springer, Heidelberg (2000). https://doi.org/10.1007/3-540-45108-0_33
2. Anderson, J.R., Corbett, A.T., Koedinger, K.R., Pelletier, R.: Cognitive tutors: lessons learned. J. Learn. Sci. **4**(2), 167–207 (1995)
3. Andrychowicz, M., Baker, B., et al.: Learning dexterous in-hand manipulation. arXiv preprint arXiv:1808.00177 (2018)
4. Azizsoltani, H., Kim, Y.J., Sanz Ausin, M., Barnes, T., Chi, M.: Unobserved is not equal to non-existent: using Gaussian processes to infer immediate rewards across contexts. In: Proceedings of the 28th International Joint Conference on Artificial Intelligence, pp. 1974–1980. AAAI Press (2019)
5. Barria-Pineda, J., Brusilovsky, P.: Making educational recommendations transparent through a fine-grained open learner model. In: IUI Workshops (2019)
6. Beck, J., Woolf, B.P., Beal, C.R.: ADVISOR: a machine learning architecture for intelligent tutor construction. In: AAAI/IAAI, pp. 552–557 (2000)
7. Chi, M., VanLehn, K., Litman, D., Jordan, P.: Empirically evaluating the application of reinforcement learning to the induction of effective and adaptive pedagogical strategies. User Model. User Adap. Inter. **21**(1–2), 137–180 (2011)
8. Chi, M., VanLehn, K., Litman, D., Jordan, P.: An evaluation of pedagogical tutorial tactics for a natural language tutoring system: a reinforcement learning approach. Int. J. Artif. Intell. Educ. **21**(1–2), 83–113 (2011)
9. Cordova, D.I., Lepper, M.R.: Intrinsic motivation and the process of learning: beneficial effects of contextualization, personalization, and choice. J. Educ. Psychol. **88**(4), 715 (1996)
10. Deci, E.L., Eghrari, H., Patrick, B.C., Leone, D.R.: Facilitating internalization: the self-determination theory perspective. J. Pers. **62**(1), 119–142 (1994)
11. Doroudi, S., Holstein, K., Aleven, V., Brunskill, E.: Towards understanding how to leverage sense-making, induction and refinement, and fluency to improve robust learning. International Educational Data Mining Society (2015)
12. Eslami, M., Krishna Kumaran, S.R., Sandvig, C., Karahalios, K.: Communicating algorithmic process in online behavioral advertising. In: Proceedings of the 2018 CHI Conference on Human Factors in Computing Systems, pp. 1–13 (2018)
13. Fujimoto, S., Conti, E., Ghavamzadeh, M., Pineau, J.: Benchmarking batch deep reinforcement learning algorithms. arXiv preprint arXiv:1910.01708 (2019)
14. Hasselt, H.V.: Double q-learning. In: Advances in Neural Information Processing Systems, pp. 2613–2621 (2010)

15. Iglesias, A., Martínez, P., Aler, R., Fernández, F.: Learning teaching strategies in an adaptive and intelligent educational system through reinforcement learning. Appl. Intell. **31**(1), 89–106 (2009)
16. Iglesias, A., Martínez, P., Aler, R., Fernández, F.: Reinforcement learning of pedagogical policies in adaptive and intelligent educational systems. Knowl. Based Syst. **22**(4), 266–270 (2009)
17. Jang, H.: Supporting students' motivation, engagement, and learning during an uninteresting activity. J. Educ. Psychol. **100**(4), 798 (2008)
18. Jaques, N., et al.: Way off-policy batch deep reinforcement learning of implicit human preferences in dialog. arXiv preprint arXiv:1907.00456 (2019)
19. Kinzie, M.B., Sullivan, H.J.: Continuing motivation, learner control, and CAI. Educ. Technol. Res. Dev. **37**(2), 5–14 (1989). https://doi.org/10.1007/BF02298286
20. Koedinger, K.R., Anderson, J.R., Hadley, W.H., Mark, M.A.: Intelligent tutoring goes to school in the big city. Int. J. Artif. Intell. Educ. (IJAIED) **8**, 30–43 (1997)
21. Koedinger, K.R., Brunskill, E., Baker, R.S., McLaughlin, E.A., Stamper, J.: New potentials for data-driven intelligent tutoring system development and optimization. AI Mag. **34**(3), 27–41 (2013)
22. Kohn, A.: Choices for children. Phi Delta Kappan **75**(1), 8–20 (1993)
23. Kunkel, J., Donkers, T., Michael, L., Barbu, C.M., Ziegler, J.: Let me explain: impact of personal and impersonal explanations on trust in recommender systems. In: Proceedings of the 2019 CHI Conference on Human Factors in Computing Systems, pp. 1–12 (2019)
24. Lange, S., Gabel, T., Riedmiller, M.: Batch reinforcement learning. In: Wiering, M., Otterlo, M. (eds.) Reinforcement Learning. Adaptation, Learning, and Optimization, vol. 12, pp. 45–73. Springer, Heidelberg (2012). https://doi.org/10.1007/978-3-642-27645-3_2
25. Mandel, T., Liu, Y.E., Levine, S., Brunskill, E., Popovic, Z.: Offline policy evaluation across representations with applications to educational games. In: Proceedings of the 2014 International Conference on Autonomous Agents and Multi-Agent Systems, pp. 1077–1084. International Foundation for Autonomous Agents and Multiagent Systems (2014)
26. McLaren, B.M., van Gog, T., Ganoe, C., Yaron, D., Karabinos, M.: Exploring the assistance dilemma: comparing instructional support in examples and problems. In: Trausan-Matu, S., Boyer, K.E., Crosby, M., Panourgia, K. (eds.) ITS 2014. LNCS, vol. 8474, pp. 354–361. Springer, Cham (2014). https://doi.org/10.1007/978-3-319-07221-0_44
27. McLaren, B.M., Isotani, S.: When is it best to learn with all worked examples? In: Biswas, G., Bull, S., Kay, J., Mitrovic, A. (eds.) AIED 2011. LNCS (LNAI), vol. 6738, pp. 222–229. Springer, Heidelberg (2011). https://doi.org/10.1007/978-3-642-21869-9_30
28. McLaren, B.M., Lim, S.J., Koedinger, K.R.: When and how often should worked examples be given to students? New results and a summary of the current state of research. In: Proceedings of the 30th Annual Conference of the Cognitive Science Society, pp. 2176–2181 (2008)
29. Mnih, V., Kavukcuoglu, K., Silver, D., et al.: Human-level control through deep reinforcement learning. Nature **518**(7540), 529 (2015)
30. Najar, A.S., Mitrovic, A.: Learning with intelligent tutors and worked examples: selecting learning activities adaptively leads to better learning outcomes than a fixed curriculum. UMUAI **26**(5), 459–491 (2016)

31. Palanca, J., Heras, S., Rodríguez Marín, P., Duque, N., Julián, V.: An argumentation-based conversational recommender system for recommending learning objects. In: Proceedings of the 17th International Conference on Autonomous Agents and Multi-agent Systems, pp. 2037–2039 (2018)

32. Precup, D., Sutton, R.S., Singh, S.P.: Eligibility traces for off-policy policy evaluation. In: ICML, pp. 759–766. Citeseer (2000)

33. Rafferty, A.N., Brunskill, E., et al.: Faster teaching via POMDP planning. Cogn. Sci. **40**(6), 1290–1332 (2016)

34. Rago, A., Cocarascu, O., Toni, F.: Argumentation-based recommendations: fantastic explanations and how to find them (2018)

35. Reeve, J., Jang, H., Hardre, P., Omura, M.: Providing a rationale in an autonomy-supportive way as a strategy to motivate others during an uninteresting activity. Motiv. Emot. **26**(3), 183–207 (2002)

36. Renkl, A., Atkinson, R.K., et al.: From example study to problem solving: smooth transitions help learning. J. Exp. Educ. **70**(4), 293–315 (2002)

37. Roll, I., Baker, R.S.D., Aleven, V., Koedinger, K.R.: On the benefits of seeking (and avoiding) help in online problem-solving environments. J. Learn. Sci. **23**(4), 537–560 (2014)

38. Rowe, J., Mott, B., Lester, J.: Optimizing player experience in interactive narrative planning: a modular reinforcement learning approach. In: Tenth Artificial Intelligence and Interactive Digital Entertainment Conference (2014)

39. Rowe, J.P., Lester, J.C.: Improving student problem solving in narrative-centered learning environments: a modular reinforcement learning framework. In: Conati, C., Heffernan, N., Mitrovic, A., Verdejo, M.F. (eds.) AIED 2015. LNCS (LNAI), vol. 9112, pp. 419–428. Springer, Cham (2015). https://doi.org/10.1007/978-3-319-19773-9_42

40. Salden, R.J., Aleven, V., Schwonke, R., Renkl, A.: The expertise reversal effect and worked examples in tutored problem solving. Instruct. Sci. **38**(3), 289–307 (2010)

41. Sansone, C., Weir, C., Harpster, L., Morgan, C.: Once a boring task always a boring task? Interest as a self-regulatory mechanism. J. Pers. Soc. Psychol. **63**(3), 379 (1992)

42. Sansone, C., Wiebe, D.J., Morgan, C.: Self-regulating interest: the moderating role of hardiness and conscientiousness. J. Pers. **67**(4), 701–733 (1999)

43. Schraw, G., Flowerday, T., Reisetter, M.F.: The role of choice in reader engagement. J. Educ. Psychol. **90**(4), 705 (1998)

44. Schwab, D., Ray, S.: Offline reinforcement learning with task hierarchies. Mach. Learn. **106**(9–10), 1569–1598 (2017)

45. Schwonke, R., Renkl, A., Krieg, C., Wittwer, J., Aleven, V., Salden, R.: The worked-example effect: not an artefact of lousy control conditions. Comput. Hum. Behav. **25**(2), 258–266 (2009)

46. Shen, S., Chi, M.: Aim low: correlation-based feature selection for model-based reinforcement learning. International Educational Data Mining Society (2016)

47. Shen, S., Chi, M.: Reinforcement learning: the sooner the better, or the later the better? In: Proceedings of the 2016 Conference on User Modeling Adaptation and Personalization, pp. 37–44. ACM (2016)

48. Shyu, H.Y., Brown, S.W.: Learner control versus program control in interactive videodisc instruction: what are the effects in procedural learning. Int. J. Instruct. Med. **19**(2), 85–95 (1992)

49. Silver, D., Huang, A., Maddison, C.J., et al.: Mastering the game of go with deep neural networks and tree search. Nature **529**(7587), 484 (2016)

50. Silver, D., Hubert, T., Schrittwieser, J., et al.: A general reinforcement learning algorithm that masters chess, shogi, and go through self-play. Science **362**(6419), 1140–1144 (2018)
51. Sweller, J., Cooper, G.A.: The use of worked examples as a substitute for problem solving in learning algebra. Cogn. Instruct. **2**(1), 59–89 (1985)
52. Tsai, C.H., Brusilovsky, P.: Designing explanation interfaces for transparency and beyond. In: IUI Workshops (2019)
53. Van Hasselt, H., Guez, A., Silver, D.: Deep reinforcement learning with double q-learning. In: AAAI, Phoenix, AZ, vol. 2, p. 5 (2016)
54. VanLehn, K., Graesser, A.C., et al.: When are tutorial dialogues more effective than reading? Cogn. Sci. **31**(1), 3–62 (2007)
55. Vinyals, O., Babuschkin, I., Czarnecki, W., et al.: Grandmaster level in starcraft II using multi-agent reinforcement learning. Nature **575**, 350 (2019)
56. Wang, P., Rowe, J., Min, W., Mott, B., Lester, J.: Interactive narrative personalization with deep reinforcement learning. In: Proceedings of the Twenty-Sixth International Joint Conference on Artificial Intelligence (2017)
57. Yeh, S.W., Lehman, J.D.: Effects of learner control and learning strategies on English as a foreign language (EFL) learning from interactive hypermedia lessons. J. Educ. Multimed. Hypermed. **10**(2), 141–159 (2001)

Recommending Insightful Drill-Downs Based on Learning Processes for Learning Analytics Dashboards

Shiva Shabaninejad[1(✉)], Hassan Khosravi[1], Sander J. J. Leemans[2],
Shazia Sadiq[1], and Marta Indulska[1]

[1] The University of Queensland, Brisbane, Australia
shiva.shabani@gmail.com
[2] Queensland University of Technology, Brisbane, Australia

Abstract. Learning Analytics Dashboards (LADs) make use of rich and complex data about students and their learning activities to assist educators in understanding and making informed decisions about student learning and the design and improvement of learning processes. With the increase in the volume, velocity, variety and veracity of data on students, manual navigation and sense-making of such multi-dimensional data have become challenging. This paper proposes an analytical approach to assist LAD users with navigating the large set of possible drill-down actions to identify insights about learning behaviours of the sub-cohorts. A distinctive feature of the proposed approach is that it takes a process mining lens to examine and compare students' learning behaviours. The process oriented approach considers the flow and frequency of the sequences of performed learning activities, which is increasingly recognised as essential for understanding and optimising learning. We present results from an application of our approach in an existing LAD using a course with 875 students, with high demographic and educational diversity. We demonstrate the insights the approach enables, exploring how the learning behaviour of an identified sub-cohort differs from the remaining students and how the derived insights can be used by instructors.

Keywords: Learning analytics dashboards · Process mining in education · Drill down analysis · Intelligent dashboards

1 Introduction

The use of online learning systems provides a rich set of data that makes it possible to extract information about student learning behaviours. This information provides an opportunity for understanding and improving education, which has motivated many universities to invest in learning analytics dashboards (LADs) [6,28,41,48]. These dashboards generally provide visualisations of student data, collected from a variety of educational systems, to assist educators in making decisions [41]. However, the increasing popularity and improvement of online

© Springer Nature Switzerland AG 2020
I. I. Bittencourt et al. (Eds.): AIED 2020, LNAI 12163, pp. 486–499, 2020.
https://doi.org/10.1007/978-3-030-52237-7_39

learning systems over the years has resulted in a significant increase data in terms of its volume, velocity and variety. Consequently, making sense of data in LADs has become more challenging compared to earlier years [43].

In some domains, a common approach to navigating large complex multi-dimensional data sets is to use drill-downs [39]. A drill-down operation, in an educational setting, allows users to explore the behaviour of sub-cohorts of students by progressively adding filters. Manual drill-down operations can generally be used by instructors to effectively investigate curiosity-driven questions that are related to student attributes. For example, it is possible to use a drill-down filter to find how international or female students have performed compared to other students. However, instructors may also be interested in finding which drill-down filters lead to insightful results. As an example, an instructor may be interested in finding drill-downs that identify a sub-cohort of students who have significantly different behaviour or performance compared to the rest of the class. Given the availability of a large number of potential drill-downs, manually finding drill-downs that provide insights is a challenging task [1,42].

In this paper, we report on extending LADs with a functionality that provides recommendations of insightful drill-downs. Our approach takes a process mining lens to examine students' learning process considering three aspects of their learning behaviour: performed learning activities, the frequency of each activity and the order in which the activities are performed. Utilising the learning process, rather than focusing on aggregated engagement metrics which is the common approach in LADs [41], is increasingly being recognised as essential to understanding and optimising learning [33,46]. In our approach, the notion of an insightful drill-down is defined as a set of filtering rules that identify a sub-cohort of students whose learning processes are most differentiated from the rest of the students. Our key contribution is the design and development of an algorithm, which we refer to as Learning Process Automated Insightful Drill-Down (LP-AID). LP-AID employs a process mining method called Earth Movers' Stochastic Conformance Checking (EMSC) [29] to compute the distance between learning processes of different cohorts to recommend insightful drill-downs.

We present a practical application of LP-AID in an existing LAD called Course Insights that provides users with a manual drill-down functionality. Specifically, we apply LP-AID to data from a course with 875 students, with high demographic and educational diversity, to demonstrate the drill-down recommendations and to explore the possible insights that can be derived from them. Our initial findings, and instructor feedback on our approach, suggest that LP-AID can be integrated into LADs to provide automated and insightful drill-down recommendations.

2   Related Work

Learning Analytics Dashboards (LADs). Several recent systematic literature reviews have been published on LADs [6,41]. Schwendimann et al. [41]

provide a comprehensive picture of the common data sources that are used by LADS, which include clickstream logs (e.g., [12, 14, 25, 34]), data related to learning artefacts (e.g., [11, 16, 20, 24, 45]), survey data (e.g., [4, 35, 40]), institutional databases (e.g., [9, 19, 23]), physical user activities (e.g., [16, 31, 44]) and data captured from external educational technologies (e.g., [10, 26, 27, 36]). To make sense of these data LADs provide a variety of visualisation options. Schwendimann et al. [41] outlines the different types of visualisations that are commonly used in LADs, which include bar charts, line graphs, tables, pie charts, and network graphs. While these visualisations simplify the process of making sense of large data sets, they naturally abstract away much of the details related to learning processes, which are essential to understanding and optimising learning [17]. We aim to address this challenge by employing process mining approaches to guide drill-down operations and identification of insightful data.

Smart Drill-Down Approaches. The concept of a drill-down operation was initially introduced in the context of OLAP data cubes. They enabled analysts to explore a large search space to identify exceptions and highlight interesting subsets of data [39]. In recent years, drill-downs have also been employed in analytical dashboards. While their use has enabled users to explore large datasets, they provide users with too many drill-down choices and also the potential for incorrect reasoning due to incomplete exploration [1]. Several attempts to address these challenges have been made. Many of the proposed methods for discovering insightful drill-downs focus on detecting anomalies in small data portions (e.g. [1, 37, 38]) while some focus on identifying interesting differences in larger data subsets (e.g. [21]). In this paper, we take a similar approach as [42] by letting LAD users request drill-down recommendations at a level of granularity they are interested in, thus reducing drill-down choices without affecting user autonomy. While [42] recommends drill-downs based on the difference between cohorts' attribute values, this paper bases the recommendations on the difference between cohorts learning processes.

Educational Process Mining. Process mining aims to derive information from historical organisational behaviour, recorded in event logs [2]. Educational process mining uses data from educational contexts to discover, analyse, and visualise educational and learning processes, for instance to analyse whether students' behaviour corresponds to a learning model, to detect bottlenecks in the educational process, to identify patterns in processes [7], to study administrative processes [18] and to study student learning through their interactions with online learning environments [3, 8, 49]. Prior work [7] indicates that current educational process mining solutions have not adequately provided support for allowing users to identify and investigate cohorts of interest.

3   Automated Insightful Drill-Down Recommendation

Next, we introduce our method for recommendation of insightful drill-down criteria in LADs, by first introducing relevant concepts and defining our problem statement formally, presenting our approach, and illustrating it with an example.

3.1   Notation and Problem Statement

Assume that a LAD has access to an event log L that captures a collection of traces $T = \{t_1, \ldots t_N\}$, each representing a student. A trace t_i has a unique identifier (e.g. a student ID), a set of features $F = f_1, \ldots f_M$ where $f_{im} = v$ presents v being assigned to feature f_i for user s_i and a sequence of events $E_i = \langle e_{i1}, \ldots e_{iL_i} \rangle$ representing the learning path taken by student s_i, where the trace length L_i can vary for each student. Each event e_{iL_i} has a timestamp and a label representing the learning activity.

A rule r expresses a condition on a feature (e.g., *'program'* = *'Computer Science'*). For a feature with numerical values in an event log L, the corresponding rule value can be a range instead of a single value (e.g., *'age'* $>$ 25). A drill-down criterion σ is defined as the conjunction of a set of rules (e.g., *'program'* = *'Computer Science'* $\wedge$ *'age'* $>$ 25). A drill-down criterion σ is said to cover a student s_n, if all rules in σ are satisfied for the corresponding features of s_n. Consequently, applying σ to L leads to the selection of a set of students $S' \subseteq S$ such that σ covers each $s_n \in S'$. We define the *coverage* of a drill-down criterion C_σ as $\frac{|S'|}{|S|}$, which is the fraction of students S covered in the resulting sub-cohort S'. Using this notation, our problem can be formalised as follows:

Formal Problem Statement: Given an event log L, a set of features $F' \subseteq F$, a constant $0 \leq \alpha \leq 1$ and a constant k, find a set of drill-down criteria $\Sigma = \{\sigma_1, \ldots \sigma_k\}$ that uses features in F' such that each criterion σ_k: (1) has a larger coverage than α (i.e., $C_{\sigma_k} > \alpha$), (2) selects a sub-cohort of students S' that deviates most from the remaining students on their taken learning path L' in terms of events, relative frequency of each different learning path and the order in which the activities have been triggered (i.e. the distance between the sub-log L' and the remaining students $L \setminus L'$).

3.2   Proposed Approach

We present our approach by first providing a high-level overview of the underlying algorithm, and then describing the automatic drill-down process using an example. Our algorithm takes the students event log as an input and returns a set of drill-down criteria annotated with the learning process distance and students' population coverage as the output. The algorithm examines all the possible drill-down actions to find the drill-downs that result sub-cohorts with the most deviated learning processes. Algorithm 1 provides the high-level pseudocode of our proposed approach. It takes four parameters as input: the event log L, the features F', the minimum coverage α and the number of drill-down criteria to be recommended k. The output of the algorithm is a set of top k scored drill-down criteria represented by Σ. The algorithm consists of three main blocks as described in the remainder of this section.

Create Drill-Down Tree. The *BuildTree* function takes two parameters as input: the event log L and the list of selected features F', and returns a drill-down tree. The function obtains all the values of each feature in F' that exist within

---

Algorithm 1. Finding a set of k smart drill-down criteria

```
function MAIN(Log L, Features F', Minimal Coverage α, k)
    T ← BuildTree(L, F')                            ▷ Create drill-down tree
    PRUNEANDSCORE(T, L, α)
    topK ← topDistances(T, k)           ▷ Sort and return the top K drill-down criteria
    return nodeToDrillDown(topK)
end function
function PRUNEANDSCORE(Log L, Node parentNode, Log parentL, Minimal Coverage α)   ▷
Score nodes and prune the tree
    for childNode ∈ parentNode.children do
        cohortSublog ← ObtainSublog(childNode, parentL)
        if (|cohortSublog|/|L| ≤ α then
            remove childNode
        else if (|L| − |cohortSublog|)/|L| ≤ α then
            remainderL ← ObtainRemainderSublog(L, cohortL)
            childNode.distance ← −1
            PRUNEANDSCORE(L, childNode, cohortL, α)
        else
            remainderL ← ObtainRemainderSublog(L, cohortL)
            childNode.distance ← computeDistance(cohortL, remainderL)
            PRUNEANDSCORE(L, childNode, cohortL, α)
        end if
    end for
end function
```

L and generates a tree-like collection of nodes T, where each node represents a splitting rule r for one feature. Each path in the tree consists of a set of feature-value pairs.

Score Nodes and Prune the Tree. The tree embodies all possible drill-down paths, of which not all will necessarily result in a cohort with the required minimum size (i.e. α). *PruneAndScore* traverses the tree recursively to examine all the possible drill-down actions. *ObtainSubLog* takes each node, which is a pair of feature/value pairs, and its parent's event log *parentL* as input and filters *parentL* to obtain a sub-log *cohortL* containing only the data of the sub-cohort. The sub-cohort's size is checked for the covered fraction of the student population to not be smaller than α and not greater than $1 - \alpha$. If the condition is met, the main event log L is filtered to obtain the event log of the rest of students *remainderL*. Otherwise, the node is pruned (if coverage $\leq \alpha$) or discarded from scoring (if coverage coverage $\geq 1 - \alpha$). For each drill-down path, *computeDistance* takes the pair of the sub-cohort and the remaining sub-logs as input and computes the distance between them using Earth Movers' Stochastic Conformance Checking [29].

Sort and Return the Top K Drill-Down Criteria. *topDistances* takes the scored drill-down Tree T and k as input and returns k recommendations. To pick the k nodes, this function uses a solution set ranking function that maximizes diversity, similar to the approach by [47]. As an alternative we could pick the k highest scored nodes. However, diversifying the recommendation allows us to provide a wider range of insightful drill-downs. Our algorithm converts the chosen nodes to a set of drill-down criteria Σ, each annotated with distance score and returns them as a recommendation to users.

3.3 Example Illustration

In this section, we illustrate our approach using an event log with a small set of 6 students, and $k = 1$ and $\alpha = 0.2$. We explain how our algorithm is used to find the most insightful drill-down criteria (namely the criteria that identify a sub-cohort with the highest distance) for the event log given in Fig. 1a,b with students $\{S1 \cdot S6\}$ and the feature set: {Residential Status, Assessment} as F'. Our example course has learning activities of: {Lecture 1, Lecture 2, Quiz A, Lecture 3, Lecture 4, Quiz B and Lecture final}, which were made available to students weekly in the mentioned order. The trace of triggered learning events by each student is shown in Fig. 1a. Each event is represented by an activity label and the timestamp.

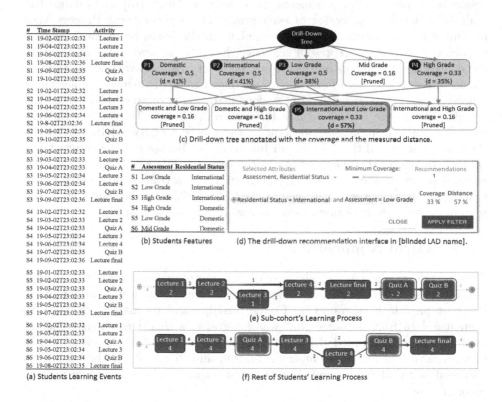

Fig. 1. Illustrative example of LP-AID applied on a sample learning event log.

Our algorithm initially extracts all values of F' that are present in the event log and generates the drill-down tree T. Next, the tree is traversed depth first; based on each node's filtering criteria, the event log is divided into the sub-cohort's sub-log and the remaining students' sub-log. The nodes covering less than $\alpha = 0.2$ of the student population are pruned. For instance, the node [Assessment='Mid Grade'] is pruned as only one student (i.e. 0.16 coverage) adheres to this criteria. As a result, 5 actionable drill-down paths remain (shown in Fig. 1c); P1: [Residential Status='Domestic'], P2: [Residential Status='International'], P3: [Assessment = 'Low Grade'], P4:[Assessment = 'High Grade' and P5: [Assessment = 'Low Grade' and Residential Status = 'International']. Our algorithm computes the distance between the sub-logs for each drill-down path and annotates each node by the distance d and the coverage (as shown in Fig. 1c). The drill-down path P5, which has the highest difference (57%), is the resulting recommendation. Figure 1d shows the LP-AID interface in Course Insights, representing the input and the resulting recommendation, including the drill-down criteria, coverage and distance.

To understand the difference between the learning behaviour of the sub-cohort and the remaining students, here we used Disco [15] to visualise the underlying learning processes of each group. Disco generates a Process Map in which: boxes represent activities, numbers in the boxes represent frequency of each activity, arrows represent sequence the activities were performed in (i.e. the control flow), numbers on the arrows represent frequency with which the two connected activities were performed, and thickness of the arrows the activities represent relative frequencies. For the demonstration purpose we highlighted the activities that were performed in a different order in red. To compare the two modelled learning processes, we look at the difference between the activities, their frequencies and their order. For instance, Fig. 1e shows that Lecture 3 was skipped by one of the two students in the cohort, while Fig. 1f shows that the remaining students have done this activity. From a control flow perspective, Quiz A and Quiz B were performed as the last activities by the cohort while the remaining students performed these quizzes during the semester.

4   Practical Application

This section presents an application of our approach using an existing LAD called Course Insights, which is equipped with manual drill-down functionality[1]. We first provide background on Course Insights and its main segments. We then use data from a course that was integrated with Course Insights to: 1) explore the recommended drill-downs generated by LP-AID; 2) visualise the process deviation for an example drill-down, and 3) report on the comments and feedback that was provided by the course coordinator upon reviewing our recommendations.

Course Insights. Course Insights (CI) is a LAD that provides filterable and comparative visualisations of students' aggregated daily activities. CI aims to provide actionable insights for instructors by linking data from several sources, including a Student Information System, Blackboard [5], edX Edge [32], and embedded learning tools such as Echo360 [13] and Kaltura [22] to create a multi-dimensional educational data set. CI is embedded in the learning management

---

[1] Approval from our Human Research Ethics Committee (#2019002181) was received for conducting this study.

system of The University of Queenslandand is available to all instructors. It is equipped with filtering functionality to enable instructors to drill-down into the data to explore the behaviour of sub-cohorts of students. Figure 2a illustrates the filter interface, which allows users to select attributes from demographic, assessment, engagement and enrolment features. When a filter is applied, statistical data and a graph representing the filtered versus unfiltered distribution of the target feature is presented (as shown in Fig. 2b).

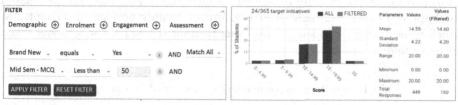

(a) Filtering Interface

(b) Demonstration of filtered vs. overall students for a target feature.

Fig. 2. The Course Insights learning analytics dashboard.

Drill-Down Recommendations in Action. We applied our technique to an introductory calculus and linear algebra course offered in 2019 to 875 undergraduate students from 16 programs. Following our data cleaning process, we were left with a dataset on 739 students. As the input for our approach, the event log includes three types of learning activities: (1) Accessing course materials: access to course materials by chapter. (2) Submission of formative quiz: submitting chapter based practice quizzes. Practice quizzes were formative assessments and thus optional. (3) Review summative assessment solutions: access to chapter based workbook solutions, released weekly. Workbooks were summative assessments, assigned weekly with a weekly requirement to submit their answer-sheets (paper based submissions).

As the features F', we selected the attributes Brand New, Final Exam, Gender, Program, and Residential Status. A total of 2447 drill-down actions were possible for this data set. Table 1 presents the recommendations generated for this course using respectively small ($\alpha = 0.05$), medium ($\alpha = 0.1$) and large ($\alpha = 0.03$) coverage.

Visualising Sub-cohort Learning Process Deviations. To investigate what insights can be derived from the recommended drill-downs, we used process discovery methods for the identified sub-cohort and the remaining students. Here, we demonstrate the insights derived from the recommended drill-down (1) (shown in Table 1). This drill-down results in a sub-cohort of: Brand new = 'Yes' and Residential status = 'International' and Final exam = 'High' and Gender = 'Male'. According to the LP-AID result, this sub-cohort's learning process is 72% different from the remaining students. To investigate the difference between the two learning processes we visualised the underlying process of the sub-cohort (shown in Fig. 3a) and the remaining students (Fig. 3b). Each box in the map is an activity which is labeled by the action type and the relevant chapter (e.g., Formative Quiz—chapter1). To more clearly visually distinguish the three types of learning activities in the process map, we use color coding. In the sub-cohort's process, the arrows in between the three different types of activities indicate switching between the types of learning tasks. Such switching can be an indication that the three types of tasks were being performed every week before the next chapter's activities were made available. In contrast, the underlying process of the remaining students shows that each activity type related to chapters 9 to 18 (highlighted in Fig. 3b) are mainly performed sequentially, which is indicative of students performing them at the end of the semester when all tasks were available.

Table 1. Resulting recommendations generated by our approach.

α	Recommended Drill-Down Criteria	Coverage	Distance
0.05	(1) [Brand new = 'Yes' and Residential status = 'International' and Final exam = 'High' and Gender = 'Male']	0.055	72%
	(2) [Brand new = 'Yes' and Residential status = 'International' and Gender = 'Female']	0.051	70%
0.1	(3) [Brand new = 'Yes' and Residential status = 'International' and Program = 'Bachelor of Engineering (Honours)']	0.10	69%
	(4) [Brand new = 'Yes' and Residential status = 'International' and Gender = 'Male']	0.12	68%
0.3	(5) [Final exam = 'High']	0.33	64%
	(6) [Brand new = 'Yes' and Residential status = 'Domestic']	0.69	63%

To further investigate our initial findings, we used Disco's Events' graph to compare the distribution of the events over the semester. Figures 3c and d demonstrate that the sub-cohort was more active during the semester compared with the remaining students. Furthermore, the average number of events per student was 36 in the sub-cohort and 25 for the remaining students, which is significantly different ($p = 0.0006$). To conclude our analysis, the identified sub-cohort had a high rate of activities throughout the semester compared to the remaining students. One of the common features of this cohort was their high performance in the final exam, which might be correlated with their developed learning process. Some other differences perceived by comparing the two process maps are that the Formative Quiz of chapter 8 was not performed by any students of the sub-cohort, Solution Review of chapters 2, 7, 8 and 9 were the highest-rated activities by the sub-cohort, and that Solution Review of chapters 1, 2, 6, 7, 8 and 9 were the highest-rated activities by the remaining students.

Feedback From the Instructor. We presented the reported drill-down recommendations and the process visualisations to the instructor of the course to capture their feedback and comments on the findings. Their feedback can be

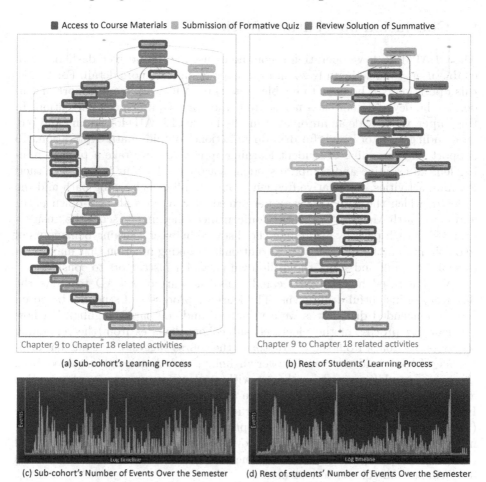

■ Access to Course Materials   ▩ Submission of Formative Quiz   ■ Review Solution of Summative

Chapter 9 to Chapter 18 related activities   Chapter 9 to Chapter 18 related activities

(a) Sub-cohort's Learning Process   (b) Rest of Students' Learning Process

(c) Sub-cohort's Number of Events Over the Semester   (d) Rest of students' Number of Events Over the Semester

Fig. 3. Learning behaviours of filtered students (by the recommended drill-down) vs. the rest of students.

summarised as follows: (1) While the instructor had access to Course Insights throughout the semester, they rarely used it and generally found it to be overwhelming. They considered the large number of potential drill-down options within the platform as the main reason that made using the platform overwhelming; (2) Findings of behaviour that have led to successful outcome can be used for positive deviance [30] purposes. The instructor indicated they would like to share Fig. 3 as a recommended pattern of successful learning with their students as evidence that consistent engagement with learning activities throughout the semester is related to better outcomes. (3) Providing the ability to receive drill-down recommendations based on a rule (e.g., 'midterm' < 50) would be useful. The instructor indicated that they would like to understand deviations in low performing and at-risk students to help them pass the course.

5 Conclusion and Future Work

The OLAP drill-down operation is commonly used in data-driven dashboards to enable users to meaningfully zoom in to explore data in more detail. For LADs, this operation can be used to enable educators to identify a sub-cohort of students who deviate from class norms and who may require special attention. In this paper, we provide an automated method called LP-AID for finding and recommending a set of insightful drill-down actions to guide data exploration. To support understanding of student learning approaches, we take a process mining lens to examine and compare student learning behaviour in terms of their learning activities, the relative frequency of each different learning path and the order in which the activities were performed. It examines all drill-down paths and uses Earth Movers' Stochastic Conformance Checking to score the 'insightfullness' of each path by examining the distance between learning behaviours of two cohorts. Furthermore, we use a solution set ranking function that maximizes diversity to rank and select the drill-down paths for instructors to consider.

We illustrated how LP-AID can be used as part of a LAD to guide the discovery of insightful drill-downs. The learning processes of students based on the recommended drill-downs were visualised and compared, highlighting how the learning process of the identified sub-cohort deviates from the remaining students. Feedback from the instructor of the course suggests that manual drill-downs without guidance can be overwhelming, and that insights gained from the recommendations can be shared with students to encourage change (i.e. application of positive deviance). Future work aims to embed LP-AID in Course Insights and to partner with course instructors through co-creation to investigate (1) the practical implications of our approach and refine it accordingly; (2) the most effective way to present the drill-down recommendations to instructors and (3) the most appropriate visualisation method(s) to present the learning process deviation of sub-cohorts to instructors.

References

1. Lee, D.J.L., Dev, H., Hu, H., Elmeleegy, H., Parameswaran, A.: Avoiding drill-down fallacies with vispilot: Assisted exploration of data subsets. In: ICII, pp. 186–196 (2019)
2. van der Aalst, W.M.P.: Process Mining - Data Science in Action, 2nd edn. Springer, Heidelberg (2016). https://doi.org/10.1007/978-3-662-49851-4_1
3. van der Aalst, W.M.P., Guo, S., Gorissen, P.: Comparative process mining in education: an approach based on process cubes. In: Ceravolo, P., Accorsi, R., Cudre-Mauroux, P. (eds.) SIMPDA 2013. LNBIP, vol. 203, pp. 110–134. Springer, Heidelberg (2015). https://doi.org/10.1007/978-3-662-46436-6_6
4. Aguilar, S., Lonn, S., Teasley, S.D.: Perceptions and use of an early warning system during a higher education transition program. In: Proceedings of the Fourth International Conference On Learning Analytics and Knowledge, pp. 113–117 (2014)
5. Blackboard Inc.: Blackboard. https://www.blackboard.com/

6. Bodily, R., Kay, J., Aleven, V., Jivet, I., Davis, D., Xhakaj, F., Verbert, K.: Open learner models and learning analytics dashboards: a systematic review. In: ICLAK, pp. 41–50 (2018)
7. Bogarín, A., Cerezo, R., Romero, C.: A survey on educational process mining. Wiley Interdisc. Rev.: Data Mining Knowl. Disc. **8**(1), e1230 (2018)
8. Bogarín, A., Romero, C., Cerezo, R., Sánchez-Santillán, M.: Clustering for improving educational process mining. In: Proceedings of the Fourth International Conference on Learning Analytics And Knowledge, pp. 11–15. ACM (2014)
9. Brouns, F., Zorrilla Pantaleón, M.E., Álvarez Saiz, E.E., Solana-González, P., Cobo Ortega, Á., Rocha Blanco, E.R., Collantes Viaña, M., Rodríguez Hoyos, C., De Lima Silva, M., Marta-Lazo, C., et al.: Eco d2. 5 learning analytics requirements and metrics report (2015)
10. Charleer, S., Santos, J.L., Klerkx, J., Duval, E.: Improving teacher awareness through activity, badge and content visualizations. In: Cao, Y., Väljataga, T., Tang, J.K.T., Leung, H., Laanpere, M. (eds.) ICWL 2014. LNCS, vol. 8699, pp. 143–152. Springer, Cham (2014). https://doi.org/10.1007/978-3-319-13296-9_16
11. Cooper, K., Khosravi, H.: Graph-based visual topic dependency models: supporting assessment design and delivery at scale. In: Proceedings of the 8th International Conference on Learning Analytics and Knowledge, pp. 11–15 (2018)
12. Dyckhoff, A.L., Zielke, D., Bültmann, M., Chatti, M.A., Schroeder, U.: Design and implementation of a learning analytics toolkit for teachers. J. Educ. Technol. Soc. **15**(3), 58–76 (2012)
13. Echo360 Inc.: Echo360. https://echo360.com/
14. Elaachak, L., Belahbibe, A., Bouhorma, M.: Towards a system of guidance, assistance and learning analytics based on multi agent system applied on serious games. Int. J. Electr. Comput. Eng. **5**(2), 344 (2015)
15. Fluxicon: Disco. https://fluxicon.com/
16. Fulantelli, G., Taibi, D., Arrigo, M.: A framework to support educational decision making in mobile learning. Comput. Hum. Behav. **47**, 50–59 (2015)
17. Ahmad Uzir, N., et al.: Discovering time management strategies in learning processes using process mining techniques. In: Scheffel, M., Broisin, J., Pammer-Schindler, V., Ioannou, A., Schneider, J. (eds.) EC-TEL 2019. LNCS, vol. 11722, pp. 555–569. Springer, Cham (2019). https://doi.org/10.1007/978-3-030-29736-7_41
18. Ghazal, M.A., Ibrahim, O., Salama, M.A.: Educational process mining: a systematic literature review. In: 2017 European Conference on Electrical Engineering and Computer Science (EECS), pp. 198–203. IEEE (2017)
19. Iandoli, L., Quinto, I., De Liddo, A., Shum, S.B.: Socially augmented argumentation tools: Rationale, design and evaluation of a debate dashboard. Int. J. Hum.-Comput. Stud. **72**(3), 298–319 (2014)
20. Išljamović, S., Lalić, S.: Academic dashboard for tracking students' efficiency. In: Proceedings of the XIV International Symposium Symorg 2014: New Business Models and sustainable competitiveness, p. 84. fon (2014)
21. Joglekar, M., Garcia-Molina, H., Parameswaran, A.: Interactive data exploration with smart drill-down. IEEE Trans. Knowl. Data Eng. **31**(1), 46–60 (2017)
22. Kaltura Software company: Kaltura video platform. https://corp.kaltura.com/
23. Kapros, E., Peirce, N.: Empowering L&D managers through customisation of inline learning analytics. In: Zaphiris, P., Ioannou, A. (eds.) LCT 2014. LNCS, vol. 8523, pp. 282–291. Springer, Cham (2014). https://doi.org/10.1007/978-3-319-07482-5_27

24. Khosravi, H., Cooper, K.: Topic dependency models: graph-based visual analytics for communicating assessment data. J. Learn. Anal. **5**(3), 136–153 (2018)
25. Khosravi, H., Cooper, K.M.: Using learning analytics to investigate patterns of performance and engagement in large classes. In: Proceedings of the 2017 ACM sigcse technical symposium on computer science education, pp. 309–314 (2017)
26. Khosravi, H., Kitto, K., Williams, J.J.: Ripple: a crowdsourced adaptive platform for recommendation of learning activities. arXiv preprint arXiv:1910.05522 (2019)
27. Khosravi, H., Sadiq, S., Gasevic, D.: Development and adoption of an adaptive learning system: reflections and lessons learned. In: Proceedings of the 51st ACM Technical Symposium on Computer Science Education, p. 58–64. Association for Computing Machinery, New York (2020). https://doi.org/10.1145/3328778.3366900
28. Kim, J., Jo, I.-H., Park, Y.: Effects of learning analytics dashboard: analyzing the relations among dashboard utilization, satisfaction, and learning achievement. Asia Pac. Educ. Rev. **17**(1), 13–24 (2015). https://doi.org/10.1007/s12564-015-9403-8
29. Leemans, S.J.J., Syring, A.F., van der Aalst, W.M.P.: Earth movers' stochastic conformance checking. In: Business Process Management Forum - BPM Forum 2019, Proceedings, Vienna, Austria, 1–6 September 2019, pp. 127–143 (2019)
30. Marsh, D.R., Schroeder, D.G., Dearden, K.A., Sternin, J., Sternin, M.: The power of positive deviance. BMJ **329**(7475), 1177–1179 (2004)
31. Martinez-Maldonado, R., Yacef, K., Kay, J.: TSCL: a conceptual model to inform understanding of collaborative learning processes at interactive tabletops. Int. J. Hum.-Comput. Stud. **83**, 62–82 (2015)
32. Massachusetts Institute of Technology and Harvard University: edx. https://www.edx.org
33. Matcha, W., Gašević, D., Uzir, N.A., Jovanović, J., Pardo, A.: Analytics of learning strategies: associations with academic performance and feedback. In: Proceedings of the 9th International Conference on Learning Analytics & Knowledge, pp. 461–470 (2019)
34. Ramos-Soto, A., Lama, M., Vázquez-Barreiros, B., Bugarín, A., Mucientes, M., Barro, S.: Towards textual reporting in learning analytics dashboards. In: 2015 IEEE 15th International Conference on Advanced Learning Technologies, pp. 260–264. IEEE (2015)
35. Rivera-Pelayo, V., Lacić, E., Zacharias, V., Studer, R.: LIM app: reflecting on audience feedback for improving presentation skills. In: Hernández-Leo, D., Ley, T., Klamma, R., Harrer, A. (eds.) EC-TEL 2013. LNCS, vol. 8095, pp. 514–519. Springer, Heidelberg (2013). https://doi.org/10.1007/978-3-642-40814-4_48
36. Santos, J.L., Verbert, K., Govaerts, S., Duval, E.: Addressing learner issues with stepup! an evaluation. In: Proceedings of the Third International Conference on Learning Analytics and Knowledge, pp. 14–22 (2013)
37. Sarawagi, S.: User-adaptive exploration of multidimensional data. In: VLDB, pp. 307–316 (2000)
38. Sarawagi, S.: User-cognizant multidimensional analysis. VLDB J. **10**, 224–239 (2001). https://doi.org/10.1007/s007780100046
39. Sarawagi, S., Agrawal, R., Megiddo, N.: Discovery-driven exploration of OLAP data cubes. In: Schek, H.-J., Alonso, G., Saltor, F., Ramos, I. (eds.) EDBT 1998. LNCS, vol. 1377, pp. 168–182. Springer, Heidelberg (1998). https://doi.org/10.1007/BFb0100984
40. Schneider, D.K., Class, B., Benetos, K., Da Costa, J., Follonier, V.: Learning process analytics for a self-study class in a semantic mediawiki. In: Proceedings of The International Symposium on Open Collaboration, pp. 1–4 (2014)

41. Schwendimann, B.A., Rodriguez-Triana, M.J., et al.: Perceiving learning at a glance: a systematic literature review of learning dashboard research, pp. 30–41. IEEE TLT (2017)

42. Shabaninejad, S., Khosravi, H., Indulska, M., Bakharia, A., Isaias, P.:Automated insightful drill-down recommendations for learning analytics dashboards (2020)

43. Sin, K., Muthu, L.: Application of big data in education data mining and learning analytics-a literature review. ICTACT J. Soft Comput. **5**(4), 1035–1049 (2015)

44. Tarmazdi, H., Vivian, R., Szabo, C., Falkner, K., Falkner, N.: Using learning analytics to visualise computer science teamwork. In: Proceedings of the 2015 ACM Conference on Innovation and Technology in Computer Science Education, pp. 165–170 (2015)

45. Tobarra, L., Ros, S., Hernández, R., Robles-Gómez, A., Caminero, A.C., Pastor, R.: Integrated analytic dashboard for virtual evaluation laboratories and collaborative forums. In: 2014 XI Tecnologias Aplicadas a la Ensenanza de la Electronica (Technologies Applied to Electronics Teaching)(TAEE), pp. 1–6. IEEE (2014)

46. Trcka, N., Pechenizkiy, M.: From local patterns to global models: towards domain driven educational process mining. In: 2009 Ninth International Conference on Intelligent Systems Design and Applications, pp. 1114–1119. IEEE (2009)

47. Ulrich, T., Bader, J., Thiele, L.: Defining and optimizing indicator-based diversity measures in multiobjective search. In: Schaefer, R., Cotta, C., Kołodziej, J., Rudolph, G. (eds.) PPSN 2010. LNCS, vol. 6238, pp. 707–717. Springer, Heidelberg (2010). https://doi.org/10.1007/978-3-642-15844-5_71

48. Verbert, K., Duval, E., Klerkx, J., Govaerts, S., Santos, J.L.: Learning analytics dashboard applications. Am. Behav. Sci. **57**(10), 1500–1509 (2013)

49. Vidal, J.C., Vázquez-Barreiros, B., Lama, M., Mucientes, M.: Recompiling learning processes from event logs. Knowl.-Based Syst. **100**, 160–174 (2016)

Using Thinkalouds to Understand Rule Learning and Cognitive Control Mechanisms Within an Intelligent Tutoring System

Deniz Sonmez Unal[1]([envelope]) [iD], Catherine M. Arrington[2] [iD], Erin Solovey[3] [iD], and Erin Walker[1] [iD]

[1] University of Pittsburgh, Pittsburgh, PA 15260, USA
{d.sonmez,eawalker}@pitt.edu
[2] Lehigh University, Bethlehem, PA 18015, USA
kate.arrington@lehigh.edu
[3] Worcester Polytechnic Institute, Worcester, MA 01609, USA
esolovey@wpi.edu

Abstract. Cognitive control and rule learning are two important mechanisms that explain how goals influence behavior and how knowledge is acquired. These mechanisms are studied heavily in cognitive science literature within highly controlled tasks to understand human cognition. Although they are closely linked to the student behaviors that are often studied within intelligent tutoring systems (ITS), their direct effects on learning have not been explored. Understanding these underlying cognitive mechanisms of beneficial and harmful student behaviors can provide deeper insight into detecting such behaviors and improve predictive models of student learning. In this paper, we present a thinkaloud study where we asked students to narrate their thought processes while solving probability problems in ASSISTments. Students are randomly assigned to one of two conditions that are designed to induce the two modes of cognitive control based on the Dual Mechanisms of Control framework. We also observe how the students go through the phases of rule learning as defined in a rule learning paradigm. We discuss the effects of these different mechanisms on learning, and how the information they provide can be used in student modeling.

Keywords: Cognitive control · Rule learning · Problem solving · Intelligent tutoring systems

1 Introduction

In ITS research, student behaviors that are associated with positive and negative cognitive and motivational states are often used within student models to design personalized adaptations. These states are often defined at a high level (e.g. gaming the system, zoning out), while in cognitive psychology, cognitive states are

© Springer Nature Switzerland AG 2020
I. I. Bittencourt et al. (Eds.): AIED 2020, LNAI 12163, pp. 500–511, 2020.
https://doi.org/10.1007/978-3-030-52237-7_40

studied at a much finer grain. We believe that identifying the parallels between the low-level cognitive structures that are studied within controlled tasks in cognitive science literature and the student behaviors associated with both positive and negative cognitive and motivational states within ITS research will improve our understanding of student learning and eventually help us design better student models and ITSs. Two such lower-level cognitive processes are cognitive control and rule learning.

Cognitive control is the basis of goal-directed behavior. It is defined as the ability to adapt behavior depending on the current goals and online maintenance of goal-related information [3]. In cognitive psychology, cognitive control's role in self-regulating behavior [16], focusing attention [19], and goal maintenance [4] have been studied within controlled tasks. These are relevant in ITS research in detecting various kinds of student behaviors. Examples include how students inhibit their will to game the system in face of temptation [11], interfering with student zoning out [12], and supporting self-regulated learning strategies [1]. Despite the fact that low-level cognitive structures that are studied in cognitive science are the underlying mechanisms of these behaviors, these mechanisms are rarely explored directly in the ITS literature. We hypothesize that identifying these mechanisms could help us better understand student behaviors and eventually help us design better detectors of them.

Rule learning consists of activities related to collecting instances of some phenomenon and identifying commonalities, relationships, and rules from these specific instances. These activities show themselves in the learning domain in the induction and refinement processes that are introduced in [17]. Some examples for these processes are perception, generalization, discrimination, categorization, and schema induction. These processes are linked to rule learning as they also require abstracting regularities and relationships, and inducing rules from them. ITSs support induction and refinement processes by giving timely feedback, guiding students' attention, and presenting worked examples in order to achieve robust learning. However, again, the underlying cognitive mechanisms of the processes are underexplored in this line of research.

As a first step, we investigate how these low-level cognitive mechanisms can be detected within an ITS. More specifically, we are interested to discover how cognitive control and rule learning present themselves within a real setting and if they have direct effects on learning, addressing two research questions: 1) How do phases of rule learning and modes of cognitive control manifest themselves in problem solving? 2) Do different operation modes of cognitive control and the different phases of rule learning have an effect on domain learning?

We designed a thinkaloud study where we instructed students to verbalize their thoughts while solving probability problems in ASSISTments [15]. Students were randomly assigned to one of the two conditions that were designed to encourage them to use different modes of cognitive control [4], and we explored differences in student behavior and learning. In addition, we designed the problems in a way that allows us to observe the phases of rule learning within a more complex educational context.

2   Background

2.1   Cognitive Control and Dual Mechanisms Framework

The Dual Mechanisms of Cognitive Control (DMC) framework [4] suggests that cognitive control operates via two distinct modes: proactive and reactive control. Proactive control is used when the goal-related information is actively maintained in order to prepare for cognitively demanding events. In contrast, in reactive control, goal-relevant information is only retrieved in a "just-in-time" manner and individuals rely on triggers to focus their attention back on the goal-relevant information. Even though proactive and reactive control are not considered to be mutually exclusive, people are likely to prefer one over the other. This preference is caused by individual factors such as age [20], working memory capacity [21,23], and external factors such as incentives [5], and the working memory load the task introduces [22].

To assess the relative use of proactive and reactive control, the AX continuous performance task (AX-CPT) has been used heavily [2,4,8]. In the AX-CPT, participants respond to letter probes based on the previous letter cue. Participants are instructed to provide a certain response if the cue-probe pair is an "AX" pair, and a different response is required for any other letter sequences. The performance of participants on specific letter sequences is indicative of their usage of proactive and reactive control. Prior research have successfully induced participants to utilize proactive or reactive control in the AX-CPT by strategy training [5,13,14,20]. The study we describe in this paper was inspired by this method. We test if a similar manipulation can successfully be applied to a realistic learning task. Further, we investigate if utilizing one mode of cognitive control influences learning.

2.2   Rule Learning

Rule learning includes investigating how humans go through phases of recognizing instances and keeping them in memory, detecting the regularities, and understanding the relationships between them [10]. The behaviors associated with the phases of rule learning were studied within different versions of a rule attainment task [6,7,10,18]. In one example, subjects are shown cards with sequentially-numbered circles. Exactly one of the circles is blue. The subjects must predict the position of the blue circle on the next card. In other words, they should respond in a certain way if the position of the blue circle is changing based on a rule. In all versions of the task, three main phases of rule learning were identified based on how subjects respond to the stimuli presented. These are rule search, rule discovery and rule following.

Rule Search. The first response with a new rule and all responses preceding rule discovery are identified as the rule search phase.

Rule Discovery. The third correct response in a row indicates that the subject discovered the rule.

Rule Following. The streak of correct responses after rule discovery corresponds to rule following.

This work investigates if students learn rules associated with mathematical problems in the same way as in the rule learning paradigm. We identify possible different patterns of rule learning that can occur in a real learning environment.

3   Task Design

We used ASSISTments [15] to design our task. It is an online tutoring system that allows teachers to write problems with solutions, hints, and feedback. Students are assisted by the system (either on demand or automatically) with hints, scaffolding (i.e. breaking the problem down to steps), and feedback. Teachers can get immediate feedback on students' performance on the problems. We built a problem set that consisted of 9 probability problems (3 calculating probability, 3 addition rule with non-mutually exclusive events, 3 multiplication rule with dependent events). All problems were divided into 3 to 4 substeps. Participants were not expected to solve the problem when they first saw it. Instead, they were asked to rate their confidence level in solving the particular problem. When the participants clicked on the "Next Problem"[1] button after confidence rating, they were shown the first substep to solve that problem in the same window (see Fig. 1). Similarly, after each substep, participants were presented with the next one until they reached the last substep that would lead them to the solution. The reasoning behind this design is to observe how the participants maintain the goal of the full problem when they needed to solve it in multiple steps.

3.1   Cognitive Control Manipulation

The participants were shown a prompt below the problem substep texts. The prompt instructed, "Think about how this step relates to the goal of the problem" in the proactive condition to encourage active maintenance of the goal of the full problem. In the reactive condition, it instructed, "Think about how you are solving this step" in order to make the participants only pay attention to what the substep tells them to do. The purpose of this is to induce proactive or reactive control through strategy training similar to [14]. This allowed us to observe how proactive and reactive control look like in a real problem-solving environment. The participants who were prompted to relate the substeps to the problem goal will be utilizing proactive control and the participants who were prompted to only react to the substeps will be utilizing reactive control. An example problem shown in Fig. 1.

---

[1] ASSISTments does not allow one to change the interface elements such as button text. Even though "next problem" sounds odd in this design as participants were going to "next step", we did not observe confusion among participants as they were given time to practice with this design.

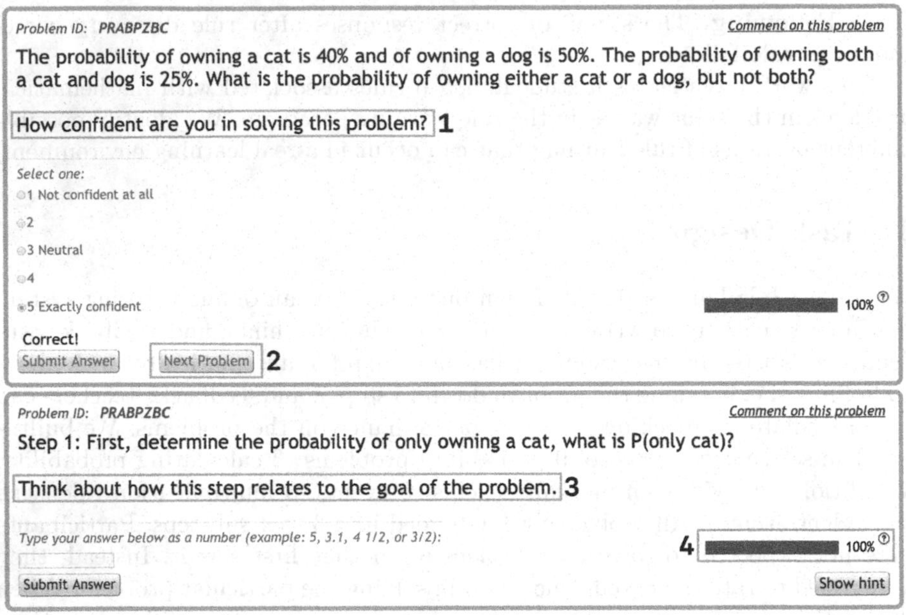

Problem ID: **PRABPZBC**   <u>Comment on this problem</u>

The probability of owning a cat is 40% and of owning a dog is 50%. The probability of owning both a cat and dog is 25%. What is the probability of owning either a cat or a dog, but not both?

How confident are you in solving this problem? **1**

Select one:
○1 Not confident at all

○2

○3 Neutral

○4

●5 Exactly confident   ▬▬▬▬▬▬▬ 100% ⑦

Correct!

[Submit Answer]   [Next Problem] **2**

Problem ID: **PRABPZBC**   <u>Comment on this problem</u>

Step 1: First, determine the probability of only owning a cat, what is P(only cat)?

Think about how this step relates to the goal of the problem. **3**

Type your answer below as a number (example: 5, 3.1, 4 1/2, or 3/2):   **4** ▬▬▬▬▬▬▬ 100% ⑦

[Submit Answer]   [Show hint]

Fig. 1. 1: Participants rate their confidence level in solving the shown problem when they first see it. The system accepts all answers to confidence ratings as correct. 2: When participant clicks on "Next problem", first substep of the problem was shown. 3: Participants see a prompt below the problem text in each substep to remember the strategy they were trained to follow based on the condition they are assigned. 4: The green bar shows if student took the available hints on the step. 100% means no hints were taken. As students take more hints, the percentage decreases. (Color figure online)

3.2   Rule Learning Manipulation

To track how students go through the phases of rule learning, every problem substep was assigned a rule. For example, for the problem given in Fig. 1, the rules assigned to the substeps are: $P(only\,A) = P(A) - P(A \cap B)$ for substeps 1 and 2, and $P(A\,or\,B\,not\,both) = P(only\,A) + P(only\,B)$ for the final substep. There were 7 distinct rules that were assigned to the problem substeps across all problems. The students may see the same rule either within a problem (as in the example) or across multiple problems. Participants saw each rule at least 3 times so that we would be able to track how they moved through phases of rule learning over multiple occurrences of each rule.

4   Study

The main purpose of this paper is to investigate how cognitive control and rule learning show themselves during problem solving and understand the effect of these mechanisms on learning with an ITS. Within this section we describe a thinkaloud study we designed in order to achieve these goals in more detail.

20 undergraduate students (6 male) from the Northeastern US, between 18 and 23 years old ($M = 19.45$, $SD = 1.27$), were recruited via emails sent to student mailing lists and flyers posted around university campuses. Our inclusion criterion was having completed no more than two university-level math courses. The study was a 1-hour session and participants were paid $10 compensation.

Participants solved the problems on ASSISTments version 1.0. They were provided a pen and a scratch paper to make the calculations on paper if they wished. They were also allowed to use the built-in calculator on the computer. We recorded the computer screen and thinkalouds while participants solved problems using a screen recording tool with audio.

After providing written consent, participants were introduced to ASSISTments. Participants first solved a simple practice problem to get used to the interface. We explained how they could submit answers and ask for hints as they solved the practice problem. After the practice, participants took a pre-test consisting of 6 probability problems. They solved these problems in "test mode" of ASSISTments (no hints available). After the pre-test, we gave another practice to the participants to prepare them for the thinkaloud session in which they were randomly assigned to one of the two conditions named "Proactive" and "Reactive". Within the second practice, participants solved an example problem with the prompts we described in Sect. 3.1 based on the condition they are assigned. After this practice, participants solved the real problems and engaged in the thinkaloud activity. After the thinkaloud session, participants took a post-test that was isomorphic to the pre-test, then filled a demographic questionnaire.

5   Data Analysis

5.1   Data Coding

We coded the video recordings from the thinkaloud sessions using Atlas.ti software. Each substep of the problem was coded. Our data had 532 substeps across 19 participants (1 participant was excluded from the analyses due to solving the pre-test in "tutor mode" of ASSISTments). The codes consisted of six labels related to the different modes of cognitive control and the phases of rule learning, and substeps could be given one or more labels. Two coders coded 20% of the data independently. Cohen's kappa was used to compare the ratings of the two coders. The agreement was $K = 0.70$ for the labels associated with cognitive control (relation to goal, saying answer, reacting), and $K = 0.82$ for the rule learning labels (rule search, rule discovery, rule following). The labels we gave the substeps are described below.

Relation to Goal. Substeps where the participant relates the current step to the goal of the problem or where they repeat the goal explicitly (e.g. "This step relates to the goal because it helps us eliminate the probability of owning both a cat and a dog.", "So, the goal of the problem is getting the probability of A or B occurring but not both.").

Saying the Answer. Substeps where the participant says the answer but never show how the answer relates to the goal of the problem (e.g. "The answer is 35.", "Total number of possible outcomes will just be number of prizes plus number of blanks because there's a possibility of getting either of those, and that is 35.").

Reacting. Substeps where the participant reacts to a mistake or a hint (e.g. "Ok it is wrong.", "Oh, I see I did not have to do the multiplication, that was just part of it.").

Rule Search. Substeps where the participant is simply guessing the answer or trying to figure out the right way to solve it (e.g. "I don't quite remember how to solve this but I'm going to try multiplying them before I take the hint.", "So, my first inclination is to do something with 0.3 and 0.4. I am going to try multiplying them or maybe I should add them.").

Rule Discovery. Substeps where the participant has just discovered a rule ("Oh! So, we add the probability of just A and just B.").

Rule Following. Substeps where the participant explains how they got to an answer. Participants being in this state does not mean they follow the correct rule. Sometimes they follow a rule they think is correct (e.g. "We multiply the two probabilities together and that is 5/44.").

5.2   Statistical Analyses

In order to test if the students in the experimental conditions are behaving as expected, we conducted two-sample t-tests for each code. The results suggested that the participants in the proactive condition related the problem substeps to the goal significantly more than the ones in the reactive condition $(t(17) = 2.49, p < 0.05)$. In contrast, participants in the reactive condition answered by simply saying the answer significantly more than the participants in the proactive condition $(t(17) = -2.66, p < 0.05)$. There was no significant difference in reacting to hints or mistakes between two conditions $(t(17) = -0.55, p = 0.59)$. Table 1 summarizes these results. Overall, the results suggest that our experimental conditions were successful.

Table 1. Mean (SD) of quotation labels between the experimental conditions. * indicates $p < 0.05$.

Condition	Relation to goal	Saying the answer	Reacting
Proactive	**7.89 (9.93)***	17.44 (9.26)	3.33 (2.12)
Reactive	0.1 (0.31)	**25.4 (1.96)***	3.8 (1.55)

We could successfully alter the student behavior in a way that reflects proactive and reactive modes of cognitive control. But does using one of these modes while problem solving result in better learning gains? We conducted a two-way repeated-measures ANOVA to compare the pre and post-test scores between conditions. Results showed that there was no significant difference in learning gain (difference between post-test and pre-test) between the proactive ($M = 0.48, SD = 0.18$) and the reactive ($M = 0.32, SD = 0.23$) conditions ($F(1, 17) = 0.17, p = 0.68$). Note that there was no significant difference in students' pre-test scores between the proactive ($M = 0.42, SD = 0.24$) and the reactive ($M = 0.48, SD = 0.18$) conditions ($t(16.44) = -0.69, p = 0.5$). However, time spent on problem substeps was significantly higher in the proactive condition ($M = 21.43, SD = 12.89$) than in the reactive condition ($M = 17.06, SD = 11.19$), ($t(661.49) = 4.77, p < 0.001$).

Next, we turn to rule learning. In our problem set, each problem substep was assigned one rule and the students may go through multiple phases of rule learning solving one substep. We identified which rule learning phases the students went through in one problem step based on the presence of the relevant labels from thinkaloud data. Then we investigated patterns of rule learning phases that the students follow across all substeps that are assigned the same rule. We extracted one sequence of rule learning phases for each participant and rule type. The unique sequences of these phases pointed out 3 different patterns (see Fig. 2 for examples) the students followed:

1) **"Search, Discover, Follow"** Students search for the rule that is assigned to the problem step and discover the rule either by thinking it through or asking for a hint in the first occurrences of a problem step that is assigned the particular rule. In the next occurrences, students would discover then follow that rule. This is the pattern we would see in the rule learning task.

2) **"Follow_wrong, Search, Discover, Follow"** Students who follow this pattern start from following a wrong rule that they think is correct. When they realize it is wrong, they search for the correct one. In the next occurrences, students would discover then follow that rule. The difference between this and the first pattern is that students already have an idea about what the rule is from the beginning. This pattern is also different than what we would see in a rule learning task. Since the rules are random in a rule learning task, the participants can only guess the rule.

3) **"Follow"** The student knows the rule assigned to the problem step already, and they continue following that rule in all occurrences of the same rule.

We identified different combinations of rule learning phases over multiple occurrences of the same rule type across all participants. Since we see no interaction between the experimental conditions and following specific patterns of rule learning, we investigate how students follow these patterns across conditions.

To see if these patterns were related to students' prior knowledge and learning gains, we first divided the students into 2 groups using a mean split on the learning gain. Similarly, both groups were divided into two using a mean split on the pre-test scores. In the end, we had 4 groups of students: high knowledge and high learning gain (HH) ($N = 6$), high knowledge and low learning gain (HL) ($N = 4$), low knowledge and high learning gain (LH) ($N = 3$), and low knowledge and low learning gain (LL) ($N = 6$). Figure 3 visualizes the proportions of the

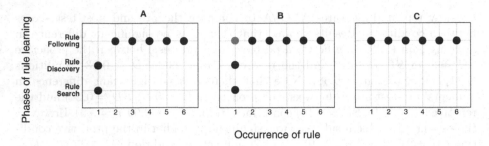

Fig. 2. A: "Search, Discover, Follow" pattern, **B:** "Follow_wrong, Search, Discover, Follow" pattern (red dot represents that the participant started by following the wrong rule), **C:** "Follow" pattern. (Color figure online)

patterns we defined earlier for each student profile. The proportion of the rule learning patterns seem similar for different student groups except students in LH seem to follow "Search, Discovery, Follow" pattern more frequently.

To explore the difference in proportion of "Search, Discover, Follow" pattern among the different student profiles, we computed confidence intervals for these proportions. For the HL, HH, LL, and LH groups, the confidence intervals were 90% CIs [.02, .24], [.04, .20], [.09, .32], and [.31, .69], respectively. These intervals suggest the proportion of students who follow "Search, Discover, Follow" pattern will be higher in LH group than it is in other groups. However, this should be confirmed with a significance test with enough sample size.

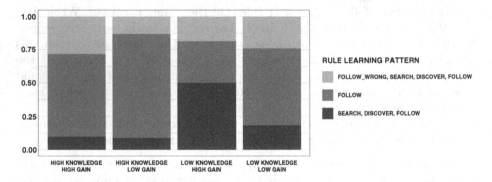

Fig. 3. Rule learning patterns by student profiles based on students' learning gains and prior knowledge.

6   Discussion and Conclusion

Most well-studied cognitive and motivational states that were associated with learning within ITSs have roots in cognitive science studies of rule learning and cognitive control. To explore the relevance of these lower level cognitive mechanisms within ITS research, we investigated how these mechanisms show themselves in a complex learning environment and their relationship with learning. We presented a study in which we induced one of the two modes of cognitive control based on the DMC framework [4] and observed how students move through the phases of rule learning within an ITS.

Our results indicated success in shifting student behavior in a way that reflects the proactive or reactive modes of cognitive control, achieving effects similar to studies that have been done with more controlled tasks [5,13,14,20]. However, we did not observe a difference in learning between the two modes. Multiple explanations could account for this result. Firstly, since this was a thinkaloud study, all participants were explaining their thought processes while they were solving the problems. The explanation practice might have helped all participants [9] and possibly hindered the effect of relating to the goal of the problem. Future studies without the thinkaloud procedure should further explore these effects. Secondly, since using proactive control is more cognitively demanding than reactive control [22], practicing proactive control might have exhausted the cognitive resources participants have and as a result they struggled with the learning tasks, cancelling out the benefits of maintaining the goal in working memory. Our finding on time data was consistent with this explanation as students in the proactive condition spent more time on the problem steps. As we show it is possible to induce proactive control, we hope future work will further explore its effects on learning.

Our analyses on rule learning revealed that students were following three main patterns of rule learning phases while they are solving problems. Results showed that the students with low prior knowledge and high learning gains followed the pattern that formal studies of rule learning [6,7,10,18] show (i.e. "Search, Discover, Follow") more frequently than the other student profiles. This result could be an indicator of a relationship between rule learning and domain learning and ITSs can benefit from this relationship in task selection by choosing tasks that support appropriate rule learning patterns based on the student's profile. However, the small sample size was a limitation for further exploration of this relationship.

To summarize our contributions, we presented a novel coding scheme in order to categorize student utterances that are indicative of mechanisms of cognitive control and rule learning within a complex learning environment and we took a first step towards understanding the underlying mechanisms of student cognitive states that are associated with learning. We believe that identifying these underlying mechanisms within such complex learning environments will open new paths in ITS research and student modeling.

Acknowledgements. This work was supported by the National Science Foundation Award No. DGE-1835251. We would like to thank the ASSISTments team for their assistance and support, and Zachary Pixley for his help with data coding.

References

1. Aleven, V.A., Koedinger, K.R.: An effective metacognitive strategy: learning by doing and explaining with a computer-based cognitive tutor. Cogn. Sci. **26**(2), 147–179 (2002)
2. Barch, D.M., et al.: CNTRICS final task selection: working memory. Schizophr. Bull. **35**(1), 136–152 (2009)
3. Botvinick, M.M., Braver, T.S., Barch, D.M., Carter, C.S., Cohen, J.D.: Conflict monitoring and cognitive control. Psychol. Rev. **108**(3), 624 (2001)
4. Braver, T.S.: The variable nature of cognitive control: a dual mechanisms framework. Trends Cogn. Sci. **16**(2), 106–113 (2012)
5. Braver, T.S., Paxton, J.L., Locke, H.S., Barch, D.M.: Flexible neural mechanisms of cognitive control within human prefrontal cortex. Proc. Natl. Acad. Sci. **106**(18), 7351–7356 (2009)
6. Burgess, P.W., Shallice, T.: Bizarre responses, rule detection and frontal lobe lesions. Cortex **32**(2), 241–259 (1996)
7. Cao, B., Li, W., Li, F., Li, H.: Dissociable roles of medial and lateral PFC in rule learning. Brain Behav. **6**(11), e00551 (2016)
8. Chatham, C.H., Frank, M.J., Munakata, Y.: Pupillometric and behavioral markers of a developmental shift in the temporal dynamics of cognitive control. Proc. Natl. Acad. Sci. **106**(14), 5529–5533 (2009)
9. Chi, M.: Self-explaining expository texts: the dual processes of generating inferences and repairing mental models. Adv. Instr. Psychol. **5**, 161–238 (2000)
10. Crescentini, C., Seyed-Allaei, S., De Pisapia, N., Jovicich, J., Amati, D., Shallice, T.: Mechanisms of rule acquisition and rule following in inductive reasoning. J. Neurosci. **31**(21), 7763–7774 (2011)
11. Dang, S., Koedinger, K.: Exploring the link between motivations and gaming. In: EDM (2019)
12. D'Mello, S., Olney, A., Williams, C., Hays, P.: Gaze tutor: a gaze-reactive intelligent tutoring system. Int. J. Hum. Comput. Stud. **70**(5), 377–398 (2012)
13. Edwards, B.G., Barch, D.M., Braver, T.S.: Improving prefrontal cortex function in schizophrenia through focused training of cognitive control. Front. Hum. Neurosci. **4**, 32 (2010)
14. Gonthier, C., Macnamara, B.N., Chow, M., Conway, A.R., Braver, T.S.: Inducing proactive control shifts in the AX-CPT. Front. Psychol. **7**, 1822 (2016)
15. Heffernan, N.T., Heffernan, C.L.: The assistments ecosystem: building a platform that brings scientists and teachers together for minimally invasive research on human learning and teaching. Int. J. Artif. Intell. Educ. **24**(4), 470–497 (2014)
16. Koch, S., Holland, R.W., van Knippenberg, A.: Regulating cognitive control through approach-avoidance motor actions. Cognition **109**(1), 133–142 (2008)
17. Koedinger, K.R., Corbett, A.T., Perfetti, C.: The knowledge-learning-instruction framework: bridging the science-practice chasm to enhance robust student learning. Cogn. Sci. **36**(5), 757–798 (2012)
18. Li, F., Cao, B., Gao, H., Kuang, L., Li, H.: Different brain potentials evoked at distinct phases of rule learning. Psychophysiology **49**(9), 1266–1276 (2012)
19. Mackie, M.A., Van Dam, N.T., Fan, J.: Cognitive control and attentional functions. Brain Cogn. **82**(3), 301–312 (2013)
20. Paxton, J.L., Barch, D.M., Storandt, M., Braver, T.S.: Effects of environmental support and strategy training on older adults' use of context. Psychol. Aging **21**(3), 499 (2006)

21. Redick, T.S.: Cognitive control in context: working memory capacity and proactive control. Acta Psychol. **145**, 1–9 (2014)
22. Speer, N.K., Jacoby, L.L., Braver, T.S.: Strategy-dependent changes in memory: effects on behavior and brain activity. Cogn. Affect. Behav. Neurosci. **3**(3), 155–167 (2003)
23. Wiemers, E.A., Redick, T.S.: Working memory capacity and intra-individual variability of proactive control. Acta Psychol. **182**, 21–31 (2018)

Remember the Facts? Investigating Answer-Aware Neural Question Generation for Text Comprehension

Tim Steuer[✉] [ID], Anna Filighera, and Christoph Rensing

Technical University of Darmstadt, Darmstadt, Germany
{tim.steuer,anna.filighera,christoph.rensing}@kom.tu-darmstadt.de

Abstract. Reading is a crucial skill in the 21st century. Thus, scaffolding text comprehension by automatically generated questions may greatly profit learners. Yet, the state-of-the-art methods for automatic question generation, answer-aware neural question generators (NQGs), are rarely seen in the educational domain. Hence, we investigate the quality of questions generated by a novel approach comprising an answer-aware NQG and two novel answer candidate selection strategies based on semantic graph matching. In median, the approach generates clear, answerable and useful factual questions outperforming an answer-unaware NQG on educational datasets as shown by automatic and human evaluation. Furthermore, we analyze the types of questions generated, showing that the question types differ across answer selection strategies yet remain factual.

Keywords: Automatic question generation · Natural language generation · Education

1 Motivation

Reading materials encode a significant amount of our human knowledge, from cooking recipes to textbooks about quantum mechanics. When we are learning, we are often relying on those reading materials as our primary source for knowledge acquisition.

Yet, learning by reading is often challenging and text comprehension depends not only on the reader but also on the text. Even advanced readers occasionally experience difficulties while reading. Texts encompassing jargon, assuming a lot of prior knowledge, or using a specific style of writing challenge even the best of readers. Consequently, providing additional text-specific help might be of great value, not only for novices but also for the intermediate and advanced.

An established reading aid is questioning the readers about the content of the text [1,14]. Depending on the type of questioning, it has different effects. Factual questions direct the attention of learners to specific aspects of the text [1], helping them to remember facts easily. Conversely, comprehension questions require

© Springer Nature Switzerland AG 2020
I. I. Bittencourt et al. (Eds.): AIED 2020, LNAI 12163, pp. 512–523, 2020.
https://doi.org/10.1007/978-3-030-52237-7_41

learners to combine different aspects of the text, supporting deeper understanding [1]. That is, to get the most benefit from asking readers, combining different types of questions is important [1,10].

Yet, posing questions is a challenging task even for humans. Authors first need to understand the underlying texts. Next, they have to identify meaningful facts and connections, which are important for the learners' understanding. Finally, they have to state a question in such a way that it actually fosters text comprehension. As a result, having well written, manually authored questions in formal learning settings is expensive, and almost impossible in informal learning settings, where the amount of reading materials is endless.

Automatic question generation is a research field investigating how to create questions without human intervention. It is used in different domains such as dialog systems, question answering or in educational settings. Ideally, to foster text comprehension, an automatic question generator receives the reading material, e.g. a text passage, as input and poses meaningful questions about this text, alleviating the need for expensive human questioning.

However, those systems are far from perfect and posing fluent and meaningful questions from unstructured text is still under active research. The current state-of-the-art systems are answer-aware neural generators (NQGs). It has been shown that such systems generate questions with excellent fluency and acceptable relevancy [7].

They are used in dialog systems and to augment question answering data, but are rarely seen in the education domain. During generation they expect two inputs (see Fig. 1). First, they generate questions given a single question-worthy sentence (context sentence) instead of the whole unstructured reading material. Second, they use an explicitly marked expected answer inside the given context sentence (answer candidate).

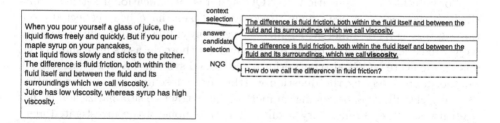

Fig. 1. Automatic question generation by selecting the context sentence (underlined) and the answer candidate (bold) from a physics paragraph before generating the actual question via an answer-aware NQG.

This paper makes two contributions. First, we apply answer-aware NQGs to texts in the educational domain and investigate the quality of the generated questions by conducting automatic and human evaluation. Furthermore, we propose two novel answer candidate selection strategies, relying on semantic graph matching, which are easily adaptable to different cases.

2 Related Work

The following section will examine the problem of question generation from different viewpoints. It aims to exemplify the challenges of the task and to motivate our design decisions. For a thorough review of automatic question generation in education we refer to Kurdi et al. [17] and for a general review of NQGs to Pan et al. [22].

The literature usually distinguishes three types of automatic question generation approaches. The most common in the field of educational research are rule-based and template-based approaches [17], while outside of the educational domain NQGs are state-of-the-art [22]. Systems in the educational domain investigate a variety of different question types such as Gap-fill questions, multiple-choice questions or Wh-questions in a variety of domains such as generic text comprehension, history or biology [17]. They rely either on text [19] or structured data such as ontologies or knowledge-bases [15] for their context and answer candidate selection. When relying on text, the answer candidate selection of the systems is mostly done via shallow semantic parsing such as semantic role labeling or named entity recognition [12,21]. Furthermore, some authors train classifiers on human-annotated data [2,16].

Looking outside the educational domain, NQGs evolved from relatively simple sequence to sequence models, relying only on the context sentence and the statistical regularities of language to generate questions [9], to sophisticated model with different facets. Subsequent systems make use of advanced neural architectures [7], take desired answers into account [7,25] and are difficulty-aware [13]. These neural approaches have been shown to be superior in terms of naturalness and grammatical correctness by automatic and empirical measures [9,22]. Current state-of-the-art systems are answer-aware NQGs, outperforming answer-unaware and non-NQG approaches [7,22].

Looking at the application of NQG systems in educational settings, relatively little work has been done. Recently, datasets have been collected, containing questions on different cognitive levels, providing more training data for NQGs in education [5,18]. Initial experiments on those datasets have shown that answer-unaware NQGs also outperform rule-based systems on those datasets [5]. Furthermore, selecting the question-worthy context sentences from text either by using classifiers [8] or relying on methods of extractive summarization [4] has been investigated. Preliminary results show that none of the investigated algorithms consistently performs best on all datasets, with LexRank [11] being one of the best performing approaches.

3 Research Questions

Our research is guided by the related work and the fact that answer-unaware NQGs outperform rule-based systems on educational datasets and answer-aware NQGs outperform all other systems on non-educational datasets. Thus we hypothesize answer-aware systems will also perform better for educational scenarios, leading to our first research question (RQ1):

1. To what extent are answer-aware NQGs more useful in educational scenarios than answer-unaware NQGs?

Aside of this direct comparison, more nuanced analysis is also important as we need to pose different question types to the learner to achieve optimal support. Therefore, the interaction between the NQG and the answer selection has to be investigated. Only asking for plain facts will not result in the best learning outcome and we hypothesise that some answer selection strategies yield more factual questions than others. Additionally, We assume that answer selection methods have a strong influence on some but not all quality criteria. We suspect that the grammaticality of the question is not altered by using different strategies but that the usefulness of the generated questions and their respective question types (e.g. what vs. why questions) is influenced by different answer selection strategies. We therefore pose our second research question (RQ2):

2. How do different answer selection strategies influence types and quality aspects of the generated questions?

We operationalize RQ1 and RQ2 by looking at the grammaticality, the answerability and the usefulness of the generated questions. Grammaticality is necessary for a question to be comprehensible at all. Furthermore, high grammaticality results in a more fluent reading of the question. We understand answerability as, how well can the answer to the generated question be given taking into account only the context sentence that was used to construct it. This score not only indicates whether the question is meaningful at all, but also whether the answer selection and question generation have worked well together. Finally, we are looking at the usefulness of the generated questions. A useful question is one that covers major concepts or fosters text comprehension whereas a useless question does not help to understand the text any better. Thus, this score informs us about the suitability of the generation process for educational purposes.

4   Experiment Setting

To investigate our research questions, we implement a question generation process comprising constant context selection and varying answer candidate selections. We compare an answer-unaware NQG baseline with three different answer-aware NQGs, yielding four different conditions in total. For the context selection in all conditions, we learn from Chen et al. [4] and use LexRank.

4.1   Answer-Unaware Condition

The answer-unaware NQG [9] is the baseline model from the related work [5]. It consists of a sequence to sequence NQG with attention. It rewrites the context sentence to a question, implicitly selecting an answer inside the sentence. Therefore it is answer-unaware, as it does not explicitly need the answer candidate as an input. We train the system on the SQuAD dataset with the same parameters as given in the authors' paper until we reach a similar performance measured by BLEU-4 [23] on the provided validation set.

4.2 Nsubj Condition

We select the subject phrase from context sentences as the answer candidate for the question. We choose this strategy because the subject is frequently correlated with the main protagonist in a sentence. Furthermore, it is a common constituent in many sentences and thus can be selected in most sentences as a plausible answer. Finally, we suspect that asking for the subject of a sentence will yield many factual questions asking for the main protagonists of a sentence or story. In other words, when answering such questions, learners are thinking about the main driving forces of a story.

To implement the strategy, the selected context sentence is dependency-parsed [6] using Stanford CoreNLP 3.9.2 [20], resulting in a semantic graph representing the grammatical relationships of the sentence. Next, we use Semgrex matching to extract relevant information from the graph [3]. This has the advantage that we do not have to write complicated graph traversal code to extract vertices that belong to a grammatical relationship. Instead, a Semgrex pattern describes subgraphs with special properties, that can easily be processed further. We apply pattern matching to all nodes under the sentences subject relation. For sentences containing multiple candidates, we heuristically select the longest, under the assumption that longer inputs are beneficial for the question generator. Note that this approach can easily be extended by changing the Semgrex pattern e.g. by matching adverbial clauses and checking the resulting subgraph to only express consequences.

To generate the actual question, an answer-aware NQG [7] based on a neural transformer [24] is used. It is pre-trained on unidirectional, bidirectional and sequence to sequence prediction tasks. For our task, we use the publicly available fine-tuned question generation model[1] provided by the authors, which is a 24-layer, 1024-hidden states, 16-attention heads 340M parameter model trained on Wikipedia and the BookCorpus and fine-tuned on the SQuAD dataset.

4.3 Dobj Condition

We select the direct object phrase from context sentences as the answer candidate for the question by using the same algorithm as in the *Nsubj* condition.

Direct objects are also common parts of sentences, allowing the application of this strategy in most cases. Yet, in contrast to the subject, direct objects are more often targets of actions. Hence, we suspect that asking for direct objects will yield questions having different purposes than in the Nsubj condition. Using direct objects as answer input may e.g. cause the NQG to focus more on the carried out action which might be favourable for understanding. The generation of the question is done with the same answer-aware NQG as in the *Nsubj* condition.

---

[1] https://github.com/microsoft/unilm.

4.4   Random Condition

We apply basic answer candidate selection by selecting one word from the given sentence at random. The sentence is tokenized[2] and a word is sampled at random. As discussed in the related work section, different neural architectures result in different performing generators. Thus, we include this strategy in the experiments to measure the influence of the different neural architectures independent of their answer-awareness. Observing high-scoring metrics when applying this strategy implies that the answer-aware generator's underlying architecture produces better results detached from the answer candidate. The generation of the question is done with the same answer-aware NQG as in the *Nsubj* condition.

5   Results

5.1   Datasets

We conduct an automatic and a human evaluation. We focus on texts given by the RACE dataset [18]. It is a publicly available educational dataset, comprising passages and questions generated by human experts for the Chinese English reading exams. It covers different domains in middle to high school difficulty.

Moreover, we also report some automatic evaluation results for the TED-ed part of the LearningQ [5] dataset which also covers a wide variety of topics. This dataset is gathered by crawling the transcripts of TED-ed, an educational video provider, and the corresponding comprehension questions posed by educational experts. Albeit we report such results for comparability, we focus on RACE because of the different nature of video transcripts compared to educational texts.

Note that we filter both datasets before conducting our evaluation. We remove all questions not ending with a question mark (e.g. fill-in-the-gap type of questions), resulting in 1089 paragraphs and 5235 gold questions for the LearningQ dataset and 19,944 paragraphs and 40,439 gold questions for the RACE dataset.

5.2   Automatic Evaluation

As a proxy for the grammatical quality of the generated questions, we compute BLEU-4 scores similar to Chen et al. [4].[3] For that, we compare the generated and the gold-standard questions in the given datasets, by only considering the maximum-scoring questions per passage (see Fig. 2).

For the RACE dataset, all answer-aware conditions slightly outperform the answer-unaware generator in terms of the BLEU-4. Yet, the differences are marginal except for the Random condition which performs best. For the LearningQ dataset, the Random condition again performs best, however, closely followed by the Answer-unaware condition.

---

[2] Using Stanford CoreNLP 3.9.2.
[3] Using https://github.com/tylin/coco-caption.

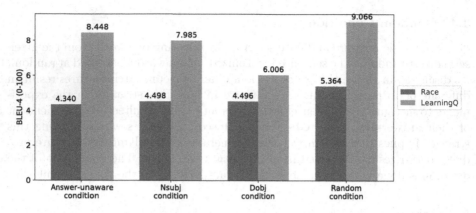

Fig. 2. BLEU-4 evaluation results only considering the maximum score per paragraph on the filtered questions of RACE and the TED-ed part of LearningQ.

To validate these results, we compared the distributions of the average sentence BLEU-4 scores per paragraph. They are narrow, with median sentence BLEU-4 scores of zero for any condition (see Fig. 3). Put differently, most questions do not overlap with the gold standard. Yet, they nevertheless might be valid as the gold standard comprises only a small subset of all plausible questions. Hence, BLEU-4 may measures little overlap, although the questions are still useful. Second, because the NSubj and Dobj conditions might fail to find an answer-candidate in a context sentence, they generate fewer questions per paragraph than the other two strategies. Only 90% of Nsubj and 65% of Dobj generation attempts succeeded. As a consequence, selecting the maximum scoring sentence per paragraph slightly favors the Random and Answer-unaware conditions, because they always generate the maximum amount of sentences

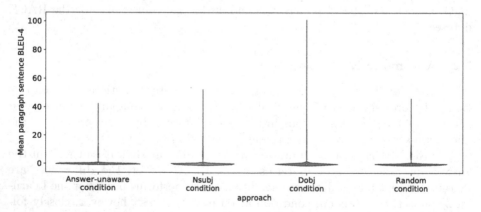

Fig. 3. Violin plot of the average sentence BLEU-4 scores per paragraph on the RACE dataset. The estimated kernel density shows that BLEU-4 scores are rarely different from zero.

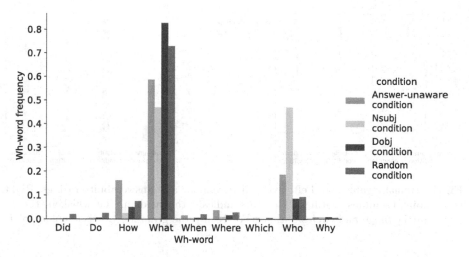

Fig. 4. Wh-word frequency on the RACE dataset for the three answer candidate conditions.

resulting in a higher chance to generate an overlapping question. In summary, although BLEU-4 is often used as a proxy measure for grammaticality, no clear statement about the grammaticality can be made from the automatic measures.

When plotting the distribution of the Wh-words we can gather some data for RQ2. The different answer-aware conditions show that they indeed influence the generated question types in our experiments (see Fig. 4). The Nsubj condition splits the generated questions almost evenly in "Who" and "What" questions whereas the Dobj and the Random condition mostly pose "What" questions. Hence, looking at these automatically computed statistics provides evidence that most of the generated questions are factual, not asking about reasons or deeper explanations. While this is also true for the Answer-unaware condition, it is worth noting that it stated more "How" questions than any other system.

5.3 Human Evaluation

We conducted a human evaluation with two annotators to get more insights into the grammaticality, answerability, and usefulness of the questions. Both annotators speak English either as a native language or at level CEF[4] B2. We included all four experimental conditions in our evaluation study. We randomly sampled 80 paragraphs from the RACE dataset and assigned each of them to one condition. For every paragraph, we generated three questions. Every annotator evaluated 80 paragraphs having 3 questions each, 240 questions in total. We presented the paragraphs to the annotators in random order. For every paragraph annotators initially saw three context sentences with their generated questions

---

[4] Common European Framework of Reference for Languages.

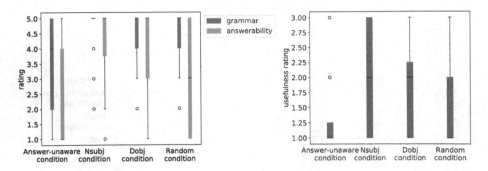

Fig. 5. Human evaluation. Left: five-point grammar and answerability ratings. Right: three-point usefulness ratings. The bars indicate the median, the whiskers the 1.5 interquartile range and circles outliers. For Nsubj, the grammar box is a single point.

and rated them in terms of answerability and grammaticality on a five-point Likert scale. Then they saw the reading passage together with the questions and rated the questions again for their usefulness (three-point Likert scale) and progressed to the next paragraph. To ensure a common understanding of the scales, an annotation guideline defining answerability, grammaticality, and usefulness was shown. The inter-rater agreement was measured by Krippendorff's $\alpha = .63$ for grammar, $\alpha = .78$ for answerability and $\alpha = .55$ for usefulness. Conflicts were resolved by preferring the native speaker's rating.

The data yields interesting insights into the performance of the different conditions. The median grammaticality rating for the different conditions is 4 in the answer-unaware condition and 5 in all three answer-aware conditions. The median answerability rating is 5 for the Nsubj and Dobj conditions, 3 for the Random condition and 1 for the Answer-unaware condition. The usefulness rating indicates that the Nsubj and Dobj conditions result in a median score of 2 whereas the two other conditions score a median of 1. As shown in Fig. 5 most ratings have a non-negligible dispersion.

6 Discussion and Future Work

Concerning RQ1, our experiments present evidence that answer-aware NQGs are more suitable for the educational domain than answer-unaware NQGs. The proposed answer selection strategies outperform answer-unaware systems in terms of grammaticality, answerability, and usefulness. For the usefulness criteria, the NSubj and Dobj conditions are the only ones that generate factual questions supporting readers in the median. In contrast, the Answer-unaware condition creates useless questions in the median often even worse than the Random condition. A possible explanation is that the answer-unaware generator mostly selects unimportant information as answers. On the answerability criteria, the answer-aware conditions also perform better, yielding readily answerable questions most of the time. We can rule out the possibility that this is only due to better grammar of the generated questions as the Random condition leads to worse results while scoring high on grammar. For the grammaticality criteria, things are a bit more complex. On the one hand, the BLEU-4 scores are inconclusive. On the other hand, human evaluation shows that the three answer-aware conditions produce more grammatically sound questions. Additionally, the BLEU-4 distributions are almost always close to zero indicating that the gold standard is rarely met. Therefore, we assume that the answer-aware systems are also performing better and that the automatic scores are not representative. However, as the random answer candidate condition also performs quite well on these criteria, answer-unaware systems might profit here from other neural architectures or more training data.

Regarding RQ2, we can see that our strategies result in better questions overall, but the data indicates that the variety of question types is still limited. In every condition, the generated questions remain mainly of factual nature. This is supported by the analysis of the Wh-word distribution, showing that determining questions are posed most often. Furthermore, the usefulness ratings of the annotators indicate that the questions are also mostly of factual nature and not connected to the main ideas of the texts. There might be several reasons for this focus on factual questions. Perhaps the most striking thing is that the whole question generation process currently works on a single sentence basis not taking into account inter-sentence relations. However, important information about the gist of the text can often only be deduced by reasoning about the whole input text. Future work may investigate such reasoning by building NQG processes working with whole paragraphs or extracted summaries, and figuring out synergies between context and answer selection steps. Finally, the used NQGs are mostly trained on data from question answering datasets and thus have most often seen factual questions during their training. In the future, one could explore ways to train or fine-tune such systems on the existing educational datasets.

In summary, this work showed that answer-aware NQGs can generate factual questions to support text comprehension. Yet, more research is needed to pose not only factual but also comprehension questions. Furthermore, we introduced two strategies for answer candidate selection to make the use of answer-aware NQGs possible, which both can easily be extended to more complex patterns.

References

1. Anderson, R.C., Biddle, W.B.: On asking people questions about what they are reading. In: Psychology of Learning and Motivation - Advances in Research and Theory (1975). https://doi.org/10.1016/S0079-7421(08)60269-8
2. Blšták, M., Rozinajová, V.: Building an agent for factual question generation task. In: 2018 World Symposium on Digital Intelligence for Systems and Machines (DISA), pp. 143–150. IEEE (2018)
3. Chambers, N., et al.: Learning alignments and leveraging natural logic. In: Proceedings of the ACL-PASCAL Workshop on Textual Entailment and Paraphrasing, pp. 165–170. Association for Computational Linguistics (2007)

4. Chen, G., Yang, J., Gasevic, D.: A comparative study on question-worthy sentence selection strategies for educational question generation. In: Isotani, S., Millán, E., Ogan, A., Hastings, P., McLaren, B., Luckin, R. (eds.) AIED 2019. LNCS (LNAI), vol. 11625, pp. 59–70. Springer, Cham (2019). https://doi.org/10.1007/978-3-030-23204-7_6

5. Chen, G., Yang, J., Hauff, C., Houben, G.J.: LearningQ: a large-scale dataset for educational question generation. In: Twelfth International AAAI Conference on Web and Social Media (2018)

6. De Marneffe, M.C., Manning, C.D.: The Stanford typed dependencies representation. In: Proceedings of the Workshop on Cross-Framework and Cross-Domain Parser Evaluation, Coling 2008, pp. 1–8 (2008)

7. Dong, L., et al.: Unified language model pre-training for natural language understanding and generation. In: Advances in Neural Information Processing Systems, pp. 13042–13054 (2019)

8. Du, X., Cardie, C.: Identifying where to focus in reading comprehension for neural question generation. In: Proceedings of the Conference on Empirical Methods in Natural Language Processing, EMNLP 2017 (2017). https://doi.org/10.18653/v1/d17-1219

9. Du, X., Shao, J., Cardie, C.: Learning to ask: neural question generation for reading comprehension. In: 55th Annual Meeting of the Association for Computational Linguistics, Proceedings of the Conference (Long Papers), ACL 2017 (2017). https://doi.org/10.18653/v1/P17-1123

10. Duke, N.K., Pearson, P.D.: Effective practices for developing reading comprehension. J. Educ. (2009). https://doi.org/10.1177/0022057409189001-208

11. Erkan, G., Radev, D.R.: LexRank: graph-based lexical centrality as salience in text summarization. J. Artif. Intell. Res. **22**, 457–479 (2004)

12. Fattoh, I.E., Aboutabl, A.E., Haggag, M.H.: Semantic question generation using artificial immunity. Int. J. Mod. Educ. Comput. Sci. **7**(1), 1 (2015)

13. Gao, Y., Bing, L., Chen, W., Lyu, M.R., King, I.: Difficulty controllable generation of reading comprehension questions. In: Proceedings of the 28th International Joint Conference on Artificial Intelligence, pp. 4968–4974. AAAI Press (2019)

14. Hamaker, C.: The effects of adjunct questions on prose learning. Rev. Educ. Res. (1986). https://doi.org/10.3102/00346543056002212

15. Jouault, C., Seta, K.: Content-dependent question generation for history learning in semantic open learning space. In: Trausan-Matu, S., Boyer, K.E., Crosby, M., Panourgia, K. (eds.) ITS 2014. LNCS, vol. 8474, pp. 300–305. Springer, Cham (2014). https://doi.org/10.1007/978-3-319-07221-0_37

16. Kumar, G., Banchs, R.E., D'Haro, L.F.: RevUP: automatic gap-fill question generation from educational texts. In: Proceedings of the Tenth Workshop on Innovative Use of NLP for Building Educational Applications, pp. 154–161 (2015)

17. Kurdi, G., Leo, J., Parsia, B., Sattler, U., Al-Emari, S.: A systematic review of automatic question generation for educational purposes. Int. J. Artif. Intell. Educ. **30**, 1–84 (2019)

18. Lai, G., Xie, Q., Liu, H., Yang, Y., Hovy, E.: Race: large-scale reading comprehension dataset from examinations. arXiv preprint arXiv:1704.04683 (2017)

19. Liu, M., Calvo, R.A., Rus, V.: Automatic question generation for literature review writing support. In: Aleven, V., Kay, J., Mostow, J. (eds.) ITS 2010. LNCS, vol. 6094, pp. 45–54. Springer, Heidelberg (2010). https://doi.org/10.1007/978-3-642-13388-6_9

20. Manning, C.D., Surdeanu, M., Bauer, J., Finkel, J., Bethard, S.J., McClosky, D.: The Stanford CoreNLP natural language processing toolkit. In: Association for Computational Linguistics (ACL) System Demonstrations, pp. 55–60 (2014). http://www.aclweb.org/anthology/P/P14/P14-5010

21. Mazidi, K., Nielsen, R.D.: Pedagogical evaluation of automatically generated questions. In: Trausan-Matu, S., Boyer, K.E., Crosby, M., Panourgia, K. (eds.) ITS 2014. LNCS, vol. 8474, pp. 294–299. Springer, Cham (2014). https://doi.org/10.1007/978-3-319-07221-0_36

22. Pan, L., Lei, W., Chua, T.S., Kan, M.Y.: Recent advances in neural question generation. arXiv preprint arXiv:1905.08949 (2019)

23. Papineni, K., Roukos, S., Ward, T., Zhu, W.J.: Bleu: a method for automatic evaluation of machine translation. In: Proceedings of the 40th Annual Meeting on Association for Computational Linguistics, pp. 311–318. Association for Computational Linguistics (2002)

24. Vaswani, A., et al.: Attention is all you need. In: Advances in Neural Information Processing Systems, pp. 5998–6008 (2017)

25. Zhao, Y., Ni, X., Ding, Y., Ke, Q.: Paragraph-level neural question generation with maxout pointer and gated self-attention networks. In: EMNLP, pp. 3901–3910 (2018). http://aclweb.org/anthology/D18-1424

Raising Teachers Empowerment in Gamification Design of Adaptive Learning Systems: A Qualitative Research

Kamilla Tenório[ID], Diego Dermeval[✉][ID], Mateus Monteiro,
Aristoteles Peixoto, and Alan Pedro

Federal University of Alagoas, Maceió, AL 57072-900, Brazil
{kktas,mms,apb,alanpedro}@ic.ufal.br, diego.matos@famed.ufal.br

Abstract. Despite the positive outcomes obtained through the application of gamification in the technology-enhanced learning context, previous studies have also reported unexpected results concerning students' engagement, learning outcomes, and motivation in gamified learning systems. To increase the chances of obtaining positive results in this context, this article proposes a "gamification analytics model for teachers". In this model, teachers are allowed to define interaction goals, monitor students' interaction with the system' learning resources and the gamification elements, and adapt the gamification design through missions to motivate disengaged students to achieve the interaction goals defined. However, the gamification analytics model-based design concepts that will be implemented to support the learning process should be well-planned to teachers' needs. Hence, one of the contributions of this paper is the validation of twenty design concepts based on the gamification analytics model for teachers by using the speed dating method. Our results suggest that teachers judged useful/relevant visualize students' interaction with gamification elements such as missions, levels to help them understand the students' status, but did not evaluate the visualization of the interaction of students with trophies relevant. Teachers also highly evaluated the creation of personalized missions for a student or a specific group as relevant to help demotivated students to engage and achieve the desired goals. Therefore, this study provides some relevant insights to guide the design and re-design of gamified adaptive learning systems.

Keywords: Gamification · Teachers · Data visualization · Adaptive learning · Gamification analytics

1 Introduction

There is a growing interest in applying gamification in the technology-enhanced learning context [1,7,10,27,28,31] to increase students' motivation and engagement [3,20]. However, despite the benefits of using gamification in users' psychological and behavioral outcomes [11], including in the educational context [24,30],

© Springer Nature Switzerland AG 2020
I. I. Bittencourt et al. (Eds.): AIED 2020, LNAI 12163, pp. 524–536, 2020.
https://doi.org/10.1007/978-3-030-52237-7_42

some studies have also reported unexpected outcomes after the implementation of gamification in technology-enhanced learning environments [9, 12, 29]. Research has pointed out that the design of gamification is one of the possible causes of negative results in educational settings [9, 19]. According to Heilbrunn, Herzig, and Schill [15], the process to design gamification should incorporate different aspects such as the personas of involved users, the application's domain, properties of the gamified application itself, or legal constraints. These diverse aspects are subject to change over time, thus, gamification design must not be a rigid artifact [15].

Therefore, monitoring and adapting data related to gamification can be an alternative solution to avoid negative outcomes related to the use of gamification and can give valuable insights to take corresponding actions towards goals achievement [13–15]. Heilbrunn, Herzig and Schill [15] named this process as gamification analytics, and defined it as "the data-driven processes of monitoring and adapting gamification designs". Nonetheless, the studies that address gamification in technology-enhanced learning environments are, in general, not concerned in monitoring and adapting gamification design during the learning process, neither through automated adaptation nor through human decision-making, increasing the risk of obtaining unexpected results [32].

Considering that we are in an era where data is being more used in the service of human decision-making and design than automated adjustment [2, 5], and that teachers should be at the heart of most ICT for education programs [34], teachers could also be in charge to monitor and adapt gamification design in gamified adaptive learning systems. In this sense, this paper proposes the *"gamification analytics model for teachers"* that can be applied in gamified adaptive learning systems to allow teachers to adapt the gamified design during learning process based on monitoring of data that show students' relevant information about their interaction with the system's learning resources and gamification elements in an intuitive and meaningful way, aiming to increase the chances in obtaining positive results related to students' motivation, engagement, and learning outcomes.

To implement this model as support for a gamified learning system, it is of utmost importance that the model-based design concepts are well designed concerning the needs of the teachers, and the target audience of the model. In this paper, we use the "Speed Dating method" – a design method for rapidly exploring application concepts and their interactions and contextual dimensions without requiring any technology implementation [6, 17] – aiming to validate the design concepts related to the Gamification Analytics Model for Teachers that we are targeting.

The remainder of this paper is structured as follows. In Sect. 2, we describe the Gamification Analytics model. In Sect. 3, we depict the Speed Dating method planning and execution. In Sect. 4, we describe the results obtained after the Speed Dating method execution. Finally, in Sect. 5, we present the discussion, concluding remarks and future works.

2   Gamification Analytics Model for Teachers

The "Gamification Analytics Model for Teachers" was developed to increase the chance of obtaining positive results concerning students' engagement, learning outcome, and motivation during the learning process in gamified adaptive learning systems. In this model, teachers can define interaction goals, monitor students' interaction with the system's learning resources and gamification elements, and adapt the gamification design through the use of missions to motivate disengaged students to achieve the defined goals. Therefore, this is the main goal of the "Gamification Analytics Model for Teachers", which is shown in Fig. 1. In the following sections, we describe this model.

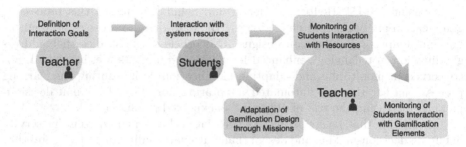

Fig. 1. Gamification Analytics Model for Teachers.

2.1   Model Components

Definition of Interaction Goals. In the Gamification literature, it is stated the importance of defining clear goals and measuring the success of gamification design towards their achievement [14,18,35]. As such, in the model presented in this paper, teachers may define interaction goals that they expect students to achieve in a given time. The interaction goals represent the number/percentage of interactions that are expected students to have with the educational resources (e.g., videos, texts, questionnaires, forums, and so on) available in the system related to a certain topic in a specific time. Therefore, the interaction goals can be represented by two elements for each topic (quantity of resources, time expected). For example, one interaction goal configured by a teacher could be: expect that students interact with at least 70% of the learning resources available in the gamified learning system related to a topic in 2 weeks.

Monitoring of Students Interaction with Resources. In the Gamification Analytics Model for Teachers, teachers are allowed to visualize students'interaction with learning resources and compare the if students' interactions occur according to the interaction goals defined by the teacher. The interaction goals previously define may serve as a metric for teachers to monitor students' learning process, since they can assess if students are at the expected pace towards the defined goal. To better present these important data for teachers, it is necessary to rely on research in Information Visualisation and Learning Dashboards. The positive effects of Information Visualisation and Learning Dashboards on teachers' decision-making processes in the technology-enhanced learning context have been reported in several studies in the literature [21,22,25,36].

Monitoring of Students Interaction with Gamification Elements. There are different objectives in showing students' interaction with gamification elements to the teachers. First, teachers can visualise students' interactions with the gamification elements implemented in the system in order to understand students' engagement with these elements, increasing teachers awareness about students' status (e.g., how many points each student accumulated so far, students' ranking and current level). Moreover, this monitoring could increase the chance of teachers perceiving the positive impact of gamification, and hence, motivating themselves towards the use of gamification. Furthermore, the adaptation of the gamification design during the learning process is performed by using the gamification element mission, thus, it is necessary that teachers can visualise which missions are more effective to motivate the students. Through these visualisations, teachers could see which missions were most successful, and assign missions properly along the learning process. This concept is based on the theoretical model of user requirements for supporting the monitoring and adaptation of gamification designs proposed by Heilbrunn, Herzig and Schill [14]. However, there is a lack of studies that explore the visualisation by teachers of students' interaction with gamification elements in the technology-enhanced learning context.

Adaptation of Gamification Design Through Missions. As previously explained, the adaptation of gamification design in educational systems can be made by teachers through the gamification element mission, e.g. when students' interaction is decreasing over time and students are not achieving the interaction goal defined by the teacher. In previous studies, missions have been also effectively used to motivate students during the learning process [25,26]. Therefore, we propose the usage of missions to adapt gamification design during the learning process because when teachers perceive students' interactions are not as expected, they can assign missions in order to motivate students to increase interaction with the educational resources available in the system. Hence, the gamification design of other gamification elements will also be adapted because when students achieve a mission, they also conquer points, badges, levels, and change their position on the leaderboard.

3   Method

To explore the wide range of feature possibilities with users, the speed dating method based on the HCI (Human-Computer Interaction) research is designed to help researchers/designers draw unmet needs and probe the boundaries of what certain users will find acceptable (initially unknown until after a technology prototype) [16,37]. The method begins with sessions in which participants receive hypothetical scenarios in rapid succession (for example, through storyboards) while researchers observe and understand participants' immediate reactions [6,23,37]. The Speed Dating method leads to the discovery of unexpected design opportunities when unforeseen needs are found, based on participants' assessment of the given scenario. Note that the Speed Dating method can reveal needs and opportunities not easily discovered through field observations or other project activities [6,8,23,37]. The method consists of two main stages - validation and user approval. In the validation step, researchers present to the target users a variety of predefined storyboards to observe the needs that users demonstrate [6,33]. Storyboards select innovation spaces and use this information to narrow the design space for the potential product. Therefore, researchers create an array of critical design problems and write short dramatic scenarios that address the permutations of these problems. As such, participants must play a specific role that they play regularly (as a teacher) while running through scenarios in a simulation [4,6,33].

3.1 Validation Through Speed Dating Method

As the gamification analytics model for teachers is a new contribution, it is still an open question on how to design gamified educational systems implementing this model. Therefore, it is of utmost importance that model-based design concepts are well designed to respect the needs of the teachers. Hence, the "Speed Dating method" was used to validate the design concepts of this model. As the target audience of the model are teachers, we recruited 15 teachers (14 post-secondary teachers and 1 secondary education teacher, all living in Alagoas, Brazil) to participate in individual sessions, through emails or requests made personally. The duration of the sessions with each teacher ranged from 30 to 60 min and 14 were performed at the university and 1 through video conference (with the help of meet.google.com).

At the beginning of each session, teachers attended a presentation made by one of the researchers, where teachers were presented with a contextualization of learning systems, gamification, and their challenges. Afterward, the "gamification analytics model for teachers" was presented. Moreover, to put all teachers on the same page regarding their understanding of gamified educational environments, a gamified educational platform (https://avance.eyeduc.com/) and its functionalities were introduced, clarifying doubts that appeared from teachers about educational environments and gamification. Therefore, it was possible to equalize the knowledge level of all teachers, thus they could formulate a more concrete opinion on the subject in the evaluation of the concepts embedded in the storyboards.

The session participants were introduced to design concepts based on the model proposed through storyboards. Teachers had time to read, reflect, and analyze each concept presented. At this time, teachers were encouraged to talk about their immediate reactions to the concept presented. Hence, the teachers evaluated the concept and classified it into three grades: grade 1 (if the teacher thought the concept would be relevant for him to use in a gamified educational environment), grade −1 (if the teacher thought the concept would not be relevant for him to use in a gamified educational environment) and grade 0 (if the teacher could not decide whether or not the concept would be relevant to him). These grades are based on the work by [17].

The first design concepts presented to teachers were developed by the author of the model. However, teachers could at any time suggest new ideas for the formulation of new concepts based on their needs. When a teacher suggested a new concept, the researchers created a new storyboard related to the concept and that storyboard would be included in the set shown to the next participant. After debating and evaluating a concept, the next concept was presented, extending that method until the last concept in the set. During this process, two supporting researchers were responsible for recording teachers' opinions, ideas, and grades for each concept for future analysis.

This research was initialized with 13 initial concepts, which were increased after the suggestion of new concepts by the teachers, resulting in a maximum of 20 concepts until the end of the research. After conducting the analysis, a table was created with the average teacher evaluation for each concept presented and recorded opinions of each teacher. The information given by each teacher will be further analyzed, so researchers can define what will be developed or adjusted in future gamified learning platforms.

4   Results

As previously explained, 20 (twenty) design concepts based on the gamification analytics model were evaluated by teachers to understand their needs in gamified adaptive learning systems. These concepts are related to the visualizations they judge most applicable to monitor students' interaction with resources and students' interaction with gamification elements, as well as the most appropriate procedures for adapting gamification design when they consider necessary. In this section, we discuss the most five well-rated design concepts in Sect. 4.1 and the most three poorly rated design concepts in Sect. 4.2. The list of all design concepts and their correspondent storyboards explored in this work can be visualized in the following site: sites.google.com.

The quantitative evaluation made by teachers about each design concept is shown in Fig. 2. The columns in this figure represent the teachers who participated in the research (listed in order of participation), and the rows represent the design concepts. The last seven design concepts listed in the figure were generated by the participants. The cells in red indicate that the teacher evaluated negatively the correspondent concept while the cells in yellow indicate that the teacher was neutral about the corresponding concept. Moreover, the cells in green show that the teacher rated positively the correspondent design concept. The overall average rating of the design concepts among teachers is listed in the

Concepts	T1	T2	T3	T4	T5	T6	T7	T8	T9	T10	T11	T12	T13	T14	T15	Average
Concept 1	1	1	1	1	1	1	-1	1	1	1	1	1	1	1	-1	0,7333333333
Concept 2	1	1	1	0	1	-1	0	-1	1	1	1	1	1	1	1	0,6
Concept 3	1	1	1	1	1	1	1	1	1	0	1	1	1	1	1	0,9333333333
Concept 4	1	1	0	1	-1	0	1	1	0	1	1	1	1	1	1	0,6666666667
Concept 5	1	1	1	1	1	1	-1	1	1	-1	1	0	0	1	1	0,6
Concept 6	1	1	0	1	0	1	0	1	-1	-1	1	0	-1	1	-1	0,2
Concept 7	1	1	1	1	-1	1	-1	-1	1	1	1	1	1	1	1	0,6
Concept 8	1	1	1	1	0	1	1	1	1	1	1	1	1	1	1	0,9333333333
Concept 9	1	-1	1	1	1	1	1	1	1	1	1	1	1	1	1	0,8666666667
Concept 10	1	1	0	1	1	0	1	1	1	-1	1	1	0	1	1	0,6666666667
Concept 11	1	1	1	1	1	0	1	0	1	1	1	1	1	1	1	0,8666666667
Concept 12	1	1	1	0	1	0	0	1	1	1	1	1	1	1	1	0,8
Concept 13	1	1	1	1	1	1	1	1	1	1	1	1	1	1	1	1
Concept 14		1	1	1	1	1	1	1	1	-1	1	0	1	1	1	0,7857142857
Concept 15		1	1	1	1	0	1	1	0	-1	1	1	0	1	1	0,6428571429
Concept 16		1	1	1	0	1	-1	1	-1	-1	-1	0	0	1	1	0,2142857143
Concept 17			1	1	-1	1	1	1	1	1	1	1	1	1	1	0,8333333333
Concept 18				1	1	0	1	0	0	1	1	1	1	1	1	0,75
Concept 19					-1	-1	-1	1	1	-1	1	1	1	1	1	0,2727272727
Concept 20					1	1	-1	-1	1	1	1	1	1	1	1	0,6363636364

Fig. 2. Validation results and average (Color figure online)

rightmost column. The average grade was calculated considering the sum of the grades the teachers assigned to the design concept divided by the number of teachers who evaluated the following design concept.

4.1   Most Well-Rated Design Concepts

Concept 3: *Visualization of the percentage of the students that reached inter-action goals (Average: 0,9333333333).*

The vast majority of participants reported that this concept is fundamental to understand the progress of the class, enabling the teacher to intervene and make a decision regarding these results (T1, T2, T4, T9, T15) since the purpose of the concept is to provide a visualization in the system showing how many of the students have already reached the interaction goals defined by the teacher. As pointed out by teacher T9, "This visualization is important for a quick overview of the class as we would know if we can move on to the next topic, or continue in the topic and intervene in the process to motivate students to achieve the goals".

Concept 8: *Visualization of each student's interaction with the resources (Average: 0,9333333333).*

From the opinions captured in the sessions regarding this concept, we understand the need for the teacher to obtain a detailed view of each student, not just the class, and visualize their interaction with each available resource in the system (T2, T9, T15). Therefore, this concept enables the teacher to visualize the interaction of each student with each resource added in the activity plan of each topic. However, some teachers reported that for classes with a small number of students this concept would be ideal, but for large classes would be impracticable.

Concept 9: Creation of personalized missions for a student or for a specific group (Average: 0,8666666667).

In this concept, we investigate the need for the teacher to have the autonomy to intervene/adapt the system when students or a specific student are not achieving an expected goal. A mission, in the teachers' view, makes it possible to motivate students to interact with the system resources and motivate the achievement of interaction goals (T1, T3, T6, T13). Some teachers believe that missions might have a more positive impact if they involve rewards that impact students' grades (T1, T6). In addition, one teacher reported, "The teacher could monitor groups by levels and could select from the most advanced group to assist the less advanced students as well, being possible to create a mission with this suggestion" (T2). By analyzing other points of view, we obtained negative opinions regarding the offering of rewards (such as trophy, points) to students who achieve a mission. As reported by teacher T15, the reward would be the learning.

Concept 11: Show the status of each mission created (Average: 0,8666666667).

This concept was considered relevant by most of the teachers who participated in the sessions. For teachers, once missions are created, it is important for them to be able to view the results of each mission they create, such as the number of students who successfully completed the mission, the number of students who tried but did not achieve the mission, and the students who have not tried. Teachers believe this visualization becomes interesting for teacher monitoring and evaluation of which assignments have the most positive impact on students (T12) and whether they are positively impacting students' level of interaction with resources (T9). In a teacher's opinion, with this concept, he can measure the difficulty of the mission, whether it is difficult, easy, or moderate. It also has the possibility to look for students who failed the mission to know the reasons for the failure (T1).

Concept 13: Help button provided for each visualization describing its functionality (Average: 1).

This concept was the most well-rated among the teachers who participated in the sessions. For teachers, the support of the system through help buttons describing the functionality of the graphics is important especially at the beginning of the teacher's interaction with the system when the teacher is not familiar with the system (T14, T11, T3). In addition, this functionality increases the possibility of joining users with few technological experiences (T1, T9).

4.2 Most Poorly Rated Design Concepts

Concept 6: Visualization of the number of students who achieved each trophy (Average: 0,2).

Some teachers see the possibility of taking advantage of this concept, given that the trophies obtained by the students correspond to the achievements and facilities in the use of the system, "can be used to compare the evolution of the class through the trophies" (T2) and "interesting to analyze the motivation or difficulty of the class with the trophies" (T4). However, the concept was poorly evaluated by most teachers, because according to teachers T3, T5, T9, T10, T13, T14, this functionality would not affect the methodology applied by the teacher. As pointed out by professor T10, "This kind of visualization would be most useful for designers or teachers with full control of course authorship, but apart from this use it can be a problem than a solution."

Concept 16: *Visualization of each student's interaction with the trophies (Average: 0,2142857143).*

The purpose of this concept is to visualize each student's trophy achievements. However, teachers show doubts regarding the achievement of trophies and their relationship with student performance, "I do not find the viewing of trophies per student as relevant", teacher (T11). However, the teacher T3 affirms the relevance of this concept, "being a way to track students' performance".

Concept 19: *Visualization of student's descriptive data (Average: 0,2727272727).*

The availability of student descriptive data (interaction with resources, trophies, missions completed) for teachers in a textual way was poorly rated due to the teachers' remarkable preference for visualizing data through graphs. For teacher T10, "presentation as the text may be a detriment to the teacher, a sensory noise."

5   Discussion, Conclusion and Future Works

In this article, we introduced the "Gamification Analytics Model for Teachers", a model that can be implemented in gamified adaptive learning systems to decrease the chances to obtain negatives outcomes concerning students' engagement and motivation. In this model, teachers are allowed to define interaction goals, monitor students' interaction with the system' resources and gamification elements, and adapt the gamification design when they judge necessary through the use of missions to motivate and engage students to achieve the interaction goals. Nonetheless, future gamified adaptive learning systems that adopt the "Gamification Analytics Model for Teachers" need to implement model-based design concepts in the system that corresponds to teachers' needs. Therefore, to validate these design concepts, in this paper, we used the "Speed Dating" method to understand teachers' needs in gamified adaptive learning systems. We present the most well-rated design concepts and most poorly rated design concepts related to the "Gamification Analytics Model for Teachers". In general, most of the 20 design concepts evaluated by the participant teachers were well accepted and judged useful.

The most well-rated concept is the concept 13 (Help button provided for each visualization describing its functionality), teachers pointed out that this functionality is mainly important at the beginning of teachers' interaction with the system, supporting and facilitating the understanding of the visualizations provided in the gamified adaptive learning systems. Other highly well-rated concept designs were the concepts 3 (Visualization of the percentage of the students that reached interaction goals) and 8 (Visualization of each student interaction with the resources). Note that there was a high acceptance rate for both more general, class level visualizations (such as concepts 2, 3, 5, 7, 11), and the more specific, more individually focused visualizations (such as concepts 8, 14, 15, 17). The first type of visualization helps teachers because it is a very compact and straightforward visualization while the second type helps teachers to act in isolated cases in the underperforming students, as stated by teacher T3.

Furthermore, the most poorly rated design concept was the concept 6 (Visualization of the number of students who achieved each trophy), followed by concept 16 (Visualization of each student's interaction with the trophies) and concept 19 (Visualization of student descriptive data). Therefore, it could be observed that the visualization of the interaction of students with the trophies available in the gamified learning system was not judged important and relevant by the teachers. However, the students' interactions with other gamification elements such as missions and levels (concepts 5, 11, 14, 15) were well-rated design concepts. Consequently, although teachers did not evaluate the visualization of the interaction of students with the trophies relevant, teachers judged useful/relevant visualize students' interaction with other gamification elements (missions, levels) to help them understand the students' status. Teachers have also demonstrated that visualizing students' data through graphs is more relevant for them than visualizing students' data through descriptive data in a textual way. During the speed dating process, some teachers highlighted how better is to visualize students' data through graphs. For example, teacher T9 stated that visualize students' interaction through descriptive data could be relevant, but visualize through graphs is more enjoyable and useful. Teachers T2 and T6 concluded that both visualizations could be relevant, but they should not be shown together, but by demand, at different levels.

This article presents some limitations such as the participants' recruitment, 93% of the participants are post-secondary teachers, implying a threat to external validity. Another limitation faced in this article is related to the subjectivity of the storytellings where the design concepts were presented for teachers, which may have caused different interpretations depending on the participating teacher. However, we tried to soften this limitation through explanations and clarifying doubts during the speed dating method conduction. Our future work includes the validation of a prototype to be developed based on the most well-rated design concepts validated by teachers regarding teachers' perceptions of perceived usefulness, perceived ease of use, behavioral intention, relevance, and perceived enjoyment. Afterward, a controlled experiment will be held in a real scenario within a gamified educational system platform based on the validated prototype to evaluate the effectiveness of the use of gamification analytics model by teachers on students' learning outcomes, motivation, and engagement.

References

1. Andrade, F.R.H., Mizoguchi, R., Isotani, S.: The bright and dark sides of gamification. In: Micarelli, A., Stamper, J., Panourgia, K. (eds.) ITS 2016. LNCS, vol. 9684, pp. 176–186. Springer, Cham (2016). https://doi.org/10.1007/978-3-319-39583-8_17

2. Baker, R.S.: Stupid tutoring systems, intelligent humans. Int. J. Artif. Intell. Educ. **26**(2), 600–614 (2016). https://doi.org/10.1007/s40593-016-0105-0

3. Borras-Gene, O., Martinez-Nunez, M., Blanco, A.: New challenges for the motivation and learning in engineering education using gamification in MOOC. Int. J. Eng. Educ. **32**(1), 501–512 (2016)

4. Buchenau, M., Suri, J.F.: Experience prototyping. In: Proceedings of the Conference on Designing Interactive Systems Processes Practices Methods and Techniques, DIS 2000, pp. 424–433. Association for Computing Machinery, New York (2000). https://doi.org/10.1145/347642.347802

5. Cukurova, M., Kent, C., Luckin, R.: Artificial intelligence and multimodal data in the service of human decision-making: a case study in debate tutoring. Br. J. Educ. Technol. **50**(6), 3032–3046 (2019). https://doi.org/10.1111/bjet.12829

6. Davidoff, S., Lee, M.K., Dey, A.K., Zimmerman, J.: Rapidly exploring application design through speed dating. In: Krumm, J., Abowd, G.D., Seneviratne, A., Strang, T. (eds.) UbiComp 2007. LNCS, vol. 4717, pp. 429–446. Springer, Heidelberg (2007). https://doi.org/10.1007/978-3-540-74853-3_25

7. Dermeval, D., et al.: An ontology-driven software product line architecture for developing gamified intelligent tutoring systems. Int. J. Knowl. Learn. **12**(1), 27–48 (2017). https://doi.org/10.1504/IJKL.2017.10009129

8. Dillahunt, T.R., Lam, J., Lu, A., Wheeler, E.: Designing future employment applications for underserved job seekers: a speed dating study. In: Proceedings of the 2018 Designing Interactive Systems Conference, DIS 2018, pp. 33–44. Association for Computing Machinery Inc., New York (2018). https://doi.org/10.1145/3196709.3196770

9. Domínguez, A., Saenz-de Navarrete, J., de Marcos, L., Fernández-Sanz, L., Pagés, C., Martínez-Herráiz, J.J.: Gamifying learning experiences: practical implications and outcomes. Comput. Educ. **63**(1), 380–392 (2013). https://doi.org/10.1016/j.compedu.2012.12.020

10. González González, C., Toledo, P., Muñoz, V.: Enhancing the engagement of intelligent tutorial systems through personalization of gamification. Int. J. Eng. Educ. **32**(1), 532–541 (2016)

11. Hamari, J., Koivisto, J., Sarsa, H.: Does Gamification Work? - a literature review of empirical studies on gamification. In: 2014 47th Hawaii International Conference on System Sciences, pp. 3025–3034. IEEE, Waikoloa (2014). https://doi.org/10.1109/HICSS.2014.377

12. Hanus, M.D., Fox, J.: Assessing the effects of gamification in the classroom: a longitudinal study on intrinsic motivation, social comparison, satisfaction, effort, and academic performance. Comput. Educ. **80**, 152–161 (2015). https://doi.org/10.1016/j.compedu.2014.08.019

13. Heilbrunn, B., Herzig, P., Schill, A.: Tools for gamification analytics: a survey. In: 2014 IEEE/ACM 7th International Conference on Utility and Cloud Computing. pp. 603–608. IEEE, London (2014). https://doi.org/10.1109/UCC.2014.93

14. Heilbrunn, B., Herzig, P., Schill, A.: Towards gamification analytics-requirements for monitoring and adapting gamification designs. In: Plödereder, E., Grunske, L., Schneider, E., Ull, D. (eds.) 44. Jahrestagung der Gesellschaft für Informatik, Informatik 2014, Big Data - Komplexität meistern, Stuttgart, Deutschland, 22–26 September 2014. LNI, vol. P-232, pp. 333–344. GI, Jahrestagung (2014). https://dl.gi.de/20.500.12116/2924

15. Heilbrunn, B., Herzig, P., Schill, A.: Gamification analytics—methods and tools for monitoring and adapting gamification designs. In: Stieglitz, S., Lattemann, C., Robra-Bissantz, S., Zarnekow, R., Brockmann, T. (eds.) Gamification. PI, pp. 31–47. Springer, Cham (2017). https://doi.org/10.1007/978-3-319-45557-0_3

16. Holstein, K., McLaren, B.M., Aleven, V.: Intelligent tutors as teachers' aides: exploring teacher needs for real-time analytics in blended classrooms. In: Proceedings of the Seventh International Learning Analytics & Knowledge Conference, LAK 2017, pp. 257–266. Association for Computing Machinery, New York (2017). https://doi.org/10.1145/3027385.3027451

17. Holstein, K., McLaren, B.M., Aleven, V.: Designing for complementarity: teacher and student needs for orchestration support in AI-enhanced classrooms. In: Isotani, S., Millán, E., Ogan, A., Hastings, P., McLaren, B., Luckin, R. (eds.) AIED 2019. LNCS (LNAI), vol. 11625, pp. 157–171. Springer, Cham (2019). https://doi.org/10.1007/978-3-030-23204-7_14

18. Huang, B., Hew, K.F.: Implementing a theory-driven gamification model in higher education flipped courses: effects on out-of-class activity completion and quality of artifacts. Comput. Educ. **125**, 254–272 (2018). https://doi.org/10.1016/j.compedu.2018.06.018

19. Kapp, K.M.: The Gamification of Learning and Instruction: Game-Based Methods and Strategies for Training and Education, 1st edn. Pfeiffer & Company, San Francisco (2012). https://doi.org/10.4018/jgcms.2012100106

20. Latulipe, C., Long, N.B., Seminario, C.E.: Structuring flipped classes with lightweight teams and gamification. In: Proceedings of the 46th ACM Technical Symposium on Computer Science Education, SIGCSE 2015, pp. 392–397. Association for Computing Machinery, New York (2015). http://doi.acm.org/10.1145/2676723.2677240

21. van Leeuwen, A.: Learning analytics to support teachers during synchronous CSCL: balancing between overview and overload. J. Learn. Anal. **2**(2), 138–162 (2015). https://doi.org/10.18608/jla.2015.22.11

22. Molenaar, I., Knoop-van Campen, C.: Teacher dashboards in practice: usage and impact. In: Lavoué, É., Drachsler, H., Verbert, K., Broisin, J., Pérez-Sanagustín, M. (eds.) EC-TEL 2017. LNCS, vol. 10474, pp. 125–138. Springer, Cham (2017). https://doi.org/10.1007/978-3-319-66610-5_10

23. Odom, W., Zimmerman, J., Davidoff, S., Forlizzi, J., Dey, A.K., Lee, M.K.: A fieldwork of the future with user enactments. In: Proceedings of the Designing Interactive Systems Conference, DIS 2012, pp. 338–347. Association for Computing Machinery, New York (2012). https://doi.org/10.1145/2317956.2318008

24. Ortiz, M., Chiluiza, K., Valcke, M.: Gamification in higher education and STEM: a systematic review of literature. In: 8th Annual International Conference on Education and New Learning Technologies, pp. 6548–6558. IATED, Barcelona (2016). https://doi.org/10.21125/edulearn.2016.0422

25. Paiva, R., Bittencourt, I.I.: The authoring of pedagogical decisions informed by data, on the perspective of a MOOC. In: Anais dos Workshops do VI Congresso Brasileiro de Informática na Educação (CBIE 2017), p. 10. Brazilian Computer Society (Sociedade Brasileira de Computação - SBC), Recife (2017). https://doi.org/10.5753/cbie.wcbie.2017.15

26. Paiva, R., Bittencourt, I.I., Tenrio, T., Jaques, P., Isotani, S.: What do students do on-line? Modeling students' interactions to improve their learning experience. Comput. Hum. Behav. **64**, 769–781 (2016). https://doi.org/10.1016/j.chb.2016.07.048

27. Paiva, R.O.A., Bittencourt, I.I., da Silva, A.P., Isotani, S., Jaques, P.: Improving pedagogical recommendations by classifying students according to their interactional behavior in a gamified learning environment. In: Proceedings of the 30th Annual ACM Symposium on Applied Computing, SAC 2015, pp. 233–238. Association for Computing Machinery, New York (2015). https://doi.org/10.1145/2695664.2695874

28. Shi, L., Cristea, A.I.: Motivational gamification strategies rooted in self-determination theory for social adaptive e-learning. In: Micarelli, A., Stamper, J., Panourgia, K. (eds.) ITS 2016. LNCS, vol. 9684, pp. 294–300. Springer, Cham (2016). https://doi.org/10.1007/978-3-319-39583-8_32

29. Snow, E.L., Allen, L.K., Jackson, G.T., McNamara, D.S.: Spendency: students' propensity to use system currency. Int. J. Artif. Intell. Educ. **25**(3), 407–427 (2015). https://doi.org/10.1007/s40593-015-0044-1

30. Subhash, S., Cudney, E.A.: Gamified learning in higher education: a systematic review of the literature. Comput. Hum. Behav. **87**, 192–206 (2018). https://doi.org/10.1016/j.chb.2018.05.028

31. Tenorio, T., Bittencourt, I.I., Isotani, S., Pedro, A., Ospina, P.: A gamified peer assessment model for on-line learning environments in a competitive context. Comput. Hum. Behav. **64**, 247–263 (2016). https://doi.org/10.1016/j.chb.2016.06.049

32. Trinidad, M., Calderón, A., Ruiz, M.: A systematic literature review on the gamification monitoring phase: how SPI standards can contribute to gamification maturity. In: Stamelos, I., O'Connor, R.V., Rout, T., Dorling, A. (eds.) SPICE 2018. CCIS, vol. 918, pp. 31–44. Springer, Cham (2018). https://doi.org/10.1007/978-3-030-00623-5_3

33. Truong, K.N., Hayes, G.R., Abowd, G.D.: Storyboarding: an empirical determination of best practices and effective guidelines. In: Proceedings of the 6th Conference on Designing Interactive Systems, DIS 2006, p. 12. Association for Computing Machinery, New York (2006). https://doi.org/10.1145/1142405.1142410

34. UNICEF: Raising Learning Outcomes: the opportunities and challenges of ICT for learning. Technical report (2018)

35. Werbach, K., Hunter, D.: For the Win: How Game Thinking Can Revolutionize Your Business. Wharton, Pennsylvania (2012)

36. Xhakaj, F., Aleven, V., McLaren, B.M.: Effects of a teacher dashboard for an intelligent tutoring system on teacher knowledge, lesson planning, lessons and student learning. In: Lavoué, É., Drachsler, H., Verbert, K., Broisin, J., Pérez-Sanagustín, M. (eds.) EC-TEL 2017. LNCS, vol. 10474, pp. 315–329. Springer, Cham (2017). https://doi.org/10.1007/978-3-319-66610-5_23

37. Zimmerman, J., Forlizzi, J.: Speed dating: providing a menu of possible futures. She Ji **3**(1), 30–50 (2017). https://doi.org/10.1016/j.sheji.2017.08.003

Far from Success – Far from Feedback Acceptance? The Influence of Game Performance on Young Students' Willingness to Accept Critical Constructive Feedback During Play

Eva-Maria Ternblad[✉] and Betty Tärning

Lund University, Box 117, 221 00 Lund, Sweden
Eva-Maria.Ternblad@lucs.lu.se

Abstract. In a learning situation, feedback is of great importance in order to help a student to correct a possible misconception. However, previous research shows that many students tend to avoid feedback regarding failures, including critical constructive feedback (CCF) that is intended to support and guide them. This is especially true for lower-achieving students, who might perceive feedback as an ego-threat, and therefore protect themselves by neglecting it. However, it has been shown that such neglect can be suppressed by using teachable agents (TA's). Another, but less studied factor that influences feedback acceptance is the degree or extent of failure when trying to solve a task. The present study explores if and how momentary performance levels influence middle school students' willingness to accept CCF when playing an educational game in history – with or without a TA. On the basis of teacher assessments of the students' general skills, data logs and analyses of sequential patterns, we concluded that the willingness to accept CCF differs between students, but also between conditions and situations. One major finding is that a TA supports the students to more readily embrace CCF, even if the effect is larger for lower-achieving students. Another finding is that indications of being far from succeeding, such as low success rates or repeated trials and revisions, have a negative impact on feedback acceptance, even if a TA mitigates some of this influence. The implications of these results are discussed in relation to meta-cognitive aspects of learning and to educational software design.

Keywords: Critical constructive feedback · Feedback neglect · Teachable agents · Lower-achieving students

1 Introduction

We know from previous studies that feedback can be an important factor for students' learning. It can provide the student with information and clues on how to proceed with a task, as well as work as a motivator, pushing the student further, into self-regulating activities and improvement [1–5].

© Springer Nature Switzerland AG 2020
I. I. Bittencourt et al. (Eds.): AIED 2020, LNAI 12163, pp. 537–548, 2020.
https://doi.org/10.1007/978-3-030-52237-7_43

Feedback on errors is especially important for students with low prior knowledge and students lacking appropriate learning strategies but must be balanced and well designed to not hinder learning [6]. Nevertheless, feedback aiming at scaffolding students to not only identify, but also to evaluate and correct errors through proper instructions, can have a significant effect on learning outcomes [4, 7]. In this text we refer to this type of feedback as *critical constructive feedback* (CCF). This feedback provides the learner with some type of assessment, pointing at the need for correction of the task, or part of task (hence critical). Further, the feedback scaffolds the learner towards improvement by providing informative hints or directions (hence constructive).

This said, for feedback to have an effect, not only does it have to be carefully formulated, it also needs to be adequately attended and responded to. And, unfortunately, the latter is not always the case.

1.1 The Problem with Feedback Neglect

Despite the beneficial learning effects of feedback in general – and CCF in particular – we also know that students neglect it to a great extent [8, 9]. In for example the study by Segedy and colleagues, the authors realized that approximately 77% of the CCF statements delivered in an educational science learning game were ignored by the students [9]. Further, in an eye-tracking study performed by Tärning et al., they found that as many as a third of the presented feedback texts in an educational history game were not even noticed [8].

The avoidance or neglect of feedback can be influenced by many factors. One is the feeling of personal failure. Critical constructive feedback indicates that the student has failed in one way or another and this might cause feelings of uneasiness [10]. CCF may also be seen as an evaluative punishment [3], and the tendency to avoid it is more frequent amongst lower-achieving students and students with low self-efficacy [11]. Not only are these individuals exposed to more negative critique due to repeated mistakes, they are also at risk for being convinced of their incapacity to succeed, whatever strategies they might apply [11].

Another factor influencing the effects of feedback is the learner's control over it. Traditionally, research on feedback has focused on situations where the feedback is provided to the learner – whether she asks for it or not [12, 13]. This is also the most common situation in an everyday classroom. When the student has no impact on the delivery of feedback, she is left with little control over her learning situation, something that often is ill correlated with motivation or other emotional states important for learning [14].

There are, however, some studies on students' control over feedback [15–17]. For example, Cutumisu and colleagues studied the effects of letting students choose between critical and confirmative feedback, provided to them in a game about graphical design principles [17]. Results showed that the students' game performance correlated significantly with both their tendency to choose critical feedback and their tendency to revise their tasks. Evidently, higher-achieving students not only have a stronger shield towards criticism than lower-achieving students, they also tend to seek this criticism voluntarily, presumably with an understanding of its importance for their own learning and development.

1.2 Protecting the Student's Ego by Using Teachable Agents

One way of addressing the problem with feedback neglect is to try to strengthen the student's ego, another one is to provide her with tools that helps her maintain attention to problems and tasks when failing. In an educational software context, both can be obtained by using a *Teachable Agent* (TA).

A TA is a type of agent based on the instructional approach of "learning by teaching" [10, 18, 19]. A student playing with a teachable agent takes the role of a teacher and hence learns for herself in order to later teach her TA. Learning on behalf of the TA has been shown to lead to a general increase in effort and motivation as well as to better learning and performance [10]. That is, having a protégé can make the student engage in behavior they otherwise might be prone to avoid, such as the up-take of critical-constructive feedback. In particular, the benefits of interacting with a TA are more pronounced for lower-achieving students [10, 20, 21]. The reasons are many, but one is that in this situation the student is positioned as the most capable, teaching someone less knowledgeable. Being in such a position can influence students positively since they view their own competence differently [22]. Lower-achieving students are less likely than higher-achieving students to take the role of a teacher in the classroom and hence, they have less experience of being the 'expert' on a subject. Consequently, such an experience is likely to be more beneficial for this group.

Another positive consequence of the TA is what is proposed by Chase and colleagues as the *ego-protective buffer*, indicating that the TA has protective qualities in that it shares the responsibilities of a possible failure with the student [10]. By letting the TA solve tasks or take tests and (perhaps) fail, the student is also transformed – from a more or less capable learner into a more or less capable teacher. And since students often treat the TA as an autonomous creature, they also – at least partially – tend to blame it for its own failures. Consequently, the ego protective buffer has also been suggested to decrease feedback neglect, since it is the TA that is being tested and hence receives critical constructive feedback and not the student [23].

1.3 Research Aims and Research Questions

Given the theoretical and empirical background presented above, studying students' inclination to accept or reject CCF during different conditions and situations, is of great interest. Working with digital educational tools gives us a unique opportunity to do so, since these conditions can be manipulated, while the students' behaviour may be evaluated in detail through data log analyses. To our knowledge, this kind of studies on feedback neglect are rare. Consequently, the study at hand focused on the probability of students accepting CCF when failing on tasks - to a larger or lesser extent. The CCF was provided to them in a teachable-agent based educational game, where the students, after receiving information about the success-rate on a task, were given an opportunity to accept or dismiss elaborations on errors and how to correct them. After this, the students were free to follow the instructions or not (see Sect. 2.1 below for a more detailed description of the game structure and experimental design). More specifically, our research questions were:

1) *When playing an educational game and failing on a certain task, does the students' momentary performance level have an impact on their inclination to accept CCF?*
2) *Does the introduction of a teachable agent influence the students' inclination to accept CCF?*
3) *Does the inclination to accept CCF differ between lower- and higher achieving students?*

2   Method

The work presented in this paper constitutes a post hoc analysis of data collected in a study performed in spring 2019 in the south of Sweden with 289 middle school children from 6 schools [23]. While the comprehensive study focused on aggregated data and general differences between conditions, this specific study utilized details in the data logs to find behavioral patterns and sequences related to the research questions. An overview of the original experimental setup, together with a description of the stimuli and a definition of the parameters relevant for this particular study is presented below.

2.1   The Educational Game

The material used in the study consists of an educational game in history, where the students visit historical scenes and persons, search for text-based information and solve tasks (on the format of a concept map, a timeline, a sorting task or a set of multiple-choice questions) (Fig. 1).

Fig. 1. (Left): An example dialogue from visiting Gutenberg and his apprentice (Right): Teaching activity where the student shows the TA "Timy" how to construct a timeline.

To be able to continue and progress in the game, the tasks (six in total) need to be completed one at a time. The students have unlimited attempts to revise the tasks, and may, if they want, revisit scenes to repeat facts or gather new information. After presenting a solution on a task, the students receive feedback in two parts: i) a general task assessment, and ii) CCF about errors together with suggestions about how to acquire useful information by revisiting relevant scenes. Depending on the level of correctness, the first part is formulated as follows:

- 100% correct (Passed): "The task is approved, everything is correct. Great work!"
- 100–80% correct (Passed): "Only some minor error. The task is approved. Great work!"
- 75–80% correct (Failed): "The major part is correct, great work!"
- 60–74% correct (Failed): "A fair amount is correct, not far to go now, great work!"
- 30–59% correct (Failed): "Some things are correct, but there is some way to go, so keep on working!"
- <30% correct (Failed): "A lot is missing or wrong, unfortunately. Keep on working!"

This verbal information is always provided, but without presenting the exact amount of errors. In other words, the student mainly receives a hint about the remaining effort necessary for success. The game can then be set to deliver the more constructive part of the feedback automatically (*automatic condition*), or to ask the student if he or she wants this information or not (*choice condition*). The subsequent CCF is structured in the following way: *"Some facts concerning Mrs X's relation to A and B are not correct. Travel back and speak to her, locate the item C on the shelf behind her and find out more."* After receiving the CCF-dialogue, which varies in phrasing and content depending on the errors made, the student can choose to act upon it, by revisiting historical places, or by simply revising the task by trying to make use of the information. The overall structure of the game is described in Fig. 2 below:

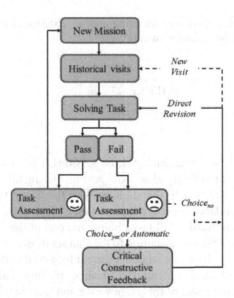

Fig. 2. Game structure with automatic or optional delivery of CCF. In the latter, the students are asked if they want the critical constructive feedback or not.

A central aspect of the game is the presence of a digital tutee, a *Teachable Agent (TA)*, whom the student is set to teach. Within a traditional learning context without a TA, the students perform tasks and tests 'themselves', and consequently they are also exposed to potential CCF. By contrast, in a setting *with* a TA it will be the agent that receives critical remarks on its performance, and not the student. Consequently, by configuring the game with and without the TA, we can evaluate its impact on the students' inclination to accept or neglect feedback.

2.2 Participants, Procedure and Instruments

Since this study focused on the inclination to voluntarily accept or dismiss CCF, the problem area only accounts for students in the choice condition. This left us with 121 students, 60 played in TA-condition and 61 in NoTA-condition. These were all equally distributed in all participating classes. Due to the game's consistently text-based content, the students' in-game performance is strongly related to their reading skills. Thus, prior to the study all teachers provided assessments (lower, mid, higher) of each student's reading proficiency. The ability to process text-based information also impacts a student's overall achievement in social science subjects. When conducting their first mission and solving their first task, it became clear that the performance levels for the 'mid-achievers' were diversified. Based on their effort in the first mission (put more accurately: the number of revisions necessary for solving the task), the students of this group were therefore allocated into either the higher- or the lower-achieving group. The final distribution of the students in different TA-conditions is shown in Table 1 below:

Table 1. Number of higher- and lower-achieving students in the used data set, assigned to the TA or the NoTA-condition (choice-condition only).

	TA	NoTA
Higher	27	29
Lower	33	32

Each class played the game during three sessions à 60 min (approximately one session per week) in their ordinary classroom setting. During this time, two researchers were present, not to directly help the students with the actual tasks but for technical support and general guidance and observation. Since all students were playing at their own pace, some of them finished all tasks before the end of third session, while others didn't finish many. The actual contribution to the data set from each student does thereby vary. In the introductory phase, the students were informed that they would be exposed to a post-test on the historical content after finishing playing. This test was distributed after the final session, the result of this is, however, not used in this study.

2.3 Defining Parameters, Categories and Hypotheses

The main research question addresses the student's willingness to attend to CCF in relation to game performance. It is hypothesized that the amount of failure and/or success during play influences the student's self-efficacy, her attitude towards trying and learning, or her general state-of-mind in a way that she either embraces more information about errors, or simply rejects it. To estimate the probability that a student accepts the CCF at a specific moment in the game, the following variables were used to formulate a logistic regression model with repeated measures and mixed effects:

Accepting offers of CCF: *CCFaccept (binary dependent variable)*. Classified as 1 if the student answered "yes" to the question *"Do you want to know more about the errors you have made?"*, and 0 if the student responded "no".

Teachable Agent Condition: *Agnt (categorical independent variable, fixed effects)*. Two conditions: TA and NoTA.

Student Achievement Level: *Achv (categorical independent variable, fixed effects)*. Two levels: Higher and Lower.

Task assessment category: *TaC (categorical independent variable, fixed effects)*. The primary measure for momentary game performance. For failed tasks, the assessment had four levels: Almost Correct (75–80%), Quite Correct (60–74%), Quite Wrong (30–59%) and Very Wrong (< 30%). See Sect. 2.1 above for verbal descriptions.

Number of previous trials on task: *Tnr (numerical independent variable, fixed effects)*. The second measure for game performance. Only the first six unsuccessful trials for each mission were included in the dataset. Students with only one single failed trial were eliminated. Hence, each student contributed with everything from 2 to 36 trials.

Proportion of pervious trials with accepted CCF's: *CCFp (numerical independent variable, fixed effects)*. A measure of possible "feedback fatigue" due to repeated feedback acceptance (%).

Student subject: *Id (categorical independent variable, randomized effects)*.

Interaction effects: The TA-condition was also hypothesized to generate interaction effects on the achievement level (*Achv*), the task assessment category (*TaC*) and on the number of previous trials (*Tnr*).

The following logistic model predicting CCF-acceptance was hypothesized:

$$\text{logit(CCFaccept)} = \beta 0 + \left[\frac{1}{Id} \right] + \beta 1 \text{Agnt} + \beta 2 \text{Achv} + \beta 3 \text{TaC} + \beta 4 \text{Tnr} + \beta 5 \text{CCFp}$$
$$+ \beta 6 \text{Agnt} : \text{Achv} + \beta 7 \text{Agnt} : \text{TaC} + \beta b \text{Agnt} : \text{Tnr}$$

3   Results

In general, the students' inclination to accept CCF was high. In total, 1316 task trials were evaluated, and 81% of these were followed by CCF-acceptance. The distribution of trials between groups and conditions (CCF-accepted or not) was the following (Table 2):

A mixed-effect binomial logistic regression model containing subject (*Id*) as random effect was fit to the data set in a step-wise-step up procedure. As postulated, the student achievement level (*Achv*) showed significant effect on the probability for feedback acceptance, revealing that higher-achieving students more often accept CCF than lower-achieving students. The general interaction effect between the TA and the achievement level was almost significant ($p = 0.055$) and had a moderate contribution to the

Table 2. Number of trials related to achievement levels in the TA or the NoTA-condition.

	TA	NoTA
H	295	327
L	354	340

model as a whole. However, as shown in Table 4, the TA had a significant positive impact on CCF-acceptance for lower-performing students, making them almost as keen as higher-achieving students to accept CCF. No other interaction effects were found.

With regard to in game performance, both the total number of previous trials (*Tnr*), and the task assessment category (*TaC*) were significant for the model, although the importance of the latter varied between categories, revealing significance only between 'Almost Correct' and 'Very Wrong'. The effect from the proportion of pervious trials with accepted CCF's (*CCFp*) was not significant. Hence, the main findings consist of a negative correlation between the number of previous trials (*Tnr*) and the willingness to accept CCF, and that a large amount of errors on a task (>70%) also influence CCF-acceptance in a negative manor. These effects are visualized in Figs. 3 and 4 below.

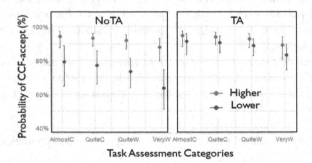

Fig. 3. Probability of CCF-acceptance in relation to TA-condition, achievement-levels and the task assessment category (Almost Correct, Quite Correct, Quite Wrong and Very Wrong).

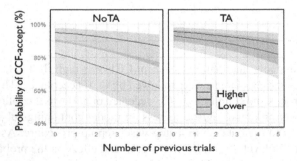

Fig. 4. Probability of CCF-acceptance in relation to TA-condition, achievement-levels and the number of previous trials on the same task (no 0–5).

The final minimal adequate model for *CCFaccept* performed significantly better than an intercept-only base line model ($\chi 2(8)$: 147.6, $p < .001$), and had a reasonable fit (C-value: 0.83, Somers Dxy: 0.65). See Tables 3 and 4 for more details and statistics.

Table 3. Summary of the final minimal adequate binomial logistic mixed-effects regression model fitted to predict CCF acceptance (*CCFaccept*).

Random effects		Variance		Std. dev.	
Id (*N = 121*)		0.77		0.88	
Fixed effects (*no of obs = 1316*)	Coeff.	OddsRatio	Std. err.	z-value	Pr(>|z|)
Intercept	2.98	19.30	0.42	7.10	<0.001 ***
Agnt[TA]	0.11	1.11	0.38	0.29	0.78 ns
Achv[Lower]	−1.42	0.25	0.33	−4.25	<0.001 ***
Agnt[TA]:Achv[Lower]	0.93	2.44	0.48	1.92	0.055.
Tnr	−0.22	0.79	0.05	−4.50	<0.001 ***
TaC[QuiteCorrect]	−0.11	0.87	0.37	−0.31	0.76 ns
TaC[QuiteWrong]	−0.31	0.74	0.34	−0.92	0.36 ns
TaC[VeryWrong]	−0.77	0.45	0.37	−2.11	0.03 *
Model statistics					Value
AIC					1147
C-value					0.83
Somers' Dxy					0.65
Likelihood ratio test	$\chi 2(8)$: 147.6, $p < .001$				

Table 4. Post-hoc analysis on the interaction effect between achievement level and TA-condition.

Linear hypothesis	Coeff.	Std. err.	z-value	Pr(> |z|)
Agnt[TA].Lower – Agnt[NoTA].Lower	1.04	0.31	3.39	0.001**
Agnt[TA].Higher – Agnt[NoTA].Higher	0.11	0.38	0.29	0.95 ns

4 Discussion

As expected, students with greater reading proficiency (in this study classified as higher-achieving students) were more inclined to accept CCF. This is hardly surprising since these students ought to be more capable of comprehending text (compared to students with lower reading skills) and therefore also should make use of the presented feedback with less effort and cognitive load.

Further, when looking at the amount of errors on a task, we saw how trials with few mistakes followed by the task assessment "The major part is correct, great work!" lead to a significantly higher probability to accept CCF than trials with many errors (followed by the formulation "A lot is missing or wrong, unfortunately. Keep on working!"). This finding is in line with previous research on feedback rejection and severe failing [11], as well as to studies on motivation and self-regulation within learning contexts [24, 25]. Additionally, research on gaming behavior reveals that gamers having 'near-wins' tend to stay highly motivated for continuing playing, even if their effort has nothing to do with the possibility to succeed – such as in using slot machines [26]. Evidently, the feeling of 'being on the right path, not far from success' is significantly more motivating and strengthening than being totally unsuccessful. It should be noted, however, that in this particular case, we do not know if it is the specific *formulation* of the CCF ("Unfortunately…") or its underlying *content* (many errors) that has an effect. It might very well be both – but that remains to be studied.

The more trials students had, the less probable it was that they accepted CCF when failing. This relates to the research mentioned above, in that repeated failure might wear the students out, convincing them of their incapacity to succeed, and that the feedback will not help them. By turning the number of previous trials to an independent numerical variable, the study is treated as an experiment with repeated measures, adding a random effect from each subject. Yet, when including this kind of order-effects, we cannot be sure of the exact reasons behind it. Perhaps the CCF accepted in earlier rounds was perceived as confusing or hard to understand, making the students negative towards it. Or perhaps a student at a later trial remembered CCF's from former trials and was trying to make use of these instead of accepting a new one.

Looking at the impact of the TA, the results are even more interesting. The group of students in TA-condition was more inclined to accept feedback compared to the group in NoTA-condition. This benefit was higher for the lower-achieving students, closing the gap between them and the higher-achieving students. Even though accepting feedback is not the same as reading it or understanding it, we know that it at least is better than neglecting it. This turns the TA into an interesting tool in educational software, not at least for empowering lower-achieving students to more easily embrace CCF and to try harder. Even though we didn't find any significant interaction effects between the TA and game performance, the diagram in Fig. 2 reveals a tendency for students without a TA to have steeper curves in relation to the number of previous trials than the students with a TA. It is quite possible that the students take a greater responsibility when teaching someone else as compared to themselves, which is in line with other research [10].

Finally, we know from research on meta-cognition, motivation and learning, that the student's knowledge monitoring has an impact on both learning outcomes and on self-regulating activities, such as spending time on delivered feedback [2]. That is, if a student is convinced that she has failed on a task, she is more reluctant to process and act on feedback messages. On the other hand, if the student thinks she has succeeded, and seeks confirmation, she is generally more receptive to negative feedback, which in this case comes as a surprise. Evidently, the importance of maintaining lower-achieving students' self-esteem, even if failing, can't be emphasized enough. Yet how feedback in educational software should be designed to deal with these matters is still not obvious and needs to be further investigated.

Acknowledgements. This research was funded by the Marianne and Marcus Wallenberg foundation. We gratefully acknowledge Agneta Gulz and Magnus Haake for help with this manuscript.

References

1. Kluger, A.N., DeNisi, A.: Feedback interventions: toward the understanding of a double-edged sword. Curr. Dir. Psychol. Sci. **7**(3), 67–72 (1998)
2. Mory, E.H.: Feedback research revisited. In: Jonassen, D.H. (ed.) Handbook of Research for Educational Communications and Technology, Mahwah, pp. 745–783 (2004)
3. Hattie, J., Timperley, H.: The power of feedback. Rev. Educ. Res. **77**(1), 81–112 (2007)
4. Shute, V.J.: Focus on formative feedback. Rev. Educ. Res. **78**(1), 153–189 (2008)
5. Van der Kleij, F.M., Feskens, R.C., Eggen, T.J.: Effects of feedback in a computer based learning environment on students' learning outcomes: a meta-analysis. Rev. Educ. Res. **85**(4), 475–511 (2015)
6. Fyfe, E.R., Rittle-Johnson, B.: Feedback both helps and hinders learning: the causal role of prior knowledge. J. Educ. Psychol. **108**(1), 82–97 (2015)
7. Black, P., Wiliam, D.: Assessment and classroom learning. Assess. Educ. Princ. Policy Pract. **5**(1), 7–74 (1998)
8. Tärning, B., Andersson, R., Månsson, K., Gulz, A., Haake, M.: Entering the black box of feedback: assessing feedback neglect in a digital educational game for elementary school students. J. Learn. Sci. (in press)
9. Segedy, J.R., Kinnebrew, J.S., Biswas, G.: Supporting student learning using conversational agents in a teachable agent environment. In: Proceedings of the 10th International Conference of the Learning Sciences, Sydney, Australia, pp. 251–255 (2012)
10. Chase, C.C., Chin, D.B., Oppezzo, M.A., Schwartz, D.L.: Teachable agents and the protégé effect: increasing the effort towards learning. J. Sci. Educ. Technol. **18**(4), 334–352 (2009)
11. Kluger, A.N., DeNisi, A.: The effects of feedback interventions on performance: a historical review, a meta-analysis, and a preliminary feedback intervention theory. Psychol. Bull. **119**(2), 254–284 (1996)
12. Evans, C.: Making sense of assessment feedback in higher education. Rev. Educ. Res. **83**(1), 70–120 (2013)
13. Geitz, G., Joosten-Ten Brinke, D., Kirschner, P.A.: Sustainable feedback: students' and tutors' perceptions. Qual. Rep. **21**(11), 2103–2123 (2016)
14. Barton, C.: How I Wish I Had Taught Maths, 1st edn. Learning Sciences International, West Palm Beach (2019)
15. D'Mello, S., Olney, A., Williams, C., Hays, P.: Gaze tutor: a gaze-reactive intelligent tutoring system. Int. J. Hum. Comput. Stud. **70**(5), 377–398 (2012)
16. Aleven, V., Roll, I., McLaren, B., Koedinger, K.R.: Help helps, but only so much: research on help seeking with intelligent tutoring systems. Int. J. Artif. Intell. Educ. **26**(1), 205–223 (2016)
17. Cutumisu, M., Blair, K.P., Chin, D.B., Schwartz, D.L.: Posterlet: a game-based assessment of children's choices to seek feedback and to revise. J. Learn. Anal. **2**(1), 49–71 (2015)
18. Bargh, J.A., Schul, Y.: On the cognitive benefits of teaching. J. Educ. Psychol. **72**(5), 593–604 (1980)

19. Blair, K., Schwartz, D., Biswas, G., Leelawong, K.: Pedagogical agents for learning by teaching: teachable agents. Educ. Technol. Sci. **47**(1), 56–64 (2007)
20. Sjödén, B., Tärning, B., Pareto, L., Gulz, A.: Transferring teaching to testing – an unexplored aspect of teachable agents. In: Biswas, G., Bull, S., Kay, J., Mitrovic, A. (eds.) AIED 2011. LNCS (LNAI), vol. 6738, pp. 337–344. Springer, Heidelberg (2011). https://doi.org/10.1007/978-3-642-21869-9_44
21. Pareto, L., Schwartz, D.L., Svensson, L.: Learning by guiding a teachable agent to play an educational game. In: Proceedings of the 14th International Conference on Artificial Intelligence in Education, Brighton, UK, pp. 662–664 (2009)
22. Riggio, R.E., Fantuzzo, J.W., Connelly, S., Dimeff, L.A.: Reciprocal peer tutoring: a classroom strategy for promoting academic and social integration in undergraduate students. J. Soc. Behav. Pers. **6**(2), 387–396 (1991)
23. Gulz, A., Silvervarg, A., Haake, M., Wolf, R., Blair, K.P.: How teachable agents influence students' responses to critical constructive feedback. J. Res. Technol. Educ. (under revision)
24. Zimmerman, B.J., Cleary, T.J.: Motives to self-regulate learning: a social cognitive account. In: Wentzel, K., Wigfield, K. (eds.) Handbook of Motivation at School, pp. 247–264. Routledge, New York (2009)
25. Fong, C.J., Patall, E.A., Vasquez, A.C., et al.: A meta-analysis of negative feedback on intrinsic motivation. Educ. Psychol. Rev. **31**, 121–162 (2019)
26. Clark, L., Lawrence, A.J., Jones, F.A., et al.: Gambling near-misses enhance motivation to gamble and recruit win-related brain circuitry. Neuron **61**(3), 481–490 (2009)

Robust Neural Automated Essay Scoring Using Item Response Theory

Masaki Uto[✉] and Masashi Okano

The University of Electro-Communications, Tokyo, Japan
uto@ai.lab.uec.ac.jp

Abstract. Automated essay scoring (AES) is the task of automatically assigning scores to essays as an alternative to human grading. Conventional AES methods typically rely on manually tuned features, which are laborious to effectively develop. To obviate the need for feature engineering, many deep neural network (DNN)-based AES models have been proposed and have achieved state-of-the-art accuracy. DNN-AES models require training on a large dataset of graded essays. However, assigned grades in such datasets are known to be strongly biased due to effects of rater bias when grading is conducted by assigning a few raters in a rater set to each essay. Performance of DNN models rapidly drops when such biased data are used for model training. In the fields of educational and psychological measurement, item response theory (IRT) models that can estimate essay scores while considering effects of rater characteristics have recently been proposed. This study therefore proposes a new DNN-AES framework that integrates IRT models to deal with rater bias within training data. To our knowledge, this is a first attempt at addressing rating bias effects in training data, which is a crucial but overlooked problem.

Keywords: Deep neural networks · Item response theory · Automated essay scoring · Rater bias

1 Introduction

In various assessment fields, essay-writing tests have attracted much attention as a way to measure practical and higher-order abilities such as logical thinking, critical reasoning, and creative thinking [1,4,13,18,33,35]. In essay-writing tests, examinees write essays about a given topic, and human raters grade those essays based on a scoring rubric. However, grading can be an expensive and time-consuming process when there are many examinees [13,16]. In addition, human grading is not always sufficiently accurate even when a rubric is used because assigned scores depend strongly on rater characteristics such as strictness and inconsistency [9,11,15,26,31,43]. Automated essay scoring (AES), which utilizes natural language processing (NLP) and machine learning techniques to automatically grade essays, is one approach toward resolving this problem.

© Springer Nature Switzerland AG 2020
I. I. Bittencourt et al. (Eds.): AIED 2020, LNAI 12163, pp. 549–561, 2020.
https://doi.org/10.1007/978-3-030-52237-7_44

Many AES methods have been developed over the past decades, and can generally be classified as *feature-engineering* or *automatic feature extraction* approaches [13, 16].

The feature-engineering approach predicts scores using manually tuned features such as essay length and number of spelling errors (e.g., [3, 5, 22, 28]). Advantages of this approach include interpretability and explainability. However, these approaches generally require extensive feature redesigns to achieve high prediction accuracy.

To obviate the need for feature engineering, automatic feature extraction based on deep neural networks (DNNs) has recently attracted attention. Many DNN-AES models have been proposed in the last few years (e.g., [2, 6, 10, 14, 23, 24, 27, 37, 47]) and have achieved state-of-the-art accuracy. This approach requires a large dataset of essays graded by human raters as training data. Essay grading tasks are generally shared among many raters, assigning a few raters to each essay to lower assessment burdens. However, assigned scores are known to be strongly biased due to the effects of rater characteristics [8, 15, 26, 31, 34, 39, 40]. Performance of DNN models rapidly drops when biased data are used for model training, because the resulting model reflects bias effects [3, 12, 17]. This problem has been generally overlooked or ignored, but it is a significant issue affecting all AES methods using supervised machine learning models, including DNN, and because cost concerns make it generally difficult to remove rater bias in practical testing situations.

In the fields of educational and psychological measurement, statistical models for estimating essay scores while considering rater characteristic effects have recently been proposed. Specifically, they are formulated as item response theory (IRT) models that incorporate parameters representing rater characteristics [9, 29, 30, 38, 42–45]. Such models have been applied to various performance tests, including essay writing. Previous studies have reported that they can provide reliable scores by removing adverse effects of rater bias (e.g., [38, 39, 41, 42, 44]).

This study therefore proposes a new DNN-AES framework that integrates IRT models to deal with rater bias in training data. Specifically, we propose a two-stage architecture that stacks an IRT model over a conventional DNN-AES model. In our framework, the IRT model is first applied to raw rating data to estimate reliable scores that remove effects of rater bias. Then, the DNN-AES model is trained using the IRT-based scores. Since the IRT-based scores are theoretically free from rater bias, the DNN-AES model will not reflect bias effects. Our framework is simple and easily applied to various conventional AES models. Moreover, this framework is highly suited to educational contexts and to low- and medium-stakes tests, because preparing high-quality training data in such situations is generally difficult. To our knowledge, this study is a first attempt at mitigating rater bias effects in DNN-AES models.

2   Data

We assume the training dataset consists of essays written by J examinees and essay scores assigned by R raters. Let e_j be an essay by examinee $j \in \mathcal{J} =$

$\{1, \cdots, J\}$ and let U_{jr} represent a categorical score $k \in \mathcal{K} = \{1, \cdots, K\}$ assigned by rater $r \in \mathcal{R} = \{1, \cdots, R\}$ to e_j. The score data can then be defined as $U = \{U_{jr} \in \mathcal{K} \cup \{-1\} \mid j \in \mathcal{J}, r \in \mathcal{R}\}$, with $U_{jr} = -1$ denoting missing data. Missing data occur because only a few graders in $\mathcal{R}$ can practically grade each essay e_j to reduce assessment workload. Furthermore, letting $\mathcal{V} = \{1, \cdots, V\}$ be a vocabulary list for essay collection $E = \{e_j \mid j \in \mathcal{J}\}$, essay $e_j \in E$ is definable as a list of vocabulary words $e_j = \{w_{jt} \in \mathcal{V} \mid t = \{1, \cdots, N_j\}\}$, where w_{jt} is a one-hot representation of the t-th word in e_j, and N_j is the number of words in e_j. This study aimed at training DNN-AES models using this training data.

3   Neural Automated Essay Scoring Models

This section briefly introduces the DNN-AES models used in this study. Although many models have been proposed in the last few years, we apply the most popular model that uses convolution neural networks (CNN) with long short-term memory (LSTM) [2], and an advanced model based on bidirectional encoder representations from transformers (BERT) [7].

3.1   CNN-LSTM-Based Model

A CNN-LSTM-based model [2] proposed in 2016 was the first DNN-AES model. Figure 1(a) shows the model architecture. This model calculates a score for a given essay, which is defined as a sequence of one-hot word vectors, through the following multi-layered neural networks.

Lookup table layer: This layer transforms each word in a given essay into a D-dimensional word-embedding representation, in which words with the same meaning have similar representations. Specifically, letting A be a $D \times V$-dimensional embeddings matrix, the embedding representation corresponding to $w_{jt} \in e_j$ is calculable as the dot-product $A \cdot w_{jt}$.

Convolution layer: This layer extracts n-gram level features using CNN from the sequence of word embedding vectors. These features capture local textual dependencies among n-gram words. Zero padding is applied to outputs from this layer to preserve the word length. This is an optional layer, often omitted in current studies.

Recurrent layer: This layer is a LSTM network that outputs a vector at each timestep to capture long-distance dependencies of the words. A single-layer unidirectional LSTM is generally used, but bidirectional or multilayered LSTMs are also often used.

Pooling layer: This layer transforms outputs of the recurrent layer $\mathcal{H} = \{h_{j1}, h_{j2}, \cdots, h_{jN_j}\}$ into a fixed-length vector. Mean-over-time (MoT) pooling, which calculates an average vector $M_j = \frac{1}{N_j} \sum_{t=1}^{N_j} h_{jt}$, is generally used because it tends to provide stable accuracy. Other frequently used pooling methods include the last pool, which uses the last output of the recurrent layer h_{jN_j}, and a pooling-with-attention mechanism.

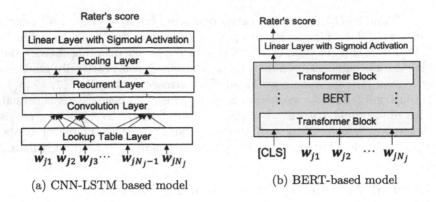

(a) CNN-LSTM based model

(b) BERT-based model

Fig. 1. Architectures of DNN-AES models.

Linear layer with sigmoid activation: This layer projects pooling-layer output to a scalar value in the range $[0, 1]$ by utilizing the sigmoid function as $\sigma(\boldsymbol{W}\boldsymbol{M}_j + b)$, where $\boldsymbol{W}$ is a weight matrix and b is a bias. Model training is conducted by normalizing gold-standard scores to $[0, 1]$, but the predicted scores are rescaled to the original score range in the prediction phase.

3.2 BERT-Based Model

BERT, a pretrained language model released by the Google AI Language team, has achieved state-of-the-art results in various NLP tasks [7]. BERT has been applied to AES [32] and automated short-answer grading (SAG) [19,21,36] since 2019, and provides good accuracy.

BERT is defined as a multilayer bidirectional transformer network [46]. Transformers are a neural network architecture designed to handle ordered sequences of data using an attention mechanism. Specifically, transformers consist of multiple layers (called *transformer blocks*), each containing a multi-head self-attention and a position-wise fully connected feed-forward network. See Ref. [46] for details of this architecture.

BERT is trained in *pretraining* and *fine-tuning* steps. Pretraining is conducted on huge amounts of unlabeled text data over two tasks, *masked language modeling* and *next-sentence prediction*, the former predicting the identities of words that have been masked out of the input text and the latter predicting whether two given sentences are adjacent.

Using BERT for a target NLP task, including AES, requires fine-tuning (retraining), which is conducted from a task-specific supervised dataset after initializing model parameters to pretrained values. When using BERT for AES, input essays require preprocessing, namely adding a special token ("CLS") to the beginning of each input. BERT output corresponding to this token is used as the aggregate sequence representation [7]. We can thus score an essay by inputting its representation to a *linear layer with sigmoid activation*, as illustrated in Fig. 1(b).

3.3   Problems in Model Training

Training of CNN-LSTM-based AES models and fine-tuning of BERT-based AES models are conducted using large datasets of essays by graded human raters. For model training, the mean-squared error (MSE) between predicted and gold-standard scores is used as the loss function. Specifically, letting y_j be the gold-standard score for essay e_j and letting $\hat{y}_j$ be the predicted score, the MSE loss function is defined as $\frac{1}{J}\sum_{j=1}^{J}(y_j - \hat{y}_j)^2$.

The gold-standard score y_j is a score for essay e_j assigned by a human rater in a set of raters $\mathcal{R}$. When multiple raters grade each essay, the gold-standard score should be determined by selecting one score or by calculating an average or total score. In any case, such scores depend strongly on rater characteristics, as discussed in Sect. 1. The accuracy of a DNN model drops when such biased data are used for model training, because the trained model inherits bias effects [3, 12, 17]. In educational and psychological measurement research, item response theory (IRT) models that can estimate essay scores while considering effects of rater characteristics have recently been proposed [9, 29, 30, 38, 42–44]. The main goal of this study is to train AES models using IRT-based unbiased scores. The next section introduces the IRT models.

4   Item Response Theory Models with Rater Parameters

IRT [20] is a test theory based on mathematical models. IRT represents the probability of an examinee response to a test item as a function of latent examinee ability and item characteristics such as difficulty and discrimination. IRT is widely used for educational testing because it offers many benefits. For example, IRT can estimate examinee ability considering effects of item characteristics. Also, the abilities of examinees responding to different test items can be measured on the same scale, and missing response data can be easily handled.

Traditional IRT models are applicable to two-way data (examinees × test items), consisting of examinee test item scores. For example, the generalized partial credit model (GPCM) [25], a representative polytomous IRT model, defines the probability that examinee j receives score k for test item i as

$$P_{ijk} = \frac{\exp \sum_{m=1}^{k} [\alpha_i(\theta_j - \beta_i - d_{im})]}{\sum_{l=1}^{K} \exp \sum_{m=1}^{l} [\alpha_i(\theta_j - \beta_i - d_{im})]}, \tag{1}$$

where θ_j is the latent ability of examinee j, α_i is a discrimination parameter for item i, β_i is a difficulty parameter for item i, and d_{ik} is a step difficulty parameter denoting difficulty of transition between scores $k-1$ and k in the item. Here, $d_{i1} = 0$, and $\sum_{k=2}^{K} d_{ik} = 0$ is given for model identification.

However, conventional GPCM ignores rater factors, so it is not applicable to rating data given by multiple raters as assumed in this study. Extension models that incorporate parameters representing rater characteristics have been proposed to resolve this difficulty [29,30,38,42–45]. This study introduces a state-of-the-art model [44,45] that is most robust for a large variety of raters. This model defines the probability that rater r assigns score k to examinee j's essay for a test item (e.g., an essay task) i as

$$P_{ijrk} = \frac{\exp \sum_{m=1}^{k} [\alpha_r \alpha_i (\theta_j - \beta_r - \beta_i - d_{rm})]}{\sum_{l=1}^{K} \exp \sum_{m=1}^{l} [\alpha_r \alpha_i (\theta_j - \beta_r - \beta_i - d_{rm})]}, \tag{2}$$

where α_r is the consistency of rater r, β_r is the strictness of rater r, and d_{rk} is the severity of rater r within category k. For model identification, we assume $\sum_{i=1}^{I} \log \alpha_i = 0$, $\sum_{i=1}^{I} \beta_i = 0$, $d_{r1} = 0$, and $\sum_{k=2}^{K} d_{rk} = 0$.

This study applies this IRT model to rating data U in training data. Note that DNN-AES models are trained for each essay task. Therefore, rating data U are defined as two-way data (examinees × raters). When the number of tasks is fixed to one in the model, the above model identification constraints make α_i and β_i ignorable, so Eq. (2) becomes

$$P_{jrk} = \frac{\exp \sum_{m=1}^{k} [\alpha_r (\theta_j - \beta_r - d_{rm})]}{\sum_{l=1}^{K} \exp \sum_{m=1}^{l} [\alpha_r (\theta_j - \beta_r - d_{rm})]}. \tag{3}$$

This equation is consistent with conventional GPCM, regarding use of item parameters as the rater parameters. Note that θ_j in Eq. (3) represents not only the ability of examinee j but also the latent unbiased scores for essay e_j, because only one essay is associated with each examinee. This model thus provides essay scores with rater bias effects removed.

5   Proposed Method

We propose a DNN-AES framework that uses IRT-based unbiased scores $\theta = \{\theta_j \mid j \in \mathcal{J}\}$ to deal with rater bias in training data.

Figure 2 shows the architectures of the proposed method. As that figure shows, the proposed method is defined by stacking an IRT model over a conventional DNN-AES model. Training of our models occurs in two steps:

1. Estimate the IRT scores θ from the rating data U.
2. Train AES models using the IRT scores θ as the gold-standard scores. Specifically, the MSE loss function for training is defined as $\frac{1}{J} \sum_{j=1}^{J} (\theta_j - \hat{\theta}_j)^2$, where $\hat{\theta}_j$ represents the AES's predicted score for essay e_j. Since scores θ are estimated while considering rater bias effects, a trained model will not reflect bias effects. Note that the gold-standard scores must be rescaled to the range $[0, 1]$ for training because sigmoid activation is used in the output layer. In IRT, 99.7% of θ_j fall within the range $[-3, 3]$ because a standard normal distribution is generally assumed. We therefore apply a linear transformation from the range $[-3, 3]$ to $[0, 1]$ after rounding the scores lower than -3 to -3, and those higher than 3 to 3.

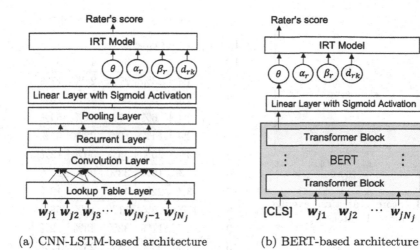

(a) CNN-LSTM-based architecture   (b) BERT-based architecture

Fig. 2. Proposed architectures.

Note that the increase in training time for the proposed method compared with a conventional method is the time for IRT parameter estimation.

In the testing phase, the score for new essay $e_{j'}$ is predicted in two steps:

1. Predict the IRT score $\theta_{j'}$ from a trained AES model, and rescale it to the range $[-3, 3]$.
2. Calculate the expected score $\hat{U}_{j'}$, which corresponds to an unbiased original-scaled score of $e_{j'}$ [39], as

$$\hat{U}_{j'} = \frac{1}{R} \sum_{r=1}^{R} \sum_{k=1}^{K} k \cdot P_{j'rk}. \tag{4}$$

6 Experiments

This section describes evaluation of the effectiveness of the proposed method through actual data experiments.

6.1 Actual Data

These experiments used the Automated Student Assessment Prize (ASAP) dataset, which is widely used as benchmark data in AES studies. This dataset consists of essays on eight topics, originally written by students from grades 7 to 10. There are 12,978 essays, averaging 1,622 essays per topic. However, this dataset cannot be directly used to evaluate the proposed method, because despite its essays having been graded by multiple raters, it contains no rater identifiers.

We therefore employed other raters and asked them to grade essays in the ASAP dataset. We used essay data for the fifth ASAP topic, because the number

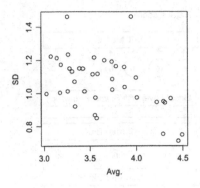

Fig. 3. Score statistics (average and SD) for each rater.

Table 1. Category usage rates.

Rater	Rating category				
ID	1	2	3	4	5
1	4%	23%	27%	28%	17%
2	4%	3%	36%	48%	10%
3	2%	6%	7%	32%	54%
4	2%	4%	10%	22%	62%
5	3%	20%	35%	30%	12%
6	6%	16%	33%	25%	21%
7	3%	22%	41%	23%	12%
8	12%	8%	11%	10%	58%
9	1%	11%	33%	43%	12%
10	9%	24%	28%	23%	17%

of essays in that topic is relatively large ($n = 1805$). We recruited 38 native English speakers as raters through Amazon Mechanical Turk and assigned four raters to each essay. Each rater graded around 195 essays. The assessment rubric used the same five rating categories as ASAP. Average Pearson's correlation between the collected rating scores and the original ASAP scores was 0.675.

To confirm any differences in rater characteristics, we plotted averaged score values and standard deviations (SD) for each rater, as shown in Fig. 3. In that figure, each plot represents a rater, and horizontal and vertical axes respectively show the average and SD values. In addition, Table 1 shows appearance rates in the five rating categories for 10 representative raters. The figure and table show extreme differences in grading characteristics among the raters, suggesting that consideration of rater bias is required.

6.2   Experimental Procedures

This subsection shows that the proposed method can provide more robust scores than can conventional AES models, even when the rater grading each essay in the training data changes. The experimental procedures, which are similar to those used in previous studies examining IRT scoring robustness [39–42], were as follows:

1. We estimated IRT parameters by the Markov chain Monte Carlo (MCMC) algorithm [30,42] using all rating data.
2. We created a dataset consisting of (essay, score) pairs by randomly selecting one score for each essay from among the scores assigned by multiple raters. We repeated this data generation 10 times. Hereafter, the m-th generated dataset is represented as $\boldsymbol{U}'_m$.
3. From each dataset $\boldsymbol{U}'_m$, we estimated IRT scores $\boldsymbol{\theta}$ (referred to as $\boldsymbol{\theta}_m$) given the rater parameters obtained in Step 1, and then created a dataset $\boldsymbol{U}''_m$ comprising essays and $\boldsymbol{\theta}_m$ values.

Table 2. Evaluations of prediction robustness.

	Kappa		Weighted Kappa		RMSE		Correlation	
	Prop.	Conv.	Prop.	Conv.	Prop.	Conv.	Prop.	Conv.
CNN+LSTM (MoT)	**0.749**	0.624	**0.778**	0.727	**0.191**	0.301	**0.937**	0.931
CNN+LSTM (Last)	**0.696**	0.459	**0.701**	0.551	**0.212**	0.400	**0.829**	0.783
LSTM (MoT)	**0.831**	0.697	**0.845**	0.779	**0.142**	0.237	**0.965**	0.958
LSTM (Last)	**0.612**	0.371	**0.624**	0.514	**0.300**	0.518	**0.804**	0.775
BERT	**0.790**	0.629	**0.808**	0.743	**0.159**	0.311	**0.960**	0.935

4. Using each dataset U_m'', we conducted five-fold cross validation to train AES models and to obtain predicted scores $\hat{\theta}_m$ for all essays.
5. We calculated metrics for agreement between the expected scores calculated by Eq. (4) given $\hat{\theta}_m$ and those calculated given $\hat{\theta}_{m'}$ for all unique $m, m' \in \{1, \cdots, 10\}$ pairs ($_{10}C_2 = 45$ pairs in total). As agreement metrics, we used Cohen's kappa, weighted kappa, root mean squared error (RMSE), and Pearson correlation coefficient.
6. We calculated average metric values obtained from the 45 pairs.

High kappa and correlation and low RMSE values obtained from the experiment indicate that score predictions are more robust for different raters.

We conducted a similar experiment using conventional DNN-AES models without the IRT model. Specifically, using each dataset U_m', we predicted essay scores from a DNN-AES model through five-fold cross validation procedures as in Step 4. We then calculated the four agreement metrics among the predicted scores obtained from different datasets U_m', and averaged them.

These experiments were conducted with several DNN-AES models. Specifically, we examined CNN-LSTM models using MoT pooling or last pooling, those models without a CNN layer, and the BERT model. These models were implemented in Python with the Keras library. For the BERT model, we used the *base*-sized pretrained model. The hyperparameters and dropout settings were determined following Refs. [2, 7, 46].

6.3 Experimental Results

Table 2 shows the results, which indicate that the proposed method sufficiently improves agreement metrics as compared to the conventional models in all cases. The results indicate that the proposed method provides stable scores when the rater allocation for each essay in training data is changed, thus demonstrating that it is highly robust against rater bias. Note that the values in Table 2 are not comparable with the results of previous AES studies because our experiment and previous experiments evaluated different aspects of AES performance.

In addition, as in previous AES studies, we evaluated score (θ) prediction accuracy of the proposed method through five-fold cross-validation. We mea-

Table 3. Prediction accuracy for IRT score θ by the proposed method

	MAE	RMSE	Correlation	R^2
CNN+LSTM (MoT)	0.431	0.546	0.719	0.499
CNN+LSTM (Last)	0.580	0.717	0.417	0.161
LSTM (MoT)	0.408	0.519	0.749	0.557
LSTM (Last)	0.509	0.640	0.584	0.340
BERT	0.400	0.511	0.763	0.562

sured accuracy using mean absolute error (MAE), RMSE, the correlation coefficient, and the coefficient of determination (R^2), because θ is a continuous variable. Table 3 shows the results, which indicate that the CNN-LSTM and LSTM models with MoT pooling achieved higher performance than did those with last pooling. The table also shows that the CNN did not effectively improve accuracy. These tendencies are consistent with a previous study [2]. In addition, the BERT provided the highest accuracy, which is also consistent with current NLP studies.

Tables 2 and 3 show that the score prediction robustness in Table 2 tends to increase with score prediction accuracy. This might be because scores in low-performance DNN-AES models are strongly biased not only by rater characteristics, but also by prediction errors arising from the model itself. With increasing accuracy of DNN-AES models, rater bias effects as a percentage of overall error increases, suggesting that the impact of the proposed method increases.

7   Conclusion

We showed that DNN-AES model performance strongly depends on the characteristics of raters grading essays in training data. To resolve this problem, we proposed a new DNN-AES framework that integrates IRT models. Specifically, we formulated our method as a two-stage architecture that stacks the IRT model over a conventional DNN-AES model. Through experiments using an actual dataset, we demonstrated that the proposed method can provide more robust essay scores than can conventional DNN-AES models. The proposed method is simple but powerful, and is easily applicable to any AES model. As described in the Introduction, our method is also highly suited to situations where high-quality training data are hard to prepare, including educational contexts.

In future studies, we expect to evaluate effectiveness of the proposed method using various datasets. Although this study mainly focused on robustness against rater bias, the proposed method might also improve prediction accuracy for each rater's score. In future studies, the accuracy should be evaluated. Our method is defined as a two-stage procedure for separately training IRT models and DNN-AES models. However, conducting end-to-end optimization would further improve the performance. This extension is another topic for future study.

Acknowledgment. This work was supported by JSPS KAKENHI 17H04726 and 17K20024.

References

1. Abosalem, Y.: Beyond translation: adapting a performance-task-based assessment of critical thinking ability for use in Rwanda. Int. J. Secondary Educ. **4**(1), 1–11 (2016)
2. Alikaniotis, D., Yannakoudakis, H., Rei, M.: Automatic text scoring using neural networks. In: Proceedings of the Annual Meeting of the Association for Computational Linguistics, pp. 715–725 (2016)
3. Amorim, E., Cançado, M., Veloso, A.: Automated essay scoring in the presence of biased ratings. In: Proceedings of the Annual Conference of the North American Chapter of the Association for Computational Linguistics, pp. 229–237 (2018)
4. Bernardin, H.J., Thomason, S., Buckley, M.R., Kane, J.S.: Rater rating-level bias and accuracy in performance appraisals: the impact of rater personality, performance management competence, and rater accountability. Hum. Resour. Manag. **55**(2), 321–340 (2016)
5. Dascalu, M., Westera, W., Ruseti, S., Trausan-Matu, S., Kurvers, H.: *ReaderBench* learns Dutch: building a comprehensive automated essay scoring system for Dutch language. In: André, E., Baker, R., Hu, X., Rodrigo, M.M.T., du Boulay, B. (eds.) AIED 2017. LNCS (LNAI), vol. 10331, pp. 52–63. Springer, Cham (2017). https://doi.org/10.1007/978-3-319-61425-0_5
6. Dasgupta, T., Naskar, A., Dey, L., Saha, R.: Augmenting textual qualitative features in deep convolution recurrent neural network for automatic essay scoring. In: Proceedings of the Workshop on Natural Language Processing Techniques for Educational Applications, Association for Computational Linguistics, pp. 93–102 (2018)
7. Devlin, J., Chang, M.W., Lee, K., Toutanova, K.: BERT: pre-training of deep bidirectional transformers for language understanding. In: Proceedings of the Annual Conference of the North American Chapter of the Association for Computational Linguistics: Human Language Technologies, pp. 4171–4186 (2019)
8. Eckes, T.: Examining rater effects in TestDaF writing and speaking performance assessments: a many-facet Rasch analysis. Lang. Assess. Q. **2**(3), 197–221 (2005)
9. Eckes, T.: Introduction to Many-Facet Rasch Measurement: Analyzing and Evaluating Rater-Mediated Assessments. Peter Lang Publication Inc., New York (2015)
10. Farag, Y., Yannakoudakis, H., Briscoe, T.: Neural automated essay scoring and coherence modeling for adversarially crafted input. In: Proceedings of the Annual Conference of the North American Chapter of the Association for Computational Linguistics, pp. 263–271 (2018)
11. Hua, C., Wind, S.A.: Exploring the psychometric properties of the mind-map scoring rubric. Behaviormetrika **46**(1), 73–99 (2018). https://doi.org/10.1007/s41237-018-0062-z
12. Huang, J., Qu, L., Jia, R., Zhao, B.: O2U-Net: a simple noisy label detection approach for deep neural networks. In: Proceedings of the IEEE International Conference on Computer Vision (2019)
13. Hussein, M.A., Hassan, H.A., Nassef, M.: Automated language essay scoring systems: a literature review. PeerJ Comput. Sci. **5**, e208 (2019)

14. Jin, C., He, B., Hui, K., Sun, L.: TDNN: a two-stage deep neural network for prompt-independent automated essay scoring. In: Proceedings of the Annual Meeting of the Association for Computational Linguistics, pp. 1088–1097 (2018)

15. Kassim, N.L.A.: Judging behaviour and rater errors: an application of the many-facet Rasch model. GEMA Online J. Lang. Stud. **11**(3), 179–197 (2011)

16. Ke, Z., Ng, V.: Automated essay scoring: a survey of the state of the art. In: Proceedings of the International Joint Conference on Artificial Intelligence, pp. 6300–6308 (2019)

17. Li, S., et al.: Coupled-view deep classifier learning from multiple noisy annotators. In: Proceedings of the Association for the Advancement of Artificial Intelligence (2020)

18. Liu, O.L., Frankel, L., Roohr, K.C.: Assessing critical thinking in higher education: current state and directions for next-generation assessment. ETS Res. Rep. Ser. **1**, 1–23 (2014)

19. Liu, T., Ding, W., Wang, Z., Tang, J., Huang, G.Y., Liu, Z.: Automatic short answer grading via multiway attention networks. In: Isotani, S., Millán, E., Ogan, A., Hastings, P., McLaren, B., Luckin, R. (eds.) AIED 2019. LNCS (LNAI), vol. 11626, pp. 169–173. Springer, Cham (2019). https://doi.org/10.1007/978-3-030-23207-8_32

20. Lord, F.: Applications of Item Response Theory to Practical Testing Problems. Erlbaum Associates, Mahwah (1980)

21. Lun, J., Zhu, J., Tang, Y., Yang, M.: Multiple data augmentation strategies for improving performance on automatic short answer scoring. In: Proceedings of the Association for the Advancement of Artificial Intelligence (2020)

22. Shermis, M.D., Burstein, J.C.: Automated Essay Scoring: A Cross-disciplinary Perspective. Taylor & Francis, Abingdon (2016)

23. Mesgar, M., Strube, M.: A neural local coherence model for text quality assessment. In: Proceedings of the Conference on Empirical Methods in Natural Language Processing, pp. 4328–4339 (2018)

24. Mim, F.S., Inoue, N., Reisert, P., Ouchi, H., Inui, K.: Unsupervised learning of discourse-aware text representation for essay scoring. In: Proceedings of the Annual Meeting of the Association for Computational Linguistics: Student Research Workshop, pp. 378–385 (2019)

25. Muraki, E.: A generalized partial credit model. In: van der Linden, W.J., Hambleton, R.K. (eds.) Handbook of Modern Item Response Theory, pp. 153–164. Springer, Heidelberg (1997). https://doi.org/10.1007/978-1-4757-2691-6_9

26. Myford, C.M., Wolfe, E.W.: Detecting and measuring rater effects using many-facet Rasch measurement: part I. J. Appl. Measur. **4**, 386–422 (2003)

27. Nadeem, F., Nguyen, H., Liu, Y., Ostendorf, M.: Automated essay scoring with discourse-aware neural models. In: Proceedings of the Workshop on Innovative Use of NLP for Building Educational Applications, Association for Computational Linguistics, pp. 484–493 (2019)

28. Nguyen, H.V., Litman, D.J.: Argument mining for improving the automated scoring of persuasive essays. In: Proceedings of the Association for the Advancement of Artificial Intelligence, pp. 5892–5899 (2018)

29. Patz, R.J., Junker, B.W., Johnson, M.S., Mariano, L.T.: The hierarchical rater model for rated test items and its application to large-scale educational assessment data. J. Educ. Behav. Stat. **27**(4), 341–384 (2002)

30. Patz, R.J., Junker, B.: Applications and extensions of MCMC in IRT: multiple item types, missing data, and rated responses. J. Educ. Behav. Stat. **24**(4), 342–366 (1999)

31. Rahman, A.A., Ahmad, J., Yasin, R.M., Hanafi, N.M.: Investigating central tendency in competency assessment of design electronic circuit: analysis using many facet Rasch measurement (MFRM). Int. J. Inf. Educ. Technol. **7**(7), 525–528 (2017)
32. Rodriguez, P.U., Jafari, A., Ormerod, C.M.: Language models and automated essay scoring. arXiv, cs.CL (2019)
33. Rosen, Y., Tager, M.: Making student thinking visible through a concept map in computer-based assessment of critical thinking. J. Educ. Comput. Res. **50**(2), 249–270 (2014)
34. Saal, F., Downey, R., Lahey, M.: Rating the ratings: assessing the psychometric quality of rating data. Psychol. Bull. **88**(2), 413–428 (1980)
35. Schendel, R., Tolmie, A.: Assessment techniques and students' higher-order thinking skills. Assess. Eval. High. Educ. **42**(5), 673–689 (2017)
36. Sung, C., Dhamecha, T.I., Mukhi, N.: Improving short answer grading using transformer-based pre-training. In: Isotani, S., Millán, E., Ogan, A., Hastings, P., McLaren, B., Luckin, R. (eds.) AIED 2019. LNCS (LNAI), vol. 11625, pp. 469–481. Springer, Cham (2019). https://doi.org/10.1007/978-3-030-23204-7_39
37. Taghipour, K., Ng, H.T.: A neural approach to automated essay scoring. In: Proceedings of the Conference on Empirical Methods in Natural Language Processing, pp. 1882–1891 (2016)
38. Ueno, M., Okamoto, T.: Item response theory for peer assessment. In: Proceedings of the IEEE International Conference on Advanced Learning Technologies, pp. 554–558 (2008)
39. Uto, M.: Rater-effect IRT model integrating supervised LDA for accurate measurement of essay writing ability. In: Isotani, S., Millán, E., Ogan, A., Hastings, P., McLaren, B., Luckin, R. (eds.) AIED 2019. LNCS (LNAI), vol. 11625, pp. 494–506. Springer, Cham (2019). https://doi.org/10.1007/978-3-030-23204-7_41
40. Uto, M., Thien, N.D., Ueno, M.: Group optimization to maximize peer assessment accuracy using item response theory. In: André, E., Baker, R., Hu, X., Rodrigo, M.M.T., du Boulay, B. (eds.) AIED 2017. LNCS (LNAI), vol. 10331, pp. 393–405. Springer, Cham (2017). https://doi.org/10.1007/978-3-319-61425-0_33
41. Uto, M., Duc Thien, N., Ueno, M.: Group optimization to maximize peer assessment accuracy using item response theory and integer programming. IEEE Trans. Learn. Technol. **13**(1), 91–106 (2020)
42. Uto, M., Ueno, M.: Item response theory for peer assessment. IEEE Trans. Learn. Technol. **9**(2), 157–170 (2016)
43. Uto, M., Ueno, M.: Empirical comparison of item response theory models with rater's parameters. Heliyon **4**(5), 1–32 (2018). Elsevier
44. Uto, M., Ueno, M.: Item response theory without restriction of equal interval scale for rater's score. In: Penstein Rosé, C., et al. (eds.) AIED 2018. LNCS (LNAI), vol. 10948, pp. 363–368. Springer, Cham (2018). https://doi.org/10.1007/978-3-319-93846-2_68
45. Uto, M., Ueno, M.: A generalized many-facet Rasch model and its Bayesian estimation using Hamiltonian Monte Carlo. Behaviormetrika **47**, 1–28 (2020). https://doi.org/10.1007/s41237-020-00115-7
46. Vaswani, A., et al.: Attention is all you need. In: Proceedings of the International Conference on Advances in Neural Information Processing Systems, pp. 5998–6008 (2017)
47. Wang, Y., Wei, Z., Zhou, Y., Huang, X.: Automatic essay scoring incorporating rating schema via reinforcement learning. In: Proceedings of the Conference on Empirical Methods in Natural Language Processing, pp. 791–797 (2018)

Supporting Teacher Assessment in Chinese Language Learning Using Textual and Tonal Features

Ashvini Varatharaj[1(✉)], Anthony F. Botelho[1], Xiwen Lu[2],
and Neil T. Heffernan[1]

[1] Worcester Polytechnic Institute, WPI, Worcester, MA 01609, USA
{avaratharaj,abotelho,nth}@wpi.edu
[2] Brandeis University, 415 South Street, Waltham, MA 02453, USA
xiwenlu@brandeis.edu

Abstract. Assessment in the context of foreign language learning can be difficult and time-consuming for instructors. Distinctive from other domains, language learning often requires teachers to assess each student's ability to speak the language, making this process even more time-consuming in large classrooms which are particularly common in post-secondary settings; considering that language instructors often assess students through assignments requiring recorded audio, a lack of tools to support such teachers makes providing individual feedback even more challenging. In this work, we seek to explore the development of tools to automatically assess audio responses within a college-level Chinese language-learning course. We build a model designed to grade student audio assignments with the purpose of incorporating such a model into tools focused on helping both teachers and students in real classrooms. Building upon our prior work which explored features extracted from audio, the goal of this work is to explore additional features derived from tone and speech recognition models to help assess students on two outcomes commonly observed in language learning classes: fluency and accuracy of speech. In addition to the exploration of features, this work explores the application of Siamese deep learning models for this assessment task. We find that models utilizing tonal features exhibit higher predictive performance of student fluency while text-based features derived from speech recognition models exhibit higher predictive performance of student accuracy of speech.

Keywords: Audio processing · Natural language processing · Language learning

1 Introduction

When learning a new language, it is important to be able to assess proficiency in skills pertaining to both reading and speaking; this is true for instructors but also for students to understand where improvement is needed. The ability

© Springer Nature Switzerland AG 2020
I. I. Bittencourt et al. (Eds.): AIED 2020, LNAI 12163, pp. 562–573, 2020.
https://doi.org/10.1007/978-3-030-52237-7_45

to read requires an ability to identify the characters and words correctly, while successful speech requires correct pronunciation and, in many languages, correctness of tone. For these reasons, read-aloud tasks, where students are required to speak while following a given reading prompt, are considered an integral part of any Standardized language testing system for the syntactic, semantic, and phonological understanding that is required to perform the task well [1–3].

This aspect of learning a second language is particularly important in the context of learning Mandarin Chinese. Given that Chinese (Mandarin Chinese) is a tonal language, the way the words are pronounced could change the entire meaning of the sentence, highlighting the importance of assessing student speech (through recordings or otherwise) an important aspect of understanding a student's proficiency in the language.

While a notable amount of research has been conducted in the area of automating grading of read-aloud tasks by a number of organizations (cf. the Educational Testing Service's (ETS) and Test of English as a Foreign Language (TOEFL)), the majority of assessment of student reading and speech is not taking place in standardized testing centers, but rather in classrooms. It is therefore here, in these classroom settings, that better tools are needed to support both teachers and students in these assessment tasks. In the current classroom paradigm, it is not unreasonable to estimate that the teacher takes hours to listen to the recorded audios and grade them; a class of 20 students providing audio recordings of just 3 min each, for example, requires an hour for the teacher to listen, and this does not include the necessary time to provide feedback to students.

This work observes student data collected from a college-level Chinese language learning course. We use data collected in form of recorded student audio from reading assignments with the goal of developing models to better support teachers and students in assessing proficiency in both fluency, a measure of the coherence of speech, and accuracy, a measure of lexical correctness. We present a set of analyses to compare models built with audio, textual, and tonal features derived from openly available speech-to-text tools to predict both fluency and accuracy grades provided by a Chinese language instructor.

2   Related Work

There has been little work done on developing tools to support the automatic assessment of speaking skills in a classroom setting, particularly in foreign language courses. However, a number of approaches have been applied in studying audio assessment in non-classroom contexts. Pronunciation instruction through computer-assistance tools has received attention by several of the standardized language testing organizations including ETS, SRI, and Pearson [4] in the context of such standardized tests; much of this work is similarly focused on English as a second language learners.

In developing models that are able to assess fluency and accuracy of speech from audio, it is vital for such models to utilize the right set of representative features. Previous work conducted in the area of Chinese language learning, of which this work is building upon, explored a number of commonly-applied features of audio including spectral features, audio frequency statistics, as well as others [5]. Other works have previously explored the similarity and differences between aspects of speech. In [6], phonetic distance, based on the similarity of sounds within words, has been used to analyse non-native English learners. Work has also been done on analysing different phonetic distances used to analyse speech recognition of vocabulary and grammar optimization [7].

Many approaches having been explored in such works, starting from Hidden Markov Models [8] to more recently applying deep learning methods [6] to predict scores assessing speaking skills. Others have utilized speech recognition techniques for audio assessment. There have been a number of prior works that have focused on the grading of read-aloud and writing tasks using Automatic Speech Recognition using interactive Spoken Dialogue Systems (SDS) [9], phonetic segmentation [10,11], as well as classification [12] and regression tree (CART) based methodologies [8,13]. Some speech recognition systems have used language-specific attributes, such as tonal features, to improve their model performances [14,15]. Since tones are an important component of pronunciation in Chinese language learning, we also consider the use of tonal features in this work for the task of predicting teacher-provided scores.

As there has been seemingly more research conducted in the area of natural language processing, such an approach as to convert the spoken audio to text is plausibly useful in understanding the weak points of the speaker. Recent works have combined automatic speech recognition with natural language processing to build grading models for English Language [16]. In applications of natural language processing, the use of pre-trained word embeddings has become more common due to the large corpuses of data on which they were trained. Pre-trained models of word2vec [17] and Global Vectors for Word Representation (GloVe) [18], for example, have been widely cited in applications of natural language processing. By training on large datasets, these embeddings are believed to capture meaningful syntactic and semantic relationships between words through meaning. Similar to these methods, FastText [19] is a library created by Facebook's AI Research lab which provides pre-trained word embeddings for Chinese language.

Similarly, openly available speech-generation tools may be useful in assessing student speech. For example, Google has supplied an interface to allow for text-to-speech generation that we will utilize later in this work. Though this tool is not equivalent to a native Chinese-speaking person, such a tool may be useful in helping to compare speech across students. The use of this method will be discussed further in Sect. 4.5.

3 Dataset

The data set used in this work was obtained from an undergraduate Chinese Language class taught to non-native speakers. The data was collected from multiple classes with the same instructor. The data is comprised of assignments requiring students to submit an audio recording of them reading aloud a pre-determined prompt as well as answering open-ended questions. For this work, we focus only on the read-aloud part of the assignment, observing the audio recordings in conjunction with the provided text prompt of the assignment.

For the read-aloud part of the assignment, students were presented with 4 tasks which were meant to be read out loud and recorded by the student and submitted through the course's learning management system. Each task consists of one or two sentences about general topics. The instructor downloaded such audio files, listened to each, and assessed students based on two separate grades pertaining to fluency and accuracy of the spoken text. Each of these grades are represented as a continuous-valued measure between 0–5; decimal values are allowed such that a grade of 2.5 is the equivalent of a grade of 50% on a particular outcome measure. This dataset contains 304 audio files from 128 distinct students over four distinct sentence read-aloud tasks. Each audio is taken as a separate data point, so each student has one to four audio files. Each sample includes one of the tasks read by the student along with the intended text of the reading prompt.

4   Feature Extraction

4.1   Pre-processing

The audio files submitted by students were of varying formats including mp3, m4a. The ffmpeg [20] python library is used to convert these audio inputs into a raw .wav format required by the speech models.

While prior work [5] explored much of this process of processing and extracting features from audio, the current work intends to expand upon this prior work by additionally introducing textual and tonal features into our grading model. The next two sections detail the feature extraction process for audio, tonal. and textual features using the processed dataset.

4.2   Audio Features

Audio feature extraction is required to obtain components of the audio signal which can be used to represent acoustic characteristics in a way a model can understand. The audio files are converted to vectors which can capture the various properties of the audio data recorded. The audio features were extracted using an openly-available python library [21] that breaks each recording into 50 millisecond clips, offsetting each clip by 25 milliseconds of the start of the preceding clip (creating a sliding window to generate aggregated temporal features using the observed frequencies of the audio wave). A total of 34 audio-based features, including Mel-frequency cepstral coefficients (MFCC), Chroma features, and Energy related features, were generated as in previous work [5].

4.3 Text Features

From the audio data, we also generate a character-representation of the interpreted audio file using openly-available speech recognition tools. The goal of this
feature extraction step is to use speech recognition to transcribe the words spoken by each student to text that can be compared to the corresponding reading
prompt using natural language processing techniques; the intuition here is that
the closeness of what the Google speech-to-text model is able to interpret to
the actual prompt should be an indication of how well the given text was spoken. Since building speech recognition models is not the goal of this paper, we
used an off-the-shelf module for this task. Specifically, the SpeechRecognition
library [22] in python provides a coding interface to the Google Web Speech
API and also supports several languages including Mandarin Chinese. The API
is built using deep-learning models and allows text transcription in real-time,
promoting its usage for deployment in classroom settings. While, to the authors'
knowledge, there is no detailed documentation describing the precise training
procedure for Google's speech recognition model, it is presumably a deep learning model trained on a sizeable dataset; it is this later aspect, the presumably
large number of training samples, that we believe may prove some benefit to our
application. Given that we have a relatively small dataset, the use of pre-trained
models such as those supplied openly through Google, may be able to provide
additional predictive power to models utilizing such features.

We segment the Google-transcribed text into character-level components and
then convert them into numeric vector representations for use in the models. We
use Facebook's FastText [19] library for this embedding task (c.f. Section 2).
Each character or word is represented in the form of a 300 dimensional numeric
vector space representation. The embedding process results in a character level
representation, but what is needed is a representation of the entire sentence. As
such, once the embeddings are applied, all characters are concatenated together
to form a large vector representing the entire sentence.

The Google Speech to text API is reported to exhibit a mean Word Error
Rate (WER) of 9% [23]. To analyse the performance of Google's Speech to Text
API on our dataset of student recordings, we randomly selected 15 student audio
files from our dataset across all the four reading tasks and then transcribed them
using the open tool. We then created a survey that was answered by the Teacher
and 2 Teaching Assistants of the observed Chinese language class. The survey
first required the participants to listen to each audio and then asked each to rate
the accuracy of the corresponding transcribed text on a 10-point integer scale.
The Intraclass Correlation Coefficient (ICC) was used to measure the strength
of inter-rater agreement, finding a correlation of 0.8 (c.f. ICC(2,k) [24]). While
this small study illustrates that the Google API exhibits some degree of error,
we argue that it is reliable enough to be used for comparison in this work.

4.4 Tonal Features

Chinese is a tonal language. The same syllable can be pronounced with different
tones which, in turn, changes the meaning of the content. To aid in our goal

of predicting the teacher-supplied scores of fluency and accuracy, we decided to explore the observance of tonal features in our models. In the Mandarin Chinese language, there are four main tones. These tones represent changes of inflection (i.e. rising, falling, or leveling) when pronouncing each syllable of a word or phrase. When asking Chinese Language teachers what are some of the features they look for while assessing student speech, tonal accuracy was one of the important characteristics identified.

To extract the tones from the student's audio, we use the ToneNet [25] model which was trained on the Syllable Corpus of Standard Chinese Dataset (SCSC). The SCSC dataset consists of 1,275 monosyllabic Chinese characters, which are composed of 15 pronunciations of young men, totaling 19,125 example pronunciations of about 0.5 to 1 second in duration. The model uses a mel spectrogram (image respresentation of an audio in the mel scale) of each of these samples to train the model. The model uses a convolutional neural network and multi-layer perceptron to classify Chinese syllables in the form on images into one of the four tones. This model is reported to have an accuracy of 99.16% and f1-score of 99.11% [25]. To use the ToneNet on our student audio data, we first break the student audio into 1 second audio clips and convert them into mel spectrograms. We then feed these generated mel spectrograms to the ToneNet model to predict the tone present in each clip. The sequence of predicted tones is then used as features in our fluency and accuracy prediction models.

4.5   True Audio: Google Text to Speech API

As a final source of features for comparison in this work, we believed it may be useful to compare each student audio to that of an accepted "correct" pronunciation; however, no such recordings were present in our data, nor are they common to have in classroom settings for a given read-aloud prompt. Given that we have audio data from students, and the text of each corresponding prompt, we wanted to utilise Google's text-to-speech to produce a "true audio" - how Google would read the given sentence. While not quite ground truth, given that it is trained on large datasets, we believe it could help our models learn certain differentiating characteristics of student speech by providing a common point of comparison. The features extracted from the true audio is particularly useful in training Siamese networks, as described in the next section, by providing a reasonable audio recording with which to compare each student response.

5   Models

In developing models to assess students based on the measures of accuracy and fluency, we compare three models of varying complexities and architectures (and one baseline model) using different feature sets described in the previous sections. Our baseline model consists of assigning the mean of the scores as the predicted value. We use a 5-fold cross validation for all model training (Fig. 1).

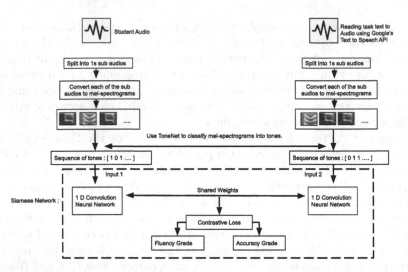

Fig. 1. The figure shows the steps involved in transforming audio to sequence of tones and feeding into the Siamese network

Aside from the baseline model, the first and second models explored in this work are the same as applied in previous research in developing models for assessing student accuracy and fluency in Chinese language learning [5]. These models consist of a decision tree (Using the CART algorithm [26]) and a Long Short Term Memory (LSTM) recurrent neural network. While previous work explored the use of audio features, labeled in this work as "PyAudio" features after the library used to generate them, this work is able to compare these additional textual and tonal feature sets. Similar to deep learning models, the decision tree model is able to learn non-linear relationships in the data, but also can be restricted in its complexity to avoid potential problems of overfitting. Conversely, the LSTM is able to learn temporal relationships from time series data as in the audio recordings observed in this work. As in our prior research, a small amount of hyperparameter tuning was conducted on a subset of the data.

In addition to the three sets of features described, a fourth feature set, a cosine similarity measure, was explored in the decision tree model. This was calculated by taking the cosine similarity between the embedded student responses and the embedded reading prompts. This feature set was included as an alternative approach to the features described in Sect. 4.5 for use in the Siamese network described in the next section.

5.1   Siamese Network

The last type of model explored in this paper is a Siamese neural network. Siamese networks are able to learn representations and relationships in data by comparing similar examples. For instance, we have the audio of the student as well as the Google-generated "true audio" that can be compared to learn features that may be useful in identifying how differences correlate with assigned fluency and accuracy scores. In this regard, the generated audio does not need to be correct to be useful; they can help in understanding how the student audio recordings differ from each other and how these differences relate to scores.

The network is comprised of two identical sub networks that share the same weights while working on two different inputs in tandem (e.g. the network observes the student audio data at the same time that it observes the generated audio data). The last layers of the two networks are fed into a contrastive loss function which calculates the similarity between the two audio recordings to predict the grades.

We experimented with different base networks within the Siamese architecture including a dense network, an LSTM and 1D Convolution Neural Network(CNN). There has been prior research showing the benefits of using CNNs on sequential data [27,28]. We wanted to explore their performance on our data. We report the results for 1D CNN in this work.

5.2 Multi-task Learning and Ensembling

Following the development of the decision tree, LSTM, and Siamese network models, we selected the two highest performing models across fluency and accuracy and ensembled their predictions using a simple regression model. As will be discussed in the next section, two Siamese network models (one observing textual features and the other the tonal feature set) exhibited the highest performance and were used in this process.

Our final comparison explores the usage of multitask learning [29] for the Siamese network. In this type of model, the weights of the network are optimized to predict both fluency and accuracy of speech simultaneously within a single model. Such a model may be able to take advantage of correlations between the labels to better learn distinctions between the assessment scores.

6 Results

In comparing the model results we use two measures to evaluate each model's ability to predict the Fluency and Accuracy grades: mean squared error (MSE) and Spearman correlation (Rho). A lower MSE value is indicative of superior model performance while higher Rho values are indicative of superior performance; this later metric is used to compare monotonic, though potentially non-linear relationships between the prediction and the labels (while continuous, the labels do not necessarily follow a normal distribution as students were more likely to receive higher grades).

Table 1 illustrates the model performance when comparing models utilizing each of the three described sets of features (See Sect. 4). From the table, it can be seen that in terms of MSE and Rho, the Siamese network exhibits the best performance across both metrics. It is particularly interesting to note that

Table 1. Results for the different models.

Model	Features	Fluency		Accuracy	
		Rho	MSE	Rho	MSE
Siamese network	Text features	0.073	0.665	**0.317**	**0.833**
	Tonal features	**0.497**	**0.497**	−0.006	0.957
LSTM	PyAduio features	0.072	1.139	−0.066	2.868
	Tonal features	−0.096	0.648	0.042	0.929
	Text features	−0.123	1.885	0.128	3.733
Decision tree	PyAudio Features	−0.005	0.749	0.011	1.189
	Tonal features	0.285	0.649	0.107	0.960
	Text features	0.090	0.794	0.261	0.998
	Cosine similarity	0.037	0.674	0.162	0.984
	Baseline	-	0.636	-	0.932

Table 2. Multitasking and ensembled Siamese models

Model	Fluency		Accuracy	
	Rho	MSE	Rho	MSE
Multitasking	0.129	0.603	0.313	0.915
Ensemble (Regression)	0.477	**0.490**	**0.34**	0.839

the textual features are better at predicting the accuracy score (MSE = 0.833, Rho = 0.317), while the tonal features are better at predicting the fluency score (MSE = 0.497, Rho = 0.497).

Table 2 shows the results for the multitasking and ensemble models. We see that the Siamese model with multitasking to predict both the fluency and accuracy scores do not perform better than the individual models predicting each. This suggests that the model is not able to learn as effectively when presented with both labels in our current dataset; it is possible that such a model would either need more data or a different architecture to improve. The slight improvement in regard to Fluency MSE and Accuracy Rho exhibited by the ensemble model suggests that the learned features (i.e. the individual model predictions) are able to generalize to predict the other measure. The increase in Rho for accuracy is particularly interesting as the improvement suggests that the tonal features are similarly helpful in predicting accuracy when combined with the textual-based model.

7   Discussion and Future Work

In [5], it was found that the use of audio features helped predict fluency and accuracy scores better than a simple baseline. In this paper the textual features and tonal features explored provide even better predictive power.

A potential limitation of the current work is the scale of the data observed, and can be addressed by future research. The use of the pre-trained models may have provided additional predictive power for the tonal and textual features, but there may be additional ways to augment the audio-based features in a similar manner (i.e. either by using pre-trained models or other audio data sources). Similarly, audio augmentation methods may be utilized to help increase the size and diversity of dataset (e.g. even by simply adding random noise to samples).

Another potential limitation of the current work is in regard to the exploration of fairness among the models. It was described that the ToneNet model used training samples from men, but not women; as with any assessment tool, it is important to fully explore any potential sources of bias that exist in the input data that may be perpetuated through the model's predictions. In regard to the set of pre-trained speech recognition models provided through Google's APIs, additional performance biases may exist for speakers with different accents. Understanding the potential linguistic differences between language learners would be important in providing a feedback tool that is beneficial to a wider range of individuals. A deeper study into the fairness of our assessment models would be needed before deploying within a classroom.

As Mandarin Chinese is a tonal language, the seeming importance and benefit of including tonal features makes intuitive sense. In both the tonal and textual feature sets, a pre-trained model was utilized which may also account for the increased predictive power over the audio features alone. As all libraries and methods used in this work are openly available, the methods and results described here present opportunities to develop such techniques into assessment and feedback tools to benefit teachers and students in real classrooms; in this regard, they also hold promise in expanding to other languages or other audio-based assignments and is a planned direction of future work.

Acknowledgements. We thank multiple NSF grants (e.g., 1931523, 1940236, 1917713, 1903304, 1822830, 1759229, 1724889, 1636782, 1535428, 1440753, 1316736, 1252297, 1109483, & DRL-1031398), the US Department of Education Institute for Education Sciences (e.g., IES R305A170137, R305A170243, R305A180401, R305A120125, R305A180401, & R305C100024) and the Graduate Assistance in Areas of National Need program (e.g., P200A180088 & P200A150306), EIR, the Office of Naval Research (N00014-18-1-2768 and other from ONR), and Schmidt Futures.

References

1. Singer, H., Ruddell, R.B.: Theoretical models and processes of reading (1970)
2. Wagner, R.K., Schatschneider, C., Phythian-Sence, C.: Beyond Decoding: The Behavioral and Biological Foundations of Reading Comprehension. Guilford Press, New York (2009)
3. AlKilabi, A.S.: The place of reading comprehension in second language acquisition. J. Coll. Lang. (JCL) **31**, 1–23 (2015)
4. Witt, S.M.: Automatic error detection in pronunciation training: where we are and where we need to go. In: Proceedings of the IS ADEPT, p. 6 (2012)

5. Varatharaj, A., Botelho, A.F., Lu, X., Heffernan, N.T.: Hao Fayin: developing automated audio assessment tools for a Chinese language course. In: The Twelfth International Conference on Educational Data Mining, pp. 663–666, July 2019
6. Kyriakopoulos, K., Knill, K., Gales, M.: A deep learning approach to assessing non-native pronunciation of English using phone distances. In: Proceedings of the Annual Conference of the International Speech Communication Association, INTERSPEECH, vol. 2018, pp. 1626–1630 (2018)
7. Pucher, M., Türk, A., Ajmera, J., Fecher, N.: Phonetic distance measures for speech recognition vocabulary and grammar optimization. In: Proceedings of the the 3rd Congress of the Alps Adria Acoustics Association (2007)
8. Bernstein, J., Cohen, M., Murveit, H., Rtischev, D., Weintraub, M.: Automatic evaluation and training in english pronunciation. In: First International Conference on Spoken Language Processing (1990)
9. Litman, D., Strik, H., Lim, G.S.: Speech technologies and the assessment of second language speaking: approaches, challenges, and opportunities. Lang. Assess. Q. 15(3), 294–309 (2018)
10. Bernstein, J.C: Computer scoring of spoken responses. In: The Encyclopedia of Applied Linguistics (2012)
11. Franco, H., Neumeyer, L., Digalakis, V., Ronen, O.: Combination of machine scores for automatic grading of pronunciation quality. Speech Commun. 30(2–3), 121–130 (2000)
12. Wei, S., Guoping, H., Yu, H., Wang, R.-H.: A new method for mispronunciation detection using support vector machine based on pronunciation space models. Speech Commun. 51(10), 896–905 (2009)
13. Zechner, K., Higgins, D., Xi, X., Williamson, D.M.: Automatic scoring of non-native spontaneous speech in tests of spoken english. Speech Commun. 51(10), 883–895 (2009)
14. Ryant, N., Slaney, M., Liberman, M., Shriberg, E., Yuan, J.: Highly accurate mandarin tone classification in the absence of pitch information. Proc. Speech Prosody 7 (2014)
15. Chen, C.J., Gopinath, R.A., Monkowski, M.D., Picheny, M.A., Shen, K.: New methods in continuous mandarin speech recognition. In: Fifth European Conference on Speech Communication and Technology (1997)
16. Loukina, A., Madnani, N., Cahill, A.: Speech- and text-driven features for automated scoring of English speaking tasks. In: Proceedings of the Workshop on Speech-Centric Natural Language Processing, pp. 67–77, Copenhagen, Denmark, September 2017. Association for Computational Linguistics
17. Mikolov, T., Sutskever, I., Chen, K., Corrado, G.S., Dean, J.: Distributed representations of words and phrases and their compositionality. In: Advances in neural information processing systems, pp. 3111–3119 (2013)
18. Pennington, J., Socher, R., Manning, C.D.: Glove: global vectors for word representation. In: Empirical Methods in Natural Language Processing (EMNLP), pp. 1532–1543 (2014)
19. Bojanowski, P., Grave, E., Joulin, A., Mikolov, T.: Enriching word vectors with subword information. arXiv preprint arXiv:1607.04606 (2016)
20. Download ffmpeg. http://ffmpeg.org/download.html. Accessed 10 Feb 2019
21. Giannakopoulos, T.: Pyaudioanalysis: an open-source python library for audio signal analysis. PloS one 10(12) (2015)
22. Zhang, A.: Speechrecognition pypi. https://pypi.org/project/SpeechRecognition/. Accessed 10 Feb 2019

23. Kim, J.Y., et al.: A comparison of online automatic speech recognition systems and the nonverbal responses to unintelligible speech. arXiv preprint arXiv:1904.12403 (2019)
24. Koo, T.K., Li, M.Y.: A guideline of selecting and reporting intraclass correlation coefficients for reliability research. J. Chiropractic Med. **15**(2), 155–163 (2016)
25. Gao, Q., Sun, S., Yang, Y.: Tonenet: a CNN model of tone classification of Mandarin Chinese. Proc. Interspeech **2019**, 3367–3371 (2019)
26. Breiman, L.: Classification and Regression Trees. Routledge, Abingdon (2017)
27. Bai, S., Kolter, J.Z., Koltun, V.: An empirical evaluation of generic convolutional and recurrent networks for sequence modeling. arXiv preprint arXiv:1803.01271 (2018)
28. Huang, W., Wang, J.: Character-level convolutional network for text classification applied to chinese corpus. arXiv preprint arXiv:1611.04358 (2016)
29. Caruana, R.: Multitask learning. Mach. Learn. **28**(1), 41–75 (1997)

Early Detection of Wheel-Spinning in ASSISTments

Yeyu Wang[1]([✉])(iD), Shimin Kai[2], and Ryan Shaun Baker[3](iD)

[1] University of Wisconsin–Madison, Madison, WI 53706, USA
ywang2466@wisc.edu
[2] Columbia University, New York, NY 10027, USA
[3] University of Pennsylvania, Philadelphia, PA 19104, USA

Abstract. Persistence is a crucial trait for learners. However, a common issue in mastery learning is that persistence is not always productive, a construct termed wheel-spinning. In this paper, we extend on prior work to develop wheel-spinning detectors in the ASSISTments learning system that distinguish between non-persistence, productive persistence and wheel-spinning. To understand how quickly we can detect each state, we use data from different numbers of practice opportunities and compare model performance across student-problem set pairs. We identify that a model constructed using data from the first nine practice opportunities outperforms models using less practice data. However, it is possible to differentiate students who will eventually wheel-spin from learners who will persist productively using data from only the first three opportunities. Wheel-spinning can be differentiated from non-persistence from the first five opportunities, and non-persistence can be differentiated from productive persistence from the first seven opportunities. These results show that early differentiation between wheel-spinning and productive persistence is feasible. These detectors relied upon hint requests, the correctness of prior opportunities, and the amount of practice and time on the skill. Identifying predictive features offer insights into the impact of in-system behaviors on wheel-spinning and guide the system design.

Keywords: Wheel-spinning · Persistence · Decision tree · Early detection · Intelligent tutoring system

1 Introduction

1.1 Persistence and Non-Persistence in Learning

Research in recent years has focused on the development of non-cognitive skills to improve student learning, such as resilience and persistence during learning. Persistence is defined as the ability to maintain an action or complete a task regardless of the person's inclination towards the task [5,7]. Recent studies have shown that persistence in educational settings is associated with academic achievement [3,19], creativity [20] and long-term academic outcomes such as later schooling and future earnings [6,19]. However, not all persistence is positive. [2] have

© Springer Nature Switzerland AG 2020
I. I. Bittencourt et al. (Eds.): AIED 2020, LNAI 12163, pp. 574–585, 2020.
https://doi.org/10.1007/978-3-030-52237-7_46

argued that some persistence may be unproductive, or wheel-spinning, defined as spending too much time struggling without achieving mastery. The definition of wheel-spinning has varied across different studies and different learning contexts. [2] defined wheel-spinning as not achieving mastery even after attempting 10 or more problems within a problem set; [14] involved two human raters to code wheel-spinning behaviors qualitatively based on a coding manual, with a Cohen's Kappa of 0.9. On the other hand, [10] defined wheel-spinning as attempting more than 10 problems but failing to achieve three consecutive correct responses in a row or demonstrate later retention of the skill.

Non-persistence, or quitting the current learning task without mastering the requisite knowledge, has also been documented in several computer-supported learning environments. For example, in the educational game Physics Playground, non-persistence was defined as quitting the level without successfully solving the problem using the physics knowledge [11, 12]. In the learning system ASSISTments, [4] looked at non-persistent behaviors in which students quit the problem set without reaching mastery of a skill, differentiating between quitting immediately and quitting after attempting a few problems. Within the same learning system, [10] defined non-persistence as attempting fewer than ten problems for a skill, but did not consider non-persistence detection in their work.

1.2 Detection of Persistence in Learning

Detection of wheel-spinning behaviors is important in identifying students who may need additional support during a learning task. Because persistence is generally defined by the number of practice opportunities a student has on a learning task, some approaches to modeling or detecting wheel-spinning have been designed to run only after the system has collected student data for a sufficiently large number of practice opportunities. For example, [2], as the first study of wheel-spinning, states that wheel-spinning could be detected as early as the eighth practice opportunity in the ASSISTments system by a logistic regression model. A follow-up study further refined this model and was able to detect wheel-spinning on the seventh practice opportunities [8]. Other machine learning methods such as neural networks [14], gradient boosting [17] and random forest [22] have also been used to enable wheel-spinning detection at earlier stages in practice. Most notably, [4] was able to identify wheel-spinning students at their third opportunity, applying Long Short Term Memory Recurrent Neural Networks. While these studies all take place in an ITS environment, there has also been work on wheel-spinning detection in educational games. [16] constructed a model to detect wheel-spinning based on the features engineered within the first 5 min, first 10 min, and first 15 min of game playing, and [15] constructed a model to differentiate wheel-spinning from productive persistence in a sequence of mathematics games.

In reviewing these prior works, we note that for a wheel-spinning detector to be practical for real-time usage, there are two important criteria to consider.

First, a detector should be able to differentiate wheel-spinning from both non-persistence (either successful or non-successful non-persistence) as well as from productive persistence, and should be able to do this at the earliest possible point. With early detection of these states, teachers and system designers may have more opportunities to create interventions to improve the learning experience for students who are at risk of unproductively persisting, or quitting early without completing a learning task. Secondly, predictions based on interpretable models, like decision trees, will offer instructors and system designers more useful insights into the factors influencing persistence and wheel-spinning. Prior work has not yet fully met both of these criteria. Currently, most detectors only account for binary prediction, by either eliminating the non-persistence cases from consideration [17] or treating all cases that are not wheel-spinning as being acceptable [8]. At the same time, recent efforts to improve prediction of wheel-spinning using gradient boosting or neural networks have improved speed and quality of prediction at the cost of interpretability, posing a challenge for educational researchers to uncover and understand the impact of learning behaviors on wheel-spinning.

In this paper, we attempt to address each of these limitations. We 1) construct multi-class detectors distinguishing the three categories discussed above states—non-persistence, productive persistence, and unproductive persistence (wheel-spinning)—so as to capture and compare specific behaviors that differentiate both between persistent vs. non-persistent students, and productively persistent vs. wheel-spinning students; 2) explore the minimum number of practice opportunities that could be used with reasonable accuracy to detect the various persistence states under these conditions, and derive specific features that may be translated into practical interventions. In doing so, in order to compare our results with the previous works on binary wheel-spinning detectors, predicting wheel-spinning vs. non-wheel-spinning [2,4,17], we also build models to make pairwise comparisons for two classes out of the three. In addition, we will summarize the predictive features used across models based on different practice opportunities, to promote better understanding of wheel-spinning. We conclude by discussing the possible impact of the features on persistence and unproductive persistence in learning.

2   Methods

2.1   ASSISTments

ASSISTments is a free online learning platform that provides immediate feedback to students and formative assessment of student performance to teachers [9]. Within the ASSISTments system, Skill Builders are a type of math problem set where students practice randomly generated problems that are based on existing templates and correspond to the same skill [9]. In a Skill Builder, students cannot proceed to the next problem until they submit the correct response. Hints are available to assist them with problem-solving. For each problem, students could make multiple attempts and request multiple hints. In general, there are two to three levels of hint per problem, followed by a bottom-out hint that provides the final answer. Students have to correctly answer three consecutive questions to complete a problem set. They are then given a single-item test after a certain period—usually a week later, though teachers can configure this—with gradually increasing space between reassessments. This test comprises one randomly selected item from a template in the completed problem set, and is delivered through the Automatic Reassessment and Relearning System (ARRS) [21]. The main objective of ARRS is to assess a student's retention of a skill over time. If the student does not answer this item correctly, and therefore fails in skill retention, they will be assigned the corresponding Skill Builder problem set to re-learn the materials.

2.2 Data Collection and Label Generation

Our research dataset is the publicly available ASSISTments Skill Builders data set from the 2014–2015 school year, which consists of 26,522 students who attempted 1,088 Skill Builder problem sets over a year. Each record in the dataset represents a student-problem set pair, which includes the log data when a learner practices a Skill Builder problem set. This data set was chosen due to its use in past research on wheel-spinning and persistence (i.e. [10]). We then constructed eight new datasets: *first-3*, *first-4*,..., *first-9*, and *first-10* (*first-1* and *first-2* were not generated, due to not being enough data to infer wheel-spinning in any previous work). Each row in one of these *first-x* datasets shows aggregate data about a student's learning in a certain problem set (i.e., a student-problem set pair), where x is the threshold number of problems over which data is aggregated. For example, *first-3* contains only data about the first 3 problems that the student attempted in each problem set, whereas *first-4*, *first-5* and *first-6* contain data about the first 4, 5 and 6 problems respectively. It should be noted that, given a problem set, a student who attempted only 3 problems would be included in *first-3* but not in *first-4* to *first-10*, while a student who completed 10 problems would be included in every dataset from *first-3* to *first-10*. More generally, the number of student-problem set pairs decreases as x increases, because there are fewer students who attempt more problems.

Table 1. Criteria of non-persistence (NP), productive persistence (PP), and wheel-spinning (WS) in the Skill Builder system.

Definition	Three Correct in a Row (Mastery) on or after the 10th Problem	First ARRS Test	Ten or More Problems
NP	Any	Any	No
PP	Yes	Passed	Yes
WS	No	Any	Yes
	Yes	No	

Next, we labeled each row of student-problem set pair as either productive persistence (PP), wheel-spinning (WS) or non-persistence (NP), according to the operational definitions in [10] (Table 1). If a student did fewer than 10 problems in a problem set, the corresponding student-problem set pair is labeled as NP. Otherwise, the pair is labeled as PP if the student reached mastery (i.e., get three correct responses in a row and pass the ARRS test) or WS if she did not.

While our definitions involve the ARRS test, some students were not assigned this test even after getting three correct responses in a row because the teachers turned the ARRS feature off. These instances, which account for 211,612 pairs from the original 287,093 student-problem set pairs, were considered out of scope and removed from further analysis. Of the remaining student-problem set pairs, 6,855 were classified as WS and 2,093 as PP; these pairs are present in every first-x dataset but take on different feature values depending on x. The number of NP pairs in the datasets from *first-3* to *first-10* are 51866, 33197, 26983, 12663, 7833, 4290, 1900 and 0 respectively. As previously noted, there are fewer NP records as x increases; the *first-10* dataset, in particular, has no NP records because students who reached the 10th problem were considered persistent.

2.3   Feature Engineering and Machine Learning

We built upon the feature set developed by [1], which consists of student actions and attributes within the ASSISTments Skill Builder platform that provides information on student persistence and learning. More specifically, we included 25 core features related to student hint usage, number of practice opportunities at a problem set, number of skill opportunities, and time between student actions. As in [10], we calculated the respective sum, minimum, maximum, average and standard deviation values of these core attributes for each student sequence and generated 125 features based on 25 core features. Next, we constructed a set of models to distinguish between NP, PP and WS. Each model is based on one of the *first-x* datasets. This process consists of three main steps:

Data splitting. We performed a student-stratified split of each *first-x* dataset into a train-validate set (90% of students) and a test set (10% of students).

Feature selection. For each value of x, we conducted outer-loop forward feature selection on the train-validate set. This routine starts with an empty feature set and, at each step, selects the feature that would generate the best performance, according to the result of cross-validation. To reduce overfitting, we set the maximum number of features to 20 and imposed an early-stopping condition: if the next candidate feature does not yield a performance improvement of more than 0.001, the routine would stop.

Model evaluation. We built a model based on the features from the previous step, and trained it on the whole train-validate set. Then we evaluated the model on the test set based on macro-average AUC and pairwise AUC between NP-WS, PP-WS, and NP-PP. In this way, we ensured that no data was used for both feature selection and model evaluation, which would bias the results.

In the above steps, our performance metric is 10-fold cross-validated AUC. Due to a class imbalance between WS, NP and PP, we oversampled the training data by randomly adding copies of records from the minority classes. To measure the goodness of the model, we adopted macro-averaging AUC for the multi-class prediction. Finally, to compare to our results with those of [10]'s binary detector that differentiates between wheel-spinning and productive persistent states, we chose the decision tree implementation from [18]. We used entropy as the splitting criterion, set the maximum tree depth as 12 and minimum number of instances per leaf as 2. While these hyperparameters could be individually tuned for each dataset model to potentially yield better performance, our goal is to use the same model construction process across all eight datasets in order to compare their performances as well as the salient features in each, and to avoid the over-fitting associated with hyperparameter tuning.

Among the 125 features, some were computed based on student actions on a certain number of past problems. *Past8BottomOut* and *Past8HelpRequest*, for example, refer to the number of bottom-out hints and help requests made in the past 8 problems. We removed these features from the feature selection process on the datasets where they are not applicable - for this example, the *first-3* to *first-8* datasets, which do not include student-skill data from more than 8 problems.

3   Results

3.1   Feature Selection Results

By applying the forward feature selection algorithm, we identified the feature sets that maximized the model performance for each *first-x* dataset. Among the eight decision tree models, six have root node features which are related to hint usage, such as the mean (*first-3, first-7, first-8*) and sum (*first-4, first-6*) of the total number of hints used, and mean of the bottom-out hint requested in the last eight opportunities (*first-10*). The root nodes of the other two models are time factors, such as sum (*first-5*) and mean (*first-9*) of the duration since the last time the student practiced the skill. While each dataset has its own feature set, we observed that there were features shared across datasets. To better represent this commonality, we summarized all the selected features into seven categories, which include the question type in the problem set, help request behaviors, hint use, scaffolding, opportunity number, amount of practice and time, and the count of failed opportunities. In Table 2, we listed three example feature categories selected with their descriptions[1]. The number list after each feature indicates which *first-x* dataset models it was selected for.

Based on forward selection, all the models from *first-3* to *first-10* include features related to hint requesting behaviors (*HintTotal*). In addition, features related to *HintTotal* are selected for the root node of five models, which indicates that features related to hint requests play a crucial role in predicting WS, NP

---

[1] The full table of features selected for each model can be viewed at https://github. com/yeyuw215/AIED_WS_2020/blob/master/FullTable2.pdf.

Table 2. Examples of selected features, categories and descriptions.

Features categories	Features and descriptions
Hint	- **HintTotal (3,4,5,6,7,8,9,10):** The total number of hint requests
	- **Past8BottomOut (9,10):** The number of bottom-out hint requests in the past 8 attempts
Amount of Practice and Time	- **TimeBetweenProblems (5,7,8,9):** The duration of time in between problems related to the skill
	- **TimeTaken (3,4,5,6):** The amount of time spent to complete the current problem
	- **TotalSkillOpportunities (5,6,7,8,9):** The total number of problems attempted that are related to the skill in the current problem set
	- **TotalTimeOnSkill (3,4):** The total amount of time spent on the skill in the system
Wrong Count	- **TotalPastWrongCount (3,4,9):** The total number of incorrect attempts made on problems within the current problem set
	- **TotalPercentPastWrong (4,5):** The percentage of incorrect attempts made on problems within the current problem set
	- **Past5WrongCount (9):** The number of attempts made that were incorrect in the past 5 attempts

Table 3. Features selected for each *first-x* dataset model. Root feature denotes the feature at the root node of each decision tree model. "*_m*" indicates the feature is aggregated as mean; "*_s*" indicates the feature is aggregated as sum.

	first-3	first-4	first-5	first-6
# of Features	10	12	11	6
Root Feature	m_HintTotal	s_HintTotal	s_TimeBtwProb	s_HintTotal
	first-7	first-8	first-9	first-10
# of Features	11	8	10	5
Root Feature	m_HintTotal	m_HintTotal	m_TimeBtwProb	m_P8BottomOut

and PP. Other features, like the number of practice opportunities and amount of time as well as the number of wrong attempts made on the previous problems, are present across different models. We will discuss the implications of these findings in the discussion section (Table 3).

3.2   Model Performance for *"first-x"* Datasets

For all *first-x* datasets, we applied the same feature selection and model evaluation procedure. In order to identify how early we can predict wheel-spinning,

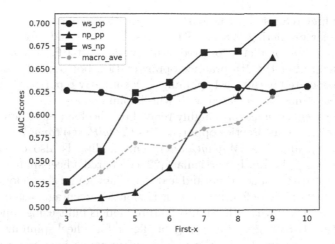

Fig. 1. AUC scores for different first-x dataset.

we calculated the macro-averaging AUC (for the multiple classes of PP, NP and WS) as goodness measurement and compared the improvement from including more problems, or practice opportunities, into consideration. We also calculated the pairwise AUC for WS-PP, NP-PP, and WS-NP predictions, to understand how well the model can differentiate between specific pairs of states.

When including more and more practice opportunities into consideration, the macro-average AUC scores of the multi-classes detector increases gradually (see Fig. 1). The model including the data for the first 9 opportunities has the best performance, with a macro-averaging AUC of 0.62. For contrasting NP-PP and WS-NP, the AUC shows an increase with more practice opportunity data. For the prediction contrasting NP and PP, including data from the first 7 practice opportunities leads to the largest increase of AUC from 0.54 (*first-6*) to 0.61 (*first-7*). Similarly, the AUC score of contrasting WS and NP increased the most after including data from the first 5 practice opportunities, from 0.56 (*first-4*) to 0.62 (*first-5*). However, the AUC for the WS-PP detector fluctuates around 0.625 and shows no rising trend from first-3 to first-10.

4   Discussion

4.1   Feature Selection Results

We observed that the hint-related features were present in all dataset models as well as at the root node of five models, which indicates these features have the most predictive power. This finding is consistent with previous studies. For instance, [8] identified features involving hints to predict wheel-spinning, such as hint use, count of previous practice opportunities with hint requests and whether students requested at least five hint requests. Another finding in our model is the effect of bottom-out hint requests for predicting WS. The average number of bottom-out hint requests for the past eight practice opportunities is selected as a root node for predicting WS and PP (*first-10*), which indicates that bottom-out hint is a strong predictor for predicting WS against PP. [2] also identified a similar finding: after the 4th practice opportunities, bottom-out hint request is positively associated with wheel-spinning. [10] similarly reported that heavy use of bottom-out hints is associated with wheel-spinning.

Another category of features highly related to wheel-spinning detection is the correctness of previous practice opportunities (*TotalPastWrongCount*, *TotalPercentPastWrong*, and *Past5WrongCount*). This finding is also consistent with previous studies [8,15,22]. In particular, [22] compared wheel-spinning detection across different tutors, algorithms and features. They found that a logistic regression model with only one feature, correct response percentage, achieved less but comparable accuracy with other multi-feature models built using random forest, indicating that correctness is a strong predictor for wheel-spinning prediction. Furthermore, according to [8], the number of previous incorrect responses on the same skill has a positive relationship with wheel-spinning. In a math learning game, [15] also found that prior knowledge measured by missing rate and nonproficiency of skills is highly related to wheel-spinning.

Features related to the amount of practice and time (*TimeTaken*, *TotalTimeOnSkill*, *TotalSkillOpportunities*, *TimeBetweenProblems*) are selected in all the *first-x* models. For models including fewer opportunities to practice the skill (*first-3* to *first-6*), *timetaken* and *totalfrtimeonskill* are predictive of wheel-spinning. However, for the models with more accumulated data (*first-5* to *first-9*), the features switched from time duration (*TotalTimeOnSkill*) to measures of the number of opportunities (*TotalSkillOpportunities*). [2] also found that response time is more predictive on the first several practice opportunities. For the later responses, fast response might indicate either the mastery of skill or gaming the system, which makes the meaning of response time ambiguous.

4.2 Model Performance of Multi-class and Pairwise Prediction

According to Fig. 1, the performance of the multi-class prediction increases as we include data from more practice opportunities. When including data from the first 9 practice opportunities, the macro-averaging AUC reached 0.62. To our best knowledge, this is the first study exploring the integrated detection of non-persistence, wheel-spinning, and productive persistence together, extending the previous research on WS detector using a decision tree classifier [10]. Therefore, it could be used as a baseline to evaluate model performance in future work.

In differentiating wheel-spinning (WS) from productive persistence (PP), we found that model performance AUC values fluctuate around 0.625 from the first-3 to the first-10 datasets, which implies that our predictive model is stable and able to differentiate between students at-risk of wheel-spinning from students who are productively persistent early on from the third practice opportunity onward. This finding may appear to contradict prior studies that find that models improve with more data [8,14,22]. This difference between studies may be due to the difference in how mastery is defined across the various studies. In prior studies, the criteria of productive mastery is defined based on in-system performance, like three-correct-in-a-row [8]. However, the stricter definition of productive persistence in our study requires students to not only meet the "three-correct-in-a-row" mastery criteria, but also pass the delayed ARRS test to demonstrate learning retention [10]. It is possible that a definition of mastery based on robust learning, a higher bar than simply achieving three correct answers in a row, might be easier to detect early. However, a contrasting finding is obtained by [22], who obtained more accurate prediction and earlier detection when using a more generous criterion of mastery than three-correct-in-a-row.

In our models generated to differentiate between wheel-spinning (WS) and non-persistence (NP), we observed that while model performance increased with the number of practice opportunities, the increase in AUC value is highest between the 4th and 5th practice opportunities. This implies that our detectors may be able to differentiate WS from NP with sufficient accuracy by the 5th practice opportunity. [4] examined the performance of Long-Short Term Memory Networks to predict wheel-spinning and non-persistence on ASSISTments in terms of how many opportunities to practice were provided to the algorithm. They found that the 3rd opportunity might be the earliest timing to predict both WS and NP, an earlier point than seen in our study. Our detectors therefore require more data than [4]. However, we are able to interpret the features in our model based on the decision tree structures to derive more general insights. This tradeoff between model performance and interpretability is also present in other areas of learning analytics such as knowledge component modeling [13].

5 Conclusion

In this study, we explore the potential for early detection of wheel-spinning, productive persistence and non-persistence in ASSISTments. By constructing decision tree models and observing the change of model performance as data about more practice opportunities is aggregated, we found that the model based on nine practice opportunities results in the best performance; the model based on the first three practice opportunities allows early detection of wheel-spinning versus productive persistence, the first five practice opportunities are sufficient for differentiation of wheel-spinning from non-persistence, and the first seven practice opportunities are sufficient for differentiation of productive persistence from non-persistence. Due to the interpretability of decision tree models, we examined the common features across models and the root node features of each. The predictive features, like hint and bottom-out hint usage, correctness and amount of time and opportunities on the previous practice, offer us insights about the factors which might lead to wheel-spinning.

Another potential area for future work, personalized intervention based on which features are predictive could be integrated into the existing learning system to better optimize student learning. Since the features which are predictive of wheel-spinning are at least somewhat consistent across studies and datasets (see discussion above), this may help us to design future intelligent tutoring systems that are more adaptive to the possibility of wheel-spinning in their early stages of learning. Such a system could encourage students to use the bottom-out hints at the first several practice opportunities, if needed; then the system could limit bottom-out hints availability in the later practice opportunities. In this way, the system could leverage what we know about wheel-spinning to help us prevent it.

Acknowledgements. We thank Neil Heffernan and the ASSISTments team, and grant NSF #DRL-1535340.

References

1. Baker, R.S., Goldstein, A.B., Heffernan, N.T.: Detecting learning moment-by-moment. Int. J. Artif. Intell. Educ. **21**(1–2), 5–25 (2011)
2. Beck, J.E., Gong, Y.: Wheel-spinning: students who fail to master a skill. In: Lane, H.C., Yacef, K., Mostow, J., Pavlik, P. (eds.) AIED 2013. LNCS (LNAI), vol. 7926, pp. 431–440. Springer, Heidelberg (2013). https://doi.org/10.1007/978-3-642-39112-5_44
3. Borghans, L., Meijers, H., Ter Weel, B.: The role of noncognitive skills in explaining cognitive test scores. Econ. Inq. **46**(1), 2–12 (2008)
4. Botelho, A.F., Varatharaj, A., Patikorn, T., Doherty, D., Adjei, S.A., Beck, J.E.: Developing early detectors of student attrition and wheel spinning using deep learning. IEEE Trans. Learn. Technol. **12**(2), 158–170 (2019)
5. Cloninger, C.R., Svrakic, D.M., Przybeck, T.R.: A psychobiological model of temperament and character. Arch. Gen. Psychiatry **50**(12), 975–990 (1993)
6. Deke, J., Haimson, J.: Valuing Student Competencies: Which Ones Predict Postsecondary Educational Attainment and Earnings, and for Whom? Final Report. Mathematica Policy Research Inc., Princeton (2006)
7. Duckworth, A.L., Peterson, C., Matthews, M.D., Kelly, D.R.: Grit: perseverance and passion for long-term goals. J. Pers. Soc. Psychol. **92**(6), 1087 (2007)
8. Gong, Y., Beck, J.E.: Towards detecting wheel-spinning: future failure in mastery learning. In: Proceedings of the second (2015) ACM conference on learning@ scale, pp. 67–74 (2015)
9. Heffernan, N.T., Heffernan, C.L.: The ASSISTments ecosystem: building a platform that brings scientists and teachers together for minimally invasive research on human learning and teaching. Int. J. Artif. Intell. Educ. **24**(4), 470–497 (2014)
10. Kai, S., Almeda, M.V., Baker, R.S., Heffernan, C., Heffernan, N.: Decision tree modeling of wheel-spinning and productive persistence in skill builders. JEDM J. Educ. Data Min. **10**(1), 36–71 (2018)
11. Karumbaiah, S., Baker, R.S., Barany, A., Shute, V.: Using epistemic networks with automated codes to understand why players quit levels in a learning game. In: Eagan, B., Misfeldt, M., Siebert-Evenstone, A. (eds.) ICQE 2019. CCIS, vol. 1112, pp. 106–116. Springer, Cham (2019). https://doi.org/10.1007/978-3-030-33232-7_9
12. Karumbaiah, S., Baker, R.S., Shute, V.: Predicting quitting in students playing a learning game. In: International Educational Data Mining Society (2018)
13. Liu, R., McLaughlin, E.A., Koedinger, K.R.: Interpreting model discovery and testing generalization to a new dataset. In: Educational Data Mining 2014. Citeseer (2014)
14. Matsuda, N., Chandrasekaran, S., Stamper, J.C.: How quickly can wheel spinning be detected? In: EDM, pp. 607–608 (2016)

15. Owen, V.E., et al.: Detecting wheel-spinning and productive persistence in educational games. In: International Educational Data Mining Society (2019)
16. Palaoag, T.D., Rodrigo, M.M.T., Andres, J.M.L., Andres, J.M.A.L., Beck, J.E.: Wheel-spinning in a game-based learning environment for physics. In: Micarelli, A., Stamper, J., Panourgia, K. (eds.) ITS 2016. LNCS, vol. 9684, pp. 234–239. Springer, Cham (2016). https://doi.org/10.1007/978-3-319-39583-8_23
17. Park, S., Matsuda, N.: Predicting students' unproductive failure on intelligent tutors in adaptive online courseware. In: Proceedings of the Sixth Annual GIFT Users Symposium, vol. 6, p. 131. US Army Research Laboratory (2018)
18. Pedregosa, F., et al.: Scikit-learn: machine learning in python. J. Mach. Learn. Res. **12**, 2825–2830 (2011)
19. Poropat, A.E.: A meta-analysis of the five-factor model of personality and academic performance. Psychol. Bull. **135**(2), 322 (2009)
20. Prabhu, V., Sutton, C., Sauser, W.: Creativity and certain personality traits: understanding the mediating effect of intrinsic motivation. Creativity Res. J. **20**(1), 53–66 (2008)
21. Wang, Y., Heffernan, N.T.: Towards modeling forgetting and relearning in its: preliminary analysis of arrs data. In: EDM, p. 352 (2011)
22. Zhang, C., et al.: Early detection of wheel spinning: Comparison across tutors, models, features, and operationalizations. In: Grantee Submission (2019)

Investigating Differential Error Types Between Human and Simulated Learners

Daniel Weitekamp, Zihuiwen Ye, Napol Rachatasumrit, Erik Harpstead[⊠], and Kenneth Koedinger

Carnegie Mellon University, Pittsburgh, PA 15213, USA
harpstead@cmu.edu

Abstract. Simulated learners represent computational theories of human learning that can be used to evaluate educational technologies, provide practice opportunities for teachers, and advance our theoretical understanding of human learning. A key challenge in working with simulated learners is evaluating the accuracy of the simulation compared to the behavior of real human students. One way this evaluation is done is by comparing the error-rate learning curves from a population of human learners and a corresponding set of simulated learners. In this paper, we argue that this approach misses an opportunity to more accurately capture nuances in learning by treating all errors as the same. We present a simulated learner system, the Apprentice Learner (AL) Architecture, and use this more nuanced evaluation to demonstrate ways in which it does and does not explain and accurately predict student learning in terms of the reduction of different kinds of errors over time as it learns, as human students do, from an Intelligent Tutoring System (ITS).

Keywords: Simulated learners · Learning curves · Apprentice Learner

1 Introduction

Simulated learners are artificially intelligent agents that simulate human learning. Simulated learners offer a powerful set of affordances to AI powered instructional technology. Prior work has demonstrated the use of simulated learners for efficient authoring of intelligent tutoring systems [9,20], building automated learning by teaching exercises [10], and automated testing and refinement of educational technologies [5,18].

Simulated learners differ from parameterized statistical models like the Additive Factors, Performance Factors, and similar models [3,14] in that they fully simulate the process of human learning, not just the patterns of performance students exhibit over the course of learning. Simulated learners work in and learn from educational technology through an inductive process of skill creation and refinement. In this study we use simulated learners built with the Apprentice Learner Architecture, a modular framework for building simulated learners and testing computational theories of human learning [8]. Unlike deep learning

© Springer Nature Switzerland AG 2020
I. I. Bittencourt et al. (Eds.): AIED 2020, LNAI 12163, pp. 586–597, 2020.
https://doi.org/10.1007/978-3-030-52237-7_47

based simulated learners [16], Apprentice Learner (AL) agents reach mastery at roughly the same rate per opportunity as human learners, and make strong commitments to the theoretical underpinnings of learning without relying on highly parameterized fitting of human data [21].

To fully deliver on their potential to aid in the testing of instructional technology, simulated learners must embody an accurate theory of learning which can both reproduce the patterns of errors that humans produce over the course of learning, and respond as humans do in different instructional conditions. Prior work has assessed the fidelity of simulated learner models by comparing simulated student learning curves of error rate by opportunity to the learning curves of human learners. MacIlellan [6] for example, presents simulated learners that shows similar learning curve patterns as humans trained under both blocked and interleaved instruction strategies. While this method has been helpful in guiding cognitive architectural decisions in the past, it has a potential to hide nuances in learners' behavior (e.g., doing a step incorrectly in different ways) that are also important for a simulation to model.

In this work, we demonstrate a method of assessing the accuracy of a simulated learner model not just by comparing overall learning curves, but also by a novel method of splitting learning curves by error type. While prior work has explored disaggregating learning curves by student subpopulations [11], our new method of generating learning curves draws two distinctions, first, between errors of *omission* whereby a learner's request for help is an indication that they do not know what do (Hint-Errors) and errors of *commission* where a student performs an incorrect action (Incorrects). Second, we make a distinction within Incorrects between actions on the wrong interface element, such as doing a step in the wrong order (Selection-Errors), and entering an incorrect value on an otherwise correct next step (Input-Errors). In the context of many tutoring systems, this distinction often appears as a difference between students putting any answer in an inappropriately selected text field (e.g., one they may use later on in the problem) and students putting an incorrect answer in an appropriately selected text field (e.g., making an arithmetic error). Tutoring systems commonly allow for multiple strategies, as is the case here, such that there may be multiple appropriate selections at some states in the solution.

An additional difficulty with modeling humans with current simulated learners [6,9], is that they use and acquire only domain-specific knowledge and, perhaps reasonably enough, they start with none. As such, they always begin learning with a 100% error rate. In principle, there is also a point at which human learners possess zero knowledge of a domain, however in the classroom setting, it is generally the case that most students have received at least some within-domain instruction prior to working with an intelligent tutoring system (ITS). Students also may possess some knowledge from previously learned domains that may sometimes provide correct solutions in the current domain of study. For the purposes of comparing the learning curves of humans and simulated learners, a comprehensive history of student learning is rarely available, and thus simulated learners must account for unobserved prior knowledge in their human counterparts. Weitekamp et al. [21], have compared several methods for accounting for prior knowledge in simulated learners. In addition to our error type analyses, we also incorporate several innovations on the best reported method of accounting for prior knowledge from this work.

Ultimately, we propose to improve learning theory by evaluating whether simulated learners that implement the computational theory of the Apprentice Learner Architecture and account for prior knowledge, can accurately predict (and thereby explain) the reduction in distinct types of errors produced by human learners; not just in overall error rate. Thus, we claim simulated learners capable of matching human learners' performance on all three of these error types (Hint-Error, Selection-Error, and Input-Error) constitute stronger models of human learning than those only capable of matching human learners on aggregate error-rates. Furthermore, we show that splitting the errors in these ways can help generate insights for how to refine simulated learner models and improve learning theory.

2   The Apprentice Learner Architecture

The simulated learners we employ throughout this work are implemented within a modular framework for generating simulated learners called the Apprentice Learner (AL) Architecture [6,8]. A single AL agent is a simulation of a single human learner, which learns as humans do through demonstrations and correctness feedback. AL agents can be trained interactively or, using an existing ITS. The Apprentice Learner Architecture's modular design consists of several independent learning mechanisms that can be swapped in and out to test different computational theories of human learning. Together, an AL agent's different learning mechanisms generate and refine production rules [1] that represent the skills of the agent. The left-hand side or if-part of each production rule is refined by *when-learning* and *where-learning* mechanisms, and the right-hand side or then-part of each production rule is generated by a *how-learning* mechanism.

In a typical AL agent, the *how-learning* mechanism is the first learning mechanism to come into play during learning. This mechanism induces a sequence of operations to explain how the action parameters (e.g. value) of a demonstrated training example were produced. *How-learning* searches over a set of domain-general operators such as addition, subtraction, multiplication, and division to find a sequence of operations that will constitute the then-part of a production rule capable of matching a demonstrated input. In this study we evaluate learning in fraction arithmetic, which only necessitates searching over singular unchained operators.

The *where-learning* mechanism is responsible for producing matching rules associated with each skill that can bind to the interface elements in an ITS interface associated with a particular use of a skill. For example, if a particular skill involves multiplying two numbers and placing the result in a text box, then the matching rule would need to bind to the text box (the selection) and to the two interface elements (the arguments) from which the solution will be computed. If there are multiple instances of a step in a problem then the *where* matching rule would need to match to all such instances. In this work we employ a simple *where-learning* mechanism that simply recalls previously seen matches.

Lastly, the *when-learning* mechanism is responsible for learning when it is appropriate for a skill to be applied. *When-learning* mechanisms are simply binary classifiers, which take the current state of the problem and, for each skill, evaluate each *where* match in the state for that skill to determine whether or not the skill should be applied for that match. *When-learning* mechanisms generalize from correct and incorrect instances of a skill being applied to determine which features of a state indicate that a particular skill should be applied. In this study we test two different classification algorithms for *when-learning*, which have been used in prior studies with the Apprentice Learner [6] the Decision Tree algorithm a common classification algorithm [2], and TRESTLE which was used in prior work to model the gradual process of concept formation from examples [7].

3   Method

We evaluate our simulated learners against human data collected from a classroom study of a fraction arithmetic ITS. This dataset consists of the work of 117 students solving fraction addition and multiplication problems. Among the addition problems some problems involved adding fractions with the same denominator meaning the numerators could simply be added together, other problems involved adding fractions with different denominators, meaning a common denominator had to be found. For the later case, the ITS enforced the 'butterfly' method where a common denominator is found by multiplying the two denominators. All three problem types, Add-Different (AD), Add-Same (AS), and Multiply (M), were solved on the same interface. This dataset was used in prior work with simulated learners [6,21] and we have chosen to use it in this work for the sake of comparison. The dataset is available as project 243 on the PSLC DataShop [4][1].

In this study, we use a novel method of learning curve analysis that categorizes student errors into several different types. Following conventions from DataShop and ITS research [4,15], we frame student actions in terms of Selection-Action-Input (SAI) triples and consider errors along each dimension of the SAI. Selection is the interface element in the tutoring system that the student interacted with during an attempted step, Action is what they did to that interface element, and Input is the value associated with that action. For example, (num3, UpdateTextArea, 5) is the SAI for placing 5 in the textbox labelled num3.

Our method for defining error types leverages the behavior graph of a CTAT example-tracing tutor to annotate each student transaction with four new binary values by comparing a student's SAI against the problem step the transaction is associated with. These four new values are "current selection" which indicates whether a student worked on a correct selection for the next step, "current

---

[1] https://pslcdatashop.web.cmu.edu/Project?id=243.

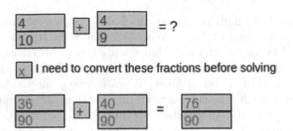

Fig. 1. An example of a fraction addition problem with different denominators (AD). The students must indicate that the fractions must be converted and apply the conversion using the "butterfly" method (multiplying the denominators together, and cross multiplying to find the new numerators). AS and M problems use the same interface but without the intermediate conversion steps.

input" which indicates if the input was correct, "downstream selection" which indicates whether the student's choice of selection is correct for a later step in the problem, and "downstream input" which indicates whether the input of the student's transaction would be correct on any step down stream in the behavior graph from the current step. Table 1 shows a few common patterns of these new values and how we group them together to get Selection-Errors and Input-Errors. Several combinations have been omitted because they are either impossible or not applicable to our data.

Table 1. Error types by SAI matching pattern

Current selection	Current input	Downstream selection	Downstream input	Error type
1	1	0	0	Correct response
1	0	0	0	Input-Error
0	0	1	0	Input-Error
0	1	1	0	Selection-Error
1	0	0	1	Selection-Error
0	0	1	1	Selection-Error
0	1	1	1	Selection-Error

In general, Selection-Errors occur whenever the student's current selection is wrong, but their input is applicable somewhere later in the problem, while Input-Errors occur when the student's input is incorrect for any step in the problem. Our motivation for encoding these distinct types of errors was to determine which characteristics of AL's learning mechanisms differed from human learners. Selection-Errors roughly correspond to issues of over-generality in the left-hand side of production rules (i.e. skills). For example, if a student does the wrong step in a problem then that is an indication that they do not fully understand the conditions under which a particular skill should be applied. Input-Errors can arise when the right-hand side of a production rule is incorrect, however, they can also occur if a student applies the wrong skill for the correct next step, in which case, the Input-Error may arise from two or more skills with underspecific left-hand sides. In the context of AL, this means that Selection-Errors are definitely issues of under specific rules generated by the *when-* or *where-learning* mechanisms. Input-Errors, on the other hand, could arise from any learning mechanism, however, we hypothesize incorrect *how-learning* is most likely to show up as an Input-Error. Lastly, Hint-Errors can occur if no learning has occurred yet, or if *when-* or *where-learning* has generated skills with overly specific left-hand sides.

Before working with an ITS, human learners generally have some prior exposure to learning materials or instruction. However, when AL agents are first instantiated they have no such prior knowledge. Weitekamp et al. [21] attempted to estimate the number of prior practice opportunities per knowledge component needed to get a set of simulated learners on par with their human counterparts by extrapolating backwards with AFM [3]. In this work, we attempt to account for prior knowledge opportunities more precisely by using a pool of simulated learners trained on randomly generated problems. We estimate the number of prior opportunities per KC by finding the opportunity at which the pool of agents' learning curves best align with the first opportunity rate of the human data. To model each student individually we perturb the log odds of the target error rate by the AFM student intercept, yielding an individualized number of estimated prior opportunities for each knowledge component per student. This estimate is then used to pretrain each agent before it practices on the set of problems solved by its human counterpart.

Whereas [21] trained using only whole problems, we developed a new training procedure capable of training individual knowledge components. For all of the knowledge components of a particular problem type we train agents on random problems up to the minimum number of estimated prior opportunities over the constituent knowledge components. Any opportunities needed beyond this point are trained by having the agent solve problems from start to finish as usual, but only providing agents feedback on steps associated with knowledge components that still need practice. This new pretraining procedure can be applied to any step-based ITS with labelled KCs [17].

4   Results

Figure 2 shows learning curves for each type of error compared across the human data and AL using the two different *when-learning* mechanisms Decision Tree and TRESTLE. In accounting for prior knowledge, we find different results across the two methods. For the TRESTLE condition the overall error rate on the first opportunity is equivalent to the first opportunity error rate in the human data. For the Decision Tree, we find that AL has a first opportunity error rate that

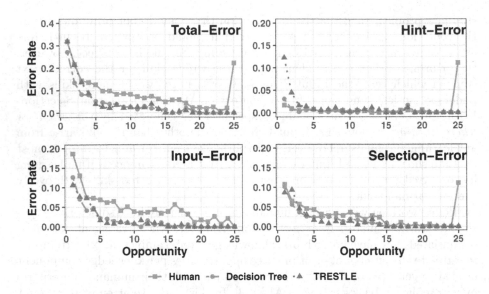

Fig. 2. Error-rate learning curves for each type of error (Total-Error, Hint-Error, Selection-Error, Input-Error) plotted by dataset (Human, AL with Decision Tree, AL with TRESTLE). Note the difference in y-axis scale between Total-Error and the others

is 4% lower than the human error rate – AL received on average too many pre-training opportunities and "over shot" the student state, indicating an imperfection in the pre-training method that we discuss below. In both conditions these results show an improvement over prior work which reported a first opportunity error rate discrepancy of 11% on the same dataset [21].

Overall, we find that AL agents with both *when-learning* methods learn more rapidly by opportunity than the human students. The AFM slope averaged over all KCs is 2.1 times greater than the humans for AL in both the Decision Tree and TRESTLE conditions. Additionally, In the Decision Tree and TRESTLE conditions the proportion of Input-Errors to Selection-Errors is roughly 1.1 whereas the human students make these errors at a ratio of 1.7. Both AL and the human students make almost all of their Hint-Errors within the first 5 opportunities. Only 5% of the human errors in the first 5 opportunities are Hint-Errors, however, TRESTLE based agents make considerably more Hint-Errors in these 5 opportunities at 26%. The Decision Tree makes 8% Hint-Errors over the first 5 opportunities, which is 60% more Hint-Errors than in the human data.

5   Discussion

We have compared AL agents with two different *when-learning* configurations to human data collected from a fraction arithmetic ITS. We have made this comparison using our novel method for splitting error curves by error type. In this section we discuss the implications of these results toward converging on a more accurate computational model of human learning. We discuss potential future features of the Apprentice Learner Architecture, and discuss how these changes would affect the trends of AL agent learning curves split by error type.

5.1   Accounting for Prior Knowledge

The pretraining method outlined in Weitekamp et al. [21] pretrained simulated learners to within 11% of the human first opportunity rate. In this study, we have used the same TRESTLE *when-learning* strategy and dataset, but have employed a new method for accounting for prior knowledge in our simulated learners which matched the human first opportunity rate to within less than 0.1%. Our strategy was however, not quite as successful with the other agent configuration, which used the Decision Tree *when-learning* mechanism. This remaining discrepancy between AL and the human data may have to do with the granularity by which we can estimate prior opportunities for each knowledge component. The first opportunity error rate for some of the knowledge components in the human data is well over 50%, but for most knowledge components the pool of AL agents trained on random fraction arithmetic problems take only 4 or fewer opportunities on average to learn beyond 50% error. This means that our pre-training strategy is still fairly sensitive to rounding. When finding the best whole number of opportunities to pretrain to get the desired first opportunity error rate, rounding to the nearest opportunity can lead to large discrepancies since the difference in error rates between early opportunities is large.

5.2   Learning Curve Comparison

The split error curves in all three conditions indicate that our AL agents' pace of performance improvement by opportunity is much higher than the human students. Thus, we would expect any method for lowering the amount of learning per opportunity to improve the fit of our simulated learners to human data. Additionally, slowing down our agents' learning in this way would alleviate some of the rounding issues we have had with estimating prior knowledge since the learning curves would be less steep overall. The issue remains of determining how learning should be slowed. Recall that a simulated learner embodies a theory of human learning, thus our objective should not simply be to make our learners fit better to human data, but to do so in a theoretically and empirically grounded manner in order to converge on a model of human learning that is predictive across a wide range of domains and conditions.

On the empirical side, our learning curves split by error type provide a few insights concerning our three configurations of AL agents. Firstly, we find that the AL agents that employed TRESTLE made considerably more Hint-Errors than human students early in the learning process. For an AL agent a Hint-Error is committed when it encounters a problem state in which it believes that none of its learned skills are applicable. When this occurs, AL agents ask for a demonstration of the next correct step. Hint-Errors generally occur early on in learning when skills either do not exist or have induced *when* and *where* conditions that are overly specific to previously seen training examples. In other words, Hint-Errors occur either when there is no appropriate *how* function induction for the then-part or when the preconditions for applying the correct skill for a step have not yet generalized to the point that they have become inclusive of all potential correct uses of that skill.

One capability which AL agents currently lack that may reduce the rate of Hint-Errors and increase the rate of Incorrect responses is the ability to make a plausible inference based on "weak methods" for more general problem solving [12] or by guessing, perhaps based on past response frequency. Human students sometimes rely on weak methods or guessing in the absence of strong hypotheses for what to do next [19]. Plausible inference may be informed by prior knowledge and involve actually taking actions similar to those in prior learned domains, or may even be slightly superstitious, (i.e., this seems like the kind of problem where the answer is 0) or based on interface heuristics (i.e., I usually operate on things that are next to each other). Further investigations are needed to select from or derive weak methods for plausible inference.

Another method for reducing Hint-Errors would be to use a *when-learning* mechanism that generalizes heavily from positive examples or incorporates negative feedback conservatively so that skills tend to be applied in spite of negative feedback. The Decision Tree appears to have this characteristic more so than TRESTLE.

One approach to plausible inference is to incorporating a memory mechanism. One weak method for plausible inference is to propose the action with the highest current memory activation (e.g., because of recency or history frequency of repetition or spacing). The AL agents tested in this work have no current means for such inference, and correspondingly, no means for forgetting skills or inferences. AL agents could incorporate methods of forgetting prior examples, features of problem states, induced internal states, or whole skills. While most existing literature on memory mechanisms pertains to the effects of memory on learning facts [1], it may be that a model like Anderson's ACT-R model of practice spacing and retention [13] is applicable to skills as well as facts. Overall a memory mechanism would likely slow down the learning rate of AL agents, although the effects of a memory mechanism on the proportion of Hint-Errors to Incorrect responses would likely depend on the implementation. The inclusion of a model of forgetting entire skills would likely further increase the number of Hint-Errors, however the spurious activation of other skills may make up for this and produce more Incorrect responses.

5.3   The Relative Rate of Input and Selection Errors

Another empirical result from our split learning curves is that among Incorrect responses human learners consistently make a larger proportion of Input-Errors than Selection-Errors over the course of learning. By contrast, AL agents consistently make these errors at about the same rate. One likely explanation for this difference is that the human students' Input-Error learning curve includes instances of arithmetic mistakes when computing the right-hand side operations of skills. Currently, AL agents employ domain general operator functions to perform arithmetic and thus are incapable of making this kind of error. It may be possible to further split out these errors as a separate type of error with their own learning curve. One possible method for separating out these sorts of errors would be to use the methods employed by AL's *how-learning* mechanism in the error type labelling process to find errors which cannot be explained by applying weak methods on the values in the interface.

5.4   Other Uses of Learning Curve Splitting

Our method of splitting learning curves likely has uses for student modeling outside of the realm of simulated learners. Analyzing the rate of Selection-Errors and Input-Errors separately may help measure the efficacy of interventions baked into ITSs. For example, CTAT tutoring systems often correct students when they are working on the wrong step of a problem (i.e., a Selection-Error). Adding elaborative feedback to these messages to explain what the correct next step is and why it is correct may improve "if" and "then" type learning differently. The relative effect of such an intervention on these two types of learning could be measured directly with split learning curves to help refine feedback messages.

In this study we have grouped several distinct patterns into just two groups, but there may also be uses for splitting errors further. For example, one pattern we encode picks out cases where students have provided a correct answer for a later step. Analyzing the rate of this kind of error may help catch instances where a tutoring system arbitrarily constrains the order that steps can be taken. It may also help identify cases where students are restricted from providing a final answer produced through mental steps.

6   Conclusion

Just as theoretical physics complements experimental physics we suggest here, a need for more computational learning science to complement experimental learning science. Simulated learners are computational theories of human learning which model inductive human learning processes by working in and learning from ITSs. Evaluating and refining simulated learners as computational theories requires measuring the accuracy with which simulated learners match the specific learning behaviors of humans. In this work, we have presented two new methods to help make this comparison more precise. We have developed an improvement on previous methods [21] for accounting for prior knowledge in simulated learners, and we have developed a new method of splitting learning curves by error type.

We have employed these two methods in a comparison of simulated learners built with the Apprentice Learner Architecture and found that when prior knowledge is accounted for, AL agents learn about twice as fast as human learners, commit more initial Hint-Errors than humans, and produce a lower proportion of Input-Errors to Selection-Errors. Finally, we have discussed several potential refinements of our current model based on these results such as alterations to *when-learning* mechanisms and the inclusion of mechanisms for forgetting, and the usage of weak methods that produce plausible inferences or guesses.

References

1. Anderson, J.R., Bothell, D., Byrne, M.D., Douglass, S., Lebiere, C., Qin, Y.: An integrated theory of the mind. Psychol. Rev. **111**(4), 1042–1044 (2004)
2. Breiman, L.: Classification and Regression Trees. Routledge, Boca Raton (2017)
3. Cen, H., Koedinger, K., Junker, B.: Learning factors analysis – a general method for cognitive model evaluation and improvement. In: Ikeda, M., Ashley, K.D., Chan, T.-W. (eds.) ITS 2006. LNCS, vol. 4053, pp. 164–175. Springer, Heidelberg (2006). https://doi.org/10.1007/11774303_17
4. Koedinger, K.R., Baker, R.S., Cunningham, K., Skogsholm, A., Leber, B., Stamper, J.: A data repository for the EDM community: the PSLC datashop. In: Romero, C., Ventura, S., Pechenizkiy, M., Baker, R. (eds.) Handbook of Educational Data Mining, pp. 43–56. CRC Press, Boca Raton (2010)
5. Li, N., Cohen, W.W., Koedinger, K.R., Matsuda, N.: A machine learning approach for automatic student model discovery. In: EDM, pp. 31–40. ERIC (2011)
6. MacLellan, C.J.: Computational models of human learning: applications for tutor development, behavior prediction, and theory testing. Ph.D. thesis, Carnegie Mellon University (2017)
7. MacLellan, C.J., Harpstead, E., Aleven, V., Koedinger, K.R., et al.: Trestle: a model of concept formation in structured domains. Adv. Cogn. Syst. **4**, 131–150 (2016)
8. Maclellan, C.J., Harpstead, E., Patel, R., Koedinger, K.R.: The apprentice learner architecture: closing the loop between learning theory and educational data. In: International Conference on Educational Data Mining Society (2016)
9. Matsuda, N., Cohen, W.W., Koedinger, K.R.: Teaching the teacher: tutoring simstudent leads to more effective cognitive tutor authoring. Int. J. Artif. Intell. Educ. **25**(1), 1–34 (2015)
10. Matsuda, N., Keiser, V., Raizada, R., Stylianides, G., Cohen, W.W., Koedinger, K.R.: Learning by teaching simstudent – interactive event. In: Biswas, G., Bull, S., Kay, J., Mitrovic, A. (eds.) AIED 2011. LNCS (LNAI), vol. 6738, pp. 623–623. Springer, Heidelberg (2011). https://doi.org/10.1007/978-3-642-21869-9_124
11. Murray, R.C., et al.: Revealing the learning in learning curves. In: Lane, H.C., Yacef, K., Mostow, J., Pavlik, P. (eds.) AIED 2013. LNCS (LNAI), vol. 7926, pp. 473–482. Springer, Heidelberg (2013). https://doi.org/10.1007/978-3-642-39112-5_48
12. Newell, A., Shaw, J.C., Simon, H.A.: Report on a general problem solving program. In: IFIP Congress, Pittsburgh, PA, vol. 256, p. 64 (1959)
13. Pavlik, P.I., Anderson, J.R.: Using a model to compute the optimal schedule of practice. J. Exp. Psychol. Appl. **14**(2), 101 (2008)
14. Pavlik Jr, P.I., Cen, H., Koedinger, K.R.: Performance factors analysis - a new alternative to knowledge tracing. Online Submission (2009)
15. Ritter, S., Anderson, J.R., Koedinger, K.R., Corbett, A.: Cognitive tutor: applied research in mathematics education. Psychon. Bull. Rev. **14**(2), 249–255 (2007)

16. Roads, B.D., Mozer, M.C.: Predicting the ease of human category learning using radial basis function networks (2019)
17. VanLehn, K.: The interaction plateau: answer-based tutoring step-based tutoring = natural tutoring. In: Woolf, B.P., Aïmeur, E., Nkambou, R., Lajoie, S. (eds.) ITS 2008. LNCS, vol. 5091, p. 7. Springer, Heidelberg (2008). https://doi.org/10. 1007/978-3-540-69132-7_4
18. VanLehn, K., Ohlsson, S., Nason, R.: Applications of simulated students: an exploration. J. Artif. Intell. Educ. **5**(2), 1–42 (1994)
19. Waller, M.I.: Modeling guessing behavior: a comparison of two IRT models. Appl. Psychol. Meas. **13**(3), 233–243 (1989)
20. Weitekamp, D., Harpstead, E., Koedinger, K.: An interaction design for machine teaching to develop AI tutors. In: CHI (2020)
21. Weitekamp III, D., Harpstead, E., MacLellan, C.J., Rachatasumrit, N., Koedinger, K.R.: Toward near zero-parameter prediction using a computational model of student learning, Ann Arbor (2009)

Studying the Interactions Between Science, Engineering, and Computational Thinking in a Learning-by-Modeling Environment

Ningyu Zhang[1]([✉]) [ID], Gautam Biswas[1], Kevin W. McElhaney[2], Satabdi Basu[3], Elizabeth McBride[3], and Jennifer L. Chiu[4]

[1] Department of EECS, Institute for Software Integrated Systems, Vanderbilt University, 1025 16th Avenue South, Nashville, TN 37212, USA
{ningyu.zhang,gautam.biswas}@vanderbilt.edu
[2] Learning Sciences Research, Digital Promise, San Mateo, USA
kmcelhaney@digitalpromise.org
[3] Center for Education Research and Innovation, SRI International, Menlo Park, USA
{satabdi.basu,beth.mcbride}@sri.com
[4] Department of Curriculum, Instruction and Special Education, University of Virginia, Charlottesville, USA
jlchiu@virginia.edu

Abstract. Computational Thinking (CT) can play a central role in fostering students' integrated learning of science and engineering. We adopt this framework to design and develop the Water Runoff Challenge (WRC) curriculum for lower middle school students in the USA. This paper presents (1) the WRC curriculum implemented in an integrated computational modeling and engineering design environment and (2) formative and summative assessments used to evaluate learner's science, engineering, and CT skills as they progress through the curriculum. We derived a series of performance measures associated with student learning from system log data and the assessments. By applying Path Analysis we found significant relations between measures of science, engineering, and CT learning, indicating that they are mutually supportive of learning across these disciplines.

Keywords: Science and engineering · Computational modeling · Log analysis · Regression methods

1 Introduction

The Next Generation Science Standards (NGSS) call for the inclusion of engineering design activities in K-12 science classrooms and propose that science investigation and engineering design be closely integrated into the curriculum [19,22]. In addition, computational modeling and analysis have become

© Springer Nature Switzerland AG 2020
I. I. Bittencourt et al. (Eds.): AIED 2020, LNAI 12163, pp. 598–609, 2020.
https://doi.org/10.1007/978-3-030-52237-7_48

a key component of scientific study [8]. We adopt an integrated approach to developing science and engineering curricula, bringing in computational thinking (CT) concepts through computational modeling activities to develop the Water Runoff Challenge (WRC) for fifth and sixth grade students [4,34].

This paper discusses the WRC curriculum, the learning environment that supports the computational modeling and engineering design activities, and the formative and summative assessments developed for evaluating student learning. We discuss the results of a study with 99 sixth-grade students. The intervention produced significant learning gains in science, engineering, and CT with moderate to large effect sizes. Given these results, we applied Path Analysis [1,33] to model the relationships between measures of student learning in science, engineering, and CT, and interpreted their relative importance. In more detail, we derived a range of measures from logs of student activities and their assessment scores to investigate (1) the relations between students' behavior and performance variables in the computational modeling and engineering design activities and (2) which of these variables contribute to the learning outcomes. Path analysis also informs us of the importance and significance of pairwise relations.

1.1 Background and Related Work

The majority of people in the U.S. are introduced to science and engineering in middle and high schools, and the experiences in these formative years shape their interest in pursuing science and engineering careers [15,25]. However, engineering had not traditionally been part of the core K-12 curriculum, instead often being offered as an elective or after-school course, where students primarily work on design projects with little discussion of the science that supports the design and implementation [6].

Recently, the "growing inclusion of engineering design in K-12 classrooms" presents students with opportunities to construct an understanding of the natural and designed world [19, p. vii]. It has been proposed that *science investigation*, which includes students' investigating scientific phenomena and *engineering design*, i.e., applying the learned knowledge to design solutions to challenges of interest should be more central to the K-12 curricula [19].

Modeling is a key practice in science and an essential mechanism to support effective engineering design [20,24,28]. A model is defined as an abstract and simplified representation of a scientific phenomenon built around the important features that explain and predict the phenomenon [9,28]. *Computational modeling* has become integral to STEM learning and practice [21,30]. Computational modeling activities can support the learning of science and engineering in virtual environments by (1) enabling learners to manipulate variables on unobservable phenomena and (2) improving the efficiency and reducing unanticipated consequences of experimental studies [7]. In other words, learners have more opportunities to conduct systematic investigations and gather more information as compared to conducting observations in a physical environment [7]. For example, chemical reactions (invisible) and geological changes (long-term) are easier to study by simulating computational models than trying to conduct physical or observational studies. Students' engagement with computational modeling activities provides instructional benefits of improved domain knowledge and problem-solving skills [2,29,31].

2   The Learning Environment in the WRC Curriculum

Our research is motivated by the trends towards integrated learning of science and engineering. Furthermore, we introduce CT and computational modeling activities as a platform for integrated engineering and science learning [30,32]. *Exploration* with models involves manipulating parameters to study the model's behaviors. On the other hand, model exploration often does not require invoking the complex cognitive processes required to build models, which includes scoping the model, developing algorithms to represent model behaviors, computing numerical outcomes, interpreting results, and validating solutions; neither do students have to fully understand the nuances of the modeling language employed [18,29]. In our *previous* work, students used a pre-built computational model for their engineering task to develop and test playground designs to mitigate flooding problems in a school [4,34]. In the present work, we introduce computational model building activities into the WRC curriculum unit. Students used the runoff computational models that they developed themselves to design a schoolyard that reduced runoff and its associated environmental impact.

Our previous runoff model was *dynamic*; the model representations needed to capture the behavior of a system over time [29]. An *agent-based approach* to modeling [5] makes the model modular and facilitates decomposition into its constituent parts. For compatibility with middle school math proficiency, the systems dynamics model was simplified to a discrete-time algebraic form [29]. This simplified representation computes the amount of rainfall, absorption, and runoff with three simultaneous equations. To make this form of modeling representation explicit and linked to the science concepts, we have created a domain-specific modeling language (DSML) to support students' computational modeling activities [10]. DSMLs specify modeling constructs at a level of abstraction that is compatible with the students' ability to build and analyze the model.

Figure 1 shows the DSML blocks created for the computational modeling activity on the left, and a correct implementation of the runoff model using these blocks on the right. The DSML, created in the NetsBlox visual programming environment [3], incorporates CT concepts, such as control structures along with the primary domain concepts to support the modeling of the water runoff processes: (1) the amount of rainfall (2) absorption of water by different surface materials, and (3) runoff. In addition, the DSML specifies key arithmetic and algebraic mathematical operations to support model-building. Using the DSML blocks, students create a rule-based computational model, which is a simplification of the system dynamics model. The runoff for a specific material is computed as the difference in the amount of rainfall and the amount of water that is absorbed by the surface material (see the example implementation in Fig. 1).

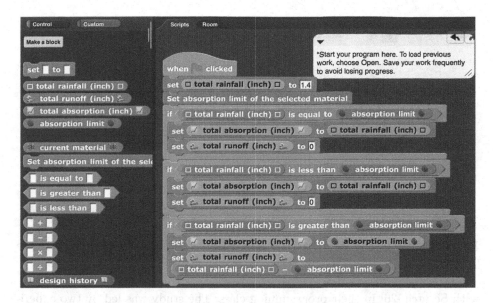

Fig. 1. DSML of the runoff problem (left) and a correct implementation of the runoff model using the DSML (right).

Students build schoolyards models for their engineering design tasks. They do this using a visual interface to populate individual squares with different surface materials (Fig. 2). The computational models that the students develop are used to calculate the total absorption and total runoff given a total amount of rainfall that the student specifies. The students can build and test multiple schoolyard designs using different combinations of materials. Their overall goal is to (1) minimize runoff, (2) remain under budget; and (3) ensure that sufficient squares in the schoolyard have accessible surface materials to meet wheelchair needs. Students need to generate multiple designs using a search process to find the *optimal* design that meets all of the constraints, i.e., minimize runoff, while meeting the cost and accessibility constraints. This design task is challenging for young learners. Typically, the more absorbent and accessible materials also tend to have high costs, so students need to analyze the trade-offs between cost, absorption, and accessibility in searching for optimal design solutions. A non-systematic *trial-and-error* approach may overwhelm a student's search. Figure 2 (right) depicts the engineering design interface. The current solution is incomplete, and students can assign any of the six available materials to the unassigned yellow square.

3   Methods

We conducted a classroom study with 99 sixth-grade middle school students in the U.S. using the WRC curriculum. All participating students had varying levels of prior programming experience with block-structured programming

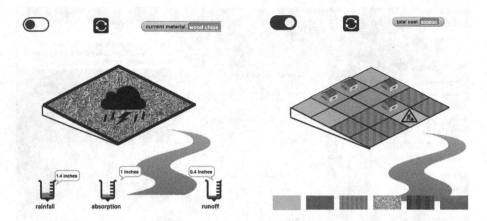

Fig. 2. The runoff simulation (left) and material selection (right) interface (Color figure online)

with Scratch [26] in their programming class. The study was led by two experienced science teachers who received four days of training before the study. Three researchers provided additional support but mostly acted as observers during the study. Students worked for 45 min per day, three days a week during their regular science classes, and 75 min, twice a week with additional personalized-learning time. The WRC curriculum was covered in 15 school days, with identical pre-post tests administered in two additional 45-min classes.

The WRC unit also includes (1) hands-on activities in which students conduct physical investigations on the absorption of different surface materials; (2) conceptual modeling of the runoff system as a pictorial representation; and (3) presenting their methods and final engineering designs. This paper analyzes the NGSS-aligned science and engineering + CT pre-post assessments and the data collected on days 8–13. This includes (1) formative assessments administered as homework that covered science, engineering, and CT topics; and (2) system logs of students' model-building and engineering design activities.

Assessments and Grading. Our science and engineering summative assessments align with a number of NGSS Performance Expectations (PEs) [16,17]. The CT assessments are derived from the concepts and practices that students perform as part of their science modeling activities. The rubrics used for coding and scoring these assessments were updated from our previous work [16]. Two researchers received 5 h of training on the rubrics, during which 5% of the test submissions were randomly selected and graded together to establish initial grading consistency. Another 20% test submissions were then graded by the two researchers independently to establish inter-rater reliability (Cohen's κ at ≥ 0.8 level on all items). All differences in the coding were discussed and resolved before the remaining 75% of test submissions were graded by a single researcher. We also designed *formative* assessment tasks that mirror the curricular tasks students worked on in the WRC. These tasks measured students' understanding of (1) the water conservation relations, (2) the relative effect of different surface materials on runoff, (3) the ability to compute water runoff and absorption under different circumstances, (4) the ability to debug incomplete or incorrect model code, and (5) the method to compare different design solutions considering trade-offs. We used students' responses to 14 items from 6 formative assessment tasks in this work.

Log Analysis. The learning environment logs individual students' actions during their computational model-building and engineering design activities. We calculated three behavioral measures from students' **computational modeling** activities: (1) the total number of add, remove, connect, or disconnect blocks actions, (2) the number of run the model actions to test the computational model, and (3) the median number of edit actions between tests (because students often perform a series of edits without testing or a series of testing without editing the model, the median number is a more robust measure given the skewness in the data). In addition to deriving behavior measures, we defined a computational model score for the student-generated models. A correct computational model scored 6 points (1 point for each correctly implemented function that calculates and assigns values to an output variable. There were two variables each in the three rules, see Fig. 1 for reference). To allow students to conduct meaningful design activities, the researchers made an effort to ensure that all students' had correct computational models before they started the design activity. Common errors were discussed with the whole class, and the students were given a chance to correct their models. The model scores reported in this work were calculated *before* the correction feedback was provided to the students.

Our measurements of students' *engineering design* quality and their learning behaviors have been discussed in our previous work [34]. The two quality measurements used are: (1) the number of satisfying designs and (2) the smallest runoff value from all of the satisfying designs created by a student. The two behavior measurements used are: (1) the number of tests conducted to evaluate designs; and (2) the total standardized Euclidean distance between a student's m consecutive tested designs, i.e., $\sum_{i=1}^{m-1} ||(V_{i+1} - V_i)^2||$ where $V = \langle runoff_z, cost_z, accessiblilty_z \rangle$. The subscript z indicates the standardized value of runoff, cost, and accessibility of a design. The total standardized Euclidean distance and the number of tested designs indicate the extent to which a learner explored the engineering design *experiment space* [12].

Path Analysis. Traditional regression methods assume that (1) only direct associations exist between dependent and independent variables and (2) errors in the dependent variable are uncorrelated with the independent variable [1,33]. When applied to intrinsically related variables, where indirect variables play a mitigating role, multi-regression or correlation analysis do not provide optimal model estimates [23]. Path Analysis addresses these problems. It can be seen as a variation of Structural Equation Modeling [13] without the latent variables. In this work, we use Path Analysis to study the effects and the relative importance

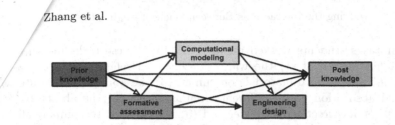

Fig. 3. Hypothesized path model.

of effects among the measured performance and behavior values. We hypothesize that students' prior knowledge and formative assessment scores influence their subsequent learning behaviors, computational model building and engineering design performance, and post-test scores in the WRC curriculum. This is represented by the causal path model shown in Fig. 3. Each arrow in the diagram indicates a direct effect on the endogenous variable from the exogenous variable.

4 Results and Discussions

4.1 Learning Performances and Behaviors

Students' pre-post test scores were compared to determine their learning gains in science, engineering, and CT. To check the normality of the scores, we first measured the skewness (z-value = -0.811, p-value = 0.417) and kurtosis (z-value = -0.567, p-value = 0.571) of the score distributions and confirmed that they were close to a normal distribution. Therefore, we used the paired t-test to evaluate the statistical significance of the pre-post score differences. Table 1 shows that all differences are statistically significant with moderate (≥ 0.5) to large (≥ 0.8) effect sizes.

Table 1. Learning gains (N = 99)

	Total points	Pre-score (*stdev*)	Post-score (*stdev*)	p-value	Cohen's d
Science	7	4.56 (1.03)	5.13 (1.04)	<0.001	0.54
Engineering	16	8.73 (2.62)	10.50 (2.67)	<0.0001	0.67
CT	13	6.23 (2.60)	8.41 (2.69)	<0.0001	0.83
Overall	36	19.52 (4.47)	24.03 (4.39)	<0.0001	1.02

Formative Assessment. The average score of the integrated science, engineering, and CT formative assessment was 19.05 points (*stdev* = 4.57) out of maximum possible scores of 31 points. This result, along with the pre-post test gains, indicates that the students were learning the domain content, CT concepts and skills, and engineering design practices through the intervention.

Computational Modeling. Students showed a large variation in their computational model-building behaviors. On average, they made 167 edits (*stdev* = 77) to build their computational models, and they performed 43 tests ($stdev = 47$) on them. The average of the median number of edits between tests was 1.11, indicating the student mostly made edits in small chunks between successive model tests. The average computational model score was 4.67 ($stdev = 1.85$), and 59% of the students created a correct computational model before the answer was disclosed in class. The model component with the least number of correct implementations ($n = 67$) was "set *total runoff* to (*total rainfall − absorption limit*)" when "*total rainfall* is greater than *absorption limit*" (c.f. Fig. 1).

Engineering Design. The students performed an average of 29.4 tests ($stdev = 22.2$) on their schoolyard designs. The average total standardized Euclidean distance was 18.6 ($stdev = 19.0$). The average number of unique designs that satisfied the criteria for cost and accessibility was 6.3 ($stdev = 4.2$). Ninety students created and tested at least 1 satisfying design, and the average amount of runoff for the satisfying design solutions, with 2 inch of rainfall, was 1.23 inch ($stdev = 0.94$). The global minimal runoff of all satisfying designs was 0.96 inch, and 29 students got at this optimal solution. These results show that most students created feasible design solutions.

4.2   Path Analysis

We created a path diagram of the measured variables using the IBM® SPSS® Amos 26 software. We modeled a total of 47 direct effects from the 15 variables in the path diagram. As a pre-analysis suggested by [27], we evaluated the assumptions of multivariate normality and then removed four outliers from subsequent analyses, leaving a sample size of 95 for the Path Analysis. 1000 bootstrap samples were generated to estimate the standard errors and calculate the confidence intervals at the 95% level. The standard errors and their critical ratios were later used to evaluate the statistical significance of the modeled causal effects while reducing the variance in the observed variables.

We also calculated model-fitting statistics of the path model as compared to the saturated model [27]: $\chi^2 = 40.89$ ($DF = 54$, p-value $= 0.91$); the goodness of fit (GFI) was 0.95 (≥ 0.95 threshold); the comparative fit index (CFI) was 0.99 (>0.9 threshold); and the root mean square error of approximation (RMSEA) was 0.01 (<0.06 threshold). These statistics indicate that the path model derived fitted the measurements well. All of the hypothesized paths in Fig. 3 were confirmed as direct or indirect effects. Figure 4 shows the statistically significant causal paths that are large ($\beta > 0.2$).

Computational Modeling. The students' learning behaviors and performance in the computational modeling activity (yellow boxes in Fig. 4) were directly affected by variables in the same category and the formative assessment score. The CT pre-test score also indirectly related to the *comp_model_ score* and *comp_edits* (via *formative*, *comp_test*, and *edit_btw_tests*) with total β's of 0.28 and 0.28, respectively (indirect effects are not shown in Fig. 4). As one of the

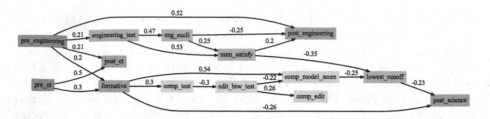

Fig. 4. Discovered causal paths with statistically significant direct effects. (Color figure online)

main learning outcomes, the students' *comp_model_score* was also significantly affected by the median number of model edits between tests (*edit_btw_test*), indicating students who edited their model in *small* chunks between tests did better in the computational model-building task. Similar results of smaller edit chunks being associated with better models have also been reported by [2]. The engineering pre-test score (*pre_eng*) also had a statistically significant but small (total $\beta = 0.12$) indirect effect on *comp_model_score* through *formative*.

Engineering Design. The number of unique satisfying designs (*num_satisfy*) and the lowest amount of runoff of satisfying designs (*lowest_runoff*) were the two variables evaluating the quality of students' designs. For *num_satisfy*, the strongest direct effects came from the number of tests on the designs (*engineering_test*, $\beta = 0.53$) and the total standardized Euclidean distance between the tested designs (*eng_euclid*, $\beta = 0.25$). The *lowest_runoff* was most strongly affected by *num_satisfy* ($\beta = -0.35$) and *comp_model_score* ($\beta = -0.25$).

These results align with our previous findings with a group of fifth-grade students in another school that students who explored a larger portion of the problem space were more likely to generate better engineering design solutions [34]. It also matched the *scientific discovery as dual search* theory [12] that successful learners connect the *hypothesis space* and the *experiment space* by making inferences with data drawn from their investigations. More importantly, these results suggest a strong connection between computational modeling (*comp_model_score*) and engineering design (*lowest_runoff*) with a total standardized effect of -0.32 ($\beta = -0.25$, total indirect effect is -0.07). The negative value indicates that students making better computational models on their own generated better design solutions, even though all students were shown the correct implementation of the computational model before the engineering design activity. It also indicates the benefits of having students develop their own computational model to use for designing and testing, relative to providing students with a model that has been developed by experts.

Post-test Scores. The **science** post-test scores (*post_sci*) were significantly influenced by *lowest_runoff* ($\beta = -0.23$), *num_satisfy* (indirectly, total β's = 0.08), *engineering_test* (indirectly, total β =0.08), and *comp_model_score* (indirectly, total $\beta = 0.04$). The **engineering** post-test scores were mostly affected by *pre_eng* ($\beta = 0.52$), *eng_euclid* ($\beta = -0.25$), and *num_satisfy* (indirectly, total β's $= 0.20$). The effect from *num_satisfy* indicates that students' success in solving the engineering design problem by searching for the optimal combinations of surface materials on the schoolyard reflected better learning outcomes. As of the **CT** post-test score, it was only significantly affected by the related pre-test scores. The variable *comp_model_score* had a relatively large total effect of 0.14 on *post_ct* yet the effect was not statistically significant.

These overall positive results suggest that the students' success with the engineering design activities can be linked to their science and engineering proficiencies, providing evidence for the benefit of integrating engineering with science learning [19]. In addition, the effect of engineering activities on the summative assessments suggested that the design goals of the WRC curriculum were achieved, and students' high learning gains (Cohen's $d = 1.02$) illustrated the benefits of integrating instruction across engineering and science.

Future Work. In the present work, we identified the connections between computational modeling, engineering design, and the learning outcomes as *effects* on the causal paths. Such connections might not be discovered by only examining the associations between the variables using model-less correlation methods [23]. For example, the correlation coefficient (Spearman's ρ) between *comp_model_score* and *lowest_runoff* was -0.11 ($p = 0.28$). This suggests that Path Analysis is an effective technique to study the relationship between related variables, such as the measures derived from the WRC.

This work can be further advanced by employing more sophisticated measures. For example, we used a simple heuristic to measure the computational modeling performance. We plan to (1) implement more sophisticated methods to study the structure of the students' models (e.g., abstract syntax trees (ASTs) [14]) and (2) include machine learning methods (e.g., sequence mining [11]) to analyze and understand their learning processes and learning strategies. These measures will help us design online feedback in the system to support student learning.

5   Conclusions

The Water Runoff Challenge is one of the first examples of NGSS-aligned curricula that support the interdisciplinary learning of science, engineering, and CT. In the present work, the curriculum is enhanced by enabling computational modeling activities for students to develop and practice CT instead of performing engineering design with a pre-built model. Results from our classroom study demonstrated the instructional benefits of using the WRC and provided empirical evidence to support the integration of engineering activities with science learning and computational model building, especially in early K-12 settings.

Our studies point to ways that using computational modeling to integrate science and engineering can merge insights from two learning research traditions: developing computational artifacts and engaging in simulation-based problem-solving. Specifically, our analysis suggests potential benefits of guiding students' development of a computational scientific model prior to using the model to solve a related engineering problem. Further research is needed to better understand the learning processes that produce such benefits and identify instructional design features that best take advantage of them.

Acknowledgment. This material is based upon work supported by the National Science Foundation under Grant No. DRL-1742195. Any opinions, findings, and conclusions or recommendations expressed in this material are those of the author(s) and do not necessarily reflect the views of the National Science Foundation.

References

1. Ahn, J.: Beyond single equation regression analysis: path analysis and multi-stage regression analysis. Am. J. Pharm. Educ. **66**(1), 37–41 (2002)
2. Basu, S., Biswas, G., Kinnebrew, J.S.: Learner modeling for adaptive scaffolding in a computational thinking-based science learning environment. User Model. User Adap. Inter. **27**(1), 5–53 (2017)
3. Broll, B., et al.: A visual programming environment for introducing distributed computing to secondary education. J. Parallel Distrib. Comput. **118**, 189–200 (2018)
4. Chiu, J., et al.: A principled approach to NGSS-aligned curriculum development integrating science, engineering, and computation: a pilot study. Paper Presented at the 2019 NARST Annual International Conference (2019)
5. Collins, A., Ferguson, W.: Epistemic forms and epistemic games: structures and strategies to guide inquiry. Educ. Psychol. **28**(1), 25–42 (1993)
6. Cunningham, C.M., Knight, M.T., Carlsen, W.S., Kelly, G.: Integrating engineering in middle and high school classrooms. Int. J. Eng. Educ. **23**(1), 3 (2007)
7. de Jong, T., Linn, M.C., Zacharia, Z.C.: Physical and virtual laboratories in science and engineering education, April 2013. https://doi.org/10.1126/science.1230579. http://www.sciencemag.org/cgi/doi/10.1126/science.1230579
8. Denning, P.J.: The profession of IT beyond computational thinking. Commun. ACM **52**(6), 28–30 (2009)
9. Harrison, A.G., Treagust, D.F.: A typology of school science models. Int. J. Sci. Educ. **22**(9), 1011–1026 (2000)
10. Hutchins, N., Biswas, G., Zhang, N., Snyder, C., Lédeczi, Á., Maróti, M.: Domain-specific modeling languages in computer-based learning environments: a systematic approach to scaffold science learning through computational modeling. Int. J. Artif. Intell. Educ. (submitted, under review)
11. Kinnebrew, J.S., Loretz, K.M., Biswas, G.: A contextualized, differential sequence mining method to derive students' learning behavior patterns. JEDM J. Educ. Data Min. **5**(1), 190–219 (2013)
12. Klahr, D., Dunbar, K.: Dual space search during scientific reasoning. Cogn. Sci. **12**(1), 1–48 (1988)
13. Kline, R.B.: Principles and Practice of Structural Equation Modeling. Guilford Publications, New York (2015)
14. Lazar, T., Možina, M., Bratko, I.: Automatic extraction of AST patterns for debugging student programs. In: André, E., Baker, R., Hu, X., Rodrigo, M.M.T., du Boulay, B. (eds.) AIED 2017. LNCS (LNAI), vol. 10331, pp. 162–174. Springer, Cham (2017). https://doi.org/10.1007/978-3-319-61425-0_14

15. Maltese, A.V., Tai, R.H.: Eyeballs in the fridge: sources of early interest in science. Int. J. Sci. Educ. **32**(5), 669–685 (2010)
16. McElhaney, K.W., Basu, S., Wetzel, T., Boyce, J.: Three-dimensional assessment of NGSS upper elementary engineering design performance expectations. Paper Presented at the 2019 NARST Annual International Conference (2019)
17. McElhaney, K.W., Zhang, N., Basu, S., McBride, E., Biswas, G., Chiu, J.: Using computational modeling to integrate science and engineering curricular activities. In: Proceedings of the International Conference of Learning Sciences, Nashville, USA (2020, in press)
18. Mehalik, M.M., Doppelt, Y., Schuun, C.D.: Middle-school science through design-based learning versus scripted inquiry: better overall science concept learning and equity gap reduction. J. Eng. Educ. **97**(1), 71–85 (2008)
19. National Academy of Engineering, National Academies of Sciences, Engineering, and Medicine: Science and engineering for grades 6–12: investigation and design at the center (2019). https://doi.org/10.17226/25216. https://www.nap.edu/catalog/25216/science-and-engineering-for-grades-6-12-investigation-and-design
20. National Research Council: Engineering in K-12 Education: Understanding the Status and Improving the Prospects. National Academies Press (2009)
21. National Research Council: A Framework for K-12 Science Education: Practices, Crosscutting Concepts, and Core Ideas. National Academies Press (2012)
22. NGSS Lead States: Next generation science standards: for states, by states (2013)
23. Pearl, J., Mackenzie, D.: The Book of Why: The New Science of Cause and Effect. Basic Books, New York (2018)
24. Penner, D.E.: Cognition, computers, and synthetic science: building knowledge and meaning through modeling. Rev. Res. Educ. **25**(1), 1–35 (2000). chap. 1
25. Pianta, R.C., Belsky, J., Houts, R., Morrison, F.: Opportunities to learn in America's elementary classrooms. Science **315**(5820), 1795–1796 (2007)
26. Resnick, M., et al.: Scratch: programming for all. Commun. ACM **52**(11), 60–67 (2009)
27. Schreiber, J.B., Nora, A., Stage, F.K., Barlow, E.A., King, J.: Reporting structural equation modeling and confirmatory factor analysis results: a review. J. Educ. Res. **99**(6), 323–338 (2006)
28. Schwarz, C.V., et al.: Developing a learning progression for scientific modeling: making scientific modeling accessible and meaningful for learners. J. Res. Sci. Teach. Official J. Natl. Assoc. Res. Sci. Teach. **46**(6), 632–654 (2009)
29. VanLehn, K.: Model construction as a learning activity: a design space and review. Interact. Learn. Environ. **21**(4), 371–413 (2013)
30. Weintrop, D., et al.: Defining computational thinking for mathematics and science classrooms. J. Sci. Educ. Technol. **25**(1), 127–147 (2016)
31. Wilkerson-Jerde, M., Wagh, A., Wilensky, U.: Balancing curricular and pedagogical needs in computational construction kits: lessons from the DeltaTick project. Sci. Educ. **99**(3), 465–499 (2015)
32. Wing, J.M.: Computational thinking. Commun. ACM **49**(3), 33–35 (2006)
33. Wright, S.: On "Path analysis in genetic epidemiology: a critique". Am. J. Hum. Genet. **35**(4), 757–768 (1983)
34. Zhang, N., Biswas, G., Chiu, J.L., McElhaney, K.W.: Analyzing students design solutions in an NGSS-aligned earth sciences curriculum. In: Isotani, S., Millán, E., Ogan, A., Hastings, P., McLaren, B., Luckin, R. (eds.) AIED 2019. LNCS (LNAI), vol. 11625, pp. 532–543. Springer, Cham (2019). https://doi.org/10.1007/978-3-030-23204-7_44

Exploring Automated Question Answering Methods for Teaching Assistance

Brian Zylich, Adam Viola, Brokk Toggerson, Lara Al-Hariri,
and Andrew Lan[✉]

University of Massachusetts Amherst, Amherst, USA
andrewlan@cs.umass.edu

Abstract. One important aspect of learning is through verbal interactions with teachers or teaching assistants (TAs), which requires significant effort and puts a heavy burden on teachers. Artificial intelligence has the potential to reduce their burden by automatically addressing the routine part of this interaction, which will free them up to focus on more important aspects of learning. We explore the use of automated question answering methods to power virtual TAs in online course discussion forums, which are heavily relied on during the COVID-19 pandemic as classes transition online. First, we focus on answering frequent and repetitive logistical questions and adopt a question answering framework that consists of two steps: retrieving relevant documents from a repository and extracting answers from retrieved documents. The document repository consists of course materials that contain information on course logistics, e.g., the syllabus, lecture slides, course emails, and prior discussion forum posts. This question answering framework can help virtual TAs decide whether a question is answerable and how to answer it. Second, we analyze the timing of student posts in discussion threads and develop a classifier to predict the timing of follow-up posts. This classifier can help virtual TAs decide whether to respond to a question and when to do so. We conduct experiments on data collected from an introductory physics course and discuss both the utility and limitations of our approach.

1 Introduction

Learning happens in many forms, including learning through self-regulated studies and learning through verbal interactions with a teacher. The latter is especially effective for problem solving [1,2] and when students experience negative emotions [3]. However, interacting with students individually requires a lot of effort from teachers, or sometimes teaching assistants (TAs), especially in large-scale educational settings such as online courses [4]. Teachers and TAs often face numerous tasks including reviewing the curriculum, teaching, creating and

B. Zylich—This material is based upon work supported by the National Science Foundation Graduate Research Fellowship under Grant No. 1938059.

© Springer Nature Switzerland AG 2020
I. I. Bittencourt et al. (Eds.): AIED 2020, LNAI 12163, pp. 610–622, 2020.
https://doi.org/10.1007/978-3-030-52237-7_49

grading assignments and exams, and answering questions in an online course discussion forum. These tasks not only put a heavy burden on teachers and TAs but also result in a slow and insufficient feedback cycle for students.

One solution to this problem is to use automated pedagogical agents driven by artificial intelligence (AI) to scale up teacher effort and interact with many students at the same time [5–8]. For example, using AI-driven *virtual TAs* in online course discussion forums such as Piazza has enjoyed some success [9–12]. However, there are many limitations to current virtual TAs and significant advances in AI must be made before they can become a reality. Below, we outline three major requirements virtual TAs have to satisfy:

– They have to be *comprehensive* and must decide whether to automatically answer a student question or to defer it to humans. This decision can be made by searching course content (e.g. textbooks, lecture notes, and supplementary materials) [13] for relevant information and evaluating their confidence in understanding the question and providing a satisfactory answer.
– They have to be *context-aware* and should decide on the best timing of an automated intervention. For duplicate questions (studied in [10]) and questions that students can discuss among themselves and resolve, virtual TAs should decide not to intervene since discussions facilitate engagement and peer learning [14]. For questions where misconceptions are formed among student responses, virtual TAs should decide to intervene immediately to clear up these misconceptions. This decision can be made by analyzing both interactions among students and topics in each discussion forum thread [15].
– They have to be *conversational* and should engage in meaningful conversations with students, such as asking a follow-up question when a student question is unclear or offering words of encouragement [6]. This requirement has been the focus of numerous existing works [5–8,16–18].

1.1 Contributions

In this paper, we explore the use of automated *question answering* methods in natural language processing to power virtual TAs in online course discussion forums. We focus on the first two requirements outlined above and restrict ourselves to studying frequent and repetitive logistical questions; our goal is to reduce the burden on teachers and TAs by automating the routine part of teacher-student interaction. First, we adopt an open-domain question answering framework [19] that consists of two steps: *retrieving* relevant documents from a pool of course materials (including the syllabus, lecture slides, announcement emails, and previous discussion forum posts), and *extracting* an answer to the question from retrieved documents via automated, neural network-based methods [20]. We also use an *answerability classifier* to decide whether a question is answerable given information from the document pool. Second, we analyze the content and timing of student posts and develop classifiers based on multi-class and ordinal classification to predict the timing of follow-up posts in a discussion thread. These classifiers can be used to identify threads where student questions are not likely to be resolved in time and thus require immediate intervention. We evaluate our system using a Piazza dataset collected from an introductory physics course. Quantitatively, we compare our system to both humans and IBM Watson on question answering performance. Qualitatively, we use several examples to illustrate where the model excels and where it falls short and discuss future advances needed for virtual TAs to become a reality.

1.2   Connections to Existing Work

Existing work on developing automated virtual TAs in course discussion forums is limited; the most relevant work is Jill Watson [9]. It requires a list of common question-answer pairs in a course; for every incoming question, it searches over all questions in the list and finds the most similar one, before deploying the corresponding answer if the similarity passes a certain threshold. The question-answer list can either be hand-crafted by teachers and TAs, which requires significant human effort, or come from discussion forum data collected in previous offerings of the same course, which is not applicable when the course is offered for the first time. On the contrary, our approach automatically retrieves relevant information from course materials and does not require human effort or prior data.

Another relevant recent work is the Curio SmartChat system [21] for question answering in self-paced middle school science courses. For an incoming student question, Curio Smartchat searches the content repository and either i) answers directly when the question is well-understood and can be matched to a question in the question-answer list, ii) recommends relevant content to the student if the question is not well-understood, or iii) responds with "small-talk" when there is no relevant content. Similarly, the Discussion-Bot system [11] retrieves relevant course documents and prior discussion posts for each discussion forum question and presents them to students after a series of rules-based post-processing steps. Despite similarities in document retrieval methods, our approach employs the additional step of automatic question answering using the retrieved documents to provide concise answers to student questions.

Most open-domain question answering systems, starting with DrQA [19], use document retrieval and answer extraction/ranking in a two-step approach. Term frequency-inverse document frequency (tf-idf) is an efficient way to retrieve documents based on their word overlap with a query, considering frequency in the document and the entire corpus. DrQA uses a tf-idf [22] look-up to retrieve documents and a recurrent neural network to extract answers from the retrieved documents. The work in [23] uses a ranking module that is jointly trained with the answer extraction module using reinforcement learning. The work in [24] explores how to better extract relevant information from documents before extracting an answer from retrieved information. The work in [25] links the document retriever with the question answering module by iteratively retrieving documents and updating the query accordingly. These systems are trained and evaluated on standard question answering datasets with highly structured text. In contrast, our goal is to explore their effectiveness on questions asked by students in online course discussion forums, which are often ill-posed or poorly written [21].

For the study of post timing in online (not necessarily course) discussion forums, relevant existing works include [26] which predicts which posts are helpful to answering a question post, [27] which predicts whether the user asking a question will accept an answer post, and [28] which predicts the timing of posts using point processes parameterized by neural networks. Instead, we use multi-class and ordinal classification for timing prediction since our dataset is not large enough for point process-based methods.

2   Methodology

We now detail our logistical question answering system. Code implementing these methods will be made available at https://github.com/bzylich/qa-for-ta.

2.1   Question Answering Framework

Our question answering framework builds on DrQA [19]. First, for each question, we retrieve a set of relevant documents using a document retriever. Then, we extract and rank short answers from each document using automated question answering methods. Finally, we add an answerability classifier to determine the probability that we are able to provide a satisfactory answer to the question.

Before retrieving documents, we split each document into paragraphs and merge short paragraphs together if they do not exceed 220 characters in total. Documents are then retrieved by calculating the inner product between the tf-idf [22,29] vector for a question and the tf-idf vectors for each document. We select the 5 documents with the highest scores as relevant sources of information for question answering. We compare variants of this retrieval approach in Sect. 3.

Following common question answering methods, we encode the text from a retrieved document and the question into a low-dimensional representation using a recurrent neural network (RNN) trained on the SQuAD [20] question answering dataset[1]. Then, we use another RNN to decode the start and end indices corresponding to the span of text in the retrieved document that best answers the question[2]. In this manner, we produce 5 candidate answers, one from each document, and rank them using their tf-idf document retrieval scores.

The document pool contains documents published by the instructor, TAs, and even other students that contain information about the course. These documents include the course syllabus, announcement emails from instructors, class notes, practice problems, the course textbook, and previous student posts on discussion forums. However, some student questions may not be answerable given the current document pool at a point in time. For example, students may ask about the time and location of the final exam during the first week of the semester

---

[1] SQuAD consists of Wikipedia articles and crowdsourced questions with answers.

[2] We extract a span of text from the document rather than generating an open-ended answer since tools for the latter are still unreliable [30,31].

when final exams are not yet set by the university. Therefore, we need an answerability classifier that can determine the probability that a question is answerable given a document in the available document pool. To train this classifier, we use the *bert-base-uncased* variant of BERT [32]. BERT is a state-of-the-art pre-trained neural language model that has been used to improve performance on a variety of downstream natural language processing tasks. We fine-tune BERT using adapters [33] with size 256 on the SQuAD 2.0 dataset [34] and the Natural Questions dataset [35] that contain human-generated answerability labels for question-document pairs. We then apply this trained classifier to filter out retrieved documents that are similar to the question but cannot be used to answer it. Specifically, we pass each question and each retrieved document separately to the answerability classifier; If the answerability classifier indicates that the question is answerable given the document with high probability, we keep that document; otherwise, it is discarded. This answerability classifier helps us to i) only answer a question when we are confident in providing a satisfactory answer and ii) improve the quality of the document retriever.

2.2 Post Timing Prediction

Automated question answering systems can potentially answer many questions immediately after they are posted, which will be effective in reducing human effort for straightforward logistical questions. However, for knowledge-related questions, there exists a clear connection between balanced collaboration in problem solving and effective student learning [1]. If the system always answers questions immediately, it will stifle useful discussion between students that promotes peer learning. Thus, there is a need for the system to decide when to automatically answer a question by predicting the length of time until the next post in a thread.

Given the sequential nature of discussion threads, we employ an RNN to predict the time until the next post of a particular thread, where each discrete time step of the network corresponds to a post. At each time step, our input to the RNN is a vector concatenating the following information: the textual embedding of the current post (generated using BERT), the time between the previous and current post, and a one-hot encoded representation of the Piazza post type. For the output at each time step, it is difficult to formulate time prediction as a regression problem since time between posts ranges from seconds to days or even infinity for the end-of-thread (EOT) post. Therefore, we formulate it as a k-class classification problem where the first $k - 1$ classes are time intervals, e.g. [5 mins, 1 hr), and the final class is for EOT posts.

We use two different loss functions to train the RNN. The first loss function, cross entropy, uses the softmax function and assumes the classes are not ordered:

$$L = -\log(e^{y_g} / \sum_i e^{y_i}).$$

In this case, the output at each time step is a length-k vector that is used to predict the probability for each output class and y_i denotes its ith entry.

g corresponds to the actual time bin the post belongs to. However, given the ordered nature of the time intervals, we also use another loss function which is a threshold-based generalization of the hinge loss [36]:

$$L = \sum_{i=1}^{k-1} \max\{0, 1 - s(i,g)(\theta_i - y)\}, \quad s(i,g) = \begin{cases} -1, i < g \\ 1, \quad i \geq g \end{cases}.$$

In this case, the output at each time step is a scalar y; $-\infty = \theta_0 < \theta_1 < ... < \theta_{k-1} < \theta_k = \infty$ denotes a set of thresholds that partition the possible values of the RNN scalar output into k bins. In other words, this loss compares the scalar output with each threshold to put it into a bin, penalizing outputs farther from their actual time bin.

3   Experiments

3.1   Dataset

Our dataset, which we dub PhysicsForum, consists of 2004 posts in 663 threads in the online discussion forum of an introductory physics course. 802 of these posts are questions asked by students (640 primary questions and 162 follow-up questions). We manually divide these questions into different types: 140 conceptual (regarding a specific concept), 250 reasoning (apply concepts to specific problems), 172 logistics (pertain to class structure, not content), 18 factual (content related, with definitive answer), 213 not answerable (needs human intervention, eg., grading related), and 9 off-topic (unrelated to course content/structure). We focus on logistics questions and content-related factual questions since automated question answering methods are mainly developed for factual questions. In addition to the discussion forum data, there are 288 course material documents including the syllabus, assignments, notes, announcement emails from the instructor, exams, and sections of the electronic course textbook.

3.2   Question Answering

Experimental Setup. To more easily judge for correctness, we use the 172 logistical questions from the PhysicsForum dataset where students ask about assignment due dates, exam locations, grading policy, etc. Since our goal is to test document retrieval and question answering performance, we retrieve documents from the entire pool of course documents and discussion forum posts, regardless of the availability at the time a question was posted. We include several variants of our proposed question answering system in an ablation study. First, we compare retrieving documents via an inner product of tf-idf vectors (our system) versus cosine similarity [29], i.e., normalizing the inner product by dividing by document length (+N). Second, we compare splitting documents into paragraphs before document retrieval (our system) versus not splitting (−P).

Table 1. Document retrieval performance for all question answering systems.

System	Human	Watson	DrQA	Ours-P+N	Ours+N	Ours
Top-1 %	*80.2%*	38.4%	17.4%	51.2%	52.9%	**61.6%**
Top-3 %	*86.0%*	–	42.4%	79.7%	75.6%	**83.7%**
Top-5 %	*86.0%*	–	55.8%	89.0%	83.7%	**90.7%**

Table 2. Answer extraction performance for all question answering systems.

System	Human	Watson	Ours
Top-1 %	*80.2%*	38.4%	**41.3%**
Top-3 %	*86.0%*	–	**66.3%**
Top-5 %	*86.0%*	–	**77.3%**

Evaluation Metric and Baselines. We use human judgment to evaluate the performance of all systems[3]; for document retrieval, we label a document according to whether or not it contains information that could be used to answer the question, and for answer extraction, we label an answer span according to whether or not it is a satisfactory answer to the question. Sometimes, a satisfactory answer is not ranked first; this situation occurs when a question has some ambiguity, which makes the answer extraction model favor generic, indirect answers. Since our system produces a list of 5 answers with their rankings, we use Top-k accuracy to characterize the percentage of questions where at least one satisfactory answer is included in the top-k ranked answers, with $k \in \{1, 3, 5\}$.

We compare our question answering system against several baselines. The first baseline is the actual performance of course staff and other students (Human) in our dataset. We note that most questions elicit between 1–3 answers from students or course staff, causing Top-1 accuracy to differ slightly from Top-3 and Top-5 accuracies. The second baseline is the IBM Watson Assistant (Watson), which is given the 15 most commonly asked logistical questions in our dataset and the corresponding answers. We expect this baseline to be a near-optimal version of Jill Watson [9] because it knows a-priori the exact questions asked by the students. The Top-3 and Top-5 metrics do not apply to Watson because Watson does not provide a ranked list of answers; Instead, Watson randomly deploys one response from a pool of possible responses to a given question. The third baseline is the unaltered version of DrQA [19].

Results and Discussion. Table 1 shows the performance of document retrieval for all systems on the PhysicsForum dataset. Here, we only consider whether the retrieved paragraph contains information that could answer the question. For

---

[3] To gauge the subjectivity of our metric, we randomly sampled 50 question-answer pairs (across questions, answer ranks, and systems) and found moderate agreement between 2 independent labelers (80% agreement, Cohen's Kappa [37] = 0.554).

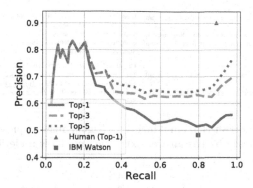

Fig. 1. Our system can use the answerability classifier to be selective in the questions it answers to improve precision at the expense of recall.

the Human and Watson baselines which do not answer every question, unanswered questions are treated as incorrect to ensure that recall is the same for all systems (since our system has 100% recall). We see that despite generally not reaching human-level performance, especially with the top-ranked answer, our system is the best-performing automated question answering method. Moreover, our system can automatically provide a satisfactory answer within its top-5 ranked answers for 90.7% of the questions, while the course staff answered only 86% of the questions. We also see that our system slightly outperforms its variants and significantly outperforms the original DrQA system that does not split documents into paragraphs in the document retrieval step. Even without this split, Ours-P+N still outperforms DrQA using the normalized cosine similarity values to rank documents instead of using inner products. These results suggest that splitting documents into paragraphs before the document retrieval process eliminates the need of normalization for the inner products between tf-idf vectors. The likely reason is that course content documents such as the syllabus and textbook sections are very long; splitting them into smaller paragraphs enables more past discussion forum posts to be selected. These threads can be highly relevant despite being relatively short.

Table 2 shows the answer extraction performance for all systems on the PhysicsForum dataset. We see that the performance on answer extraction is significantly worse than document retrieval, which means that the short span of text extracted from the document often fails to capture key information. This observation is not surprising since current answer extraction methods are designed for well-structured documents and questions with simple answers, while questions asked by real students often require complex answers using information from different pieces of the document. Therefore, if our system is to be deployed in real online course discussion forums, it is necessary to provide the entire retrieved document in addition to the short answer in case the answer itself is not satisfactory but its context still contains relevant information.

Question: How is our grade impacted if we forgot to do the catme team evaluation...
Top Answer: ...There will be two team evaluations during this semester, one after the first three labs, and one after the last three. Each team evaluation will be <u>worth 5%.</u>
Source: Lab syllabus

Question: Does anyone know if we can still get credit for late Perusall comments?
Top Answer: ...<u>no extensions will be given." No credit for late homework.</u>
Source: Forum post

Question: I did not receive full credit for the exam 1 corrections and there were no comments on moodle. How do I find out where I lost points?
Top Answer: ...there will be a correction aspect to the exams...you will, <u>after the exam be able to turn</u> in some corrections to regain 15% of your lost points back...
Source: Course syllabus

Question: Where can I find the SI materials from the review session?
Top Answer: ...There is a link on your moodle under "Supplemental Instruction" called "Location of SI materials"... <u>Tuesdays and Sundays</u> are used to go over class material... I upload worksheets 2 hours before every session...
Source: Forum post

Fig. 2. Examples of correct (left) and incorrect (right) answers provided by the system. The short answer chosen by the answer extraction model is underlined.

To improve the precision of our question answering system (at the expense of recall), we can use our answerability classifier's confidence value output to select questions to answer. Figure 1 shows the precision-recall curves with varying confidence threshold values for our system. The Human and Watson baselines are represented as points on the plot because neither supports multiple thresholding values. The precision shown for these baselines is higher than that in Table 1 since we are now using their actual recall values. We see that despite not reaching human-level performance, our system is capable of achieving 80% precision at 20% recall, which decreases to 50% at 80% recall. Moreover, our system slightly outperforms the IBM Watson-based system that was developed with knowledge of the questions (and corresponding answers) that were actually present in our dataset. This result means that our system can be readily used to enhance existing dialogue-based question answering systems that require non-trivial effort by instructors and TAs. Moreover, our system does not need to be warm-started using discussion forum data from previous offerings of the course; instead, all the instructor has to do is upload materials into the document pool.

Figure 2 shows several example questions and answers both when our system performed well and poorly. Figure 2(a) shows that our system can harness both course content documents and other forum posts to answer student questions. Figure 2(b) shows two cases where our system fails to extract a satisfactory answer. In one case, the text similarity-based document retriever finds a document about exam corrections, but the document does not answer the question of how to determine why the student did not receive full credit on their corrections. In the other case, the document contains relevant information about how students can access materials from a review session; this information is distributed throughout the document. However, existing answer extraction methods can only select a single short span in the text, causing the model to select a span that addresses the related (but different) question of when review sessions are held.

Question: How do you determine the direction of an electric field?
Top Answer: The electric field from a positive charge points away from the charge. The electric field from a <u>negative charge points towards the charge</u>.
Source: Forum post

Fig. 3. Beyond logistical questions, our system may also be used to answer content-related factual questions.

In addition to logistical questions, we also applied our system to the 18 questions we labeled as factual [38] in the PhysicsForum dataset. On these questions, our document retrieval system had Top-1, Top-3, and Top-5 accuracies of 44.4%, 88.9%, and 88.9%, respectively. Figure 3 shows an example where the system answers correctly. This example and the system's performance suggest that our system may be applicable beyond the limited domain of logistical questions, which we will explore in future work.

3.3   Post Timing Prediction

Experimental Setup. For the next post timing prediction task, we consider all threads in the PhysicsForum dataset. Using RNNs as the base model, we compare several variants of our method, including varying the number of discrete time bins as $k \in \{4, 8\}$, using the two different loss functions, cross entropy (C) and ordinal hinge loss (O), and the addition of two input features (A). These two additional features are derived from the answerability classifier; one is the maximum predicted probability of a satisfactory answer to the main question across all available documents, and the other is the maximum predicted probability of a satisfactory answer across only previous answer posts in the thread. We select bin boundaries such that EOT posts make up their own bin while the remaining posts are evenly placed into the other $k - 1$ bins. We train the RNN on a subset of 522 randomly sampled threads of the PhysicsForum dataset and evaluate it on the remaining 141 held-out threads. We evaluate the model using the time bin prediction accuracy (ACC) metric, which is simply the portion of correct predictions, and accuracy within one bin (ACC1), which is the portion of predictions that differ from the the actual time bin by at most 1. We repeat our experiments over 10 randomly sampled training and test sets.

Results and Discussion. Table 3 shows the mean performance across all training and test sets for all variations of our model. For reference, a majority-class model (EOT posts) achieves an ACC of 33.1%. We see that the ordinal loss provides a slight advantage over the cross entropy loss on both metrics under almost all settings. This observation suggests that the ordinal loss function that considers bin ordering by penalizing predictions farther from their actual bin more heavily is more effective than the cross entropy loss that does not consider bin ordering. We also see that the use of the answerability classifier improves the timing prediction performance but only marginally. This observation suggests that knowing whether the question in a discussion forum thread is answerable or whether it has already been answered can benefit next post timing prediction. However, this benefit is limited by the performance of the answerability classifier, which is not as accurate on the PhysicsForum dataset as it is on the standard SQuAD and Natural Questions datasets since real student questions are often ill-posed or poorly written. Nevertheless, the next post timing predictor can help virtual TAs to predict whether a student question is likely going to be answered by other students soon and decide whether to answer it immediately.

Table 3. Comparison between variants of the RNN using the cross entropy loss (C), ordinal loss (O), and the answerability classifier features (A) for predicting the discrete time bin of the time until next post.

System	$k = 4$				$k = 8$			
	RNN-C	RNN-O	RNN-CA	RNN-OA	RNN-C	RNN-O	RNN-CA	RNN-OA
ACC	75.2%	76.6%	75.4%	74.7%	69.8%	72.0%	70.0%	72.3%
ACC1	89.3%	91.9%	89.5%	92.3%	78.1%	79.5%	77.8%	80.6%

4   Conclusions and Future Work

In this paper, we have developed an automated system for logistical question answering in online course discussion forums and discussed how it can help the development of virtual teaching assistants. In addition to analyzing students' interactions with our system in a live course setting, avenues of future work include i) exploring what type of course content-based questions can be answered, ii) improving our system by fine-tuning neural language models on course content to adapt to student-generated text, and iii) developing methods that can automatically identify misconceptions in student posts.

References

1. Graesser, A.C., Person, N.K., Magliano, J.P.: Collaborative dialogue patterns in naturalistic one-to-one tutoring. Appl. Cogn. Psychol. **9**, 495–522 (1995)
2. Heffernan, N.T., Koedinger, K.R., Razzaq, L.: Expanding the model-tracing architecture: a 3rd generation intelligent tutor for algebra symbolization. Int. J. Artif. Intell. Educ. **18**, 153–178 (2008)
3. Lehman, B., Matthews, M., D'Mello, S., Person, N.: What are you feeling? Investigating student affective states during expert human tutoring sessions. In: Woolf, B.P., Aïmeur, E., Nkambou, R., Lajoie, S. (eds.) ITS 2008. LNCS, vol. 5091, pp. 50–59. Springer, Heidelberg (2008). https://doi.org/10.1007/978-3-540-69132-7_10
4. Gaebel, M.: MOOCs: Massive Open Online Courses. EUA, Geneva (2014)
5. Leelawong, K., Biswas, G.: Designing learning by teaching agents: the Betty's brain system. Int. J. Artif. Intell. Educ. **18**, 181–208 (2008)
6. Karumbaiah, S., Lizarralde, R., Allessio, D., Woolf, B., Arroyo, I., Wixon, N.: Addressing student behavior and affect with empathy and growth mindset. In: Proceeding of the International Conference on Educational Data Mining, pp. 96–103, June 2017
7. Benedetto, L., Cremonesi, P., Parenti, M.: A virtual teaching assistant for personalized learning. arXiv preprint arXiv:1902.09289 (2019)
8. Adamson, D., Rosé, C.P.: Coordinating multi-dimensional support in collaborative conversational agents. In: Cerri, S.A., Clancey, W.J., Papadourakis, G., Panourgia, K. (eds.) ITS 2012. LNCS, vol. 7315, pp. 346–351. Springer, Heidelberg (2012). https://doi.org/10.1007/978-3-642-30950-2_45
9. Goel, A., Polepeddi, L.: Jill Watson: a virtual teaching assistant for online education. Georgia Institute of Technology. Technical report (2016)

10. Bilgrien, N. et al.: PARQR: augmenting the piazza online forum to better support degree seeking online masters students. In: Proceedings of the Sixth (2019) ACM Conference on Learning at Scale, pp. 1–4 (2019)

11. Feng, D., Shaw, E., Kim, J., Hovy, E.: An intelligent discussion-bot for answering student queries in threaded discussions. In: Proceedings of the 11th International Conference on Intelligent User Interfaces, pp. 171–177 (2006)

12. Wang, C.-C., Hung, J.C., Yang, C.-Y., Shih, T.K.: An application of question answering system for collaborative learning. In: 26th IEEE International Conference on Distributed Computing Systems Workshops. (ICDCSW 2006), p. 49. IEEE (2006)

13. Ramesh, A., Goldwasser, D., Huang, B., Daumé III, H., Getoor, L.: Understanding MOOC discussion forums using seeded LDA. In: Proceeding of the Workshop on Innovative use of NLP for Building Educational Applications, pp. 28–33, June 2014

14. Chiu, T.K., Hew, T.K.: Factors influencing peer learning and performance in MOOC asynchronous online discussion forum. Australas. J. Educ. Technol. 34(4), 16–28 (2018)

15. Lan, A.S., Spencer, J.C., Chen, Z., Brinton, C.G., Chiang, M.: Personalized thread recommendation for MOOC discussion forums. In: Berlingerio, M., Bonchi, F., Gärtner, T., Hurley, N., Ifrim, G. (eds.) ECML PKDD 2018. LNCS (LNAI), vol. 11052, pp. 725–740. Springer, Cham (2019). https://doi.org/10.1007/978-3-030-10928-8_43

16. Benedetto, L., Cremonesi, P.: Rexy, a configurable application for building virtual teaching assistants. In: Lamas, D., Loizides, F., Nacke, L., Petrie, H., Winckler, M., Zaphiris, P. (eds.) INTERACT 2019. LNCS, vol. 11747, pp. 233–241. Springer, Cham (2019). https://doi.org/10.1007/978-3-030-29384-0_15

17. Reyes, R., Garza, D., Garrido, L., De la Cueva, V., Ramirez, J.: Methodology for the implementation of virtual assistants for education using Google dialogflow. In: Martínez-Villaseñor, L., Batyrshin, I., Marín-Hernández, A. (eds.) MICAI 2019. LNCS (LNAI), vol. 11835, pp. 440–451. Springer, Cham (2019). https://doi.org/10.1007/978-3-030-33749-0_35

18. Niranjan, M., Saipreethy, M., Kumar, T.G.: An intelligent question answering conversational agent using Naïve Bayesian classifier. In: 2012 IEEE International Conference on Technology Enhanced Education (ICTEE), pp. 1–5. IEEE (2012)

19. Chen, D., Fisch, A., Weston, J., Bordes, A.: Reading Wikipedia to answer open-domain questions. In: ACL 2017 55th Annual Meeting of the Association for Computational Linguistics, Proceedings of the Conference (Long Papers), vol. 1, pp. 1870–1879. Association for Computational Linguistics (ACL) (2017)

20. Rajpurkar, P., Zhang, J., Lopyrev, K., Liang, P.: SQuad: 100,000+ questions for machine comprehension of text. In: EMNLP 2016 - Conference on Empirical Methods in Natural Language Processing, Proceedings, pp. 2383–2392. Association for Computational Linguistics (ACL) (2016)

21. Raamadhurai, S., Baker, R., Poduval, V.: Curio SmartChat: a system for natural language question answering for self-paced K-12 learning. In: Proceeding of the Workshop on Innovative Use of NLP for Building Educational Applications, pp. 336–342, July 2019

22. Rajaraman, A., Ullman, J.D.: Mining of Massive Datasets. Cambridge University Press, Cambridge (2011)

23. Wang, S. et al.: R 3: reinforced ranker-reader for open-domain question answering. In: Thirty-Second AAAI Conference on Artificial Intelligence (2018)

24. Lin, Y., Ji, H., Liu, Z., Sun, M.: Denoising distantly supervised open-domain question answering. In: Proceedings of the 56th Annual Meeting of the Association for Computational Linguistics (Volume 1: Long Papers), pp. 1736–1745 (2018)
25. Das, R., Dhuliawala, S., Zaheer, M., McCallum, A.: Multi-step retriever-reader interaction for scalable open-domain question answering. arXiv preprint arXiv:1905.05733 (2019)
26. Halder, K., Kan, M.-Y., Sugiyama, K.: Predicting helpful posts in open-ended discussion forums: a neural architecture. In: Proceedings of the 2019 Conference of the North American Chapter of the Association for Computational Linguistics: Human Language Technologies, Vol. 1 (Long and Short Papers), pp. 3148–3157 (2019)
27. Jenders, M., Krestel, R., Naumann, F.: Which answer is best? Predicting accepted answers in MOOC forums. In: Proceedings of the 25th International Conference Companion on World Wide Web, pp. 679–684 (2016)
28. Hansen, P., et al.: Predicting the timing and quality of responses in online discussion forums. In: Proceeding IEEE International Conference on Distributed Computing Systems, pp. 1931–1940, May 2019
29. Singhal, A., et al.: Modern information retrieval: a brief overview. IEEE Data Eng. Bull. **24**(4), 35–43 (2001)
30. Yin, J., Jiang, X., Lu, Z., Shang, L., Li, H., Li, X.: Neural generative question answering. arXiv preprint arXiv:1512.01337 (2015)
31. He, S., Liu, C., Liu, K., Zhao, J.: Generating natural answers by incorporating copying and retrieving mechanisms in sequence-to-sequence learning. In: Proceedings of the 55th Annual Meeting of the Association for Computational Linguistics (Volume 1: Long Papers), pp. 199–208 (2017)
32. Devlin, J., Chang, M.-W., Lee, K., Toutanova, K.: Bert: pre-training of deep bidirectional transformers for language understanding. arXiv preprint arXiv:1810.04805 (2018)
33. Houlsby, N. et al.: Parameter-efficient transfer learning for NLP. arXiv preprint arXiv:1902.00751 (2019)
34. Rajpurkar, P., Jia, R., Liang, P.: Know what you don't know: unanswerable questions for SQuAD. In: ACL 2018 56th Annual Meeting of the Association for Computational Linguistics, Proceedings of the Conference (Long Papers), vol. 2, pp. 784–789. Association for Computational Linguistics (ACL) (2018)
35. Kwiatkowski, T.: Natural questions: a benchmark for question answering research. Trans. Assoc. Comput. Linguist. **7**, 453–466 (2019)
36. Rennie, J.D., Srebro, N.: Loss functions for preference levels: regression with discrete ordered labels. In: Proceedings of the IJCAI Multidisciplinary Workshop on Advances in Preference Handling, vol. 1. Kluwer Norwell, Norwell (2005)
37. Cohen, J.: A coefficient of agreement for nominal scales. Educ. Psychol. Measur. **20**(1), 37–46 (1960)
38. Wang, Z., Lan, A.S., Nie, W., Waters, A.E., Grimaldi, P.J., Baraniuk, R.G.: QG-net: a data-driven question generation model for educational content. In: Proceedings of the ACM Conference on Learning at Scale, pp. 1–10, June 2018

Correction to: SoundHunters: Increasing Learner Phonological Awareness in Plains Cree

Delaney Lothian, Gokce Akcayir⬤, Anaka Sparrow,
Owen Mcleod⬤, and Carrie Demmans Epp⬤

Correction to:
Chapter "SoundHunters: Increasing Learner Phonological Awareness in Plains Cree" in: I. I. Bittencourt et al. (Eds.): *Artificial Intelligence in Education*, **LNAI 12163,** **https://doi.org/10.1007/978-3-030-52237-7_28**

The chapter was inadvertently published with errors in the reference numbers 28 and 34. The authors' names of the cited contributions were corrected.

The updated version of this chapter can be found at
https://doi.org/10.1007/978-3-030-52237-7_28

© Springer Nature Switzerland AG 2020
I. I. Bittencourt et al. (Eds.): AIED 2020, LNAI 12163, p. C1, 2020.
https://doi.org/10.1007/978-3-030-52237-7_50

Author Index

Abdi, Solmaz II-3
Ahmed, Umair Z. I-106
Ahuja, Rohan II-301
Akcayir, Gokce I-346
Al-Doulat, Ahmad I-3
Aleven, Vincent I-240, II-92, II-124
Al-Hariri, Lara I-610
Alhazmi, Sohail II-10
Al-Hossami, Erfan I-3
Allen, Laura K. II-197
Alshaikh, Zeyad II-15
Amadi, Chukwudi E. II-224
An, Haokang II-273
An, Sungeun II-20
Andres-Bray, Juan Miguel L. II-208
Andrzejewska, Magdalena II-25
Arrington, Catherine M. I-500
Azad, Sushmita I-16
Azevedo, Roger I-67

Bae, Chan II-69
Baek, Jineon II-69
Bailey, James I-296, I-423
Baker, Ryan I-411, II-329
Baker, Ryan Shaun I-228, I-423, I-437,
    I-574, II-208
Banerjee, Ayan I-29
Baraniuk, Richard G. II-424
Barnes, Tiffany I-472
Basu, Satabdi I-598
Bates, Robert II-20
Belfer, Robert II-140, II-387
Benedetto, Luca I-43
Benedict, Aileen I-3
Bengio, Yoshua II-387
Bennani, Samir II-114
Beydoun, Ghassan II-168
Biswas, Gautam I-411, I-598, II-296, II-352
Bittencourt, Ig Ibert I-79, I-448, II-376
Bogart, Christopher II-273
Bonnin, Geoffray II-203
Bosch, Nigel I-204

Botarleanu, Robert-Mihai II-31
Botelho, Anthony F. I-562
Boyer, Kristy Elizabeth II-240
Brown, Paul S. II-395
Brusilovsky, Peter II-424
Buckingham Shum, Simon I-360
Buttery, Paula II-358

Cader, Andrzej II-37
Caines, Andrew II-358
Camus, Leon II-43
Cappelli, Andrea I-43
Carlstedt-Duke, Jan II-214
Carpenter, Dan I-55, I-67
Carvalho, Paulo F. I-460
Castagnos, Sylvain II-203
Chalco Challco, Geiser II-312
Challco, Geiser Chalco I-79
Chambel, Teresa II-98
Chanaa, Abdessamad II-49, II-54
Charlin, Laurent II-387
Chatterjee, Rishabh I-92
Chen, Binglin I-16
Chen, Guanliang II-174
Chen, Jiahao I-269
Chen, Penghe II-59, II-185
Chen, Shiping II-168
Chhatbar, Darshak I-106
Chi, Min I-472
Ching-En, Chou II-400
Chiu, Jennifer L. I-598
Chklovski, Tara II-427
Chng, Edwin I-118, II-64
Cho, Junghyun II-69
Choi, Youngduck II-69
Choffin, Benoît II-417
Cohn, Anthony G. II-395
Conati, Cristina I-282
Condor, Aubrey II-74
Courville, Aaron II-387
Couto, Marta II-346
Cremonesi, Paolo I-43

Cristus, Miruna   II-371
Crossley, Scott A.   I-437, II-31, II-329
Cui, Tingru   II-168
Cukurova, Mutlu   II-135

Daniel, Ben K.   II-224
Dascalu, Maria-Dorinela   II-80
Dascalu, Mihai   II-31, II-80, II-228
Del Bonifro, Francesca   I-129
Demmans Epp, Carrie   I-346
Dermeval, Diego   I-524, II-312
Derr, Tyler   II-130
Desmarais, Michel C.   II-191
Dhamecha, Tejas I.   II-214
Di Mitri, Daniele   I-141
Dillenbourg, Pierre   II-346
Dimitrova, Vania   II-395
Ding, Wenbiao   I-269, II-162, II-340
Dorodchi, Mohsen   I-3
Doroudi, Shayan   II-86
Dou, Wenwen   I-3
Dowell, Nia   I-333
Drachsler, Hendrik   I-141

Echeverria, Vanessa   I-360
Effenberger, Tomáš   I-153
El Faddouli, Nour-Eddine   II-49, II-54
Elizabeth Richey, J.   II-208
Emara, Mona   II-296
Emerson, Andrew   I-55, I-165
Engel, Don   II-301

Fancsali, Stephen E.   II-92
Filighera, Anna   I-177, I-512, II-43
Fonseca, Manuel J.   II-98
Fowler, Maxwell   I-16
Frank, Kenneth A.   II-130
Friedman, Leah   II-318
Fu, Weiping   I-269
Fung, Gabriel Pui Cheong   II-364

Gabbrielli, Maurizio   I-129
Gagnon, Paul   II-214
Gao, Hongli   II-180
García Iruela, Miguel   II-98
Gašević, Dragan   II-174

Gautam, Dipesh   I-191
Gauthier, Andrea   II-103
Geden, Michael   I-67
Glazewski, Krista D.   I-55
Gliser, Ian   I-204
Goel, Ashok   II-20
Gong, Jiaqi   II-157
Goodell, Jim   II-420
Graesser, Art C.   I-321
Gu, Lin   I-309
Guo, Yuqing   II-409
Gupta, Sandeep K. S.   I-29
Gupta, Varun   II-140, II-387

Hallifax, Stuart   I-216
Hamilton, Margaret   II-10
Hammock, Jen   II-20
Hanegbi, Nathan   I-296
Harpstead, Erik   I-586
Hart, Glen   II-395
Hasan, Sahil   II-273
Hayashi, Yusuke   II-109
Hayati, Hind   II-114
Heffernan, Neil T.   I-562, II-263
Heintz, Fredrik   II-427
Henderson, Nathan   I-165, I-228
Henry, Julie   II-427
Heo, Jaewe   II-69
Herodotou, Christothea   II-119
Hijón-Neira, Raquel   II-98
Hilton, Michael   II-273
Hinze, Scott R.   II-197
Hirashima, Tsukasa   II-109
Hlosta, Martin   II-119
Hmelo-Silver, Cindy E.   I-55
Hoareau, Lara   II-203
Holland, Jay   I-386
Holstein, Kenneth   I-240, II-92
Hoppe, H. Ulrich   II-382
Hossain, Sameena   I-29
Hou, Xinying   I-255
Hu, Xiangen   II-180, II-420
Huang, Changqin   II-364
Huang, Gale Yan   I-269
Huang, Yuchi   II-252
Huang, Yun   II-124

Huang, Yuqi   II-376
Hutchins, Nicole   II-352
Hutchins, Nicole M.   II-296

Indulska, Marta   I-486
Isotani, Seiji   I-79

Jay, Michael   II-420
Johal, Wafa   II-346

Kai, Shimin   I-574
Kandimalla, Siddharth Reddy   II-273
Kandlhofer, Martin   II-427
Kar, Purushottam   I-106
Karduni, Alireza   I-3
Karimi, Hamid   II-130
Karumbaiah, Shamya   I-437, II-329
Kashima, Hisashi   II-417
Kennedy, Gregor   I-423
Khalidi Idrissi, Mohammed   II-114
Khan, Daniyal   II-301
Khan-Galaria, Madiha   II-135
Khosravi, Hassan   I-486, II-3
Kim, Byungsoo   II-69
Kiu, Kai   II-180
Kleinsmith, Andrea   II-157
Kochmar, Ekaterina   II-140, II-387
Koedinger, Kenneth   I-460, I-586, II-124
Koenig, Sven   II-427
Koprinska, Irena   I-374
Kumar, Amruth N.   II-147
Kurzum, Christopher   I-309

Labrum, Matthew   I-437
Lallé, Sébastien   I-282
Lamrani, Imane   I-29
Lamtara, Jesslyn   I-296
Lan, Andrew   I-610
Lan, Andrew S.   II-424
Lang, Charles   II-152
Lang, David   II-174
Langner-Thiele, Angela   II-382
Lavoué, Elise   I-216
Lee, Heera   II-157
Lee, Seewoo   II-69
Lee, Seung   I-165
Lee, Youngnam   II-69
Leemans, Sander J. J.   I-486
Lehman, Blair   I-309

Lemos, Bruno   II-312
Lester, James   I-67, I-165, I-228, II-240
Lester, James C.   I-55
Li, Guoliang   I-269
Li, Haiying   I-321
Li, Hang   II-162
Li, Li   II-168
Lin, Jiayin   II-168
Lin, Jionghao   II-174
Lin, Yiwen   I-333
Lisanti, Giuseppe   I-129
Liu, Haochen   I-269
Liu, Jiefei   II-59
Liu, Yulin   I-309
Liu, Zitao   I-269, II-162, II-340
Llorente, Ana María Pinto   II-405
Lobczowski, Nikki G.   I-460
Long, Zhou   II-180
Lothian, Delaney   I-346
Lu, Xiwen   I-562
Lu, Yu   II-59, II-185, II-376
Lubold, Nichola   II-318
Luckin, Rose   II-135
Luo, Dehong   II-180

Ma, Xingjun   I-296
Madaio, Michael   I-92
Maher, Mary Lou   I-3
Mandalapu, Varun   II-157
Mangaroska, Katerina   I-360
Maniktala, Mehak   I-472
Manske, Sven   II-382
Mareschal, Denis   II-103
Martinez-Maldonado, Roberto   I-360
Marwan, Samiha   II-246
Mbouzao, Boniface   II-191
McBride, Elizabeth   I-598
McBroom, Jessica   I-374
McCarthy, Kathryn S.   II-197
McElhaney, Kevin W.   I-598
McLaren, Bruce M.   I-255, II-92, II-208, II-409
McLaughlin, Elizabeth   II-124
Mcleod, Owen   I-346
McNamara, Danielle S.   II-31, II-80, II-228
Medeiros Machado, Guilherme   II-203
Mendoza, Red   II-214
Meng, Qinggang   II-185
Mills, Caitlin   I-204
Min, Wookhee   I-165, II-240

Minogue, James I-165
Mishra, Shitanshu I-411, II-296, II-352
Mitrović, Antonija I-386
Mogessie, Michael II-208
Mondal, Sneha II-214
Monteiro, Mateus I-524
Moore, Russell II-358
Moore, Steven I-398
Morales-Urrutia, Elizabeth K. II-220
Mott, Bradford II-240
Mott, Bradford W. I-55
Mouta, Ana II-405
Muldner, Kasia II-306
Munshi, Anabil I-411
Murray, R. Charles II-273

Nascimento, Pedro II-312
Nawaz, Sadia I-423
Ndukwe, Ifeanyi G. II-224
Nguyen, Huy A. I-255, I-398, II-409
Nicula, Bogdan II-228
Niu, Xi I-3
Nkomo, Larian M. II-224
Nomura, Toshihiro II-109
Nur, Nasheen I-3

O'Leary, Stephen I-296
Ocaña Ch., José Miguel II-220
Ocumpaugh, Jaclyn I-411, I-437, II-329
Oertel, Catharine II-234
Ogan, Amy I-92
Okano, Masashi I-549
Olsen, Jennifer K. II-234
Ostrow, Korinn S. II-263
Ou, Lu II-252

Pacifici, Valentino II-371
Paiva, Ana II-346
Paiva, Ranilson I-448
Pan, Shimei II-301
Papathoma, Tina II-119
Paquette, Luc I-228, I-411
Park, Kyungjin II-240
Park, Seoyon II-69
Pathak, Smriti II-214
Paudyal, Prajwal I-29
Pedro da Silva, Alan II-312

Pedro, Alan I-524
Peixoto, Aristoteles I-524
Pelánek, Radek I-153
Peng, Yan II-59
Pérez-Marín, Diana II-220
Perret, Cecile A. II-228
Pian, Yang II-376
Pineau, Joelle II-140, II-387
Piromchai, Patorn I-296
Pizarro-Romero, Celeste II-220
Popineau, Fabrice II-417
Porayska-Pomsta, Kaśka II-103, II-400
Price, Thomas W. II-246
Pritchard, David II-168
Pu, Shi II-252

Qu, Jing II-180

Rachatasumrit, Napol I-586
Radu, Iulian II-257
Razzaq, Renah II-263
Redd, Brandt II-420
Rensing, Christoph I-177, I-512
Rice, Andrew II-358
Richey, J. Elizabeth I-255, I-460
Ritter, Steven II-92
Robson, Robby II-420
Rosé, Carolyn II-273
Rowe, Jonathan I-67, I-165, I-228
Rubio, Miguel A. II-268
Rugaber, Spencer II-20
Rummel, Nikol I-240
Rus, Vasile I-191, II-15
Ruseti, Stefan II-80

Sadiq, Shazia I-486, II-3
Sakr, Majd II-273
Saleh, Asmalina I-55
Sánchez, Eva Torrecilla II-405
Sandbothe, Michael II-92
Sankaranarayanan, Sreecharan II-273
Santos, Rodrigo II-312
Sanz Ausin, Markel I-472
Schiano, Michael I-309
Schneider, Bertrand I-118, II-64, II-257
Schneider, Jan I-141
Schulte, Jurgen I-360

Schulten, Cleo   II-382
Serban, Iulian Vlad   II-140, II-387
Serna, Audrey   I-216
Seyam, Mohamed Raouf   I-118
Shabaninejad, Shiva   I-486
Shahrokhian Ghahfarokhi, Bahar   II-279
Shen, Jun   II-168
Shibani, Antonette   I-360, II-285
Shin, Dongmin   II-69
Shrier, Ian   II-191
Sivaraman, Avinash   II-279
Sjödén, Björn   II-291
Skawińska, Agnieszka   II-25
Smilek, Daniel   I-204
Smith, Shelby   I-204
Snyder, Caitlin   II-296, II-352
Solovey, Erin   I-500
Sopka, Sasa   I-141
Sosnovsky, Sergey   II-424
Sparrow, Anaka   I-346
Specht, Marcus   I-141
Srivastava, Namrata   I-423
Stacey, Simon   II-301
Stamper, John   I-398, II-409
Steinbauer, Gerald   II-427
Steuer, Tim   I-177, I-512
Stranc, Samantha   II-306
Sun, Geng   II-168
Symonette, Danilo   II-301

Täckström, Oscar   II-371
Tahir, Sara   II-301
Talks, Benjamin   I-296
Tamang, Lasagn   II-15
Tan, Lingyi   II-371
Tang, Jiliang   I-269, II-130, II-162
Tang, Yong   II-364
Tanner Jackson, G.   I-309
Tärning, Betty   I-537
Tazouti, Youssef   II-203
Tenório, Kamilla   I-524, II-312
Ternblad, Eva-Maria   I-537
Thevathayan, Charles   II-10
Thomas, Aude   II-203
Tian, Xiaoyi   II-318
Toggerson, Brokk   I-610
Tong, Hanshuang   II-324

Torphy, Kaitlin T.   II-130
Trausan-Matu, Stefan   II-80
Trebing, Kevin   I-141
Tsuprun, Eugene   I-309
Tu, Ethan   II-257
Turrin, Roberto   I-43
Tywoniw, Rurik   II-329

Uchida, Yuto   II-334
Unal, Deniz Sonmez   I-500
Uto, Masaki   I-549, II-334

VanLehn, Kurt   II-279
Varatharaj, Ashvini   I-562
Vie, Jill-Jênn   II-417
Viola, Adam   I-610
Vu, Dung Do   II-140, II-387

Walker, Erin   I-500, II-318
Wammes, Jeffrey D.   I-204
Wang, Deliang   II-185
Wang, Magdalene   II-301
Wang, Yeyu   I-574
Wang, Zhen   II-324
Wang, Zhiwei   II-162
Weigel, Emily   II-20
Weitekamp, Daniel   I-586
West, Matthew   I-16
Wiebe, Eric   II-240
Wijayarathna, Gayathri K.   II-214
Wijewickrema, Sudanthi   I-296
Williams, Joseph Jay   II-246
Winters, Michael   II-246

Xie, Haoran   II-174
Xu, Dongming   II-168
Xu, Qi   II-59
Xu, Shiting   II-340

Yacef, Kalina   I-374
Yadollahi, Elmira   II-346
Yang, Songfan   I-269
Yao, William   I-118
Ye, Zihuiwen   I-586
Yett, Bernard   II-296, II-352
Yu, Ji Hyun   I-423

Yu, Renzhe   I-333
Yu, Weihao   II-364
Yudelson, Michael   II-252

Zaidi, Ahmed   II-358
Zeylikman, Sofya   II-64
Zhang, Ningyu   I-411, I-598, II-352

Zhao, Jing   I-309
Zheng, Zetao   II-364
Zhou, Yun   II-324
Zhu, Jia   II-364
Zilles, Craig   I-16
Zingaro, Stefano Pio   I-129
Zylich, Brian   I-610

Printed in the United States
By Bookmasters